PRAISE FOR *IN SEARCH OF CHRISTIAN ORIGINS*

"Much of everything you've ever wondered about Christian history is summarily answered in *In Search of Christian Origins*. J. Steven Paul has compiled a treasure trove of forgotten roots and historical milestones bookended by his own illuminating reflections. An invaluable reference book to understand how Christian beliefs, practices, and movements originated and evolved. Will help many rethink Christianity and distinguish man-made religion from Jesus' love ethic. Highly recommended."

—Michael Camp, author of *Craft Brewed Jesus: How History We Never Knew Taps a Spirituality We Really Need* and podcaster at The Spiritual Brewpub

IN SEARCH OF
CHRISTIAN
ORIGINS

J. Steven Paul

IN SEARCH OF
CHRISTIAN
ORIGINS

A Timeline of the Good,
the Bad, and the Ugly

PUFFINLAND
PUBLISHERS

This book is dedicated to the unfortunate millions of people whose lives were ruined or ended for the sole reason that they had different religious views than their oppressors.

Published by Puffinland Publishers

Cover design: Emily Weigel
Project management: Mari Kesselring and Reshma Kooner
Production: Abi Pollokoff
Image credits: cover © Shutterstock/Kamira, Shutterstock/Don Mammoser, Shutterstock/Arkady Mazor, Shutterstock/Gregor Buir

Scripture quotations taken from the *Holy Bible, New International Version.* Copyright © 1973, 1978, 1984 by International Bible Society. Used by permission of Zondervan Publishing House.

ISBN (paperback): 979-8-9857309-0-6
ISBN (e-book): 979-8-9857309-1-3

Library of Congress Control Number: 2022905337

CONTENTS

INTRODUCTION

All national institutions of churches, whether Jewish, Christian or Turkish, appear to me no other than human inventions, set up to terrify and enslave mankind, and monopolize power and profit.
—Thomas Paine

It is not reason which turns the young man from God; it is the flesh. Skepticism but provides him with the excuses for the new life he is leading.
—Aurelius Augustine

Religion is the impotence of the human mind to deal with occurrences it cannot understand.
—Karl Marx

MY BACKGROUND

When I was a child, my Sunday school teachers introduced me to a compassionate, forgiving, wise, and humble Jesus, the tender of his sheep and the Prince of Peace. In my naive, young mind I assumed that if someone became a Christian, that was a commitment to emulate the morality of this concept of Jesus, because I wasn't aware of any other way to follow him. Those characteristics of Jesus resonated with me personally and I admired anyone who was able to model the loving and self-sacrificing behavior he taught.

As I matured, I began to understand that the best most people, including myself, could achieve was a weak imitation of him. When I became aware of Christians who didn't even seem to try to live that way, it was hard for me to reconcile their behaviors with what I'd assumed it should be.

I eventually became skeptical of what I'd been taught in church because much of it conflicted with what logic and reason informed me about reality. If I was supposed to believe in angels, demons, nine-hundred-year-old men, and talking snakes, I wanted to see one first. Like Jesus's doubting disciple Thomas, I needed some real evidence before I could believe those seemingly unbelievable things. I also saw many contradictions and incompatibilities in the Bible.

Through all this doubt, no matter how absurd certain biblical stories seemed to me on a conscious level, another part of my mind couldn't stop thinking that I might be wrong. After all, I'd been taught by respected adults that those stories about Adam and Eve and the great flood of Noah's time were true. I couldn't totally disregard those unless I found other people who doubted them also. I didn't trust myself enough to be able to say they weren't true without good evidence, and I never sought out others to confirm my doubts. How could a high school kid like me contradict two thousand years of Christian belief that was endorsed by very wise men? I was very confused, and I basically stopped thinking about religion altogether.

During my college years I found all the spirituality I needed in nature, and all the philosophical meaning and ethereal music I required from the early albums of the British symphonic-rock band, the Moody Blues. In my last year of college, my roommate's father, the first fire-and-brimstone pastor I'd ever encountered, condemned me to hell during our only brief conversation. He apparently was full of condemnation for anyone who didn't live up to his personal standards of belief and behavior, and my crime was not attending church on a regular basis; in fact, at that time, I didn't attend at all. If college had "corrupted" me, it was because it helped me further develop my senses of skepticism and reason. This man's whole approach of threatening me seemed to be his default mode in trying to "save" my soul, and I found it extremely offensive. I was still the same considerate, compassionate, and innocent person I'd always been, but he didn't even care about any of that. I couldn't understand why not showing up weekly at a church was enough to justify my being sent to a place of eternal suffering. In the long run, though, the incident proved positive because it demonstrated that Christians can be horrible people, despite their belief in Jesus. I closed the door on a religion that I had to be frightened into believing. Give me evidence, give me encouragement, throw in some compassion and love, but don't try to scare me into believing something I can't believe. I had enough anxiety and fear in my life already without him piling on the extra baggage of roasting in hell. By the time I was out of college, I was basically a Deist but retained my admiration for Jesus and the kindness that he symbolized to me.

Later, as a parent in my late thirties, my wife and I had to decide how much religion to expose our own daughter to. We finally decided to give her an introduction to Christianity for a few years, as much for socializing with other children as anything else, and then let her decide her future. The thought never crossed our minds to introduce her to other religions because we were cultural Christians; that was the only religion we knew and the most practical one for living in the United States. We began to attend church again, but for me it was also for social reasons because we had recently relocated and didn't know many people in our new town. I always went to church reluctantly, being suspicious of what those people might try to make me believe, or them discovering that I was a skeptic.

By the time Kristin was in high school, she had not only been introduced to Christianity but was completely immersed in it. She served as a leader of a church youth group and sang in the youth choir; she attended a private Christian school where she organized and conducted the chapel sessions; she spent her summers on the staff of a Christian summer camp. To my chagrin, her school taught her that there were dinosaurs on Noah's ark, that the theory of evolution was bunk, and that if she couldn't speak in tongues, she wasn't a "real Christian." She even informed us that she had to get her Christian guidance elsewhere because we weren't spiritual enough.

I still couldn't take church seriously as a route to an anticipated heavenly salvation, but I'd seen her grow into a compassionate and responsible person, with a strong devotion to God. I'd met her teachers, friends, and fellow students, and they were the kind of people we wanted her to associate with, even if some of them had some whacky religious ideas. Instead of thinking we might be largely responsible for her maturing morality, I couldn't help thinking it was mainly due to her association with other Christians. At that time, she was in their company much more than ours.

As I became more curious about what effects Christianity was having on Kristin, my interest in the religion began to seep out of its long dormancy. I had forgotten about the people and dogma that had driven me away years before and wanted to focus more on real world topics such as how to make the best of a stressful life. I wanted to relate to Kristin better since she was a teenager and you know how parents and teens often get along. Instead of just going through the motions of sitting in a pew for an hour each Sunday morning, I decided to give church a thorough evaluation this time around and see what I might have missed in my earlier years. As I was doing that, Kristin went off to a Presbyterian college.

Another thing that caused me to give Christianity a second try was continuing to see people who I judged to be more confident and intelligent than I accept the sin and salvation story. My confusion about why they believed it and I didn't returned. I put my doubts and suspicions aside and decided to learn more about Christianity and its God, this time with the mind of an adult.

If this was all real, I sincerely wanted to feel the presence of Jesus, experience the guidance of the Holy Spirit, and know God on a more personal level. Was God kind and loving like the New Testament God or vindictive, wrathful, and seemingly unpredictable like the Old Testament God? I didn't want to miss out on a life-changing experience just because I was too resistant to it when I was younger. My basic problem was that I could conceive of Jesus in my mind but not in my heart.

The fact that Kristin's commitment to Christ was challenged because she didn't speak in tongues prompted me to wonder what the difference was between a "real Christian" and what I assumed had to be a fake Christian, or an imposter. I wanted to know what the true litmus test was for a Christian and when and how that test was revealed to humankind. Did being a Christian all boil down to the declaration of belief in a god named Jesus and an association with other Christians, or was there more to it than that? This book is as much as anything the result of my quest for that answer. Based on the beliefs and behaviors of historical Christians, I wanted to determine what a real Christian was and how to recognize one when I saw one.

Jane and I joined a home group and really enjoyed the discussions, but although the group was very friendly, we always felt that everything we said was being judged and we couldn't speak honestly with them. We met for years, but I finally had to break my bonds when I became frustrated that I couldn't express my doubts and questions without disapproving stares. One time I mentioned that I was reading a book on universalism since I'd never heard the term used and wanted to learn what it meant. When I told them what I was learning, they obviously disapproved and were concerned, telling me that I might need some counseling to purge that knowledge from my mind. Later I admitted to reading a book about Jesus written by Deepak Chopra to see a different perspective, and I got the same reaction, like how dare I read anything about spirituality other than what was written by approved Christian authors. My breaking point with the group came when I mentioned that the verses about women remaining silent in church in First Corinthians may not have been written by Paul. Even though the commentary in one of our group member's Bible supported me, a major confrontation ensued. I'd had enough, and Jane and I decided to start another home group that would not put any limits on discussions. Judging others was banned in our new group.

The next year, we were asked to join a mission team going to Africa. Once we determined that this team might have some real impact on improving people's physical lives, we became very enthusiastic. Getting involved with the other team members, their weekly prayer meetings, and their occasional overnight prayer retreats took us deeper into Christian life than ever before. We participated in extended prayer sessions rather than just short prayers like we'd recited most of our lives. We laid hands on fellow team members and anointed them with oil to bless and heal them. We learned about spiritual warfare and spiritual mapping; things I'd never even realized existed. The strangest of all our new experiences was witnessing people speaking in tongues. I learned that the practice was common in our church, but only in private gatherings, and I found it very creepy.

A spark was lit. I became very interested in where all these strange traditions originated. I supposed they were from the Bible and began to wonder what else was in there that I wasn't aware of and might be interesting to know. If Christianity had changed since the time of Jesus, as I knew it had, I wanted to know when, why, and how. I'd always loved to study history, and I was curious to know how three hundred years after the Roman army executed Jesus, they would be praying to him as their God and fighting under his banner. I wanted to find out how the so-called Bible Belt of our country, which sounded very Christ-like to me, could be the same region that endorsed slavery, instituted Jim Crow laws, and gave birth to the Ku Klux Klan. I wanted to know the evidence for the existence of heaven and hell. If there was a hell or heaven, where exactly would they be? Our most powerful microscopes and telescopes had so far failed to locate them. I wanted to learn why people believed in the audacious stories in Genesis and if there was any truth to the rumors that Christians caused the fall of the Roman Empire, led Europe into the Dark Ages, or were responsible for the Holocaust.

Of the Ten Commandments, the one which seems of utmost importance to pro-life Christians clearly states, "thou shall not kill." Jesus taught us in the Gospels to love our enemies as well as our neighbors, meaning to love and respect everyone. I wanted to learn how Christian monks become symbolic of medieval European torture chambers, and how they rationalized what they did. The popes, I assumed, were the world's most righteous Christians, but they clearly ignored one of the most important teachings of their faith in ordering the crusades and inquisitions. If Christian crusaders could go off on sprees of mass murder in the name of Jesus, how does that represent Christianity? I really wanted to know how those popes interpreted the scriptures to justify what they were doing. If they could twist scripture to justify whatever they wanted to do, then was there any consistency in Christianity? Were we supposed to follow just those biblical verses that justified our own actions? If we can ignore certain verses, I'd like to know which ones they are.

Over the course of my life, I had sat through maybe a thousand church services. I'd read most of the Bible, served as an acolyte, earned the God and Country Award as a Boy Scout, taken optional adult classes at church, discussed issues with my pastor, and participated in various home groups. I had been a short-term missionary overseas on six occasions, associated almost exclusively with other believers, and prayed regularly. But, in all that exposure to Christianity, I had still never met God, nor had God ever spoken to me. Like most people, I had experienced a sense of awe and wonder when looking at the night sky, a scenic vista, or a newborn baby but had never associated them with a divine being the way I was told to.

I assumed, like most other people, that there must have been at least a creator God. But I racked my brain to understand how that Creator might have been created. If I assumed that everything came from nothing, how could anything, including God, exist at all? This caused me great consternation, and none of my efforts ever helped me get close to answering those kinds of questions. I couldn't find the answers I sought on my own or through church groups, and the only resource I hadn't tapped into was the brilliant minds from the past and present. With the revolution in information, I had Amazon as my bookstore, iTunes as my source for hundreds of podcasts, Netflix for documentary films, and my search engine for articles and blogs about any subject in the universe. I also began to attend lectures and debates to see both sides of a given issue, such as Young Earth Creationism versus Old Earth Creationism or atheism versus belief in God. Little did I know that due to advances in archeology, genetics, linguistics, critical Bible study, and the findings and translations of ancient texts, more was known about the ancient than ever before, and it was all available to anyone who wanted to know.

Not only were there very intelligent people who believe in Christianity, miracles and all, but two billion people around the world identify as Christians. It seemed impossible that so many people could have been deluded into believing something that wasn't true. But why was Christianity any more likely to be true than the many other religions that people have followed passionately? I became obsessed with learning everything I could about the foundation of the religion of my culture. I felt that if I didn't begin to learn these things at that point in my life, I never would, and the idea of never knowing didn't sit well with me.

THE PROJECT

Around 2008, I read the book *Pagan Christianity?: Exploring the Roots of Our Church Practices* by Frank Viola and George Barna, and, for the first time, began to understand Christian traditions from an entirely new perspective. I was shocked by the number of practices that Christianity had taken from paganism, and I began to wonder if that was true for Christian doctrines as well.

In 2010, I devoted myself to a serious study of Christianity and its antecedents, searching for clues to better understand not only Christian origins but also how its doctrines have affected people, not just spiritually, but psychologically and sociologically. I studied writings from everyone I could find, from hard-core fundamental apologists to freethinkers and atheists. I wanted to hear everyone's opinion before I made up my mind about what to believe.

I decided to press the reset button and flush all the knowledge I had learned from the Bible and my religious experiences out of my mind. I wanted to relearn Christianity with a completely clean slate. In rebuilding my knowledge of the religion, I still planned to use the Bible, but only as one of many resources.

One thing that really struck me when I began this project was how little I knew about the history of Christianity. Like most other Christians in the US, I was led to believe that the Bible was an accurate, historical document. Through my church, the only history that seemed to matter was what happened thousands of years ago in Palestine and how the good news of Jesus radiated out from its place of origin. In grade school and high school, I learned of the Crusades, the Reformation, the Dark Ages, and the Renaissance. But what of the period from AD 60, roughly when the book of Acts seems to end, to the First Crusade in AD 1095? That was a thousand-year period that I knew almost nothing about, except for vaguely remembering someone named Constantine becoming the first Christian Roman emperor and monks building monasteries and copying scripture by candlelight. From the Crusades to the Protestant Reformation was another period of several centuries about which I knew almost nothing. Finally, from the Reformation to the twentieth century was a four-hundred-year gap in my knowledge. Yet, I absolutely loved studying history, and if

I knew so little about Christian history, what did that say about other Christians? What information were we missing that would be valuable for us to know?

The only way for me to find the answers I sought was to break this extremely complex history down into small pieces and learn what I could from each piece individually. Then I could link pieces and events together into trends. The process was like solving an eight-thousand-piece jigsaw puzzle without the final picture of how it would look, where one piece tells you almost nothing, but by fitting the pieces together, they form recognizable patterns, and then those patterns begin to reveal previously unassociated information.

I wanted to dig into the bedrock of Christianity—not just back to the Hebrew Bible (the Christian Old Testament) but even further, to the roots of those Old Testament writings in the religions and cultures that preceded the Hebrews. Who were the writers of pre-Hebrew texts, and why do we assume they knew more about God than anyone else? If they were "inspired" prophets or mystics, I wanted to know what the term *inspired* really meant. I wanted to learn if they had made up their stories, took them from ancient mythology, or received direct messages from God. I wanted to know their true agendas. I didn't know if I could ever learn the answers to my questions, but I was sure going to try.

With a timeline format in mind, I first searched for existing timelines of important events in Christian history. That was a start, but the skeletal information, obvious biases, generalities, unexplained terms, and lack of reference material left me unsatisfied. I decided to compose my own timeline that would hopefully be more useful to me. I originally didn't expect it to be very long, and when it reached about twenty pages, I thought I was doing well. By putting events in chronological order, I'd already made progress toward my goal of relating events in Christian history to one another. As I became absorbed in my research, my timeline grew in complexity. Then my progressive Christian home group decided to study the first thousand years of Christianity over the course of a year. In conjunction with a DVD series, I filled in what I thought were the important events the documentary left out. Even to the most well-churched and history-loving members of our group, most of what I related to them was new and often astonishing. Their enthusiasm inspired me to keep researching, and my page count kept increasing. I decided not only to jot down brief facts, like other time-lines I'd seen, but to give at least some background or context and offer some human interest when I could.

First, I had to decide what were the truly significant events in Christian history. I couldn't do that on my own, so I had to turn to many reliable sources such as other timelines. I didn't want to leave out any pivotal events. If I found something questionable as to its his-toric probability, I searched through multiple sources to confirm it. After that, if the entry was still questionable, I either stated the con-troversy in the timeline or deleted the entry.

The wonderful thing about history is, like science, findings are always open to revision when someone discovers new evidence and modifies or disproves an accepted hypothesis. Every fragment of pa-pyrus unearthed by archeologists, every archaic writing translated by linguists, and every new theory about the history of Christianity or the historical Jesus must be evaluated by projecting it onto the back-drop of past findings to see what overlaps or what extends beyond the former limits of accepted knowledge.

Most of the events I recorded were the consequence of decisions made by influential leaders who were invested in their positions and represented Christian populations. It was very difficult to find stories about individual Christians unless they were victims of the Church. The first problem was that common Christian folk didn't leave many historical records because before the nineteenth century, most of them were illiterate. The second problem was that it was relatively easy to discern the motivation of powerful people, but not so much for the average Christian. For example, how could I recognize the true moti-vation for a Christian woman who started an orphanage for poor chil-dren? Unless she specifically mentioned that she helped others out of a compassion inspired by the teachings of Jesus or for the glory of God, it's hard to discern whether her motivation came from her religion. Secular humanists are also compassionate people, but they aren't mo-tivated by religion. Instead, they are motivated by instinct. Some peo-ple just want to help others. It happened everywhere in every culture, religion, and era.

My point is that it is much easier to determine what motivated someone like Constantine the Great, Augustine of Hippo, Emperor Theodosius I, or Pope Gregory I—all of whom dramatically changed Christian history—than what motivated the average person raised in a Christian culture. Also, the history of Christianity as recorded is primarily the history of one victorious sect and how they justified their superiority over other sects they perceived as competitors. Bottom line, the average Christian wrote their stories in deeds, not words, so are mostly unremembered.

CONSIDERATIONS AND INCLUSIONS

Often, especially in the distant past, no one knows exactly which year an event occurred. In those cases, I did my best to make an educated guess and entered *c.* (circa) before the entry to indicate that it is an approximate date.

All the dates in the Old Testament era and many in the first millennium of Christianity are best estimates by historians. Archeologists and scholars of antiquity have confirmed very few Old Testament events before the Assyrian and Babylonian conquests of Judah and Israel, beginning around 700 BC. Before that time, biblical characters, places, and events are almost entirely based on unconfirmed traditions that were included in the Hebrew Bible, and sometimes even based on pre-Jewish myths and fables.

The Jewish people are prominently mentioned in the timeline because there is no way to honestly portray the history of Christianity without also telling the story of its parent religion, Judaism. The histories of Christians and Jews since the time of Jesus have been intertwined like twin strands of DNA and seemingly impossible to separate.

My timeline also includes a significant amount about Christianity's sister religion, Islam. This is because I want to shed light on the complicated past relations and competition between these two groups and, hopefully, provide a better understanding of each based on their history, not just on current animosities and assumptions. Current relations between the two cultures are the culmination of a long history of adverse and sometimes cooperative interrelationships.

In the early chapters, I mention non-Christian gods. This may seem strange in a book about Christianity, but there are a surprising number of similarities between those gods and Jesus Christ. Most of those resemblances are still open to debate, but I suspect that at least some of the oral and literary characteristics of Jesus may have been influenced by those older gods. In the days of Jesus, having certain specific attributes, such as a resurrection or a virgin birth, seemed to be prerequisites for divinity. The Gospel writers may have incorporated previous god legends into their writings to better understand and glorify Jesus.

As far as my featuring empires, it's important to recognize that the Roman Empire after AD 381 (also known as the Byzantine Empire, which overlapped and outlived the western Roman Empire until AD 1453) and the Holy Roman Empire (which lasted from AD 800 to around AD 1800) were thoroughly Christian empires. Their leaders ruled and administered those empires based on their interpretation of Christian scriptures and doctrines. Those empires were experiments in Christian theocracy, demonstrating what Christians, given absolute power over society, government, and territory, would do with that power.

Although Christianity didn't begin in Europe, the story of European Christianity is in many ways the story of world Christianity. Since the fifteenth century, European Christian nations have influenced every part of the world through trade, colonialism, wars, and missionary efforts. The Age of Discovery was extremely important to the spread of Christianity because the explorations were undertaken by Christian countries with the goal of conversion. Admittedly, this exploration was not usually carried out in the name of Christianity, but it was often combined with a public commitment to Christianize the world, and colonists and missionaries always followed in the wake of the explorers.

I didn't sugarcoat how Christians or Christian countries acted toward others. For instance, American slavery was both defended and condemned based on selected passages from the Bible, making it a very Christian issue to me. I bring up many social issues for two reasons. The first is because I wanted to determine who took the lead in pioneering humanitarian care to the average person and because much of the divisiveness in our country today is the result of a clash of moral values, exemplified in these social issues.

I also included much information about militarism in the Roman, Byzantine, Holy Roman, and Islamic empires. These may not seem like landmarks in Christian history, but they all are relevant in understanding the full context in which Christian history unfolded, how the religion became militant, and where that militarism has led it.

I often mentioned the extraordinary events in the geographical region known as Palestine (basically the same region as modern-day Israel) because of its geographical position at the crossroads between Asia, Africa, and Europe, the only three continents known until around AD 1500. Many ancient Christian scholars considered Jerusalem the true center of the world because of its geographical location as the hub of the three continents and the concept of a flat earth. Understanding Palestine and the Middle East helps immensely to understand and sympathize with the people who lived there in the past and who live there now. Not only were they the victims of endless invasions, but they were the recipients of many new ideas and innovations from other cultures. The dynamic region was the birthplace of Judaism and Christianity and, indirectly, Islam. I also included Jerusalem, Rome, Constantinople, Alexandria, and Antioch whenever I saw something significant happening in those cities because they were the five holy cities of Christianity, the five patriarchates, and because what happened in those cities was fundamental to the development of this originally urban religion.

The term *Christian* will be used often, and I want to distinguish between types of Christians in the United States today. When I use the term *evangelicals,* I mean the 25 percent of mainly white, Christian Americans who basically believe the Bible is inerrant and contains all the truth we need to live by. I might also occasionally refer to them as conservative Christians because of their rejection of modernism, science, and critical analysis of the Bible. When I use the terms mainstream or progressive, I'm referring to the more liberal Christians who do not take the Bible literally but put more emphasis on emulating Jesus. I know these terms are confusing, and we may not all completely

agree on them, but I had to distinguish between these two current theologies. There is another major group of American Christians, and this
is the African American churches. I refer to them occasionally also.

I will mention scientific advancements a lot because I found it interesting to see how conservative Christians reacted to scientific progress (i.e., understanding and applying reality to the physical world) and
to learn how and why Christian leaders shut down the study of science
during most of its history. I also mentioned some examples of evolutionary evidence that are difficult to refute.

In this book, the dates remain based on the present BC/AD dating
in which Jesus was born in the year AD 1, although it is most likely he
was really born around 5 BC.

Whenever I quote from the Bible, I'll be using the Life Application
Bible-New International Version.

THE GOALS OF MY SEARCH

To be clear, these are my intentions:

1. To trace the evolution of Christianity from its roots to
    the present day. This will encompass the predecessors,
    origins, and refinements of Christianity's traditions, doc-
    trines, and political influence.
2. To try my best to determine what a "real Christian" is and
    if Christians are primarily known by the love and forgive-
    ness they show each other and their neighbors, as I'd been
    taught.
3. To trace the behavior of selected empires that professed
    Christianity as their imperial religion and see how they
    compared to other empires of their times.
4. To trace Christianity in the United States and try to
    determine if this is a "Christian nation" like so many
    evangelical Protestants say it is.
5. To determine if the world is a better or worse place
    because of the existence of Christianity.

This book has the potential to offend almost everyone in one way or another but I'm just attempting to honestly study history and then draw my own conclusions. Those who take the Bible literally will see that I don't. Very patriotic Christians, who may think the United States can do no wrong, may not like that I point out not just the good that our country has accomplished but also the cruelty that many of its leaders and their followers have inflicted on others. Agnostics, atheists, other non-Christians, maybe even some progressive Christians, may see my interpretation of events as not going far enough to condemn the hypocrisy and savagery that they believe characterize Christianity. True historians may grumble that I don't have an advanced degree in their field, don't use the right terminology, don't focus on the same events they would, or don't interpret events as they would. There certainly are many different ways to interpret the same events, and I am just an amateur historian. I study history as a hobby because it fascinates me, and I want to learn from it.

I see myself in the role of what's been called "Napoleon's idiot." Before a campaign or battle, French general Napoleon Bonaparte would run his plans past an average man, someone who saw things from outside the box, to see if Napoleon's plans made sense to him. This person wasn't an actual idiot, of course, but someone unacquainted with military logistics and warfare. He was an outsider. That's the role I see myself in since I'm not a trained theologian, historian, sociologist, or mental health professional.

More than any other motive, I want to present little-known but what appear to me significant historical facts and make them accessible to anyone who is interested. I think it's the responsibility of any religious person to know their religion thoroughly, warts and all, and I want Christians to have another source of information other than the echo chambers of many churches and websites. Progress and growth come through dissatisfaction with what has been tried in the past and found to have failed. People need to know what failed and why.

I suppose my true motivation is to make some effort to nudge Christianity back on the course that I originally saw it on when I was young. I may not make much of a difference, but I want to try because much of today's Christianity, especially in the United States, has become too unloving for me.

This complex religion has brought us magnificent, other-worldly cathedrals; many of the world's most treasured works of art and music; and many millions of compassionate believers inspired by the love and compassion of the Jesus they found in the Gospels. But history reminds us that Christians also introduced the horrors of inquisitions, the savagery of crusades, and a two-thousand-year-long persecution of the Jewish people and many other groups.

CHAPTER 0: THE BC ERA

In the beginning, God created the heavens and the earth. Now the earth was formless and empty, darkness was over the surface of the deep, and the Spirit of God was hovering over the waters.

—Genesis 1:1:2

If the gods listened to the prayers of men, all humankind would quickly perish since they constantly pray for many evils to befall one another.

—Epicurus

This chapter sets stage for Christianity, focusing on pre-Jewish civilizations and Jewish traditions and culture out of which Christianity was eventually born. It shows that Jesus was not as unique as we might believe but shared many characteristics with other miracle workers, itinerant preachers, prophets, and even gods of ancient Europe and Asia. It introduces the strategic and tumultuous region of the Levant, which included the land of Palestine, in order to understand its importance in the origination of three major world religions: Judaism, Christianity, and Islam. The chapter also discusses the main events of the Old Testament and shows where they supposedly fit into the historical chronology.

30000

c. Eurasian Paleolithic cave art shows evidence of shamanism, the world's first religion. It was practiced in different forms predating the entry of humans into the Americas. Shamanism involves a practitioner or shaman who interacts with the spirit world, usually in an altered state of consciousness. The name is based on a Siberian word *saman*, meaning "one who knows." Hunter-gatherer societies believed in a three-tiered cosmos—an upper spirit world and middle and lower worlds of material beings.

5000

c. There is geological evidence that catastrophic floods occurred around this time in the region of the Black Sea due to melting of glacial ice and rising sea levels. A former shoreline has since been discovered approximately four hundred feet below today's current water level. There is a high probability that this was the flood that inspired the story of Noah and the great flood.

4004

This was the year that Irish Bishop James Ussher, in 1650, calculated for the creation of the universe, Earth, and life on Earth—October 23 to be exact. He studied the Bible extensively for clues and calculated the date based on Old Testament stories that he considered historically accurate. This date is still trusted by those living today who believe in Young Earth Creationism. There is tremendous controversy with his calculations because with modern scientific discoveries, Bishop Ussher's date must be revised. The overwhelming majority of scientists now believe that the universe has existed for approximately 13.7 billion years, Earth for 4.5 billion years, and life on Earth for 3.8 billion years. The first anatomically modern humans lived around two hundred thousand years ago, and our species, *Homo sapiens*, probably emerged from sub-Saharan Africa only in the last hundred thousand years to spread throughout the world.

4000

c. By biblical dating, meaning based on the timeline of events that Bishop Ussher derived from the Old Testament, the Fall of man and the expulsion from the Garden of Eden would have occurred at this time.

3500

c. The Sumerians are the earliest known civilization in Mesopotamia. In modern times, this is southern Iraq and is regarded as the "cradle of civilization." The Sumerians began to worship the goddess Inanna. In later cultures of that region, such as Babylon, Akkad, and Assyria, Inanna was known as Ishtar. According to mythology, three days after she was killed, she was brought back from the underworld. This may have been the earliest surviving record of a god who died and was resurrected. The idea of ancient gods being resurrected was believed to be derived from interpretations of the natural world and the cosmos, where ancient observers noticed the "death" of the sun, moon, planets, constellations, and vegetative life, followed by endless cycles of renewal.

3100

c. The Egyptians began to worship Horus, the son of Isis and Osiris. They believed Horus to have been born of a virgin mother. His mother, Isis, was said to have resurrected her husband Osiris before producing Horus. Celestial numbers derived from studying the cosmos played into his life as they later would with Jesus. At age twelve, he was believed to have taught at a temple, and then at age thirty, he was consecrated without any accounting of the intervening years. He was also said to have had twelve followers, as ancient sun gods usually did. It may not be just coincidence that there are twelve lunar cycles a year, each around thirty days. Also, the earth takes around 360 days to make a revolution of the sun through twelve zodiac quadrants of thirty degrees each. There were many primitive cultures trying to make sense of the cosmos and attributed its characteristics to their gods. One other interesting note is that Isis and Horus were often pictured as mother and infant son, just as images of Mary and baby Jesus would later be depicted.

3000

c. Archeological evidence shows that there was human settlement at the site of present-day Jerusalem by this time.

c. The Sumerians produced the first written clay tablets, and their cuneiform script was later adopted by the Babylonians and Assyrians. Some of these early writings show an obsession with the heavens, describing the movements of the sun, moon, and planets, all associated with messages from the gods to shape their behaviors.

2780

c. The Egyptians introduced a twelve-month annual calendar based on the twelve lunar cycles each year. Other ancient cultures, such as the Babylonians and Chinese, also devised twelve-month calendars.

2560

c. The Egyptians constructed the first of the pyramids of Giza near what would become Cairo. They are a symbol of the advanced civilization in Egypt at the time. Many Jewish traditions can be traced back to that culture, which is not surprising considering there are only 263 miles separating Jerusalem and Cairo, about as far as Boston is from Philadelphia.

2400

c. Sargon of Akkad was the first ruler of the Akkadian Empire (Assyria and Babylon), which stretched through modern-day Iraq. He instituted a seven-day week, presumably based on the number of observable celestial bodies: the sun, moon, Mars, Mercury, Jupiter, Venus, and Saturn. His birth legend told that he was put adrift on a river in a basket made of rushes, previewing the story of Moses in the book of Exodus.

2348

c. By Biblical dating, this was when the worldwide flood of Genesis would have occurred. An interesting fact is that at that time, there were only about a hundred species of animals known to Middle Easterners, so it was conceivable to them that all those animals could fit on one enormous boat. These days we know of more than a million species across the seven continents that would have needed an ark ride to survive this magnitude of flood. That, and other evidence, such as the implausibility of a worldwide flood in the first place, make the story appear mythical.

2300

c. The Egyptians began to write the *Pyramid Texts* on the walls of sarcophagi, or stone coffins, placed in Egyptian pyramids. The texts mention Atum, one of the most important deities of that era. The Biblical Adam could have stemmed from Atum. Atum was the first god to arrive on Earth, both he and Adam were naked, and like Adam, Atum's wife was said to have been extracted from him. The texts also contained a collection of incantations to help a pharaoh's soul merge with his mummy in order to be reborn.

2200

c. The Adam and Eve cylinder seal dates from this time. It is a Sumerian stone cylinder depicting two people, a serpent, and a tree. At first thought to be a scene from the Garden of Eden, it is now believed to be a scene of worship with the serpent serving as a symbol of fertility.

2100

c. The Sumerians wrote the *Code of Ur-Nammu*, the oldest surviving code of law. It was written in the Sumerian language and wasn't translated until 1952. Like the later Babylonian *Code of Hammurabi*, it was probably a forerunner to Judaic Law. It included a version of the Ten Commandments, not dictated by a god, but by the government.

c. By biblical dating, this was the era in which the Tower of Babel was built by descendants of the worldwide flood's survivors. It was a story of the origin of the world's languages and a warning for humans not to try to become like gods.

2080

c. By biblical dating, Abraham would have led Semitic nomads from Sumer, in Mesopotamia, to Canaan, in present-day Israel, and become the patriarch of the Hebrews. An interesting bit of trivia is that circumcision was already being practiced in Canaan and Egypt before Abraham arrived, demonstrating that it was not a Jewish invention.

2060

c. By biblical dating, the destruction of Sodom and Gomorrah occurred at this time. The location of these towns is uncertain, but the legend seems to point to a volcanic eruption. One theory is that the story originated in southern Syria, where towns were found to have been destroyed by a volcanic eruption around 3000 BC.

2000

c. The Mesopotamians produced the earliest surviving great work of literature, the *Epic of Gilgamesh*. Like other writings of this time and place, it was carved into clay tablets. It mentions several stories that parallel and predate Jewish ones, such as a garden similar to Eden, a worldwide flood, and a story similar to Samson and Delilah.

1950

c. The Babylonians began to write the *Enuma Anu Enlil*. It is a collection of supposedly supernatural omens and their earthly consequences, such as lunar eclipses foretelling the death of a king.

1934

c. The *Code of Lipit-Ishtar* was written in Sumer, dealing with civil issues such as personal rights, marriages, successions, penalties, property, and contracts. It is one of the earliest surviving legal documents.

1900

c. The Babylonians began to produce the *Enuma Elis*, their creation myth. There is strong evidence that the Genesis creation story was significantly inspired by this work, as possibly were the creation stories of Egypt, Phoenicia, and India. Creation myths confirm that people of the Paleolithic and Neolithic periods saw events on Earth and in the sky intertwined, where humans and animals could ascend to the sky or heavenly bodies could interact with earthly creatures. By interpreting signs from the cosmos correctly and carrying out the appropriate rituals, priests could help their communities avoid dire consequences. Since signs in the sky could be witnessed by all, they were thought to address the fate of the entire community, its harvest, wars, and politics.

1875

c. By biblical dating, the sons of Jacob would have settled in Egypt, where their brother Joseph was portrayed as one of the most influential people in the empire.

1800

Canaanites, from the region of Palestine, appeared in Egypt and established themselves in the eastern Nile Delta.

1750

Hammurabi was the King of Babylon. Under his rule, the Babylonians wrote his book of laws, called the *Code of Hammurabi*. It contained groups of laws with scaled punishments. Like the *Code of Lipit-Ishtar* (see 1934 BC), it appears to be the source for other Near Eastern codes of law, including the Torah, the first five books of the Hebrew Bible. It is one of the earliest decipherable writings of significant length to be discovered.

1700

c. The Greeks formulated their mythology. They considered Zeus the supreme god and Perseus as the son of Zeus and the human virgin Danae. The Perseus story was similar to that of Jesus in that they were born to virgins to reconcile people to a god because they had drifted away from him. Another Greek god, Asclepius, the god of medicine, was also born of a human (Koronis) and a god (Apollo). Heracles was Perseus's great-grandson, and his legend is thought to predate that of Samson in the Hebrew Bible. Like folk heroes in other ancient cultures, both he and Samson were superhuman; both had unnatural strength, wrestled lions, were in some way associated with haircuts, and died violently and partly voluntarily.

1650

The Hyksos, a Semitic tribe from the north, invaded Egypt. The Hyksos introduced the horse, chariot, and other innovations and established Egypt's Fifteenth Dynasty. The Hyksos may have been the predecessors of the Jews.

1626

c. The oldest known copy of the Sumerian *Atra-Hasis* tablets were written at this time. They included a creation myth, a rebellion against a god, and a flood account similar to the one depicted in the Hebrew

Bible. In this epic, Atra-Hasis was a Noah-like character. Most of these tablets were only discovered in 1965.

1600

c. The Greek island of Santorini blew apart in a devastating volcanic explosion, and the effects would have been experienced in Palestine and Egypt. Even though the events were not chronologically concurrent, the explosion may have inspired the catastrophic plagues represented in the Book of Exodus, as well as the legend of Atlantis.

1550

c. The Egyptians drove the Hyksos out of Egypt. Josephus, the first century AD Jewish historian, wrote that the Hyksos first entered Syria and then detoured to Judea, founding, or at least settling, at the site of Jerusalem. This could well be the basis for the story of Moses and the migration of the Israelites out of Egypt, which appears in the book of Exodus. It seems to have been passed on as oral history for as long as a thousand years before being written down, so the story would have evolved significantly and clouded the original events.

c. The Egyptians were using the *Book of the Dead*. The description of the Egyptian creation story closely parallels the one in Genesis. One of the consistent themes in the book is that every act of creation involved an expression of words, such as was the case in the book of Genesis with God speaking words and triggering life into existence, or in the beginning of the Gospel of John, where Jesus is said to be the Word of God. The *Book of the Dead* also mentions a final judgment at the end of life. The book included ways to help people weigh their hearts to see if they deserved to enter heaven. The Egyptians may have been the first culture to see a divine realm in the sky as the ultimate destination for righteous souls.

1500

c. The Sumerians produced their *Farmer's Almanac*, and it was not discovered by archeologists until 1949. This, along with the Egyptian *Instruction of Amenhotep*, are the first known writings to discuss ethics for commoners. Both advised farmers to show compassion by setting aside a portion of their harvest for the poor and said their gods would favor them for this action. This was a turning point in literary history because past literature almost exclusively celebrated the ethics of valor, the military success of heroes, and gods as entities to be feared because of their unpredictability.

c. The Greeks began to worship Dionysus, the god of the grape harvest, later known by the Romans as Bacchus. There were many similarities between Dionysus and Jesus in the legends of their lives, deaths, and returns to life.

1458

In the Battle of Megiddo, Egyptian forces under Pharaoh Thutmose III defeated a large Canaanite coalition under the king of Kadesh. The Greek word *Armageddon* comes from the Hebrew name Har-Megiddo, meaning Mount of Megiddo.

1450

c. According to biblical dating, the Exodus of the Israelites from Egypt would have begun at this time. To date, there has been no archaeological confirmation that any large group of people lived in the Sinai Desert for forty years at this, or any, time.

1406

c. According to biblical dating, Moses died, and the Israelites crossed the Jordan River into Canaan. If the Hyksos people mentioned in 1550 were the historical Israelites, this 150-year gap in dating could be explained by the lack of accurate historical knowledge of the Bible writers, who lived many centuries after this event.

1336

c. Pharaoh Amenhotep IV of Egypt died. He had abandoned ancient Egyptian polytheism and introduced the worship of Aten, in a religion called Akhenaten. This was perhaps the first example in history of a civilization worshipping a single god. After Amenhotep died, Egypt reverted to its polytheistic roots, but monotheism would make a comeback in the neighboring land of Israel centuries later.

1250

c. The cult of Attis began in Phrygia, modern-day Turkey. Attis was said to be a god who died and was resurrected. His mother was Cybele, an archetype of the Christian Virgin Mary. Attis and Cybele were worshipped on the Vatican Hill outside of Rome before Christian times.

c. A Middle Eastern tribe known as Israelites worshipped celestial bodies, with Yahweh as their chief god, possibly a sun god, and his wife Asherah, associated with Venus.

1208

c. The Egyptians created the Merneptah Stele in Thebes, Egypt, providing the first known mention of a nation called Israel. Archeologists and historians theorize that around this time the Israelite tribes coalesced into a culture in present-day Palestine.

1200

c. The Philistines were among the "sea peoples" who migrated from the Aegean Sea to the coast of Canaan or Palestine.

1100

c. According to biblical dating, Samson would have lived at this time. Interestingly, he was one of the first recorded suicide killers.

1050

c. By biblical dating, the Philistines defeated the Israelites and captured the Ark of the Covenant, the container with the two stone tablets on which the Ten Commandments were engraved.

1043

c. By biblical dating, Saul became the first king of Judah.

1012

c. According to biblical history, Ish-bosheth (or Eshbaal), one of the Saul's sons, became the second king of Israel after his father and his brothers died at the Battle of Mount Gilboa.

1010

c. According to biblical history, David became the third king of Israel. He captured Jerusalem about three years later and made it his capital. David is the first person mentioned in the Bible for whom there is external archaeological evidence.

1000

c. Persians began collecting the skeletal remains of the departed and placing them in stone boxes, known as ossuaries. This was continued by the Jewish people in the form of separate boxes for the bones of each individual. This practice has evolved to the point where many Catholic and Eastern Orthodox sites contain the bones of thousands of people, intermingled, stacked, and even used to create artistic displays.

970

c. According to biblical dating, Solomon succeeded David as king, and a few years later, he began to build the first Temple in Jerusalem.

c. By biblical dating, the Queen of Sheba, or Saba, of southwestern Arabia or Yemen, journeyed to visit King Solomon in Judah. Ethiopian tradition traces its Jewish heritage back to her son, Menilek I.

957

c. The first Jewish Temple was completed on Mount Moriah in Jerusalem.

930

King Solomon died and the kingdom of Israel was divided. Israel, in the north, held ten of the original twelve tribes and had its capital in Samaria. Judah, in the south, consisted of two tribes and established its capital in Jerusalem.

c. The Egyptians, under Pharaoh Sheshonk I, captured and sacked Jerusalem. The city was destined to be captured and heavily damaged two more times in a little over a century.

853

The combined forces of King Ahab of Israel and Hadadezer of Damascus fought the invading Assyrian army of Shalmaneser III at the Battle of Qarqar. The outcome is unknown, most likely indecisive, but it was a preview of things to come as the Assyrians sought to expand their empire westward.

850

c. An allied army of Philistines, Arabs, and Ethiopians sacked Jerusalem and looted King Jehoram's palace.

830

Hazeael, the king of Damascus, conquered most of Palestine.

786

King Joash's army of Israel sacked Jerusalem, taking King Amaziah prisoner.

753

c. The inhabitants of central Italy founded Rome about this time. Romulus was the legendary founder and first king of Rome, considered by the Romans to be the son of God. They believed that he was born to a virgin, was killed by corrupt leaders, then appeared after his resurrection and ascended into heaven.

722

After conquering Damascus twelve years earlier, Assyria conquered Israel and took much of the population into exile. The southern kingdom of Judah was allied with Assyria at this time, so they were not affected. This exile was the beginning of the first diaspora, or dispersion of the Jews, whose people became known as the "ten lost tribes of Israel."

701

Assyrian forces attacked Judah and the important city of Lachish. Refugees fled to Jerusalem, the region's main economic center.

700

c. Homer, the Greek author, was credited with writing *The Iliad* and *The Odyssey*. Some of the stories in *The Odyssey* were similar to those told by biblical authors, including the author of the Gospel of Mark. The main characters, Odysseus and Jesus, both suffered greatly, both were carpenters, and both had inept companions of questionable faith. Anyone who read or wrote in Greek at the time the Gospels were written in first century AD would have been very familiar with the writing of Homer, since the biblical Gospels were also written in Greek.

689

Archeologists are not certain when the enormous Babylonian ziggurat Etemenanki was built, but it was destroyed this year by Neo-Assyrian King Sennacherib. The Hebrew Bible's depiction of the Tower of Babel may have originated with this event.

650

c. What is believed to be the earliest book in the Old Testament, the book of Job, was written. The book was based on millennia-old legends and dealt with God's justice and human suffering. In the book, Satan (Hebrew for *adversary* or *accuser)* acted in cooperation with God, not as any embodiment of evil. The story was said to take place in the "land of Uz," which is sometimes identified with Edom, or northern Arabia, so scholars think it suggests an earlier source from that region.

c. The religion of Jainism may have originated at this time in the Ganges basin of Eastern India. Like Buddhism, Jainism renounced the physical world and promoted asceticism as the way to spiritual enlightenment through one's own efforts.

639

Josiah became the king of Judah. This was considered a bright age in the history of the Jews because of Josiah's true devotion to his god.

622

During Josiah's reign, the Temple in Jerusalem was cleaned and repaired. The *Book of Law,* most likely what is now known as the Deuteronomic writings, was said to have been discovered in the

Temple. This was one of the four strains of writing interwoven to create the Torah, also referred to as the books of Moses. This discovery
of the *Book of Law* is controversial because the documents may have
been written at this time and said to have been "discovered" because
the older they were made to appear, the more authority they would
carry.

612

Allied Persian and Babylonian armies invaded Assyria and sacked
its capital, Nineveh. They completed their conquest of the Assyrian
Empire a decade later. The Assyrian Empire had lasted almost two
thousand years and was well-known for inflicting horrendous brutality on the people they conquered.

609

King Josiah died in battle against the Egyptians at Megiddo when he
and his army tried to block the Egyptians' route to Mesopotamia.
With his death, Judah became part of the empire of the Twenty-Sixth
Dynasty of Egypt.

605

Babylonian forces under Prince Nebuchadnezzar II defeated the
Egyptians in Syria. They then besieged Jerusalem, forcing Judah's king
Jehoiakim to pay a tribute.

600

c. The Israelites discontinued the practice of human sacrifice. Child
sacrifice was mentioned in the book of Genesis with Abraham and
Isaac and in the books of Micah and Isaiah. It may not have been a
common practice, but it was part of the culture until it was forbidden.

c. Aesop's fables were collected and written down for the first time.
The story collection is credited to Aesop, a Greek storyteller, who lived

possibly as early as 1500 BC. The fables were originally transmitted orally and meant to instruct adults in religious, social, and political themes, but later they evolved into guides for the moral education of children. There are many similarities between these fables and morality stories in the Old Testament, especially the book of Proverbs.

c. The religion of Zoroastrianism took root in Persia at this time or maybe even centuries earlier. It was a monotheistic religion based on the teachings of the prophet Zoroaster. It included themes of messianism, the Golden Rule, heaven and a fiery hell, angels and demons, an eschatological end-times war between good and evil, resurrection of the dead, an evil anti-God, and a virgin-born future savior. This religion would greatly influence Judaism when the Jews became captives of the Babylonians and later the Persians. From Judaism, most of these concepts would find their way into Christianity and Islam.

After Jehoiakim stopped paying tribute to the Babylonians, they invaded Judah and captured Jerusalem, replacing Jehoiakim with King Zedekiah.

587

Zedekiah, the king of Judah installed by Nebuchadnezzar II, revolted against the Babylonians by entering an alliance with Pharaoh Hophra of Egypt. Nebuchadnezzar's army returned to Judah, defeated the Egyptians, and besieged and vandalized Jerusalem and its temple. Judah became a Babylonian province, and the Babylonians took between eight thousand and ten thousand high officials, military commanders, priests, and other members of the Jewish upper class back to Babylon. This initiated what is known as the "Babylonian captivity," which would last for almost seventy years.

c. The Babylonian captivity is believed to have been the time when the Priestly writers, known to modern scholars as the P writers, created the Torah as it exists today by combining their P writings with the contemporary Yahweh or J documents, which refer to God as Yahweh; the Elohim (E) writings, most likely from around the eighth century BC, which refer to God only as Elohim; and the Deuteronomic (D) writings from the time of Josiah. The Priestly writers would have been the elites who controlled the Temple. There is also evidence that during this time, the Jews, believing that God was punishing them for not being faithful to him, destroyed their idols and became, for the first time, truly monotheistic.

585

The philosopher-scientist Thales, of Asia Minor, was said to have predicted an eclipse of the sun. Whether he did or not, by around 460 BC, Anaxagoras successfully predicted a solar eclipse. They and other Greek naturalists detected an underlying order in the cosmos that could be used to predict future natural events. This accurate prediction of the eclipse reinforced the belief that gods did not interfere in the workings of the cosmos and world. Observation and reason were the keys to the amazing scientific advancements the Greeks were beginning to make.

560

c. The Babylonians recognized the seven-day week. The Jewish people who were captives at that time adopted the tradition. Later it would spread to the Greeks and Romans. As mentioned, the days were named after the seven observable celestial bodies. Later, in English, Sunday continued as the day of the sun and Monday as the day of the moon, but Tuesday would be named after the Anglo-Saxon god Tiu, Wednesday for the Norse god Odin, Thursday for the Norse god Thor, Friday for Odin's wife Freya, and Saturday would continue to be the day of Saturn.

539

Persian king Cyrus the Great conquered Babylon. Soon after, he allowed the Jewish people to return to their homeland, but he continued to rule Judah as a vassal state. The Persians were reportedly sympathetic to the Jews because their religions were compatible. When the

Jews returned to Israel, it's probable that most of the descendants of the original Jewish exiles remained behind in Persia.

c. Jews of Judah recognized Yahweh as the creator of the universe and the only god that should be worshipped. This god was outside of time and space and no longer bound by physical rules or limits, unlike previous chief gods like Zeus, who faced limits to his actions because of the restraints imposed on him by other gods. This monotheistic sect came to control Judaean religion and assembled and edited the documents that became the Hebrew Bible.

538

c. Buddhism may have entered Japan as early as this time. It wouldn't be until the nineteenth century AD that Shintoism would evolve as a separate polytheistic religion incorporating elements of Buddhism, Confucianism, and Taoism.

535

c. Since Cyrus didn't allow the Jews to have a king, priests ruled in Palestine, and the Sadducee party that supervised the Temple emerged as the party of the elites.

525

Persia conquered Egypt, and the emperor, Darius, claimed the title of Pharaoh of Egypt.

521

Darius, the new Persian emperor, facilitated the rebuilding of the Jewish Temple. The work had begun under Cyrus the Great but had been halted briefly by non-Jewish inhabitants who had remained in Jerusalem during the exile. The restoration replaced Solomon's Temple, which had been destroyed by the Babylonians in 586 BC. The new Temple was completed in 516.

500

c. The Babylonians invented the zodiac, a belt surrounding Earth, composed of imaginary creatures dictated by the positions and patterns of stars, what we today call constellations. This was the path that the sun, moon, and planets traveled through and was divided into twelve equal segments of thirty degrees. The zodiac figures gained widespread usage by cultures from Egypt to India, spawning multitudes of myths with the constellations coming alive and playing the central figures. The heavens were so prominent in the lives of ancient people that all twenty-four of the brightest stars, and many of the constellations, were referenced in the Bible.

c. About this time, the Greeks recognized the importance of freedom of speech as a better way to solve conflicts than war.

c. Some Greek scientists began to understand that thunder and lightning were the results of air masses colliding, not dire warnings or threats from gods. They were just another predictable cycles of nature that had an explainable cause.

c. The Song of Songs, later known as the Song of Solomon, was compiled. It was a book unlike any other in the Jewish scriptures since it is a collection of love poems from earlier centuries. It was written in Aramaic, which had recently been replacing Hebrew as the spoken language of the Jews during and after the Babylonian exile. It unlikely had anything to do with Solomon.

480

c. The Eleusinian Mysteries were the earliest mystery cult. Mystery cults would last for over a millennium in the Greco-Roman world and survive to compete with Christianity. These cults were characterized by secrecy, initiations, dues, rituals of the death and rebirth of various deities, and purification by direct contact with gods.

479

Confucius, a Chinese teacher and philosopher, died. His teachings emphasized personal and societal morality, correctness of social relationships, justice, and sincerity. Like the Golden Rule we know, he said: "Do not impose on others what you do not wish for yourself."

450

c. The Hebrew Torah was most likely compiled between this time and 350 BC. Palestine was still under Persian control, and the Persians allowed their client states to create their own societal laws.

425

c. Historian Herodotus wrote of Zalmoxis, most likely the supreme deity of the monotheistic Getae people of the lower Danube, around present-day Romania. Zalmoxis was said to have gone into an underground chamber for three years and was thought to be dead. He emerged in the fourth year, showing that death was not irreversible.

407

The Persian governor of Judah wrote the *Petition to Bagoas*. It was a request for help in rebuilding the Jewish temple in Elephantine, Egypt, which had been damaged by anti-Jewish riots. The location of this island in the Nile River in southern Egypt gives some idea of the extent of the Jewish dispersion in that direction.

400

c. People in India began worshipping the god Krishna as a master communicator and a god of compassion, tenderness, and love. He was killed, then transcended death and his human incarnation, and returned to his heavenly home.

c. Either Babylonians or Persians wrote the folktale "The Story of Ahikar." It was a story like the biblical Job or Mark's Jesus—a just man whose righteousness was sorely tested and ultimately rewarded by God. This is a literary trope referred to as "the suffering and vindication of the innocent righteous one," a storyline for many novels and movies even into the present time. The writings were discovered in 1907 in the ruins of the Jewish settlement in Elephantine, Egypt.

c. Buddha—the ascetic sage on whose teaching Buddhism was founded—lived and taught in eastern India. Despite the distance, Buddhism was not isolated from the Middle East. In the gnostic sect of Manichaeism, the Buddha is listed among the prophets who preached the word of God prior to their founder Mani.

c. Over the next two centuries, the writings of the Torah came to be regarded as holy scripture by the Jews.

c. The roots of Taoism go back at least to this time in China. The religion differs from Confucianism by not emphasizing rigid rituals but rather learning everything from nature. Its "Three Treasures" are compassion, frugality, and humility. The Taoist's main book is *Tao Te Ching*, which is attributed to Laozi (Lao-Tzu), who like Jesus was an ethical teacher who experienced an extraordinary birth. Interestingly, *Tao* means "the way," which is also what Jesus's followers called early Christianity.

370

c. Greek philosopher Democritus died. In one of his numerous writings, he had formulated an atomic theory. This was handed down to us by other Greek writers since none of Democritus's works were preserved. It has been said that the loss of his works was the greatest intellectual tragedy in the extinguishing of classical Greek civilization by Christians seven centuries later.

360

c. The Greek philosopher Plato wrote *Timaeus*, which would later have an immense impact on early Christian philosophers. It presented an account of the formation of the universe and reasons for its order and beauty. It described the universe as a product of a rational, purposeful, and beneficent creator. Plato suggested that humans had immortal souls which originated in the realm of the stars.

347

Plato died. He had founded the Academy in Athens, the first institution of higher learning in the Western world devoted to a rational study of nature. Along with his mentor Socrates and his most famous student Aristotle, Plato helped lay the foundations of Western philosophy and science. He popularized the notion that we have a sense of alienation in this material world and need to move beyond it to discover the perfect and unchanging reality.

332

Alexander the Great conquered Phoenicia and Gaza on his way to Egypt, where he was proclaimed the son of the god Amun. The following year he defeated the Persian Empire. His vast Greek or Hellenic Empire would create a cultural network and introduce people to many different religions. People in some regions began to worship the gods of their choosing.

Due to the conquests of Alexander, the Jewish people were exposed to Greek culture. Apparently, one of the ideas passed on to them was the concept of Tartarus as a part of Hades, where bad people went after they died. This was a refinement of Sheol, where everyone went after they died. Within the next few centuries, the concept of hell as a torture chamber would be established.

323

Alexander the Great died, and his empire, stretching from Greece to India, was divided between his heirs and generals. A year later the First War of the Diadochi, (Latin for *successors*) broke out among the competitors in Egypt. Four more wars would follow, and it wouldn't be until 275 BC that invasions by outsiders forced a semblance of order to the region.

One of Alexander's former generals and historian, Ptolemy I Soter, became the ruler of Egypt. He founded a dynasty that would last for three centuries, turning Alexandria into a major center of Greek culture.

c. Within the next hundred years, the Jewish books of the Prophets were canonized, thus joining the Torah as holy scripture.

322

After Macedonian troops subdued an uprising in Athens, the world's first sustained experiment with democracy came to an end. It had lasted, off and on, for close to two centuries.

Aristotle, the prominent Greek philosopher and scientist, died. His writings covered a wide variety of subjects from zoology to music to logic. Aristotle had studied at Plato's Academy and tutored the young Alexander the Great. His views on science, especially the use of physical evidence to draw conclusions, would be lost to Western Europe but would reemerge after Greek texts were translated into Latin in the late Middle Ages and greatly influence the Renaissance and the Enlightenment. He had concluded that the heavens had to be structured in a perfect way—spherical—including a spherical Earth. He imagined a system of concentric spheres around Earth, consisting of the sun, the moon, and the five visible planets, which inspired the idea of "seven heavens."

312

Another of Alexander's chief generals, Seleucus I Nicator, established the Seleucid Empire, based in Babylon and extending from the Aegean Sea to India.

300

c. The mystery cult of Mithraism existed in Persia at this time, devoted to the god Mithras. It had many similarities to the future Christianity, including eating flesh and drinking blood. With Christians it was the flesh and blood of Jesus through transubstantiation; with Mithraism, it was those from a bull. When Mithraism later spread to the Roman Empire, Christian apologists would say that Mithraic rituals were evil copies of Christian ones, but it may have been the reverse.

By this time, Jews of the diasporas had established communities in the Aegean Islands, Greece, Asia Minor, Cyrenaica (Libya), Italy, and Egypt.

c. From this time forward, the Jews ceased to use the name Yahweh for their god and began to call him Elohim, the common noun for a god or gods.

291

The Romans erected a temple to the Greek healer-god Asclepius in Rome. At such shrine-medical centers, doctors treated patients for various infirmities with the best-known treatment at the time. These healing centers were the first known hospitals in Europe.

280

c. The Greeks founded the Museum of Alexandria to study music, poetry, anatomy, and astronomy. It was connected to the Library of Alexandria and served as a meeting place and think tank for scholars, with more than one hundred living there at times. Most of these philosophers believed that understanding the natural order was possible for the human mind and thanked their gods for the gift of intellect.

279

Ptolemy II Philadelphus, the king of Egypt, claimed that his parents were gods, and therefore, he was also divine. This was most likely the earliest example of a Greek ruler claiming to be a god while still alive. This tradition would continue with Hellenistic and Roman emperors.

273

c. The Buddhist king of India, Ashoka, sent representatives as far west as Egypt, Syria, and Greece. These missions help explain any Asian influence on Western civilization and religions.

270

Greek philosopher Epicurus died. He had founded the Epicurean philosophy based on attaining contentment through the absence of pain and fear. He found no evidence of supernatural beings or an afterlife and considered religion only irrational fantasies. He wrestled with the mystery of evil: if a god is all-loving and all-powerful and allows suffering, either he is not powerful enough to prevent it or doesn't want to. As a scientist, he theorized the existence of atoms and some form of evolution of life forms.

260

c. Ptolemy II Philadelphus asked seventy-two scholars to translate the Hebrew Bible into Greek. The resulting book, created in Alexandria, is known as the Septuagint, based on the Greek word for "seventy." It would be widely used in Greek-speaking Jewish diaspora communities. The Septuagint would also become the basis for the Old Latin, Slavonic, Syriac, Old Armenian, Old Georgian, and Coptic versions of the Christian Old Testament.

247

King Devanampiya Tissa of Sri Lanka established the world's first-known wildlife sanctuary. This came about due to a Buddhist monk teaching the king that all mammals, birds, and other creatures deserve an equal right to live as humans. This concept of guardianship or stewardship over Earth would be seen in the book of Genesis but interpreted in various ways, from the Buddhist concept of protecting and admiring nature to the materialistic concept of exploitation of Earth for its resources.

225

Writers compiled the earliest of the Dead Sea Scrolls. Others would be written as late as the first century AD. This was the stash of Jewish writings that began to be discovered in 1947 in caves near the Dead Sea in Palestine and provided many new insights into ancient Jewish culture.

217

The Egyptians under Ptolemy IV crushed the Seleucid army under Antiochus III at Raphia, near Gaza, thereby taking control of most of Palestine. This conflict was known as the Fourth Syrian War.

200

c. Antiochus III defeated Ptolemy V of Egypt at the Battle of Panium, and Judah became part of the Seleucid Empire centered in Syria. This battle ended the Syrian Wars.

c. At this time, the symbol of the cross was being used by people in Egypt, Assyria, Greece, Persia, and Africa as an emblem and an ornament. In many cases, the cross was connected to a form of worship; in others, it was just a design. The pre-Christian cross was either the tau cross, shaped like the capital T, or the swastika type, which was used as a symbol of divinity in some American Indian religions. Egyptian

Christians later adopted the tau version, but the cross as we know it today wouldn't become the universal symbol of Christianity until fourth century AD.

168

In the quest for uniformity in his empire, Seleucid King Antiochus IV Epiphanes appointed a Hellenized Jew (one who had adopted the Greek culture and language) as the high priest of the Jewish Temple. Antiochus also placed a pagan idol on the Temple's altar and may have vandalized it to some degree. He decreed death sentences for circumcision, studying the Torah, and observing the Sabbath, and he mandated the worship of Greek gods. His actions unsurprisingly provoked an armed revolt by the Orthodox Jews, although many other Jews welcomed some degree of Hellenization.

167

Mattathias the Hasmonean, a Jewish priest, refused to offer sacrifices to the Greek gods and instead fled to the desert with his five sons. His family led a revolt against the Seleucids, with Judas Maccabeus taking over control of the revolt after Mattathias's death the following year. This uprising led to Jewish independence from Seleucid rule, the nation being referred to as Judea, and the rededication of the Second Temple, initiating the Jewish celebration of Hanukkah. The Hasmonean family would rule until 63 BC.

c. The *Book of Daniel* was most likely written at this time, centuries after the events it describes. This book was the last writing to be included in the Hebrew Bible. It emphasized the idea that the faithful could expect to join God in heaven. Daniel 12:3 states "those who are wise will shine like the brightness of the heavens, and those who lead many to righteousness like the stars for ever and ever." This concept of the righteous rising to heaven would be echoed in Christianity and Islam.

160

The earliest date speculated by scholars for the writing of the *Book of Jubilees*, a Jewish text, considered canonical by the Ethiopian Orthodox Church and Ethiopian Jews.

150

c. A Jewish sect known as the Essenes established a settlement at Qumran, near the Dead Sea, and at other relatively isolated locations throughout Judea.

139

The Jewish population was expelled from Rome most likely because of their proselytizing or a suspected connection with the Roman cult of Jupiter Sabazius, a god of the Phrygians of Anatolia. The Jupiter cult worshipped a sky god and was popular with Indo-European tribes north of the Black Sea. Apparently, the religion had an element of prophesy that the Roman rulers especially disliked because it might foretell of their demise and put ideas in people's heads about helping it along.

134

Antiochus VII Sidetes led his Seleucid army into Judea, where he captured Jerusalem. According to the Jewish writer Josephus, Hasmonean leader John Hyrcanus paid tribute to the Seleucids to spare the city. He remained their vassal and ruled semi-autonomously.

113

John Hyrcanus, taking advantage of the Seleucid war with Parthia and the death of Antiochus VII, sought to expand his realm eastward into Jordan. He overran Samaria and Galilee and subjected many of the conquered people to slavery.

100

c. Jewish scholars wrote the *Book of Wisdom,* or *Wisdom of Solomon.* It taught that wisdom was with God through all eternity as the perfection of knowledge and was a gift from God. This book offered the concept that Cain's murder of his brother Abel was the first sin committed in the world, not the eating of the fruit of knowledge by Adam and Eve.

93

Alexander Jannaeus, the Hasmonean high priest and king, lost all the newly acquired territories to the Arab Nabataeans at the Battle of Gadara. This incited a civil war that lasted six years and resulted in the death of over fifty thousand Judeans. Jewish historian Josephus reported that Jannaeus had eight hundred Pharisee rebels crucified in Jerusalem.

86

c. The Antikythera mechanism was lost when the ship carrying it sunk in the Aegean Sea, not to be rediscovered until 1900. The machine had working gears to track the movement of the sun through the signs of the zodiac and could predict the position of the planets, phases of the moon, and solar and lunar eclipses. It further demonstrated the advanced astronomical knowledge of the Greeks at that time, and no machine that complex would be seen again until the fourteenth century AD.

64

c. Jewish writers completed the final part of the *Book of Enoch,* an important noncanonical book. It had probably been compiled over the previous century, and New Testament authors were familiar with it as demonstrated by its mention in the epistle of Jude.

63

Roman general Pompey captured Jerusalem. The forces on the Temple Mount, the high ground on which the Temple was built, held out the longest. Pompey took the Jewish ruler Aristobulus II and his son Antigonus II Mattathias to Rome as prisoners and incorporated Palestine into the Roman Empire.

57

The Romans founded the Sanhedrin in Jerusalem as the supreme court of justice for the Jewish people.

55

The Greek philosopher and poet Titus Lucretius Carus died. In his six-volume *On the Nature of Things*, he asserted that not only are humans made up of atoms like every other thing on the planet but that a form of natural selection works to change species over time. These ideas were not acceptable to his contemporaries and would also lead to much controversy almost two thousand years later between the Christian Church and Charles Darwin's theory of evolution.

50

c. Scholars believe the Egyptian *Book of the Dead* was completed by this time. Since its origin around 1550 BC, it had been continually edited by priests. As previously mentioned, there are many similarities between the god Horus in these writings and Jesus as depicted in the New Testament.

c. The bulk of the *Corpus Hermeticum* dates from this time until the fourth century AD. These are Egyptian-Greek books of wisdom, and the religious and philosophical tradition of Hermeticism is based on these writings. Their doctrines are based on the existence of one true theology that is present in all religions. One of their tenants was that nature could be controlled, so these writings would catch the attention of scientists during the scientific revolution in Europe. The original writer was named Hermes Trismegistus, a pagan, who was later the subject of many Christian writers who said he predicted the future religion of Christianity.

48

The Library of Alexandria, the scholastic center of the ancient world, was largely destroyed by fire. It had housed the most extensive collection of literary works in the ancient world. The prevailing understanding of the disaster's cause was Julius Caesar ordering his men to burn Egyptian ships in the harbor, but the fire became uncontrollable and burned much of the city. Estimates suggest that up to four hundred thousand papyrus scrolls were stored in the library at this time, and many tens of thousands of them were destroyed, including writings by scholars such as Sophocles, Euripides, Aeschylus, Plato, Ptolemy, and Aristotle. Many of the surviving writings were transferred from the library to a magnificent temple known as the Serapeum. As a comparison to its size, the great Sorbonne library in Paris in AD 1338 held only 1,728 documents.

44

After Roman conspirators assassinated Julius Caesar, his adopted son Octavian witnessed what has become known as "Caesar's comet"; he claimed his father had ascended into heaven, proving he was a divine being. Octavian came to believe that he was the son of a god, and this idea would carry over to future Roman emperors, who were also worshipped as gods.

40

Antigonus II Mattathias, who had escaped from the Romans seventeen years earlier, seized power in Judea with the aid of the Parthians of Persia.

39

The Romans sent Herod, an influential Jew of Edomite heritage, from Rome to his native Palestine to confront Antigonus. He defeated Antigonus two years later and handed him over to the Romans for execution. This ended Hasmonean rule forever. Herod took the title of king of Judea and began the Herodian dynasty.

28

c. Unknown authors in Egypt wrote the *Treatise of Shem*. It is thought to reflect Jewish astrological concerns in the first century BC. In that era, on the vernal equinox, the sun transitioned from rising in the constellation Aries—to Hebrew astronomers, a sacrificial lamb—to rising in Pisces, the fish. This is where it has risen ever since and will remain until the Age of Aquarius dawns around AD 2600. This treatise also gave an important glimpse into the intertestamental, or pre-Christian, period of Jewish history.

27

c. The Romans built the Pantheon in Rome as a temple to honor all their gods.

20

Herod began to restore and expand the Jewish Temple and its foundation, the Temple Mount, in Jerusalem. He also initiated many other massive building projects throughout the country, including Caesarea Maritima, the largest artificial harbor in the Mediterranean; the fortress of Masada; the palace fortress Herodium; and synagogues for diaspora Jews in cities outside Palestine. He heavily taxed the Jewish people to fund these projects, which resulted in Herod's extreme unpopularity.

12

Octavian became known as Augustus, or Caesar Augustus, the "re-vered one" and the first Roman emperor. With the military backing him, he dominated the Roman Senate.

Augustus ordered the retrieval of all circulating prophetic books in Latin and Greek and burned two thousand of them. The rest were kept in an official collection of Rome.

8

Caesar Augustus had the eighth month of the Roman year named after himself. In 44 BC, his adoptive father, Julius Caesar, had the seventh month named for himself. Otherwise, the original Roman names were still in use. January was named after the Roman god Janus; February for *februum*, the month of purification; March for the god Mars; April for *Aprilis*, meaning "second" because it was originally the second month of the year; May for the Greek goddess Maia; June for Juno, the wife of the Roman god Jupiter; July for Julius; August for Augustus; September, October, November, and December just mean the seventh, eighth, ninth and tenth months from the older Roman calendar.

5

c. According to the Gospel of Luke, a baby boy named Jesus was born to Mary and Joseph, a young Jewish couple from a small town in Galilee, a region of northern Palestine. The Gospel of Matthew says nothing about Nazareth until after Jesus was born and his parents returned from Egypt following the death of Herod. Both Gospels agree that he was born in Bethlehem, known as "the city of David," because King David was believed to have been born there and maybe even anointed as king in that town. To the authors of the Gospels, fixing Bethlehem as Jesus's place of birth would link him to the lineage of King David and justify his royal pedigree. In Matthew, after Herod died, the family moved to Nazareth to fulfill the prophesy that Jesus would be called a Nazarene. Jesus is the English name derived from the Hebrew *Yeshua* or the Greek *Iesous*, with a root meaning of "to deliver or to rescue." The name Joshua is also derived from the same word, and in the Bible, both men with those names fit the role of deliverer. After his death, Jesus would later be called Christ, which is a Greek title meaning "the anointed one" and, in the Bible, is applied to the Jewish Messiah or anticipated liberator. If Jesus was really born around 5 BC, every future date concerning him and his followers would shift five to six years earlier, but to avoid confusion I'll stay with prevailing belief that he was born in AD 1.

4

After Herod the Great died, Augustus divided Herod's realm among his three surviving sons but allowed none of them to bear the title of king. Herod Antipas took control of Israel, including Galilee; Archelaus ruled Judea; and Philip became the ruler of territories north and east of the Jordan River. The Temple reconstruction was not completed at the time of Herod's death, but it was already one of the great tourist attractions in the empire.

CHAPTER 1: FIRST CENTURY AD

A new command I give you: Love one another. As I have loved you, so you must love one another.
—Jesus Christ (John 13:34)

This is my simple religion. There is no need for temples; no need for complicated philosophy. Our own brain, our own heart is our temple: the philosophy is kindness.
—Dalai Lama XIV

Those who say religion has nothing to do with politics do not know what religion means.
—Mahatma Gandhi

This was the century of Jesus, from his ministry to the writing of the last canonical Gospel. The chapter focuses on his life, death, reported resurrection, and legacy. It demonstrates characteristics of original Christianity and how diverse the religion was from the beginning. An apostle and mystic named Paul of Tarsus carried the Christian message to non-Jews, or Gentiles. The first century was a time of escalating conflicts between Christians and Jews and the arrival of other messianic figures. Evidence from this period shows how little was really known about the biblical Jesus outside of Galilee.

1

c. At this time, the Jews from the diasporas far outnumbered the Jews in Palestine. Because of this, the geographical centers of Jewish culture shifted from region to region. In the first century, the center was Jerusalem, but by the second, it would be Alexandria. The community still living in Babylon was the only major Jewish population outside the Roman Empire.

6

Since the Romans had recently taken over the direct governing of Palestine, Quirinius, the governor of Syria, ordered a census in Judea for the purpose of determining taxation. There is little doubt that this was the census in the Gospel of Luke that caused Joseph and Mary to travel to Bethlehem for the birth of Jesus. This census is one of the clues to estimate when Jesus was born, but Herod was not king at this time; therefore, the generally accepted birth date of Jesus has been shifted to the BC era when Herod ruled.

Judas of Galilee led an uprising against the Romans after the census was ordered. His followers refused to pay taxes to any ruler because they thought that action violated the First Commandment to not honor other gods, and the Roman emperor was considered a god in the Roman pantheon. Judas was killed during the revolt and his followers dispersed. First-century Jewish historian Josephus would later write that Judas established a fourth sect of Judaism, known as the Zealots. The other three were the Sadducees, the keepers of the Jerusalem Temple; the Pharisees, the legalists who strictly observed Jewish law; and the Essenes, the ascetics who lived in isolated communal groups.

9

The *Letter of the Proconsul to the Cities of Asia* honored Emperor Caesar Augustus, calling him the savior who would put an end to war, set all things in order, and fulfill the hopes of earlier times. It proclaimed that he was a god himself. A few years later, an inscription was carved near Sparta, Greece, referred to "the God Caesar Augustus, son of the god, our Savior and Deliverer." This kind of statement would echo later in how Christians described Jesus.

14

When Caesar Augustus died, one senator said that he had seen his spirit rise out of the funeral pyre toward heaven. From this, the Senate confirmed that Augustus was truly a god like his father.

26

c. A man known as John the Baptist attracted a large following in the Jordan River Valley, preaching about God's impending final judgment. John's importance in Christianity is paramount since the Gospels said that he was the one who baptized Jesus.

Emperor Tiberius appointed Pontius Pilate the fifth Roman governor of Judea.

30

c. According to the Gospels, Jesus's ministry would have begun when he was about thirty years old, following his baptism by John the Baptist. He was apparently motivated by the urgency of the approaching apocalyptic period he referred to as the Kingdom of God or Kingdom of Heaven. His tenure as a roving preacher and miracle worker lasted from one to three years, depending on which canonical Gospel is referenced.

c. Jesus made his base in Galilee. He had twelve men who served as traveling companions and disciples. They were Simon Peter; Andrew; James and John, sons of Zebedee; Philip; Nathaniel; Matthew Levi; Thomas Didymus; James and Judas, sons of Alpheus; Simon the Zealot; and Judas Iscariot. There is still much uncertainty about these men since the canonical Gospels include three different lists of disciples or apostles and little is recorded about most of them.

c. According to the Gospels, Herod Antipas had John the Baptist beheaded.

33

c. The Romans crucified Jesus of Nazareth in Jerusalem, most likely for the crime of sedition since his followers referred to him as the "King of the Jews" and "Lord." To the Romans, he was only another trouble-making traveling agitator. After his death, Jesus's cult of Jews seemed to come to an end but was reinvigorated by reports of his resurrection and even an ascension into heaven. Jesus's poverty, morality, and unjust suffering became models for many Christians to emulate. At the time of Jesus's death, it's estimated that he had only about twenty committed followers, and they were convinced that he was a divine incarnation who came to Earth to show the way to salvation.

c. The Pentecost, meaning "fifty days after Passover," was the day that the book of Acts described the disciple Peter addressing a crowd in Jerusalem. This was the beginning of the public ministry of the apostles. According to Acts, Peter was said to have won over thousands of followers with that one speech, but there is no historical evidence of this, and the number of true believers in the resurrection of Jesus grew at a very slow pace.

35

c. According to the book of Acts, God killed the Christian couple Ananias and Sapphira for not turning over all of their property to the Christian community.

36

c. According to the Gospels, Herod Antipas had executed John the Baptist around the time Jesus's ministry began. However, other historical evidence places John's execution closer to this time.

c. According to the book of Acts, Orthodox Jews executed Stephen, a vocal supporter of Jesus, for blasphemy, while Saul of Tarsus, a persecutor of Christians, watched approvingly. This event seems to have caused much of the Christian core in Jerusalem to move elsewhere to avoid a similar fate.

Syrian governor Lucius Vitellius relieved Pontius Pilate of duty after Pilate's violent suppression of a Samaritan uprising.

c. Saul of Tarsus became a follower of Jesus Christ. His conversion story, as recorded in the book of Acts, tells that while on his way to Damascus to persecute Christians, he encountered an apparition of Jesus that spoke to him. At some point, he decided to change his name to Paul, a more Roman-sounding name. Later, the new apostle wrote in his canonical letters that he learned about Jesus Christ from mystical revelations from Christ himself, not from any of Jesus's disciples. After experiencing his vision of Christ and recovering from temporary blindness, he was said to have gone into the East, mentioning Damascus and Arabia in particular. Canonical books tell almost nothing about this time of his life.

37

The rule of Caiaphas, the high priest of the Jewish Temple, ended with his death. The Gospels would later portray him as interrogating Jesus before his crucifixion.

Yosef ben Matityahu, better known as Titus Flavius Josephus, was born in Roman Judea. He would become a leader in the later Jewish-Roman War and a much-quoted historian of first-century Palestine and the history of the Jewish people.

In Antioch, followers of Jesus established a "church," literally meaning "gathering" of Jesus followers, derived from the Greek word *ekklisia*. This church would later send Paul and Barnabas to the Gentile, or non-Jewish, mission field.

39

c. Paul later wrote of visiting Jerusalem at about this time and meeting with the apostle Peter and James the Just, the brother of Jesus. James is believed to have joined the followers of Jesus after Jesus's resurrection and is thought to have been the leader of the church in Jerusalem. The reason for this meeting was apparently to meet the Christian leaders and learn more about their experiences with Jesus. Paul's report of this encounter was one of the few times he ever acknowledged that Jesus was once a human being, since he mentioned Jesus's human brother.

42

c. The first Christians came to Antioch in the wake of the stoning death of Stephen, and this year they began to be referred to as *christianoi*, meaning Greek-speaking Christians, to distinguish them from the Aramaic-speaking Nazarenes.

c. James, the son of Zebedee, brother of John the Apostle and one of Jesus's original disciples, was reported in Acts to have been executed by Herod Agrippa. He is considered the first of the original apostles to be martyred, but there is no canonical mention of any others.

45

c. Paul began his first journey to spread Christianity to the Gentiles, traveling with Barnabas to Antioch, Cyprus, Pamphilia, Pisidia, and Lycia. He was challenged with finding ways to explain Christian doctrines by using concepts and terms that were understandable to Greeks, so his version of Christianity was somewhat different from the Jewish version from the very beginning.

46

c. Theudas, a Jewish rebel thought by some Palestinian Jews to be the long-awaited Messiah, led his followers in a short-lived, sparsely documented revolt against the Romans.

48

c. According to Christian tradition, Mark, who had been a companion of Peter, founded a church in Alexandria, Egypt. By the early second century, scriptures would be translated into Coptic, the native language of Egypt. By the third century, Christianity would be the majority religion in the region.

c. Paul, according to his reports in the epistles, traveled south from Antioch to attend the first Christian church council in Jerusalem. This was a pivotal and hotly contested event since many of the Pharisee followers of the Jesus movement insisted that converts adhere to Jewish customs such as dietary restrictions and circumcision. The leaders finally decided that Gentiles were not required to follow Jewish cultural customs in order to be Christians and endorsed Paul taking the Christian message to the Gentiles. The other Jewish Christian leaders apparently continued to evangelize the Jews. If Paul had been overruled and submitted to the will of the others, Christians might have remained a sect within Judaism.

49

Paul began his second missionary journey, which lasted two years. He was accompanied by Timothy and Silas and visited Phrygia and Galatia in Asia Minor and various towns in Greece.

50

c. Paul wrote his first epistle to the Thessalonians and his epistle to the Galatians. These are his earliest surviving letters and the earliest writings chosen as part of the Christian New Testament. Paul was the first and possibly only contemporary of Jesus to write what became holy scripture, yet he never knew Jesus in human form. Paul's epistles taught a very different Christianity than the Gospels, which were written later in the century. Unlike the Gospels, Paul's letters mentioned almost nothing about the life or teachings of a human named Jesus but focused on a spiritual presence he called Jesus Christ. In Galatians, he wrote of disunity in the church and confusion about what resurrection really meant. This points to confusion and divisions in Christianity from the very outset.

Philo of Alexandria, a Hellenized Jewish philosopher, died. One of his interests was studying the religious sects of his time. Although Philo's family was intimately involved in affairs in Jerusalem, there is no mention of Jesus or Christians in his surviving writings. This shows that there were contemporary writers who didn't seem to know about Jesus.

c. Someone wrote the proposed Gospel source known as Q around this time. Q stands for *Quelle*, the German word for "source." Q and the Gospel of Mark were frequently mined by the writers of the Gospels of Matthew and Luke.

c. By this time there were probably more non-Jewish or Gentile Christians than Jewish Christians, thanks to Paul's missionary work.

51

c. This was the earliest date for the writing of the second epistle to the Thessalonians. While there is much debate over the actual authorship, it is attributed to Paul.

52

c. The apostle Thomas was reported to have sailed to southern India to spread the good news of Jesus to Jews who had lived in Kerala for centuries. Today, the sect, which traces their founding back to him, are known as the Saint Thomas Christians and are mostly former Hindus.

54

c. Paul left on his third missionary journey, which lasted five years. He visited many towns and regions in Turkey, Greece, and the Levant, including Ephesus, Corinth, Macedonia, Philippi, Athens, Phrygia, Galatia, and Caesarea.

c. Paul wrote the first epistle to the Corinthians. By this time, Paul had turned against the Greek traditions of learning by one's senses and rational thought, with sayings such as "I will destroy the wisdom of the wise" (1:19). Later Christians would use this kind of comment to help justify Christian belief without the need for wisdom or evidence.

55

c. Paul wrote his letter to the church in Philippi. In Philippians 2:6–11, he quoted a hymn which mentioned that Christ took the form of a slave and was born in human form and human likeness. These lyrics implied support for the concept that Christ had only seemed to be human but was truly a spiritual being. This concept is known as Docetism.

c. Paul wrote his epistle to Philemon and second epistle to the Corinthians.

58

c. Paul wrote his epistle to the Romans. In the letter, he mentioned his desire to travel to Rome and then possibly even to Spain.

Paul made his final journey to Jerusalem. The book of Acts states that he brought an offering to the poor from several Gentile churches. About that time, he was apparently arrested by the Jewish Temple police.

60

c. Paul is believed to have arrived in Rome as a prisoner. He was possibly held in Caesarea Maritima for as long as two years before being shipped to Rome and possibly spending another two years under house arrest there. Outside the book of Acts, details of this imprisonment are hard to come by.

c. Noncanonical writings presented the apostle Peter as traveling to Rome to focus his efforts at the heart of the empire and build a strong Christian community there. However, there is no mention of this in the New Testament and no proof that Peter ever set foot in Rome. Many scholars believe that in the second century, Peter was literarily retrojected into first-century Rome to legitimize his position as the first bishop of Rome. From this, Rome could claim to be the world's predominant Christian church.

c. The total estimated number of Christians was between 1,000 and 1,500. This meant that the churches in many towns were extremely small.

c. The Mandaeans, a quasi-Christian sect devoted to John the Baptist, left Palestine and migrated to Mesopotamia to escape persecution. The Koran later identified them as Sabians and other "people of the book" but apparently didn't consider them Christians or Muslims. They eventually became known as the Saint John Christians by the Carmelite missionaries who discovered them in Iran in the sixteenth century.

62

c. Josephus reported that James the Just, the brother of Jesus and leader of the Christian church in Jerusalem, was executed by the high priest Annas. Simon is believed to have succeeded him as the leader of the church.

This is the earliest date that the epistle to the Ephesians was written. It was originally attributed to Paul, but beginning in 1792, with the evolution of a more critical approach to scripture, many biblical scholars consider this letter written by a later author.

64

After a fire swept through Rome and caused extensive damage, many Romans suspected Emperor Nero of starting it. He deflected the blame to the small sect of Christians, a group he disapproved of because they didn't respect Roman authority or conform to its religion. Until this time, most Roman officials, if they knew of Christianity at all, had likely perceived it as a sect of Judaism, which was a legal and respected religion.

c. The apostles Peter and Paul were rumored to have been executed in Nero's purge of Christian leaders, but there is no historical record of this, and neither death is mentioned in the New Testament. Many of these executions took place on the Vatican Hill across the Tiber River from Rome, and Peter was later said to have been buried there. In Latin, *vaticanus mons* means "hill of prophesy."

c. An unknown author who went by the name John wrote some of the book of Revelation. By the third century, Bishop Dionysius of Alexandria doubted that the author of the writing was the same John as the author of the Gospel of John. Many scholars think this book is a symbolic or coded attack on the Roman Empire, with Emperor Nero being the Anti-Christ.

65

Seneca, the greatest Roman ethics writer of his time, wrote *Naturales Quaestiones*, in which he recorded unusual natural phenomena. In his writings that were preserved, he had nothing to say about Jesus or the observable supernatural events associated with him, such as the star of Bethlehem or an earthquake and the emergence of the dead from their tombs at the time of Jesus's death, as recorded in Matthew 27.

c. There is some evidence that one of Jesus's more obscure disciples, Simon the Zealot, may have died at this time. Not much is known about him other than his name. Mark 6 said that Jesus had four brothers and one of them was named Simon. Another tradition said that Simon became the head of the church in Jerusalem after James was martyred.

66

The Roman procurator of Judea, Gessius Florus, plundered money from the Jewish Temple, then whipped and crucified anyone who demonstrated against him. The Jews of Palestine revolted against the Romans, beginning what became known as the First Jewish-Roman War, one of the greatest uprisings against Roman rule in the entire empire. In the conflict, Christians mainly chose to stay neutral.

Palestinian Christians had to go into hiding to survive the war, and sects like the Ebionites carried on their Jewish version of Christianity elsewhere, reportedly in Pella, Jordan. The centers of Christianity begin to shift from Jerusalem and Antioch to Rome and Alexandria. The Essene sect of Judaism viewed the Jewish revolt against the Romans as the final end-time struggle before the arrival of their expected Messiah.

68

c. Christian tradition holds that the Romans executed the apostle Mark, the supposed author of the Gospel of Mark in Alexandria.

70

c. Most biblical scholars believe this was the earliest date that the epistle of James could have been written. The letter was intended for Jewish Christians who were dispersed outside of Palestine. Although supposedly written by Jesus's brother, the letter makes no mention of Jesus's death, resurrection, or divinity. Also, other sources report that James was martyred before this time. The earliest manuscript of this letter is dated to the mid to late third century.

c. A Christian writer in an unknown location wrote the earliest canonical Gospel, the Gospel of Mark, but it wouldn't carry that name for centuries. The preponderance of biblical scholars has concluded that it was written during the Jewish-Roman War. In the Gospel of Mark, Jesus was portrayed as a human who seemed to be adopted by

God at his baptism and later abandoned while on the cross. This was the first known book to give significant details of a historical human called Jesus, since Paul mentions almost none of that in his epistles. In the earliest-known version of Mark, there was no physical resurrection. Post-resurrection appearances were only added later. Other interesting information: Jesus's father Joseph was not mentioned at all, Mary was not identified as a virgin, nor was there any mention of Jesus's nativity. In this book, Jesus spoke in parables and predicted the coming Son of Man. As with all New Testament Gospels, the fact that they were written in Greek, not Aramaic, and none of the authors claimed to be eyewitnesses, or even wrote as if they were eyewitnesses, gives strong indications that they were written decades after the events they told.

Simon bar Giora, a self-proclaimed messiah, was the leader of a powerful rebel faction during the Jewish-Roman War. The citizens of Jerusalem invited him into the city to overthrow the despotic Zealot ruler, John of Giscala. Simon was said to have entered Jerusalem as a deliverer and protector, like other would-be messiahs. Rival Jewish factions fought each other inside the city even while the Romans besieged it from the outside. The Romans later captured and killed Simon.

The Romans destroyed much of Jerusalem and the Jewish Temple, ending the Second Temple era in Jewish history. Jerusalem would not be rebuilt as a civilian settlement for another sixty years. With the destruction of the city, Christians abandoned the idea that the Second Coming of Christ would take place on the Mount of Olives, just east of Jerusalem. Despite that, the early Christians continued to pray toward the east and the rising sun and interpreted the destruction of the Temple as God's judgment on the Jewish people.

c. After the Jewish-Roman War, Christians increasingly separated themselves from Jews. They claimed to represent the true religion of God and, therefore, claimed the Hebrew Bible or Old Testament and the covenant of Abraham as theirs. Since the Hebrew scriptures were ancient documents—and to Christians unquestionably pointed to Jesus as the future Messiah or Christ—they claimed that he had been anticipated since antiquity and that "their" scripture predated any pagan writings. Christians hoped that would deflect the accusation that they were a recently established religion. The Jews rejected Jesus when most Christians considered him their savior and even a god. To Jews, calling Jesus *God* had the same significance as rejecting the one true God, and they considered it blasphemy. To Christians, Jews rejecting Jesus was unforgivable, and therefore, many Christians believed they eclipsed Jews as God's chosen people.

72

c. Indian tradition tells of the apostle Thomas being killed this year after founding seven churches on the Malabar coast of southwest India.

73

The besieged Jewish fortress of Masada fell to the Romans after seven years of resistance. When the Romans entered Masada, they found that 960 of the 967 defenders had committed suicide rather than surrender. This was the symbolic end to the First Jewish-Roman War.

After the war, Flavius Josephus, a former Jewish military leader then living in Rome, wrote *The Jewish War* in the Aramaic language to discourage further revolts against Rome in the eastern Roman Empire. It was followed by an account written in Greek of the same events for the Greco-Roman readership. Interestingly, in book six, he wrote of a Jesus ben-Ananias, a doomsday prophet from around AD 66. In Josephus's account, the Jewish authorities took this Jesus before the Roman procurator, who whipped him severely and then released him. Josephus also noted that this Jesus, like the biblical Jesus, said nothing in his own defense. It all sounds very much like the Jesus of the Gospels, but the dating confuses the issue.

79

Pliny the Elder was a Roman author, natural philosopher, and friend of Emperor Vespasian. He wrote *Naturalis Historia*, which became a prototype for all other encyclopedias or collections of various knowledge. In his writings, he never mentioned any natural abnormality, such as an earthquake while Jesus was on the cross, the darkening of the daytime sky, or the star of Bethlehem, as portrayed in the Gospels. He died shortly after the book's publication while observing the eruption of Mount Vesuvius.

80

c. The Gospel of Matthew is dated to this time and used the Gospel of Mark as a resource. Its Christology, or status of Christ, is more developed, and a reference to the destruction of Jerusalem in the twenty-second chapter most likely applies to the Jewish-Roman War. There are peculiarities compared to other canonical Gospels, such as Jesus being interpreted in the context of Jewish scripture and as a modern version of Moses. This was the first text that mentioned Jesus being born to a virgin. Mathew's belief that Mary was a virgin came from Isaiah 7:14, as a supposed prediction of the coming Messiah: "The virgin will be with child and will give birth to a son and will call him Immanuel." The word *virgin* in the Greek Septuagint version of Isaiah was a mistranslation of the Hebrew word for young woman or woman of child-bearing age.

Matthew also wrote that Jesus said, "I am not sent but unto the lost sheep of the house of Israel" (15:24), and he spoke of the end of the world as imminent. The Great Commission in 28:19 ("Go ye therefore, and teach all nations, baptizing them in the name of the Father.") is considered by some biblical scholars to have been an addition to the original ending of the Gospel after the world did not end when expected. It authorized a Christian mission to the Gentiles in addition to "lost sheep of the house of Israel."

In Mathew's Sermon on the Mount (chapters five through seven), Jesus was said to have blessed the poor in spirit, those who mourn, the meek, those who hunger and thirst for righteousness, the merciful, the pure in heart, the peacemakers, and those who are persecuted for righteousness—in other words, those who were not the elites of society. Jesus went on to condemn anger, lust, divorce, oaths, retaliation, fear, and judgment. He recommended loving enemies, giving to the needy, forgiving, and practicing the Golden Rule. Matthew also wrote that a prophet foretold that "he shall be called a Nazarene" (2:23), but that was not found in the Hebrew Bible. He was the first Gospel writer to describe Mary and Joseph fleeing Egypt to live in Nazareth.

c. Justus of Tiberias, a Jewish author and historian, lived in Galilee, very close to Nazareth. His writings were not preserved, and only fragments of *Chronicle of the Kings of the Jews* survive today. In the ninth century, Photius, the patriarch of Constantinople, having access to this writing, wrote "this Jewish historian does not make the smallest mention of the appearance of Christ, and says nothing whatever of his deeds and miracles." Photius thought that was odd because living so close to Jesus's hometown, and in the same era, Justus should surely have mentioned something about Jesus in a book bearing that title.

c. The earliest date assigned by scholars to the *Infancy Gospel of Thomas*. It told miraculous, anecdotal stories about the childhood of Jesus and is the oldest source known to assert the perpetual virginity of Mary.

c. An unknown author wrote the epistle to the Colossians. Modern critical analysis shows that it was most likely not written by Paul.

c. An unknown author wrote the Gospel of Luke. Like Matthew, it used the Gospel of Mark and Q as its main sources. In the Gospel, the nativity story was presented with Jesus being born in Bethlehem and then his family returning to their home in Nazareth a month after his birth, not going to Egypt as Matthew describes. The two accounts contain several other contradictions and are basically two different birth legends. There is a great deal of evidence that this book was not written by Luke, the companion of Paul, as believed. It was the first of two works probably written by the same author, the other being the book of Acts.

c. The earliest date for the pastoral epistles (the first and second epistles to Timothy, and the epistle to Titus) and the general epistles (first, second, and third epistles of John; the epistle of Jude; and the epistle to the Hebrews). The true authors of all of these letters are unknown. A recurring theme in many of these first-century writings, including the epistles of Paul, was a warning not to believe false prophets or teachers or anyone saying anything contrary to the claims of trusted apostles. This was another indication that there were many forms of Christian theology even at this early time. The problem was: how were people to know who the true and false prophets were and where these prophets obtained their knowledge? From the start, it seems that Christians, like all people, could be persuaded by charismatic and convincing preachers to believe what they said was the truth. An interesting fact was that the first and only mention of an Anti-Christ was in the epistles of John; it wasn't found in Revelation.

c. The Jewish writer of the Gospel of Luke wrote the book of Acts. There is little evidence that this was a true historical account. In the book, the author mentioned the failed uprisings of two more messianic pretenders, Judas of Galilee and Theudas the Magician. Also, to confuse the messiah situation even more, in *Antiquities of the Jews*, Josephus mentioned Athronges the Shepherd and Simon of Peraea, two other messiah figures who tried to lead revolts after the death of Herod the Great and around the time of Jesus. This makes it very perplexing to distinguish between the Jesus of the Gospels and other would-be messiahs. Some biblical scholars believe that the name "Jesus, the one from Nazareth" was first mentioned in writing in the book of Acts. In the Gospels, Jesus was referred to as "Jesus the Nazarene" or "a prophet from Nazareth." It was after the Gospels that Jesus became known as "Jesus of Nazareth." The point to this is the confusion over what "Nazarene" meant. Its meaning is very significant because there is archeological evidence that the town of Nazareth in Galilee was not even inhabited during Jesus's lifetime, and if he may not have been from Nazareth, the title "Nazarene" is puzzling. Acts also mentions that Christians met on the first day of the week, which is Sunday, the day of Jesus's resurrection, as opposed to the Jewish Sabbath.

c. The Persian religion of Mithraism became popular in the Middle East. Scholars have drawn many parallels between the god Mithra and Jesus. The religion of Mithraism was attacked by early Christians, such as Justin Martyr, as a competitive and counterfeit religion. The legends of the two religions both related a miraculous birth, salvation accomplished by the shedding of blood, marks on their foreheads in the sign of a cross, and later a shared birthday on December 25. In addition, several Christian churches in Rome were built over Mithras shrines.

c. This is the earliest date for the merging of the three sections of the *Ascension of Isaiah*, a text of unknown origin. The subject matter was apocalyptic and focused on Isaiah's prophetic vision of Jesus. Many later Christians referred to this document in their writings.

c. The Old Testament was translated into Sahidic, the literary version of the Coptic language.

c. The Jewish Council of Jamnia met in Palestine. It is thought that here, Jewish authorities decided to exclude Christians from synagogue attendance.

81

c. Unknown authors wrote the first and second epistles of Peter. The text of the first identifies Peter as its author, but the language, style, structure, and dating have led many scholars to the conclusion that they were written by someone else.

85

Roman religion had no personal relationship with a god, no concept of salvation, and no moral principles to live by and was turning into a religion of emperor worship. This year, Emperor Domitian began to require exultation from all citizens and began signing documents as "Lord and God."

90

c. Anonymous authors wrote what became known as the Gospel of John. In this portrayal of Jesus, he was the "Word of God" and a divine being from before the beginning of time. This was a significant progression in his status from the Gospels of Mark, Matthew, and Luke. John carried on the solar imagery that had been introduced in Luke, Matthew, and Revelation, such as calling him "the light of the world." Another significant theme was the authors' antisemitism in 8:44, calling the Jews children of the devil and liars. It was the most anti-Jewish of the canonical Gospels, and the consequences of this portrayal of Jewish people would haunt them for millennia.

c. Gnosticism was becoming a popular Christian sect. There were many versions of Gnosticism, but they all seemed to agree that the material world was the result of some disaster in the spiritual world and that humans didn't belong to the material world. They believed salvation was only possible through learning the correct secret knowledge. Gnostics were said to believe in the divinity of Jesus but denied his incarnation and the physical resurrection because they believed that matter was evil and that Jesus, if divine, could not have inhabited a human body. Some scholars think that Gnostic ideas may have come from Buddhism, and it is possible that they in part stemmed from Paul's mention of his secret revelations from the spiritual Christ.

The noncanonical epistles written after this time had much more biographical information on Jesus than the earlier ones. This is additional evidence that scholars who believe Jesus was not a historical person use to bolster their case for the legend of Jesus evolving over time.

This was the earliest date proposed by biblical scholars for the *Epistle of Barnabas*, a book that was later seriously considered for inclusion in the New Testament. It was not written by Barnabas, who had been a missionary companion of the apostle Paul much earlier. Like the writings of other renowned Church Fathers, such as Clement of Rome and Polycarp of Smyrna, the author made no mention of the torture and crucifixion of Jesus, although the author did believe Jesus lived a physical life and performed miracles. The letter contained a section on moral teaching but did not attribute any of it to Jesus. The author also believed that the Jews had forfeited their covenant with God when Moses smashed the engraved tablets containing the Ten Commandments.

93

c. Jewish historian Flavius Josephus wrote his book *The Antiquities of the Jews*, an account of the historical books in the Hebrew Bible. In the fourth century, Christian historian Eusebius of Caesarea used the book as evidence that Josephus knew of Jesus being the resurrected Messiah. One reference Josephus made, which scholars believe to be authentic, was his mention of the stoning of "James, the brother of Jesus." If Josephus wrote this and if it referred to the Jesus of the Gospels, it would be the only mention of Jesus in any surviving Jewish or pagan writing other than the Bible from the first century. The other reference in Josephus's writing, known as the Testimonium Flavianum, was much longer but was very likely to have been inserted by a Christian editor, possibly Eusebius, in a later century.

95

c. According to Eusebius of Caesarea, Papias, the bishop of Hierapolis, was the first writer to mention the Gospel of Mark. If so, this would have been the first mention of any Christian Gospel by its current name.

96

According to some historians, Christians and Jews may have been persecuted toward the end of Domitian's reign. Also, some historians believe that this may have been the persecution alluded to in the book of Revelation, which was believed to have not yet been completed.

Clement, the bishop of Rome, wrote the *First Epistle of Clement*, instructing the congregation in Corinth to reinstall elders who had been dismissed from the church. This was the first document known to address the separation of clergy and laity. Also, when Clement described the suffering of Jesus, he reproduced sayings from Isaiah 53 and Psalms, implying that he had no knowledge of the Gospel accounts of Jesus's final days. The epistle also never proclaimed Jesus as equal to God, but instead understood him as a chosen intermediary.

CHAPTER 2: SECOND CENTURY AD

I am writing to all the churches to let it be known that
I will gladly die for God if only you do not stand in my
way. . . . Let me be food for the wild beasts, for they are
my way to God.

—Ignatius of Antioch

Christians, needless to say, utterly detest one another;
they slander each other constantly with the vilest
forms of abuse, and cannot come to any sort of agreement in their teaching. Each sect brands its own, fills
the head of its own with deceitful nonsense.

—Celsus

This century, most of Christianity's noncanonical scripture was written by authors mostly unknown to us. Some of these writings were
considered sacred scripture in their time, but most have been consigned to the scrap pile of history. The first canon of scripture was
proposed by Marcion. Christians grew in number but not as rapidly
as we might think, and Christian sects bitterly opposed each other as
one sect sought to dominate the others. Male Christian clergy continued to gain power, and women church leaders gradually faded into
oblivion. This century also saw the first unequivocal mention of Jesus
Christ in non-Christian writing.

100

c. Apollonius of Tyana died, and some of his written works still survive. He was a pagan philosopher, orator, and teacher of morality from Anatolia (modern-day Turkey). In his time, people often compared him with Jesus. There were many parallels between their lives and legends, such as both having miraculous births, gathering disciples, performing miracles, and ascending to heaven. He is said to have traveled extensively throughout Syria, Israel, Egypt, Greece, and even India, and many considered him the greatest religious figure of the first century.

The estimated worldwide Christian population was probably between seven thousand and ten thousand.

c. The Writings (Psalms, Lamentations, Proverbs, Ecclesiastes, Esther, Ezra, Nehemiah, and Chronicles) were the final part of the Hebrew Bible to be canonized. From this point to the present, the Hebrew Bible (later adopted as the Christian Old Testament) has remained in this form, except for the inevitable scribal changes due to copying by hand. The Hebrew Bible didn't say much about what happened after death. It suggested that human life comes to an end, except for a few exceptional people, a theme that Calvinism would share 1,500 years later.

Cerinthus, an Egyptian theologian, popularized the idea that Jesus was a man possessed by a divine force at his baptism and that the power gained by this infusion abandoned Jesus at his crucifixion. This was very similar to how the Gospel of Mark portrayed him. This theology is called Adoptionism because it seemed that God adopted Jesus as his son at either his birth or baptism and then departed from him when he died.

c. An unknown writer wrote the noncanonical *Gospel of Peter*. It was widely known and popular in the early Church. It contained incredible claims about Jesus's resurrection, including a gigantic cross following him from the tomb and Jesus grown to a thousand feet tall.

c. This is the earliest estimated date for the writing of *Odes of Solomon*, a collection of forty-two poetic songs attributed to the former king. It was probably written in Edessa, Syria, and is referred to as the first Christian songbook. In it, the Holy Spirit is referred to as a woman, which was not unusual in those days. It was similar to wisdom being feminized by the Greeks into the female Sophia.

c. Unrevealed authors wrote the little-known, noncanonical scriptures known as the *Acts of Peter, Acts of Paul, Acts of Andrew,* and *Acts of John.*

c. Unknown authors wrote the *Didache,* also known as *The Teaching of the Twelve Apostles.* This is the oldest surviving written catechism and dealt with Christian ethics and sacraments such as baptism and the Eucharist. Some sects of Christians considered it holy scripture. In this manual, two chapters warned against the many false preachers who were "trafficking upon Christ," further demonstrating the large number of religious teachers at that time.

c. Due to overcrowding and scarcity of land for burials, Jews in Rome began to bury their dead outside the city in excavated underground chambers known as catacombs. The Christians followed this Jewish tradition because they didn't believe in burning their dead and didn't want above-ground burial sites desecrated. The Christians wanted to leave a physical body, or at least part of one, preserved in anticipation of a bodily resurrection. These catacombs consisted of immense corridors and rooms. Recesses in the walls, one above the other, contained the bodies, grouped by families.

101

c. Clement, the leader of the church in Rome, died. He was a very influential "father" of the Church. He increased the authority of the emerging Christian clergy by decreeing that whoever disobeys divinely ordained church leaders disobeys God himself.

c. The word *catholic*, derived from the Greek *katholikos*, was first used by Ignatius of Antioch to describe the "universal," rather than local, scope of the Christian Church.

Martial, a well-known Roman satirist, died. He had written about the most diverse characters in the contemporary Roman Empire. There is no mention of Jesus or any Christians in his surviving writings.

c. Ignatius, the leader of the church of Antioch and a former disciple of the apostle John, was very influential in the early days of Christianity. He declared that observance of the Jewish Sabbath on Saturday, the seventh day of the week, was no longer necessary for Christians.

110

The Romans arrested Ignatius, possibly for disturbing the peace, and sent to him to Rome. He pleaded with his followers not to try to free him because he welcomed a martyr's death. En route to Rome, he wrote a series of letters that have been preserved as examples of very early Christian theology. Important topics addressed in these letters included the sacraments, the consolidation of home churches into organized units under a male bishop, and the structuring and decoration of churches. Ignatius was also the first noncanonical writer to mention basic information about the birth of Jesus by Mary and his death under Pontius Pilate, yet he didn't refer to the names of any Gospels to support his statements. In none of the seven letters written while he was being brought to Rome for execution did Ignatius quote a single teaching of Jesus, refer to one of his miracles, or mention any specific detail of Jesus's treatment by the Romans. This is evidence that Ignatius may not have been familiar with any specific Gospel accounts, although it is clear he thought martyrdom was extremely important. He emphasized that Jesus was both God and man, and this concept would later become the *orthodox*, meaning "correct," but not the universal, understanding of Jesus's nature.

c. Papias, the bishop of Hierapolis, wrote the five-volume *Expositions of the Sayings of the Lord*. The work mentioned various accounts of

Jesus's life and speculated on the coming Kingdom of God. One of the sayings refers to a future messiah and closely parallels a passage from *Second Baruch*, a Jewish apocalyptic work written about this time. The Jews still expected their first visit by the Messiah, but Papias used his statement to forecast the return of Jesus, who he considered the true Messiah. This is an example of both religions sharing a similar text but deriving two different meanings from it. In the fourth century, the historian Eusebius of Caesarea would dismiss Papias as not worthy of attention, explaining why his writings were not copied nor preserved.

112

Pliny the Younger, the governor of Bithynia, in Anatolia, wrote to Emperor Trajan seeking advice on how to deal with Christians in his region. Trajan instructed him that they "must not be sought out, but if they are denounced and proven guilty, they are to be punished." He said that they should then be pardoned if they agreed to worship the Roman gods. Trajan also said that anonymous accusations against Christians should be ignored. Outside the questionable paragraph from Josephus in AD 93, this was the first time Christians were mentioned in a surviving, non-Christian source.

115

c. Papias wrote that the authorship of the Gospels and the way they were composed was already confusing and that the chain of oral stories about Jesus was preferable to the more recent written ones. This seemed to indicate that oral legends about Jesus were changed when put into a written form. There was also the problem that too many writings were available from which to choose, and they were wildly at odds with one another. This confusion over which writings were authoritative caused many problems because if there was no authoritative body of holy scripture, it would be impossible to demonstrate what an orthodox Christian should believe.

116

c. In his work entitled *Annals*, Roman historian and senator Tacitus wrote that Nero dispelled rumors that he had ordered the city of Rome torched by accusing others of the crime: "a class of men loathed for their vices, whom the crowd styled Christians." Tacitus also gave a one-page background on Jesus, his execution, and the Christian movement. This was only the second or possibly third time that there was mention of Christ or Christians in a surviving non-Christian document, indicating that Christians still were not considered very significant or threatening to the empire.

117

Basilides began a teaching and writing career in Alexandria. He wrote the *Gospel of Basilides*, and the *Exegetica*, which was possibly the first commentary on the Gospels by a Christian writer. Being a Gnostic, he was viewed by the preorthodox Christian sect as a heretic and nonconformist, and like most others who were declared heretics, his writings no longer exist. His followers persisted for at least two centuries after his death.

The Romans crushed anti-Roman rebellions by Jewish communities. The rebellions had begun two years earlier while the Romans focused on a war with the Parthians on their eastern border. As a result of the rebellions, the Romans expelled Jewish communities from Cyrene, Alexandria, and Cyprus. These rebellions were known as the Kitos War, derived from a corruption of the name of the Roman general Quietus.

120

In his *Lives of the Twelve Caesars*, Suetonius, a Roman historian, referred to Chrestus, who was the leader of a Jewish sect that was expelled from Rome. This was thought to be one of the earliest mentions of Christ in Roman literature, but it is questionable whether Suetonius was referring to Jesus Christ or someone else.

c. This is the earliest proposed date for the writing of the *Shepherd of Hermas*. It consisted of a series of end times and prophetic sayings and was one of the most widely read documents by some early Christian sects. It was considered canonical scripture by several of the early Church Fathers and would be bound as part of the New Testament in fourth-century *Codex Sinaiticus*, one of the oldest surviving copies of the Greek Bible.

125

c. This is the earliest date for the writing of the oldest surviving piece of papyrus containing any part of the New Testament, specifically John 18. The papyrus fragment is known as P52 and was acquired at an Egyptian market in 1920. Aside from P52, the next oldest documents would be dated from around AD 150, but most of the oldest remaining copies of scriptures are from the late second century to early third century.

c. The earliest proposed date for the *Gospel of Mary*, a Gnostic writing found in Egypt in 1896. The main character was Mary Magdalene, and it is the only known early Christian gospel whose main subject was a woman.

128

c. The Latin hymn "Gloria in excelsis Deo," or the *Greater Doxology*, came into use. It's a short hymn that is still a part of many Christian church services.

c. The Pantheon in Rome was rebuilt after being ravaged by fire. It's been demonstrated that the sunlight passing through the circular opening in the roof could indicate solar equinoxes and solstices. All original pagan statuary or items of significance were later stripped away by Christians in the fourth century.

130

c. An anonymous author wrote *Epistle to Diognetus*, stating that God sent the Logos, his Son, down to earth, but it identified no time, place, or name for this incarnation.

c. An unknown author wrote the Gnostic *Gospel of Thomas*. The author presented himself as the brother of Jesus and was obviously being dishonest. However, the sayings of Jesus recorded in this gospel may be accurate. This gospel wouldn't be discovered until 1945.

132

Emperor Hadrian announced plans to establish a Roman colony named Aelia Capitolina and build a temple to the god Jupiter on the site of the former Jewish Temple in Jerusalem. This led to another Jewish revolt—instigated by another messiah figure, Shimon Bar Kokhba—which the Romans extinguished three years later. After that, Jews were permanently expelled from Jerusalem, many moving into Mesopotamia, and Jerusalem became a pagan city.

135

Greek stoic philosopher Epictetus died. He had promoted a "brotherhood of man" doctrine, aiming his message at the poor and humble masses. It is uncertain whether he was influenced by or even aware of his Jewish humanitarian predecessor, Jesus, since he made no mention of him in his surviving writings.

c. Marcion, a Christian theologian from Sinope, Anatolia, traveled to Rome to propagate the Christian faith. He and his followers rejected the Hebrew Bible and the God Jehovah, who they saw as the unreasonably wrathful tribal god of Israel, not the real God of whom Jesus spoke. They focused on the god of love they found in their chosen gospel, later named the Gospel of Luke, with Jesus as the savior God sent to earth and Paul as his chief apostle. The Marcionites allowed women to serve as priests and bishops, countering the prevailing preorthodox trend of that time. For this, they attracted much criticism.

c. Montanus founded the sect of Montanism—known to its members as the New Prophecy—in Phrygia, Anatolia. It was a prophetic movement that called for reliance on the spontaneity of the Holy Spirit and focused on personal ethics and asceticism. Like the Marcionites, many of their most influential members were women, and preorthodox Christians used this as a criticism of Montanism. Tertullian, one of the most well-known early Christian theologians, eventually joined the Montanist movement, undermining the moral attacks on the sect. Montanism spread across the Middle East, North Africa, and into Gaul and lasted into the eighth century.

136

c. Valentinus, a Gnostic, taught in Alexandria and later in Rome. He was influenced by Paul's epistles and was said to have inherited secret wisdom that Paul had received from the risen Christ. Valentinus had expected to become bishop of Rome, but when he was passed over, he broke from the Roman Church and went to Cyprus. Like the other nonorthodox sects, he and his followers were condemned, but his movement lasted into the third century.

138

c. Juvenal, a popular Roman poet and satirist, died. In his extensive writings, he never mentioned anything about Christianity, continuing the trend of written evidence that Christianity was still not significant to the Romans.

140

c. An unknown author wrote *The Pseudo-Clementine Recognitions and Homilies* and attributed them to Clement, the first-century leader of the church of Rome. The works only quoted from the Old Testament and non-Christian sources. The fact that Clement couldn't have written it is another example of deception in the early Church, only detected with more modern forensic methods of study. By assigning a famous name to a written work, it guaranteed undeserved notoriety.

c. The Marcionites compiled the first Christian canon. It was known as the *Bible of the Marcionites* or the *Gospel of Marcion* and contained an abbreviated *Gospel of Luke*, called the *Evangelium*, which cut out all of Jesus's references to the Old Testament and most of the first four chapters of Luke containing Jesus's genealogy, birth narrative, and the mention of John the Baptist as his cousin. It did include ten of the thirteen epistles thought to have been written by Paul, known as the *Apostolicon*. Marcion's collection of scripture was another impetus for preorthodox Christians to establish their own canonical scripture to differentiate them from the Marcionites.

c. Aristides wrote one of the earliest surviving "apologies," or defenses, of Christianity. He wrote it in the Syriac language to Emperor Antoninus Pius. Since it is clearly dependent on a canonical Gospel story, it seems that the Gospels we're familiar with were becoming well-known. His apology had nothing to say about the Logos, or other Greek philosophical concepts, as the writings of other contemporaries did.

c. This was the earliest mention of a sect known as the Ebionites, a Jewish-Christian group that became established in Syria, Anatolia, and Egypt. They were descendants of the early Christian Church in Jerusalem, revered James the Just, and rejected Paul of Tarsus and his epistles. They regarded Jesus as Messiah, used the Gospel of Matthew as their main scripture, and insisted on the necessity of following Jewish law and rites. They did not believe in a virgin birth and did believe that Jesus, a human, was adopted by God for a specific purpose. The Hebrew root of their name means "the poor ones," evidence that they placed a special value on voluntary poverty. Like other sects, they were eventually driven out of existence by the preorthodox Christians. Their writings no longer exist, but the sect was active for centuries.

144

c. After the Roman Church accused Marcion of heresy and excommunicated him, he and his followers migrated to Syria.

145

c. An unknown author wrote the *Gospel of James*, also known at the *Protoevangelium of James* and the *Infancy Gospel of James*. It was extremely popular with certain groups of Christians, even into the Middle Ages. It mainly concerned Jesus's mother Mary's birth and early life and the conception and birth of Jesus. The book introduced Anne and her husband Joachim, the parents of Mary. In the earliest versions of the gospel, Mary was conceived without sexual intercourse. It was written long after Jesus's brother James lived, but the author used the name James, apparently to pass himself off as the real first-century James and thereby promote his story to a wider audience.

147

c. Justin Martyr became one of Christianity's most important defenders, explaining aspects of the religion to non-Christians in convincing terms. He wrote his *Major Apology* to Emperors Antoninus Pius and Marcus Aurelius. In it, he compared the worship of Jesus to the worship of Roman gods Jupiter and Mercury. He compared Jesus being born of a virgin with the god Perseus, who was also said to have had a virgin birth. He also declared pagan oracles and miracles valid and true and wrote that he was only saying similar things about Jesus. In other words, Justin Martyr seemed to say that Christianity wasn't so different from paganism so there was no reason to be suspicious of Christians. Justin Martyr and Aristides became the first of Christianity's elite scholars.

150

c. The estimated population of Christians worldwide was probably around forty thousand. Around this time, Christians were spreading into Bulgaria, Portugal, and along the Black Sea.

c. From this time onward, it became somewhat easier for modern scholars to deduce the authenticity, completeness, and reliability of Christian writing. That's because of the wealth of intact material left from the late second century. All that survives from the early second century is an occasional scrap of papyrus, and no written material at all survives from the first century.

c. This is the earliest estimated date for any surviving writings of Paul and is known as Papyrus 46. Other estimates of the same papyrus are as late as AD 250. This means that any alterations or additions made to any of Paul's writings before this time could never be detected by modern scholars.

c. Justin Martyr was the first early Christian writer to quote from a Gospel that was included in the New Testament. He didn't mention the name of the Gospel or its author, referring to it as the "memoirs of the apostles." It appears that names may have been assigned to the Gospels soon after this time. Whoever named them used the names of apostles Matthew, Mark, Luke, and John to give them substantial authority.

c. Justin Martyr mentioned *The Acts of Pontius Pilate* in his writing. This document has never been found, but later books about Pilate written by unknown authors were in circulation.

c. The Marcionites settled in Edessa on the edge of the Syrian desert where they formed a separate Christian community that lasted into the fifth century. Preorthodox Christianity would not arrive in that region until the last decades of the third century.

c. Earliest date for Greek astronomer and mathematician Claudius Ptolemy's *Almagest*. This was a treatise on the apparent motions of stars and planets around Earth and expressed the geocentric view of the cosmos that lasted for the next 1,500 years.

155

The Romans burned Polycarp, the bishop of Smyrna, who was said to be a former disciple of the apostle John. Tradition states that his crime was atheism. That was a charge brought against various people who wouldn't sacrifice to the Roman gods. Many Christians of the time believed that along with Clement of Rome and Ignatius of Antioch, he was another Church Father who received his authority through a direct line of disciples leading back to Jesus. In his surviving epistle, Polycarp used sayings found in the Gospels but never attributed them to a specific written document.

Justin Martyr mentioned some of the events in the book of *Acts*, but it was only later that the first clear reference was made to that book by name.

160

Members of the Church of Rome built a monument on the Vatican Hill on what was believed to be the burial site of Saint Peter. A historic dilemma is that neither Acts, nor the epistle to the Romans, nor *1 Clement* mentioned Peter being in Rome. The legend that Peter visited Rome apparently first appeared in the noncanonical *Acts of Peter*, which was written sometime after AD 150.

Tatian, a pupil of Justin Martyr, wrote *Apology to the Greeks*, urging pagan readers to turn to Christianity. In his description of Christian truths, he didn't use the names Jesus, Christ, or even the term Christian. He instead focused on Logos, the creative power of the universe, derived from Greek philosophy. There were a few allusions to Gospel sayings, but no specific reference to any written Gospel by name. Tatian didn't seem to believe that Christ or Logos could assume a human body.

c. This is the earliest date that an unknown author wrote the *Acts of Paul*. The writing was based on oral tradition of Paul's missionary work, providing personal information about Paul of Tarsus not found in the Bible. It had three parts: *The Acts of Paul and Thecia*, the *Epistle of the Corinthians to Paul*, and the *Third Epistle to the Corinthians*.

Tertullian first mentioned the writings and found them heretical in that they encouraged women to preach and baptize.

165

A devastating plague swept through the Roman Empire. Most pagans, fearing for their lives, tried to distance themselves from those who were sick, but many Christians, not afraid of martyrdom, cared for the sick and saved lives, sometimes by sacrificing their own.

166

c. Christian historian Hegesippus traveled from the East to Rome, documenting and comparing the teachings of the various churches he visited. He wrote against the heresies of his time, such as Marcionism and Gnosticism. His works are now entirely lost except for what Eusebius of Caesarea quoted in the fourth century.

167

Melito, the bishop of Sardis, gave a sermon entitled "Homily on the Passover." He argued that in crucifying Jesus, the Jews had murdered God. Additionally, he provided the first list of books that he thought Christians should borrow from the Hebrew Bible and coined the term *Old Testament*. In his proposed canon of scripture, he excluded the books of *Esther*, *Nehemiah*, and any book written after *Daniel*.

c. Lucian, an extremely popular Greek satirist, died. He wrote *On the Death of Peregrinus* about a Christian philosopher who burned himself to death at the Olympic Games. It is one of the earliest preserved writings to mock Christians, portraying Peregrinus as an adulterer and a murderer who had risen to a high position in the Church. The document stated that after his suicide, Christians honored him as a god. Lucian satirized the Christians for their gullibility in accepting beliefs without proof and for being naive enough to be tricked by sorcerers and alleged miracle workers, such as Jesus and Simon Magus. He was also criticizing public and voluntary martyrdom, which many early Christians sought.

170

c. Celsus, a Greek philosopher, began a bitter attack on Christianity entitled *On the True Doctrine*. He was very familiar with Christian scripture and its defenders but loathed the religion for its absurdity and the danger it presented to society. He was greatly troubled by the Christian lack of intellectual curiosity. To him, it seemed that they were proud of their ignorance. In the writing, he mentioned other gods beside Jesus who rose from the dead and sarcastically asked the Christians if they believed their story was the only one that was convincing. Another criticism was that Christian writings were falsified and revised when copied. His writings were refuted by Christian apologists centuries later, most famously by Origen in his third-century, eight-volume work *Against Celsus*.

Apuleius, a Christian writer in North Africa, wrote of the cult of Isis and Osiris, who, like Christians, had a ceremony of rebirth or resurrection in their religion. The theme of rebirth continued in the "mystery religions" that were popular at this time.

Apart from Clement, the bishop of Rome in AD 90, there is no evidence that a Christian writer mentioned Nero's persecution of Christians until Bishop Melito did so at this time. This may mean that the persecution hadn't been well-known to Christians outside Rome.

c. The earliest proposed date for the writings known as the *Apocryphal Acts of the Apostles*. These were widely circulated writings about the individual apostles of Jesus and included many stories of miracle working by them. By this time, it was too late for anyone to examine any historical records to confirm or deny these events.

c. The Alogi were a group of heretical Christians in Asia Minor who rejected the doctrine of the Logos, as expressed in the Gospel of John. They attributed the Gospel of John and the book of Revelation to the Gnostic writer Cerinthus.

Tatian harmonized the four canonical Gospels into one, which became known as the *Diatessaron*, meaning "four." Written in Syriac, the compilation facilitated the spread of Christian doctrine outside the Greek-speaking cities and further into Asia, where in the early fourth century, the Diatessaron became very influential to what would become the Church of the East.

171

c. Dionysius, the bishop of Corinth, was reported to have said that his own writings "had been falsified by apostles of the devil," seemingly to imply that his writings had been revised by copiers. At that time, no writing could be guaranteed to remain as originally written.

176

c. Athenagoras, a Greek Christian philosopher, wrote *Embassy for the Christians*, addressed to Emperor Marcus Aurelius. It was a plea for justice for Christians, refuting charges that they were atheists, cannibals, infant killers, or incestuous. He wrote that Christians were in fact more moral and had more of an ancient tradition than other religions. He justified this with his belief that Christ originally helped the Jewish God "create man in our image." Interestingly, the book did not, in thirty-seven chapters, mention that the Logos was incarnated in the person of a historic man.

177

The Romans executed forty-eight Christians in Lyon and Vienne, in Gaul. This persecution was precipitated after the Romans seized two pagan servants of Christians. Fearing torture, the servants accused their masters of incest and cannibalism. The charge of cannibalism was based on the Eucharist, or communion, in which Christians believed they ate the body of Jesus and drank his blood. At this time, Roman emperors were largely content to treat Christians as a local problem and let their subordinates deal with them if necessary. Until the reign of Decius in AD 249, persecution was conducted only regionally and enforced sporadically.

180

c. Irenaeus, the bishop of Lyon, wrote a five-volume set, *Against Heresies*. It was a detailed attack on Gnosticism, especially the form that Valentinus taught. Irenaeus alluded to the beliefs that Jesus's ministry extended over ten years and that he didn't die until he was fifty years old. Papias also believed that Jesus may have lived to old age. Even in those early days, knowledge of the historical Jesus was hard to discern. Irenaeus also mentioned the *Gospel of Judas*, which was the only evidence that this gospel existed until an antiquities dealer discovered it in Egypt in the 1970s. Out of all the gospels available at that time, Irenaeus was the first to choose Mark, Mathew, Luke, and John as the only ones that he thought were truly orthodox. Irenaeus noted that the Ebionites preferred Matthew's Gospel, the Marcionites preferred their abbreviated version of Luke, the Valentinian Gnostics preferred John's Gospel, and the Docetists found Mark's Gospel more to their liking.

c. An anonymous author wrote the *Apocryphon of John*, or *Secret Book of John*, no later than this time. It told of Christ's appearance to the apostle John after his resurrection and recounted what John learned from him. In *Against Heresies*, Irenaeus labeled this book a forgery.

c. Theophilus of Antioch wrote the *Apology to Autolycus*. He was the first writer to use "Trinity" to refer to "God, his Word (Logos), and his Wisdom (Sophia)." He is also the first writer known to mention the name John as a Gospel author. When asked what the meaning of Christianity was, he answered, "being anointed with the oil of God," never mentioning Jesus or Christ. He said that his sect's doctrines and knowledge of God came through the Holy Spirit.

The Scillitan Martyrs were twelve Christians from Numidia, present-day Algeria, who were executed for their religious beliefs. According to Tertullian, a Christian writer in Carthage, this was the earliest Roman persecution of Christians in North Africa. *Acts of the Scillitan Martyrs*, a record of their trial, is the earliest surviving document from the Church of North Africa and the earliest specimen of Latin writing in Christian literature.

Irenaeus wrote that Peter founded and organized the church at Rome and appointed Linus to be bishop of Rome in AD 67. This information was not found in the New Testament but had been mentioned in Clement of Rome's letter to the Corinthians in AD 96. This statement was later used to further justify the succession of the line of popes, starting with Peter. This is confusing because there was already a church in Rome when Paul wrote his epistle to the Romans in the late '50s, and this would have been well before Peter or Paul would have gone there. The Gnostics already had a tradition of apostolic succession, the chain of apostles traced back to Jesus, from whom they received their spiritual authority. The same process was adopted by the preorthodox Christians to gain credibility for their line of authority. In addition, the earliest list of popes and their dates in office has been found to be inaccurate.

c. A man named Pantaenus was later recorded by Eusebius and Jerome as being sent by his bishop from Alexandria to India, where he encountered Christians.

182

c. Irenaeus, still writing in Greek even though he lived in Gaul, wrote about the observance of Lent as a time of self-examination and penitence by the denial of pleasures. In his time, Lent lasted one or two days, possibly only forty hours, but not forty days, as it is today.

185

c. Irenaeus was the first writer known to mention anything about the pastoral epistles, (first and second epistles to Timothy and the epistle to Titus), which would eventually be canonized in the New Testament. These writings were originally attributed to Paul but were later found to be written by other unknown authors. The verse that is often used by today's evangelical literalists to support the doctrine of biblical inerrancy and infallibility is Second Timothy 3:16: "All scripture is God-breathed and is useful for teaching, rebuking, correcting and training in righteousness." This was not written by anyone who is known, but some Christians rest their entire worldview and belief system on this statement by taking the Bible literally.

A mob of Christians arrived at the home of Arrius Antoninus, the governor of Asia, and demanded to be executed as martyrs. Antoninus was said to have executed a few and then sent the rest away, telling them, "You miserable wretches, if you want to die, you have cliffs to leap from and ropes to hang by."

188

Clement of Alexandria wrote *Miscellanies*. These three volumes contained the most thorough examples of the synthesis of Christian doctrine and Greek philosophy at the time. When Christianity moved from the Middle East into areas more influenced by Greek culture, it had to adapt to be understandable to the inhabitants. By doing so, it adopted elements of Stoicism and Platonism. Clement wrote, "Philosophy has been given to the Greeks as their own kind of Covenant, their foundation for the philosophy of Christ . . . the philosophy of the Greeks . . .

contains the basic elements of that genuine and perfect knowledge which is higher than human . . . even upon those spiritual objects."

190

c. Christianity spread easily in the region of Edessa (present-day eastern Syria). Since the people there had worshipped one god, Marilaha, they were prepared for another monotheistic belief. Christianity mainly followed the paths of the Jewish diaspora.

c. Irenaeus and Clement of Alexandria both wrote against the Carpocratians, a Gnostic sect that believed Jesus was not divine but had been able to free himself from the powers of the material sphere. They believed that they, too, could transcend the material realm. They rejected Mosaic law, and critics reported that they did not hold to sexual morality. They also were said to have believed in reincarnation.

Theodotus, a Roman preacher, used logical analysis derived from Greeks Aristotle and Euclid to conclude that while the Holy Spirit was involved in the conception of Jesus, this did not give Jesus a status of divinity. Theodotus was excommunicated for his teaching, but his congregation continued in this belief for almost another century.

c. Scholars translated the writings that would make up the Bible into Latin from the original Greek, and the compilation became known as the Vetus Latina. These writings were later made obsolete by Jerome's fourth-century Bible translation, the Vulgate. Only at this time, after Paul's epistles had been translated into Latin, did Paul's authority in the Church of Rome increase.

c. Egyptian Gnostic followers of Basilides commemorated Jesus's baptism on the Epiphany, January 6, the same date thought to have been the visitation of the Magi to the baby Jesus. Over the first centuries of Christianity, this date was also used by many Christians to commemorate Jesus's birth.

c. In Egypt, variants of the books that would be included in the New Testament were translated into Sahidic, the leading Coptic dialect.

c. Christian art first consisted of allegorical symbolism, such as a lamb, fish, dove, anchor, or vine. At this time, the first depictions of human images appeared in the catacombs to help Christians understand biblical stories.

193

Septimius Severus became the Roman emperor. It's uncertain if there were persecutions of Christians during his reign. If so, the persecutions were local and apparently not initiated by the emperor. Severus even employed a Christian as his personal physician.

194

c. An unknown Christian theologian compiled the *Muratorian Canon*. It is the oldest-known list of New Testament writings but is somewhat different from the current list in that it did not contain James, Hebrews, and the two letters of Peter. It did, however, contain the *Wisdom of Solomon*, the *Shepherd of Hermas*, and the *Apocalypse of Peter*.

195

c. The threefold hierarchy of bishop, presbyter, and deacon was becoming widespread in the preorthodox Church by this time.

196

Byzantium, the Greek city, which in AD 330 would be renamed Constantinople, took the wrong side in a dispute between Roman emperors Pescennius Niger and Septimius Severus. The army of Severus inflicted major damage to the city.

c. Tertullian of Carthage began the writings that would earn him the reputation of "Father of Latin Theology" since he was the first

Christian writer to produce extensive writings in Latin. He had the
onerous task of translating a religion that was deeply rooted in the
Middle Eastern and Greek world and infusing it with concepts that
Latin readers could understand. This would make the most confusing
concepts of Christianity even more difficult for the Greeks and Latins
to agree on. Tertullian's condemnation of Marcion in *Against Marcion*
provided a glimpse into two basic types of Christianity at the time.
One was the rational, optimistic view that believed love and compassion were sufficient, and the other was the pessimistic view that was
convinced of the essential corruption of human nature and the need
for a mechanism for damnation and salvation. Tertullian represented
the latter group and set the stage for Augustine to make his mark on
Latin theology two centuries later. When Tertullian joined the stringent Montanist movement, it was due to the issue of remission of sins
after baptism.

197

c. Tertullian mentioned a document written by Pontius Pilate to
Emperor Tiberius. Later, this and other correspondence supposedly
written by Pilate were said to have been discovered and were publicized. What was believed to be the letter Tertullian mentioned was
discovered in Italy in 1309. In it, Pilate presented himself as innocent
of Jesus's death, calling himself "unwilling and afraid" and writing
that the Jews gave him no choice but to carry out the execution of this
"ambassador of truth." This is a very controversial document, clearly
designed to shift the responsibility for the death of Jesus from Pilate
to the Jews. Other similar letters were the *Letters of Pilate and Herod*,
dating from the seventh century, and the *Letter of Tiberius to Pilate*,
written no earlier than the eleventh century. This entire body of literature appears to have been produced in order to make Pilate appear
blameless of the death of Jesus, and even possibly a secret Christian.

CHAPTER 3: THIRD CENTURY AD

Having refuted, then, as well as we could, every notion which might suggest that we were to think of God as in any degree corporeal, we go on to say that, according to strict truth, God is incomprehensible, and incapable of being measured.
—Origen

The blood of the martyrs is the seed of the church.
—Tertullian

All religion, my friend, is simply evolved out of fraud, fear, greed, imagination, and poetry.
—Edgar Allen Poe

In this century, Christians were still struggling to define who and what Jesus Christ really was and were divided into feuding camps in the process. This century also saw the further rise in power and prestige of the clergy, the Virgin Mary taking a more prominent role in the religion, and the refining of the concept of "apostolic succession" to justify which churches and bishops were most authoritative. The first Christian hermits, the first empire-wide persecution of Christians, Christianity's spread into rural areas, and the rising popularity of Christian art and iconography were other significant themes.

200

The estimated number of Christians worldwide was between 140,000 and 170,000 out of the approximately sixty million inhabitants of the Roman Empire. This was less than one percent of the empire's population. By this time, there were also Christian enclaves as far east as the Caspian Sea, outside the Roman Empire.

c. Tertullian wrote that the Jews called Christians "Nazarenes," but the origin of that title is unclear. The name may not have referred to the city of Nazareth but to the Hebrew root word *nazara*, meaning "the Truth" or "strong defender of the Mosaic Law."

c. Marcus Minucius Felix, a Latin Christian apologist, wrote *Octavius*, which was designed as an argument between a Christian and a pagan. The names Jesus or Christ never appeared, and Felix, himself a Christian, ridiculed the idea that the object of Christian worship was a mortal human who was executed as a criminal. This was more evidence of the multitude of Christian theologies in circulation.

c. Tertullian wrote that the forger of the *Third Epistle to the Corinthians* was convicted by Church authorities for falsely composing the letter and attributing it to the apostle Paul.

c. Because of the ancient Jewish dispersions, the tradition of oral scholarship could not be maintained, so the rabbis wrote discourses. By this time, there was a form of the *Mishnah*, a codification of non-biblical laws and customs. The *Mishnah* and the *Gemara*, the rabbinical commentaries on the Mishnah, eventually comprised the *Talmud*.

c. The *Martyrdom of Polycarp* was the first well-known text to develop the theology of martyrdom. In the writing, Polycarp's suffering closely paralleled that of Jesus. Polycarp's bones and the relics of other saints became valuable to Christians, who preserved them for protection against evil because of their assumed miraculous powers. Relics inspired Christians to be more courageous when facing the challenges of life.

c. By this time, the Jewish-Christian sects that understood Jesus as purely human were becoming rare and isolated.

c. The *Sophia of Jesus Christ* was a Gnostic writing of this time later discovered at Nag Hammadi, Egypt, in 1945. It was said to have reflected the true sayings of Jesus. The wording is highly mystical and concerns the creation of gods, angels, and the universe.

c. The earliest known artistic representation of the crucifixion of Jesus was graffiti in Rome depicting a donkey being crucified, apparently a mockery of Christians. At this time, most Christians were horrified by the symbol of crucifixion, so it didn't appear in their art.

201

c. It is recorded that King Abgar of Osroene, in Anatolia, converted to Christianity, making him the world's first Christian monarch. His capital of Edessa would later play an important role in Christian history by being a launching site to evangelize the East. Archeologists have discovered a church from this time that was destroyed in a flood, making it the first known Christian house of worship.

c. Available evidence shows that the preorthodox brand of Christianity didn't move into Egypt until about this time. Before this, Gnosticism was the predominant form of Christianity.

c. This is the earliest date that the *Papyrus Bodmer X* would have been written. It contained the *Third Epistle to the Corinthians*, purportedly written by Paul, and was designed to correct certain misunderstandings in the first and second epistles to the Corinthians. The third epistle was not considered canonical by the western Church but was by some in the Syriac-speaking Church.

c. The *Acts of Thomas* was in circulation and described the apostle Thomas's missionary activities. Written in Greek, it refers to Thomas as Jesus's brother, as do the writings the *Gospel of Thomas* and the book of *Thomas, the Contender*, also written in this era. All of this adds more confusion to an already confused history of Jesus. Could Thomas really have been Jesus's brother? A twin brother? One can only speculate. The *Acts of Thomas* also described Thomas traveling to India and provided glimpses of hell that previewed Dante's vision centuries later.

202

c. Perpetua, a twenty-two-year-old mother with an infant child, was believed to have been executed in the arena in Carthage because she was a Christian and most likely didn't sacrifice to the Roman gods. She not only refused to recant but was said to have welcomed martyrdom. She became well-known through a book that she partly wrote or dictated while in captivity, entitled *The Passion of Saints Perpetua and Felicitas*. It became a prototype for literature documenting Christian martyrs.

c. Emperor Severus seems to have followed Trajan's tolerant attitude toward Christians but may have issued an edict to prevent pagans from converting to Judaism or Christianity. It is known that Bishop Clement of Alexandria fled the city to avoid arrest at this time and never returned to Alexandria.

206

Tertullian included the first explicit rationale against infant baptism in *On Baptism*. He distinguished baptism, unction, and laying on of hands in the Christian initiation rites. His concept of baptism involved elaborate preparation, including confession of sin, renunciation of the devil, fasting, and anointing and could only be undertaken by an adult.

212

Origen had been a pupil of Clement of Alexandria at Clement's Catechetical School. He was a convert to Christianity who was influenced by Greek philosophical tradition and was one of the more progressive Christian thinkers and writers of his time. Like seemingly all Christians of his time, he used anti-Jewish rhetoric, writing that the Jews "have committed the most abominable of crimes" in conspiring against Christ, and for that reason "the Jewish nation was driven from its country, and another people was called by God to the blessed election."

215

From this time until the reign of Decius in AD 250, there were few accounts of persecution against Christians.

Clement of Alexandria died. He had denounced the idea of voluntary martyrdom as something done only by heretics, not by true Christians. He also equated voluntary martyrdom with suicide, not anything that God desired.

220

Sabellius, a priest and theologian who taught in Rome, was a Modalist, holding a theology that considered the Father as the creator, the Son as redeemer, and the Holy Spirit as the inspiration to humanity. They were different modes of one entity, not three persons in one. This kind of hairsplitting was a characteristic of theological disputes for centuries.

224

The Persian ruling House of Sassan founded the Sassanid Empire. It would be the last Persian empire before the rise of Islam. Bordering the Roman Empire on the Euphrates River, there would be almost constant strife between the Sassanids and the Romans over the next four centuries. The Sassanids revived Zoroastrianism as the state religion and resisted the influence of other religions.

225

c. In his *Homilies on Ezekiel*, Origen discussed Tammuz, a Babylonian god who he associated with the Phoenician and Greek god Adonis. It's interesting that Origen stated that after Tammuz died, he was raised from the dead. So it's confusing whether Origin believed there were other gods beside the Hebrew God.

230

Sextus Julius Africanus wrote his *Chronographia*, estimating that the Creation event took place 5499 years before the birth of Christ, a date that was later adopted by many eastern Churches. He estimated March 25, or around the spring equinox, as the day of Creation and also the day of Jesus's conception, so he estimated that December 25, around the winter solstice, was Jesus's birthday. Five years later, Hippolytus of Rome confirmed this date. As seen earlier, December 25 was the traditional birthdate of sun gods.

c. The Christian treatise *Didascalia Apostolorum*, or *Teaching of the Apostles*, first appeared in Syria. It belonged to the genre of the Church orders and presented itself as being written by the twelve apostles at the time of the Council of Jerusalem in the first century. *Didascalia Apostolotum* has since been declared a forgery, written by unknown authors and intended to increase the status of the clergy. It was modeled on the earlier Didache and exalted bishops to nearly absolute power over the laity. This concept made God inaccessible to most people without the clergy to mediate for them. In the fourth century, the *Didascalia Apostolorum* would be used as a source for books of the *Apostolic Constitutions*, which presented supposedly authoritative guidelines on moral conduct.

Urban I, the bishop of the Church of Rome, died. His reign was the first of that office that can be dated with accuracy. Every bishop mentioned before him, including the apostle Peter, was questionable as to either their filling that role or their dates in office.

The Church of Lyon was the only Christian church founded in the region of what is now Belgium, France, and Germany, despite many claims made a few hundred years later that many churches in the region could be traced back to the time of the apostles. There are legends about the early martyrs of Gallic Christianity, such as Saint Benignus of Dijon. Even though a church was built to honor Benignus, he may have never existed.

232

Heraclas, the bishop of Alexandria, was the first Christian bishop to be called "pope." The name was derived from the Greek word *pappas*, an affectionate term for father. This was three centuries before the title would apply exclusively to the bishop of Rome.

236

Against all odds, the electors of Rome chose the unlikely candidate Fabian as their new bishop. The story is told that he was chosen primarily because during the deliberations, a dove flew into the room and landed on his head. This was seen as a sign that God had chosen this man the same way he had chosen Jesus at his baptism.

240

Roman historian Herodian finished writing the history of the Roman Empire, including the sixty years of events during his lifetime. In it, he listed the most significant threats that emperors had to confront during this period. Christianity was not mentioned as one of them.

c. Tertullian, the first notable Christian Latin writer, died. This quote summarized his intellectual philosophy, "What concord is there between the Academy [the place in Athens where philosophers and scientists met] and the Church? . . . Away with all attempts to produce a mottled Christianity of Stoic, Platonic, and dialectic composition! We want no . . . inquisition after enjoying the gospel! With our faith, we desire no further belief." This statement reinforced the tradition that one should unquestioningly accept and submit to whatever was handed down through the clergy and not use reason or Greek philosophy to understand the world.

241

c. This is the second-earliest known evidence for what we would call a church building. Discovered in Dura-Europos, Syria, the church is proof that Christianity was openly practiced at that time, at least in some regions. It even contained the earliest known baptistry. Prior to this, most baptism was probably carried out in natural streams and lakes.

242

c. Mani, a Persian prophet who had been raised with Zoroastrian, Jewish, and Christian influences, came to believe that he was destined to help end world suffering. He had taught his new religion in Persia and India, and at this time, he received permission from Shapur I to spread his teachings in the Sassanid Empire. His religion, called Manichaeism, was focused on purifying the soul, not the corrupted body. The Manichaeans criticized Old Testament scripture for its contradictions and rejected its prophets. They considered women as temptations and the earthly pleasures of sex and family to be part of Satan's plan. Mani accentuated pacifism, asceticism, and disconnection with the physical world. He was also said to have had twelve disciples and seventy-two bishops. Manichaeism had been described as a Christian Zoroastrianism, and it also incorporated ideas from Buddhism, Taoism, and Gnosticism. Mani preserved his own revelations in writing.

245

Origen wrote his eight-volume *Against Celsus*, an apologetic work aimed at the first-century pagan philosopher who objected to the supernatural and exclusivist claims of Christianity. Ironically, we would now know almost nothing about Celsus's writing if Origen hadn't kept it alive by paraphrasing it to sustain his arguments.

249

Cyprian became the bishop of Carthage. In his *Unity of the Church*, he wrote that the Church was a divine institution, that only within the Christian Church could people have spiritual life, and that individual lay people could not be saved by direct contact with God but only through the intercession of the clergy. Whereas many pagans thought it ridiculous that a god would be interested in the unimportant activities of the average human, devout Christians were being taught that God was monitoring their every word, deed, and thought.

A great plague swept through the empire, killing an estimated 25 percent of the population of the Mediterranean region. Christian leaders such as Cyprian called for Christians to help the sick, and inflicted Christians had a much higher survival rate because they weren't abandoned. This compassion was said to have won them much respect from the non-Christian population.

250

The estimated worldwide Christian population was six hundred thousand to seven hundred thousand, and Rome may have been home to thirty thousand to forty thousand Christians.

c. Cyprian claimed that other Christians were forging letters to discredit him.

c. Gregory Thaumaturgus, a bishop from Asia Minor, wrote his *Exposition of Faith*. According to eastern Church tradition, the apostle John and the Virgin Mary presented teaching to him in a vision. This was the earliest recorded incidence of someone witnessing an apparition of Mary.

c. Christians in Caesarea, Judea instituted the *Caesarean Creed* of faith and belief. Based on the fourth-century writings of Eusebius of Caesarea, he introduced the creed to the Council of Nicaea in AD 325 as the prototype for the Nicene Creed.

Paul of Thebes retreated to the Egyptian desert and became the first known Christian hermit. His motivation for this seemingly masochistic lifestyle was to escape the temptations of civilization, women being prominent in that regard, and to become better acquainted with God through prayer and ascetic denial of comfort. He is remembered through Jerome's biography *Life of Saint Paul the First Hermit*, written around AD 375.

c. The earliest surviving papyrus containing parts of the Gospels of Matthew, Mark, Luke, John, and the book of *Acts* was written at this time and became known as P45.

c. The Church of Rome was so well-established that it could support a staff of 155 clergy as well as 46 presbyters, 7 deacons, 7 sub-deacons, 42 acolytes and 52 exorcists, readers, and doorkeepers. It had a charity list of over 1,500 people.

According to Gregory of Tours, writing in the sixth century, this year the Roman bishop Fabian sent out seven bishops to spread Christianity to the Gauls. Martial of Limoges succeeded in converting the inhabitants of the region where he was assigned. His burial site in Limoges would later become the site of the Abbey of Saint Martial, which contained a magnificent library, second only to the one in Cluny Abbey. As Martial's legends were passed on, this abbey became one of the most visited pilgrimage sites in Europe.

Although many Christians had been killed in isolated persecutions, there were few true martyrdom accounts found in Christian literature until this time. This year, however, Emperor Decius issued a decree forcing every citizen to sacrifice to the Romans gods. Many Christians refused, and although Decius had in the past shown tolerance, his attitude changed. He blamed many of the empire's problems, whether military setbacks or plagues, on those who disrespected the Roman gods. Decius instituted the first empire-wide persecution which affected many Christians, and many were executed during the next decade, starting with prominent bishops. Fabian, the bishop of Rome, Babylas of Antioch, and Alexander of Jerusalem all fell victim. The other patriarchs, Dionysius of Alexandria, and Cyprian of Carthage went into hiding. One result of this persecution was its effect on non-Christians. Observing Christians willingly, and on occasion cheerfully, welcoming martyrdom made many pagans wonder what kind of God these Christians worshipped to allow them to be so courageous in the face of death. Others thought Christians were crazy to seek death. In the long run, Christianity prospered because they represented the anti-government sentiments shared by many pagans. This persecution was ended after eighteen months.

c. The first known physical depiction of Jesus was a fresco showing him beardless, youthful, and with short hair. Since there were no physical descriptions of him in the Gospels, all artistic depictions of him came from people's imaginations. Previously, the commandment prohibiting graven images had prevented such works of art, but Christian artists were pushing the limits at this time.

c. The first known reference of Jesus descent into hell, as part of the circa AD 180 Apostles' Creed, was from this time. In his book *The Secret Lore of Egypt: Its Impact on the West*, Dr. Erik Hornung theorizes that the visit to hell comes from the Christian Copts incorporating the ancient Egyptian belief that the sun god Ra made a nightly journey to the netherworld to be rejuvenated and rise again in the morning.

Many Christians began to flee Roman persecutions by migrating to the Sassanid Empire.

251

Novatian, a Roman priest, opposed the election of Cornelius as bishop of Rome because he thought Cornelius was too accepting of Christians who had denied their faith during the persecution. Novatian allowed his followers to appoint him as a rival bishop or in this case, antipope. The Novatians were later declared schismatics and heretics.

252

Cyprian of Carthage wrote *On Mortality*. In this work, he asserted that plagues should be welcomed because they would send Jews and pagans to hell quicker and the Christians would arrive in heaven that much sooner. This statement was significant because it demonstrated the way disease was understood by people in those days—not as something that should be studied and cured but rather as a divine reward or punishment for one's beliefs. *On Mortality* made it clear that hell was the place that all non-Christians would go when they died.

253

Origen died of aftereffects of being tortured during the Decian persecution. He had argued for equality of the sexes, for the necessity of good deeds in addition to faith, against celibacy, and against those who willingly sought martyrdom. He was one of Christianity's greatest philosophers and writers. He had insisted on going back to the original Greek writings and rethinking the conclusions that the preorthodox Christians had developed. He created the science of biblical theology, whereby every sentence of the scripture was explored for metaphor and hidden meaning, and he warned against the literal interpretation of the Bible. Origen was a humanist and optimist who believed in the gradual improvement of humans based on Jesus's guidance. He was also a universalist who believed salvation was offered to all of humanity and that ultimately all people would be reconciled to God. Debate over his theory of reincarnation would continue until the sixth century.

Antioch, one of the major centers of Christianity, was sacked by the Sassanids.

254

c. Roman Bishop Stephen I tried to establish the primacy of Peter as the first bishop of Rome by using Jesus's words in Matthew 16:18: "And I tell you that you are Peter, and on this rock, I will build my church." At this time, the Church of Rome was distancing itself from any connection to the apostle Paul because that was who the Marcionites admired. Also, using Peter as the head of apostolic succession took the first bishop of Rome one step closer to Jesus than Paul, since Paul never knew Jesus in life.

255

Cyprian invited North African bishops to the Council of Carthage. There, they opposed the validity of baptisms by formerly heretical priests who had recanted. The bishops also rejected Roman Bishop Stephen's claim to be the "bishop of bishops."

256

Emperor Valerian introduced a renewed persecution of Christians. Valerian issued an edict that Christian clergy sacrifice to the Romans gods or face banishment. The following year he ordered the execution of Christian clergy who refused to sacrifice. Valerian demanded that Christians stop meeting in Rome's cemeteries, that high-ranking Christians in government be downgraded, and finally, that if Christians did not recant from their religion, they should be put to death. The fact that there were high-ranking Christians at the heart of the imperial establishment demonstrated that the persecutory actions taken by Decius in AD 250 had not been entirely successful. Cyprian and many other prominent Church leaders were executed, and this persecution would last three and a half years.

258

After Roman authorities executed Bishop Sixtus II, they tasked Lawrence, one of seven deacons at the Church of Rome, with collecting the Church's treasures and turning them over to the emperor. Lawrence was said to have given the Church's possessions to the poor and arrived at the prefect's office instead with poor, disabled, blind, and otherwise pitiful people and presented them as the true treasures of the Church. In the legend, the prefect was said to have been so furious that he roasted Lawrence on a gridiron. In actuality, he was probably decapitated, like the pope and other deacons.

260

When Emperor Valerian was captured by the Sassanids, his son Gallienus became emperor. Gallienus, whose wife was a Christian, ended his father's persecution. This inaugurated another long period of toleration during which the Church expanded, and many Christians rose to, or regained, positions of status in the empire.

c. The doctrine of the Trinity faced opposition at this time by both Sabellianism and Tritheism. Sabellianism was the belief that the Father, Son, and Holy Spirit were three modes of one god, not three distinct persons, and Tritheism was the belief that there were three gods in Christianity.

Paul of Samosata, the bishop of Antioch revived the Adoptionist doctrine, insisting that Mary was the mother of a man, not the mother of a god. Paul's theology declared that Jesus became Christ only when the spirit of God descended on him due to his purity and sanctity. The bishop said that the apostle Paul taught that ordinary believers could and must emulate Jesus, and so Jesus had to be a human, or else aspiring to be like him would have been impossible. He believed the man Jesus had died on the cross, but the divinity of Christ did not.

Sassanid emperor Shapur I had conquered Syria, Cilicia, Cappadocia, and Antioch and deported tens of thousands of Christians to Mesopotamia, where he built the city of Gondishapur. Since these Christians were Greek-speaking, they didn't integrate with the Syrian-speaking Church of the East and began their own congregations.

268

c. The Greek word *homousios* was being used to compare Jesus to God, saying that both were made of the same substance. At the Synod of Antioch, the bishops dismissed the idea as heretical nonsense. Surprisingly, only sixty years later at the Council of Nicaea, *homousios* would become the key word used to define the orthodox concept of Jesus Christ.

269

Valentine of Terni died. He was reported to have been martyred in Rome, and his death was commemorated on February 14. There is not much known about Valentine's death because no persecution was recorded at this time. Many of the legends about him were apparently pieced together in England in the fourteenth century, leading to what we now celebrate as Saint Valentine's Day. Valentine of Rome may have been the same person, or their legends were possibly interwoven.

270

When his parents died, Anthony, an apprentice to the hermit Paul of Thebes, gave away his family lands, sold his remaining property, and donated his money to help the poor. He began life as a hermit near his hometown in Egypt. Anthony the Great would eventually be regarded as the "Father of All Monks."

272

Roman emperor Aurelian mounted a major campaign to bring the Syrian Desert region around Palmyra and Mesopotamia back into the empire. These areas had been taken by Arab Queen Zenobia in the first recorded incident of Arabs exerting military power on the fringe of the empire.

273

The Sassanid government began to suppress Manichaeism because its pacifism and asceticism were not in sync with the empire's agenda, but Christianity was allowed to flourish.

274

Emperor Aurelian instituted the cult of Sol Invictus, a newer sun god, to replace the worship of Jupiter. The day of the sun's death was regarded as the winter solstice, December 21, but the day that the sun was reborn and visibly began to rise in the sky was considered December 25. This was the day the sun appeared to be born anew and began its seasonal path of rising higher in the sky each day. This was celebrated as the sun god's birthday, as it was for Mithra and Dionysus.

280

By this time, the western Church had evolved a formula designed to avoid presenting Christ as being too human or too divine. In Latin terms, Jesus Christ was said to be one person in whom there were two substances.

c. Greek Neoplatonic philosopher Porphyry of Tyre wrote the fifteen-volume series, *Against the Christians*. In his criticism, he targeted the Old Testament prophecies, blind faith, and lack of rationality demonstrated by Christians. He was confused as to why God would have waited so long to send a savior to the earth and what happened to all the innocent souls in the millennia before Jesus arrived. He admired Jesus as a great philosopher and teacher but didn't believe he was a god. In AD 435, Christian emperor Theodosius II would order all copies of Porphyry's books book burned.

284

Diocletian became the Roman emperor and raised Maximian to the office of caesar, or second in command. The next year he divided the

Roman Empire into eastern and western halves, each with one augustus and one caesar who would be the heir to the augustus. At this time, the four imperial capitals on the frontiers of the Roman Empire were Trier in northwestern Germany, Milan in central Italy, Sirmium on the Danube, and Nicomedia near Byzantium. From those cities, military campaigns were planned and executed.

285

Quintus of Phrygia died. Rufus, the local governor, had tortured him for not sacrificing to the Roman gods. Quintus survived his captivity, and Rufus released him because he believed Quintus had freed him from demonic possession. Quintus was known as a miracle worker and had gone about the rest of his life healing the sick and aiding the poor.

c. Anthony the Great left his dwelling place to move further into the wilderness, where he lived a life of asceticism in an abandoned Roman fort near the Nile River. Eventually, a colony of hermits established themselves in his locale, and he eventually yielded to pleas to be their spiritual guide.

286

Emperor Maximian transferred a Roman legion containing Coptic Christians from Egypt to Gaul. When they arrived, they refused to fight against the local peasants because they were Christians. The Romans executed their leader, Maurice, and seventy of his men for refusing to follow their orders. They are remembered as the Theban Legion.

290

c. The Church of the East appointed its first bishop in the Sassanid capital of Ctesiphon, and although linked to the Church of Antioch, the Church of the East was never subordinate to them.

293

Constantius, the father of later emperor Constantine, became the deputy emperor, or caesar in the West.

295

Maximilianus became the first recorded Christian conscientious objector when he told the proconsul in Numidia that his religious beliefs would not allow him to serve in the Roman army. Because of his objection to military duty, he was executed and later venerated as a saint.

Marcellinus was the first bishop of Rome to prefer the title "pope." The bishop of Alexandria had previously gone by that name, and any Christian bishop could be referred to that way. It wasn't until the sixth century that the title was used exclusively for the bishop of Rome.

c. Bishop David of Basra (present-day Iraq) was sent to southern India and established the first official contact between the Church of the East and the Thomas Christians of India.

297

With the expansion of the Sassanid Empire into Armenia and Georgia, the Church of the East was able to make headway in those regions.

298

Galerius, the caesar in the East, subdued the Sassanids by sacking their capital of Ctesiphon.

CHAPTER 4: FOURTH CENTURY AD

If you must break the law, do it to seize power: in all other cases observe it.

—Julius Caesar

And as the world of the Christian Fathers became the world of the Church Triumphant, while fluid and contested mythologies hardened into dogmatic theology, certain fundamental characteristics of Christianity, often derived from the teaching of Paul, came to express themselves in fanatical form.

—David E. Stannard

These impious Galileans not only feed their own poor, but ours also; welcoming them into their *agape*, they attract them, as children are attracted, with cakes. . . . Whilst the pagan priests neglect the poor, the hated Galileans devote themselves to works of charity and by a display of false compassion have established and given effect to their pernicious errors. See their love feasts and their tables spread for the indigent. Such practice is common among them and causes a contempt for our gods.

—Emperor Julian

I spend a lot of time in the early part of this chapter telling stories of Roman emperors because understanding who they were and what they did helps to understand the most pivotal point in Christian history. One cannot appreciate Constantine's reshaping of Christianity without learning about the legend of his heavenly vision and the civil wars he fought to achieve sole control of the Roman Empire. The center of Roman power moved to Byzantium, where the dominant orthodox church was relocated. Theodosius I established Christianity as the empire's only legal religion, thus changing Western civilization forever. Also, for us to appreciate the Great Persecution, it's necessary to be familiar with Diocletian. Each emperor in this tumultuous century had his role to play, either in favor of Christians or against them, and most made significant impacts in shaping the radically changing religion. The first Church Council of Nicaea defined Christian theology, and despite early setbacks, the Arian Church achieved great success with their different concept of Jesus.

300

The population of the Roman Empire was around sixty million, and between two million to six million were Christians. About 2 to 10 percent of the Latin-speaking West were Christians, and Christians dominated the population of the Middle East and North Africa. Despite sporadic Roman persecutions, the religion continued to grow. It offered the hope of salvation, an escape from the fear of death and eternal punishment, and the belief in a benevolent, all-loving God. People also gravitated to the message of equal rights and compassion for all people, including women, slaves, and outcasts.

c. The *Clementine Recognitions* was written in Greek, but the only surviving writing is a Latin translation. In this text, a writer purporting to be Clement, the first-century bishop of Rome, gave a firsthand account to James the Just, the bishop of Jerusalem, concerning his religious questions and doubts. It also tells of Clement's travels to Palestine, where he supposedly met Peter and asked that he accompany him back to Rome. The author is known as Pseudo-Clement.

c. Christian missionaries from Syria spread the religion up the Nile River Valley, all the way into Nubia (Sudan) and Abyssinia (Ethiopia).

Abyssinia would become a hotbed for Christianity, continuing into our present time.

c. An anonymous author wrote the *Apocalypse of Paul*, and it became part of New Testament Apocrypha. Its descriptions of heaven and hell helped to shape Christian beliefs concerning the afterlife. It stated that the worst torture imaginable was reserved for those who said the bread and wine of the Eucharist were not the real body and blood of Christ.

c. The oldest version of the Gospel of Matthew, written in the Syriac language, is contained in *Codex Sinaiticus Syriacus*. It taught that Joseph, not the Holy Spirit, begat Jesus. Jesus did not acquire a virgin birth in Syriac scripture until the fifth century.

c. Christians were producing copies of the Jewish scripture in codices, or bound books, which would eventually become the Old Testament. The earliest surviving texts that contain the bulk of the Greek New Testament are the Codex Sinaiticus and Codex Vaticanus, also written about this time.

c. The *Book of Mary's Repose* offered insights into Mary's piety and the rise of her cult within Christianity. It was the first writing to mention the assumption of Mary into heaven at the end of her life.

301

Gregory the Illuminator, the head of the Armenian Apostolic Church, had been confined to a dungeon for thirteen years. When Armenian King Tiridates III needed someone to cure him of a serious illness, he had called for Gregory, who is said to have cured the illness and given credit to the miraculous powers of his God. Tiridates was so grateful that he converted to Christianity, sparking a mass conversion of the Armenian people. Armenia became the first significant state to embrace Christianity, and it has been a strong Christian bastion ever since.

c. The earliest date for the writing of the *Acts of Peter and Paul*, also known as the *Passion of Peter and Paul*. Like almost all the pseudo-scriptures, the author is unknown. The writing describes Paul's travel to Rome and his execution there. It portrays Paul and Peter as brothers and seems to be based on the *Acts of Peter*, with Paul being written into the plot. Some copies later in the century would include a letter said to have been written by Pontius Pilate, known as the *Acts of Pilate*. These titles are very confusing because so many similar book titles have focused on these people.

In this century, the dress of Christian clergy began to deviate from the normal attire worn by common people. Vestments, especially for use during church services, continued to evolve and become more elaborate to the point where a bishop could be mistaken for Roman or Greek royalty.

303

Emperor Diocletian, believing the empire had lost the favor of the Roman gods, ordered a general sacrifice by all his subjects. Christians again had to choose between loyalty to their religion or loyalty to Rome and the emperor. In the regions where this decree was enforced, some Christians were able to avoid the sacrifice with bribery, some made the required sacrifice, some went into hiding, and many refused. Refusal led to imprisonment, torture, even execution. Diocletian issued edicts against Christianity, declaring it an illegal religion. He ordered Christian places of worship to be destroyed, their scriptures confiscated, and those of high social status in the army or civil service to be expelled. A few months later he ordered the arrest of prominent Christian clergy, but they were freed if they made the sacrifice. Since Diocletian ruled from Nicomedia, in Anatolia, his persecution affected primarily the eastern Roman Empire, and even there it was not uniformly enforced. The persecution lasted in the West until AD 306 and in the East until AD 311. It was the empire's last, longest, and worst persecution of Christians.

c. Damian and Cosmas, twin brothers and physicians living in Syria, became Christian martyrs during the persecution. They were believed to have accepted no payment for their medical services during their careers. They became the patron saints of medicine.

305

Diocletian abdicated his position as augustus due to poor health. Maximian also abdicated his corresponding office in the West, leaving Maxentius, Licinius, and Constantius to maneuver for control of the empire. There would be vicious power struggles over who would succeed the rulers, often leading to civil war, as was the case in many of these successions.

The Synod of Elvira was one of the frequent meetings of Spanish bishops. It banned marriage between Christians and non-Christians, condemned willful martyrdom and suicide, declared that no paintings of Jesus should be displayed in churches because such art was considered idolatry, denounced abortions, and reaffirmed that clerics should remain unmarried and celibate, untainted by sexual relations so as to better focus on their relationship with God.

When Constantius, also known as Constantius Chlorus, became augustus in the West, he summoned his son Constantine from Nicomedia to campaign with him in Gaul and Britain. Constantius was reported to have circulated only the first of Diocletian's decrees requiring Christians to sacrifice to Roman gods and made little effort to enforce the anti-Christian persecution in the western empire.

306

Upon the death of Constantius Chlorus, Constantine's army proclaimed him augustus at York, in Britannia. Galerius, Diocletian's heir in the east, refused to recognize Constantine as augustus and instead named him caesar, appointing Valerius Severus above him. Maxentius, the son of Maximian, was envious of Constantine's new authority and declared himself augustus in the West. Galerius refused to recognize him but couldn't unseat him. This forced Galerius to send western augustus Severus and his army against Maxentius. Severus's army defected to Maxentius, and Severus was captured, later dying in captivity.

Constantine and Maxentius ended persecution of Christians in the western empire, granting Christians in Britain, Gaul, Spain, and North Africa religious freedom and calling for the restoration of their confiscated property.

Diocletian's persecution had ended with his abdication. Meletius, the bishop of Lycopolis, in Egypt, broke from the orthodox church over the ease with which lapsed Christians could reenter the Church following the persecution. He refused to accept the return of those who renounced their faith during the persecution and had repented afterwards. His followers were known as the Meletians, a sect that existed into the fifth century.

307

Maximian returned from retirement after his son's rebellion and met with Constantine in Gaul. He offered his daughter Fausta in marriage to Constantine and acknowledged him as the augustus of the West. In return, Constantine reaffirmed the family alliance between his father Constantius, Maximian, and his son Maxentius, who currently controlled Italy.

308

c. Roman Christian philosopher Lactantius completed *The Divine Institutes*, an apologetic work that pointed out the futility of pagan beliefs and the reasonableness of Christian "truths." Many historians consider this the most insightful apology by a Christian writer up to that time. Two topics he argued against were religious violence and forced conversions, and he provided a Christian rationale for the toleration of all religious beliefs.

Galerius called Diocletian out of retirement, and they met with Maximian in Carnuntum, Austria. They forced Maximian to abdicate again, and again reaffirmed Constantine as caesar. Galerius appointed his former military companion, son-in-law of Constantius and brother-in-law of Constantine, Licinius, as augustus in the East. Constantine refused to accept being subordinate to Maxentius.

309

Firmilian, the Roman governor at Caesarea Maritima, in Judea, ordered the deaths of several prominent Christians. Among them were Pamphilus, a scholar and presbyter from Caesarea; Valens, who was deacon of the Church of Jerusalem; and Paul of Jamnia. Firmilian even crucified or beheaded onlookers who appeared sympathetic to the victims. All of the victims would be venerated as saints.

310

The aging Maximian was still refusing to accept retirement and attempted to seize Constantine's army while Constantine was campaigning in Gaul. When he learned of this attempted coup, Constantine marched his army south to Marseille, where, with the assistance of the town's population, he captured Maximian and forced him to commit suicide. Maxentius, residing in Rome and still claiming to be the rightful augustus, vowed to avenge his father's death. Maxentius fortified northern Italy against Constantine and attempted to gain the loyalty of Italian Christians by allowing them to elect the next bishop of Rome. They chose a man named Eusebius, who must be differentiated from the historian Eusebius of Caesarea.

Constantine, realizing that he couldn't rely on his family's connection to the now dead Maximian to legitimize his power, tried to resurrect his image by publicizing a previously unknown dynastic connection between himself and the popular third-century emperor Claudius II. Constantine added to his authority by describing the divine vision he'd had of the gods Apollo and Victory granting him health and a long reign. These revelations served to increase his popularity in Gaul and made him appear destined to rule the empire. From this time, most of Constantine's coins featured Sol, who was described as the "companion and guardian deity of the emperor."

311

Eastern Augustus Galerius issued an Edict of Toleration, realizing that the attempt to eradicate Christianity in the East had not been practical and that Christians were doing their part to help Rome by worshipping their own god. He died that year and Maximinus II divided the eastern empire between Licinius and himself. A committed pagan, Maximinus II renewed the persecution of Christians in Egypt, Palestine, and Asia Minor.

With the death of Galerius, the era of the four rulers ended. Since Maxentius had declared war on Constantine, Constantine formed an alliance with Licinius, his brother-in-law and now augustus in the East. Maximinus II viewed this as an affront to his authority and offered recognition to Maxentius in Rome in exchange for military support. The empire was becoming full of armed camps ready for civil war.

The monk Anthony, who was still living in the desert at this time, was said to have traveled to Alexandria in the hope of being martyred. He was unable to fulfill his wish and returned to the desert.

Eighty North African bishops declared the ordination of Caecilian as bishop of Carthage to be invalid. They accused him of being a traitor because during the persecution, he had handed over holy books to the Romans for burning. The bishops then elected Donatus Magnus, or Donatus of Casea Nigrae. His native Berber followers, who became known as Donatists, resented the Romanized, upper-class church leaders who had renounced Christianity during Diocletian's persecution and decreed sacraments performed by these men were nullified. The Donatists believed themselves to be the true church of North Africa since they had not submitted to the Romans. The Donatist Church rejected the world of imperial politics and sided with the native poor, whom the Romans viewed as second-class citizens.

312

The estimated worldwide Christian population was three to four million.

Christians made up almost half the population in Asia Minor, Armenia, and Cyprus. They were very prevalent around Antioch, parts of Egypt, parts of Italy, and Spain but were sparse in Palestine, Arabia, and Phoenicia (Lebanon). They hardly existed in northern Italy, mid to northern Gaul, Germany, or the British Isles.

Constantine's army arrived outside Rome. Eusebius of Caesarea, the historian, later wrote that Constantine was praying when "he saw with his own eyes the trophy of a cross of light in the heavens, above the sun, and an inscription, Conquer by This, attached to it." Eusebius wrote that Constantine understood this as a sign from the Christian God and carried the symbol of the Chi Rho cross, the first two letters of the Greek title Christ, on his army's battle flags and shields. Constantine won a tremendous battle over the forces of Maxentius at the Milvian Bridge in Rome. Maxentius drowned in the Tiber River along with a mass of fleeing soldiers, but Constantine had him fished out and paraded his head through the streets of Rome. This battle would be of little importance to modern Christians if not for Constantine's reported vision and what he did after receiving it. This became Christian legend, and he exemplified a new model for Christians as literal warriors for Christ, greatly conflicting with Jesus's model of pacifism and his being known as the Prince of Peace. There is a strong possibility that the story of the vision was another version of the Apollo vision story from AD 310 retold by Eusebius for a Christian audience.

This was the major turning point in Western Christianity with the Church submitting to Constantine in exchange for enormous financial gain, exulted status of the clergy, and insurance against further persecution.

Candlemas began as a feast celebrating Luke's story of the Virgin Mary's presentation of baby Jesus at the Temple in Jerusalem. It was a Christian celebration that occurred at the same time as the Celtic celebration of Imbolc, forty days after Christmas and anticipating the return of light, and the arrival of spring. The Germans would transplant their version of the holiday to America where it would evolve in 1887 into Groundhog Day.

313

Constantine and Licinius issued the Edict of Milan, an endorsement of Galerius's Edict of Toleration, that officially ended the sporadic ten-year persecution of Christians. It returned Christianity to legal status, which allowed it to be practiced openly. Constantine decreed that any property taken from Christians during the persecution was to be restored. This was the West's first written charter of religious freedom and toleration. Its sincere gesture would not last long.

In the Roman Empire, every citizen was required to perform various services or provide resources to the emperor, all grouped under the category of compulsive public services. One of Constantine's first actions was releasing the Christian clergy from this obligation.

From this time until AD 450 would be the only period in their entire history that the Coptic Christians in Egypt would live under a government that was not hostile toward them.

Eusebius of Caesarea wrote the fifteen-volume *Praeparatio Evangelica*, or Preparation for the Gospel, as an introduction to Christianity, explaining its superiority over other religions. He wrote that any truths that the pagan Greeks taught were stolen from the ancient Hebrews. *Preparation for the Gospel* is a valuable work that recorded much information by contemporary writers that was not preserved elsewhere.

314

Constantine called the Council of Arles to determine how to handle the Donatist situation in North Africa. The bishops condemned Donatism as a heresy, excommunicated Donatus Magnus, and reinstalled Caecilian as the bishop of Carthage. This action was taken for practical reasons since the North African Church was in turmoil at the time. The council also passed other measures such as mandating that conscientious objectors to war be excommunicated, essentially making pacifism a sin; setting the date of Easter on the same day for all Christendom, no longer decided by individual churches; participation in chariot races and gladiatorial fights be punished by excommunication; and those clergy who had turned over sacred books during the persecution be deposed, though the sacraments that they had administered remained valid.

315

Lactantius completed his *On the Death of the Persecutors*. This book, along with Eusebius's *Church History*, gave the impression that Christians were under almost constant persecution since the religion began, rather than the ten or so years that there were empire-wide persecutions and sporadic local discrimination.

Constantine decreed that any Jew who stoned another Jew for converting to Christianity should be burned to death. He also declared that anyone who converted to Judaism should receive the "appropriate punishment." This vague statement allowed local jurisdictions to enforce the law as they wished.

Builders of the Arch of Constantine completed their work in Rome. The arch featured much pagan iconography and absolutely no Christian symbols. The arch was offset to reveal a view of a giant bronze statue dedicated to the sun. The sun gods were among the most prominent gods in ancient culture. The word "deity" is derived from the Hittite word *dsius*, meaning "shining in the sky." This and other evidence, such his coins containing pagan imagery of the sun god, indicate that Constantine was not a fully committed Christian at this time and worshipped other gods in addition to the Christian god. On the arch, Constantine was depicted with a nimbus or halo for the first time, indicating the radiation of cosmic light. It was only after this that Jesus Christ began being depicted in the same way.

317

Constantine issued an edict calling for the confiscation of all Donatist property and a death sentence to anyone who disturbed the peace. In Carthage, the local governor sent troops to suppress Donatus and his followers. They killed some of the Donatists and exiled their clergy, but outside the city of Carthage, the Donatists were mostly unaffected.

318

Arius, an Alexandrian priest, began preaching that Jesus could not be equal to God since he was God's Logos, and although he was begotten before time began, he was still begotten and therefore was subordinate to God the Father. His followers, known as Arians, could back their theology with scripture, such as John 14:28 ("I go unto the Father: for my Father is greater than I"). Arius's bishop, Alexander I, totally disagreed with him, countering with John 10:30 ("I and the Father are One") and John 14:9 ("If you have seen me, you have seen the Father"). Arius reasoned that if Jesus Christ was not truly God himself, then he could not forgive sins. Since both sides of the debate used the Bible to support their cases, the conundrum of how to use a self-contradictory source to resolve theological problems continued.

Constantine gave Christians the right to take their legal cases before an ecclesiastical court rather than a secular court. The rulings of the bishops would carry the same weight as those of secular court judges.

c. Half the population of Egypt may have been Christian by this time. This figure would rise to around 75 percent by midcentury and close to 90 percent by the beginning of the fifth century.

c. After living under the guidance of another hermit for several years, Pachomius organized the first Christian monastery in Tabennisi, Upper Egypt. Until that time, most hermits tended to live solitary lives in huts or caves, meeting only occasionally. Many hermits were physically or mentally ill and needed a community, so Pachomius organized their various cells into a single entity.

c. The oldest inscription ever found on a Christian church was written in Syria. It referred to *Chrestos*, which in Greek meant "the Good," not *Christus*, meaning "the anointed one" or Messiah. The name *Chrestos* also described other gods in this region.

320

Licinius, who defeated Maximinus II to become the augustus in the East and had previously joined Constantine in issuing the Edict of Milan, became less tolerant of Christians and was said to have renewed persecution of them at this time.

Constantine ruled that Church clerics were exempt from paying taxes, as were their wives, children, and servants. This created even more incentive for educated people to join the Christian clergy and be able to either give extra money to the poor or stash it away.

Constantine initiated the construction of Old Saint Peter's Basilica on Vatican Hill, the traditional site of Peter's crucifixion and burial. It would not be completed for another forty years.

With the recognition of the primacy of the bishop of Selucia-Ctesiphon in Sassanid Persia, the Church of the East was established.

321

Constantine, realizing that he couldn't unite the churches of North Africa by force, asked the local Roman bishops to show moderation and patience with the Donatists. The sect would not escape future persecution but continued to exist in the rural areas of Tunisia until the Arab invasion in the seventh century.

c. The *Minor Doxology*, "Glory Be" or "Gloria Patri," took the form that we have today. The Roman version is: "Glory to the Father, and to the Son, and to the Holy Spirit; as it was in the beginning, is now, and ever shall be, world without end. Amen."

Constantine declared Sunday, the day of the sun, to be a day of rest for all judges, city dwellers, and craftsmen, but farmers remained free to work. He also decided that new Christian churches should be built with an orientation so that the congregation faced the sunrise in the east.

Constantine decreed more laws: if any slave was freed in the presence of a bishop, they would be granted Roman citizenship; every person would have the right to leave property to the Church in his will; and all soldiers were required to gather on Sundays and recite a prayer that Constantine composed to an "Almighty God." It became mandatory for pagan and Christian soldiers to publicly worship this same god.

323

Constantine declared that if a pagan forced a Christian to participate in a pagan practice, he would be publicly beaten or fined. This put an end to Christians in the Roman Empire ever having to sacrifice to a pagan god.

324

The *"Testimonium Flavianum,"* the name scholars applied to a small section of Flavian Josephus's first-century book *Jewish Antiquities*, was quoted for the first time by Eusebius of Caesarea. It stated that Jesus was the Christ, and maybe not a human at all, and that he was resurrected as prophets had foretold. The late date of first hearing of this statement, as well as evidence that it may have been inserted into the document, indicate that the *"Testimonium Flavianum"* paragraph was likely created or altered by Eusebius to support Christian beliefs. Eusebius was also the first to write about Constantine's vision of the sign in the sky before his victory in Rome, and he also admitted that truth wasn't important if deception served his purposes.

According to Eusebius, when Constantine learned that Licinius was renewing the persecution of Christians in the East, Constantine saw it as an opportunity to unify the empire under his sole control. Constantine went to war with Licinius, defeated him, and sent him into exile.

Constantine began placing Christian symbols on his coins, but of all the coins issued during his reign, only about one percent had Christian symbology.

Constantine started to build a new imperial capital on land he gained from Licinius. He selected the site of the ancient Greek city of Byzantium at the strategic position where Europe meets Asia, the same place where Emperor Severus built a colony in AD 197. It was a place Constantine knew well, having lived only forty miles away in Nicomedia as a child. In building Constantinople, the "city of Constantine," he expanded the old city to fit the acreage needed for a capital city. Rome would remain the capital of the empire in name, but Constantinople would be the seat of government and the home of the emperors, who tended to live far from Rome anyway to be near military centers on the frontiers. From this point onward, except on campaign, emperors mainly resided in Constantinople, which would often itself be the frontier due to the number of invasions it had to fend off. Both pagan priests and Christian clergy publicly gave their blessings to the endeavor. Constantinople obtained much of its building materials and statues by stripping and razing pagan temples throughout the empire.

Constantine granted permission to restore or enlarge the churches in the eastern provinces that had been damaged in the recent persecutions. He ordered local governors to assist in these efforts.

Constantine proclaimed that the worship of idols, prophecies, and sacrifices to pagan gods were illegal. He also decreed that all exiled or enslaved Christians in the East should be restored to the positions they
held before Licinius's persecution. In effect, he ended centuries-old
Roman traditions and equalized the rights of Christians throughout
the empire, not just in the West.

325

Constantine saw Christianity as a way to unite the vast and troubled Roman Empire and apparently felt he had a duty to help define
and preserve orthodox belief. He called all bishops to Nicaea, near
Constantinople, to end the Arian controversy and finally settle the
issue of how Jesus was related to God. Constantine set a precedent
for emperors and the government being involved in Church issues by
presiding at the council. The Council of Nicaea proclaimed that Jesus
was equal to God and part of a Holy Trinity. In describing Christ,
there was great controversy over one *iota*, the letter *i*: with *homoousios*
meaning "same substance" as opposed to *homoiousios*, meaning "similar substance." The emperor and bishops introduced the Nicene Creed
as the definitive statement of Christian beliefs. The creed's only mention of the human Jesus was his birth to a virgin and his death on the
cross, ignoring his entire earthly life and all his teachings. It was the
cosmic Christ of Paul they worshipped, the Christ whose earthly existence was apparently of little significance. Arius arrived with twenty-
two supporting bishops, but things didn't go well for him, and he was
exiled to Illyricum, on the east shore of the Adriatic Sea. The bishops
also established a method of calculating the date of Easter based on
astronomical criteria tracing back to Babylonian times and carried on
by the Jewish Passover. Easter was based on the solar calendar, the
first full moon after the spring equinox, whereas the Passover is based
on the Jewish calendar and the lunar cycle. This, along with Jesus's
birth on the winter solstice, identified Christ's birth and death with
the annual cycle of the sun. At the council, Constantine quoted from
pagan poets and oracles to demonstrate that Christ and Christian
doctrine had been prophesied by both Hebrew and pagan prophets.

He mentioned that the Erythraean Sibyl, a pagan prophetess, had also foretold the coming of Jesus.

c. Constantine assigned Eusebius, the bishop of Caesarea, to create fifty copies of "the sacred scriptures". According to Eusebius, there was general agreement that the four canonical Gospels, the letters of Paul, the book of Acts, 1 John, and 1 Peter were authentic and therefore sacred. Disputed books were Hebrews, James, Jude, 2 John, 3 John, 2 Peter, and Revelation. Those clearly not genuine according to Eusebius were the *Acts of Paul*, the *Shepherd of Hermas*, the *Apocalypse of Peter*, the *Epistle of Barnabas*, and the *Didache*.

Ethiopians established a Jewish kingdom of Beta Israel, later known as the kingdom of Gondar. The new kingdom included more than five hundred small villages. Shortly after this, Athanasius of Alexandria appointed a Christian bishop to the region. An armed dispute between Christians and Jews followed. Whatever the results of that conflict, Beta Israel became an independent state and did not submit to Christian invaders until 1627.

326

Constantine ordered the cruel executions of his wife, Fausta, and eldest son, Crispus. The reasons for these are not certain, but their names were even chiseled off of engravings to further remove their names from memory.

Constantine's mother, Empress Helena, traveled to Palestine to locate Christian relics and sites of significance from the life of Jesus. She chose sites for two important churches, one to commemorate Jesus's birth in Bethlehem and the other to commemorate his ascension in Jerusalem. In Jerusalem, she ordered the destruction of a magnificent temple of Venus on the site where the Church of the Holy Sepulchre was to be built. A legend began that while she was in Jerusalem, she was presented part of the True Cross, the actual cross from which Jesus was hung. The cross, a Roman symbol of violent execution, was on its way to becoming the main symbol of Christianity, replacing the peaceful symbols such as fish, lamb, shepherd, or Greek letters.

Constantine commissioned the construction of the Church of the Holy Sepulchre in Jerusalem. The tradition of Christian pilgrimages to that region began with its construction, as well as that of other churches in the Holy Land, including the Church of the Nativity commemorating Jesus's birth in Bethlehem. At this time, Christians showed an immense interest in discovering the homeland of Jesus, his disciples, and the early martyrs. By the end of the century, almost every New Testament site of significance was said to have been discovered and commemorated.

c. Eusebius of Caesarea wrote a chapter in the book *Evangelical Preparation* entitled "How It May Be Lawful and Fitting to Use Falsehood as a Medicine, and for the Benefit of Those Who Want to Be Deceived." It spelled out how deceit and lies could be justified to induce someone to become a Christian. By accepting Christianity, he believed they would be saved from hell, so anything at all that caused them to convert to Christianity was acceptable.

327

c. Arius and Euzoius wrote a letter to Emperor Constantine that included a creed to demonstrate the orthodoxy of their position.

328

Helena, the emperor's mother, brought the Holy Stairs, the twenty-eight marble steps leading to the praetorian where Jesus was said to have been judged by Pontius Pilate, from Jerusalem to Rome. They were installed leading into the Church of Saint Lawrence, the personal chapel of the early popes.

c. Athanasius, the new bishop of Alexandria, succeeded in having Arius denounced as a heretic, but around this time, Constantine recalled Arius and allowed him to return to Alexandria.

330

Constantine inaugurated Constantinople as the new imperial city of the Roman Empire. On a tall column, he erected a statue of himself, naked with a radiate crown and facing east toward the rising sun. It carried the inscription "For Constantine who is shining like the Sun." It's been said by prominent historians that he never gave up his pagan worship but joined paganism to Christianity, seeing the Christian deity as a supreme solar god whose radiance was spread on Earth by Christ. By clouding the differences between the worship of Sol and the worship of Christ, including the insertion of pagan holidays into Christianity, Constantine made it less objectionable for pagans to convert to Christianity.

c. The Circumcellions, a fanatical group of Christian Berbers in North Africa, allied with the Donatists. They were uncontrollable peasants who ignored the law, attacked their enemies, and vandalized their property. They were concerned with social and class grievances and weren't afraid to bring about their own martyrdom or even commit suicide for their faith. Their support of the Donatist cause greatly harmed the reputation of the Donatists.

332

Constantine forbade all so-called heretical Christian groups from meeting and decreed that all of their property must be turned over to the orthodox Christian Church. Orthodox Christianity was evolving, and its doctrines were solidifying in Constantinople. As the sect of orthodox Christians grew in influence, one of their main goals was to obliterate all evidence of what they considered heretical groups.

333

The anonymous Pilgrim of Bordeaux wrote the *Jerusalem Itinerary* about his journey to and return from the Holy Land. It is the oldest known writing in Christianity in the form of a travelogue.

335

Constantine gradually became sympathetic to the Arians because of their harsh treatment by the Trinitarian, or orthodox, Christians. With Constantine in agreement, the Council of Tyre exonerated Arius and the next year exiled Athanasius, who was Arius's bishop and chief accuser. Athanasius would spend a total of seventeen years in five different exiles.

The Church of the Holy Sepulchre, built over the believed remains of Jesus's burial site, was completed in conjunction with Constantine's veneration of burial sites of the saints, which included Saint Peter's and Saint Paul's Basilicas in Rome.

c. Didymus the Blind began his professional career in Alexandria as a student of the theology of Origen. He went on to teach Christian theology in the Church of Alexandria for the next half century. Not much is known about his writings because in AD 553 he fell out of favor with the Church, and his writings were not preserved. Like Origen, he interpreted scripture allegorically and symbolically, not literally. He honestly confronted his doubts and the inconsistencies he saw in the scriptures. He imagined God as transcendent and beyond description, and like Origin, he believed in universal reconciliation.

c. Constantine declared that December 25, the traditional birthday of Mithra and Sol Invictus, should also be celebrated as the birthday of Jesus Christ.

336

Donatus held a council in Tunisia that was attended by 270 bishops, demonstrating that the Donatists were still a force to be reckoned with in North Africa.

Arius died in Constantinople the evening before a ceremony that was to restore him to his former standing in the Church.

337

c. Constantine abolished the practice of crucifixion in the Roman Empire in honor of Christ's death.

Eusebius of Nicomedia, the bishop of Berytus (Beirut) and a supporter of Arius, baptized Constantine before he died. Constantine's body was placed in a gold coffin in the Church of the Holy Apostles in Constantinople. His sarcophagus was surrounded by twelve empty tombs, apparently for the twelve apostles, but also symbolic of the sun surrounded by the twelve signs of the zodiac. The memorial coin issued after his death showed him in a chariot, wearing a radiate crown and rising into the sky. Constantine had never outlawed paganism nor publicly condoned the persecution of pagans. Most of his life he had apparently continued to worship the sun god Sol Invictus along with the Christian God. With his conversion to Christianity, the predominant understanding of the universe was changing from a divine living entity, as it was to the pagans, to a product of a greater creator.

Constantine was succeeded by his three remaining sons born to Fausta, Constantine II, Constantius II, and Constans. Constantine II had been caesar for twenty years, and he decided that he should rule the empire with his brothers, as a triumvirate, each responsible for a different region. Before long, they were quarreling about their shares of the empire.

Constantine II allowed Christian clergy to use the imperial transport system at no cost when traveling on official journeys.

The Republic of Georgia established orthodox or Nicaean Christianity as the country's official religion.

340

Constantine II was killed in a civil war against his brother Constans.

c. Ulfilas, a Greek bishop and missionary, was credited with converting the Goths to Christianity. He invented an alphabet for them and
translated the Bible into Gothic. Since subordination of Jesus to God,
or Arianism, was the dominant belief in the Roman Empire at that
time, Ulfilas passed Arian theology to the Goths, and the Goths would
mostly remain Arian for the next three centuries.

Eusebius of Caesarea died. One of his many bequeaths to the Christian
world was to do his best to see that any literary work that didn't support orthodox Christianity was "consigned to silence," meaning not
copied, not passed on to future generations, or just destroyed. His
written version of Christianity was the only one that he wanted to
preserve.

c. King Ezana of Axum (Ethiopia) converted to Christianity, and within
a few years, he issued the first known coins other than Constantine's
to bear any Christian symbol, in this case a cross.

343

The Council of Sardica, in what is now Bulgaria, tried to reform the
quality of the post-Constantine church by requiring bishops to have
at least a "moderate" amount of church experience before taking over
their jobs. In the past, that hadn't been a prerequisite, and a position
in the clergy entailed mainly prestige, power, and fringe benefits, with
spiritual guidance being of low priority. This council proved totally ineffective, and it remained common for state or private interest groups
to maneuver their nominees into key Church positions. The process
of selecting bishops was never uniform. In these early centuries, there
was continued wrangling about whether archbishops, bishops, or secular leaders had the authority to install clergy. At this council, echoes
of the Arian controversy never faded from background discussions.

344

c. Shapur II of Persia executed a hundred Christian bishops and priests
on Good Friday. He was persecuting Christians whom he suspected of

potentially aiding the Roman Empire, which he perceived was becoming a Christian empire. Over the next decades, tens of thousands of Christians would be cruelly and sadistically killed in Persia as state oppression turned into massacres by uncontrolled mobs. This persecution of Christians wouldn't end until AD 383, but isolated pogroms continued after that. This victimization of Christians would play out every time the Persians were at war with the Christian Byzantine Empire.

345

c. Before the monastic pioneer Pachomius's death, he supervised eight monasteries and was the spiritual leader of several hundred monks. His example was copied and replicated rapidly throughout Egypt and the Middle East.

The Donatists asked Emperor Constans to declare theirs as the only legitimate church in North Africa. They argued that as indigenous Berbers they had a better case for representing North African Christians than the Romanized Church in Carthage. Constans refused to see things their way.

Bishop Joseph of Edessa visited Kerala, India, and integrated the Thomas Christians into the hierarchy of the East Syrian Church, or Church of the East.

c. Pope Julius I of Rome made official policy the celebration of the nativity or birthday of Jesus on December 25.

346

c. In his apology *The Error of Pagan Religions*, Firmacus Maternus condemned anyone who was not a Christian and asked that emperors do everything they could to suppress pagans, as brutally as necessary.

Emperor Constantius issued an order for all pagan temples to be closed and access to them forbidden. Anyone who violated this decree would face capital punishment. He continued to forbid all sacrifices and decreed that any governor who failed to enforce the law would be punished.

347

The Roman Church ordered the Donatists to reconcile with them and accept their authority. Those who refused were to be exiled or killed. Donatus was exiled to Gaul, where he died in AD 355, but his sect lasted at least into the next century.

348

c. By this time, missionaries and captured Christians had converted many Goths to Arian Christianity because of the Goths' desire to be on a par with Roman society. On occasion, Christian Goths were persecuted by pagan Goths, and between AD 348 and 378, several prominent Christian Goths were martyred.

350

c. It was about this time that artists began depicting Jesus with a halo, or nimbus, around his head. Painting a radiant circle around the head of a holy person was a pagan Greek and Roman tradition used for the sun god Helios and Roman emperors such as Constantine the Great. By the sixth century, the halo was also being used for the Virgin Mary and, later, for angels and saints.

c. An anonymous author wrote the *Gospel of Nicodemus*, also known as the *Acts of Pilate*. The book presented itself as being written by Nicodemus, a biblical follower of Jesus some 320 years in the past. It declared Pilate to be totally innocent of Jesus death and was one of the noncanonical books that blamed Jews for Jesus's crucifixion.

c. Nubia, the area near the ancient Biblical land of Kush, and present-day southern Egypt and northern Sudan, was invaded by the kingdom of Aksum, in present-day Ethiopia, and Nubia was split into three Christian kingdoms.

c. Half of all Christians worldwide belonged to a group that the Trinitarian, or orthodox, Church regarded as heretical or schismatic.

c. Up until this time, Christians had rejected the depiction of winged angels because the angels were being confused with pagan winged goddesses and cupids.

c. Bishops became de facto judges, and sins were viewed as breaking God's law. To satisfy the demands for divine justice, confessing sins to a priest became a requirement for forgiveness by God.

Cyril of Jerusalem created the first list of the books of the New Testament, but the only one not included was Revelation.

The school of Nisibis in present-day Iraq was founded as a center of learning. It was established by the Church of the East. Teaching theology, philosophy, and medicine, it is often referred to as the world's first university. When Nisibis fell to the Sassanids in AD 363, the Church of the East's center of learning moved to the school of Edessa.

351

Jews in Palestine, under Isaac of Diocesarea, revolted against the Roman rule of eastern caesar, Constantius Gallus. The Jewish people were furious over being repressed by Christians, which was like the way Christians were treating pagans in that region. By the following year, the revolt ended with the execution of several thousand rebels.

Emperor Constantius II attempted to bring some order to the Church by seeking agreement on a new *Sirmium Creed*. This creed was based on the Arian belief in Jesus being subordinate to God, so it was popular with the Arians, but not with the orthodox.

354

Aurelias Augustine was born to a Christian mother and a pagan father in Hippo, Algeria. His parents wanted him educated in classical philosophy, and he would later become one of the main theological influences on the Roman Catholic Church.

Illustrator Furius Dionysius Filocalus produced the *Philocalian Calendar*, or *Chronography of 354*, for a wealthy Christian named Valentius. It was the first codex to contain full-page illustrations and the first literary work that associated the birth of Jesus with the new official date of December 25.

356

Anthony the Great, the most prominent Christian hermit and monk, died. Athanasius of Alexandria wrote his biography the following year, and it became extremely popular reading. It inspired Christians throughout the empire to emulate Anthony's example of asceticism and began a new genre of Christian literature in which ascetics achieved the status of celebrities.

Less than fifty years after his father Constantine issued the *Edict of Tolerance*, Constantius II decreed it a capital offense to worship images of pagan gods. No matter how magnificent, historical, or valuable they were, he demanded the destruction of Greek and Roman temples along with their statues and decorations. The Christian clergy didn't consider these acts of vandalism, but instead, the will of their God.

357

Constantius II issued edicts concerning harmful magic and divination (prophesy or fortune telling), which emperors tended to perceive as a threatening. Constantius II eliminated Greek oracles, whose sole purpose was to predict the future, and by AD 392, all of the oracles would be put out of commission.

The third Council of Sirmium was the high point of Arianism. The words *homoousios*, meaning "one substance," and *homoiousios*, meaning "similar substance," were considered unscriptural, and the bishops declared the Father greater than the Son.

359

Constantius II ordered two church councils, one in the East and one in the West, to resolve the Arian controversy. The western Council of Ariminum drew three hundred to four hundred bishops. The bishops confirmed the Nicene Creed but were constrained by the emperor and had to accept a pro-Arian compromise, possibly the Sirmium Creed. Jerome of Stridon, a prominent Latin theologian and historian, wrote: "The whole world groaned, and was astonished to find itself Arian." Bishop Liberius of Rome rejected the new creed, and as a result, Constantius deposed him and sent him into exile. Felix was installed as antipope, but eventually Liberius was recalled, and Felix was driven out of office by the Roman citizens.

c. According to Roman historian Ammianus Marcellinus, Constantius II initiated a court at Scythopolis, in northern Palestine, halfway between Antioch and Alexandria. Many pagans were said to have been brought to that place, which was basically a concentration camp, to await trial. Their stay there would have included torture or execution for violating the emperor's recent edicts.

360

c. Apollinarius, the bishop of Laodicea, in Anatolia, opposed Arianism in his writings, going so far as to remove almost any human nature from his description of Christ. Apollinarius became a spiritual ancestor to the fifth-century Monophysites, or those who believed Christ had no human nature and was solely divine, and possibly to the Miaphysites, who believed in a blending of human and divine essences into one nature. Because of his theology, Apollinarius would later be declared a heretic by the Dyophysite orthodox Christians who came to believe Christ had two natures, fully human and fully divine.

Bishops from the East and West attended the Council of Constantinople. The council declared that Christ and God were made of the same substance, thus supporting the Trinitarian view.

Martin of Tours founded the first monastery north of the Alps, in Gaul. At first, his monks lived in huts, but with time, the community evolved into the influential Liguge Abbey.

361

After the death of Constantius II, Bishop Liberius of Rome annulled the pro-Arian decrees of the recent councils in towns under his jurisdiction.

Constantine I's nephew Julian, who was raised as a Christian, became emperor. Julian was disillusioned by the in-fighting between various Christian groups and tried to steer the Roman Empire back to its pagan roots. He never persecuted Christians and allowed them to worship in public. He noted how much less violence there was among Christians after the empire stopped supporting the Roman Church in its war against perceived heretics. Julian presented Christians as positive examples of how the empire should provide social welfare to all citizens, but at the same time, he diminished the roles of bishops and did not allow avowed Christians to serve as teachers. He passed tax laws that transferred much of the wealth of the Christian clergy back to the state. Julian tried to undermine the claim that Christianity had replaced Judaism, reopening Jerusalem to the Jews, allowing them to govern themselves and rebuild their Temple. The Jews would barely begin work on the Temple before Julian was killed during his invasion of Persia a year and a half later, and the work was stopped by his successor.

Alexandrians murdered the city's tyrannical bishop, George of Cappadocia, and two of his officers. Those responsible were unknown, but the city's Christians blamed pagans. The effect of Julian's efforts to repaganize the empire had exacerbated tensions, and many Christians began to fear renewed persecution.

Roman historian Ammianus Marcellinus made the earliest mention of the Epiphany, or Three Kings Day, as a day of Christian feasting. The holiday commemorated the visit of the Magi to the baby Jesus and the end of the winter festive season, the twelfth day of Christmas. Epiphany is still recognized and celebrated on January 6 by many Christian denominations.

362

At the Council of Alexandria, the bishops struggled to properly translate important theological concepts into Latin. The Greek word *ousia*, meaning "essence or substance," was translated into the Latin as *substantia*, and the Greek *hypostasis*, the underlying or indispensable part of something, was translated to *persona*. It was necessary to define and agree on those terms in order to understand Jesus and his relationship to God.

363

Emperor Jovian restored the empire to Christianity. He ordered the destruction of the Royal Library of Antioch, which had been founded around 220 BC. It was burned along with its treasure of books. Not only pagans but many educated Christians considered this a barbaric act.

Basil of Caesarea wrote a document to young Christian men entitled *Address to Young Men on the Right Use of Greek Literature*. In it, he gave advice on which classical pagan authors were safe to read based on his subjective scale of their sinfulness. Pagan literature, he said, was riddled with idolatry, blasphemy, lust, murder, vanity, and whatever other sin that could be imagined. The irony is that he could attack pagan literature for the same vices that the Old Testament contained. Basil's document had a lasting effect on classical studies by Christians for many centuries.

365

Emperor Jovian revoked some of Julian's anti-Christian policies, but he only ruled for a year before he died and was replaced by Valens, an Arian Christian. Valens ruled in the East, and Valentinian, an unbiased Christian, ruled in the West. Both emperors continued to tolerate paganism.

c. Emperor Valens tried to revive Arianism throughout the empire. As Constantius II had done, he appointed an Arian patriarch in Constantinople and sent Arian missionaries to the lands of the barbarians.

366

After the death of Bishop Liberius of Rome, rival factions resorted to violence to determine who should succeed him. At that time, it was usually the consensus of citizens and clergy that determined who the next bishop would be. Eventually Damasus emerged as the new Roman bishop, but over a hundred people were said to have been killed in these riots.

Damasus I began to use the old pagan priestly title of pontifex, or pontiff, to imply his superiority over all other bishops.

367

Athanasius, the bishop of Alexandria, was the first known person to list all twenty-seven books that became the New Testament. He strongly condemned many gospels and other religious writings that he considered noncanonical, and this led to the concealment or destruction of many of them.

370

c. The Copts in Egypt assembled the texts that would make up the Nag Hammadi Library, which included the *Gospel of Thomas*.

These Gnostic writings became a sensation following their redis-covery in 1945.

Basil became bishop of Caesarea Mazaca in Cappadocia. He wrote a "rule," basically meaning constitution, which still serves as the basic guide for Eastern Orthodox monastic life. He also organized a soup kitchen and a hospital and distributed food to the poor. He, like many other Christians who rejected materialism, gave away his personal family inheritance because of his belief that worldliness was a sin. Around this time, Leonitus, the bishop of Antioch, established hostels to help the poor, and Bishop Eustathius of Sebaste built a poorhouse. These are some of the earliest known Christian charitable institutions.

The bones of Saint Thomas were said to be transferred to Edessa, greatly raising its prestige as the "mother city of Syrian Christianity."

372

Gregory became bishop of Nyssa. He, his brother Basil of Caesarea, and Gregory of Nazianzus would become known as the Cappadocian Fathers. Gregory of Nyssa was a theologian who made significant con-tributions to the doctrine of the Trinity and the Nicene Creed. He was influenced by Origen and, like him, believed in universal reconcilia-tion, a common belief at that time, which would later be declared a heresy.

373

Ephraem the Syrian mentioned All Saints' Day, or the Feast of All Saints, for the first time in writing. The holiday celebrated the spiritual bond between the living and the heavenly saints and was first cele-brated on May 13 in Edessa.

374

Ambrose of Milan, one of the most influential Christian figures of the century, was baptized and consecrated as bishop of Milan, all within a week. He would later be the theological mentor to Augustine, who was also ordained directly from lay status.

c. This was the earliest plausible date for the creation of the *Old Roman Creed*, or *Old Roman Symbol*, which was the baptismal creed of Rome and precursor to the Apostles' Creed.

c. Epiphanius, the bishop of Salamis, began compiling the *Panarion*, which became one of the best sources for understanding the diversity of early Christian beliefs and documented the religion's growing obsession with heresies. It focused on eighty sects from the time of Adam to Epiphanius's own time, summarizing their histories and refuting their heretical beliefs. In the book, he mentioned Christians as being called Jessaeans and Nazoreans before being called Christians.

Emperor Valentinian I repealed the *patria potestas* law that gave men the power of life or death over their wife and children. Infanticide became a capital offense in Roman law, though it was rarely enforced. The Jewish people had enforced a similar prohibition since the first century.

376

The Goths were tribes of Germanic and Scandinavian origin who had gradually been converted to Arian Christianity. They arrived in great numbers at the Danube River, the border of the Roman Empire, seeking asylum from the invading Huns. Gothic envoys traveled to Antioch to plead with the emperor for a place of refuge. Emperor Valens, who was focused on the Sassanids in the East, allowed them to enter the empire, but only under Roman escort. Due to mismanagement by the escorts, the underfed and weary Goths soon rebelled and went their own way.

c. The Church of the East established a monastery in the city of Gondishapur in the Sassanid Empire. In the sixth century, the school they founded there would grow into the main university of the empire.

377

c. Ambrose, the bishop of Milan, wrote *Concerning Virgins*, a series of letters that he sent to his sister. The three-volume set extolled the superiority of Christian women who denied fashion and beauty enhancements and lived their entire lives as virgins.

378

A Gothic army defeated the Romans at the Battle of Adrianople, in what is now European Turkey. Emperor Valens died in the battle, and the eastern empire nearly collapsed. Theodosius I, whose name literally means "giving to God," became the new eastern emperor.

379

Basil of Caesarea died. In discussing the intellectual climate of his time, he lamented, "Now we have no more meetings, no more debates, no more gatherings of wise men in the agora, nothing more of all that made our city famous." At this time, secular knowledge was increasingly being seen as useful only under the umbrella of biblical interpretation.

380

Emperors Theodosius I, Gratian, and Valentinian II issued the *Edict of Thessalonica*. It was instigated by Pope Damasus I and made Nicene or Trinitarian Christianity the official religion of the Roman Empire. In his Codex Theodosianus, Theodosius declared "the rest [heretics], however, whom we adjudge demented and insane, shall sustain the infamy of heretical dogmas, their meeting places shall not receive the name of churches, and they shall be smitten first by divine vengeance and secondly by the retribution of our own initiative." Never in the Greek or Roman world had there been such an imposition of a single religious belief along with the suppression of all others. Theodosius withdrew state support from the increasingly poorly attended pagan temples, and since they were public property, he either closed them, sold them, or turned them over to Christians. An era of strict religious intolerance would follow, and Theodosius reportedly did little to nothing to control or punish Christian mobs that destroyed pagan temples and centers of pagan scholarship. Christians seemed to have forgotten the days when they, as a minority, had pleaded with the Romans for equal rights so they could worship as they wished. Now, the Christians were persecuting the minority pagans out of existence, and in doing so, Theodosius had abruptly changed the course of Western civilization.

Pelagius, an ascetic from Britannia, who was fluent in Latin and Greek, moved to Rome. He worked as a church reformer who, against the prevailing trend of his age, looked back to Origen and the idea of Christianity as a great moral changing force that would improve society. He taught that rich Christians should give away their money to the poor and live exemplary lives. Like Origen, he wrote that there was no completely lost soul. The Catholic Church, especially Augustine, bitterly attacked him for his views. Augustine accused him of denying the need for divine aid in performing good works. Pelagius would challenge Augustine's doctrines of predestination and original sin, which were ripe for attack because of their denial of human free will and the innate morality of humans. Pelagius's interpretation of the doctrine of free will became known as Pelagianism.

c. With interest in the apostle Paul greatly increasing in the Latin world, a huge basilica was built around his humble shrine in Rome. This dramatic elevation can be traced back to the AD 360s when Marius Victorinus produced the first Latin commentary on Paul. Five other Latin authors, including Jerome and Augustine, would write commentaries on Paul by AD 410. Augustine became obsessed with the apostle but was unable to read Paul's original Greek epistles, so he had to rely on translations and interpretations of the linguistically complex and poorly translated originals.

c. With Christianity as the favored religion of the empire, most Christians in Rome were being buried publicly in church cemeteries instead the catacombs.

c. John Chrysostom, who had spent several years as an ascetic, was ordained as a deacon in Antioch. He wrote his treatise *Virginity*, based largely on his interpretation of Paul's epistles. He wrote that Adam and Eve were initially an asexual couple, but the Fall corrupted them, and sex was one of the "vices" that all humans inherited from them.

c. At least part of the Bible was translated into Gothic by this time.

381

Theodosius attacked the quasi-Christian sect of Manichaeans, ordering that no Manichaean of either sex should bequeath or inherit property. The following year he decreed the death penalty for membership in certain Manichaean sects and started a system of informers to identify them. While the emperor himself was somewhat restrained in the persecution he directed, he established a framework that fanatical Christians were able to exploit. In the West, the increasing power of the Church would be imposed not by an emperor but mainly by Ambrose, the bishop of Milan. Theodosius was so obsessed with Christian unity that conversion from Christianity was not an option, and those who wouldn't convert to Christianity were severely persecuted.

Theodosius convened the *Council of Constantinople* to finally resolve the Arian controversy. This council of exclusively eastern bishops affirmed the divinity of the Holy Spirit and the Trinity, placing Jesus on a par with the creator God, and officially issued the Nicene Creed as the proper creed for all Christians. This council also condemned Apollinarianism, which was the belief that Christ had a human body but a divine soul and mind, which the council judged an even worse heresy than Arianism. The patriarchate in Constantinople was elevated to the same status as the one in Rome, above Antioch and Alexandria. This was an extremely controversial decision and caused much resentment because the patriarchates in Rome, Alexandria, and Antioch were thought to have been founded by Peter or his disciples and therefore should have had more authority than the one that was merely the seat of government.

c. Before Christian domination, Alexandria had nearly 2,500 pagan shrines and temples, and there may have been as many as a million in the entire Roman Empire, and Rome observed 117 religious holidays each year. There was so much pagan infrastructure in the 90 percent pagan empire that it would not be entirely dismantled for decades.

382

Theodosius agreed to a peace treaty with the Goths and focused on extinguishing paganism. Many of his laws reinstated the prohibitions of Constantius II from the AD 350s.

Theodosius I declared heresy a capital crime and ordered that heretics be revealed to the authorities by everyone, even by the heretics' personal servants and slaves. He ordered the burning of heretical books and the denial of inheritance to children of heretics.

Pope Damasus I presided over the Council of Rome, which issued the official canon of Christian scripture. The centuries-long and divisive struggle to create a New Testament was officially over, but various sects chose their own body of scripture to supplement these twenty-seven books.

Damasus I commissioned priest and theologian Jerome to revise the *Vetus Itala*, a poorly translated collection of Latin manuscripts based on the Septuagint and various Greek manuscripts of the New Testament and dated from the second century. Jerome's translation of the Bible became known as the Vulgate, and it would remain in common use in the Roman Catholic Church until the twentieth century.

Western augustus Gratian came to power after the death of his father Valentinian I. Due to Bishop Ambrose's influence, Gratian ordered that the pagan Altar of Victory, which had stood in the Roman Senate for centuries, be removed due to its offensiveness to Christians.

383

Eunomius, a defrocked Arian bishop who resided in Constantinople, taught that Jesus and God were of two dissimilar materials and there was only a moral resemblance between them. He decided to change the baptismal formula from three immersions representing the Trinity to one, representing the death of Jesus. Theodosius I decreed that Eunomius be banished and his followers no longer be allowed to assemble. Their property was confiscated, their writings were destroyed, and their clergy was expelled.

For the next four years, Christian mobs periodically attacked Rome's synagogues, often after local priests incited them with anti-Jewish sermons. These raids resulted in forced conversions, exiles, and deaths. These incidents were repeated in Callinicum in AD 388, Edessa in 411, Alexandria in 414, Minorca in 418, and in Syria and Palestine in 419-422. This was just a preview of the much more serious Christian persecution of Jews to come. Imperial edicts supposedly protected synagogues but plundering by these mobs was for the most part ignored.

384

Theodosius I dispatched imperial prefect Maternus Cynegius to the eastern provinces to close pagan temples. He was accompanied not only by soldiers but also by fanatical monks. They rampaged through Syria, Lebanon, Palestine, and Egypt. Libanius, a pagan teacher of rhetoric in Antioch, would complain to Theodosius that "utter desolation [followed], with the stripping of roofs, demolition of walls, the tearing down of statues, and the overthrow of altars," in addition to physical violence against pagans.

385

Priscillian, the bishop of Avila, Spain, had started a hyperascetic and highly moralistic sect. Other Spanish bishops accused him of Gnosticism, Manichaeism, and sorcery. He was tried in Bordeaux and brought to the imperial court in Trier, where under torture, he and his companions confessed to heresy. Despite protests by Martin of Tours, the leading bishop in Gaul, Roman governor Magnus Maximus ordered Priscillian and his companions beheaded. This was the first time since Constantine I's grant of religious toleration that a court condemned a Christian to death primarily for his religious beliefs.

In Milan, the bishop Ambrose defied Empress Justina after she ordered him to provide a church for Arian worship. When Justina tried to establish such a place herself, Ambrose rallied a mob to stop her. His success helped establish the precedent of the Church being more authoritative than secular leaders when confronting perceived immorality or heresy. God was the highest authority, the Church represented God, and Ambrose represented the Church.

c. Unknown authors wrote a collection of eight treatises called the *Apostolic Constitutions*, or *Constitutions of the Holy Apostles*. They were passed off as the actual legislation of Jesus's apostles about how to organize and conduct churches. These canons would be used by the Church as references for centuries but later be proven forgeries.

c. Tormented by thoughts of sin, Evagrius of Ponticus, a very influential theologian in Constantinople, decided to become an ascetic monk in Egypt. To help his fellow Christians confront the demons they believed tempted them to sin, he wrote *Talking Back*. In this writing, he selected passages from the Bible to be used against demons for five hundred different temptations, such as gluttony, fornication, and pride.

386

Emperor Valentinian II, the western emperor, permitted the Arian version of Christianity to remain legal, in opposition to Theodosius I, who had outlawed it in the East.

In a series of sermons, John Chrysostom of Antioch, later archbishop of Constantinople, denounced Jews and Christians who associated with them. He used the term *deicide* when holding Jews collectively responsible for killing Jesus, thereby killing God himself for

Trinity-believing Christians. Jews and Christians had lived together peacefully in Antioch for centuries before Chrysostom began cutting those ties with his "golden mouth," which is what his last name literally meant because of his speaking eloquence.

Bishop Ambrose was in the process of completing the Basilica Ambrosiana in Milan—incidentally, the first Christian church to be named after its founder—and he wanted the bones of a saint for the basilica's consecration. Ambrose reported that he had a dream or vision that told him where to dig for the required bones, and sure enough, the relics of Gervasius and Protasius were found exactly where he was told they would be. He then staged a demonstration of their authenticity by exposing demonically possessed individuals to these relics, and every afflicted person was miraculously purged of their demons. Thus, Ambrose set a precedent for the relic industry, which consisted of obtaining bones and other artifacts of saints, often by way of dreams and visions, "proving" the miraculous curing powers of the relics, and then, as a bishop, serving as the initiator and guardian of the shrine bearing the saint's relics.

In one of his early letters, Augustine wrote of the many Christians who were passionate about becoming martyrs. If they couldn't find someone to kill them for their religious beliefs, he told of some who committed suicide with the hope of eternal glory. One group he was probably referring to was the Circumcellions, who were active in his region of North Africa.

387

Augustine traveled to Italy to study Manichaean doctrines and learn how to synthesize Christian scripture with Latin philosophy. While he was there, he converted to orthodox Christianity and was baptized by Bishop Ambrose. He wrote *Soliloquia*, in which he stated "I desire to know God and the soul. Nothing besides? Nothing whatsoever." As one of the most influential and intelligent men in early Christian history, he apparently considered curiosity about the natural, physical world unhealthy, even sinful, because it diverted attention away from an understanding of the spiritual God.

The Romans abandoned their ancient imperial capital of Trier, in modern-day Germany, because it became indefensible against the numerous Germanic tribes that continued to migrate into the western Roman Empire.

388

Augustine returned to North Africa at a time when the Donatists still outnumbered the Roman Catholic clergy in the region.

The bishop of Callinicum in Mesopotamia led a mob that destroyed a Jewish synagogue. When Emperor Theodosius I learned of this, he ordered the synagogue to be rebuilt. Ambrose protested the blasphemy of sympathizing with Jews and was able to block the synagogue's reconstruction.

Theodosius I issued a decree that made Jewish-Christian marriages punishable by death. He also prohibited any public discussion of religious topics.

390

Theodosius issued an order for monks to remain in the desert and keep away from cities and large shrines because of their recent unruly behavior.

The first known mention of the *Apostles' Creed* was in a letter from Ambrose to Siricius, the bishop of Rome. This creed did not originally contain the now-familiar phrase "maker of heaven and earth" and said nothing about the divinity of either Jesus or the Holy Spirit. It was therefore acceptable to the Arians who believed both Jesus and the Holy Spirit were created by God.

Fabiola, a nurse who renounced her family's wealth, established a hospital in Rome. This was the first documented hospital in Europe since those established by the ancient Greeks in the second century AD.

Jovinian, a monk from Rome and former ascetic, renounced asceticism and celibacy as being spiritually meaningless. He also denied the perpetual virginity of Mary and supported his position with numerous scriptural references. Regardless, he was found guilty of heresy, flogged, and exiled to Milan. There he had to suffer the verbal attacks by Ambrose who was a strong advocate of the superiority of virginity over marriage.

c. John Chrysostom proposed that Jesus's mother Mary was a perpetual virgin, since her body had not been altered by the birth of her son, and that she maintained her virginity her entire life. The Lateran Council in AD 649 solidified this concept into Church doctrine.

Diodore of Tarsus died. He had founded the great Christian scholastic tradition in Antioch and had attracted church-wide attention as a leading critic of Arianism and Apollinarianism. A century later, a Christian council would declare Diodore himself a heretic.

Augustine became the bishop of Hippo in his native Algeria.

The Romans consecrated the Basilica of Saint Paul Outside the Walls. It was one of the first Christian churches to use the transept design, creating a cross-shaped floor plan. This design would eventually become the norm in the large churches and cathedrals of Western Europe.

Philastrius, the bishop of Brescia in modern-day Italy, compiled a list of 156 Christian groups who did not support the Roman Empire's chosen Trinitarian theology. Philastrius also proposed that searching for empirical evidence to confirm a doctrine was itself a heresy.

In Thessalonica, a Roman commander named Butheric arrested a popular charioteer on charges of homosexuality. As a result, the city's race fans revolted and killed Butheric. Emperor Theodosius I, enraged at the action, issued an order that resulted in the massacre of thousands of Thessalonians. Since Theodosius resided in Milan at the time, Bishop Ambrose refused to allow him to attend Mass until he repented for the murders. Theodosius eventually submitted and performed his penance.

Serapion, the bishop of Thmuis, in lower Egypt, wrote the biography *Life of John the Baptist*, and it became part of New Testament Apocrypha for Egyptian Christians.

Prudentius, a Christian Spanish poet, wrote *"Crowns of Martyrdom,"* which focused on Christian martyrs and their horrible deaths. This was an era that also spawned graphically detailed paintings of the agonizing deaths of martyrs.

Theodosius issued a law that reaffirmed that homosexual practices were illegal. Depending on the jurisdiction, anyone found guilty could be castrated or put to death.

391

The laws issued by Theodosius effectively created a death sentence for paganism in the Roman Empire and ended any degree of religious freedom.

The magnificent temple dedicated to the Greek god Serapis, known as the Serapeum, held the literary remnants of the great library in Alexandria since it was destroyed in 48 BC. At this time, a mob of fanatical Christians under the leadership of Bishop Theophilus destroyed the temple, its statuary, and most likely its entire collection of books and scrolls. Augustine, John Chrysostom, Martin of Tours, and other Christian leaders fired up their followers to do the same to other pagan temples. Destruction of remnants of paganism became an obsession, and the most passionate Christians invaded private homes to haul out and burn or otherwise destroy pagan statues and images.

The marble debris from the temples was made available for Christian construction material.

392

After Valentinian II, the emperor in the West, died, Eugenius, the Christian usurper to the throne, became the last emperor to demonstrate any tolerance of Roman polytheism or paganism. Like Julian, he had tried to restore support for other religions, but his reign was also a short one, lasting only two years. One can only imagine how Christian history would have changed if Julian or Valentinian II had had long reigns.

Jerome produced the *Gallican Psalter*, a revision of the old Latin Psalms, the translation of the book of Psalms. He also wrote *On Illustrious Men*, a compilation of 135 Christian authors who he thought had superseded Greco-Roman authors.

Theodosius I repealed his edict restricting monks to the deserts, opening the door for them to again join in the destruction of pagan shrines in urban regions and create havoc.

With the death of Valentinian II, Theodosius I, who had been the eastern emperor since AD 379, became emperor of the entire empire.

393

Jerome was the first writer to mention a correspondence between the apostle Paul and the Roman philosopher Seneca. All available evidence now shows that these letters were forgeries.

Epiphanius, the bishop of Cyprus, verbally attacked Origen, who had died in AD 257. Origen had believed that Jesus was the mediator of God but not his equal. Epiphanius gained the support of Jerome, and with their rejection of Origen, they also rejected the tradition of free and creative scholarship, which was his trademark. Church doctrine was becoming firm and unyielding, with an increasingly narrow definition of orthodoxy. By AD 553, the Church would declare Origen a heretic because of his evolved theology.

Due to the persecution of pagans, the Greeks celebrated the Olympic Games for the last time. The games had been held every four years for the last one thousand years in honor of the Greek god Zeus, but since Zeus was a pagan god, any semblance of worship of him could no longer be tolerated.

394

The Battle of the Frigidus marked the last serious attempt to contest Christianity and revive paganism in the western empire. The battle was fought in northeastern Italy between the army of Theodosius I, who was allied with the Goths, and the army of the western Emperor Eugenius, who had strong pagan sympathies. Theodosius's forces defeated Eugenius and executed him. This was another potentially major turning point in Christian history.

395

Upon the death of Theodosius I, the Roman Empire was divided between his two sons, with eighteen-year-old Arcadius ruling in the East and ten-year-old Honorius in the West. As was traditional, their borders fell between the predominately Latin-speaking and Greek-speaking regions. These two sister empires would never be reunited, and doctrinal differences between the Roman Catholic Church and the Eastern Orthodox Church would never be fully resolved. In the East, the emperor would still be seen as God's representative on Earth, and the eastern empire would survive and expand. In the West, with a weakening central government, bishops would gain more independence from secular authority, and Western Europe would be increasingly administered by an alliance of princes, counts, and bishops, and that arrangement would remain in place for another thousand years.

c. Emperor Arcadius was quoted as saying, "Those persons who may be discovered to deviate even in a minor point of doctrine, from the tenets and path of the Catholic religion are included within the designation of heretics and must be subject to the sanctions which have been issued against them." Over the next few years, the treatment of heretics would take up a significant part of the government's time and resources, and since there was no end to the blurred boundary between orthodoxy and heresy, local rivalries evolved into mutual accusations of heresy.

397

c. Augustine developed his pessimistic concept of "original sin," which Irenaeus had first put forth in the second century. Augustine theorized that Adam and Eve eating the fruit of the Tree of Knowledge was a serious enough sin that God transferred their guilt to all humanity by way of sexual intercourse. Unless they repented, humans, even including unborn infants, would be punished after death by never-ending torture in hell. This concept likely came from a misinterpretation of Romans 5:12 because of the poor translation to which Augustine had access. It stated, "just as sin entered the world through one man, and death through sin, and in this way, death came to all men, because all sinned." In the original Greek, Paul, the writer, did not appear to mean that all humans were guilty because of Adam's sin but that they had all sinned because it is impossible for a human not to sin.

The former hermit, Martin of Tours, a monastic pioneer and the bishop of Tours, died. The city of Tours secured possession of his body, and the town became the chief pilgrimage destination in Gaul for miracle cures.

John Chrysostom was chosen bishop of Constantinople. He gained popularity with the common people by presenting Christ's simple message of love and criticizing wealth and immoral behavior, such as the chariot races in the Hippodrome. Chrysostom continued to demonstrate an intense hatred for Jews. His anti-Jewish sermons were translated into Russian in AD 1100, at the time when the first Russian pogroms against Jews were taking place, and later into German in the twentieth century to be used by the Nazis.

398

The fourth Council of Carthage decreed that bishops were forbidden to read books written by pagans.

c. Non-Christian historian Ammanianus Marcellinus wrote of the Christian purge of Antioch's intellectuals, which included public torture, beheadings, and burnings of pagan philosophers. This was all accompanied by the burning of their books. Marcellinus said that throughout the eastern provinces, prominent owners of pagan libraries would burn their valuable collections to avoid the fate of the philosophers. John Chrysostom, commenting on the scarcity of ancient pagan books, proudly declared, "Every trace of the old philosophy and literature of the ancient world has vanished from the face of the earth."

399

The anti-pagan laws were now more enforceable than ever due to the willing bands of young Christian fanatics ready to do the dirty work. Emperor Arcadius issued an edict for the destruction of all pagan temples in rural districts. Libanius—a pagan teacher, writer, and former mentor of John Chrysostom—protested at the highest levels of government. He said the temples gave hope to the farmers and provided a place to pray for their crops. His pleas apparently were ignored.

CHAPTER 5: FIFTH CENTURY AD

I most certainly believe that it is a gift of God that I
am what I am. And so I dwell amongst barbarians, a
proselyte and an exile, for the love of God.
—Saint Patrick

Faith is to believe what you do not see: the reward of
this faith is to see what you believe.
—Saint Augustine

Compassion is not a popular virtue. Very often when I
talk to religious people, and mention how important it
is that compassion is the key, that it's the sine-qua-non
of religion, people look kind of balked, and stubborn
sometimes, as much to say, what's the point of having
religion if you can't disapprove of other people?
—Karen Armstrong

This was another monumental century in solidifying the doctrines of
the only acceptable religion of the entire Roman Empire. Paganism,
including its temples, shrines, and libraries, was being entirely erad-
icated, and the Jews were barely tolerated. Augustine of Hippo, supported by like-minded, influential people in the empire, found himself
in a position to define a multitude of orthodox beliefs that remain in effect to this day. The western Roman Empire was overrun by barbarian
tribes, and Rome itself was sacked by the Goths. Orthodox Christians
continued in their attempt to eliminate all heretical texts from the

face of the Earth. Due to the destruction of literature and the centers of learning, literacy rates and scholarship sharply declined throughout Christian Europe. Orthodox Christians continued to battle against the Arians, the Donatists, and the Pelagianists, and as a result of the Council of Chalcedon, orthodox Christianity further divided into two additional rival camps.

400

The estimated worldwide Christian population was twenty-five to thirty-five million, approximately half the population of the Roman Empire. This enormous increase in the fourth century was the result of the policies of Constantine I and Theodosius I, not any spiritual breakthrough.

Before Constantine's conversion, there had been twenty-eight public libraries and many private libraries within the city of Rome, but they no longer existed by this time. Discussions of pagan philosophy and religion were illegal, and any pagan literature that deviated from orthodox Christian belief or sensitivity was destroyed. This Christian control of all European literature lasted until the seventeenth century before very gradually eroding.

c. Churches increasingly began to exert independence from the secular courts in the cities of the Roman Empire. The empire recognized the Church's independence by giving clerics a stronger separate justice system. In the West, the system applied to all clergy, but in the East, it pertained only to bishops.

c. With the growth of monasticism and the solitary life of monks, masturbation began to be mentioned as a sexual offense, although it was never mentioned specifically in the Bible or by the early Church fathers.

c. The Praeconium Paschale, better known in English as the *Exultet*, was a prayer written for Easter observance, possibly written by Ambrose. In the prayer, Jesus was referred to as the light-bringer and "the bright morning star." The Latin word for morning star, light-bringer, or the planet Venus was *lucifer.* The mythology gets interesting when Lucifer, or Venus, seen by its movements as falling from the heavens, is equated with the Satan of Christianity falling from God's grace and being cast into the underworld.

Supporters of the theological schools of Antioch and Alexandria differed in their starting points in understanding Jesus. The Antioch school focused on the historical Jesus of the Synoptic Gospels and how he could be God, while the Alexandrian school began their Christology with the "Word of God" in the Gospel of John and how it became flesh and blood. The scholars from Antioch spoke of two natures of Christ and therefore were known as Dyophysites. The scholars from Alexandria interpreted the Bible allegorically, imagining a blend of human and God in Christ's one nature, and were called Monophysites by the Byzantines, although the Coptics of Egypt and the Syrians preferred the more accurate term Miaphysite because they didn't see Christ as fully divine.

c. John Chrysostom encapsulated the dilemma of who Jesus was in this way, "Hell will spit out those who assert that our Lord Jesus Christ has only one nature. Now, which nature do they destroy? If the divine, then there is no salvation. If the human, then humanity loses all hope of eternal life."

401

When John Chrysostom found six bishops guilty of simony—using bribery to obtain their posts—he refunded their bribes and didn't allow them to serve. When he left office, these persistent men finally became bishops.

Chrysostom told his congregation to spy on each other in order to uncover hidden un-Christian influences, like enjoyment of the theater or the chariot races. If someone was discovered having attended a theater, they should be shunned. He preached that if someone was serious about saving a friend's eternal life, they should report that person to their bishop. According to Chrysostom, this was done not to control an individual's life but to save their soul. If someone refused to act as an informer, Chrysostom said they would be punished, either in this world or the next.

Christians inspired by Chrysostom destroyed the last part of the magnificent Temple of Artemis in Ephesus, one of the seven wonders of the ancient world. Much of its marble was burned in lime kilns to make cement, and the rest was reused in various construction projects.

c. Tribes from the area that became the Netherlands moved south into the western Roman Empire, where they united and formed a confederacy of Franks. This group would play an important role in European and Christian history for many centuries to come.

c. The *Doctrine of Addai* was written in Syriac. It described a request by King Abgar of Edessa to Jesus to come to Edessa and heal him of his leprosy. After that, he wanted Jesus to stay there because it was much safer for him there than in Palestine. Jesus apparently couldn't make the journey, so instead he dried his face, leaving an image of his face on the towel. Jesus then sent the towel to Abgar, and this began the legend of the miraculous Image of Edessa, later known as the Mandylion.

Visigoth leader Alaric and his forces marched on Rome. The Roman army under General Stilicho attacked and defeated them while the Visigoths were observing Easter Sunday.

Augustine wrote his *Confessions*, possibly the world's first modern-style autobiography. In the book, he admitted his sins and his self-loathing, giving a glimpse into why he believed in original sin.

402

When the Visigoths entered northern Italy, Emperor Honorius moved his capital from Milan to Ravenna, which was easier to defend but not as well situated for Roman forces to protect central Italy. Ravenna would remain the capital until the western empire finally collapsed in AD 476.

404

The provincial Synod of the Oak ousted John Chrysostom as the patriarch of Constantinople after he fell out of favor with Empress Eudoxia. His ouster was followed by a popular revolt by Chrysostom's loyalists and the burning of the Hagia Sophia Church.

Emperor Honorius ended gladiator fights in Rome, reportedly after the Egyptian monk Telemachus was killed, either by gladiators or angry members of the audience, while trying to stop the fighting. Reformist Christians said that these fights, like the Olympic Games in Greece, had originated to honor pagan gods, so it was time for them to end. For the many spectators who loved to watch bloodshed, they still had public executions and *venationes* for their entertainment. The *venationes* involved the hunting and killing of wild animals in arenas and evolved into present-day bull fights.

405

Emperor Honorius issued an imperial edict against the Donatists, again ordering them to rejoin the Roman Church in North Africa. He also demanded that the Donatists' property be confiscated, and their clergy exiled.

406

The winter was so cold that the Rhine River froze solid. The western Roman Empire was thrown into upheaval by the arrival of tens of thousands of barbarians from the eastern shore. Vandals, Alans, and Suevi sacked the former imperial capital of Trier and wreaked havoc across Gaul, eventually crossing into Spain. In the process, the province of Britannia was cut off from the rest of the empire and would remain so for centuries.

407

Honorius, the augustus in the west, again forbade pagan festivals and declared that participation in them could lead to execution. He decreed, "If any images stand even now in the temples and shrines, . . . they shall be torn from their foundations . . . The temples situated in cities or towns shall be taken for public use. Altars shall be destroyed in all places."

408

Visigoth leader Alaric and the leading Roman general Flavius Stilicho had become allies in the defense of Italy from outside forces. After political opponents murdered Stilicho and Rome still owed money to Alaric, Stilicho's thirty thousand Roman troops and forty thousand freed Gothic slaves allied with Alaric. He marched on Rome, which had been weakened by the loss of their best general, Stilicho and a regional famine. Once in Rome, Alaric extracted a ransom but spared the city.

Augustine began writing his *Tractates on the Gospel of John*. In these 124 writings, he still had to deny that Christianity was a religion of sun worship, as many pagans observed it to be.

409

Marcellinus, Emperor Honorius's emissary in Carthage, proclaimed the Donatists heretical and demanded they give up their churches. The declaration was based partially on the Donatist view that any Catholic that joined their sect must be rebaptized. In opposing the Donatists, Augustine set forth the principle *Cognite intrare*, ("Compel them to enter"), his interpretation of the parable in Luke 14:23: "Then the master told his servant, 'Go out to the roads and country lanes and make them come in so that my house will be full.'" Augustine interpreted the parable as it being allowable to force people to confess their sins and repent. This interpretation would become Church doctrine used throughout the Middle Ages to justify the Church's violent suppression of dissenters. Between Augustine's theological condemnation of the Donatists and the emperor's military actions against them, the Donatists were severely weakened.

Alaric again besieged Rome. His demanded to be granted a territory in the Balkans for him to rule and wanted to be named commander-in-chief of the Roman army. Since Emperor Honorius was in Ravenna and wasn't willing to oblige him, Alaric set up a rival emperor in Rome.

Emperor Honorius ordered the burning of books written by heretics and decreed that anyone discovered to be hiding any such book in their personal library would be executed.

410

The Council of Seleucia-Ctesiphon met in the capital of the Sassanid Empire. King Yazdegerd I, a Zoroastrian, extended official recognition to the empire's Christian community and allowed them to establish a bishopric there. Christians were allowed to worship openly and rebuild destroyed churches but were not allowed to proselytize to Zoroastrians. They were permitted to convert pagans in northern Iran. The same liberties were given to Manichaeans and Marcionites.

On his third siege of Rome, Alaric and the Visigoths broke into the city and looted for three days. They did not violate the Christian churches, which served as places of sanctuary.

Roman forces withdrew from the province of Britannia due to the increasing difficulty of defending northwestern Europe against barbarian attacks. One result of the withdrawal was that literacy rates in Britainnia would sharply decline.

Synesius was a rich and influential envoy to the imperial court and a former disciple of Hypatia, the renowned pagan scholar in Alexandria. The peoples of Ptolemais, in Libya, offered Synesius the position of bishop, even though he was not a Christian. He agreed to take the position but said he would not comment on the soul's creation, Jesus's literal resurrection, or the final destruction of the world, all of which were important Christian doctrines.

411

Emperor Honorius called the Council of Carthage, again trying to end the Donatist schism. After long persecution, the Donatist Church still produced three hundred bishops for their attempt at compromise.

412

Cyril was elected bishop of Alexandria after a show of force by a mob of his followers. His *parabalani*, or peasant troops, incited such terror that the emperor tried to limit their number to five hundred. Cyril was relentless in his pagan-hunting to the point of conducting house searches to discover pagan literature or paraphernalia. Cyril's main opponent for power was Orestes, the Roman prefect and a Christian, but one who was tolerant of other religious practices.

414

When Cyril led a mob to attack Jewish synagogues and to rob and expel Jews, Orestes protested to the emperor. In response, monks from the Nitrian Desert stormed Alexandria and denounced Orestes as a pagan idolater. They attacked his headquarters and drove away his military guard before the citizens of Alexandria rallied and drove the monks out of the city.

On the advice of his persuasive older sister Pulcheria, Emperor Theodosius II expelled the last pagans from Roman civil service. Pulcheria would continue to have a great influence over the empire's policies until her death in AD 440.

415

The priest Lucian had a dream that revealed the location of the remains of Saint Stephen, Christianity's first martyr. The relics were found at that precise location, twenty miles from Jerusalem, and later a church was built on that site to honor Stephen.

After much debate, the Synod of Diospolis exonerated Pelagius from the charge of heresy. As seen repeatedly, someone who was orthodox one day could be a heretic the next, or the opposite.

John Cassian had lived in monasteries in Palestine and Egypt and sought to reform Christian monastic life. He believed that true believers didn't need to separate themselves from other humans and didn't need to be fanatical about denying bodily and psychological needs such as proper diet, shelter, and conversation. He proposed using monasteries as hospitals and schools to help the poor, and he is best known for bringing monastic ideas and practices to the West.

Hypatia was the pagan Greek scientist, philosopher, and leader of the Neoplatonic school in Alexandria. Citizens of Alexandria regarded her as a considerable moral authority, and she sided with Orestes in his opposition to Cyril. A Christian mob sought her out and murdered her, then mutilated and burned her body. Cyril said that she was killed because she was an immoral female who had presumed, against the Christian God's commandments, to teach men. Her murder could be designated as the beginning of the Dark Ages for science because no further significant scientific advancement took place in Christian North Africa or Europe until the sixteenth century.

416

A letter written by Pope Innocent I to the bishop of Gubbio argued for the subordination of all churches to Rome. It stated that because Saint Peter was the only apostle to have worked in the West and Peter was the first bishop of Rome, all churches in Italy, Spain, Gaul, Sicily, Africa, and the Mediterranean islands must have bishops appointed by Peter's successors. This was all based on the theory that Peter was the first bishop of Rome.

Two church councils in North Africa condemned the Pelagians, and a year later, a council in Jerusalem had also condemned them, but another one had endorsed their views. Augustine wrote to Pope Innocent I and poisoned him against the Pelagians by reminding him that too much emphasis on free will would undermine the authority of the bishops.

Paulus Orosius, a Christian theologian and historian in North Africa, wrote *Historiae adversus paganos*, a historical comparison of present Christians and past pagans from the time of Noah's flood until his own time. He showed how the world had improved through God's guidance of Christians, and he rejected the idea that the Roman Empire was faltering because it became Christian.

417

Pope Innocent I died, and his successor, Zosimus, with no loyalty to Augustine, was sympathetic to the Pelagians, who pleaded their case to him personally.

418

Emperor Honorius, disturbed by rioting in Rome that had been blamed on the Pelagians, condemned them in a special edict and ordered them to leave the city. Although the Pelagians were not heretics, the emperor wanted to restore order. This edict was then endorsed by another synod of North African bishops who were aligned with Augustine and the Roman Church and were successful in winning Pope Zosimus over to their side. There was further disagreement when eighteen Italian bishops refused to support the pope against the Pelagians. Zosimus condemned and excommunicated Pelagius and sought to locate and disband Pelagian cells in Britain, Spain, Sicily, Rhodes, and Palestine. Regardless, Pelagius's optimistic theology remained popular, even into our present time.

419

The Council of Carthage accepted Jewish scriptures that were considered helpful for reading and teaching in the churches. These became the Christian Old Testament, consisting of thirty-nine to fifty-one books depending on what regional churches preferred.

420

Augustine, in his *De trinitate*, tried to explain the Trinity. He relied heavily on Latin authors such as Tertullian, who had first applied the Latin word *trinitas* to God. Augustine's interpretation of certain biblical passages differed from those of the Greek Church. In what became known as the "double procession," he said that the Holy Spirit proceeded from both the Father and the Son, whereas the Eastern Church thought it came only from the Father. This was based on John 15:26: "When the Counselor comes, whom I will send to you from the Father, the Spirit of truth who goes out from the Father, he will testify about me." This concept would become a major point of contention between the western and eastern Churches.

c. After being expelled from a monastery for being too austere, living in a hut for a year and a half, and then living in a narrow crevice, Simeon Stylites decided to live atop a pillar near Aleppo, Syria. He remained on a one-square-meter platform fifty feet above the ground for thirty-seven years, inspiring many Christians because of his perceived devotion to God.

Augustine wrote his second treatise against lying, titled *Contra mendacius*, because lying and forgery were so prevalent in Christian writing at that time. He believed that the presence of a single lie in scripture could call into doubt the truth of all passages.

421

Yazdgerd I deposed the Christian patriarch Ma'na because he wouldn't carry out the rebuilding of sacred Zoroastrian fire temples that

Christians had destroyed. This began a rebellion among bishops who gained the support of Zoroastrians in the military, and they appointed an antipatriarch. Eventually the true patriarch, Dadisho, was released from prison and retired to a monastery.

To avenge the execution of a Christian bishop who had reportedly destroyed a Zoroastrian altar, Pulcheria influenced her younger brother, Emperor Theodosius II, to declare war on the Sassanids. It ended the next year with Theodosius II being victorious and crediting Pulcheria's vow of virginity for his victory.

422

After the sacking of Rome twelve years earlier, criticism of the empire's new religion intensified. One of Augustine's most famous works, *The City of God*, was written as a defense of Christianity against accusations that the plight of Rome was the result of the Romans embracing Christianity. The treatise concerned Christianity's special place in world history. In the book, he seemed to revel in the punitive and unforgiving nature of God and provided little evidence for what he believed was God's ultimate rejection of most of mankind. His views were accepted by the Church almost without debate and became embedded in orthodox belief.

424

The Church of the East declared its independence from the church of the Roman Empire.

425

Aelia Galla Placidia, the mother of six-year-old western Emperor Valentinian III, became his regent. Along with the general Aetius, she ruled the empire for the next decade and held great power until her death in AD 450. She was involved in the building and restoration of many churches, especially in Ravenna.

428

Bishop Theodore of Mopsuestia, in Anatolia, died. In his writing, he argued that Jesus had been conceived twice, once in human form and again in divine form, and that after these conceptions, the body and soul were united in one person or nature. The Church of the East, although not agreeing with everything he said, would later consider Theodore's writings very valuable to their church.

Nestorius became the patriarch of Constantinople. In his first day in office, his anti-Arian inaugural speech managed to alienate and enrage not only Gothic soldiers stationed in the capital but also much of the nobility. It wasn't a good start for him, and things would get worse.

429

The Vandals swept from Spain into North Africa and reached the gates of Hippo near the time of Augustine's death.

430

c. Novatian had been a priest, scholar, and antipope who died in AD 258. This year, in Rome, Alexandria, and elsewhere, orthodox Christians seized Novatian churches and forced the congregations to go into hiding. Even being dedicated Christians was no longer enough to keep one safe, as the Donatists and Pelegians had already discovered. One had to precisely follow the correct form of the faith, as laid down by the Church and with the approval of the emperors.

Augustine of Hippo died. He is remembered not only for his wisdom and devotion to God, but also for his pessimistic view of humanity and how that view influenced Church doctrine for the next 1,600 years. His views contradicted a loving and forgiving God and encouraged priests to use the threat of hell to scare people into converting to Christianity and almost guarantee their obedience once they were Christians. With his themes of just war, forced conversions, antisemitism, acceptance of slavery, original sin, and the sinfulness of sexual intercourse, Augustine provided the necessary theology to allow the Church to consolidate its authority in the empire. Historians consider Augustine to have been the most influential Latin voice in the history of the religion and possibly more important than Jesus in his influence on how future Christians believed and behaved. Because he wrote in Latin, Augustine's writings made less impact in the Greek-speaking eastern empire.

c. An English teenager named Patrick was captured by Irish pirates and taken to Ireland as a slave. He lived there for six years before escaping and returning to England. He would later return to Ireland as a missionary.

431

The Third Ecumenical Council met in Ephesus. The bishops concluded that Jesus was only one person but possessed both human and divine natures. It also affirmed that Mary was *Theotokos*, the "God-bearer." This was a defeat for Nestorius, the archbishop of Constantinople, who claimed that Christ's two natures meant that Mary was not the mother of God, only the mother of the human Jesus. After the council allowed Mary to be worshipped as Theotokos, temples and sacred sites once dedicated to pre-Christian goddesses were rededicated or replaced with sites and churches dedicated to Mary. Mary had attained the equivalent status of a goddess, which Christianity seemed to need, even though very little information about her appeared in the entire New Testament. Like the human Jesus, Mary was transported from the world of humans and made into a spiritual entity. The council also accepted the Twelve Anathemas of Cyril, a list of requirements that if not followed would lead to anathema, or condemnation. As an example, the first condemnation from this document states, "If anyone does not confess that Emmanuel is God in truth, and therefore that the Holy Virgin is the mother of God, for she bore the Word of God made flesh, let him be anathema."

Pope Celestine I sent Palladius to Ireland as its first bishop. Once there, however, the king of Leinster banished Palladius, who then traveled to Scotland where he had better success.

432

Patrick, the former slave, returned to Ireland as a Christian missionary. He would have tremendous influence on the island, and many legends would be told of the miracles he performed to achieve conversions. Ireland is said, by Thomas Cahill in *How the Irish Saved Civilization*, to be "the only land into which Christianity was introduced without bloodshed."

435

The orthodox Christians banished Patriarch Nestorius for life, sending him into exile in Upper Egypt, where he would defend his theology until he died in AD 450. His enemies ordered his writings burned and insisted that his followers not call themselves Christians. This was a major schism in orthodox Christianity, with the Nestorians destined to link with the Church of the East.

The Huns were warlike nomadic people from Central Asia and were approaching the northern border of the Roman Empire. The Romans met with Attila and his brother Bleda, the leaders of the Huns, and agreed to pay a tribute to keep peace. Theodosius II realized this was only a temporary peace and used the time to strengthen the walls of Constantinople and build up defenses along the Danube River.

438

The *Codex Theodosianus* was published. It was a compilation of approximately 2,500 laws of the Roman Empire since the time of Constantine, and it provided stronger penalties for ethical violations that became crimes only after the empire adopted Christianity. It also established Christianity as the official religion of the empire, resulting

in the exclusion of Jews from public office and the forbiddance of any
new synagogues.

439

The Vandals had broken their treaty with the Romans four years earlier and captured Carthage, the second most important Christian
city in North Africa after Alexandria. Their king, Gaiseric, an Arian
Christian, set about confiscating all the Catholic churches in the area
under his control. They were either turned into Arian churches or
destroyed. He banished, imprisoned, enslaved, or killed the Catholic
clergy in the vicinity.

440

c. Officials of the Roman Empire closed the Athenian Parthenon, one
of the major temples still being used. Pagans were not unified to resist the Christians because they were split into innumerable factions
based on whichever gods they worshipped. Thus, the pagans were
steamrolled by the unified Christian efforts to wipe out all gods but
their own.

The eunuch Chrysaphius dominated the Byzantine court and used his
power to promote Monophysitism, or the One Nature of Christ doctrine, which stated that Christ was a divine being, not a human.

442

Pigol founded the White Monastery in Egypt with thirty other monks.
Under the leadership of his nephew Shenouda, it would grow to cover
fifty-one square kilometers and see its population increase to 2,200
monks and 1,800 nuns by the time Pigol died in AD 466.

Child abandonment had been practiced for various reasons throughout human history. The Council of Vaison was the first to stipulate that
unwanted children should be left at a church for protection, though it
required the church to protect them for only ten days.

443

c. In Constantinople, Palestinian Christian historian Sozomen completed his second major work on Christian history. The nine volumes covered the period from the Council of Nicea to Sozomen's present time. His first work covering the period from the ascension of Jesus to the defeat of Licinius has been lost. His books were extensively researched, using Eusebius of Caesarea, the *Clementine Homilies*, Hegesippus, and Sextus Julius Africanus as sources.

445

Emperor Valentinian III of the West, issued *Novel 17*, a decree that recognized the primacy of the Roman bishop over other churches in the West.

Sassanid king Yazdgerd II tried to eliminate all religions other than Zoroastrianism in his empire and conducted persecutions for the next twelve years. The worst massacre occurred in modern-day Kirkuk in which ten bishops and an estimated 153,000 Christians were said to have been killed. This persecution only ended with the ascension of Hormizd III to the throne.

448

The Nicene, Trinitarian, or orthodox Christians found it difficult to refute the many sayings of Jesus that supported the Arian view that suggested he was subordinate to God the Father, so they started to reference Church councils instead of the Gospels. This practice of basing doctrines on tradition more than scripture would be addressed by the Protestant Reformation a thousand years later.

Eastern Emperor Theodosius II reimposed a law that ordered the execution of anyone owning or reading a heretical book. Pagan and non-orthodox Christian books became less available, causing scholarship to further decline in the empire.

449

Theodosius II convened what would become known as the Robber or Gangster Synod in Ephesus. The president of the council, Dioscorus of Alexandria, coerced attending bishops into agreeing that Christ had one nature, both human and divine. Flavian, the patriarch of Constantinople, who believed Christ had two natures was attacked and killed by a mob of monks who disagreed with him.

The Huns ravaged the countryside around Constantinople but were unsuccessful at breaching the walls. They settled for the payment of a tribute and withdrew from the region.

450

After Emperor Theodosius II died, his older sister Pulcheria married an army general named Marcian in an arranged marriage. The new emperor Marcian immediately revoked all treaties with Attila, ending the payments of tribute to the Huns.

c. Pagan Anglo-Saxons from Germany and the Netherlands began to migrate to Britain and settle there.

c. By this time, much of Western Europe was under the political control of Arian Vandal and Visigoth warlords, whose subjects were overwhelmingly Catholics.

Rome had a population of about 350,000, a steep decline from the near 800,000 who lived there in the fourth century. It would further drop to 60,000 by AD 530. In AD 330, the empire's central axis had led through Rome and Carthage—now, it was through Constantinople and Alexandria. Speaking Latin, the Church of Rome was increasingly cut off from church debates in the Greek-speaking East.

By prohibiting and burning nonorthodox writings, the Roman Catholic Church gave the impression that the Bible with its four canonized Gospels, represented the only Christian views of Jesus. Yet, Theodoret of Cyrrhus said that at this time, there were at least two hundred different gospels circulating in his own diocese.

The Theodosian walls of Constantinople were completed, ringing the city and extending twelve miles. They would protect the city, and therefore Christianity in the eastern empire, for over a thousand years.

451

Emperor Marcian called the Council of Chalcedon to "end disputations and settle the true faith more clearly and for all time." It was headed not by church leaders but by the emperor and his senior officials. The counsel reversed the findings of the council of AD 449 and declared that Jesus Christ was one person with two natures, truly God and truly human. Pope Leo I of Rome had issued a letter, or *Tome*, which was used as a compromise between the opposing sides. Mary was reconfirmed as Theotokos, the bearer of God, and Jerusalem was formalized as a fifth patriarchate. It was the first time Rome had taken a determining role in establishing universal Church doctrine, and Emperor Marcian insisted that his officers swear allegiance to the new creed. As a result of monks' disruption and murder of Flavian two years earlier, Marcian ordered monks to "embrace peace and occupy themselves only with their fasting and prayer, and remain in the place assigned to them, and involve themselves in none of the business of the church nor the secular world." This decision on the nature of Jesus marked another schism, this time between the orthodox Byzantine and Roman churches and Christians in Egypt and Syria, who would retain their Monophysite beliefs and become two of what became known as Oriental Orthodox Churches and be persecuted as heretics.

At the Battle of the Catalaunian Plains in France, a coalition of Roman and Visigoth forces stopped the army of Attila the Hun. The Huns had pillaged Gaul and weakened the Roman forces, but the Huns did not try to advance further west.

452

Aquileia, the most prosperous city in northeastern Italy, one of the world's largest cities and a patriarchal seat said to have been founded by Saint Mark, was overrun by the Huns. When they were finished with it, the city no longer existed, and most of the refugees fled to the marchlands and islands to the south, where they would eventually establish the town of Venice.

When Attila's army assembled outside Rome, Pope Leo I and two officials rode out to meet him. After a brief conference, Leo persuaded the Huns to call off their attack and depart. It's not known what Leo said to Attila, but the pope's reputation soared after his show of courage.

Honoria, the sister of Valentinian III, the western emperor, was confined to a monastery following a failed plot against her brother. She wrote to Attila and offered to marry him if he freed her. This would have made it legitimate for Attila to rule the western empire, but he died before he could resume any campaign against the Romans.

454

The Huns' empire was finally ended after an alliance of tribes, including the Ostrogoths, defeated them at the Battle of Nedao in the Balkans. The Ostrogoths were tribes related to the Visigoths but had left their eastern homeland later than the Visigoths.

455

After Petronius Maximus murdered western emperor Valentinian III and claimed his throne, Valentinian's widow, Empress Licinia Eudoxia, was so enraged that she summoned Gaiseric—the "King of Africa"— and his Vandal army to attack Rome. Gaiseric did as she requested and invaded the city. His army looted the palace of everything of value but left the city intact and spared the inhabitants. The Vandals carried off many important citizens, including an apparently willing Eudoxia and her daughters, to Carthage, and Maximus died at the hands of an angry Roman mob.

456

Eutyches of Constantinople died. He had devised a theology known as Eutychianism, which, by leaning toward a Monophysite belief, caused controversy within the orthodox Church. This confusing concept forced the Council of Chalcedon to distinguish between the person-hood and nature of Jesus, stating that Christ was one person with two natures, but the natures were "without confusion, without change, without division, without separation."

457

c. This was a dangerous time, and tensions between Monophysites and Dyophysites ran high. An enraged mob killed Alexandrian patriarch Proterios in his baptistry. The Coptic Church, attempting to protect its beliefs, broke away from the Church of Constantinople.

Rome changed to the Alexandrian method for calculating the date of Easter. It was fixed on the first Sunday after the first full moon follow-ing the spring equinox, an event deeply rooted in traditions originat-ing from the worship of sun gods.

460

Leo I, the bishop of Rome, proclaimed universal leadership of the Church and immunity from civil control. As recently as AD 370, the pope's jurisdiction had been confined primarily to Italy.

461

Patrick of Ireland died. His church saw tremendous growth during his lifetime and included many women in leadership positions. By this time, Ireland was overwhelmingly Christian, with a vast network of monasteries. To a large extent, Irish monks tended to demonstrate their devotion by studying scripture and copying manuscripts. It's been said that we would have little of the writing from the first thousand years of Christianity without these monks because at this time, barbarian attacks were destroying European monasteries on the continent along with their libraries. In fact, it's been noted that the only place western Christianity survived undisturbed for the next century was on the remote islands of Ireland, before Irish monks brought Christianity to the barbarians on the continent.

The colossal bronze statue of Athena, which had stood on the Acropolis for almost a thousand years, was removed by Christians and shipped to Constantinople as a trophy. In 1203, crusaders would destroy the statue when they invaded Constantinople.

466

Euric, an Arian Christian, became king of the Visigoths, the tribe that then controlled the area between southern France and northern Spain. Being an Arian, the Roman Catholic population hated him because of his persecution of them. He refused to allow them to elect their bishops and closed many Catholic churches, handing them over to Arians.

468

The Romans made another attempt to recover North Africa from the Vandals but were defeated off the coast of what is now Libya.

470

c. The king of the Himyarites, who lived in the southwest part of the Arabian Peninsula, converted from Christianity to Judaism.

475

Orestes, the German commander of the Roman army in Ravenna, bestowed the name Romulus Augustulus on his ten-year-old son and made him the new emperor. This was legitimized by Orestes having a Roman noblewoman as his wife. This made Orestes his son's regent and ruler of what was left of the western empire, which included Italy, Sicily, the eastern coast of the Adriatic Sea, and a portion of north-western Gaul.

476

The western Roman Empire fell when Germanic chieftain Odoacer deposed the boy-emperor Romulus Augustulus, captured Ravenna, and took the title of king of Italy. Odoacer shipped Romulus's royal possessions—consisting of his purple robe, gold crown, and jeweled scepter—to Byzantine emperor Zeno in Constantinople. Odoacer was content to serve as Zeno's administrator of Italy, and with the western emperor and his court no longer in existence, the pope played a much greater role in city and regional leadership. After the fall of Rome, Constantinople became the capital of what would be known as the Byzantine Empire, although the emperors would continue to call their empire the Roman Empire until Constantinople fell in the fifteenth century.

480

c. The Church of Hosios David was built in Thessaloniki, Greece. Its artwork has been compared to the earlier church in Dura-Europos, Syria, to demonstrate the change in the status of Christ. Whereas the Dura-Europos church showed Jesus wearing a simple tunic, tending his sheep, or healing a paralyzed man, the Greek church built over two hundred years later showed him dressed in purple robes with a golden halo, sitting on a celestial throne composed of rainbows.

482

The patriarchs of Alexandria and Constantinople wrote the *Henotikon of Zeno*, an attempt to reconcile differences in the churches and reassert the Nicene Creed and the Twelve Anathemas of Cyril. The document never took a stand on the number of the natures of Christ. The work was widely accepted in the East but rejected in the West.

The edict intended to unite the Christians but instead initiated a new schism that lasted thirty years.

484

At the Synod in Beth Lapat, the Persian Church accepted Nestorianism and became known as the Apostolic Church of the East. Although Nestorius personally had little to do with the Church of the East, it would become known as the Nestorian Church, and its adherents would become known to the rest of the world as Nestorians.

Pope Felix III excommunicated Emperor Zeno and the patriarch of Constantinople, Acacius, due to Felix's opposition of the *Henotikon*, and this "Acacian schism" lasted until AD 519 when Emperor Justin revoked the document.

486

Patriarch Acacius of the Church of the East, not the one in Constantinople, called the second synod of Seleucia-Ctesiphon. It adopted a creed, reasserted the authority of bishops over monks and hermits, and reaffirmed the Church's independence. The bishops also attested to their allegiance to the traditions of Nestorius and Theodore of Mopsuestia. The synod not only limited celibacy to monks but required all clergy to marry and produce children. This requirement was in alignment with the culture of the Zoroastrians. This marriage requirement would be annulled in AD 544.

489

Emperor Zeno ordered the Nestorian theological and scientific center in Edessa closed. The Nestorian and Hellenistic scholars migrated to Nisibis, where they were protected by the Sassanid emperor.

493

Theodoric the Great, leader of the powerful Ostrogoths, took Italy from Odoacer after a three-year siege of Ravenna. He established his kingdom there and ruled Italy during its most peaceful and prosperous time since AD 375.

A hermit by the name of Daniel the Stylite died this year. During his life, he had spent thirty-three years living on a column near Constantinople after being inspired by Simeon Stylites. Both men were later declared saints of the Church.

496

The Saint Thomas Christians in India renewed their affiliation with the Church of the East and remained connected for over a thousand years, receiving support from Persian bishops.

Clovis I united the Frankish tribes and founded the Merovingian dynasty, which would rule for the next two centuries.

Pope Gelasius I established the Feast of Saint Valentine on February 14 to commemorate Saint Valentine, who died on this day in AD 269.

497

Emperor Anastasius I recognized Theodoric, the Ostrogoth king, as the ruler of Italy. He shipped him the robes and palace ornaments Odoacer had sent to Constantinople twenty years earlier.

The pagan Shah of the Sassanids decided that he would determine the true Christianity taught in his empire. In the debate of whether Christ was of one or two natures, he chose the Nestorian two-nature version.

498

The head of the Church of the East took the title of patriarch of Babylon and, with the title, authority over all nonorthodox Christians in Asia.

Symmachus became pope, and during a dispute with a papal rival named Laurentius, his supporters wrote what became known as the Symmachian forgeries. These were documents supposedly reporting historical incidents that distinguished the papacy as an independent office, free from criticism and judgment by any clerical law.

CHAPTER 6: SIXTH CENTURY AD

I am surrounded by priests who repeat incessantly
that their kingdom is not of this world, and yet they lay
hands on everything they can get.
                              —Napoleon Bonaparte

The Christian resolution to find the world ugly and
bad has made the world ugly and bad.
                              —Friedrich Nietzsche

The world is by no means averse to religion. In fact, it
is devoted to it with a passion. It will buy any recipe for
salvation as long as that formula leaves the responsibility for cooking up salvation firmly in human hands.
                              —Robert Farrar Capon

In the sixth century, orthodox Christians continued to eradicate any
evidence of paganism or what they considered heresies. With the destruction of ancient pagan and heretical literature by Christians and
as a result of war, scholasticism continued in sharp decline, and curiosity was being understood as the sin of pride, an analogy to trying to
eat from the Tree of Knowledge. Saint Benedict founded his monastic order and issued his Rule for the conduct of monks. The Catholic
Church became the dominant power in the West, and the bishops of
Rome, now known as popes, assumed leadership in the former western
Roman Empire. Emperor Justinian I survived a revolt and attempted
to regain control of the western empire from barbarian tribes, and

Christianity experienced a very successful expansion into Asia and Africa. With Italy and much of Europe in ruins, one of the main bastions of Christianity became the remote island of Ireland, where a strong monastic system developed.

500

c. At the age of fourteen, Benedict of Nursia withdrew from what he viewed as an immoral society. He later became one of monasticism's true reformers, founding the Benedictine Order.

c. Based on the sympathetic way they were portrayed in many gospels, Pontius Pilate and his wife, Claudia Procula, were elevated to sainthood by the Ethiopian Orthodox Church.

c. The earliest indisputable reference to "Jesus of Nazareth" or "Jesus the Nazarene" in any Jewish literature was found in the *Bavli*, which was compiled about this time. Earlier Jewish references to the Jesus of Christianity were vague, and Jewish scholars were uncertain as to who the various Jesuses mentioned in their scriptures really were. It's said that Josephus mentioned nineteen different Jesuses in his writings, most around the time of the Christian Jesus. Since Jesus, or Yeshua in Hebrew, means "savior," this name could have been applied to any messiah figure.

c. Caesarius of Arles, in his volumes of writing titled *Sermons*, considered any sexual longing or self-stimulation to be a serious sin on a par with adultery or excessive marital sex.

c. This is the earliest date for the writing of the *Cave of Treasures*, a book of New Testament Apocrypha attributed to Ephrem Syrus, a Syrian theologian. It is a collection of fables that roughly parallel the Bible from the time of Adam until the crucifixion of Jesus. It was an attempt to trace Jesus Christ back to Adam and show how he had been foretold in history.

c. At this time, more than two-thirds of Christians still lived outside Europe, mainly in the Middle East and North Africa.

c. Sixteen volumes of medical texts written by the second-century Greek physician Galen were still in use, and his theories and methods would remain basically unquestioned for over a thousand years because of the Church's suppression of scientific scholarship.

c. Christian theologian, mystic, and philosopher, who was known as Pseudo-Dionysius the Areopagite, wrote the *Corpus Dionysiacum*. The writer identified himself as Dionysius, the pagan Athenian converted by the apostle Paul in the book of Acts. These writings were not confirmed as forgeries until the nineteenth century. During all that time, the *Corpus Dionysiacum* carried authority among Christian leaders because it was believed to have been written by an eyewitness to the very beginning of Christianity.

c. Irish abbots wrote the *Penitentials*, which listed every sin they could imagine, and the appropriate penance a priest should impose upon the confession of that sin.

c. Parchment became the chosen writing material for Christian scribes. With the fall of the western empire, papyrus from Egypt was less available, and parchment or vellum became more commonly used. Parchment was more durable and smoother than papyrus if processed carefully and could be bound in codices or books which were more durable and took up less room than papyrus scrolls. The process of making parchment from animal hides was messy and time-consuming, so parchment was very expensive and used almost exclusively for Bibles and other religious writings copied in monasteries. A single Bible could consume the skins of 170 sheep.

c. Ethiopians created the *Garima Gospels* in the Ge'ez language, making them the world's first-known Christian illuminated manuscripts. These were Bibles and scriptural writings decorated with colorful and intricate designs and using gold and silver leaf. The illustrations reflected light, thus illuminating the text. Illumination not only beautified the text but added easily understood illustrations to enhance what was described.

By the end of this century, the Bible had been translated into Armenian, Syriac, Coptic, Old Nubian, Ethiopic, and Georgian. Over time, due to scribal errors and omissions, all of the Bible's versions would come to differ a great deal.

501

This is the earliest date for the writing of the *Syriac Infancy Gospel*, or *Arabic Infancy Gospel*. Scholars believe this writing was partly based on the *Infancy Gospel of Thomas* and the *Protevangelium of James*. It was written in the Arabic language and depicted fanciful stories from Jesus's youth. Some of these stories also found their way into the Koran.

508

Legend tells that after Clovis, the king of the Franks, prayed to the Christian God, a battle turned in his favor. He was baptized on Christmas Day. His adoption of Catholicism. as opposed to Arianism. led to widespread conversion of the Frankish people to Roman Christianity. It was recorded that after he became a Catholic, he remained just as cruel, immoral, and deceitful as ever.

512

The *Trisagion*, or "Thrice Holy," is a hymn chanted in Eastern churches to the Holy Trinity. This year Emperor Anastasius I requested a change of one lyrical phrase to make it more about Christ and thus more appealing to Monophysites. The change was acceptable in Antioch but was seen as heretical in Constantinople. The reaction led to an uprising of the orthodox Christians, known as the Trisagion Riots, which resulted in many deaths and Emperor Anastasius nearly being deposed.

Severus, a founding father of Syria's Monophysite Church, became the patriarch of Antioch. He was appalled by the luxurious living of his predecessors and stripped himself of as many comforts as he could to live an ascetic lifestyle.

513

A Greek bishop asked Pope Symmachus for an authoritative explanation of the real nature of Jesus. He wanted to know: if Jesus were fully human, how could he be sinless, referring to the concept of original sin? The request apparently caused Symmachus great consternation, and since he regarded this subject a matter that had been conclusively settled by councils, he reportedly referred the bishop to council records.

519

The Roman Catholic and Eastern Orthodox Churches reconciled when Emperor Justin I withdrew the *Henotikon*, the document that began the Acacian Schism. In Justin's effort to reestablish Church unity, he had to gain the favor of the pope and did this by revoking the *Henotikon*, recognizing the Council of Chalcedon, and deposing the patriarch of Antioch and fifty-five of his Monophysite bishops.

Emperor Justin's persecution of Monophysites caused some to resettle in Najran, on the southwest of the Arabian Peninsula, in the region of present-day Yemen.

520

c. The *Decretum Gelasianum* was written at this time in the name of Pope Gelasius I, who died in AD 496. It listed false information about Christian writings that had been supposedly declared canonical by a council in Rome in the fourth century and then published this information in the name of a dead pope to influence Christian doctrine.

521

With increased persecution of the Monophysites over the next forty years, many of them immigrated to the Sassanid Empire, where they came into conflict with the Church of the East. Since they had lost their bishops, they had to reorganize themselves in a way that was independent of the Byzantine Church.

523

c. Yusuf As'ar Yath'ar, a Jew, seized power in Yemen. At that time, the region had a significant Christian population under the protection of Ethiopia, a Christian country across the Red Sea. Yusuf burned Christian churches and reportedly killed over four thousand Christians who would not renounce their religion. The persecution finally ended in AD 525 with the intervention of the Ethiopians, who killed Yusuf and reestablished a Christian kingdom in Yemen.

Hilderic became king of the Vandals of North Africa. His wife Eudocia was the daughter of Roman Emperor Valentinian III and Licinia Eudoxia, who had accompanied the Vandals to Africa after their attack on Rome. Because his wife was an orthodox Christian, Hilderic ended his predecessor's persecution of Catholics. Hilderic was also on friendly terms with Justinian, who was the heir to the Byzantine throne.

525

Theodora, an ex-actress and dancer, who had recently converted to Monophysite Christianity, married Justinian, himself a former peasant. Theodora would become a rags-to-riches prototype for stories such as Cinderella.

526

Theodoric the Great, the ruler of the Ostrogoths of Italy, sent Pope John I to Constantinople to protest Justin's persecution of Arians.

Justin backed down after Theodoric threatened war with the Byzantine Empire. Upon Pope John's return to Ravenna, Theodoric imprisoned him on the suspicion that he had conspired with Justinian against him. Pope John eventually died in his cell.

527

Justinian and Theodora ascended to the throne. Theodora was very concerned with women's rights and the protection of prostitutes and orphans. She had pimps arrested and bought their prostitutes from them, freeing the women and helping them to a fresh start in life.

Justinian believed that agents of the government had to enforce existing laws against pagans, even if their sinful behavior was in their private homes. With the Church's network of spies, suspected individuals were targeted if they didn't conform to Christian behavior. Just one anonymous accusation could ruin someone's life.

Justinian closed the last of Egypt's temples to Isis on the island of Philae.

529

Justinian issued a decree that anyone who lived "under the insanity of paganism" had to be baptized as a Christian immediately or face exile and the confiscation of their property. He also declared that anyone who was baptized a Christian and then reverted to paganism was to be executed. After years of persecution, this was the death knell of paganism. In AD 300, an overwhelming percentage of the Roman Empire had been pagan, but now, not one pagan was allowed to exist in the empire. This persecution had been implied by Constantine, toughened by Theodosius I, and now finally enforced by Justinian.

Due to Justinian's decrees, Plato's Academy, which had operated for nine hundred years, was permanently closed and the philosophers dispersed. Many of these pagan scholars were invited to Persia, seeking freedom of thought and speech, but were disappointed with their treatment there. They returned to Greece and lived in hiding until the last of them died.

The Council of Orange accepted Augustine's theology that denied human free will and agreed that humans were tainted by original sin. This was a blow to the Pelagians, who believed in a loving God who granted his children free will and would never brand newborn babies with sin. The council did not uphold Augustine's theory of strict pre-destination. The council's conclusions would reverberate throughout Europe even after the Protestant Reformation in the sixteenth century.

c. It was hard to distinguish between those who followed Christ be-cause it was the law, because it was necessary for self-preservation, or because they had real faith in him. As a result, many devout Christians sought to separate themselves from the masses by withdrawing from society and surrounding themselves with other devout Christians. To this end, Benedict of Nursia became the abbot of a group of monks known as the Benedictines. His strict *Benedictine Rule*, which called for poverty, chastity, and obedience, set a precedent for guiding mo-nastic life, which had in the past often crossed over into fanaticism or lapsed into sinfulness. His order founded a monastery on the grounds of a pagan temple on Monte Cassino, south of Rome.

530

Gelimer became king of the Vandals and Alans in North Africa after removing Hilderic from the throne. An Arian Christian like most Vandals, Gelimer renewed the persecution of Catholics. This led Emperor Justinian I to declare war on the Vandals.

531

After a plea from his sister Chrotilda, Childebert, king of the Franks, invaded Spain, which was still under the control of the Visigoths. Chrotilda was the wife of Visigoth king Amalaric and a Catholic, and she claimed that her Arian husband was preventing her from worship-ping in the way she chose.

Under the rule of Sassanid emperor Khosrau I, the center of learning and national university for his empire became the Nestorian School of Gondishapur. Here, not only Greek and Syriac scholars met but also Indian and Chinese scholars. It basically became the world's think tank.

532

Since there was no mention in scripture of the year in which Jesus was born, Scythian monk Dionysius Exiguus, at the request of papal chancellor Bonifatius, calculated the date by using clues from the Gospels and other historical records. He determined the exact year and introduced a new dating system beginning with the incarnation of Christ. The Christian dating system was inaugurated using AD from the Latin *anno Domini* or "in the year of our Lord." The BC we use today stems from *ante Christum natum*, which translates into English as "before the birth of Christ." Dionysius fixed year zero at the Roman year 753. Not until AD 1000 would his system become popular in Europe, and later, as Europeans colonized every part of the world, this Christian system would become the dominant dating system throughout the world.

In Constantinople, government forces arrested fans of the Green and Blue chariot teams after a brawl in which many were killed. Those found guilty were executed, causing fans to rebel against Emperor Justinian I. Aided by aristocrats who opposed Justinian, the mob declared a new emperor and threatened to move en masse from the Hippodrome and assault the adjacent royal palace. During what was called the Nika Revolt, Justinian seriously considered fleeing the city, but Empress Theodora convinced him to stay and fight for his crown. The riot ended when Justinian's agents entered the Hippodrome and managed to separate the Green from the Blue fans. As the Blue fans left, imperial troops led by General Belisarius attacked anyone who was left inside. It's estimated that thirty thousand rioters, mostly the fans of the Green team, were massacred that day.

Justinian commissioned mathematicians Anthemius of Tralles and Isidore of Miletus to rebuild the Hagia Sophia Basilica after it was heavily damaged again during the Nika riots.

533

Byzantine General Belisarius led an invasion fleet to the western Mediterranean to attack the Vandals in North Africa and try to restore that region to the empire.

534

Vandal King Gelimer fled before the Byzantine army, and Belisarius entered Carthage. It was too late to restore Hilderic to the throne because he had recently been killed. During this campaign, Belisarius also reclaimed Corsica, Sardinia, and the Balearic Islands for the empire.

Justinian updated the empire's law codes, deleting obsolete edicts and bringing a thousand years of Roman law into one consistent body. The laws were issued in the joint names of the Lord Jesus Christ and the emperor and became the foundation of the system of law of modern Europe.

Under the Justinian code of laws, life became much worse for Jews in the eastern empire. One law decreed that in Byzantine society, Jews were not allowed to read their sacred books in the Hebrew language in their synagogues. They had to be read in Greek. The Mishnah and other rabbinic interpretations of Jewish scripture were banned altogether. Despite this, the Jews were still treated better than pagans and heretics.

Many Jews migrated to Khazaria, in the vicinity of the Caspian Sea, where they eventually joined Jewish refugees who had fled the Sassanid Empire. The Jews who remained in the Byzantine Empire were largely assimilated into the population by conversion.

535

Empress Theodora, a passionate Monophysite, brought her Christology back into favor in the eastern empire to the extent of having the Anthimus, a Monophysite, installed as the patriarch of Constantinople.

At the start of what became known as the Gothic Wars, Justinian launched an invasion of Italy via Sicily. General Belisarius captured Naples and then marched on Rome, where he was welcomed by the population. Unfortunately, due to the depopulation and destruction of Rome, the city was no longer fit to serve as a capital.

536

Justinian imposed a Chalcedonian creed that only strengthened the resistance of the Monophysite Churches.

538

The Third Synod of Orléans decreed that Jews could not walk the streets during Passover because during this emotionally charged week aligning with the death of Jesus, even the sight of a Jew was enough for some Christians to take revenge for the death of Jesus.

Damascius, known as "the last of the Neoplatonists," died. He was a Greek philosopher and one-time leader at the Academy in Athens, which had been the pinnacle of scholasticism in Europe for centuries. He had first been driven out of Alexandria by Christians, and later he was driven out of Athens when Emperor Justinian closed Plato's Academy. Few of his written works survived.

540

With a resurgence of Gothic power in Italy, the second phase of the Gothic Wars began. The Goths were not suppressed until AD 553, and several northern Italian cities would not be reclaimed by the empire until AD 562. The first phase of this prolonged war ended with the fall of the Ostrogoth capital in Ravenna, which was occupied by Byzantine forces under General Belisarius and was ruled directly by the Byzantine emperor.

The Sassanids, under King Khosrau I, broke the "eternal peace" and invaded Roman territory, sacking and burning Antioch and taking a hundred thousand prisoners of war to Persia.

541

A plague spread from Egypt to the Middle East and beyond, killing hundreds of thousands of people in the Byzantine Empire. Those least affected by the plague were the nomads in the Arabian Desert. Many church leaders in the affected regions sermonized that the plague was God's punishment for the sin of not obeying Church authority. They condemned Greek and Roman medicine, which had been ineffective in curing the plague. After the pandemic ran its course, the Church and monasteries basically ran any health care systems until the sixteenth century. Since they believed sickness was caused by evil entities, Christian treatment was often spiritually based, and physical attempts to drive demons out of someone's body could weaken or kill the patient. The popular procedure of bloodletting, modeled on the natural process of menstruation, rarely helped and instead killed untold numbers of patients.

Emperor Justinian I dispatched John of Ephesus to dismantle paganism in western Asia Minor. John found many pagans still living there despite all their years of persecution.

542

The king of the Ghassanid tribe that ruled East Syria requested two bishops for his people. Empress Theodora arranged for the patriarch of Alexandria to send them. They were Theodore the Arab and Jacobus Baradaeus. Jacobus, or Jacob, was consecrated as bishop of Edessa and began the Monophysite Syrian Orthodox Church. His influence reached from Egypt to Persia, where he ordained bishops and priests for the growing clandestine church, which became known as the Jacobite Syrian Christian Church. He was the leading Monophysite proponent of his time and, over his career, was said to have won more Christian converts than Paul of Tarsus.

No further persecution of Christians occurred in the Sassanid Empire due to the large Christian population in the empire and the leaders trying to avoid revolts.

543

At the request of his spiritual advisors, Emperor Justinian condemned Origen, the former distinguished Christian theologian, for what he judged as heretical beliefs, including universal reconciliation. With this action, people were basically left with only two alternatives concerning the afterlife, either they spent eternity in heaven or in hell.

544

The Sassanids defeated a Byzantine army and besieged Edessa. The siege was unsuccessful, and the next year the two sides agreed to a truce, but only for the southern region of the conflict.

c. Cassiodorus, a Roman statesman and writer, founded the Vivarium Monastery in Calabria, Italy. There, he revived and improved the quality of manuscript copying. By this time, many treasured ancient writings were disappearing and the Vivarium became a place of preservation for classical literature. One of the most notable works the Vivarium produced was the Codex Grandior, a single volume of the Bible written in Old Latin.

Emperor Justinian tried to win the favor of the Monophysites with an edict known as The Three Chapters. This was basically a condemnation of the writings of three scholars, one of them being Theodore of Mopsuestia, a father of the Church of the East. This, in effect, turned the entire Church of the East into a heresy.

545

Pope Vigilius was said to have promised Empress Theodora that he would favor a form of Monophysitism if he became the bishop of Rome, but he reneged on his promise after coming to power in AD 537. At this time, after failing to sign a condemnation of three chapters of theology selected by Emperor Justinian I, the emperor summonsed Vigilius to Constantinople. Justinian imprisoned him there for almost ten years until he accepted the emperor's demands. Vigilius died during his return to Rome.

546

Ostrogoth King Totila sacked Rome, which was mostly depopulated after a year-long siege. The Ostrogoths demolished imperial palaces and forums and, in the process, destroyed many more thousands of literary works.

547

The Byzantines, still calling themselves Romans, recaptured their beloved city of Rome but would lose it to the Goths again three years later.

550

The Byzantines used the Christian Ghassanid and Lakhmid tribes to patrol their eastern borders and control any bothersome Arab nomads.

c. Hephthalites in present-day south Uzbekistan and Afghanistan asked for a Nestorian bishop to be sent to them.

552

c. Abraha, the Christian Ethiopian ruler of Yemen and southern Arabia, led a military expedition against the Quraysh tribe in Mecca to avenge the desecration of a Christian church. It was said that Abraha planned to reciprocate and desecrate the Ka'ba, their most holy site in Mecca. On his way, his army was ambushed and destroyed by the warriors of Mecca.

553

After a decade of warfare between the Byzantines and the Goths in Italy, the city of Rome was again under Roman control, and again the peninsula's Catholic population was freed from Arian rule.

Justinian called the Fifth Ecumenical Council in Constantinople to soothe differences between Christian factions and appease the Monophysites by condemning the writing of certain long-dead theologians. In response to the council's decision to honor the Council of Chalcedon's two-nature formula, the Monophysites further tried to distance themselves from the Church of Constantinople. Those Monophysite churches were the Coptic Church in Egypt, the Syrian Orthodox Church, the Malankara Orthodox Church in India, the Ethiopian Orthodox Church, the Eritrean Orthodox Church, and the Armenian Apostolic Church. Now, there were three main Christian Churches, the one of Rome, Constantinople, and Jerusalem; the Monophysite churches; and Church of the East.

555

Justinian sent an aide, Amantius, to suppress a revolt in Palestine and stamp out any heretical sect in Antioch. Amantius was said to have mutilated and killed those who resisted him on his way to Antioch and then terrorized the population once he arrived. He arrested and imprisoned many pagans, atheists, and astrologers. He collected and burned a vast number of their books on science and philosophy and desecrated pagan idols.

561

Portuguese bishops called the First Council of Braga. Only eight bishops attended, but they passed twenty-two canons, or decrees.

One stated that anyone who committed suicide would be denied a Christian burial, including the singing of psalms or bringing the body into a church. Another decree was issued against the Priscillianists, the followers of Priscillian, who was executed in AD 385. Since they refused to eat meat or drink wine, the decree stated that any priest who abstained from eating meat should eat vegetables cooked in meat juices.

562

In Constantinople, the restoration and expansion of the Hagia Sophia, the Church of the Holy Wisdom, was completed. This became the paramount church in the Christian world and still is one of the crowning achievements in Christian architecture.

563

Irish abbot Columba and twelve companions sailed from Ireland to the Isle of Iona off western Scotland. There he founded a monastery from which he evangelized Scotland and northern England. Columba and his followers copied and preserved a significant number of books throughout the Middle Ages. Columba made 150 monks the upper limit for his abbey, and when that was exceeded, he'd send off a monk and twelve companions to establish a new monastery. In this way, but the time of his death near the end of the century, his followers would create sixty new monastic communities in Scotland, and they would send missionaries to the continent.

565

John, the patriarch of Antioch, publicized the collection of decrees known as the *Apostolic Constitutions*. This collection of forged decrees dated back to AD 375-380 and were dusted off and reused for centuries when someone needed their authority.

Justinian I, the last Latin-speaking emperor of the Roman Empire, died. He left the empire's treasury in a fragile condition after excessive taxation to support his wars and construction projects. The empire had been enlarged to the extent that the borders could not be adequately defended. It wouldn't be long before the western provinces slipped back under barbarian control and Rome again became isolated from the rest of the Christian world.

The Byzantines had been paying tribute to the Avars, a tribe of equestrian warriors similar to the Huns and originally from Central Asia, who were raiding the land of present-day Hungary. An Avar envoy arrived in Constantinople shortly after Justin II's coronation to collect his tribute, but Justin II refused to pay. The Avars would counter by attacking Byzantine territory in the Balkans.

567

The Second Council of Tours proclaimed the sanctity of the twelve days from Christmas on December 25 to Epiphany on January 6. The bishops also declared that it was the duty of all Catholics to fast before Christmas.

568

The Lombards of Central Europe invaded Italy where war and pestilence had left the northern part of the country almost uninhabited. The Byzantine Empire permanently lost control over most of the Italian peninsula except for isolated outposts such as Verona and Pavia. The centers of Christian monasticism, learning, and document preservation had shifted to Ireland and would remain there for the next three centuries.

570

A Sassanid army landed in Yemen and defeated the Christian inhabitants.

571

Emperor Justin II refused to pay the required tribute to the Sassanid Empire, thus renewing the war with them. By AD 573, a Sassanid army sacked the important provincial capital of Apamea, in Syria.

c. When the Lombards destroyed the Benedictine monastery at Monte Cassino in Italy, the monks fled to Rome, bringing with them their Benedictine Rule. They remained in Rome for more than a century and brought the body of Saint Benedict to Fleury Abbey in France. The abbey of Monte Cassino would be rebuilt around AD 718.

575

Monophysite unity was fractured in a dispute between Coptics and the Syrian Orthodox.

584

Hermenegild, the son of Visigoth King Liuvigild of Spain, converted from Arianism to Catholicism. He led a rebellion against his father but was defeated and executed. A few years later, Pope Gregory I's *Dialogues* mentioned him as a martyr.

585

The bishops at the Synod of Mâcon embedded tithing 10 percent of one's earnings to the Church into canon law.

Emperor Maurice destroyed the Monophysite Ghassanids on the Arabian Peninsula.

The Church of the East held a synod and rejected the Monophysitic understanding of Christ.

587

Realizing that the Visigoths could never successfully rule Spain without adopting the religion of the population, the new Visigoth ruler Reccared I converted from Arianism to Catholicism. When the king converted, so did many of the Visigoths, but there were several rebellions against Reccared by recalcitrant Arians.

589

The Third Council of Toledo celebrated the entry of Visigoth Spain into the Catholic Church. It also approved the forced baptism of children of mixed Jewish-Christian marriages and forbade Jews from holding public office. Jews still had some allies and protectors among Arian Spaniards who refused to convert to Catholicism.

590

Gregory I became pope. He had once served as a prefect in the Roman government but sold his properties to provide relief for the poor and to establish monasteries. In Rome, where the aqueducts had been destroyed, many influential families had left the city, and large parts of the city were still deserted, Gregory did not inherit an ideal situation. He would rule more as a governor than a bishop.

After his army mutinied against him, the Sassanid emperor Khosrau II fled to the Byzantine Empire where Emperor Maurice received him and even presented his daughter to Khosrau in marriage. Maurice colluded with his new son-in-law to overthrow the usurper and restored Khosrau to his rightful throne. He did this the following year with a combined Byzantine-Armenian army.

591

Pope Gregory I identified Mary Magdalene not only as the anonymous sinner who washed Jesus's feet with perfume in Luke's Gospel but also as the sister of Martha and Lazarus. This became known as the "composite Magdalene." It was during this time that she also came to be regarded as a former prostitute. This weaving together of legends seemed to be unavoidable in Christian history and probably any tradition of that time. John, James, Judas, Josaphat, Valentine, and possibly even Jesus himself are each now remembered as one person, but their stories seem to be derived from memories of many historical people.

593

Sassanid emperor Khosrau II had the Christian king of the Lakhmid tribe, Nu'man III, murdered. As a result, both the Christian Lakhmids and Ghassanids were greatly weakened and that would become extremely significant in the early seventh century.

594

Gregory of Tours died. He was a historian, bishop, and writer, and he was convinced that relics had the ability to heal those who came near them. He wrote extensively about saints, martyrs, and the miraculous powers of the relics.

597

At this time, with very few Christians in England, Pope Gregory I sent the Benedictine monk Augustine to Canterbury, England, with the goal of converting their king.

598

Dallán Forgaill, an Irish poet, died. The Christian hymn "Be Thou My Vision" is attributed to him.

599

Byzantine emperor Maurice campaigned against the Avars and was the first emperor to take an army across the Danube River in two centuries.

CHAPTER 7: SEVENTH CENTURY AD

Every other sect supposing itself in possession of all truth, and that those who differ are so far in the wrong—like a man traveling in foggy weather, those at some distance before him on the road he sees wrapped up in the fog, as well as those behind him, and also the people in the fields on each side—but near him, all appears clear, tho' in truth he is as much in the fog as any of them.

—Benjamin Franklin

Philosophy is questions that may never be answered. Religion is answers that may never be questioned.

—Unknown

Do not suppose that I have come to bring peace to the earth. I did not come to bring peace, but a sword.

—Jesus (Matthew 10:34)

Due to the weakened Byzantine and Persian empires, the armies of Islam faced little opposition as they astonished the world with their military conquests. Jews continued to be forced into exile and migrated to unanticipated regions. As civilization in Europe declined, the Arabs experienced their golden age in Baghdad, and along with the Arabs, the Christian Church of the East prospered.

600

c. The economy of western Arabia was growing through the increased mining of precious metals.

At the beginning of the seventh century, Byzantine authority in Italy was limited to a band that ran from Ravenna to Rome and south to Naples. The Byzantine seat of power was located at Ravenna, and the Pope ruled from Rome.

Pope Gregory I equated the four great councils—Nicaea in 325, Constantinople in 381, Ephesus in 431, and Chalcedon in 451—with the four Gospels as the cornerstones of Christian orthodoxy, even though those councils had been subject to imperial pressures and in many cases were unrepresentative of the Church as a whole. Except for Ephesus, the emperors who called the councils played a large part in molding Christian doctrine and incorporating it into the empire's legal system. For instance, heretics were condemned by the Church but punished by the state if found guilty.

This is the earliest date that the *Acts of Thaddeus* could have been written in Greek. Like the Syriac *Doctrine of Addai*, it described a fictitious correspondence between King Abgar V of Edessa and Jesus.

c. An unknown author wrote the *History of Joseph the Carpenter*. It depicts the story of the family of Joseph and Mary, with Joseph having children by a previous marriage and Mary being a perpetual virgin. Today only the Coptic and Arabic versions of this work survive.

By this time, half the population of the Sassanid Empire was Christian. Their breakdown was approximately 75 percent Nestorian, 20 percent Monophysitic Jacobites, and 5 percent Chalcedonians, loyal to Constantinople.

c. The Apostles' Creed attained its current form in France. One of the provisions in the creed was the resurrection of the body, and from this came the hesitancy to injure a body in such a way as to prevent a physical resurrection. This was an idea that had been inherited from Egyptians by way of the Greeks and Romans. This dictate would prevent dissections in the study of anatomy and hamper the advance of medicine until the sixteenth century. These restrictions drove true scientists out of medicine and narrowed its practice to those lesser qualified or outright frauds. Of course, Jews and Muslims were excluded from this decision and were the leaders in medical advancements.

By this time, it had been around a century and a half since there was any formal communication between the Roman Church and the Christians in Britain and Ireland.

Additionally, all the great libraries of Europe had vanished, and except in the Vivarium monastery in Italy, the profession of copyist had basically disappeared on the continent. The wandering Irish monks who came from a copyist tradition were in high demand due to Europe's shortage of scriptures and other Christian writings.

601

c. Pope Gregory I moved the beginning of the Lent season from Sunday to Wednesday, creating a forty-day period of fasting that did not include Sundays since those were considered days of celebration. He is also said to have marked the foreheads of his congregation with ashes, a biblical symbol for penance, thus instituting the Ash Wednesday tradition.

602

After his own generals assassinated Byzantine emperor Maurice, the usurper Phocas took power. Sassanid King Khosrau II, Maurice's son-in-law, used this coup as an excuse to renew their war.

603

The wife of Lombard King Agilulf persuaded him to abandon Arianism for Catholicism. His son was baptized as a Catholic, and the king later built a cathedral in Monza, Italy.

604

Pope Gregory I died. Among his many accomplishments, he regained much of Spain, Italy, and Britain for Catholicism. He also standardized what became known as the seven deadly sins, the worst being pride, and to Gregory, pride came largely from secular learning. He wrote about the saints and encouraged their veneration; in the future, no church would be consecrated without a relic of a saint to display. He defined purgatory as a halfway house where sins were purified before the soul could advance to heaven. And he believed that the clergy should be free to marry if it was too difficult for them to remain celibate. The Gregorian chant was also introduced during his reign.

Roman Catholic bishoprics were established in London and Rochester, England, and Augustine of Canterbury tried to force Celtic churches to submit to the authority of Rome but had little success.

Pope Sabinianus officially sanctioned the use of church bells, which had first been introduced in a Catholic church around AD 400 in Nola, Italy.

607

The Sassanids had achieved success in their war against the Byzantine Empire and occupied Mesopotamia, Syria, and much of Asia Minor. The Avars struck in the Balkan territories and were able to gain footholds there.

609

After a successful rebellion, the unpopular Byzantine leader Phocas was overthrown and killed. Heraclius became the strong emperor that the empire needed to wage the necessary wars on two fronts. Being raised in Cappadocia, in Asia Minor, he made Greek the official language of the empire.

Pope Boniface IV consecrated the Pantheon in Rome to the Blessed Virgin and all the martyrs, ordering a feast on each anniversary of the dedication. The feast was celebrated on May 13 as All Saints' Day, or All Hallows' Day.

610

Muhammad, an Arabian man of commerce, said that he had received revelations from the angel Gabriel over a twenty-two-year period during spiritual retreats in the desert. Those revelations would eventually be compiled and become the Koran. It is known that he was already very familiar with Judaism and Christianity, and it's believed that he was familiar with the Diatessaron and the *Gospel of Thomas.* Muhammad acknowledged that the messages he had received were similar to those that had been given to the Jews and adopted by the Christians but argued that that Jews had rejected them and Christians had confused and corrupted them in their scriptures. For example, Muhammad believed Jesus was not a god but rather a highly respected prophet and a servant of God. He rejected original sin and did not believe that Mary was the mother of God. He and his followers believed in salvation through knowledge.

613

A Sassanid army invaded Syria and defeated the Byzantines at the Battle of Antioch. They also captured and ravaged Damascus. Egyptian and Syrian Christians, bitter about high taxes and resistant to the concept of the two natures of Jesus being forced on them, welcomed the

Sassanids as liberators, and the Sassanids responded by giving these Christians important positions in the new government.

Muhammad began preaching his new understanding of God's message and appealed to the disenfranchised, just as Jesus and the early apostles had. His main themes were devotion to God, the resurrection of the dead, God's final judgment, the tortures of hell and the pleasures of paradise, the forgiveness of sins, the importance of frequent prayers, the requirement to help those in need, the rejection of cheating and greed, remaining morally chaste, and not committing female infanticide.

At the insistence of Catholic bishops, Sisebut, the Visigoth ruler of Spain, began an aggressive persecution of Jews, making them choose between orthodox Christianity or punishment. Many fled Spain, but some returned during a tolerant reign eight years later.

At this time, the Jewish population of Palestine was concentrated in Galilee with Jews still banned from Jerusalem. Due to their harsh treatment by the Byzantines, the Jews joined the Sassanids and revolted against the Byzantines. This was the last serious attempt by the Jewish people to gain independence from the Roman Empire.

614

The Sassanids, reinforced by their Jewish allies, captured Jerusalem, and the Persians handed the city over to the Jews. After a few months, Christians in Jerusalem revolted and briefly regained control of the city before Sassanid forces returned and defeated them. Ninety thousand Christians were said to have been killed in Jerusalem, and many more were deported to Mesopotamia. The Sassanids found the True Cross of Jesus in Jerusalem and took it to Persia. This was the fragment of wood that Constantine's mother, Helena, had found in AD 324 and one of Christianity's holiest relics.

When the hundreds of thousands of Byzantine prisoners of war were deported from Syria, they encountered Jacobite Christians there and many joined them. At the time, the Monophysite Jacobites were in strong competition with the Church of the East.

615

The Sassanid army reached Chalcedon, on the shores of the Bosporus across from Constantinople. They captured Chalcedon two years later but then withdrew most likely to focus on their campaign in Egypt.

617

Donnan, a Gaelic priest, attempted to convert the Picts of northwestern Scotland. On the island of Eigg, pirates attacked and killed him and fifty-two of his monks.

The Sassanid army entered Egypt, pillaging Christian monasteries along the way. They took Alexandria from the Byzantines, which gave the Sassanids control of all Egypt.

The Sassanids and Byzantines signed a truce that returned Palestine to Byzantine rule. The Palestinian Jews refused to accept this peace agreement, but the Sassanids forced them to comply.

619

The bishops at the Second Council of Seville decided that baptism only required dipping in water. The bishops also concurred that Christian hymns didn't have to use text directly from scripture, as had been the case in the past when hymns were basically singing from the Bible.

622

The citizens of Mecca forced Muhammad out because his teachings were undermining the social balance of what was then a pagan city. He was advocating the cleaning of the pagan shrine, known as the Ka'ba, of idols and consecrating it to Allah alone. He migrated to the Jewish city of Yathrib, later known as Medina, where he was welcomed because of his abilities as a negotiator with neighboring tribes. His religious teachings were well-received in Medina, especially after his followers expelled the Jewish tribe of Banu Qaynuqa from their own city and executed the leaders of the Jewish Qurayzah tribe. Eventually the entire town converted to his new way of belief, and the religion spread rapidly. This marked the beginning of Islam as a formal religion, and the Islamic calendar dates from this year.

Armenians established an independent and self-governing patriarchate in Jerusalem. The Armenian Quarter of Jerusalem's Old City still exists to this day.

624

The forces of Medina went to war against Mecca. Records of the Battle of Badr are thought to be the first to mention that soldiers who died in the cause of Islam became martyrs and had glorious afterlives.

625

c. When Christians first encountered Muslims, they thought they might be another Christian sect, but what convinced them otherwise was that Muslims resisted the Eucharist, the cross, and religious images, all staples of Christian sects.

626

With the renewal of the Byzantine-Sassanid War, and after receiving blessings and miracle-working icons from Patriarch Sergius, Byzantine emperor Heraclius led his army into the heart of the Sassanid Empire. He defeated them at the Battle of Nineveh, in present-day Iraq, opening the way to the Sassanid capital of Ctesiphon.

Constantinople was besieged by allied Sassanid, Avar, and Slavic forces who wanted to end the Roman Empire once and for all. With Emperor Heraclius on his way to Persia, Patriarch Sergius organized religious processions along the city walls with citizens of Constantinople carrying an icon of the Virgin Mary. The siege was ultimately unsuccessful due to the strength of the Byzantine navy, which defeated the Avar fleet, but the Virgin Mary was credited with protecting the citizens of the city.

627

Paulinus of York attempted to suppress the Celtic Church in northern England and make it subservient to the Roman Catholic Church, but his plans dissolved when a pagan king came to power.

628

As the army of Heraclius moved closer to Ctesiphon, members of the Sassanid army overthrew and killed their king, Khosrau II. His son and heir, Sheroe, better known by the dynastic name Kavad II, agreed to a truce with Heraclius and returned Byzantine lands, prisoners, and the True Cross, which had reportedly been taken from Jerusalem in AD 614. Heraclius negotiated the withdrawal of Sassanid forces from Egypt and Syria and set about restoring Byzantine rule and religious conformity in those regions. Syria, for example, had been out of Byzantine control for seventeen years and greatly resented the renewal of forced religious conformity and the closing of their Monophysite churches.

Babai the Great, the leader of the Assyrian Church of the East, died. He had been a reformist monk before being chosen as patriarch. He reformed the Church, revived the Church's monastic orders, and formulated the Church's Christology in a more understandable way.

629

Palestinian Christian leaders demanded that the Jews be punished for their earlier role in assisting the Sassanids. The Byzantines launched new campaigns to convert the Jews, executed thousands, and drove many into Persian territory. The Byzantines massacred the Jewish population of Jerusalem and again banned Jews from the city.

To bridge the gap between the Monophysite and Dyophysite churches, Heraclius and his advisors came up with a compromise called Monothelitism, meaning that Jesus had two natures but only one will. This compromise was rejected by both sides and in AD 681 was denounced as heretical.

Arabs began to make their first scouting incursions into Syria, looking for booty in the turmoil that followed the withdrawal of Sassanid forces. The region was important to them due to its proximity to Arabia and because they considered Jerusalem the site where Muhammad had ascended to heaven and met the early prophets and God. It was the holy city to which they focused their prayers before Mecca took its place.

630

Mecca and Medina declared a truce in their war. Muslims from the smaller town of Medina had conquered Mecca with the assistance of other tribes. Muhammad's army destroyed the pagan idols but reportedly did not take revenge on the civilian population.

c. Muhammad called for an interfaith council to be held in Medina. The next year, local rabbis, as well as a delegation of sixty Christians from the city of Najran, Yemen, attended. At the council, Muhammad forced the Najrans and the Nestorians in the region to submit to him. He granted them freedom of worship if they paid an annual tribute. Other Christian tribes converted to Islam.

Sassanid queen Boran, the daughter of Khosrow II, sent her Nestorian patriarch, Ishoyahb II, to lead a peace delegation to the Byzantines, and Emperor Heraclius returned the True Cross to the Church of the Holy Sepulchre.

631

Heraclius sent Cyrus to Alexandria to serve as governor. Although Cyrus was unfamiliar with Egyptian culture, he was determined to enforce the doctrines of orthodox Christianity over the majority Monophysite Coptics.

632

Before the Arab conquests, there were approximately one million Christians in Persia, three million Coptic Christians in Egypt, and two hundred thousand Christians in Asia Minor. In addition, about 80 percent of the six and a half million Berbers in western North Africa were Christian.

Before Muhammad died, he urged his followers to spread Islam throughout the world. Islam had already spread throughout the Arabian Peninsula by military conquests and treaties. Jihad was taken up as a religious requirement, and Arab tribes united under the flag of Islam. The new religion exploded in growth, in part because people welcomed a religion without a dominant clergy that attempted to intervene between them and God while becoming wealthy in the process. In Islam, God was of one nature and one substance; there was no trinity, no confusion about who was divine and who was human, and no argument about how many natures or wills Jesus had. God was a god, and Jesus was a human. This made it easier for the average Miaphysite to identify with Islam more than Dyophysite theology.

The Arab campaign in Syria began in earnest. Since the Council of Chalcedon's declaration that Christ had two natures, resistant Monophysite churches had continued in Egypt, Armenia, Ethiopia, and Syria. Rural tribal areas resisted the orthodox doctrines that were being forced on them and most welcomed Islamic rule.

633

The Fourth Council of Toledo was called to debate the problems of compulsory baptism and Jews who pretended to be Christians. The bishops decided that if a baptized Christian was determined to practice Judaism, their children would be taken from them and raised in a monastery or a Christian household.

Umar ibn al-Khattab became the second caliph of Islam. He was known as a just and pious leader as well as a military conqueror. By the time he was assassinated ten years later, his empire extended from Libya to India and included over four thousand captured towns and cities. Umar is credited with issuing the Pact of Umar, which specified the treatment of non-Muslims in conquered areas. By abiding with the pact, non-Muslims were granted security for their families and possessions and freedom of religion.

There are reports that Caliph Umar rescinded the pact that Muhammad had made with the Najran Christians and deported them, although this didn't seem to apply to all Christians in the area. Most of those deported went to al-Hira, a Christian city on the Euphrates River.

634

Arab forces conquered Damascus and invaded Palestine, while another Arab army invaded Persia. Without the Lakhmid and Ghassanid peoples as a buffer, the Arabs were able to exploit this former defensive line and drive unopposed into Syria and the Levant. The Sassanids and the Byzantines had destroyed the only allied forces in the way of the Arabs.

635

Irish monk Aidan had left Iona and founded a monastery on the island of Lindisfarne off the coast of northeastern England. From there, Aidan spread the Christian faith among the Anglo-Saxons at the request of King Oswald of Northumbria.

Alopen, a Nestorian missionary, was reported to be the first Christian missionary to reach Chang'an, now Xi'an, China, at that time a city of over one million inhabitants. Alopen had done his homework and emphasized the Chinese values of honoring their emperor, their family, and their ancestors. Since the emperor approved of his version of Christianity, Alopen was allowed to establish a Christian presence there that would last for many centuries. In fact, Alopen was believed by many Chinese to be the return of the wisdom of Laozi (Lao-Tzu), the founder of Taoism, to the region. He established a monastery near a Taoist temple and was granted the privilege to establish other monasteries in one hundred cities. While in residence there, he translated the Bible into Chinese.

636

The Arabs crushed the Byzantine army at the Battle of Yarmouk in the Golan Heights of Syria. The defeat was catastrophic for the Byzantines, and the resulting panic spread throughout the Christian world. Byzantine emperor Heraclius traveled from Antioch to Edessa to organize the defense of northern Mesopotamia. He eventually returned to Constantinople after a ten-year absence and reportedly visited Jerusalem and removed the True Cross and other holy relics to take them to Constantinople for protection.

638

Antioch and Jerusalem surrendered to Caliph Umar, and the Syrian, Greek, and Armenian patriarchates went into exile. In the peace agreement, at Christian request, Jews were not allowed to resettle in Jerusalem. It is said that Umar was invited to pray at the Church of the Holy Sepulchre but refused, saying that if he did, it would be taken over by the Muslims as a shrine. The church has remained in Christian hands ever since.

640

All of Syria, except for the coastal cities of Caesarea and Tripoli, was under Muslim rule. Caesarea probably fell the next year, but Tripoli may have held out for four years. In the end, the Byzantines lost the last of their seaports in the eastern Mediterranean, and the northern boundary of the Arabian Empire was established at Antioch.

641

c. An Arab army entered Egypt after Heraclius refused to pay tribute to them, and he replaced his governor, Cyrus, with a military governor. The Arab campaign was bogged down by Alexandria's strong defenses, but after a six-month siege, the city fell. Byzantine troops who surrendered were able to leave and sail to Constantinople unmolested.

After two centuries of existence, the White Monastery in Egypt would slowly decline due to the heavy taxes imposed on it by the Arabs.

Heraclius died, and a crisis of succession followed.

644

Arab Caliph Uthman ibn Affan noticed differences in the memorized recitations of the Koran in different regions of his conquered territory. He ordered a committee to create a standardized version of the holy book. The challenge was to create the written scripture from oral versions and written pieces that often were inconsistent. Obviously, like in Christianity, it was an enormous job to reconcile all the oral and written histories into one book of scripture since someone had to decide which of the oral or written histories were authoritative and which were not.

645

A Byzantine fleet under the command of General Manuel landed at Alexandria and recaptured the city, forcing the Arabs to quickly assemble another invasion force.

646

The Arabs again drove the Byzantines out of Alexandria. This time there was much destruction and widespread slaughter. A thousand years of Greek and Roman rule in Egypt ended.

647

Muslim forces moved not only westward from Egypt, but also north-ward into Cappadocia, sacking Caesarea Mazaca, an important Byzantine city in central Anatolia.

648

Constantinople society was being torn apart by religious feuds, espe-cially after paying for almost fifty years of constant warfare. The Arab wars were also greatly troubling, and Constans II, who became em-peror in AD 641, desperately sought to unify Christianity. He tried to achieve peace by issuing the *Typos of Constans*, which forbade the mention of either the single or double will, not nature, of Christ. This replaced the Monothelite leaning of Heraclius's Ecthesis, issued in AD 638. The Typos wasn't destined to work any better than past compromises—it only made both sides angrier and further poisoned relations between them.

649

Pope Martin I called a Lateran Council in Rome to condemn the *Typos of Constans*, Monothelitism (the belief that Christ has one will), Monophysitism (the belief that Christ has only one nature), and all associated writings, declaring them heretical and calling Constans's edict blasphemous and irreverent.

650

The Koran was completed in its present form and organized into 114 chapters. It's considered the pinnacle of classical Arabic literature. Jesus, known in the Koran as Isa, was mentioned in seventy-one verses, making him one of the most mentioned people in Koranic scripture.

Most of North Africa, Syria, Palestine, Persia, and Mesopotamia had fallen under Arab control. The relatively unopposed conquests had been greatly facilitated by the lack of Christian unity and by recent debilitating wars between the Byzantines and Sassanids, which had exhausted both sides. In most places they conquered, Muslims did not destroy churches or force Christians to convert to Islam. In Egypt, after the conquest, there were probably only about a hundred thousand Muslims among a mostly Christian native population of three million. In fact, it would not be until the tenth or eleventh century that the majority of the population in those conquered regions was Muslim.

By this time, the Church of the East was established along the entire Silk Road from Damascus to Xi'an, China.

651

Landry, the bishop of Paris, founded the Hôtel-Dieu de Paris as a symbol of charity and hospitality. It was the only hospital in Paris until the Renaissance.

652

The Arabs invaded Sicily, where they looted churches and monasteries. There was a range of ways that the Arabs, like any other conquerors, treated the defeated populations. Sometimes they showed leniency, and sometimes they imposed severe punishment. This was based on a multitude of factors, including who the conquering general was and what limits his superiors had set for him.

653

The king of Hispania, modern-day Spain, called the Eighth Council of Toledo. The bishops forbade all Jewish rites and decreed that any converted Jews who relapsed should be executed by stoning or burning by converted Jewish Christians.

For his condemnation of Monothelitism in AD 649, Pope Martin I was arrested in Rome, along with his advisor, the scholar Maximus the Confessor. They were transported to Constantinople, where Martin felt the wrath of the emperor. He only escaped execution because of pleas by the patriarch, Paul II. After his imprisonment and public humiliation, he was banished to the Crimea, where he died four months later.

660

An Armenian named Constantine-Silvanus combined Manichean, Adoptionist, and canonical Christian doctrines to vigorously oppose the orthodox Church. His sect became known as the Paulicians, named after Paul of Samosata, the third-century bishop of Antioch.

661

Mu'awiyah I became the Arab caliph and founded the Umayyad Caliphate. He moved his capital from Medina to Damascus, which was a Christian region, and from this center, he ruled the entire Muslim world.

663

Emperor Constans II became the first emperor in two centuries to visit Rome. Pope Vitalian received him with great honor, but while Constans was there, he ordered buildings—including certain churches and the Pantheon—stripped of their ornaments, which were to be shipped to Constantinople for safe-keeping. He then established his court at Syracuse, on the island of Sicily, to try to prevent the Arab conquest of the island.

664

The Synod of Whitby was held in England to resolve differences between the Celtic and Roman Churches. Their agenda included such items as the ultimate authority for their Church, the date of Easter, the limits of the pope's authority, the appointment of bishops, and women in the clergy. In this synod, the Roman Catholic doctrines prevailed.

669

Caliph Mu'awiyah sent his son Yazid to lead an army into Asia Minor. Yazid was so successful that he reached the Asian shore of the Bosporus across from Constantinople.

670

After a twenty-year hiatus in their North African invasion, due to a civil war among political factions, the Arabs resumed their westward advance along the North African coast.

673

Theodore, the archbishop of Canterbury, called the Council of Hertford. It was the first Anglo-Saxon Church council and helped unify the fragmented English Church.

674

While the Byzantines were focused on their own survival, the Lombards tried to extend their control further into northern Italy, and Slavic tribes moved into Greece.

678

An Arab army had been besieging Constantinople for four years but failed to take the city. They did, however, capture the island of Rhodes and secure naval bases to isolate Constantinople. This year the Byzantines launched an attack on Arab forces in Asia Minor, forcing them to retreat into Syria. In a coordinated effort, the Byzantine navy, although outnumbered, sailed out to confront the Arab fleet. They were victorious with the aid of "Greek fire," an early version of a ship-borne flame thrower. The Arabs signed a truce in which they returned Rhodes and neighboring islands to the Byzantines.

680

The Sixth Ecumenical Council was held in Constantinople. It condemned Monothelitism, proclaiming that Christ had two wills as well as two natures, thus reaffirming the Chalcedon definition. The council also prohibited any future representation of a symbol of a lamb on the cross. It ordered that "instead of the lamb, our Lord Jesus Christ will be shown hereafter in His human form in images so that we shall be led to remember His mortal life, His passion, and His death, which paid the ransom for mankind." From then on, the use of the crucifix (the image of Jesus on the cross) became widespread.

681

The Twelfth Council of Toledo ordered the burning of the Talmud and other Jewish books.

The Khazars pushed the Bulgarians out of the region north of the Black Sea. When the Bulgarians met the Byzantines in the Balkans, they signed a peace treaty that marked the establishment of the first Bulgarian Empire.

683

A second Arab civil war slowed their conquest in North Africa for another nine years.

684

Constantine-Silvanus, the founder of Paulicianism, was stoned to death on the orders of Constans II.

685

Muslims built the Dome of the Rock, one of the most important shrines in the Islamic world, on the Jewish Temple Mount in Jerusalem. This shrine is regarded as the third most holy place in Sunni Islam, after

Mecca and Medina, because legend says that Muhammad ascended to heaven from that hill, taken by the angel Gabriel to pray with Abraham, Moses, and Jesus.

Umayyad caliph Abd al-Malik decreed that Arabic was to be the new administrative language of the Islamic Empire. It replaced the predominant language of Greek in Syria and Egypt and Latin or native languages in North Africa.

689

An Irish monk Kilian was a missionary in Würzburg, Germany. After Kilian told Duke Gozbert that the duke had violated sacred scripture by marrying his brother's widow, the duke's new wife Geilana had Kilian beheaded.

690

c. The ancient homily from Ireland discussed three types of *martyrdom*, or "witness" for Christ. The first was red martyrdom referring to a violent death; white martyrs did not shed blood but were persecuted for their faith. Green martyrdom focused on extreme penance and fasting, common with the Egyptian and Irish monks who sought out extreme weather and solitude.

692

The Quinisext Council was held in Constantinople to draw up disciplinary canons. Two hundred and fifteen bishops attended from the eastern empire, and possibly one papal legate from the West.

The *Codex Amiatinus*, the oldest surviving manuscript of the Latin *Vulgate*, was produced in the Anglo-Saxon kingdom of Northumbria, England, as a gift for the pope.

Not only were Constantinople's pantomime theaters closed because of Church disapproval and city budgeting, but a Church edict also banned street performers.

693

The Sixteenth Council of Toledo continued the harsh treatment of Jews. It prevented Jews from conducting commerce with Christians. However, if they converted, recited creeds, and ate nonkosher food, they were allowed to trade with Christians. Another canon reaffirmed castration as the appropriate punishment for homosexuality.

695

Under Emperor Justinian II, a full-face image of Jesus Christ was added to the imperial gold coins. This change caused the Caliph Abd al-Malik to end his use of Byzantine coins. The caliph then began to mint Islamic coins with no human images on them.

After the Arabs conquered Carthage, in modern-day Tunisia, the Byzantines launched an amphibious attack and recaptured the city.

696

c. Local pagans drove Rupert, the bishop of Worms, Germany, from office. Rupert then responded to a request from Duke Theodo of Bavaria to aid him in converting his subjects. Rupert would successfully convert the Bavarians to Roman Catholicism and establish the bishopric in Salzburg.

697

Adomnán, the abbot of the Iona Abbey off the coast of Scotland, promulgated the *Cain Adomnán*, or the *Law of the Innocents*. This guaranteed the safety and immunity of noncombatants during times of warfare and provided sanctions against the killing of people on Church lands, the commission of rape, and the failing to become

involved when seeing a crime being committed. This was a predecessor to the Peace of God and the Truce of God, which would be enacted
in the tenth century.

698

Muslim forces again drove the Byzantines out of Carthage, in the process destroying the city and killing most of its Christian inhabitants.
Once Carthage was retaken, the native Berbers, under the leadership
of Kahina the Sorceress, rebelled against the Muslims and reportedly
drove them back. In all North Africa, the only territory left in Byzantine
control was Ceuta, an autonomous city, on the Mediterranean coast.

CHAPTER 8: EIGHTH CENTURY AD

The role that blood plays in Christian iconography is huge—the washing of the blood, the shedding of blood, the blood of the cross, the crucifixion, the violence of that imagery. These are horrific, and yet they are at the center of the Christian faith. There is a place where beauty and terror merge, and it's at the cross.
—Scott Derrickson

Fathers and guardians, bishops of our Church, you ought to minister to the poor, or rather to Christ in them, and not to seek after vanities. But now you act quite contrary to this and are vainglorious and avaricious beyond all other men.
—Charlemagne

If it shall be clearly established that he professes belief in another world and other people existing beneath the earth, or in [another] sun and moon there, thou art to hold a council and deprive him of his sacerdotal rank, and expel him from the Church.
—Pope Zachary

Iconoclasm controversies rocked the orthodox Christian world, the Holy Roman Empire was born, and the Papal States of Italy were granted to the pope. Charlemagne rose to power in the Frankish Empire, where he oversaw a short renaissance and introduced

Christianity to the pagan world through military conquest. The Arab Empire continued to expand as the western Roman Empire further diminished, but the advancing Arab armies were stopped in France, Spain, and Constantinople.

700

c. This is the earliest date for the writing of *On the Life and the Passion of Christ*, an Apocryphal account of Jesus, which implied it was written in the fourth century.

Bede, or the Venerable Bede, as he was known, was an English Benedictine monk of great renown, especially for his interest in Christian history. He translated the *Gospel of John* into Old English, but unfortunately his translation did not survive.

c. In Mesopotamia, Arabic largely replaced Syriac as the language of the Church of the East.

701

c. In Christian art, Jesus began to be depicted on the cross wearing a *perizoma*, or loincloth, instead of being fully clothed. Since it was the Roman custom to crucify their victims naked, that is most likely what happened to Jesus.

709

With the fall of Ceuta and Tangier, the Arabs controlled the entire North African coast.

711

The Moors, who were Arab-Berbers from Morocco, landed at Gibraltar in southern Spain at a time when both Spain and Portugal were still ruled by the Visigoths. In eight years, the Moors conquered the Iberian Peninsula as far north as Barcelona.

716

Boniface, an English Benedictine monk, set out to evangelize the Germanic peoples along the North Sea. He spent almost forty years as a missionary, and with the support of the popes and Frankish rulers, he achieved remarkable success.

717

Caliph Umar II sent a fleet to support his new attack on Constantinople. Most of the crews of these ships were Christian slaves, and once they arrived, many defected to the Byzantine side, where they provided important information about the location of Arab forces.

718

Constantinople survived a second well-planned and well-funded Arab siege. The Bulgars, who were allied with the Byzantines, attacked the Arabs, killing over twenty thousand. This was the largest Muslim army ever assembled, and its defeat was monumental. This siege was the last serious attempt by a Muslim army to attack Europe through the Balkans for more than six centuries.

721

Caliph Yazid II ordered Christian churches to remove images of Jesus, Mary, and the saints in Muslim-held territories. If a church was to be turned into a mosque, all the frescos and mosaics were plastered over and painted in Muslim symbology or patterns with no human depictions.

Muslim forces besieged the city of Toulouse in southern France. Duke Odo of Aquitaine set out to find allies to help defend the city and region. He returned three months later with a large force and devastated the invaders. The number of casualties is uncertain, but this was a major battle that halted the Muslims in their attempt to conquer the coastal region of France.

722

Christian forces defeated the invading Moors at Covadonga, Spain, and formed the Christian kingdom of Asturias in the mountainous region of northwestern Spain. This would become a bastion for Christian resistance against the Moors for centuries.

723

Bede wrote *On the Reckoning of Time*, which was very influential during the Middle Ages. In it, he described a spherical Earth and how the shape influenced daylight and tides. He computed the date of Easter and traced the origin of the word back to Eostre, the Anglo-Saxon name of a Teutonic goddess of spring and fertility. The festival of Eostre was said to have included rabbits and colored eggs. In this work, Bede made an educated guess about the age of Earth, calculating from biblical references, and determined that Christ had been born 3,952 years after the creation of the world.

726

c. The Iconoclast Controversy engulfed Christianity when Emperor Leo III outlawed the use of icons in the empire's churches. The word iconoclasm refers to the destruction of icons, which include depictions of Jesus or other holy persons such as the Virgin Mary and the saints. Iconoclasm has generally been motivated by the interpretation of one of the Ten Commandments that condemned worshipping graven images. To Leo, icons also accentuated the humanness of Christ, and the fact that Christians had started to worship and pray to the icons themselves did not sit well with him. The Muslims forbade sacred images in their holy places and remained incredibly successful, so Leo might have thought that Christians needed to do the same to regain God's favor.

727

Pope Gregory II condemned iconoclasm, broke ties with the Byzantine Church, and took control of the remaining Byzantine lands in Italy. Emperor Leo III would respond to the pope's resistance to iconoclasm by removing Balkan and southern Italian dioceses from papal control.

Taking advantage of the rift between Rome and Constantinople, King Liutprand of the Lombards conquered Bologna and other northern Italian cities.

730

Emperor Leo III continued his icon destruction and prohibited worshipping of images, calling it superstitious and blasphemous. He ordered the removal of all holy statues and the whitewashing of intricate and beautiful frescos and mosaics on church walls, sending Byzantine troops to churches and monasteries to obliterate the images. This was an abomination not only to the pope but to Italian and Greek monks who had to smuggle smaller icons to safe places to protect them from destruction. As a result of Leo's iconoclasm, the only Christian artwork that can be seen before his time in Constantinople-Istanbul had to be uncovered from the plaster or paint that concealed it.

731

The Venerable Bede completed his *Ecclesiastical History of the English People*, chronicling the history of England from the days of Julius Caesar to Bede's own era, with the chief focus on Christianization and the decline of paganism in England. Bede was the first well-known writer to use the new dating system based on Jesus's birth. With this book, the system of *anno Domini* (AD) became more widely used in Europe, with Jesus's incarnation as the central event in human history.

Gregory III became pope. He founded a chapel in Saint Peter's Basilica for the relics of the "holy apostles and all saints, martyrs and confessors." Gregory changed the date of All Saints' Day from May 13 to

November 1 to coincide with the dedication of the chapel, and it has remained on that day ever since. Today, we call the night before All Saints' Day Halloween, derived from Hallows' Eve.

732

Frankish forces under Charles Martel defeated Muslim invaders in the Battle of Tours, in present-day France. This was the high-water mark of the Muslim advancement into Western Europe, and it was only by a twist of fate that Islam didn't take over Europe. At that time, Christianity had only slightly penetrated into Germany and the Netherlands. If the Moors had conquered the Franks, they would have had no Christian forces to stop them, only pagan tribes. This was exactly a century after Muhammad's death, and the Muslims had conquered two-thirds of the Christian world and the entire Persian Empire.

Emperor Leo III launched a fleet toward Italy to recover imperial lands and arrest the pope, but a storm destroyed the fleet in the Adriatic Sea.

740

c. After expulsions of the Jews by Roman, Byzantine, and Persian emperors, a large Jewish population had been established in the Khazar Khaganate in the region north of the Black and Caspian Seas. The Khazars followed the example of their royalty and nobility and converted to Judaism.

A Berber rebellion against the Muslims in North Africa began in Tangiers and resulted in the first successful cessation from the Arab caliphate, which ruled from Damascus. The revolt spread across North Africa, and the caliphate would never regain some of the land they lost.

745

Pope Zachary convened a synod in Rome to discourage the worship of angels and the assignment of names to angels, which didn't appear in scripture. Boniface, the missionary to the Germans, presided over the synod and brought with him a list of various clerical abuses that needed to be addressed. One of the changes Boniface addressed was the need for more spiritual passion from the Frankish clergy, which was composed of members of the nobility and more interested in world rewards. He also wanted to fill vacancies in bishoprics and parishes.

747

At the Council of Clovesho in England, the Gaelic English churches agreed to conform with Roman liturgy and holidays.

749

Syrian monk, scholar, and priest John of Damascus died. He wrote *An Exact Exposition of the Orthodox Faith*, in which he explained that the bodies of saints can produce miracles because they were not dead, only asleep. Since these people were saints, he said God dwelt in them while they slept.

Ratchis, the king of the Lombards, besieged Perugia, one of the few remaining cities in Italy still controlled by the Byzantines. Pope Zachary visited Ratchis's camp to plead for peace, and Ratchis unexpectedly not only lifted the siege but gave up his crown and retired to a monastery.

750

There were almost no remaining Christian bishops in Algeria or Tunisia, whereas before the Arab invasion, there had been nearly five hundred.

c. The lack of papal authority outside Italy meant that bishops in Western Europe established their own new dioceses, resulting in many localized versions of Christianity. There would be attempts to correct this in later centuries when European Christendom became controlled by the church in Rome.

c. The earliest surviving fragment of an Old Testament writing in Arabic is Psalm 77, dating from this time. It was discovered in the Umayyad Mosque in Damascus in 1901.

c. A document known as the *Donation of Constantine* was reportedly discovered in Rome. It stated that when Emperor Constantine moved to Constantinople in the fourth century, he granted control of the western empire to the popes. The donation made the pope a quasi-emperor and allowed him to reside in the Lateran Palace; to wear the diadem, collar, and purple cloak of an emperor; to carry the scepter; and to be attended by a body of chamberlains, officials who manage his affairs. The pope was to ride a white horse and receive honors from the senate, including the practice of kissing his foot. Centuries later, this document would be found to be a forgery. Nevertheless, it was used extensively by popes even after its authenticity was disproven.

The Abbasids overthrew the Muslim Umayyad dynasty. They were more interested in the world at large than the Umayyads and would convert the Arab empire into an Islamic empire.

751

The Carolingian dynasty began when Pepin, the son of Charles Martel, became king of the Franks. The name Carolingian stems from the family name Karling. Pepin and his son Charles would bring the Frankish Empire to its zenith.

Muslims of the Samarkand region of Uzbekistan defeated an invading Chinese army at the Battle of Talas River. During this campaign, Muslims captured artisans who brought wood pulp papermaking skills to the Middle East. This papermaking would allow the Muslims to attain their golden age of scholarship, which was centered in Baghdad.

Aistulf, king of the Lombards, conquered Ravenna, the last vestige of the Roman Empire in northern Italy, and then he demanded the submission of the pope.

753

After meeting with Aistulf, who refused to return Ravenna, Pope Stephen II crossed the Alps to meet with Pepin of the Franks. Pepin's nobles consented to the pope's request for a campaign against the Lombards.

754

Emperor Constantine V convened the Council of Hieria, near Constantinople. Three hundred eighty-three bishops attended, but not the patriarchs from the major sees of Rome, Alexandria, Antioch, or Jerusalem. The council supported the iconoclast position and gave the emperor license to hunt down image-worshippers and punish them not just as rebels, but as heretics. These rulings were later rejected by the Church as illegitimate, but in the meantime, using this decree, Constantine V cracked down on the monastic orders. He considered monks and nuns the most superstitious of all Christians and shirkers of the duties of ordinary citizens.

Pope Stephen II anointed Pepin the Short and his sons, Charles and Carloman, in Paris. It was the first time a pope had crowned a king, demonstrating that God's authority flowed through his spiritual representative on Earth, the pope.

c. Boniface repeatedly accused clergyman and astronomer Vergilius of Salzburg of offenses against the Church, including teaching the heretical doctrines that the world was round and that people lived on the other side the world. To Boniface, that meant that those on the other side of the world may not have been descended from Adam and therefore may not have original sin to be redeemed by Jesus. Pope Zachary threatened Vergilius's expulsion from the Church if the charges against him were proven true. Later that year, bandits killed

Boniface and his companions in the province of Frisia, and the charges against Vergilius were not pursued. Vergilius later became the bishop of Salzburg and a saint.

756

King Aistulf of the Lombards besieged Rome for three months before being forced to break off the siege when news arrived that Pepin and the Franks were on their way south from Gaul.

Pepin the Short wrote a promise to the pope to transfer certain territories to him after Pepin took them from the Lombards. This document was called the *Donation of Pepin* and provided the authority for the establishment of the Papal States in Italy. The pope most likely coerced Pepin by using the forged *Donation of Constantine*. For the first time, the pope became the legal ruler over earthly territories. This donation was confirmed by Pepin's son Charlemagne in AD 774 and would prevent Italian unity for over a thousand years.

After Constantine V refused to pay further tributes to the Bulgars, they invaded the empire, reaching the walls of Constantinople before Constantine's fleet defeated them at the Battle of Marcellae. The two sides then agreed to another truce.

759

Pepin and his Frankish army drove the Moors out of Narbonne, in Gaul, and then occupied all territory north of the Pyrenees Mountains.

760

The stunningly illustrated *Book of Kells* was created in a monastery somewhere in the British Isles. It contained the four canonical Gospels along with other sacred texts. Today, it is on display at Dublin's Trinity College and is one of the most visited tourist attractions in Dublin.

762

The Abbasids founded Baghdad on the site of a Christian village. The new city would quickly become the scholastic center of the world. Arab and Christian scholars translated Greek texts to Syriac and then to Arabic. The Abbasids also made great advances in science and medicine, including establishing hospitals to treat the sick and injured.

764

Stephen the Younger, who founded of a monastery near Constantinople, refused to accept the decisions of the Council of Hieria in AD 754. Emperor Constantine V decided to use Stephen as an example of what could happen to someone who resisted his authority. He had Stephen clubbed to death, but his skull was rescued and taken to the Dius Monastery as a relic.

768

Charles, the son of Pepin the Short and the grandson of Charles Martel, became king of the Franks. He is better known as Charles the Great or Charlemagne. He continued the family duty of protecting Christian Europe from the Muslims, Slavs, and Saxons and converting as many pagans as he could subdue by force.

772

Charlemagne's army entered Saxony to confront and convert the pagan Saxons. Charlemagne would fight eighteen battles over thirty years in northeastern Germany, eventually resulting in the forced conversion of the Saxons to Catholicism.

773

Nestorian Patriarch Hnanisho II moved his patriarchate from Seleucia-Ctesiphon to Baghdad for logistical reasons. It remained in Baghdad for the next five centuries until the Mongol invasion.

778

c. Upon the death of Hnanisho II, Timothy I was elected as the Nestorian patriarch through various chicanery, for instance, showing potential supporters bulging bags of money as bribes. After he was elected, those bags were found to contain stones. He angered so many influential people in the ways he won his office that Metropolitan Joseph of Merv, Turkmenistan, held a synod somewhat later and had him excommunicated. This led to a counter-excommunication and rioting by the Christians of Baghdad until the situation was brought under control by the intervention of 'Isa ibn Quraysh, the Christian doctor to the caliph. In the end, Timothy would guide the church for four decades and become one of its most accomplished patriarchs.

Pope Hadrian I made the earliest preserved mention of the *Donation of Constantine* in a letter to Charlemagne encouraging him to follow the example of his father Pepin the Short, and Constantine I, in endowing the popes with territories, but Charlemagne resisted.

781

Nestorian Christians in China erected the Xi'an Stele to commemorate 150 years of Christianity in China.

782

Charlemagne introduced a code of laws to Saxony, demanding the death sentence for any Saxon who sacrificed to the god Woden, burned their dead, robbed a church, ridiculed church ceremonies, refused baptism, refused to fast during Lent, or failed to conform with church discipline.

After a rebellion by the defeated Saxons and a subsequent Frankish crackdown, Charlemagne massacred 4,500 Saxons in one day at Verdun (in present-day France) because they refused to convert to

Christianity. This act served only to ignite the Saxons into fury, lead-ing to two more years of revolt.

783

c. The king of the Karluk Turks of Central Asia is believed to have con-verted to Christianity.

785

Charlemagne issued the *Capitulatio de partibus Saxoniae*, which as-serted, "If anyone of the race of the Saxons hereafter concealed among them shall have wished to hide himself unbaptized, and shall have scorned to come to baptism, and shall have wished to remain a pagan, let him be punished by death."

786

The Indian Buddhist missionary Prajna asked Nestorian monas-tic scholar Qing Qing to help translate the *Satparamita Sutra* into Chinese. Qing Qing did this, but the translation was not acceptable to the emperor, possibly because the translation Christianized the sutra too much.

787

The Seventh Ecumenical Council met at Nicaea. The bishops tried to end the violent split within the Church over icons and images. Irene, the regent for her son, Constantine VI, and a future empress herself, reversed imperial policy and denounced iconoclasm as heresy. The council decided that it would allow icons to be venerated but not worshipped, which was a fine line determined by the belief that since Jesus Christ was fully human, his human nature could be expressed in icons, but his divine nature could not.

789

The earliest recorded Viking raid on Britain and Ireland occurred in Dorset, England. Lindisfarne monastery was raided four years later. Monasteries were easy picking due to their isolation and valuable religious objects available to loot.

790

After the secret of Chinese papermaking seeped into the Middle East, a paper mill was established in Baghdad. Paper would revolutionize the world in unanticipated ways. It was much less expensive than parchment and provided a high-quality writing surface. The availability and inexpensiveness of paper allowed scholarship to expand from exclusively religious writing into science, medicine, philosophy, and poetry.

The Monophysites in al-Hira in Mesopotamia converted to the Church of the East.

794

Charlemagne called the Council of Frankfort to condemn Adoptionism, the idea that Jesus was God's son in a spiritual nature but that his human form was adopted by God. In response to the Nicene Council of 787, the bishops condemned both the destruction of icons and their veneration but decided that they could be used as educational tools.

797

Emperor Constantine VI fell out of favor with the Church when he divorced his wife and married his mistress. As his level of unpopularity rose in both the empire and the Church, he was arrested, blinded, and imprisoned. Irene, his mother and former regent, seized power for herself and was crowned empress, becoming the first woman to rule the empire.

799

Enemies attacked Pope Leo III in Rome after he was accused of adultery and perjury. He was rescued and taken to France, where he asked Charlemagne for help. Charlemagne had Leo escorted back to Rome and reinstalled as pope.

CHAPTER 9: NINTH CENTURY AD

On Earth, God has placed no more than two powers, and as there is in Heaven but one God, so is there here one Pope and one Emperor. Divine providence has specially appointed the (Holy) Roman Empire to prevent the continuance of schism in the Church.

—Emperor Frederick I

The worship of God is a duty, the hearing and reading of sermons may be useful; but, if men rest in hearing and praying, as too many do, it is as if a tree should value itself on being watered and putting forth leaves, though it never produced any fruit.

—Benjamin Franklin

You can safely assume that you've created God in your own image when it turns out that God hates all the same people you do.

—Anne Lamott

Charlemagne continued his quest to expand Christendom into pagan northern and eastern Europe. Once believed resolved, the iconoclasm controversy entered a new phase and then finally ended in compromise. Relic and pilgrimage sites became more commonplace, and the Latin and the Greek Churches separated again in the Photian schism. Christian Europe was invaded by pagan Vikings from the north, Muslims from the south, and pagan Magyars from the east.

800

In Rome, Pope Leo III crowned Charlemagne as Holy Roman emperor. Now Charlemagne was not only king but "crowned by God" as the guardian of Christian morality and protector of the Church. As a result, a strong bond was formed between the Catholic Church and the Franks that broke the eastern Roman Empire's control over Italy. This set a precedent for Frankish kings to be crowned by popes, and at this time, Charlemagne ruled more of Europe than anyone since Emperor Theodosius in the fourth century.

The *Charter of Charlemagne* was the first official secular document dated by the AD dating system, but the new system would not come into general use until two centuries later.

c. Nestorian patriarch Timothy I listed the fundamental doctrines shared by all Christians, whether Nestorian, Monophysite, Catholic, or Eastern Orthodox. They included faith in the Trinity, baptism, adoration of the cross, the holy Eucharist, the two Testaments, the resurrection of the dead, eternal life, the return of Christ in glory, and the final judgment.

Charlemagne gifted the Holy Prepuce, the supposed foreskin from Jesus's circumcision to Pope Leo III, saying it had been brought to him by an angel. This became one of the most important and controversial Christian relics.

801

c. Charlemagne, who was fascinated with learning, began to encourage the reestablishment of public libraries, something that had been missing in Europe since the fall of Rome over three centuries earlier. The return of literacy was said to be impossible without the infusion of Irish codices into the continent.

Sergius-Tychicus founded the Paulician Church of the Colossians in Anatolia and later led a mission to Cilicia where he founded the

Church of the Ephesians. This sect embarked on major evangelical campaigns across the eastern empire and even established their own state in Armenia. They were a mix of Adoptionists, Gnostics, and quasi-Manichaeans named after Paul of Samosata. They had a knack for survival and could still be found in Armenia in the nineteenth century.

Louis the Pious conquered the Muslim-ruled city of Barcelona and added the region to the Frankish Empire.

c. Satan began to appear in Christian artwork. He was often shown with hooves and horns, the physical features of a goat. This may be because of his association with the parable of the sheep and the goats (Matthew 25:31–46), in which Jesus separated the saved sheep from the doomed goats. Christians borrowed from pagan art and used the image of the rustic human-goat Greek god Pan to depict Satan.

c. Biblical angels Gabriel and Raphael joined Michael as saints in the Roman Catholic Church.

802

With the backing of the Roman Catholic Church which resented any woman in a leadership position, Byzantine conspirators deposed Empress Irene in a palace coup. She lived out the remainder of her life in a monastery she had founded on the island of Lesbos.

804

The Byzantine Empire still held footholds in Naples, Reggio, Brinidisi, and semiautonomous Venice and began to clash with the Frankish Empire in Italy. Emperor Nicephorus I resented the intrusion of the Franks into Italy and Charlemagne's assuming the title "emperor." Six years later, with Venice securely back under Byzantine control, the two empires signed a peace agreement, giving the Franks several coastal cities in Istria, modern-day Croatia.

807

The *Book of Armagh*, also known as the *Canon of Patrick*, was written in Ireland. It contained early stories about Saint Patrick and an almost complete New Testament. It is one of the oldest surviving specimens of the Old Irish language and a wonderful example of an illuminated manuscript.

810

Hindu forces defeated the attacking Muslims in the battles of Rajasthan, checking the eastward expansion of the Islamic Empire.

811

Byzantine emperor Nicephorus I invaded the Bulgarian Empire, defeated their army in two battles, and then sacked their capital. This was recorded as a particularly brutal invasion, with the Byzantines committing multiple atrocities. During Nicephorus's withdrawal, Bulgarian khan Krum ambushed Nicephorus's army and captured the emperor. It's said that Krum used Nicephorus's skull as a drinking cup.

813

After defeating the Byzantines at the Battle of Versinikia, Krum approached Constantinople, where he laid waste to churches, monasteries, and palaces outside the city walls. Krum died before he could carry out his final assault on the city.

c. Persian caliph al-Ma'mum chose a Nestorian, Yuhanna Ibn Masawayh, to run his new state library.

814

Charlemagne died after uniting much of Europe under the Christian banner. Upon his death, Western Europe was mostly at peace and exhausted by war. The Holy Roman Empire, with its Frankish leadership, was greatly weakened when the territories were divided among Charlemagne's grandchildren.

815

Emperor Leo V convened another council at the Hagia Sophia in Constantinople. Just before the council, he removed the icon-worshipping Eastern Orthodox patriarch Nicephorus I (same name as the late emperor), and replaced him with Theodotos I, who immediately reestablished iconoclasm. It's said that Theodotos had to nearly starve several abbots to death to acquire their consent.

817

Claudius became the bishop of Turin. He was known as a maverick in his time for not only attacking the veneration of images but also relics, crosses, and pilgrimages. He had little regard for the authority of the pope.

822

Frankish king Louis the Pious extinguished a rebellion led by his nephew, Bernard. For his treachery, Louis had Bernard blinded, and he died two days later. Louis's guilt led him to perform public penance and admit all the things for which he felt shame. In his orgy of repentance, he also released dangerous enemies from monastic confinements and put them in powerful roles. Although many of his subjects were in awe of his excessive Christian devotion, his enemies saw it as a weakness to exploit.

Adalhard, a Benedictine abbot in Germany, was the first known writer to mention adding hops to beer, which greatly added to its flavor.

Pope Paschal I wanted to relocate the remains of Saint Cecilia, who was thought to have been martyred around AD 177, but he didn't know exactly where to look for the grave. He reported that in a dream, Cecilia revealed her burial place, and when found, her body was said to be incorruptible, meaning it didn't decompose. This was the first claim of incorruptibility for a saint, but Saint Cecilia's entire existence may have been a fabrication.

823

Timothy I, the Nestorian patriarch, died. He had been an excellent administrator, who had greatly strengthened his Church and left an extensive written record. Being interested in expanding the Church of the East, he sent bishops—also known as metropolitans—to Azerbaijan, Tabaristan, and deep into China. He had planned also to send one to Tibet.

824

Patriarch Michael II of Constantinople sent a letter to the Frankish emperor Louis the Pious condemning image veneration and other practices such as using icons as baptismal godfathers to infants. He reiterated the decrees of the first iconoclast council in AD 754.

825

A western monk accompanied a Sogdian trader to visit the king of Tibet. The Sogdian language was the language of trade in that region, and the trader served as guide and translator.

826

Agobard, the archbishop of Lyon, made the earliest known mention of the *Toledot Yeshu*, a Jewish text that offered an alternative and un-complimentary biography of Jesus and how he led to the downfall of the Jewish people. Some scholars speculate that it is a parody of a lost gospel. It was widely circulated in Europe and the Middle East during medieval times. Christian anti-Semites later used it to demonstrate Jewish disrespect for Jesus.

827

The new basilica in Michelstadt, Germany, needed a relic, so the bones of Peter and Marcellinus, both Christian martyrs, were transferred from the catacombs of Rome to Michelstadt. Unfortunately, the relics were unhappy there and failed to produce miracles. They were then moved to Mulinheim, where they were much happier, and miracles began to occur.

829

At the request of the Swedish king Björn, the Holy Roman emperor sent Flemish monk Ansgar to Sweden to evangelize Björn's people. Ansgar was rewarded two years later with the archbishopric of Hamburg and the commission to evangelize Scandinavia.

Two Venetian merchants decided to steal the body of Saint Mark from Alexandria and take it to Venice. Since Venice had a church named after him, they thought they should possess the relics. To them, it was a rescue, not a theft. They and two accomplices went to his tomb, removed the body, and replaced it with another. On their ship, they placed the body in a large basket and covered it with raw pork to repel Muslim inspectors who might search the vessel.

830

c. A legend had circulated for centuries that after the resurrection of Jesus, the apostle James had traveled to Spain as a missionary, and that after his execution in Jerusalem around AD 44, his bones were miraculously transported to Spain on an unmanned boat made of stone. At this time, eight hundred years later, a shepherd reported rediscovering James's bones in northern Spain. A cathedral was later built to contain the remains, and it would become one of the major pilgrimage sites in Europe. It has been speculated that the discovery of the bones and the Church's embrace of the new city of Santiago de Compostela as a pilgrimage site were related to the Muslims expanding occupation of the Iberian Peninsula and the Spanish Catholic population's need for a sign of hope.

831

Paschasius Radbertus published *On the Body and Blood of the Lord*, agreeing with Ambrose of Milan that the Eucharist contained not just bread and wine as symbols of Jesus's body, but they literally turned into his body and blood.

832

The *Utrecht Psalter*, a volume containing the book of Psalms was published. The people of the Netherlands consider it their most valuable manuscript. It included 116 intricate pen illustrations and the earliest western image of a dead Jesus on the cross.

The Bayt al-Hikma, or House of Wisdom, was the name of the Grand Library established in Baghdad. It was an intellectual center where scholars assembled texts and translated a broad range of non-Islamic works into Arabic. A Nestorian ran the school and Christians dominated the initial translation phase, thanks to their skills with Greek and Syriac languages. The main translator was Hunayn ibn Ishāq, a Nestorian Christian. He and his pupils translated 129 works of Galen alone into Arabic. When the Latin west recovered these long-lost Greek works in the fifteenth century, they would help launch the Italian Renaissance.

Emperor Theophilus issued an edict against representations of Jesus in the form of pictures, statues, and mosaics. He sought them out for destruction in monasteries, public places, and private residences. Painters caught working on images in secret had their hands mutilated. Patriarch John the Grammarian supported Theophilus by excommunicating any clergyman accused of creating or worshipping images.

835

Pope Gregory IV confirmed the new date of All Hallows' Day as November 1, the same day as the pagan festival of Samhain. Pagan practices were intermixed with the Christian celebration of dead saints, martyrs, and ancestors, giving us our current version of Halloween. In Mexico, All Hallows' Day is known as Day of the Dead.

837

In Egypt, Muslims prohibited Christian education and the celebration of Christian festivals. New churches were demolished, and Christians were said to have been ordered to wear five-pound crosses from their necks. This kind of persecution was unusual in Egypt, and the Copts remained the majority religion of Egypt into the fourteenth century.

The Abbasid caliph moved his capital from Baghdad to Samarra, a strongly Nestorian region with eight monasteries. In AD 889, the capital would return to Baghdad.

838

Byzantine emperor Theophilus provoked a war with the Abbasids of Anatolia and invaded their empire. Caliph Al-Mu'tasim led a large army against him and defeated Theophilus at the Battle of Dazimon. The Abbasid army then besieged the Byzantine city of Amorium. After they broke through the walls, they sacked the city and slaughtered thousands of inhabitants.

840

A chapel was built in Oviedo, Spain, to house the reliquary containing the shroud of Jesus. This shroud was believed to have been the cloth that was wrapped around Jesus's head when he was placed in his tomb, as mentioned in John 20:6–7, but should not be confused with the Shroud of Turin.

842

Empress Theodora II, the wife of Byzantine emperor Theophilus and soon to be regent for their son Emperor Michael III, was a secret worshipper of images. After the death of Theophilus, she appointed a new patriarch, deposed iconoclastic bishops, and taught her children to reject their father's icon policies. A Church council in Constantinople ended the period of iconoclasm.

c. Chinese Taoist emperor Wu-Tsung conducted the most severe persecution of Buddhists in Chinese history. At the time, Buddhism was viewed as a foreign religion in China, unlike native Taoism and Confucianism. The emperor thought Buddhist monasteries were gaining too much political power and were corrupting the government. He saw monasteries as refuges for those who wanted to avoid paying taxes and participating in society. The Zoroastrians, Nestorians, and Manichaeans were also caught up in this suppression, as Wu-Tsung tried to raise war funds and cleanse his country of foreign influences. He was said to have destroyed or closed 4,600 monasteries and some 40,000 temples and ordered 260,000 monks and nuns to return to secular lives. He basically destroyed Zoroastrianism and Manichaeism in China, and Nestorian Christianity, which had been on the rise in China, suddenly fell into a gradual decline.

843

A Frankish civil war ended with the Treaty of Verdun. This treaty split the Frankish homeland into three parts and led to the formation of the country of France and German states straddling Burgundy and the Low Countries.

Viking raiders attacked Nantes, France, where they killed the town's bishop and many clergy and plundered the surrounding region.

Empress Theodora II instituted a devastating persecution of the Paulicians in Asia Minor. A hundred thousand Paulicians were said to have been killed in this purge.

After the restoration of icon veneration, Emperor Michael III had the body of previous iconoclastic emperor Constantine V exhumed and the remains burned. This dramatically signified the end of the controversy.

844

After the death of Pope Gregory IV, the Roman populace installed John VIII, a popular deacon, as the new pope. The city's aristocratic laymen then elected the more nobly born Sergius II as the new pope. Sergius removed John VIII, considered an antipope by the aristocracy, from office but spared his life and had him confined to a monastery.

845

The Vikings, under the chieftain Ragnar, invaded France and sacked Paris. They finally left after being paid a ransom.

846

Arab raiders from Africa invaded Italy and attacked Rome, sacking Old Saint Peter's Basilica, the Tomb of the Fisherman (the tomb dedicated to Saint Peter), and the Basilica of Saint Paul's Outside the Walls. The defenders kept the raiders from entering the city itself.

847

The Moors captured the Byzantine city of Bari in southern Italy, and the Berber Kalfun became the first ruler of the Emirate of Bari.

848

Pope Leo IV enclosed Vatican Hill, across the river from Rome, within city walls to protect Saint Peter's Basilica from future attacks. The district was called Leonine City.

849

A Muslim pirate fleet from Sardinia set out to take Rome. Pope Leo IV organized a naval force to meet them, and the two forces engaged at the Battle of Ostia. With the aid of a storm that scattered the Muslim fleet, the Christian armada easily defeated the invaders.

850

A monk named Eulogius of Cordoba began encouraging public declarations of faith in Muslim-ruled Spain, but the bishop of Cordoba advised against it. In the next nine years, following his example, forty-eight Christians, mostly monks, were martyred, including Eulogius, for speaking about their faith or for criticizing Muhammad.

The Abbasid caliph al-Matawakkil persecuted Christians in his realm. They were discriminated against in almost any conceivable way, even forced to wear distinctive clothing, as Jews were to differentiate themselves from Muslims. This brought an end to the regional prosperity of the Church of the East.

Uigurs in eastern Turkistan founded a Manichaean kingdom.

c. Ibn Nusayr was expelled from Arabia, and his followers, a sect of Shia Muslims, settled in Turkey and northern Lebanon. They developed a syncretistic religion with elements of Christianity and Gnosticism and are still in existence, now known as Alawites.

852

This was the first mention of texts attributed to someone, or several writers, using the pseudonym Isidore Mercator. The documents had supposedly been found in Spain and became known as the Pseudo-Isidorian Decretals. They were a set of cleverly forged letters, supposedly written by notable bishops and popes from the first to the sixth century. They were designed to extend papal power, essentially transforming the papacy into an absolute monarchy and preparing the way for Europe's conversion to a theocratic popedom. These documents would be freely used until 1140.

855

King Aethelwulf of Wessex, England, granted English churches the right to receive tithes and gave one-tenth of his land to the Church. He also promised to make a pilgrimage to Rome with his youngest son.

857

Since his infancy, Emperor Michael III had been designated as co-ruler with his father, Theophilos. Now, at age seventeen, he banished his regent-mother Theodora II and his sisters to the Gastria Monastery. His uncle, Bardas, to whom Michael gave the title caesar, became the most influential person in the empire.

858

Michael III removed Ignatios, the patriarch of Constantinople, from office due to his criticism of Bardas and selected Photius, a layperson of great intellect, to replace him. Photius began Christmas week by becoming a monk and ended it as archbishop of Constantinople. The next year a local council confirmed his appointment.

859

Pope Nicholas I and the western bishops supported Ignatios over Photius during the controversy in Constantinople. They believed that a formal church trial was necessary before a patriarch could be removed from office.

Fatima al-Fihri, an Arab woman, founded a mosque in Fez, Morocco. Her mosque developed into a teaching institute—al-Qarawiyyin—credited with being the world's first university. It was founded two centuries before the first European university.

860

The Filioque Controversy, the unresolved problem of eternal procession, began anew. Photius maintained that the procession of the Holy
Spirit was "from the Father alone," as had been determined at the First
Council of Constantinople in AD 381, and Ignatios opposed him. In
the late sixth century, some Latin churches had added "and from the
Son" to the phrase. This would later be made foundational in Rome in
the eleventh century but rejected by the Eastern Orthodox Church.

862

Prince Rastislav of Moravia requested that the emperor and patriarch
in Constantinople send missionaries to his country. They sent two
brothers, Cyril and Methodius, to evangelize the Slavic people. The
missionaries learned the native language and eventually translated
scripture and church liturgy into Slavonic. Cyril invented a new alphabet based on Greek letters that would be called Cyrillic.

863

In what became known as the "Photian schism," Pope Nicholas I's objection to the selection of Photius as patriarch of Constantinople and
the failure of the pope's envoys to terminate this appointment caused
Nicholas to call a synod in Rome. He deposed Photius and said that
Ignatios was the rightful patriarch. This created a further breakdown
in relations between the Eastern Orthodox and Roman churches. In
867, Photius would respond by calling a council and excommunicating
Pope Nicholas on the grounds of heresy and schism.

864

Boris, the king of Bulgaria, was secretly baptized along with his family.
Bulgaria became a Christian kingdom the following year. The king had
wanted to convert his population to Christianity in order to resolve
the disunity between Slavs and Bulgars within the Bulgarian Empire.

866

c. Irish scholar John Scotus Eriugena had immigrated to France (no longer called Gaul) and taught at the Palatine School established by Charlemagne. In his time, Eriugena was one of only two people in Western Europe known to be fluent in Greek, and in his book *The Division of Nature*, he reawakened ancient Greek philosophy. His philosophy was that all of reality was a continuum and offshoots of God himself and that true reason should be the basis of any authority. Since all humans were continuations of God, he believed that in the end, all would be saved. In 1225, Pope Honorius III would order all copies of this book burned in a bonfire.

867

Basil the Macedonian seized power in Constantinople after killing Emperor Michael III and his caesar, Bardas. He then deposed Photius and reinstalled Ignatios as patriarch since Basil sought an alliance with the pope. Later, Photius and Ignatios reconciled, and when Ignatios died the following year, Photius was returned to office.

869

When a slave revolt broke out in the Abbasid empire, Egypt, Yemen, Tunisia, and the eastern part of Iran declared their independence.

871

The Emirate of Bari was an Islamic state in southern Italy ruled by Berbers from North Africa. After a Byzantine fleet swept the Adriatic of Muslim raiders, a combined army of Lombards, Germans, and Franks, aided by a Croatian fleet, captured Bari and took the sultan prisoner.

872

Frankish emperor Louis II had been crowned king of Italy in AD 839 at the age of fourteen and then crowned co-emperor by Pope Sergius at the age of nineteen. This year Pope Adrian II crowned him Holy Roman emperor. He led a successful military campaign and drove the Muslims out of southern Italy.

The Paulicians, who had transformed into a militant, religious-political organization, had sacked Ephesus four years previously. At this time, Emperor Basil the Macedonian sent a Byzantine army into Anatolia and defeated the Paulicians, who had allied themselves with the Arabs, and eliminated them as a military power. The Byzantines beheaded their leaders, and many others were relocated to the Bulgarian frontier to provide a buffer between the Byzantines and the Bulgars. The Paulicians eventually gave rise to future Christian sects such as the Waldensians and Cathars.

The Abbasid governor built a hospital in Cairo and mandated the licensing of physicians. This was many centuries before any kind of licensing of doctors would be considered in Europe.

875

Lindisfarne monastery, off the coast of England, had been raided and destroyed by the Vikings often enough that the survivors abandoned the island. About thirty years later, Iona was abandoned along with other remote monasteries for the same reason. Any valuable items had to be hidden or smuggled out to be preserved, and the *Book of Kells* was one of them.

876

The Moors returned to Bari. The pope and local nobles again asked the Franks for aid, but when the Franks didn't send forces, they turned to the Byzantines. Emperor Basil's forces drove the Moors from Bari, and it returned to Byzantine control.

877

John Scotus Erigena, an Irish theologian and philosopher, died. He was one of the few Western Europeans who knew the Greek language and had translated literary works from Greek to Latin. He wrote *On the Division of Nature*, which was a synthesis of fifteen centuries of philosophical thought, but all his works would be declared heretical four centuries later.

878

After a nine-month siege, Arab forces captured the Byzantine fortress city of Syracuse on Sicily, slaughtering most of the Christian population.

879

The Fourth Council of Constantinople was convened to confirm the reinstatement of Photius as patriarch. It included all five patriarchates and 383 bishops, and they confirmed Photius without incident. The bishops also agreed that the Bulgarian Church would be under the Eastern Orthodox Church.

882

This was the cultural golden age for Jews in Moorish Spain. The Moors gave them the freedom to flourish, and there was an influx of Jews from other regions, initiating a proliferation of Jewish literature, art, science, and medicine. Jews translated many texts from Hebrew, Greek, and Arabic at a time when academic progress was basically nonexistent in the rest of Europe.

889

Moors from Spain founded a colony called Fraxinet on the southern coast of France. From there, they raided along the coast and the alpine passes of France and northern Italy.

891

A biographical account of all known popes, called the *Liber Pontificalis* or the *Book of the Popes*, was first published. Saint Jerome was thought to be the original author, but it had been updated since then. The first edition covered popes from Peter to Adrian II in AD 872, but many accounts from before the sixth century were compiled long after their suspected reigns and were not accurate.

Photius, the patriarch of Constantinople, wrote *The Library*, a review of several hundred important books. He reviewed a book named *A Chronicle of the Kings of the Jews* by Justus of Tiberias, who lived at the time of Josephus in first-century Galilee. Photius wrote that he was disappointed there was no mention of Jesus in that book.

897

The year after Stephen VI became pope, he had the rotting corpse of his predecessor, Pope Formosus dressed in papal vestments, seated on a throne, and put on trial. This became known as the Cadaver Synod. Various political charges were presented against Formosus's corpse, with a deacon answering questions for it. The former pontiff was found guilty, all of his ordinations were annulled, and all his acts were declared invalid. His body was subjected to further humiliation, then thrown into the Tiber River, from which it was later retrieved by a monk. Angry clerics imprisoned Pope Stephen, and he was strangled while in confinement. What was left of Formosus was again buried with full honors in Saint Peter's Basilica, and a ban was instituted on any further trials of deceased persons.

899

Magyar tribes separated from the Khazars and left their homeland in the Ural Mountains. They entered Italy and pillaged the Lombard territory as far south as Bologna and Verona and were finally stopped during their approach to Venice.

CHAPTER 10: TENTH CENTURY AD

Religious wars are not caused by the fact that there is more than one religion, but by the spirit of intolerance . . . the spread of which can only be regarded as the total eclipse of human reason.

—Montesquieu

If it weren't for Christians, I'd be a Christian.

—Mahatma Gandhi

If anyone comes to me and does not hate his father and mother, his wife and children, his brothers and sisters— yes, even his own life—he cannot be my disciple.

—Jesus (Luke 14:26)

This century saw the decline of the Frankish Carolingian Empire but the preservation of a Germanic Ottonian Holy Roman Empire and the continuing erratic relationships between Holy Roman emperors and the papacy. Monastic orders and reform movements spread throughout Europe. Christianity was established in Poland, Hungary, Denmark, and the Ukraine, while Magyars, Vikings, and Muslims continued as threats to Christian Europe. Jews continued to migrate due to their seemingly endless persecution by Christians.

900

c. By this time, Nestorian Christians were almost always the personal physicians to the caliphs and occasionally even served as their pastors. Every major city in the Abbasid Caliphate had a hospital by this time.

901

c. This was the earliest date that western churches began to use organ music in their liturgy. By the fifteenth century, organ music would be widely accepted in the Roman Catholic Church, though it never became popular in the Eastern Orthodox Church.

c. After centuries of declining use and desecration by Vandals and Lombards, Christians abandoned the Roman catacombs and transferred holy relics to above-ground basilicas. These underground burial sites, covering hundreds of kilometers, would not be rediscovered until almost seven hundred years later.

902

Taormina, the last Byzantine stronghold on Sicily, fell to the Muslims. The Muslim invasion of the island began in AD 827, and the last of the isolated Christian outposts on the island would fall in AD 965.

904

Pope Sergius III endorsed decisions made by Pope Formosus, who died in AD 896, and reordained the bishops consecrated by Formosus but later annulled by Pope Stephen VI.

906

c. The *Canon Episcopi*, a body of church law, decreed that belief in witchcraft was heretical. The Church would have to confront, modify, or ignore this canon centuries later to justify its persecution of suspected witches.

907

The Tang dynasty fell in China, and Nestorians were cut off from their patriarch in Baghdad.

The Magyars invaded as far west as the Holy Roman Empire, present-day Hungary, and Austria, burning many churches and monasteries as they advanced.

909

The Fatimid Caliphate began in Egypt. It extended from the Atlantic Ocean, across North Africa to the Red Sea. The caliphate would make its capital in Cairo and last until 1171.

910

William the Pious established an abbey at Cluny, France, for those who sought a stricter adherence to Benedict's Rule. It grew into the most prestigious, influential, and financially secure abbey in Europe and became the site of the largest church building in western Christendom. The abbey supported the local economy, as well as providing hospitality to the poor and to pilgrims. Even the pope had a very loose grip on Cluny. By 1100, the abbey may have supervised as many as two thousand other monasteries and abbeys. Because of Cluny, the competency of the clergy improved as their devout monks became bishops and even popes.

911

Viking leader Hrolfr Ragnvaldsson, or Rollo, became a vassal of the Frankish king Charles the Simple. He was allowed to keep the land he conquered if he buffered the Franks from invasions by other Viking tribes. This region of France would become known as Normandy, named after the Norsemen.

915

The Christian League, an alliance of Christian armies led by Pope John X, met the Saracens at the Battle of Garigliano, north of Naples. After a three-month siege of their fortress, the Saracens attempted to escape, but all were captured and executed.

After John X crowned Berengar I as Holy Roman emperor, in Rome, Berengar went to northern Italy to try to control the Magyars.

917

At the Battle of Achelous, north of the Black Sea, the Bulgarians destroyed a Byzantine army. The number of casualties is unknown, but it was one of the bloodiest battles of that time and led to a forty-year truce between the two adversaries.

The Magyars crossed the Rhine River, attacked Basel, and moved into Burgundy. In recent years, they had defeated three large Frankish armies and destroyed the Bavarian army.

927

After the long period of war between the Bulgarians and the Byzantines, the patriarch of Constantinople recognized the Bulgarian Orthodox Church as fully independent of the Eastern Orthodox Church.

944

After capturing Edessa from the Arabs, Co-emperor Romanus I returned to Constantinople with the Mandylion, the cloth image of Jesus said to have miraculous properties, such as protecting Edessa from the Sassanids in AD 544.

945

Olga, the ruler of Rus (Russia), converted to Christianity. Her grandson Vladimir I would later establish Christianity as the official religion of their people.

949

The Buyid dynasty began in the Persian Empire. It was a very peaceful time for the Nestorians, and Emir Adud named a Christian, Nasr ibn-Harum, as his vizier, his chief counselor who basically ran the business of the empire for him.

950

The Byzantines reoccupied most of Syria and Mesopotamia and threatened Jerusalem and Baghdad.

c. The House of Habsburg rose to prominence in Switzerland, the family name derived from a Swiss fortress. The influential dynasty of Count Radbot of Klettgau would later rule the Holy Roman Empire for almost three hundred years and in different eras would rule Austria, Bohemia, Croatia, Galicia, Portugal, and Spain, retaining power until the end of World War I.

The Viking raids had ended in the British Isles, and the Norsemen and their families had settled down and established towns along the Irish coast. But their past raids had been so devastating to Irish culture that Ireland would never regain the level of European cultural leadership that it held in the past.

951

Godescalc, the bishop of Le Puy, made the earliest known pilgrimage from France to Santiago de Compostela in northwestern Spain. After his trek, the route became extremely popular, and today this web of trails is known as the Way of Saint James, or the Camino de Santiago, Europe's most popular pilgrimage routes.

955

The Franks defeated the Magyars at the Battle of Lechfeld. This stemmed the tide of Magyar raids into Western Europe. Once the Magyars settled into what is now Hungary, their leaders accommodated themselves to their neighbors in the Holy Roman Empire, and they gradually converted to Christianity beginning in AD 975.

Ottaviano, who was between eighteen and twenty-four years old at the time, was elected Pope John XII due to the political influence of his powerful father, Alberic II of Spoleto.

960

c. King Harald Bluetooth of Denmark converted to Christianity, possibly to avoid an invasion by the Holy Roman Empire. The rest of his realm followed.

The Seljuk Turks of Central Asia converted to Islam. They would later conquer most of the Middle East and establish a large empire there.

962

Pope John XII crowned German King Otto I as Holy Roman emperor. The *Diploma Ottonianum* confirmed John as the spiritual head of the Church, and Otto as its secular protector. The *Diploma* granted the clergy and people of Rome the exclusive right to elect future pontiffs.

963

After Otto conquered Italy, the Pope John XII began to fear his rising power. The pope formed alliances and plotted against Otto. After Otto discovered the conspiracy, he besieged Rome to depose the pope, but John XII had already fled the city. Otto installed Leo VIII in his place.

964

Pope John XII returned to Rome and deposed Leo VIII, but John XII was assassinated the same year, and Benedict V was elected pope by the Romans.

The people of Rome rebelled against Otto's reinstated puppet pope Leo VIII, but Otto's deputy compelled the Romans to accept Otto's appointee and exiled Benedict V.

965

The Khazars, who had dominated a vast region around the Black and Caspian Seas for three centuries, were defeated by the Kievan Rus (Ukrainian Russians). Khazaria had recently been ruled by leaders who had converted to Rabbinic Judaism, so many Jews had sought asylum there. After the Khazars were defeated, many of the region's Jews migrated westward into Hungary, Romania, and Poland and would become known as Ashkenazi Jews.

Muslim forces took the last Byzantine stronghold in Sicily and would retain full control of the island until 1091.

Pope Leo VIII died, and it was not possible to reinstate Benedict V, so John XIII, with the approval of Otto I, was elected as the new pope. John was disliked by the local population, and they arrested him. He escaped a few weeks later and sought Otto's help to depose his replacement and restore him to his rightful seat.

966

Emperor Otto I led his army south to Rome where he reinstalled John XIII as pope and hanged the leaders who had deposed him. Otto lived in Rome for the next six years to better control the papacy.

Duke Mieszko I of Poland converted to Christianity, but it would be subsequent rulers who converted the population and created a Kingdom of Poland under the protection of the pope.

969

c. Córdoba, Spain became another great Muslim center of scholarship and the most prosperous city in Europe. Within a few years, it would house seventy libraries and seven hundred mosques.

The Byzantines recovered the strategically important city of Antioch from the Arabs. They refortified the city and then moved on to sack the Arab-occupied city of Aleppo.

c. Gero, the archbishop of Cologne, commissioned a cross that depicted Jesus in a new way. In the past, he had usually been shown holding his head erect, looking straight ahead or looking down at the Virgin Mary, but always alive. Gero's was the first Western crucifix to depict a dead Jesus.

At the Battle of Tourtour, William I of Provence drove the Muslims out of their colony of Fraxinet on the French Riviera. The alpine passes, which Muslims had held, were reopened and contact resumed between Italy, France, and Germany.

975

Byzantine emperor John I Tzimiskes took Baalbek, Damascus, Tiberias, Nazareth, Sidon, Beirut, Byblos, and Tripoli from the Arabs, but failed to take Jerusalem.

976

c. The body of Saint Mark was lost in a fire in Venice. In 1094, when the magnificent Saint Mark's Basilica was completed, the body of Saint Mark was said to have been miraculously found and given a new place to rest.

978

Construction began on Saint Mark's Basilica in Venice, intended to house the holy relics of Saint Mark. It would be renowned for its architecture and was said to be a copy of the Church of the Holy Apostles in Constantinople which would be destroyed by the Ottomans in 1461.

979

Stained glass was installed in the Basilica of Saint-Denis in Paris. Stained glass had first been used in some English churches in the seventh century and by this time had improved to provide a stunning visual effect and a creative way to teach biblical stories to those who were illiterate.

980

When Nestorian monks were sent from Baghdad to China, they reported that "Christianity in China has become extinct. The native Christians have perished, and their churches have been destroyed."

987

Muslim rulers in Iraq proclaimed the right to appoint the patriarchs of the Nestorian Church, and the Nestorian bishops were in no position to resist.

988

Vladimir, prince of Kievan Rus, wanted to unite his people under one religion. He was said to have considered Islam and Judaism, but when the Byzantine emperor Basil II offered his sister in marriage, Vladimir decided to convert to Eastern Orthodox Christianity. With his conversion, his entire realm of Russia became Christian after Vladimir ordered all his subjects to be baptized.

989

The Synod of Charroux enacted the *Peace of God,* a declaration that threatened to excommunicate anyone who attacked or robbed a church, church official, pilgrim, woman, child, peasant, defenseless person, or property such as cattle and horses. In 1033, merchant and their goods would be added to this list. The *Truce of God* also originated about this time. It was a temporary suspension of hostilities during Sundays and holy days, which added up to many days each year. These practices spread to most of Western Europe over the next century.

992

Many Christians believed the end times would occur within three years because Good Friday coincided with the Feast of the Annunciation, and clerics taught that this was the event that would expose the Anti-Christ.

993

Pope John XV canonized Ulrich, the former bishop of Augsburg, as a saint. Before that, cults dedicated to certain saints had been regional and came into existence spontaneously. For a pope to be involved in canonizing a saint was something new.

995

Olaf Tryggvason returned home from raiding England and built the first Christian church in Norway. Christianity had previously been introduced and rejected in his country, but when Olaf became king, Norway became nominally Christian. Olaf was said to have found no problem with using torture to force conversions.

996

Otto III, the king of Germany, became the king of Italy and Holy Roman emperor. He appointed his cousin as the first pope of German heritage, Pope Gregory V. After Otto left the city, Crescentius, a Roman aristocrat, led a rebellion and deposed Gregory.

998

Otto III returned to Rome, reinstalled Gregory V as pope, and had Crescentius and his appointed pope, John XVI, executed. Otto's actions strengthened imperial control over the Catholic Church.

999

Sylvester II, who became pope upon the death of Gregory V, predicted the end of the world, the Millennium Apocalypse, at the end of this Christian millennium.

CHAPTER 11: ELEVENTH CENTURY AD

Relics are a very important part of the expression of religious faith, as well as of cultural importance in the way that people cling to a souvenir from a person they've loved or a place that they've been to. And what that conveys is the connecting of this moment with the treasured moment of the past. And if that connection is made through an object which maybe forensically won't stand up to the test, that's of secondary importance to the spiritual and emotive power that the object can contain and does contain.
　　　　　　　　　　　　　　　　　　—Vincent Nichols

Ever since the Crusades, when Christians from western Europe were fighting holy wars against Muslims in the near east, western people have often perceived Islam as a violent and intolerant faith: even though when this prejudice took root Islam had a better record of tolerance than Christianity.
　　　　　　　　　　　　　　　　　　—Karen Armstrong

It was not alone the spectacle of headless bodies and mutilated limbs strewn in all directions that roused the horror of all who looked upon them. Still more dreadful was it to gaze upon the victors themselves,

> dripping with blood from head to foot, an ominous
> sight which brought terror to all who met them.

—William, Archbishop of Tyre, commenting on Jerusalem

The Cathars became a sect that the Church could not allow to exist. Events in the Holy Land paved the way for a series of papal-inspired and papal-sanctioned incursions that are known as the Holy Land Crusades. Christian demonization of Jews continued and even intensified, while heresies became more commonplace. Shifting relationships between the popes and Holy Roman emperors continued, and the Cistercian monastic order ventured into what we know as capitalism.

1000

c. The Nestorian Church of the East was the world's largest Christian denomination by geographical area, with two hundred and fifty bishoprics and as many as twenty million followers. At this time, about three million Christians remained in Africa, mostly Coptic Christians in Egypt. There were approximately forty million Catholics and Eastern Orthodox Christians in Europe. Additionally, there were independent denominations in Ethiopia, India, Syria, and Armenia.

King Olaf of Norway converted Leif Erikson to Christianity and gave him the mission to introduce Christianity to Greenland, a colony the Norwegians established in AD 986.

Iceland became Christianized when pagans and Christians agreed that the island should have only one religion. Baptism and conversion to Christianity became required. The traditional law allowing newborn children to be abandoned and die of exposure remained in force.

Hungary was recognized as a Catholic apostolic kingdom under King Stephen I. Six years later, Stephen solidified his power and began making sweeping reforms, including forced conversions. Latin became the official language of the country and remained so until 1844.

c. Many of the laity across Europe were disgusted with the increasing power of the clergy and demanded reform, as well as a return to the teachings and apostolic poverty of the Gospels. The Church continued to brand these potential reformers as heretics and silenced their voices.

c. Communion bread began to be pressed into wafers, which were easier to administer and avoided crumbs; every crumb was considered part of the body of Jesus.

1001

c. A Christian sect known as Cathars began to appear in Western Europe, with their presence and theology emerging concurrently in several regions. They believed in the good God of the New Testament and an evil God of the Old Testament, who created the physical world and was even identified as Satan by many Cathars. The Cathars' spiritual ancestors were the Paulicians of Armenia, and the movement came to Europe by way of Armenia, Bulgaria, and Croatia.

1003

Athanasius the Athonite died when the cupola of his church collapsed on him. He is remembered for bringing monasticism to the hermits at Mount Athos, Greece, where today there are twenty monasteries.

1009

The Nestorians converted the khan of the Keraites, one of the five dominant Turco-Mongol tribes, to Christianity. The metropolitan of the city of Merv sent a priest and deacon who baptized the khan and two hundred thousand of his people.

Fatimid Caliph Al-Hakim, who was described as mentally unbalanced, launched a systematic persecution of Christians and Jews in his domain. He destroyed or converted to mosques hundreds of churches including the Church of the Holy Sepulchre in Jerusalem, Christendom's most important church. Popes late in this century would use this event to stir up hatred for the Muslims and launch the Crusades to the Holy Land. At this time, a rumor spread among Christians that the Jews incited the caliph to destroy the church, and Jews, always conveniently cast as demons conspiring against Christians, would face renewed attacks and expulsions.

1015

After Vladimir of Kiev died, his sons competed for the throne. Vladimir's son Svyatopolk had his brothers, Boris and Gleb, assassinated, and the dead brothers became the first saints of the newly established Russian Orthodox Church.

1020

c. Saint Romuald of Ravenna, the founder of the Camaldolese order and a dedicated ascetic, was said to have been visiting France when he heard that he was in peril due to the value of his bones for the use of potential relics. He fled back to Italy in fear for his life.

1022

At a heresy trial in Orléans, France, King Robert II ordered the burning of fourteen clerics who had challenged the validity of the ordained priesthood, the sacraments, and the miracles of Christ. This is believed to be the first state-sponsored execution of heretics in medieval Western Europe and the first serious heresy persecution in five centuries.

1023

Gerald Thom founded the Amalfitan Hospital in Jerusalem to provide care for sick, poor, and injured pilgrims. During the Crusades, this organization may have spawned the monastic order known as the Knights of the Hospital of Saint John of Jerusalem, or Knights Hospitaller.

1024

c. Gerard of Florennes, the bishop of Cambrai, called a synod in Arras, France, to confront the heresy of Gundolfo. Gundolfo's teachings denied the benefit of the sacraments and claimed that righteousness alone could lead to salvation. As a result of the synod, the Gundulfians were believed to have renounced their heresy and reconciled with the church.

Pope John XIX was twenty-one years old when elected pope, being elevated from layman to pope in a single day. Eight years later, his successor Benedict IX was also a layman in his twenties when elected. Both were from powerful aristocratic families.

1025

Cunegunde, the wife of Holy Roman emperor Henry II, moved to Kaufungen Abbey in Germany one year after her husband's death. She insisted on being treated as an average woman, not as a former empress, and remained there caring for the sick and performing charitable acts until her death in 1040.

Persian scholar Avicenna completed work on *The Canon of Medicine*, a medical encyclopedia that would be used extensively by European universities until the mid-seventeenth century.

1027

Richard of Verdun, the abbot of Saint Vanne Monastery, led seven hundred pilgrims to Palestine. He was an avid relic collector and saw nothing contradictory or immoral about the theft or falsification of relics. Like others of his time, since relics were a living conveyance of the saints, a relic itself decided who would acquire it. Therefore, if someone thought the relic would be "happier" somewhere else, they felt justified in relocating it to a new location.

With the issuance of the *Truce of God*, princes, nobles, and knights swore not to conduct war from Saturday to Monday or during holy seasons. The penalty for breaking this law would be the denial of last rites, Christian burial, and forgiveness of sins.

1028

The militia of Milan's Archbishop Ariberto of Intimiano stormed the castle at the Cathar town of Monforte, Italy. They captured much of the population and took them to Milan. When the Cathars were forced to choose between conversion to Catholicism or death at the stake, the majority chose death over becoming a Catholic.

1033

Following the failure of the prediction of January 1, 1000, as the Second Coming of Jesus, some end times theorists proposed that the end would occur a thousand years after Jesus's supposed resurrection, which was this year.

1046

Henry III, king of Germany, Italy, and Burgundy, traveled to Rome. It was another time of turmoil for the papacy with three popes vying for power. Henry deposed all three and appointed Suidger of Bamberg, a German, to the throne. On Christmas Day, the new pope, who had taken the name Clement II, crowned Henry as Holy Roman emperor. Within the next two years, Henry would install two other German popes to refocus the Church on spiritual and ecclesiastical matters.

1048

The text of the story *Barlaam and Josaphat* was translated from Greek into Latin, and their legends spread throughout Europe. These men ended up on the list of saints in both the Roman Catholic and Eastern Orthodox Churches. It was later discovered that through various misunderstandings, the legend of Josaphat, also known as Saint Josaphat, was based on the life of Siddhartha Gautama, better known as the Buddha.

Caliph Ali az-Zahir, the son of the Caliph Al-Hakim who destroyed the Church of the Holy Sepulchre in Jerusalem, allowed the Byzantines to rebuild and redecorate the church. When the repairs were completed, Christians were allowed to resume their normal pilgrimages to the site.

1049

Pope Leo IX convened the Council of Reims and demanded that all bishops and abbots declare whether they had paid bribes to obtain their offices. He also condemned priests who did not practice celibacy. Leo became a traveling evangelist at a time when few priests preached in public and almost no non-clerical person had ever laid eyes on a cardinal, let alone a pope.

1051

Anthony, an Eastern Orthodox monk, founded the Kiev Monastery of the Caves after returning from a monastery at Mount Athos in Greece. He selected the cave and organized a community of disciples.

In Goslar, Germany, a group of Manichaeans were executed for their unusual beliefs, including the refusal to kill chickens or eat meat.

1054

The Great Schism occurred when the patriarchs of Constantinople and Rome excommunicated each other. This began when, as part of his defense against the Normans who were threatening southern Italy, Pope Leo IX took the few Greek churches in Italy under his control. The pope also reminded Patriarch Michael Cerularius of Constantinople that the Eastern Orthodox Church had neglected to send him a letter of congratulations when he became pope six years earlier. Leo viewed the Byzantine Church's lack of submission as an affront to his

supremacy and even invoked the *Donation of Constantine*, maybe believing it was genuine. In retaliation, Cerularius demanded that Latin
churches in the East conform to Greek standards. When the churches
refused, he shut them down. This and other unresolvable differences
eventually led to a permanent break between the two churches.

Pope Leo IX's *Ad splendidum nitentis* officially condemned the practice of masturbation as a grave moral disorder. Even if scripture
didn't condemn the practice by name, Church tradition understood
it to be condemned in New Testament terms such as *impurity* and
unchasteness.

1055

The Seljuk Turks, whose first leader may have been Christian or Jewish,
arrived from the East and conquered Baghdad.

1058

French Abbot Baudillon received the pope's appraisal that his relics,
the physical remains of Mary Magdalene, were indeed authentic. The
remains were placed in Vezelay Abbey, which was on the pilgrimage
route between Germany and Santiago de Compostela in Spain. This
location allowed many more pilgrims to visit Mary's shrine, and many
miracles were attributed to the relics. Another body would be discovered in 1267, and after examination, that one would be declared to be
the real remains of Saint Mary Magdalene. Over the years, three more
of "Mary's" bodies would be found.

1059

Nicholas II became the fourth consecutive pope who sought major reforms in the Church. He ordered Christians to boycott masses and
sacraments performed by priests who kept concubines or had purchased their offices. Disputing Augustine, he believed that the morality of the clergy affected the validity of their sacraments. He reformed
the process by which popes were elected—instead of being chosen

by powerful secular families, they would be elected by a College of Cardinals.

1060

c. By this time, Christianity was firmly established in Sweden—although to people in Uppland, the east-central part of the country, and some other regions, it was still considered a foreign religion.

1062

Wulfstan II became the bishop of Worcester, England. He was a social reformer who campaigned vigorously against the slave trade based in Bristol and Dublin, consisting mainly of Irish men and women who could not pay their debts.

1063

Pope Alexander II organized an army to drive the Muslims out of Spain. On their way to fight the Moors, the crusaders paused in France and Spain to attack Jewish settlements. This would set a precedent for future crusades.

1064

German Catholic bishops led between seven thousand and twelve thousand pilgrims across Europe on their way to Palestine. Due to the group's size, they were not welcomed by the people in the lands they passed through. Their treatment became worse the further south they progressed, and many were killed. In Palestine, they were eventually rescued by the Fatimid governor, who arrived with a large force and drove away the Arabs who were harassing the pilgrims. After a period of rest, the pilgrims finally arrived in Jerusalem.

1066

The Normans of France, no longer Vikings but Frenchmen of Nordic descent, invaded Britain. Their king, William the Conqueror, won the Battle of Hastings and took control of the island.

In Spain, the Granada massacre occurred when a mob of Muslims stormed the royal palace where the unpopular Jewish vizier to the Berber king had sought refuge. They crucified him and massacred much of the Jewish population of the city, possibly as many as four thousand men, women, and children.

1070

The Seljuks Turks captured Jerusalem from the Egyptian Fatimids.

c. A copy of the sixth-century manuscript *The Digest of Justinian's Law Code* was discovered in Padua, Italy. It included the laws issued by Justinian and Theodosius I. After that, the states that followed Roman law, such as the Holy Roman Empire, began to more seriously defend Christian orthodoxy.

1071

The Seljuk Turks won a momentous victory over the Byzantines at the Battle of Manzikert in eastern Anatolia, during which they captured the Byzantine emperor, Romanos IV Diogenes. Sultan Alp Arslan kept the emperor as his guest for a week and then had him escorted back to Constantinople. The defeat of the Byzantines led to a mass migration of Seljuk Turks into central Anatolia, and after the battle, they were within a hundred miles of Constantinople. They apparently settled down in their new land and broke apart into smaller, more isolated principalities. That loss of centralized government would benefit the crusaders when they arrive in Anatolia twenty-six years later.

With Normans taking the town of Bari on the heel of the Italian boot and the Turks defeating the Byzantines, Constantinople was in great peril. The emperor appealed to Pope Gregory for help, but Gregory VII was too preoccupied with other matters to be able to assist.

1073

Gregory VII was elected pope and became one of the great reformers of the Church. He wrote, "I find everywhere bishops who have obtained their office in an irregular way, whose lives and conversations are strangely at variance with their sacred calling—who go through their duties not for the love of Christ, but from motives of worldly gain." He reasserted the papacy's control over Western civilization by claiming the right of the Church to intervene in every aspect of human society. He rigorously enforced the Church's policy of celibacy, forcing many clergy to leave their wives, and he had some success in limiting the widespread practice of simony, the selling of clerical offices for bribes.

Pope Gregory VII declared that many of his predecessors as the bishops of Rome were saints and that sainthood should be assumed for all popes unless proven otherwise.

1075

Robert of Molesme left his Abbey of Molesme and settled with a band of hermits in Sèche-Fontaine, France. Years later, they would begin the Cisterician monastic order, which would have dramatic and lasting effects on Western civilization.

1076

Because of disagreements about who should appoint bishops in Germany and the Papal States, Henry IV, king of Germany, Italy, and Burgundy, convened the Synod of Worms. In agreement with Henry, the bishops demanded that Pope Gregory VII abdicate his office and that German bishops renounce their allegiance to the pope. Because of this affront, Pope Gregory excommunicated Henry.

1077

Henry IV traveled to Italy to do penance and plead for Pope Gregory VII to grant him deliverance from his excommunication. He was in dire straits due to a civil war that was not going well for him. He was said to have stood for three days barefoot in the snow before the pope would pardon him.

1079

Hildebert, the archbishop of Tours, was the first bishop to use the now-accepted term *transubstantiation* to describe the physical transformation of simple bread and wine into the actual body and blood of Jesus. This concept had been formulated in the first century but never been known by this term before.

1080

Gregory VII excommunicated the Henry IV again, but Henry did not accept it humbly this time. He deposed the pope and elevated Wibert of Ravenna to the papal throne to become what is now known as an antipope. His papal name was Clement III.

For decades, Berengar of Tours, archdeacon of Angers, had confronted the highest levels of the Church concerning his views on the Eucharist. He denied that the physical change, or transubstantiation, really occurred. He had been condemned and excommunicated and had recanted, then retracted his recantation, was tried again, and finally recanted once and for all, at least publicly. This year he retired to Saint-Cosme Priory to live in ascetic solitude.

1081

The Seljuk Turks arrived in the western Anatolia and captured Nicea, only about a hundred miles south of Constantinople. There they established their new Sultanate of Rum (meaning Rome, since they hoped to establish a new Turkish Roman Empire).

1084

Bruno of Cologne founded the Carthusian monastic order in Chartreuse, France. The movement included both monks and nuns and became widespread throughout Western Europe.

King Henry IV marched his army south and deposed Pope Gregory VII at his castle in Tuscany. Henry then proceeded to Rome to ensure that his choice, Clement III, was solidly enthroned as pope. Clement then crowned Henry as Holy Roman emperor. Following that, Henry had to flee Rome because of the advance of Gregory's military allies intending to reinstall him as pope.

Venice came to the aid of the Byzantines, and after several sea battles and a plague had decimated the Norman army, the Normans ended their quest to conquer Constantinople. The Byzantines rewarded Venice with favored trading status, but it would be a very rocky relationship between Venice and Constantinople over the following centuries.

1085

The Seljuk Turks captured Antioch, the last Byzantine bastion in Syria.

Pope Gregory VII died. He had been very influential as a reformer and the first pope to promote the idea of a great military expedition to regain the Church of the Holy Sepulchre in Jerusalem, which by this time had already been rebuilt and reopened to Christian pilgrims.

Christian forces under King Alfons VI of Castile captured the former Visigoth capital of Toledo in central Spain from the Moors, beginning the four-century-long Christian reconquest of Spain. Toledo was in the Caliphate of Cordoba, the European center of Islamic scholarship. Once the Latin-speaking Castilians obtained the works of the Nestorian and Arab translators, they were in turn able to translate them into Latin and later stimulate the minds of European

scholars such as Peter Abelard and Thomas Aquinas and lead the way
to European universities.

1086

c. At this time, the possessions of the Church amounted to approximately 27 percent of the cultivated area of England, and the Church
held as much as one third of all the land in Europe. This vast wealth
was mostly due to gifts from monarchs who sought to use the Church
as a counterweight to the nobility and from nobles who sought to save
their souls. The Church also had the great advantage of not paying
taxes.

1087

A group of merchants wanted to establish Bari, Italy, as a pilgrimage
site, but in order to do so, they needed relics. They stole the bones
of Saint Nicholas, the former bishop of Myra, from his resting place
in Constantinople. Thereafter, these merchants exchanged gifts on
the anniversary of Nicholas's death on December 6, presaging Saint
Nicholas's significant part in the celebration of Christmas. Bari became the center of the Saint Nicholas cult, which eventually spread
to northern Europe where the Saint Nicholas legend was embellished
and merged with Norse legends of their god Odin on a flying horse,
wearing heavy winter clothing.

The leaders in Speyer, Germany, issued a charter to their Jewish population. One article stated that in order to protect them, the town had
to surround the Jewish population with a wall. The treatment of Jews
in Speyer was apparently very progressive and seemed to have good
intentions, but it would result in the concept of a Jewish ghetto.

1088

The University of Bologna, Christian Europe's first university, was
founded in Italy. It began as a mutual aid society for foreign students,
protecting them against laws that imposed collective punishment for

the crimes and debts of their countrymen. These students hired scholars to teach them, and the university concept gradually evolved.

1090

c. By this time, the Jews in northern Europe were being squeezed out of international trade and into forbidden occupations such as banking, moneylending, and currency exchange, which were also taboo for Christians and Muslims. All three religions regarded charging interest on a loan as usury, which they considered a sin. Because of this, Jews were pushed even further to the fringes of society and would become stereotyped as greedy moneylenders.

Henry IV, the Holy Roman emperor, issued a document that affirmed the rights listed in the Speyer charter for all his Jewish subjects. Five years later, Pope Urban II would call for a holy war against the Muslims, and this brief, relatively optimistic period for German Jews would come to an end when they were caught up in the Christian frenzy of eliminating anyone who was their supposed enemy.

1091

The Normans, who were becoming a powerful force in the Mediterranean region, drove the Muslims out of Sicily.

1093

Anselm became the archbishop of Canterbury. He took a rational and philosophical approach to theology, and he has been called the founder of Christian Scholasticism. He put forward the "satisfaction theory of atonement," which basically stated that sin was an injustice to God that must be balanced; therefore, Jesus had to die in order to correct the injustice of human sin and satisfy God's sense of justice. This theory was somewhat different than the several other atonement theories that earlier Christians had developed to explain why Jesus had to die. Anselm also presented the ontological argument for a belief in God. He taught that since human reason can imagine a perfect being, that perfect being had to exist. He listed the characteristics of God that most Christians are familiar with today—that he is all knowing, all present, all loving, and all powerful. During his career, Anselm was exiled twice from England and spent much of his life in Rome as an advisor to the pope.

1095

The right to grant indulgences (inducing people to pay money to spend less time in purgatory) was extended to bishops, and soon bishops were underbidding each other in the generosity of their forgiveness.

Byzantine emperor Alexius I Komnenos asked Pope Urban II for assistance in stopping Turkish incursions into his empire. The pope escalated the mission, calling for an army of knights to free the Holy Land from Muslim control. During a sermon in Clermont, France, he demonized the Turks, saying they were much worse than the Arabs, who had demonstrated respect and toleration for Christians. He accused the Turks of killing priests, nuns, and pilgrims and destroying the Church of the Holy Sepulchre. Urban said that the knights should use their skills in warfare to their spiritual advantage by regaining Jerusalem for Christianity. He promised the remission of sins, reduced time in purgatory, and a guarantee of heaven to anyone who joined this venture as long as they avoided carnal sins. He also allowed the knights to keep their spoils of war. In sermonizing at Clermont, Urban revived Pope Leo IX's example of preaching in public, prompting many other clergymen do the same.

1096

Peter the Hermit and Walter the Penniless, anxious to get involved, rushed to organize the People's Crusade, or Peasants' Crusade, an unorganized affair not sanctioned by the pope. Ten thousand to forty thousand peasants plundered their way across Europe toward the Holy Land. Their crusade began with what are called the Rhineland massacres, led by Count Emicho of Leiningen, who felt they were fulfilling end-times prophecies. This assault on Jews gave them a choice of conversion or execution and involved many thousands from Cologne to Mainz, the main centers of Jewish intellectual and cultural vitality in Germany. Some Christian clergy reportedly tried to protect Jews but were powerless against the large and unruly mob. Still other clergy refused to protect Jews who rejected conversion. More than a thousand Jews were murdered in Mainz, Germany, alone, and as many as eight thousand to twelve thousand were killed or chose to commit suicide. Later, the mob killed four thousand Hungarians and pillaged and burned the city of Belgrade. Local troops killed several thousand of the pseudo-crusaders, and the crusade finally ground to a halt when the Turks annihilated most of the crusading mob neared Nicea.

The knights of the first papal-sanctioned Crusade arrived in Constantinople. Emperor Alexius originally hoped for several hundred knights to come to his aid, but sixty thousand crusaders appeared outside his walls, and he was said to have felt threatened by their enormous numbers. Alexius agreed to supply necessities to the crusaders and transport them across the Bosporus if their leaders signed an oath of loyalty to him and ceded all lands that they conquered to him. Godfrey of Bouillon, the overall leader, insisted on food and transportation without any loyalty oath. While camping outside the city, the crusaders became frustrated with the emperor, pillaged the suburbs, and even attacked the city. After they were brought under control by Byzantine forces, they agreed to Alexius's oath.

1097

When the Holy Roman emperor Henry IV returned from Italy, he issued an edict allowing Jews who had been forced to convert during the recent crusade to return to Judaism. He also ordered that all Jewish property taken in the attacks be returned to the rightful owners, but as can be imagined, most of the guilty never paid for their crimes.

The first battle of the First Crusade occurred at Nicea, which was the sultanate of the Seljuk Turks. While the crusaders had the city under siege, the Turks secretly surrendered to the Byzantine forces who accompanied them in order to keep the city from being looted. This infuriated the leaders of the crusade and caused them to renege on their loyalty oath to the Emperor Alexius.

The wife of one of the crusade's leaders, Baldwin of Boulogne, died while he was on crusade, and with her death came the loss of his inheritance. He detached himself and his knights from the crusade to seek financial gain and set his sights on Edessa, a Christian city in eastern Syria. There, the inhabitants welcomed Baldwin and his knights because they had recently been under frequent attacks by the Turks. Baldwin plotted to take control of the city and instigated the murder of the city's ruler. He established the first crusader state, and to solidify his rule, the widowed Baldwin married the daughter of the ruler from a neighboring city.

The crusaders, minus Baldwin, arrived at Antioch and began a nine-month siege. Before the crusade, the Muslims had granted the Christians in Antioch the freedom to gather and worship in their churches. Non-Muslims had to pay a tax, but otherwise, they usually were not harassed. That tolerant policy didn't deter the crusaders, who wanted to rid the Holy Land of all Muslims. The crusaders were recorded to have treated Nestorian Christians not as fellow followers of Jesus, but as heretics.

1098

Antioch fell to the crusaders, who went on a killing rampage, massacring Christians along with Muslims. Soon after their conquest, a powerful Turkish army surrounded the city. After a vision of Saint Andrew, the mystic, Peter Bartholomew, discovered the Holy Lance, the one said to have pierced Jesus's side as he hung on the cross. There were skeptics, but to those who believed this was that historical lance, they would gain a powerful psychological comfort and see it as a sign from God. The crusaders carried the Holy Lance into battle and drove off the forces that besieged them. Antioch was retained as a Crusader possession under the rule of Bohemond and was never returned to Emperor Alexius as promised.

Count Stephen of Blois, one of the leaders of the crusade, had not been present for the capture of Antioch, and when he arrived there, the city was surrounded by a huge army. It appeared that the situation was hopeless, and he set out for home. On his way north, he met Alexius leading a Byzantine army south to join in the campaign. Stephen warned him of the risk he was taking, and after hearing what he had to say, Alexius returned to Constantinople, and Stephen returned to France. The crusaders thereafter always viewed Alexius as a traitor.

Twenty-two monks left the Molesme Abbey to establish their own monastery in Citeaux, France. There, they founded the Cistercian Order, a stricter more ascetic order, emphasizing physical labor, silence, and self-discipline. They would locate their monasteries in challenging locations and develop innovative methods to drain swamps, clear forests, breed farm animals, and raise crops.

Crusaders laid siege to the city of Maarat because winter was approaching, and they were low on supplies. They captured the city in two weeks, using a siege tower to breach the walls. Bohemond, the crusade's leader, had promised the Muslims safe conduct if they surrendered, but after the city's capture, the crusaders massacred the entire population of as many as twenty thousand inhabitants. Some crusaders resorted to cannibalism in Maarat.

1099

The crusaders arrived at Jerusalem, which the Fatimids of Egypt had recaptured from the Seljuk Turks the previous year while the Turks were focused on the Latin invaders. The crusaders laid siege and eventually captured the city, slaughtering up to thirty thousand Muslims and Jews. They reportedly burned the Jewish synagogue where hundreds of Jews had taken shelter and killed all Muslims who took refuge in the Al-Aqsa Mosque. Little is known of the fate of the native Christian population.

Following the conquest of Jerusalem, most crusaders returned to Europe, but twenty thousand knights and soldiers remained in the

Holy Land to control the newly won territories. The crusaders established a Latin patriarchate in Jerusalem and four crusader states in the region. The states became known as the Kingdom of Jerusalem, the Princedom of Antioch, the County of Tripoli, and the County of Edessa.

Paschal II became pope. He was said to have appointed the first bishop to America, Erik Gnupsson, who was given the bishopric of Greenland and Vinland, which included Newfoundland.

The Knights Hospitaller were approved as a military order charged with the care of patients and the defense of the Holy Lands. They would take an active role in European warfare until the late eighteenth century.

Peter Bartholomew, who had discovered the Holy Lance in Antioch, had many skeptics who suspected he was not being truthful about his vision. Peter demanded a trial by fire, which was a medieval method of determining innocence or guilt. When he walked into the corridor of flames, he was hideously burned and died shortly later. The crusaders lost faith in the Holy Lance, but it would play an important role in later European legends.

CHAPTER 12: TWELFTH CENTURY AD

The death sentence is a necessary and efficacious means for the Church to attain its end.
—Pope Leo XIII

The key to wisdom is this—constant and frequent questioning, for by doubting we are led to question and by questioning we arrive at the truth.
—Peter Abelard

I was called before the king's tribunal like a layman and was deserted in the quarter where I had looked for support. My brethren, the bishops, sided with the court and were ready to pronounce judgment against me.
—Thomas Becket

This century highlighted Christianity's continued intolerance of non-Christians and the established Church's struggle to stomp out the various divergent views of Christianity that pointed out hypocrisy within the Church. The founding of the University of Paris and the writings of Peter Abelard demonstrated a move toward the use of rationalism and scholasticism while men like Peter Waldo and Henry of Lausanne promoted a return to Christianity's humble beginnings. It was obvious Church reform was needed. All the while, popes declared more crusades; profiteering resulted from Christians using relics to seek cures and blessings; Gothic architecture was introduced; new military monastic orders were established; and the Catholic Church continued to use forged documents to achieve its ends.

1100

At this time, the largest cities in Western Europe were Rome and Venice; each had a population of around fifty thousand. As a comparison, Constantinople had over four hundred thousand citizens just within the city walls. Constantinople was by far the largest concentration of Christians in the world.

After completing a church in honor of Saint Nicholas and wanting his relics to protect it, Venetian crusaders claimed to have recovered the bones of the saint, which they said were unwittingly left behind by the tomb raiders from Bari in 1087. The Venetians eventually started their own reliquary to the saint. Later, leaders in Myra, the hometown of Nicholas, reported that both Italian groups had stolen the wrong bones and that the true ones were still safe in Myra.

c. Christian theaters began to produce plays based on the Bible. Public theater had disappeared since the time of the western Roman Empire, so this was a significant cultural development.

1101

c. Middle Eastern mathematicians introduce the numerical system developed in India during the sixth or seventh centuries to Europe. Before this time, Roman numerals were the accepted method of expressing numbers.

c. An Italian religious order known as the Humiliati was founded. The pope approved their ultra-ascetic way of life but forbade them from holding private meetings or preaching in public, since the Church was intolerant of competition in the public sphere. The fraternity spread rapidly and persisted into the sixteenth century before the Church finally suppressed it.

1111

The Synod of Ráth Breasail was held in Ireland. It marked the transition of the Irish Church from a monastic to a diocesan and parish-based Church.

1115

c. Bernard of Clairvaux, a French abbot, led thirty other monks from his order to Citeaux, France, and joined the Cistercian abbey. He devoted his energy to expanding the abbey, and by the time Bernard died in 1153, there were over sixty-five other Cistercian monasteries.

French knight Hugues de Payens proposed the establishment of a monastic order to protect pilgrims traveling to sacred sites in the Holy Land. King Baldwin II and Patriarch Warmund of Jerusalem agreed, and the following year, the Poor Fellow-Soldiers of Christ and of the Temple of Solomon, better known as the Knights Templar, was founded. Their duties would expand to include establishing banks to protect the money and other valuables of those on pilgrimage or crusades and protecting Jewish people whenever possible.

1120

c. Peter Abelard, a prominent French philosopher and theologian, and one of the most brilliant scholars of the twelfth century, wrote *Sic et Non*—meaning "Yes or No" or "For or Against"—pointing out 158 apparently contradictory statements in the Bible and other writings of the early Church fathers. None of the statements gave a reader any definitive answers to theological questions. An example was his first question: "Must human faith be completed by reason, or not?" He then quoted scripture or authoritative writings to show that there was no consistent answer to this question. He applied reason to theology, and as a result, the following year, the Synod of Soissons charged him with heresy. His students sought to defend the Trinity based on reasoning and logic, going beyond traditional Church doctrines and returning to classical ideas.

c. Hugh of Saint-Victor, a French theologian and writer, contradicted the prevailing belief that the accumulation of knowledge about the natural world threatened the authority of God and the Church. His ideas led to the founding of some of the first universities.

Guibert of Nogent, a Benedictine historian and theologian, wrote his treatise on relics. His main targets were the churches that made profits from their relics and the mobs that swarmed the shrines where the relics were kept. He berated the laity for accepting the authenticity of relics without evidence that they were real, and he pointed out how ridiculous it was that there were multiple examples of the same relic, such as two heads of John the Baptist.

At the request of Pope Calixtus II, Norbert of Xanten, a German bishop, founded the Premonstratensian order to give active priests an ascetic and contemplative retreat. His adherents were active in Germany, France, Belgium, and Transylvania, and they established many monasteries in those regions. Many of these cells, or canons, are still active.

c. A Roman-era cemetery was discovered in Cologne, Germany, in which the remains of a probably fictional Saint Ursula were thought to be buried along with her retinue of eleven thousand virgins. The real number of virgins in the legend was eleven, but someone had mistranslated the Roman numeral. Believing that there were eleven thousand, the grave diggers excavated the entire cemetery over the next three centuries to collect the relics that are now on display in Basilica of Saint Ursula in Cologne.

Prompted by the First Crusade, Pope Calixtus II issued the papal bull *Sicut judaeis* to protect Jews. It threatened excommunication for anyone forcing Jews to convert, harming them, disturbing their festivals, or taking their property. It would be reaffirmed by many future popes, but also easily ignored.

1122

The Investiture Controversy, a conflict over who would appoint church officials, ended when Emperor Henry V and Pope Calixtus II agreed on the Concordat of Worms. It differentiated between royal and spiritual powers and gave emperors a limited role in selecting bishops. This ended one of the most significant conflicts between the Church and the Holy Roman Empire in medieval Europe. The forged *Donation of Constantine* was again dusted off to support the pope's position.

1123

Anglo-Norman priest and monk Rahere founded Saint Bartholomew's Hospital in London. It was essentially a hostel or hospice, lacking any resident medical providers. So little was known about medicine in those days that medical treatment mostly consisted of allowing patients to rest and let their bodies heal on their own.

The First Lateran Council was convened in Rome. It accomplished little but marked the first time a significant church council was held in the West. The bishops did decide that unmarried priests should not marry after ordination, so apparently some priests were allowed to be married at that time.

1124

When Germans threatened to invade France, Louis VI convened an assembly at Saint-Denis Church in Paris and placed the relics of Saint Denis on display. The assembled audience called on Saint Denis for protection. When the invasion failed to occur, they believed that it was the result of their prayers to Saint Denis. After that, the crowds visiting these relics grew so enormous that the humble Frankish abbey built in AD 630 had to be rebuilt and enlarged to provide access to relics. This reconstruction resulted in the world's first Gothic-style cathedral.

Returning from the Crusades, a Venetian fleet raided the Aegean Islands belonging to the Byzantines, looting, burning, and stealing relics. Because the Byzantines had no substantial navy at the time, they were unable to resist.

1126

An angry French mob tossed the popular French priest Peter of Bruys into a bonfire that he set for burning Christian icons. He had raised the ire of the Church for dismissing all of the New Testament, except the Gospels, as of little value. He furthermore rejected the authority and most traditions of the Roman Catholic Church.

1129

The Council of Troyes endorsed the Knights Templar, and this monastic order became one of the most skilled fighting units of the Crusades. The order would go on to amass enormous wealth and political power due to being a favored charity.

1130

After the death of Pope Honorius II, two popes, Innocent II and Anacletus II, were elected and consecrated on the same day by two different groups of cardinals. Since Anacletus had the support of most Romans, Innocent was forced to flee to France. However, Anacletus was the great-grandson of a converted Jew, so Bernard of Clairvaux and other prominent reformers wanted someone else elected. Bernard was quoted as saying, "It is an insult to Christ that the offspring of a Jew has occupied the chair of Peter." The irony that both Jesus and Peter were Jewish must have been lost on Bernard, and Anacletus remained pope until 1138.

1131

Pope Innocent II recognized the autonomy of the Maronite Patriarch in Antioch. The Maronite Church had been separated from the Eastern Orthodox Church since the seventh century.

1134

Henry of Lausanne, considered an apostate Benedictine monk, was brought before Pope Innocent II and accused of many charges, including rejection of Church doctrines such as the intercession of saints and the disciplinary authority of the Church. Henry advocated reading the Gospels openly as the sole foundation of truth and condemned both infant baptism and the Eucharist. Not much is known about him, but he was extremely popular in southern France, and his followers were known as Henricians. It is thought that he died in prison in 1148.

1135

c. Patriarch Gabriel ibn Turayk mandated that Coptic services be conducted in Arabic because by then that had become the predominant language in Egyptian society.

1139

The Second Lateran Council met in Rome. Its canons included condemnation of marriage and concubinage among clergy, excommunication of laity who failed to pay their tithes, and modifications to the Truce of God. Pope Innocent II also condemned heretics and deposed clergy who had been ordained by Anacletus II, the antipope who had recently died.

1140

Gratian, an Italian canon lawyer, wrote *Gratian's Decretum*, an attempt to use the scholastic method to solve contradictory canons from past centuries. It became the main text used by masters of canon law at universities and the code of canon law used by the Roman Catholic Church until 1918.

An author known as pseudo-Calixtinus wrote the *Codex Calixtinus*. It contained a guidebook to the Camino de Santiago, the pilgrimage route to the shrine of Saint James in Santiago de Compostela in northern Spain.

c. The Cistercians founded La Trappe Abbey in Normandy, France. Today's abbey ale lovers are very familiar with the Trappist breweries, established by the monks beginning in 1664.

1141

Pope Innocent II issued a bull excommunicating Peter Abelard and his followers. Peter's crime was the use of logic to interpret scripture.

1143

Pope Celestine II ordered the Knights Hospitaller to take over management of a German hospital in Jerusalem. This responsibility eventually shifted to Germans, who could better communicate with their patients, and gave birth to the monastic order of Teutonic Knights.

1144

The new Basilica of Saint-Denis was completed in Paris. It was so magnificent that many other bishops wanted spectacular buildings like that for their own towns and cities and would try to outcompete each other in their grandeur.

Turks, under their new leader Zengi, captured the remote crusader state of Edessa following a four-month siege. They executed the Latin prisoners, but the native Christians may have been spared.

1145

Pope Eugene III organized the Second Crusade to the Holy Land in response to the fall of Edessa. The call to arms was answered by King Louis VII of France and King Conrad III of Germany.

c. German Historian Otto of Freising chronicled a myth-like story of a Prester John, who defeated a Muslim king in far-off Asia and intended to liberate Palestine. Otto of Freising must have certainly been referring to the Nestorians, who European Christians knew almost nothing about.

1147

Pope Eugene III sent a member of the clergy, known as a papal legate, to the Cathar district of Languedoc, France, to contain the perceived Cathar threat to the Church. The mission was generally unsuccessful, and other similar efforts would be carried out in 1178 and 1180, but the Cathars resisted these attempts to submit to Catholic authority.

A Christian army of Danes and Saxons launched the Wendish Crusade, in conjunction with the Second Crusade to the Holy Land. It would result in the Christianizing of the Wends, Sorbs, and Obotrites of eastern Germany and western Poland by way of the sword.

The German army of the Second Crusade arrived outside the walls of Constantinople and camped there to await the French army's arrival. The Germans were belligerent, and this led to fighting between them and the Byzantines, who subdued them and sent them on their way across the Bosporus. The German and French armies traveled independently, and the Seljuk Turks defeated both armies in Anatolia. The remnants of their armies reached Jerusalem, and later the French participated in an unsuccessful attack on Damascus. The only successful part of this crusade occurred when a force of Flemish, Frisian, Norman, English, Scottish, and German crusaders, on their way to the Holy Land, landed in Lisbon and assisted the Portuguese army in driving out the Moors. When King Louis VII finally returned to France, he blamed Byzantine emperor Manuel for the crusade's failure. He even began to discuss the idea of a crusade against Constantinople.

1149

c. The Swedish Crusades involved Christian Swedes invading pagan Finland. There would eventually be another crusade in 1293 that would complete the conquest of Finland.

The monk Thomas of Monmouth began writing a book entitled *The Life and Miracles of Saint William of Norwich* about a boy named William whose body was found near Norwich, England, five years earlier. The forester who discovered the body had accused Jews of the murder. Since there was no proof of this accusation, local Jews were protected until the passion for revenge subsided. The crime was eventually forgotten until Thomas arrived at the local abbey. His intent was to have William declared a martyr and a saint and to create a pilgrimage site for him in Norwich. Thomas described visions he had experienced and arranged for false testimony against Jews by fake witnesses. This is thought to have been the first accusation of the crime of "blood libel," which was rumored to be the ritual sacrifice of a Christian child. As Thomas hoped, by 1150, crowds of pilgrims began to visit William's tomb, and a saint cult was established in his honor.

1150

A university was founded in Paris as a place of learning independent of the Church. The curriculum was mostly based on newly translated classical works seeping into the rest of Europe from Spain and the Middle East.

Papermaking began in Europe when the Moors opened a paper mill in Xativa, Spain. From there, the process spread to the rest of Europe and facilitated the development of the new universities. With scholarship expanding beyond the monasteries, the demand for paper increased enormously.

Hildegard of Bingen—a German mystic, writer, and composer—founded a monastery at Rupertsberg. She would establish another one at Eibingen fifteen years later. This was an unusual endeavor for a woman during this era.

c. Necromancy, or the practice of communicating with the dead, was becoming more popular in Europe. It was accompanied by the infiltration of Islamic texts on magic and the demonic world. The perceived magical powers of an ordinary person could be easily attributed to a pact with Satan and that set the stage for belief in witches.

1154

Nicholas Breakspear became Pope Adrian IV, the only Englishman ever to serve as pope.

1157

Holy Roman emperor Frederick I Barbarrosa issued a charter of protection to Jews living in Worms, Germany. It was intended to gain the loyalty of the Jewish residents and to deflect legal claims on them by the nobility and the Church. By 1236, Jews and their possessions would not only be protected but become the "property" of the king.

1160

c. The concept of an actual place called purgatory was becoming established as a temporary transitional site following death. To the Catholic Church, this where the soul did penance for its sins before being allowed to enter the afterlife. By promising that purchasing indulgences could influence the destiny of departed souls, the Church would add to its wealth during the Middle Ages.

1162

Thomas Becket became archbishop of Canterbury thanks to his patron King Henry II. Becket, however, disappointed Henry by not helping the king gain control of the English Church. Instead, Becket defended the rights of the Church.

1163

Five Flemish Cathars were burned at the stake in Cologne after refusing to repent for heresy. In the past, there had not been many burnings for heresy, but it became much more frequent after this. Burning had been a means of execution since the Babylonians in 1800 BC, and it appealed to Christians to publicly execute heretics and Jews based on their interpretation of John 15:5–6. "I am the vine; you are the branches. If you remain in me and I in you, you will bear much fruit; apart from me you can do nothing. If you do not remain in me, you are like a branch that is thrown away and withers; such branches are picked up, thrown into the fire and burned."

The Council of Tours banned all surgical treatment by monks. It was seen as more appropriate to heal people through prayer and other supernatural means.

1164

Holy Roman emperor Frederick Barbarossa took the relics of the three Magi from a church in Milan and gave them to the archbishop of Cologne. The container in which they were stored, known as a reliquary, was the largest one in Christendom, and Cologne became one of the most popular pilgrimage sites. According to legend, the three wise men, by visiting the baby Jesus, had been the first pilgrims in Christian history. In 1245, the pope would grant a reprieve of forty days in purgatory for anyone who visited the relics. Today, the reliquary lies in the Cologne Cathedral. Surprisingly, the Gospel of Matthew never mentioned the number of magi; the number three was derived from the number of gifts they brought.

1165

Holy Roman emperor Frederick Barbarossa pressured Pope Paschal III into canonizing Charlemagne. The pope stopped short of making him a saint, designating Charlemagne "blessed" instead. Charlemagne's remains were placed in a shrine in Aachen, Germany.

c. The legend of Prester John was becoming more popular throughout Europe. It was a story of a Christian king who ruled over an isolated outpost in far-off Asia, possibly China. These stories found their way into the two most popular travel books of the Middle Ages, *The Travels of Marco Polo* and *The Travels of Sir John Mandeville*. The legend certainly must have referred to the Nestorians.

1170

Knights loyal to King Henry II, possibly intending to arrest Thomas Becket, confronted and murdered him in Canterbury Cathedral. All signs pointed to King Henry as being responsible for the murder.

Pope Alexander III established new rules for the canonization of saints. After this, only popes could decree someone a saint in the western Church.

The Chivalric Code, also known as chivalry, was adopted as a code of conduct among European knights, who were soldiers that had been honored for their bravery in service to the Church or their king. There were ten commandments of chivalry, including "thou shalt respect all weaknesses, and shalt constitute thyself the defender of them"; "thou shalt never lie, and shalt remain faithful to thy pledged word"; "thou shalt defend the church"; "thou shalt make war against the infidel without cessation and without mercy"; "thou shalt believe all that the Church teaches and thou shalt observe all its directions"; and "thou shalt be everywhere and always the champion of the Right and the Good against Injustice and Evil."

1171

The townspeople of Blois, France, accused Jews of blood libel, or ritual murder. Even though a body of a victim was never found, all adult Jews in the city were imprisoned, and their children were baptized as Christians. Eventually the Jews in prison were given the choice of converting or being executed. Between thirty and forty of them were herded into a hut and burned alive.

Saladin became sultan of Egypt. He ended the Fatimid Caliphate and realigned the region's allegiance to the Sunni Abbasid Caliphate based in Baghdad.

1172

The Compromise of Avranches removed guilt from Henry II for the murder of Thomas Becket. The conditions were that Henry had to pledge to go on crusade, defer all appeals to the pope, and agree that secular courts had no jurisdiction over clergy, except for high treason. This last canon was called the *Benefit of Clergy* and was not repealed in Great Britain in 1827.

1174

By this time, Becket had become a popular Christian martyr throughout Europe. Since Henry II showed no interest in going on crusade, Pope Alexander III forced him to perform public penance by walking barefoot to Becket's tomb at Canterbury Cathedral and once there, being whipped by monks who had witnessed the murder. The pope excommunicated Becket's murderers and sentenced them to fourteen years in the Crusades to gain the Church's forgiveness.

After peacefully entering Syria at the request of its governor, Saladin launched his conquest of the region, defeating his former Zengid lords based in Baghdad. He was proclaimed the Sultan of Egypt and Syria by the Abbasid Caliph al-Mustadi.

1176

c. Peter Waldo, a rich merchant from Lyon, France, commissioned a translation of the Bible into French so he could learn for himself what the Gospels said. He later gave away his wealth and began preaching apostolic poverty. He rapidly attracted followers, mostly people who were disgusted with the worldliness of the Church. They rejected relics, pilgrimages, holy water, clergy vestments, purgatory, and saints' days like the Protestants would do in the sixteenth century. Because his followers were laymen, they were not allowed to preach without a bishop's approval, and that was not forthcoming. The Waldensian movement, also a derivative of Paulicianism, emerged as a monastic movement within the church; whereas the Cathars, who were their spiritual cousins, were outside the church and therefore considered heretics. Nevertheless, the Church treated both sects with extreme cruelty.

Byzantine emperor Manuel I Komnenos sought to steal glory from the crusaders and attacked the Turks, but the Seljuks ambushed the Byzantines and handed them a shattering defeat at the Battle of Myriokephalon.

1179

Pope Alexander III proclaimed a crusade against the Cathars in France, promising two years of indulgences to all who would take up arms and eternal salvation for anyone who died. This offer failed to stir enough interest against the Cathars, who were popular in southern France.

The pope called the Third Lateran Council in Rome. The bishops approved many canons, including the election of popes exclusively by cardinals; declaring ordinations by antipopes null and void; setting age limits for various offices; forbidding clergy to charge fees for normal services such as burials and marriages; requiring masters to teach theology in every cathedral; holding princes responsible for repressing heresy; forbidding tournaments; declaring several Christian sects heretical; forbidding Jews and Muslims from having Christian servants; and excommunicating any Christian who was found lodging with Jews.

Waldensian representatives traveled to Rome to seek official recognition for their sect, but instead, they stirred up anxiety among the Roman clergy. As one chronicler wrote: "They go about two by two, barefoot, clad in woolen garments, owning nothing, holding all things in common like the Apostles . . . If we admit them, we shall be driven out." The pope blessed their lifestyle but continued to forbid them from preaching.

1180

The city of Zara on the eastern coast of the Adriatic Sea won its independence from Venice and became the only region on the entire Dalmatian coast not controlled by Venice.

1182

By this time, Jews had been living in France for over a thousand years. In order to add to his treasury, the fifteen-year-old French king Philip II seized Jewish property and expelled Jews from his domain. In doing so, he captured the admiration of both the Church and anyone who owed money to the Jewish moneylenders.

After Byzantine emperor Manuel I died in 1180, his eleven-year-old son Alexius II became emperor with his Norman mother Maria of Antioch as his regent. This was a time of strong anti-Western feelings in Constantinople, and Maria was seen as a Westerner. The Byzantines considered them arrogant, rich, and uncouth. This year, Andronikos I Komnenos seized the throne and coordinated an attack on the city's Italian Quarter and the massacre of as many as sixty thousand Catholics. The rest of the Westerners were imprisoned or sold as slaves. Andronikos led a reign of terror in the city, targeting any potential political rival, including the royal family. He ordered the death of Maria but kept Alexius II alive and served as the boy's regent.

1184

At the Synod of Verona, Pope Lucius III required all bishops to investigate the faith of their congregants, and if they suspected anyone of heresy, they were to turn them over to secular authorities. The synod declared that Arnoldists, Cathars, Humiliati, Josephini, Paterenes, Passagini, and Waldensians were heretics, but they still gave them a path to orthodoxy, and therefore salvation, if they repented. This opened the door for medieval Inquisitions, the beginning of a series the Church would conduct over the next seven centuries.

1185

By this time, the people of Constantinople bitterly resented the regent Andronikos I. He neglected the city while enjoying the pleasures of life. Since the Byzantine navy had been neglected in recent years, he released imprisoned Venetians in return for a naval alliance. Andronikos returned from one of his vacations to find the city in a full-scale riot, incited by a young aristocrat named Isaac Angelus. Andronikos disguised himself, collected what treasure and concubines he could, and fled the city. He was captured and returned to the city, where his former subjects publicly humiliated and horribly mutilated him. He died from his innumerable wounds.

1187

Raynald de Châtillon broke the truce in Palestine by attacking an Arab caravan and killing many Muslims. In response, Saladin mobilized his enormous army and drove toward Jerusalem. Saladin's army encountered the crusaders at the Battle of Hattin and annihilated their army. It was reported that the sultan also captured the True Cross, which then disappeared from historical records.

After a ten-day siege of Jerusalem by Saladin's forces, the Christian defenders agreed to a truce. They agreed to pay a ransom and promised not to destroy the Al Aqsa Mosque. In exchange, they were permitted safe passage out of the city and an escort to the coast. Jerusalem again became a city open to all faiths, and Saladin appointed Franciscans to guard the Church of the Holy Sepulchre and the Knights Hospitaller to aid any pilgrims who made the journey to Jerusalem.

c. The papacy again came under the control of the Italian aristocracy and would remain so for generations to come. The papacy became a badge of honor and power instead of a positive spiritual influence, which changed the entire nature of the office.

Returning crusaders, frustrated with their setbacks in the Holy Land, attacked the Jewish community of Mainz, Germany—a community that had been repeatedly harassed.

Pope Gregory VIII decided that the loss of Jerusalem was a message from God, and his interpretation was that God wanted the holy city back in Christian hands, so he called for another crusade. King Philip II of France, the Holy Roman emperor Frederick Barbarossa of Germany, and King Henry II of England answered the call.

1189

King Henry II of England died. He and the French-speaking Norman aristocracy had usually protected the mostly French-speaking Jews in England, but with the increasing charges of ritual murder, the Jews faced renewed persecution throughout the country. Many Jews took refuge in York Castle and committed mass suicide when their position became hopeless. Mobs destroyed records of the debts that were owed to Jewish bankers. With Henry's death, the new king, Richard I, pledged himself to the new crusade.

Byzantine emperor Isaac II Angelus had signed a treaty of non-aggression with Saladin. When Frederick Barbarossa approached Constantinople, his disgust for Isaac's treaty with the enemy caused him to divert his army and capture the Byzantine city of Adrianople. He eventually agreed to leave the city in return for supplies and the transportation of his army across the Bosporus Strait. Barbarossa soon after drowned when his horse fell while crossing a river in Anatolia, and King Richard "the Lionhearted" took overall command of the crusade.

1190

German knights founded the Order of Brothers of the German House of Saint Mary in Jerusalem, better known as Teutonic Knights. They would operate a field hospital during the siege of Acre, and their monastic order would be recognized by the pope two years later.

1191

Guy of Lusignan, a crusader leader who had been captured and re-leased by Saladin after the Battle of Hattin had Acre under siege when King Richard's army arrived. Richard took control of the siege, and the city fell soon after. When Richard was unable to exchange his Muslim prisoners, he ordered all two thousand of them executed. Leopold V of Austria, Frederick Barbarossa's successor in the crusade, and King Philip II of France returned to Europe. Richard marched the remainder of his army down the Palestinian coast, pursued closely by Saladin's army most of the way. When the crusaders were within twenty miles of Jerusalem, Richard surprisingly decided not to attack and instead returned to Acre.

French poet Robert de Boron wrote *Joseph of Arimathea*, which gave the Celtic legend of the Holy Grail an explicitly Christian rendition. The Grail was said to be the cup that Jesus drank from at the Last Supper and with which Joseph of Arimathea had used to collect the blood of Jesus at his crucifixion.

c. Pope Celestine III crowned German king Henry VI as Holy Roman emperor.

Construction began on a new Chartres Cathedral in France. Four pre-vious cathedrals had stood on the site but had all been destroyed by fire or war. This pilgrimage site would become one of the most magnif-icent examples of French Gothic architecture.

1192

King Richard I finalized a treaty with Saladin. Jerusalem would remain in Muslim hands but unarmed Christian pilgrims and merchants would be allowed to visit the city. After leaving Palestine, Richard captured Cyprus from the Byzantines and used it as a supply base for the crusades. Then he sailed to Corfu disguised as a Knight Templar to avoid notice by the Byzantines. His ship was wrecked near Corfu, and he was faced with a land journey through central Europe. Near

Vienna, he was captured by Leopold of Austria, who held a personal grudge against him.

1193

Richard was turned over to the Holy Roman emperor Henry VI, who held Richard for ransom. Pope Celestine III nearly excommunicated Emperor Henry VI for keeping King Richard I prisoner in Austria, but it wasn't until 1194 that Richard was freed to return to England.

1195

Byzantine emperor Isaac II's power-hungry brother, Alexius Angelus, had him imprisoned and blinded. Alexius took over the throne and became Emperor Alexius III.

1196

Future Mongol emperor Ghengis Khan was a vassal to the Nestorian khan Toghril, and at the time, at least seven Turko-Mongol tribes were completely or partially Nestorian. If one powerful Nestorian leader had been able to unite the tribes, Nestorian Christianity had a good possibility of becoming their state religion.

1198

A crusading expedition landed in Livonia, present-day Latvia, but the crusaders were repulsed. Two years later, the archbishop of Bremen would send another expedition. By 1212, the crusaders would accomplish their goal, and the Livonian leader and his subjects were forced to convert to Christianity.

John de Matha founded the Trinitarian monastic order in France with the primary intention of ransoming Christians held captive by non-Christians, a consequence of the many crusades and many Muslim pirate attacks.

Pope Innocent III pointed out nine types of forgeries that he had noticed and attempted to establish criteria for the detection of fraudulent
papal documents.

The king of Aragon, Spain, gave the Waldensians and others who had
been declared heretics a deadline to leave his dominion. If they failed
to leave, they were threatened with arrest, confiscation of their property, and the possibility being burned at the stake.

Ibn Rushd, better known to the Christian world as Averroes, died.
Although a Spanish Muslim, his philosophical works contained many
commentaries on Aristotle, and once translated into Latin, they inspired Christian scholars in the next century. The classical philosopher's contention was that certain theological concepts were beyond
human understanding, and this conflicted with the Church's confidence that it held all truths. To Christian writers, Averroes became
known as "The Commentator," and those interested in his commentaries would become known as Averroists.

CHAPTER 13: THIRTEENTH CENTURY AD

In truth, they were exposed as frauds. Seeking to avenge the Holy Sepulchre they raged openly against Christ and sinned by overturning the Cross with the cross they bore on their backs, not even shuddering to trample on it for the sake of a little gold and silver.

—Nicetas Choniates, Constantinople aristocrat

For they who are supposed to serve Christ rather than themselves, who should have used their swords against the infidel, have bathed those swords in the blood of Christians. They have not spared religion, nor age, nor sex, and have committed adultery and fornication in public, exposing matrons and even nuns to the filthiness of their troops.

—Pope Innocent III

I think we must fully face the fact that when Christianity does not make a man very much better, it makes him very much worse . . . Conversion may make of one who was, if no better, no worse than an animal, something like a devil.

—C. S. Lewis

More crusades targeted not only the Muslims in the Holy Land but also the Cathars in France, the Moors in Spain, the Eastern Orthodox Christians in Russia, and even the Roman Catholic Stedingers in

Germany. Conflicts and cooperation with the Nestorian-influenced Mongols in the Holy Land occurred. Astonishingly, Latin crusaders conquered Constantinople, the capital of Eastern Orthodox Christianity, but were eventually driven out of the Middle East. This century continued the gradual seepage of scholasticism and rational thought into Christian theology, represented by Roger Bacon, Bonaventure, and Thomas Aquinas. This was the century of the Dominicans, Franciscans, Cathars, and Waldensians, and the Church of the East reached its pinnacle.

1200

c. Stone benches began to be installed along the side walls of English churches. Before this time, there had probably been no seating inside churches, and it would be another century before seats were transferred to the center of the nave and, even later, affixed to the floor. Wooden benches with backs, or pews, would gradually begin to replace the stone benches. The word *pew* is derived from the French and Latin word for a raised platform or balcony.

c. Poland had been ravaged repeatedly by invasions of Tartars, Huns, Magyars, Mongols, and other nomadic tribes from Central Asia. The Poles needed immigrants to help rebuild their society and economy, and so they signed charters to protect immigrants, including Jews, who came mainly from Germany.

c. At the Basilica of Saint-Denis in Paris, a priest began to add a theatrical flourish to the consecration of the host during communion. The priest turned away from the congregation to conceal the host from view until he was certain it had become the actual body of Christ, then he raised it overhead to the sound of bells.

c. Marie of Oignies adopted a devout life, devoted to helping the poor and sick and marked by strenuous asceticism and manual labor. She may have inaugurated the sect known as the Beguines, who lived in semimonastic communities mainly in the region of Belgium and the Netherlands and did not take formal religious vows. They were either condemned or praised, depending on who was pope, and some Beguine communities still exist.

c. When the pope saw a noticeable decline in pilgrims traveling to Rome, he offered four years of indulgences to anyone who went to see the heads of Peter and Paul on the days they were on display.

c. Slavery was abolished in northern Europe, but serfdom continued. In southern Europe, slavery would continue into the nineteenth century.

1201

c. At this point, the attire and regalia worn by Roman Catholic clergy was fully established and would be carried over to the present time.

c. The grandest library in Europe was in Paris, but it held only 1,017 books because of the centuries-long purge of non-Christian literature, as well as near constant warfare and destruction. As a comparison, the monastery library on the island of Patmos contained 330 texts, of which only sixteen did not deal with theological issues. This modest size was not unusual for Christian libraries of the time.

c. In paintings of the crucifixion of Jesus, it became common for the artist to add depictions of their patrons to the crowd.

Alexius Angelus, the twenty-year-old son of former Byzantine emperor Isaac II, secretly traveled to Germany to visit his sister, Irene, who was married to King Philip of Swabia. While there, he met Boniface I, the Marquis of Montferrat and the chosen leader of the next crusade to recover Jerusalem. Boniface had already arranged for a large Venetian fleet to transport his army to Egypt, but Alexius explained to Boniface that he was the rightful Byzantine emperor and that if Boniface diverted his fleet to Constantinople and installed him, the people would rebel against his uncle and deposer of his father, Emperor Alexius III and welcome the crusaders. Boniface seemed to like the idea.

The planning for the Fourth Crusade involved sailing to the Holy Land instead of traveling by land. Venice was chosen as the port of embarkation for the crusaders. In negotiations with Venice, the crusaders convinced the Venetians to build possibly the largest war fleet assembled. To carry the 20,000 soldiers, 4,500 knights, 9,000 squires, 10,000 horses, and all their war provisions, the fleet would require 50 warships, 500 transport ships, and 30,000 sailors and marines.

1202

Alexius Angelus traveled to Rome to meet with Pope Innocent III. He promised that if he became emperor, he would use the wealth of the Byzantine Empire to support the holy work of the Crusades and force the patriarch of Constantinople to submit to Innocent and future popes. The pope refused to lend his support to Alexius's plans because Jerusalem was his main priority.

In Venice, only about ten thousand crusaders had arrived by the date specified for departure to Egypt. Enrico Dandolo, the duke, or doge, of Venice, refused to transport the army unless they paid the shipping costs that had been agreed on. The crusade stalled for four months while waiting for enough soldiers to arrive. Dandolo said that he would defer the payment for the ships and supplies if the crusaders attacked Zara, the renegade- and pirate-infested city on the eastern Adriatic coast that had rebelled against Venice.

1203

Genghis Khan gave his son, Tolui, a Nestorian Christian wife named Sorghaghtani Beki. Tolui and Sorghaghtani would become the parents of Mongke and Kublai. Since their own mother was a Christian, the two future Khans would be especially receptive to Christianity.

The Fourth Crusade set out from Venice. The crusaders first sailed to Zara, a Catholic city, and, after conquering it, spent the winter there. Envoys from Alexius Angelus arrived in Zara and told the crusaders that if they helped Alexius seize the throne, he would finance the

crusade with fifty-one tons of silver and furnish their needed supplies. Not only that, but he would join the crusade with an army of
ten thousand knights. Most crusaders wanted nothing to do with this
deal, realizing that their duty was in the Holy Land and the pope had
threatened excommunication to anyone who attacked Constantinople,
but the leaders, including Boniface, accepted Alexius's offer, and bishops on the crusade offered a general absolution for their future sins.

After demolishing Zara, the crusader fleet reached Constantinople
and the residents were amazed by the largest naval force to enter the
Sea of Marmara in centuries. The crusaders, in turn, were in awe of
the enormous and majestic city before them. The crusade's leaders demanded that Alexius III relinquish his throne to the rightful emperor,
young Alexius Angelus. When the Byzantines refused, the crusaders
attacked but were driven back to their ships in a counterattack. The
invaders managed to set some fires that destroyed a large section of
the city. Emperor Alexius III took what possessions he could and left
the city to seek reinforcements. As soon as the citizens realized he was
gone, they restored the blinded ex-emperor, Isaac II, to power. Isaac
opened the city to the crusaders, but after friction began between the
crusaders and the Greek population, he asked them to camp on the
eastern shore of the estuary called the Golden Horn. Alexius Angelus
was crowned Emperor Alexius IV and ruled with his enfeebled father, Isaac. Negotiations for young Alexius's promised funding of the
crusade failed, leading the crusaders to realize they would have to
take control of the city by force in order to get what they needed and
expected.

1204

After a rapid series of coups left Alexius IV dead and Constantinople
in anarchy, the crusaders attacked the city in earnest. By chance, the
attackers found a sealed gate and broke through. As the crusaders entered the city, the Byzantine soldiers, most of whom were not loyal
to the city, fled. One by one, the crusaders captured the towers along
the wall and were able to open the city gates. The city's last leader,

Constantine Laskaris, fled to Nicea, where he and his brother Theodore would start a government in exile known as the Nicean Empire.

The crusaders and Italian refugees ruthlessly sacked Constantinople, removing everything of value, including church adornments and holy relics. They destroyed countless ancient scrolls and codices; stole or damaged many of the city's statues; and ran amok murdering, raping, and looting.

The crusaders established the Latin Empire of Constantinople, and much of the population abandoned the city. Over the next fifty-seven years of Catholic rule, the population of the city fell from four hundred thousand within the walls alone to around thirty thousand in the entire region. The crusaders chose Baldwin of Flanders as the new emperor, and he was coronated in a Catholic ceremony in the Hagia Sophia. Venetian Thomas of Morosini was chosen as patriarch.

Following its defeat, most of the Byzantine Empire was divided between Venice and the crusaders. Venice acquired an empire consisting of much of Greece and many eastern Mediterranean islands while the crusaders took control of Constantinople and its vassal states in Greece and northern Anatolia. The Greek "successor states" still in Byzantine control were the Despotate of Epirus in western Greece, the Empire of Nicea in northwest Anatolia, and the Empire of Trebizond, on the Black Sea, in northern Anatolia.

Domingo de Guzmán traveled through France and encountered the Cathars, also known as Albigensians because of the Albi region they inhabited. Domingo began a campaign to convert the Cathars and held public debates with them in several cities. Domingo later expressed that the only way to make Cathars adopt Catholicism was for Catholic leaders to live in austerity that rivaled the Cathars.

Pope Innocent III gave his legates the authority to modify churches in any way they judged necessary, destroying what remained of the independence of local churches.

Genghis Khan defeated the Nestorian Keraites and unified the Mongol people. He took a Nestorian wife and married two of his sons to Nestorian wives. He did not establish a state religion and left religion a private individual matter.

1206

c. According a Dominican legend, Domingo de Guzmán saw an apparition of the Virgin Mary, who gave him a rosary to use against heretics. This apparition became known as Our Lady of the Rosary and is thought to be the beginning of the use of the rosary, also known as "crown of roses," or "garland of roses." However, threads of this practice can be traced back to the fourth century. Rosary beads were used to count the various creeds, prayers, and adorations of Jesus and Mary.

A group of hermits were living on Mount Carmel in Palestine, the traditional home of the prophet Elijah. They petitioned the patriarch of Jerusalem for recognition as a monastic order and became known as the Carmelites.

Francis of Assisi, the son of a prosperous silk merchant, gave away his family wealth and adopted a life of complete poverty. His simple gospel of love and service to others generated a faithful following, which became the Franciscan Order.

1208

In Italy, Pope Innocent III consecrated Stephen Langton, an English cardinal, as archbishop of Canterbury without seeking the consent of the English king. The previous year the pope had rejected two choices for the office including King John's favorite, John de Grey. This initiated a bitter struggle between King John and Innocent. The pope placed England under "interdict," which meant a prohibition of certain rites and the invalidation of sacraments by King John's archbishop. The king yielded to the pope in 1213, but only after Philip II of France threatened to overthrow him.

Pope Innocent III sent Pierre de Castelnau to act as legate and inquisitor to Raymond, the Count of Toulouse, and to investigate Catharism. While in France, an assassin killed Pierre de Castelnau. The pope then excommunicated Raymond and began planning for an Albigensian Crusade.

The crusaders in Livonia (Lithuania) turned their attention to Eastern Orthodox lands further to the east. The Talavan Principality converted to Roman Catholicism without bloodshed, but this was the only peaceful conquest of the Nordic Crusades, which lasted until 1224, and was concurrent with a campaign against the Estonians.

1209

Pope Innocent III, in collusion with Philip II of France, launched the Albigensian Crusade to eliminate Catharism from southern France. Innocent offered indulgences and eternal salvation to participants, but it took the additional offer of Cathar lands and property to induce enough knights from northern France to join.

The Cathar-controlled city of Béziers fell to the crusaders, and it was reported that they slaughtered every inhabitant of the city. Twenty years later, Caesarius of Heisterbach wrote that when the crusaders discovered that there were Catholics mixed with the Cathars, one crusader asked Abbot Arnaud Amaury, a papal legate and their leader, "Sir, what shall we do, for we cannot distinguish between the faithful and the heretics." The abbot—afraid that many Cathars, in fear of death, would pretend to be Catholics and, after the crusaders' departure, would return to their heresy—is said to have replied, "Kill them all for the Lord knoweth them that are His." They burned the city, and the abbot later boasted of killing twenty thousand men, women, and children.

Francis of Assisi wrote *Regula primitiva (Simple Rule)*, a monastic rule derived mainly from the words of Jesus. The original wording has been lost, but the essence was vows of obedience, chastity, and poverty, along with necessary rules of conduct. This rule would be updated at various times in the future. Pope Innocent III recognized the Franciscan order of friars.

1211

The Nestorian Kuchlug seized control of the huge Qara Khitai Empire in Central Asia and China. Seven years later he would be killed, and the Qara Khitai absorbed into the Mongol Empire. Kuchlug is believed to be the last Nestorian Mongol head of state.

Catholic officials arrested and burned more than eighty Waldensians in Strasbourg, France, beginning several centuries of persecution against the sect.

1212

The Children's Crusade began in northern France. There is little information about this crusade, but it may have been led by an eloquent shepherd boy who said he had been visited by Jesus. His goal was not to conquer Muslims but to convert them, and he inspired others to follow him by giving them certain expectations such as the parting of the Mediterranean Sea for their convenience while traveling to the Holy Land. There may have been additional groups following other boys from France and Germany, but none of them would ever leave Europe.

The Battle of Las Navas de Tolosa was fought between Christian forces under King Alfonso VIII of Castile and the army of the Almohad Caliphate. This was an important victory and a turning point for the Christians in their reconquest of Spain.

1213

c. The term *crusade* came into usage in the English language. It meant "taking up the cross," or in Latin *crucis*. The term was used to refer to armed incursions into various regions to destroy the enemies of God and spread Christianity. Originally, these expeditions had been called journeys or pilgrimages.

King John of England signed the Golden Bull with a papal legate, surrendering the Kingdom of England to the pope in exchange for a payment. Following the agreement, Pope Innocent III became a supporter of John.

1215

The traveling Spanish priest Domingo de Guzmán founded the Dominican Order of friars with the approval of Pope Innocent III. They were called the Order of Preachers because they were not cloistered but rather went directly to the people.

The Great Charter was issued in England as a peace agreement between King John and rebellious barons. This charter limited the king's powers and protected the rights of the barons. It ultimately failed as a peace treaty but was revised almost annually and became a model for later constitutional documents. It eventually became known as the *Magna Carta* and served as a symbol for those who wished to show that the king was bound by secular law and not by the Church.

Since Pope Innocent III claimed control of England, he opposed the Magna Carta and the weakening of the king's power, calling it "not only shameful and demeaning, but illegal and unjust." He also excommunicated all the rebel barons who had forced John to sign it. This led to the First Baron's War in which John died of dysentery the following year.

The faculty of the University of Paris forbade the study of anything written by Aristotle, whose works were said to conflict with Church doctrines. Aristotle didn't believe that God interfered in the created world and did believe in the use of logic and reason to understand the natural world. Subjects banned by the Church included metaphysics, physics, and natural sciences. However, shortly later the Italian scholar Thomas Aquinas incorporated Aristotelian philosophy into Christian theology. His writings must have nudged Christianity back its pre-Constantine reasoning.

Pope Innocent III called the Fourth Lateran Council in Rome. It laid the groundwork and responsibilities for more inquisitions by authorizing state governments to punish heretics and confiscate their property. Local rulers were urged to swear a sacred oath that they would exterminate all heretics in their regions. The council also banned the creation of new monastic orders, condemned counterfeit relics and the exaggerated claims about them, prohibited the sale of relics, and decreed that all relics be placed in containers or reliquaries. The council threatened to excommunicate any physician who performed medical treatment without spiritual advice from the clergy, since it was still believed that illness was attributed to God's punishment for sin or of demonic origin. The council further confirmed that no new saint could be recognized without the pope's approval. As for Jews, the council again accused them of blasphemy against Christ and treachery and cruel oppression by charging interest on loans to Christians. The bishops decreed that Jews must wear clothing that distinguished them from Christians and that they were not to appear in public during the last three days of Holy Week or on Easter Sunday. The bishops decreed that Christians should have no commerce with Jews, and this led in time to the creation of more Jewish ghettos. Finally, the council declared that Jews would roast in hell for all eternity. Most of these anti-Jewish canons were not rescinded until six centuries later. This council basically defined the Catholic Church that would dominate Europe until the Reformation three centuries later.

1216

Pope Innocent III died. He had been one of the most powerful and influential popes in history, and some of his philosophy was summed up in his quotes: "Anyone who attempts to construe a personal view of God which conflicts with Church dogma must be burned without pity" and "Every cleric must obey the Pope, even if he commands what is evil; for no one may judge the Pope."

1217

The Fifth Crusade to the Holy Land began. No crusader army had reached Jerusalem unscathed since 1099. The first strike was coordinated by King Andrew II of Hungary and Duke Leopold VI of Austria, whose armies sailed from the Adriatic Sea to Acre in Palestine. Despite an initial victory over Sultan Al-Adil I, they were unable to attack fortresses since not all of their siege equipment had arrived.

1218

A German army led by Oliver of Cologne and a mixed army led by William I, count of Holland, attempted to reach Jerusalem and the Holy Land by first conquering Egypt. They landed and occupied the port of Damietta before being disastrously defeated in the Nile Delta. The two sides then agreed to an eight-year truce.

1219

c. Pope Honorius III prohibited priests from studying Roman civil law and forbade its teaching at the University of Paris. Instead, the Church preferred its own system of canon laws.

1220

Frederick II was crowned Holy Roman emperor in Rome. He reigned over the empire at its territorial peak, also serving as the King of Sicily, Germany, and Italy.

1223

After receiving permission from Pope Honorius III, Francis of Assisi staged the first nativity scene in a cave in the Italian village of Greccio. He used it as a visual aid while he preached. It displayed two live animals, an ox and an ass, and a manger of hay. It may also have included people playing the roles of Mary, Joseph, and baby Jesus. The nativity display evolved from there to include Luke's shepherds and Matthew's wise men, but the farm animals were never mentioned in the Gospels.

1224

Frederick II decreed that anyone found guilty of heresy was to be burned to death. However, if the judge was merciful, the victim could only have his tongue cut out for slandering the Catholic faith.

During a forty-day fast, Francis of Assisi saw an angel. When the vision evaporated, he was purportedly left with marks on his hands, feet, and side that were similar to Jesus's crucifixion wounds. This was thought to be the first incident of a phenomenon called "stigmata," but two years before, *The Dunstable Annals* in England reported the case of a man who "made himself out to be Christ and . . . perforated his hands and feet." That man was tried for blasphemy by the Council of Oxford and sentenced to jail for the rest of his life.

1225

King Henry III updated the Magna Carta in exchange for the English barons' aid in retaking lost French provinces.

After first accepting the service of the Teutonic Knights in 1211, King Andrew II of Hungary expelled them because of their growing power.

Pope Honorius III issued a bull that permitted Dominican friars to establish a mission in Morocco to serve Christians there. By 1246, Pope Innocent IV would appoint a bishop there to lead the Church of Africa.

1226

Duke Konrad I of Poland had sought the aid of the Teutonic Knights in his ongoing attempt to conquer the Baltic kingdom of Prussia, which was still partly pagan territory. The Teutonic Knights were no longer very active in the Holy Land and could now negotiate with other states on an equal footing.

1227

Stephen Langton, the archbishop of Canterbury, divided the Bible's books into numbered chapters in order to help locate and convey passages. The division of chapters into verses would come later.

Pope Gregory IX excommunicated Holy Roman emperor Frederick II for failing to honor his crusading pledge. The pope had expected him to travel to Egypt as part of the Fifth Crusade, but Frederick had not participated and was thereafter blamed by Pope Honorius III and many crusaders for the defeat.

1228

The Sixth Holy Land Crusade began. Although excommunicated, Holy Roman emperor Frederick II, already bearing the title of king of Jerusalem through family ties, arrived with his army at Acre by way of Cyprus. Except for the military monastic orders such as the Knights Templar and Knights Hospitaller, his support had dwindled due to his excommunication. He realized that if he was going to accomplish anything of value on this crusade, he would have to do it through diplomacy. The Egyptian sultan, occupied with putting down a rebellion in Syria, agreed to open Jerusalem, Nazareth, Sidon, Jaffa, and Bethlehem to the Franks. The Muslims retained control of all of Palestine's castles and fortifications and Islamic holy sites in Jerusalem. This arrangement resulted in a ten-year truce.

1229

Emperor Frederick II returned from the crusade and routed a papal army that had been sent to invade Sicily, which was under his control. Following the battle, he agreed to a truce with the pope.

The Council of Toulouse prohibited everyone except clerics from reading translations of the Bible. It also ordered that every parish should be monitored for heretical thinking and actions in response to the growing Cathar movement in the region.

1230

The Teutonic Knights, along with the duke of Masovia, launched the Prussian Crusade with the intention of Christianizing the stubborn Prussians. Those who didn't convert were suppressed, exiled, or killed. The conquest would take fifty years and lead to an independent Monastic State of the Teutonic Knights on the Baltic Sea.

1231

Physicians began to attend patients at the Hôtel-Dieu in Paris. They still had almost no effective medical treatment to offer, but the facility provided a place of physical comfort and emotional and dietary support and performed whatever surgical treatment the physicians could, including eye surgery, trepanation, bloodletting, tumor removal, bone setting, and bladder stone removal.

1233

A crusade was launched against the Stedingers, peasants on the German-Dutch border who refused to pay tithes to the archbishop of Bremen. The first crusade against them failed, but the following year a second campaign defeated them. This was a crusade against fellow Roman Catholics, not pagans or heretics.

Officials in Montpellier and Paris ordered the burning of Hebrew books, and some twelve thousand volumes of the Talmud were collected and burned.

Pope Gregory IX issued the bull *Licet ad capiendos*, which introduced an inquisition as the way to root out heretics. The French Inquisition would be a separate tribunal, independent of bishops and prelates, and operated by Dominican and Franciscan monks who were answerable only to the pope. Gregory insisted that those found guilty should suffer death by fire and the penitent be imprisoned. Burning at the stake became the preferred mode of execution for anyone who would not confess to a crime, failed in their previous penance, or relapsed into heresy.

Pope Gregory IX issued an edict entitled *Vox in Rama*. This was in response to a grand inquisitor, Conrad of Marburg, who was concerned about satanic cults in Germany. This document was the first to associate cats with witchcraft and vilify them as agents of the devil. Cats, especially black ones, were hunted down and killed as a result, which would haunt Europe in the next century when the bubonic plague struck and there were fewer cats left to kill the plague-spreading rats.

1234

The Council of Tarragona ruled that "no one may possess the books of the Old and New Testaments in the Romance language [Spanish, Portuguese, Italian, French, Romanian], and if anyone possesses them, they must turn them over to the local bishop within eight days after promulgation of this decree, so that they may be burned."

1235

Friar Julian and a group of Dominicans left Hungary to contact pagan Magyars who had remained in their homeland in what is present-day Ukraine. Julian was successful in finding them, but two years later, on a second journey, he learned that they had been overrun by Mongols.

1236

After being energized by the preaching of a new crusade, mobs in Bretagne, Anjou, and Poitou, in France, murdered three thousand Jews.

Mongols sacked the Christian stronghold of Ani, in Armenia, and left it in ruins. It had once been called the "City of 1001 Churches."

Pagan Samogitians and Semigallians defeated the Christian Livonian Brothers of the Sword at the Battle of Saule in present-day Lithuania and reclaimed territories that had taken Christian forces thirty years to conquer. Later, the defeated Livonian fighters would ally with the Teutonic Knights, who were soon to control much of the Baltic region.

1239

Using the forged *Donation of Constantine* to back his claim, Pope Gregory IX excommunicated Emperor Frederick II for the second time when he felt Frederick was threatening the Papal States. The pope called Frederick a heretic and organized a council to condemn him. Frederick responded by trying to capture or sink ships carrying bishops to the council.

Jesus's supposed crown of thorns, which was looted from Constantinople, arrived in Paris, and the city proclaimed itself "the second Jerusalem." Louis IX paid more than half of his annual budget to obtain the crown, and he built the magnificent Sainte-Chapelle to house it.

1240

Muslims had been living in Sicily for centuries, the remnants of Arabs, Persians, Berbers, and Sicilians who had converted. Holy Roman emperor Frederick II ordered that around sixty thousand of them be resettled on the Italian mainland, mostly around Lucera and Apulia.

King Louis IX of France, who later became Saint Louis, ordered an investigation of the Jewish Talmud in Paris, which would become known as the Trial of the Talmud. The Jewish holy book was convicted of heresy and blasphemy against Mary and Jesus Christ.

1241

The Council of Regensburg declared Frederick II the Anti-Christ, but Pope Gregory IX died this year, ending their feud.

A Mongol army reached Eastern Europe, pillaging Hungary and Poland and probing the borders of the Holy Roman Empire. They withdrew when the Great Khan died in Mongolia, and a successor had to be named.

Pope Celestine IV died sixteen days after being elected, and another pope would not be elected until 1243.

1242

More than twenty-four wagonloads of Jewish sacred books, about ten thousand volumes, were burned in a public square in Paris.

1244

Innocent IV became pope and renewed Gregory IX's demands for the return of Lombardy to the Papal States. Frederick II refused, and his agents encouraged plots against the pope's authority in the Papal States. Innocent had to flee Rome in disguise and found sanctuary in Lyon, France.

After the truce in the Holy Land expired, the Khwarezmian Turks took control of Jerusalem. The Mongols had driven them out of Persia, and the Turks were on their way to ally with the Egyptians.

A Mongol army under Yisaur attacked Syria. The Christian states of Aleppo and Antioch submitted to them and agreed to pay a tribute.

Hundreds of Cathar leaders were burned at the stake in Montsegur, France, after making their last stand against the pope's crusaders.

The Council of Narbonne ordered that in the sentencing of heretics, no husband should be spared because of his wife, nor wife because of her husband, nor parent because of helpless children, and no sentence should be mitigated because of sickness or old age.

1245

Pope Innocent IV granted inquisitors and their assistants the right to carry weapons and gave inquisitors the right to absolve their assistants from any acts of violence.

Innocent IV convened the First Council of Lyon, the Thirteenth Ecumenical Council, to deal with what he called "the five wounds of the church." In attendance were 150 bishops, three patriarchs, and the Latin emperor of Constantinople. The five wounds consisted of the inadequacies of the Church, the failure to recapture the Holy Land, the invasion of Hungary by the Mongols, the schism with the Eastern Church, and the conflict between the Church and the Holy Roman emperor. The pope also began to organize another crusade to the Holy Land.

c. Innocent IV sent the first Catholic mission to the Mongols to learn more about their intentions. Franciscan monk John of Plano Carpini was hosted by the khan of the Mongol Golden Horde and attended the inauguration of the Great Khan Guyuk in Karakorum. Two years after he set out, Carpini returned and reported that he was amazed by how many Christians attended the inauguration and that they held some of the highest state offices.

1246

The Mongols reduced Kiev, the capital of Russia and a prosperous city, to ruins.

1247

Dominicans Ascelin of Cremona and Simon of Saint-Quentin met with Mongol general Baiju in Armenia. Baiju found them so arrogant that he sentenced them to death, but they were saved by the intervention of the Baiju's superior, Eljigidei, who sent them back to Rome with a letter for the pope.

1248

The forces of King Ferdinand III of Castile captured Sevilla from the Moors. In 1236, Cordoba, less than one hundred miles away, had also fallen to the Christians.

Eljigidei, the viceroy of the Mongol Empire in the Near East, sent Nestorians to meet with King Louis IX of France and ask for an alliance in attacking Baghdad. By the time Louis's Dominican envoy arrived in Mongolia in 1250, the Great Khan had died, and his wife and regent wanted nothing to do with the plan, instead calling for a tribute from them.

The Seventh Crusade began with Louis IX of France leading a well-organized army from France to Cyprus. Once there, the Latin Empire in Constantinople requested the crusaders' aid against the Byzantines of the Nicene Empire. The Knights Templar also requested help in Syria against the Mongols. Louis, however, kept to his original plan of invading the Holy Land by way of Egypt. He landed in Damietta and had some initial success, but his army became bogged down for six months by the flooding Nile River. When he was able to take the offense again, he met defeat, and the Egyptians took him prisoner. He was later ransomed and eventually returned to the crusader city of Acre.

1249

The Teutonic Knights defeated the pagan Prussians in the Prussian Crusade. The Knights then moved against the Lithuanians.

Prince Birger Jarl of Sweden led an expedition into Finland, which became known as the Second Swedish Crusade. It was designed to root out the last remnant of paganism there.

1250

By this time, the Nicene Empire had defeated Greeks, Latins, and Bulgarians in the remnants of the Byzantine Empire, and the Byzantine government in exile had their sights set on recapturing Constantinople. The Nicene emperor was also trying to prevent a new crusade against him by publicly supporting a reunion of the divided eastern and western Churches.

c. At this time, if a priest spilled any wine during communion, he could be suspended from performing Mass. If wine fell on any cloth, that cloth had to be preserved as a relic, since it was believed to contain the actual blood of Jesus.

The Order of Saint Paul the First Hermit was founded to unite the hermits living in the forests of Hungary and Croatia.

c. The Christian world outside Europe spanned from Constantinople to Samarkand in Uzbekistan and from Alexandria, Egypt, on the Mediterranean Sea, to the border of Somalia, almost on the equator. Unfortunately, Christian territory would gradually shrink to insignificance in most of those regions over the next six centuries.

The Mamluk Sultanate came to power in Egypt and Syria. The Mamluks were a warrior class composed of mostly Christian children who had been enslaved during Egyptian conquests and converted to Islam. They would hold power in Egypt until the time of Napoleon's invasion six centuries later.

When Holy Roman emperor Frederick II died, his son Conrad IV became king of Germany, Italy, Sicily, and Jerusalem. Frederick's other son Manfred was named Prince of Taranto, a principality in southern Italy. While Manfred was trying to extinguish rebellions in southern Italy that were instigated by Pope Innocent IV, Conrad and his army became involved and limited Manfred's authority solely to his principality.

1251

Genghis Khan's grandson, Möngke Khan, had grown up with a Christian mother and grandmother, and during his rule, Christianity was the greatest religious influence in the empire. This Christian influence carried over to China during the Yuan dynasty. But Möngke, like his grandfather, believed in many paths to truth and that all religions were valuable in some ways and no one religion should criticize others and say they were the only way to truth.

While King Louis IX was believed to still be held prisoner in Egypt, the first Shepherds' Crusade was originated in France to rescue him. A disorganized rabble of thousands of peasants revolted against the Church and the nobility, who they thought had abandoned their king. They went on a rampage, attacking Christian clergy, Jews, and whomever else got in their way. They were rounded up and excommunicated before they even left France.

Hoping to end the crusader attacks on Lithuania, King Mindaugas, his wife, his court and many of his subjects converted to Christianity. Most citizens did not follow his example, and the entire country would not become Christianized until much later.

1252

In response to the killing of Peter of Verona, the papal inquisitor in Lombardy, Pope Innocent IV issued the papal bull *Ad extirpanda*, which sanctioned the use of torture and burning of heretics and witches. He also created an armed militia to enforce the rulings of the Inquisition.

1253

For the last two years, Pope Innocent IV had gradually been making his way south from Lyon. With Frederick II gone, he thought it was safe to return to Rome.

William of Rubruck, a Flemish Franciscan friar, departed Constantinople on a mission for Louis IX of France. Louis had heard that Sartak, the son of the Mongol leader Batu, was a Christian and decided to try to make contact and encourage him to attack the Muslims from the east. In the Ukraine, William discovered that neither Sartak nor Batu were interested in conversion, but they sent him on to Mongolia with two Nestorian priests. The Great Khan allowed William to preach but reportedly became tired of him because of his forcefulness and sent him home.

Robert Grosseteste, an English Franciscan bishop and theologian, died. He was reported to be the first Christian to suggest the use of the modern scientific method by which theories are proven experimentally by isolating and controlling variables. He may not have carried out experiments, but he did inspire Roger Bacon, who became one of the greatest medieval scientific scholars.

1254

The king of Armenia, Hethum I, traveled to Karakorum, the Mongol capital, to recognize Möngke Khan and form an alliance against the Muslims. Upon his return he encouraged the Frankish rulers in the Middle East to follow his example and submit to the Mongols.

Pope Innocent IV sent an army to the Castle of Gatta in Italy, where Roberto Patta da Giussano allowed heretics, most likely Cathars, to live under his protection. After Roberto surrendered, the papal forces burned his castle and all the heretics' houses. They also dug up the bones in the cemetery and burned them.

When his brother, Holy Roman emperor Conrad IV, suddenly died of malaria, Manfred of Taranto refused to surrender Sicily to the pope as Conrad had wanted. He also accepted the regency over Conrad's infant son Conradin. The pope then excommunicated Manfred. When Manfred tried to negotiate through papal emissaries, he became suspicious of their intentions and also of the papal military occupation of Campania in southern Italy. He fled south to Lucera, where he allied with the Saracens. When the pope sent an army south, Manfred defeated them at Foggia. Manfred then had control of Sicily and its possessions on the mainland.

The French expelled Jews from France and confiscated their property. They would eventually allow Jews to buy their way back into the country. The French Church and government would find this process profitable for them and repeat it over the next two centuries.

1255

A small boy was found dead in a well in Lincoln, England. Some of the townsfolk were convinced that he had been killed by Jews, although there was no supporting evidence. They arrested a local Jewish man and tortured him until he confessed to ritual murder, then arrested all the other Jews in the city and hanged at least eighteen of them. Like William of Norwich a hundred years earlier, young Hugh was proclaimed a saint. It was most likely the boy fell into the well while playing there.

1256

The pope granted inquisitors absolution if they used instruments of torture against their suspects.

1257

After years of intrigue and warring, Manfred crushed the papal army and brought the rebellions throughout Italy to an end. The following year, when a rumor circulated that the boy-king Conradin was dead, Manfred was crowned King of Sicily. When the rumor proved false, he chose not to abdicate and, over the next nine years, strengthened his influence.

1258

In this era, the Mongols were attacking along a vast front that extended from Lithuania to Korea. This year they destroyed Baghdad, the world's largest and most prosperous city, and ended the Abbasid Caliphate. They slaughtered at least ninety thousand people and burned the city's priceless library, the House of Wisdom. Since Cordoba had already fallen to the Christians, the intellectual innovations of the Islamic Golden Age came to an end. With Arabia no longer the center of the Muslim world, the region of Andalusia in southern Spain was the last refuge for free Saracens who traced their history directly to Muhammad.

1259

Michael VIII Palaiologos became the ruler of the Nicene Empire, the Byzantine government in exile. He revoked his predecessor's order of forced baptism and awarded Jews religious and economic liberties in return for their loyalty.

A combined force of Mongols and Christian Georgians, Armenians, and Franks led by Bohemond VI of Antioch captured Aleppo from the Muslims. Later, the Mongols seized Damascus, at this time, the capital of the Ayyubid dynasty.

The Mongol army moved westward and captured Damascus and Aleppo, where the local Christians welcomed them as liberators from the Muslims. The Christian's fantasy was a triple alliance—between the Mongols, the Byzantine Empire, and the crusaders—that would finally remove Islamic domination. When the Mongol khan died and the rival Mongol Golden Horde threatened their homeland in Persia, the army returned home, leaving behind Nestorian General Kitbuqa and an army of around ten thousand in Syria.

1260

With Kitbuqa's Mongol army in the region, the Mamluks assembled an army and moved north to meet them. The crusaders around Acre were caught between the two armies and pressured for an alliance on both sides. The crusaders opted to remain neutral but allowed the Mamluks to pass through their region unmolested. The Mamluks met the army of Kitbuqa at Ain Jalut, in Palestine, and the Mamluks crushed the Mongol army and forced them and their allies to retreat. The Mamluks seized the coastal cities from the crusaders and continued to Damascus, where they carried out a massacre of Christians.

The forces of the Nicene Empire, under Michael VIII Palaiologos, attacked Constantinople but were easily defeated. Michael realized he needed more naval forces to defeat the Venetian fleet that defended Constantinople. He turned to Genoa, which was already an enemy of Venice.

Gerard Segarelli sold his possessions and became an ascetic who announced that the Kingdom of Heaven was at hand. He eventually gathered a large following known as the Apostolic Brethren, who walked through Italian towns while singing hymns, subsisting on whatever people gave them to eat. This movement spread throughout Western Europe.

Archbishop of Genoa and Italian historian Jacobus da Varagine wrote the *Golden Legend*, a collection of hagiographies, or writings about the lives of the saints. It was extremely popular reading in medieval Europe and outsold previous best sellers about the saints.

1261

Constantinople was still in crusader hands and the seat of their Latin empire. Nicene forces were still active in the surrounding regions such as Nicea, Trebizond, and Epirus. Nicene emperor Michael VIII Palaiologos sent Alexios Strategopoulos to reconnoiter Constantinople with a force of about eight hundred men. Unexpectedly, they arrived when most of the Latin garrison and the Venetian fleet were raiding the Nicene-controlled Island of Daphnousia in the Black Sea. They gained entrance into Constantinople through a little-used gate, defeating the small Latin force that met them, and suddenly they had control of the city. The Latin residents fled in terror to the harbor, and the Nicenes set fire to the Venetian Quarter. The heart of the Byzantine Empire was restored, although the capital city was in ruins.

Michael VIII Palaiologos put an end to a rival bloodline and co-emperor by having eleven-year-old John IV Laskaris kidnapped and his eyes gouged out. This was the method used repeatedly in the Byzantine Empire to keep someone from serving as emperor. Palaiologos reported the kidnapping but shifted the blame elsewhere. When the truth came out, Patriarch Arsenius excommunicated Michael, but he stubbornly held on to power.

1264

Duke Boleslaw the Pious of Poland issued a charter to the Jews in his domain that stated that they would not be accused of ritual murder or blood libel. He also instituted punishments for anyone making such false accusations against a Jewish person. In return, Jews were obligated to defend Boleslaw in battle.

Pope Urban IV instituted Corpus Christi as an official feast day for the Catholic Church. This feast was to commemorate the joy of the Eucharist being the body and blood of Jesus Christ. The celebration was said to have been inspired by a priest who visited Oviedo, Spain, the previous year and witnessed the miracle of a bleeding communion wafer, or host. The word *host* is derived from the Latin *hostia*, meaning "sacrificial offering."

1265

Thomas Aquinas completed his four-volume *Summa contra Gentiles*, written to aid missionaries to the Muslims, Jews, and pagans. Aquinas avoided using scriptures as references because he didn't think his intended audience was familiar with Christian scripture.

c. The Mamluks, led by their Sultan Baibars, captured Caesarea from the Franks and destroyed this valuable seaport. Baibars then attacked the crusaders at Haifa, Ascalon, Safad, Jaffa, and Arsuf, capturing each city. The Franks fled to Acre to make their last stand.

The ring worn by popes, called the Ring of the Fisherman, was first mentioned in a letter written by Pope Clement IV. The ring was intended to be used to seal the wax on the pope's private correspondence, and today is an ornament infrequently worn, but the custom of kissing a pope's ring when meeting him carries over.

1266

Pope Clement IV still claimed Sicily and sold the kingship to Charles I of Anjou. His army met Manfred's at the Battle of Benevento, where Manfred was killed and his army defeated.

1267

Church leaders gathered for a synod in Breslau, Poland, with the goal of restricting the rights that Duke Boleslaw had recently bestowed on the Jewish population. The bishops ordered the Jews of Silesia to wear horned skullcaps as a distinguishing piece of clothing.

Baldwin II, still considering himself the rightful Latin emperor of Constantinople, transferred his title to Charles I of Anjou. With the pope's support, Charles began planning a new crusade to recover Constantinople but was thwarted when Byzantine emperor Michael VIII Palaiologos wrote to Charles's brother, King Louis IX of France, and convinced Louis to focus on retaking the Holy Land.

1268

The Mamluks captured the crusader state of Antioch. The city had been weakened by recent battles and power struggles and was not well defended. The result was the slaughter of some fourteen thousand Christians and the enslavement of another hundred thousand.

English Franciscan monk and philosopher Roger Bacon sent his most important work, *Opus Majus*, to his protector, Pope Clement IV. Since the pope died the same year, it is not known if he received it or read it. The book was a plea for church reform and explored how to incorporate Aristotelian science and logic into Christian theology. Bacon later spent as many as fourteen years in prison for his progressive ideas.

The Holy Roman Empire reached its largest geographic size and included Germany, Belgium, the Netherlands, eastern France, Switzerland, northern Italy, Corsica, Sardinia, and parts of what are now the Czech Republic, Austria, and Poland.

1269

The Polo brothers, Niccolo and Maffeo, were Italian merchants who had just returned to Venice from China where they had met Kublai Khan, the ruler of the Mongols. The khan, already partial to Christianity, had asked them to convince the pope to send a hundred teachers of science and religion to instruct the Mongols in the traditions of Europe. He said that if the teachers convinced him of the truth of their religion, he and his people would become Christians. He also requested a sample of oil from a lamp in the Church of the Holy Sepulchre.

1270

King James I of Aragon passed a law requiring his people to turn over for burning any Bibles that had been translated into Spanish. If anyone refused, they would be declared a heretic and subject to the appropriate punishment.

King Louis IX of France, who had been captured in the previous crusade, launched the Eighth Crusade to the Holy Land by landing an army in Tunisia. Many crusaders soon became sick from drinking contaminated water, and soon Louis died. Since he was already regarded as a saint, there was a struggle for his remains. Eventually, his son received his bones, and his brother received his entrails. This ill-fated crusade achieved some success in the form of a free trade agreement and a guarantee of protections for monks and priests who lived in North Africa.

c. A sect of Christians known as the Free Spirits had coalesced in central Europe. The most notable of their beliefs was that a perfected soul could attain oneness with God by reliance on the Holy Spirit alone, not through Christ.

1271

The Mongols returned to Syria and captured Aleppo but withdrew when the Mamluks marched against them.

The North African front of the Eighth Crusade continued as Prince Edward of England led an army from Tunis to Acre, but he arrived too late to break the siege against the French defenders. Later, a combined English and French army marched to Tripoli, (present-day) Lebanon, where tens of thousands of Christians had taken refuge, and successfully broke the siege there. Emboldened by new forces from England and Cyprus, Edward tried to form an alliance with the Mongols against the Mamluks and sent an army into northern Syria that displaced the Muslim population from the region. Baibars counter-attacked against Cyprus, but his fleet was defeated in a naval battle. The two sides signed a ten-year truce, and Edward returned to England, where he was crowned king.

The Polos, including seventeen-year-old Marco, returned to China. They brought the oil from the Church of the Holy Sepulchre as requested, along with a letter from the pope. But the Great Khan's main request was unfulfilled. Instead of a hundred educated men, only two friars had set out on the expedition. The journey proved too difficult for them, and both turned back before reaching China. Not fulfilling the khan's request may have been a colossal, missed opportunity in the history of Christianity, but there also were many risks involved if the pope did attempt to fulfill it, such as the clergymen not being able to survive the ordeal, the holy men not making the right impression on the khan, or possibly the khan dying before they arrived, and the Polos and their entourage being received by a hostile khan. Marco reportedly commented that "if the Pope had sent out persons duly qualified to preach the gospel, the Great Khan would have embraced Christianity, for which, it is certainly known, he had a strong predilection."

1272

Benita Zita, a very pious and much-abused servant, died in Italy. After her death, over a hundred miracles were attributed to her. In 1580, her body was exhumed and declared "incorrupt," and in 1696, she was venerated as the patron saint of maids and servants. She serves as an example of how certain noninfluential persons could become saints if miracles were attributed to them.

1274

The Dominican friar, priest, philosopher, and theologian Thomas Aquinas died. The previous year he had completed *Summa Theologica*, the theological masterpiece of the Middle Ages, which sought to reconcile Christian theology with classical Greek philosophy. He was often compared to Augustine for the significance of his contributions to Christian thought, but he was positive about the human condition, whereas Augustine was convinced of the basic depravity of humans. Aquinas was largely responsible for restoring faith in the power of reason by teaching that reason was a gift from God and intended for the purpose of understanding God. After he died, his body was decapitated, and his flesh was boiled away so monks could save his bones as relics.

The Second Council of Lyon was called to act on the pledge by Byzantine emperor Michael VIII Palaiologos to reunite the eastern and western Churches. Michael sought to prevent another crusade against Constantinople, so he agreed to all of Pope Gregory X's conditions. The council agenda also included the pope's call for another crusade to the Holy Land, but he was unsuccessful in gaining enough support. The Eastern Orthodox clergy never accepted the decisions of this council and did all they could to undermine them.

Giovanni di Fidanza, later known as Saint Bonaventure, died. He was a Franciscan theologian and philosopher, who had served at the highest level of Church leadership. He presided over the Franciscan order and played a significant role at the Council of Lyon in the attempt to unify Greek and Latin churches.

1275

When the people of Florence argued with Pope Gregory X's representatives over tribute payments, the pope excommunicated the entire city. When he died the next year, so did his excommunication of Florence.

A Nestorian archbishopric was established in the capital of the Yuan dynasty, Khanbaliq. The city had been founded by Kublai Khan and is now known as Beijing.

1276

In the "Year of Four Popes," after the death of Gregory X, Innocent V became pope, but died of natural causes 153 days later. Then Adrian V, not even an ordained priest, served for 38 days before succumbing to old age. Then, the fourth, John XXI, would serve only for 254 days before his apartment collapsed on him. It was not until Nicholas III in 1277 that a pope again reigned for more than a year.

1277

French crusaders took control of Acre after disputes with Hugh III of Cyprus, the Knights Templar, and the Venetians. Any hope of a united stand against the Muslims collapsed because the Venetians were only interested in retaking Constantinople.

Pope John XXI sent word to Stephen Tempier, the bishop of Paris, to investigate reported "errors" being taught at the University of Paris and discover who was at fault. Tempier, in the *Condemnations of Paris*, responded by prohibiting the teaching of 219 philosophically and theologically progressive ideas. His list was believed to have been directed at the Aristotelian teachings of Thomas Aquinas, who died three years earlier. One subject the bishop did not censor was the possibility of life existing elsewhere in the universe, even though his understanding of the universe was very rudimentary.

1280

c. Witch hysteria was on the rise, along with the first images of witches flying on broomsticks. The Church portrayed witches in league with the devil, stealing children, and engaging in inhuman practices. These characteristics were like the ways Jews were often portrayed. In fact, it is very likely that the pointed black hat imagined to be worn by witches, had antisemitic roots since in 1215, the Fourth Lateran Council had issued an edict for Jews to wear identifying clothing and headgear, and one form was the pointed Judenhat.

Pope Martin IV, a former French cardinal and a favorite of Charles of Anjou, was elected. When Michael VIII Palaiologos could not convince his clergy to unify the Church, the new pope excommunicated him and authorized Charles to begin planning a new crusade against Constantinople. Charles began to assemble a large army.

1281

There is evidence that a Nestorian military officer was in Japan. This is based on the finding a silver cross on a Mongol steel helmet there.

1282

Michael VIII Palaiologos instigated a revolt in French-controlled Sicily to draw the attention of Charles I of Anjou somewhere other than Constantinople. In the ensuing rebellion, the French were expelled from Sicily with great loss of life. The Sicilians were aided by Peter III of Aragon, who was declared King of Sicily.

With the death of Michael VIII, his son Andronikos II Palaiologos became emperor. He immediately repudiated the agreements of the Council of Lyon and restored Patriarch Joseph, who had been deposed by his father.

1283

After an accusation of ritual murder in Mainz, Germany, mobs attacked Jews, killing ten.

1284

Pope Martin IV launched the Aragonese Crusade against Peter III of Aragon to avenge Peter's recent conquest of Sicily. Martin's justification was that the island was a papal territory. The next year, Peter's forces would defeat the retreating French papal army at the Battle of the Col de Panissars in the Pyrenees Mountains of northern Spain.

The Mongolian Khan of Persia offered Pope Honorius IV an alliance against the Egyptians in the Holy Land, but nothing came of it.

1287

Kublai Khan defeated Manchurian Prince Nayan's army, which had gone into battle with a flag that displayed a Christian cross.

1288

Pope Nicholas IV ordered Dominican inquisitors in France to treat relapsed Jewish converts the same as heretics.

1290

King Edward I expelled all Jews from England. This ruling would not be overturned until 1655 when the Puritans came to power.

In Paris, a rumor started that the Jewish people were desecrating the communion host. Knowing that the host was the body of Jesus Christ, the accusation stemmed from the belief that Jews could torture Jesus endlessly by damaging holy bread. This charge became common not just in France but also in Germany and led to riots in which many Jews were killed.

1291

c. Khan Arghun of Mongolia sent envoys to King Edward I of England and King Philip the Fair of France. The envoys reported that Arghun wanted to aid Pope Nicholas IV in driving the Mamluks out of Syria and that when Jerusalem again fell into Christian hands, Arghun would become a Christian himself. He even named one of his sons Nikolya, after Pope Nicholas IV. Unfortunately for the Mongols, the last crusaders were being evicted from the Holy Land, and Europe was tiring of crusades.

The Mamluks defeated the Frankish crusaders at Acre and ended the Christian Crusades in the Holy Land. There was a mass evacuation of the city, with the Knights Hospitallers and Knights Templars moving to Cyprus and the Teutonic Knights migrating to Venice.

Raymond Lull, a Franciscan friar, traveled as a missionary to Tunisia and engaged in evangelism among the Muslims. He taught in Arabic, which he encouraged other European missionaries to learn. He also encouraged the conversion of Muslims by prayer, not by military force. Because of his efforts, the universities of Europe began to create programs for the study of the Hebrew, Arabic, and Aramaic languages.

Oliver of Tréguier justified the dismemberment of suspected saints by asserting that offering more relics to Christians would generate more prayers and a multitude of shrines where the relics could be displayed. Another reason for dismembering the bodies, according to Oliver, was to look for marks of sainthood. By the fifteenth century, it was normal to present evidence from an autopsy at the canonization of a saint. Any sign of sanctity that the examiner found unnatural could be a sign that the body was marked with holiness. Examples were an image of a cross somewhere inside the body, an enlarged heart being interpreted as full of God's love, a resistance to decay, or a sweet odor.

1293

With their Mongol and crusader wars ended, the Mamluks were free to launch a sixty-year persecution of Christians in their lands as revenge for Christian collaboration with the Mongols.

In Naples, Dominican priests spread anti-Jewish propaganda and forced Jews to convert or be expelled.

1294

Pope Nicolas IV sent Franciscan John of Montecorvino to the court of Kublai Khan. He arrived in China by way of India, becoming the first Roman Catholic missionary in China. He found the Nestorians already well-established in the region, but eventually he converted a Nestorian king, built Catholic churches, and translated the Bible into Uyghur, the common language of the Mongol ruling class. He directed his mission more at the Nestorian Christians than people of Eastern religions, but this rivalry apparently turned off the Mongols and most supported their Nestorian version of Christianity.

The hermit Peter de Murrhone had founded the order of Celestines, a branch of the Benedictines. This year he was elected Pope Celestine V, but he abdicated his office after just five months because he preferred monastic life. He may have been the first pope to abdicate because he also issued the edict that allowed a pope to do so.

1295

Mongol ruler Ghazan took the throne in Persia. To gain popular support, he converted to Islam, the religion of the Persians. Future Mongol khans would become Muslims, and they began a persecution of Christians and Buddhists that lasted for the next forty years.

Marco Polo returned from the Orient. He'd kept an extensive journal during his twenty-four years there, which became the basis for the popular book, *The Travels of Marco Polo*. He mentioned that he had encountered many communities of Christians living in the Far East.

1296

Former pope Celestine V died in prison. Since his resignation in 1294, his successor, Pope Boniface VIII, had kept him imprisoned in a castle to prevent him from being installed by schemers as an antipope.

1298

After Dominican friar Giordano da Rivalto accused Jews of host desecration, enraged Christians killed some twenty thousand Jews in a murderous spree throughout southern Germany.

1299

A papal bull prohibited crusaders from dismembering and boiling bodies to retrieve bones to be used as relics.

Invading Turkish tribes founded a state in Anatolia that would become the birthplace of the Ottoman Empire.

Bernard Délicieux, a Franciscan friar, led a revolt against inquisitors in Carcassonne, France. He was arrested and, under torture, confessed to obstructing the Inquisition. He was defrocked and sentenced to life in solitary confinement.

CHAPTER 14: FOURTEENTH CENTURY AD

As editor to the largest newspaper in West Virginia, I scan hundreds of reports daily and I am amazed by the frequency with which religion causes people to kill each other. It is a nearly universal pattern, undercutting the common assumption that religion make people kind and tolerant.

—James Haught

All religion seems to need to prove that it's the only truth. And that's where it turns demonic. Because that's when you get religious wars and persecutions and burning heretics at the stake.

—John Shelby Spong

Nation shall rise against nation, and kingdom against kingdom. There will be great earthquakes, famines, pestilences in various places, and fearful events and great signs from heaven.

—Jesus Christ (Luke 21:10–11)

This century appeared to be a sequel to the horrible events of the thirteenth century. The crusaders lost their last base within striking distance of the Holy Land. A major famine struck northern Europe, and the Black Death overwhelmed most of the continent, turning once fertile farmland into forests that spawned legends of demons, witches, and werewolves. Anti-Jewish hysteria filled Europe in the wake of the plague, and Christians conducted massive killing sprees against Jews and Muslims. Muslims reciprocated against Jews and Christians, and peasants revolted in Flanders, France, England, and Tuscany. Authorities became more brutal in their law enforcement, and more liberal in their use of torture, while burning people alive became more commonplace. As wars, taxes, poverty, famines, indulgences, and hereditary guilt took their toll on the average Christian in Europe, saints were called on more often for rescue, and saint shrines and relics became omnipresent. The Ottoman Turks rose to power in Asia Minor, Lithuania became the last European region to be coerced into accepting Christianity, and the Alexandrian and Nicopolis Crusades again targeted Muslims.

1300

Gerard Segarelli and his Apostolic Brethren had been banned from Parma, Italy, in 1286, but Gerard returned and was taken before the grand inquisitor of Parma. He was found guilty of relapsing into forbidden behavior and burned at the stake.

Christian forces sacked the Muslim colony at Lucera in southern Italy, and the residents were either exiled or sold into slavery. Many who escaped found asylum in Albania. French soldiers and farmers were brought in to replace the Muslims.

Pope Boniface VIII promoted the idea of a "jubilee" year, or holy year. It was the thirteenth centennial of Jesus's birth and the first such celebration to take place in Rome. His motive is uncertain, but he granted full indulgences for those who traveled to Rome and attended the city's basilicas for fifteen consecutive days. Citizens of Rome were required to visit the sites for thirty days for similar pardons, and offerings were expected at every shrine.

c. The earliest known depiction of the legend of the Pied Piper of Hamelin was installed in a stained-glass window in the church in Hamelin, Saxony. The story is thought to have originated from a local rat infestation and fear of the plague. The Pied Piper lured the rats out

of town to protect the townspeople, but when he wasn't paid for this
service, he returned and lured the town's children away.

1301

King Philip IV of France sent reformers to Languedoc to curb the excesses of Foulques de Saint-Georges, the inquisitor of Toulouse. These
included arresting women for no apparent reason other than to sexually abuse them.

c. Due to the persecution of Christians, Egypt's population became
predominantly Muslim.

c. Painted scenes of the crucifixion of Jesus began to reflect the more
graphic and emotional aspects of Jesus's suffering, such as being nailed
to the cross or entombed. They also began to show a swooning or
fainting Mary at the scene.

1302

Pope Boniface VIII issued the papal bull *Unam sanctam*, which laid
out the necessity of belonging to the Catholic Church to achieve eternal salvation, the status of the pope as supreme head of the Christian
Church, and the necessity to submit to the pope in order to belong
to the Church. The pope gave himself the power to prohibit the distribution of sacraments within the secular realm, to excommunicate
anyone, and even to depose royalty. This was a haughty agenda, but
nothing new for the papacy.

The encroaching Ottoman Turks defeated the Byzantines at the Battle
of Bapheus near Nicea. In effect, the Byzantines had lost Asia Minor,
and the Ottomans began to set down roots there.

1303

The Mamluks defeated an allied army of Mongols and Christian
Cilician Armenians at the Battle of Shaqhab in Syria. The Mamluks

made the Armenians pay dearly for their alliance, and by 1375, the Armenian kingdom of Cilicia no longer existed.

The last remaining Latin foothold in the Middle East was lost with the fall of the crusader garrison on Ruad Island off the coast of Syria.

King Philip IV of France levied heavy taxes on the French clergy, but Pope Boniface VIII resisted Philip's efforts to transfer church property to the French government and excommunicated him. Philip then had Boniface arrested and beaten, and shortly later he died of his wounds.

1304

Ephesus surrendered to the Ottoman Turks, but the Turks didn't observe the terms of surrender. They massacred or deported all Christians and pillaged the church of Saint John. The emerging power of the Ottoman Empire began to allow them to influence events on the Mediterranean coast.

In Zhenjiang, near the Yellow Sea in China, Taoists accused Nestorians of converting other Taoists to Christianity. At this time, there was a growing Buddhist resentment toward the Nestorians, and this helped precipitate a decree in 1311 to transfer Nestorian monasteries to Buddhist monks.

1305

With the aid of King Philip IV, Frenchman Raymond Bertrand de Got became Pope Clement V. He was coronated in Lyon, France, and one of his first acts was to appoint nine new French cardinals. He refused to move to Rome.

1306

After Boniface's treatment by the king of France, Clement V nullified the *Unam sanctam*, the papal bull from four years earlier that asserted papal supremacy over secular rulers.

c. Philip IV seized all Jewish property and expelled Jews from France, likely so he could use their assets to finance his wars. He did the same to Lombard bankers.

1307

The Inquisition executed Friar Dolcino, the leader of the Apostolics, a reformist movement in Italy. He had taken over leadership after Gerard Segarelli was executed. The Dulcinians fiercely opposed ecclesiastical hierarchy and the feudal system and advocated for human rights for the poor. The Church had branded them heretics and sent crusaders against them. The Dulcinians turned to guerrilla warfare in their battle against Catholic forces.

Pope Clement V issued a bull for the arrest of the Knights Templar. King Philip IV of France arrested hundreds of Templars—including some to whom he owed money—ostensibly for the crimes of devil worship, heresy, and conspiracy.

1309

French-born Pope Clement V established his papacy in Avignon, France. This was in response to what he saw as a chaotic environment in Rome, and it would place him closer to his protector, King Philip IV. The Avignon papacy would last for sixty-seven years and through seven popes. The move led to a great loss of revenue for Rome and a decline in influence for the bishops in Rome.

In a dispute over Italian territory, Pope Clement V excommunicated all the citizens of the city-state of Venice, and when Venitian troops refused to withdraw from the conquered city of Ferrara, Clement declared a crusade against Venice. Ironically, Venice had been the state that had answered the calls to crusade more than any other in Europe. When disease struck the Venetians in Ferrara, they were easily defeated and three years later bought absolution from their excommunication.

1310

The Knights Hospitallers conquered the island of Rhodes and established it as their new headquarters.

During a persecution of non-Muslims, the Assyrian Christian inhabitants of Erbil, in northern Iraq, retreated to the city's citadel for protection. The governor of the region took the citadel and massacred every defender and refugee.

King Philip IV was anxious to punish the imprisoned Knights Templars, so he took the initiative of having dozens of them burned at the stake in Paris.

c. Marguerite Porete, a French mystic and a member of the semimonastic Beguines, wrote the book *The Mirror of Simple Souls*, about achieving oneness with God through love. It was written in Old French, not common Latin like most religious texts. The book explained the mystical "heresy of the Free Spirit," which was denounced by the Church. Some bishops judged Marguerite's book heretical and condemned it, and Marguerite was tried and burned at the stake. Her book had many adherents at the time and gained renewed popularity after being rediscovered in 1946.

1311

Pope Clement V accused the Beguines and their male counterparts, the Beghards, of heresy and immorality. They would be suppressed under the next three popes until rehabilitated by Pope Eugene IV in the next century.

Pope Clement V called the Council of Vienne to decide the fate of the Knights Templar order. The bishops voted against suppressing the Templars, and those outside France were found innocent of the charges against them. Templar survivors fled to Portugal, where they founded the Order of Christ in 1319, which is still active.

1315

In Bologna, Italy, Mondino de Liuzzi conducted the first officially sanctioned public dissection since Herophilus in third century BC. The fact that the Church did not object was a sign of the gradual influence of scholasticism. Latin was the language of scholasticism, so scientific knowledge spread easily throughout Europe, and Latin is still the world's scientific language.

King Louis X ended slavery in France and declared that any slave who set foot on French soil would be freed.

1317

Pope John XXII issued a bull ordering Jews to wear badges on their chests. Since he was an Avignon pope, his decrees may not have been observed outside France.

1318

The Fraticelli, or Spiritual Franciscans, revolted against the authority of the Church. They were radical proponents of the rule of Saint Francis of Assisi, especially with regard to poverty, and they regarded the wealth of the Church as scandalous. The pope declared them heretics and excommunicated them. Later, he had their villages burned, and executed many of them.

1319

The bishop of Rochester, England, required a man caught in adultery to provide a three-pound candle each year for Saint Andrew's feast day and to make a pilgrimage to Thomas Becket's shrine in Canterbury. These actions would absolve the man from his sins and serve as an interesting example of the creative ways that church leaders assigned penance.

1320

Pope John XXII authorized the Inquisition to prosecute witches and sorcerers. He also banned all Jewish writing and carried out a new round of Jewish book burning.

A second Shepherds' Crusade began when a teenage French shepherd said he had been visited by the Holy Spirit and told to fight the Moors in Iberia. A mob under his influence traveled to Paris to ask the king to lead them. After he refused, the peasants pillaged their way south, attacking and killing Jews in several cities and even ransacking some Christian churches. When they crossed into Spain and began killing Jews there, King James II of Aragon executed their leaders and sent the rest home.

c. Bernard Gui, a French Dominican friar, bishop, and papal inquisitor, wrote an Inquisition manual concerning witches. Magic had always been accepted in most cultures, but this was the first time the Christian Church distinguished between good magic and harmful magic. Gui accused witches of working for the devil, changing shapes, and flying at night, which caught the attention of many uneducated and superstitious people, including clergymen.

1321

In France, during the Shepherds' Crusade, rumors circulated that lepers were poisoning wells in order to kill Christians. Under torture, authorities forced a leper to confess that Jews were behind the conspiracy, and as a result, some lepers and Jews were burned, and many lepers and foreigners were arrested or expelled.

Muslim mobs looted and destroyed Coptic churches and monasteries across Egypt. The riots began in Cairo and spread throughout the country.

Dante Alighieri completed his book *The Divine Comedy*, in which he described the soul's path to God and his fictitious journey through purgatory, hell, and into paradise. He portrayed the eternal destiny of various classes of people, and his description of a fiery hell, known as "Dante's inferno," still captures the imagination of Westerners to this day.

The Inquisition executed Guillaume Bélibaste, the last known Cathar leader in southern France, and thereafter, no Cathars exist in the historical record.

1322

Thirty of Friar Dolcino's disciples, the Dulcinians, we burned alive in the marketplace in Padua, Italy.

1323

The incongruity of an extravagantly wealthy Church representing the ideals of Jesus Christ, the poor carpenter, prompted John XXII's papal bull *Cum inter nonnullos*, which proclaimed it heresy to say that Jesus and his apostles owned no property.

1324

Italian scholar Marsilius of Padua published one of the most important books of the late Middle Ages, titled *Defender of Peace*. In this book, he argued that the purpose of the state was to guarantee peace and the Church should not have power over secular affairs. There was more freedom to voice such ideas in Italy's relative safety since the popes were residing in Avignon.

After Alice Kyteler was accused of having sex with a demon, she fled Ireland. Her maidservant Petronilla de Meath was then arrested, tortured, and made to confess to witchcraft. The maidservant was the first recorded person to be convicted of witchcraft in Ireland and was burned at the stake.

1326

The Ottomans captured the city of Bursa in Anatolia, about a hundred miles from Constantinople. They established their seat of government there and began plans for an invasion of Europe.

Meister Eckhart was a prominent German theologian, preacher, and mystic. The archbishop of Cologne turned him over to the Inquisition because of Eckhart's various mystical teachings, which the archbishop thought contradicted scripture. After an investigation, Eckhart was determined to have orthodox beliefs, but his detractors wouldn't relent. He traveled to Avignon to have the pope judge his case but died before a verdict was reached.

1327

Cecco d'Ascoli was a scholar and empirical researcher who was at odds with the Church on several important issues. He was arrested on the accusation of impiety for apparently trying to determine the birthday of Jesus by examining the savior's horoscope and also for failing to believe in miracles. He was declared guilty and burned in Florence. He was the first university scholar to be burned by the Inquisition.

Richard of Wallingford became the abbot of Saint Albans monastery in England. It was tradition, based on Benedict's Rule, for the monks to pray seven times a day, and keeping track of those times was the original incentive for the invention of clocks. There had been other clocks in England, dating back to Dunstable in 1283, with no hands, only a device to ring bells. But Richard's was different. His was the most sophisticated machine since the Antikythera mechanism of late second century BC. It tracked the position of the sun, moon, planets, and stars; predicted lunar eclipses; and even forecast the tides in the River Thames. It was meant to demonstrate the divine order of the cosmos and was still running two centuries later.

1328

After being driven into an anti-Jewish frenzy by the preaching of Franciscan monk Pedro Olligoyen and others, mobs in Navarre, Spain, attacked and killed more than five thousand Jews.

After a long-running feud with Pope John XXII over who had authority over the other, Holy Roman emperor Louis IV led his forces into Rome and installed Nicholas V as his antipope. John XXII remained in Avignon.

The pope excommunicated William of Ockham, a Franciscan friar, and one of the major theological thinkers of his time. His misdeeds included leaving Avignon without permission and arguing that Pope John XXII was a heretic for attacking both the doctrine of apostolic poverty and the Rule of Saint Francis. Luckily, William was protected by the Holy Roman emperor in these disputes. His reputation within the Church was restored after he died, and he is remembered today for his philosophical theory known as "Occam's razor," which states that if there were two ways to explain a certain concept, the one involving the fewest variables (in other words, the simplest) is most likely the correct explanation. The term *razor* refers to the shaving away of unnecessary assumptions to distinguish between different hypotheses.

Andronikos III Palaiologos became the Byzantine emperor. His empire was so weak, and he was so desperate for help that he turned to the Turks for aide in fighting the Serbs and Bulgarians.

1330

Pope John XXII sent Dominican missionary Jordanus to Quilon in southern India to convert the people and try to bring the Thomas Christians into the Catholic flock.

c. It's estimated that only 5 percent of Europeans received any form of education at this time, and the individuals who did were mainly the sons of the wealthiest citizens. The Church still provided most of the education because there were still very few universities.

1336

Pope Benedict XII in Rome, issued *Benedictus Deus,* redefining the path to heaven by stating that departed souls were transported directly to heaven without waiting in any kind of limbo.

1337

The Hundred Years' War began. This was a series of separate engagements, marked by multiple truces, fought between England and France and their various allies for control of the French throne. The war would separate England and France politically for the first time in three centuries, and the English language would become the official language of England in 1362, after almost three centuries of the ruling class speaking French.

1338

People in Alsace, France, blamed Jews for failed crops, bad weather, pestilence, and whatever else they could think of. John Zimberlin, who was considered a prophet, said he received a divine calling to murder Jews to avenge the death of Christ. He led a band of outlaws known as *Judenschlaeger* ("Jew-beaters"), who rampaged through Alsace for weeks, evading the imperial troops sent to contain them. They were said to have attacked over 120 Jewish communities and murdered over 1,200 Jews.

1339

The *Gottesfreunde,* or Friends of God, was a lay group of mystics organized this year in Germany. Growing out of the teachings of Meister Eckhart, their beliefs were similar to the Free Spirit groups, such as the Beghards. The Friends of God movement was very popular but lasted only until around 1393, when its leaders were burned at the stake in Vienna for heresy.

1342

Franciscan friars took over custody of the Christian shrines in the Holy Land and popularized the "stations of the cross," commemorating various events that the Gospels and Church tradition portrayed happening to Jesus on his way to his death on Calvary Hill. The hill received its name due to its contours. Calvary comes from the Latin word *calva*, meaning "skull." The hill is also sometimes called *Golgotha*, the Aramaic word for skull.

1343

Pope Clement VI issued the bull *Unigenitus Dei filius* (Only Begotten Son of God) in which he declared the power of the pope to issue indulgences. The bull also reduced the time between Great Jubilees from one hundred years to fifty years.

1347

Refugees from Genoese colonies on the Black Sea are thought to have brought the bubonic plague to Western Europe. The disease eventually killed up to one third of the European population, as many as twenty-five to fifty million people. Many Christians were taught that God was punishing them for allowing Jews to live in Christian lands. Between the wars, famine, papal schism, and then the "Great Pestilence," it was easy to think the Apocalypse was approaching. This spurred the sense of urgency in some to convert Jews to Christianity to fulfill prophesy.

1348

Officials in Savoy, Italy, became the first to formally accuse Jews of causing the plague by poisoning wells. Every Jew in the town was arrested, and their property was confiscated. Officials tortured prisoners until they confessed to crimes they had not committed and then burned eleven of them alive. As news spread, mobs of Christians in other towns began dragging Jews from their homes and treating them similarly.

Having first appeared in Italy in 1259, the Flagellants, a Christian zealot sect, peaked at this time in reaction to the spread of the plague. They traveled from village to village reciting prayers. When they entered a town, the men would strip to the waist and whip themselves brutally to atone for sins. They also were known to incite mobs to attack and murder Jews. In the eyes of some of their observers, they took on the status of heroes, even saints.

In Strasbourg, the townspeople dragged the Jewish population of more than two thousand to the Jewish cemetery, and unless they converted to Christianity, the townspeople burned them. Only a few submitted to baptism. In a similar event hundreds of Jews were also burned at Chillon Castle in Switzerland after admitting under torture to poisoning wells. More than 60 large and 150 small Jewish communities were destroyed as a result of these spurious accusations. Jacob von Königshofen, a German chronicler of the time, said, "The money was indeed the thing that killed the Jews. If they had been poor and if the feudal lords had not been in debt to them, they would not have been burnt."

In Bavaria, ten thousand Jews were killed and nearly eighty Bavarian Jewish communities were eliminated. Their synagogues were turned into churches.

Pope Clement VI issued the papal bull *Quamvis Perfidiam*, which condemned the violence against the Jews and stated that those who blamed the plague on them had been "seduced by that liar, the devil." The pope ignored his advisors and stayed in Avignon during the outbreak, supervising care for the sick, coordinating burials, and providing pastoral care of the dying.

When the plague hit Venice, the leaders came up with a plan to place the sick on a separate island for forty days. If they were healthy after that time, they could return to the city, but few of the thousands sent there ever returned. The forty-day waiting period was known in Italy as *quaranta,* and that's the root of the English word *quarantine.* This number was significant. It was like the forty-day or forty-year waiting periods often referred to in the Bible, thought by some to have been derived from the celestial cycle, since there are about forty days of waiting after the solstices and equinoxes before the weather changes significantly.

1350

Saint Bridget of Sweden and her entourage went to Rome for the jubilee year. Bridget was a mystic who founded the Brigittine Order of nuns and monks. She would remain in Rome for twenty years before receiving the pope's approval for her order. She was extremely popular in Rome because of her kindness and charitable works. Her visions of the birth of Jesus greatly influenced later artistic depictions of the nativity, such as showing Jesus emitting light.

The Nestorian expansion across Asia reached its zenith with more than fifteen million Nestorian Christians living there.

Pope Clement VI granted remission of sins to all who had died of the plague. Since keeping up with burials was impossible, he also sanctified the water of the Rhône River in France so that bodies thrown into the river would be considered to have had a Christian burial.

The Black Death pandemic had run its course in Europe. Societies in many countries, such as Italy, were so devastated that they had to be recreated. This was one of the factors leading to the Italian Renaissance.

1351

A civil war began for control of the Byzantine Empire. Co-emperor John VI Kantakouzenos shipped ten thousand Ottoman Turks to Europe to fight for him. He defeated the forces of Emperor John V Palaiologos, but once safely in Europe, the Turks would not return to

the Asian side of the Bosporus and were in the perfect position to invade Eastern Europe.

1354

Islamization of Egypt reached its peak when Muslim mobs demanded
that Coptic Christians and Jews agree to the Muslim pledge of faith or
be burned alive.

Emperor John V Palaiologos deposed John VI Kantakouzenos after another Byzantine civil war.

1355

c. The first known appearance of the burial cloth of Jesus, with his
image mysteriously imprinted on it, was seen in a church in Lirey,
France. Knight and author Geoffrey de Charny was the owner and
proclaimed it to be the Holy Shroud, later known as the Shroud of
Turin. Apparently, no one ever learned how or where he acquired
it, but rumors indicated that the shroud was found during the sacking of Constantinople. The shroud was said to produce miraculous
cures. Modern carbon dating revealed that the fabric and image—
showing how Jesus would have been depicted in the fourteenth
century—originated at about this time.

1357

An unknown author published *The Travels of Sir John Mandeville.*
This book documented the travels of an Englishman journeying to
Jerusalem. It was both a travel and a spiritual guide that linked the
events in the life of Jesus with the places where they happened.

1365

The Alexandrian Crusade was launched by King Peter I of Cyprus. He
landed an army in Egypt and sacked Alexandria, then withdrew. This

was most likely a preemptive strike to prevent an Egyptian invasion of Cyprus.

An anonymous English author wrote *The Cloud of Unknowing*, a mystical guidebook for those dedicated to a life of contemplation, in which God is discovered only after emptying one's mind of any conception or image of a god. The work became increasingly popular centuries later, even into the twentieth century.

1366

Damascus became the seat of the Eastern Orthodox Church of Antioch, also known as the Antiochian Orthodox Church, where it remains today.

The rulers of Florence decided that all captives of infidel origin, even if they had converted to Christianity before their arrival, could be legally held as slaves.

1368

The Yuan dynasty ended, and the Ming dynasty began with the overthrow of the Mongol regime founded by Kublai Khan in Khanbaliq (now Beijing), China. The Chinese then began to persecute religious minorities, including Nestorians, and they destroyed Nestorian monasteries in the process.

c. After his parents died, a young Frenchman named Roch declined to serve as governor of Montpellier and sold his worldly goods and went to Rome as a pilgrim. After arriving in Italy at the time of the plague, he devoted himself to tending to the sick and is credited with many miraculous cures. He later became ill himself and returned to France, where he was arrested as a spy and sent to prison until he died around the age of twenty-eight. He was later venerated as a saint.

1369

The Ottomans captured Adrianople, the important city about two hundred miles northwest of Constantinople and made it their European capital. At the time, Byzantine emperor John V Palaiologos was in Venice seeking support against the Turks but found himself under house arrest until he paid the Venetians what he owed them.

1370

Pope Urban V returned the papacy to Avignon, France, after a three-year hiatus in Rome.

The Turko-Mongol leader Timur, aka Tamerlane, took power. He possessed a thorough hatred of Christians and Jews and began his quest to rid Asia of them in probably the world's most brutal ethnic cleansing.

1372

With Constantinople surrounded by Turks, John V Palaiologos, who had returned from Venice, did as the Bulgars and Serbs had done; he declared himself and his city a vassal of the Ottoman Empire. The once great capital of the Byzantine Empire was being controlled primarily by the Turks and wealthy Genoese and Venetian merchants. The only lands the Byzantines still ruled were a few ports in Thrace, northern Greece; part of the Greek Peloponnesian Peninsula; and a few islands.

1374

Francesco Petrarch, an Italian poet, scholar, and priest, and the recognized founder of humanism, died. Humanism challenged the withdrawal of men and women from society for religious fulfillment and restored the ancient classical ideal of their active involvement in city life. Petrarch's rediscovery of the letters of first century BC Roman statesman and scholar Cicero, written to various influential people, was credited with helping to initiate the Italian Renaissance. Petrarch was the first person to refer to a "Dark Age" of superstition and ignorance, which Europe was gradually trying to climb out of. He wrote: "Amidst the errors there shone forth men of genius; no less keen were their eyes, although they were surrounded by darkness and dense gloom."

1375

The War of the Eight Saints began between Pope Gregory XI and a coalition of Italian city-states led by Florence. The war started because Florence resisted the expansion of the Papal States but ended with a treaty in the pope's favor three years later.

1376

Nicholas Eymerich, a Spanish inquisitor, wrote the *Directorium Inquisitorium*. In this book, he wrote, "In our days there are no more rich heretics . . . it is a pity that so salutary an institution as ours should be so uncertain of its future," apparently implying that the inquisitions were running out of wealthy people to target.

Against the wishes of the king of France—and largely because of the pleas, demands, and threats of Catherine of Siena—Pope Gregory XI left Avignon to reestablish the papacy in Rome. He was the last of the popes of French descent.

1377

John Wycliffe, an Oxford theologian, preached that the Church had fallen into sin. He urged the Church to give up its property and the clergy to live in poverty. He attracted the attention and condemnation of Pope Gregory XI.

In retribution for small Italian city-states revolting against papal control, Pope Gregory XI sent a band of mercenaries to punish them. Cardinal Robert, the leader of the mercenaries, swore an oath to be lenient to the people of Cesena, but once inside the city walls, his men killed five thousand townspeople, all fellow Christians. The following year Cardinal Robert was rewarded by being elected as Antipope Clement VII.

1378

After Frenchman Pope Gregory XI died in Rome, a Roman mob surrounded the conclave to pressure the cardinals to elect an Italian pope. Shortly after the forced election of Urban VI, who was an Italian, most of the cardinals fled town. Based on his temperament and actions in the ensuing months, many cardinals judged Urban VI mentally unstable. Five months later, the cardinals proclaimed Urban VI's election invalid and withdrew from Rome to Fondi where they elected Robert of Geneva, the militant cleric, as the new pope. He became Pope Clement VII and started a new line of Avignon popes. Thus, began the Western Schism with two separate lines of popes, one living in Rome and the other in Avignon, and secular leaders had to decide which claimant to support. This division would last until the Council of Constance in 1417.

During the schism, Catherine of Siena, still only thirty years old and said to possess a remarkable ability at reconciliation, was summoned by Pope Urban VI to Rome. She was somewhat of a celebrity papal advisor and envoy, besides being a compassionate caregiver. She remained in Rome working for Church reform and helping the afflicted and destitute.

1380

Catherine of Siena withered away and died by denying herself food and water. She had been obsessed with Jesus, and it's suspected that she brought on her own death at the age of thirty-three since that was the age Jesus was when he died. She also modeled her life on a legend of Mary Magdalene, which claimed that Mary engaged in intensive fasting to purify herself. Catherine hoped fasting would end her menstrual cycles and also allow her body to be light enough to more easily float up to heaven. Her relics are still on display in Siena, Italy.

c. The Ottoman Empire formed an elite corps of infantry known as the Janissaries. The corps was composed of Christian boys who had been captured and then raised as Muslims, very similar to the Mamluks in Egypt. They were renowned for their unit's cohesiveness and strict discipline.

1381

Oxford University dismissed John Wycliffe for his criticism of the Church and the doctrine on the Eucharist. His followers were known as Lollards, a term of uncertain origin but probably meaning uneducated. Their ideas and passion would later influence reformers such as Jan Hus and Martin Luther.

1382

John Wycliffe's English translation of the Bible became available. His translators had worked from the Vulgate, the standard Latin Bible of the time, and the Wycliffe Bible was the first new one to use Stephen Langton's concept of numbered chapters.

1383

After a church burned in Wilsnack, Germany, the priest had a dream that directed him to search a certain location in the ruins. There he said he found three white hosts, still intact despite the fire and subsequent rain, each with a drop of blood in the center. Because of this miracle, Wilsnack became a pilgrimage site, drawing as many as a hundred thousand pilgrims a year by 1470. This made it the fourthmost visited pilgrimage site after Rome, Jerusalem, and Santiago de Compostela. Later reformers such as Jan Hus and Nicholas of Cusa discouraged this pilgrimage, suspecting fraud. The sacred hosts would be destroyed in 1552 during the Protestant Reformation.

The rulers of the Spanish kingdoms of Castile and León ordered a change to their dating system, which was based on the birth year of Jesus being 38 BC. The edict required them to align with the dating system of the rest of Europe, but neighboring Portugal wouldn't adopt Europe's system until 1422.

1384

John Wycliffe died. He had been a champion of challenging the hierarchy and the wealth of the Church, the power and historical authority of the popes, Church tradition, the widening division between clergy and laymen, the corruptions of monasticism, and immorality of priests that should have invalidated their office and sacraments. He was popular enough to escape the wrath of the Church until he died.

1385

Grand Duke Jagiello of Lithuania was baptized. This made Lithuania the last country in Europe to convert to Christianity, ending paganism in Europe except for those who practice their religion in secret. It had taken almost exactly a thousand years to accomplish what Emperor Theodosius I had set out to do in making Christianity the official religion of the Roman Empire and almost six hundred years since Charlemagne set out to bring most of Europe under the Christian banner.

1386

English author Geoffrey Chaucer wrote *The Canterbury Tales*, the still-popular stories describing a group of pilgrims journeying to the shrine of Thomas Becket.

1389

c. Reports spread that a sealed sample of the blood of Saint Gennaro (aka Januarius), who was believed to have been martyred during the Diocletian persecution of the fourth century, had spontaneously liquified. Over the next two centuries, the blood would continue to "melt" twice a year, and later, even three times a year. There are reports that several vials of congealed blood from other saints still occasionally liquify in the region around Naples.

1390

c. The Church of the East in Mesopotamia collapsed as it had in Mongolia, China, central Asia, and Persia. After this, it survived in only Kurdistan, Azerbaijan, Armenia, and Kerala, India, where it had been able to escape Mongolian Timur Khan's fury.

Archdeacon Ferrand Martinez, the administrator of the diocese of Sevilla and confessor to the queen mother, called for the razing of synagogues and the destruction of the Jews. His anti-Jewish fervor spread to most of Spain. In Sevilla alone, as many as four thousand Jewish people were executed, and the entire persecution may have resulted in as many as fifty thousand Jews being killed. Jews were easy to distinguish due to the brightly colored badges that they had been forced to wear on their outer clothing.

Bishop Pierre d'Arcis wrote to Antipope Clement VII, stating that the burial cloth of Jesus, now believed to be the Shroud of Turin, was a hoax and that the artist had confessed. This may have been true, or it may have been a ploy to lower the number of pilgrims visiting the shroud and increase the number visiting Pierre's cathedral instead.

1392

Leaders in Bern, Switzerland, expelled Jews from the city after the city government permitted Christians to engage in moneylending.

1396

During the Nicopolis Crusade in Bulgaria, the Ottomans devastated an ill-disciplined and overconfident Christian army.

1399

The Turko-Mongolian conqueror Timur led a bloody military campaign into the Middle East. His intent was to reestablish Mongol
rule over the entire former empire of Genghis Khan. Once entering
Anatolia, his enemy was the Ottoman Turks, who were also Muslims.
His military campaigns are estimated to have caused the deaths of
more than seventeen million people, and he took great satisfaction in
marking his route of destruction with pyramids made from his victims' severed heads.

CHAPTER 15: FIFTEENTH CENTURY AD

The City can expect help neither from inside or outside. Funds and men are lacking since the City has been
tortured for so long by its great poverty, lack of men,
attacks of the enemy, and fear of the bitter realization
of what is to become of us. Our only hopes are the merciful and compassionate God, should He return, spare,
and defend us, and the pure, ever-Virgin Mother of God.
—Theodore Agallianos of Constantinople

I hope, by God's grace, that I am truly a Christian, not
deviating from the faith, and that I would rather suffer
the penalty of a terrible death than wish to affirm anything outside of the faith or transgress the commandments of our Lord Jesus Christ.
—Jan Hus

Christianity was practically a failure. . . . The Church . . .
instead of elevating man it had been dragged down to
his level.
—Henry Charles Lea

The sovereigns before three years, will undertake and
prepare to go conquer the Holy Sepulchre; for thus I
urged Your Highnesses to spend all the profits of this
my enterprise on the conquest of Jerusalem.
—Christopher Columbus

Popes launched crusades to Varna, Belgrade, Bohemia, and Otranto. The Latin monopoly on the Bible was broken in Western Europe. The printing press was invented and led to a quantum leap in communication. After a thousand years of Roman control, the capital city of Constantinople was conquered by the Turks. The Age of Discovery began with the loss of a land route to the Far East, the continued desire for spices and precious metals, the commission to spread Christianity throughout the world, and the quest for personal fame in discovering new lands. Columbus reached America, and Spain began a reign of terror, including forced conversions of the native inhabitants. Jews continued to be terribly mistreated. The Christian Church in Asia went into a downward spiral, and Jan Hus left the Church and introduced his form of Protestantism in Bohemia.

1400

c. With the decline of Christian churches in Asia due to intolerant rulers, Western Europe, for the first time, became the epicenter of the Christian world.

1401

The English statute De Heretico Comburendo authorized the burning of heretics who preached or held beliefs contrary to the Church. It was specifically aimed at the Lollards, the followers of John Wycliffe.

c. The need to copy illustrations in books led to the pictures being carved in wood. When dipped in ink and pressed onto paper, this created the first primitive printing presses.

A combined Turko-Mongol and Bedouin army under Timur destroyed Baghdad after a forty-day siege, slaughtering every inhabitant. The city would change hands several times in rapid succession.

1402

Ottoman sultan Bayezid I withdrew from an eight-year campaign of besieging Constantinople in order to turn his attention to Timur.

In Bohemia, priest and scholar Jan Hus began denouncing corruption in the Church and the papacy and promoting many of the same reformist concepts of John Wycliffe.

Mongol leader Timur captured Smyrna, the last Christian stronghold in modern-day Turkey. He had already defeated the Egyptians, Indians, Russians, Turks, and Syrians and sacked Baghdad. As was Timur's normal methodology, he seized Smyrna and massacred everyone inside, including some Knights of Rhodes, the former Knights Hospitaller.

1406

Ptolemy's second-century book *Geographia* was translated into Latin and changed the Western view of the world. The world had been depicted by European Christians with Jerusalem at its center and the three continents of Europe, Asia, and Africa radiating out from the city. From Ptolemy's book, it was readily seen by his calculations that those three continents only took up a small part of the spherical surface of the world, and no one knew what lay beyond.

Emperor Wenzel of Bohemia and Germany ordered that from this time forward, the practice of surgery should no longer be considered dishonorable.

1409

Neither Antipope Benedict XIII of Avignon nor Pope Gregory XII of Rome attended the Council of Pisa. As a result, the council deposed both and elected Alexander V as another antipope.

The archbishop of Canterbury ordered that Christians worship the cross, images of the crucifix, and other images of the saints with processions, kneeling, frankincense offerings, kisses, monetary offerings, candle lighting, and pilgrimages.

1410

Father Juan Gilberto-Jofre founded a medical facility called Hospital of the Innocents in Valencia, Spain. It is believed to be the first hospital for the mentally ill in the Christian world.

The Teutonic Knights had been attacking pockets of pagans in Lithuania for years. After the Lithuanian king converted to Christianity, the Knights claimed that his conversion wasn't sincere and continued their attacks. When the two armies met at Grunwald, the Lithuanians defeated the Teutonic Knights, sending them into decline.

After the Church excommunicated Jan Hus, the Bohemian reformer, riots broke out in Prague. He opposed the sale of indulgences and the worldliness of the popes, and he claimed that the Church was a human invention, not originating with Christ. Hus is credited with starting the Bohemian Reformation, which along with John Wycliffe, pioneered the way for Martin Luther and other reformers a century later and produced the first non-Catholic national church in Western Europe in modern times.

Pierre d'Ailly was a French cardinal, theologian, and astrologer. He wrote *Imago Mundo*, a book of Christian-tinged geography and cosmology that would later be used by Christopher Columbus to wrongly calculate the size of Earth.

1411

Spanish Dominican friar Vincent Ferrer incited mobs to attack synagogues and convert them into churches. He was said to have overseen twenty thousand forced baptisms and pressured the king of Castile into expelling all Jews who refused to convert.

1414

The Council of Constance gathered to settle the schism of the three popes. It ended four years later after deposing or accepting the resignation of the remaining papal claimants and electing Pope Martin V. The bishops also condemned Jan Hus as a heretic and ordered the body of John Wycliffe to be exhumed and burned.

Holy Roman emperor Sigismund lured Jan Hus to Constance with an offer of safe passage. There, Hus hoped to defend his reformist views and win allies, but he was seized on arrival. The following year he was burned as a heretic. Despite the attempts to stamp out his movement, it continued as the *Unitas Fratrum*, or Unity of the Brethren. The future Hussite Wars were named after Jan Hus and his followers.

1415

The knights and nobles of Bohemia condemned the execution of Jan Hus in the strongest possible language, enraging Sigismund, who in turn sent threatening letters to the Bohemians, vowing to wipe out the Hussites and Wycliffians. Chaos broke out, and Bohemians assaulted Catholic churches and drove many Catholic priests out of Bohemia. They also expelled many German Catholics from Bohemian cities.

1416

Jerome of Prague, a follower of Wycliffe and an associate of Jan Hus, was burned for heresy in Germany.

1417

Construction began on the Sistine Chapel at the Vatican. It would not be completed until 1484.

Sir John Oldcastle, a Lollard leader, was hung and then burned in England for his Wycliffian religious views.

Italian author Poggio Bracciolini discovered Titus Lucretius Carus's first-century BC tribute to Epicurus, *On the Nature of Things*, in a German monastery. This was an important find since almost all of Epicurus's own writings had been lost. Examples of his thoughts were "fear was the first thing on Earth to create gods" and "the nature of the universe has by no means been made through divine power, seeing how great are the faults that mar it." Bracciolini distributed copies to European intellectuals, spurring subtle changes in thinking that would help trigger the Renaissance and Enlightenment periods.

1419

Prague was in turmoil due to the letters from the Council of Constance. The nobles, still furious about what had been done to Hus, prepared to resist the Church even though some Hussites were pacifists. They were joined by Beghards, who were attracted by Bohemia's reputation for religious freedom.

1420

In the first battle of what would become the Hussite Wars, the Bohemians defeated the forces of the Holy Roman emperor at the Battle of Sudomer in southern Bohemia.

Pope Martin V invaded Bohemia again. This time the Hussites defeated the Catholic forces at the Battle of Vitkov Hill. By the end of the year, almost all of Bohemia was in the hands of the Hussites.

c. Thomas á Kempis wrote *The Imitation of Christ*, which became the most widely read Christian devotional work of its time other than the Bible. Kempis was involved in the Brethren of the Common Life, a sect in the Netherlands and northern Germany that spread the ideals of godliness and charitable service.

1421

Giacomo Colonna was said to have found a letter supposedly written by a Roman at the time of Jesus, giving physical and personal descriptions of Jesus that had not previously been revealed. The document was called the Letter of Lentulus and is now regarded as a fraud.

A large Catholic army arrived in Bohemia from Germany and laid siege to Zatec. The Hussites defeated them at the Battle of Deutsch Brod the following year.

Sultan Murad II and an Ottoman army of one hundred thousand warriors failed to capture Constantinople. Constantinople for centuries had massive defensive walls and a once-powerful navy, but they also had phenomenal luck, and this led the populace to believe they had miraculous help from their icons, statues, and angels.

1425

At the age of thirteen, Jeanne d'Arc, a girl from a peasant family in northeastern France, began to experience visions and hear voices. She came to believe they were saints and angels, and they told her that she was the one God had chosen to drive the English out of France and help the rightful heir become king. From this humble beginning, the teenage woman we know as Joan of Arc would go on to convince any doubters that God was working through her.

1426

At a time when the Hussite army was said to be twenty-five thousand strong, the Catholics launched a fourth crusade against them but were defeated again at the Battles of Aussig and Tachov. Throughout these wars, the Hussites had been conducting their own raids into the neighboring countries of Germany, Poland, and Hungary, which still held Catholic loyalties.

The Mamluks of Egypt forced Cyprus, the last bastion of the crusaders in the eastern Mediterranean region, into vassalage.

1428

Joan of Arc had convinced enough influential French leaders God was guiding her that she was given control of the French forces that lifted the six-month-long English siege of Orléans. From then on, the French increasingly considered her guided by supernatural powers. To them she was a mysterious saint, but to the English, who would have controlled almost all of France if they had taken Orléans, she was a witch working black magic against them.

1430

Bohemian followers of Jan Hus composed the first hymnbook written in a language other than Latin. It was named the Jistebnice hymn book, and it contained eighty-nine Czech hymns, Czech translations of Latin liturgy, and Czech Christmas carols.

The Ottoman Turks drove the Venetian forces from Thessalonica, Greece, and captured and burned the city.

Joan of Arc was reported to have dictated a letter to the Hussites threatening to invade Bohemia and defeat them if they did not return to orthodoxy. The letter still exists, but since Joan was illiterate, it's uncertain if she dictated it.

After helping King Charles VII of France win independence from England, Joan of Arc was taken captive by Burgundians when she was locked out of the town of Compiégne while retreating from an engagement with them. The Burgundians then sold her to the English.

1431

Pro-English Bishop Pierre Cauchon prosecuted Joan of Arc in a civil court on a variety of charges including heresy and witchcraft. This court had no legal authority to try someone for heresy since it was a secular court, but it did so anyway. The court wanted a theological justification to execute Joan and make it appear she was working for the devil. She was charged with blasphemy for having worn men's clothing during her military activities in violation of Deuteronomy 22:5, which states, "A woman must not wear men's clothing, nor a man wear women's clothing, for the Lord your God detests anyone who does this." She was reportedly tricked into wearing men's clothing again during her trial, and Cauchon charged her as a relapsed heretic. She was burned at the stake in Rouen at the age of nineteen.

This year ended a dry spell of canonizations. Whereas between 1199 and 1276, there were twenty-three canonizations of saints, between 1276 and 1431, there were only twelve. This difference was due to a difference in the interpretation of the miracles that were requirement for sainthood.

A German army accompanied by papal legate Cardinal Cesarini entered Bohemia. A combined Bohemian and Polish Hussite army routed the Catholics at the Battle of Domazlice.

Pope Martin V convened the Council of Basel to address the Hussite heresy, the Ottomans, and the question of papal supremacy, which was being rejected by a group of bishops known as Conciliarists. The council ran into trouble from the beginning as few bishops attended, making Cardinal Cesarini decide to adjourn the assembly. The assembled bishops however refused any postponement and proceeded with their business.

1433

Bohemian emissary Pavel Kravar traveled to Saint Andrews, Scotland, to gain support for the Hussite cause. The bishop of Saint Andrews accused him of spreading the heretical ideas of Jan Hus and John Wycliffe, then had him tried and executed.

1436

c. Metallurgist Johannes Gutenberg, who would later invent the movable-type printing press, produced small convex mirrors of polished metal to pin onto hats. They were called pilgrim mirrors, and they were intended to capture the holy rays of light radiating from religious relics. The mirrors could then be used to benefit others by sharing that captured light.

1438

The Council of Ferrara, Italy, began under Pope Eugenius IV with the goal of resolving differences between the Latin and Greek Churches. He threatened those bishops still meeting in Basel with excommunication if they did not attend. Eastern Orthodox and Roman Catholic clergy tried to resolve their differences with Byzantine emperor John VIII Palaiologos and all the Christian patriarchates represented.

1439

The council moved to Florence when a plague hit Ferrara. The council lasted another ten years and was somewhat successful in reuniting the two churches. They also affirmed the seven sacraments of baptism, Eucharist, confirmation, reconciliation or penance, matrimony, anointing the sick or extreme unction, and holy orders.

The papal bull *Laetentur Caeli* (*Let the Heavens Rejoice*) united the Roman Catholic and the Eastern Orthodox Churches. Unfortunately for the pope and the emperor, this arrangement was not acceptable to the eastern bishops.

The Hussite Wars ended due to internal struggles in Bohemia and the defeat of their Polish Hussite allies. The Bohemian population remained overwhelmingly Protestant and would ally itself with the Protestant movement in Germany when it emerged in the next century.

1440

c. Johannes Gutenberg, the German goldsmith and blacksmith, invented movable type using letters made of metal. The type was movable because the various letters could be rearranged to form any word, sentence, or page of type. This was a phenomenal invention. His press would be in operation by 1450, and the technology spread rapidly throughout the major cities of Europe, creating a revolution in the dissemination of information. Many scholars consider this the end of the Middle Ages because of its vast effect on European culture.

Lorenzo Valla proved that the *Donation of Constantine* was a forgery; the document had been used repeatedly to support the popes' claims to a legal right to control basically all lands and policies in Europe. Despite this finding, the Church continued to use the document until 1870, when the popes lost their territorial control in Italy.

1441

With the closure of ancient trade routes to the Far East due to the Ottoman expansion, the Portuguese accelerated their exploration of a sea route to the eastern Asia. The first step was exploring Africa with the hope of finding precious metals. This year, for the first time, they brought captured African slaves back to Portugal. By 1454, the Spanish would bring African slaves to Spain.

1444

The crusade that the pope had counted on to drive the Turks out of Europe and free Constantinople came to a disastrous end. In Varna, Bulgaria, near the Black Sea, Turks routed the crusader army, killing over fifteen thousand in battle and beheading thousands of captives.

Portuguese explorers reached Senegal and Equatorial Guinea on the West African coast. With every new territory, they explored and investigated for resources; they also paved the way for future Christian missionary activity.

1445

To bring unity to the Christian world and halt the advancing Turks, Pope Eugenius IV signed alliances with the Armenian, Jacobite, Nestorian, and Maronite Churches in Asia.

1448

The Russian Orthodox Church elected Bishop Jonah as the metropolitan of Kiev and all Russia. Since he was elected without the approval of the patriarch of Constantinople, a rift developed that led to the independence of the Russian Orthodox Church.

In France, Franciscans claimed to have the true blood of Christ in their possession, supposedly collected by Nicodemus and Joseph of Arimathea. A fierce debate ensued between those who possessed the relics and those who insisted that it was theologically impossible for Jesus to have left any human blood behind. Five professors at the University in Paris were assigned to resolve this impasse, and they decided that the idea that some of Jesus's blood remained on Earth was conceivable.

At the Second Battle of Kosovo, the Ottomans crushed a Hungarian army, leaving Constantinople surrounded by Ottoman Turks, with no hope of rescue except by sea.

1449

When the king of Spain ordered Christian tax collectors of Jewish descent to collect an unpopular tax in Toledo, a riot broke out. The people attacked not the king who taxed them, but the tax collectors and other converted Jews still suspected of retaining the Jewish faith.

1450

c. The era of witch hunts was in full swing. Witches took on the roles of scapegoats for any personal misfortune, bad harvest, famine, or plague—just as pagans, heretics, and Jews had previously. Suspected witch activity expanded to include trampling on crosses, flying in the sky, committing cannibalism, controlling the weather, having mystical experiences, and placing curses on others. The accused were mostly women, and it is estimated that by the end of the witch hysteria three hundred years later, thirty-five thousand to one hundred thousand unfortunate people were executed as witches in Europe.

1452

In the last imperial coronation conducted in Rome, Nicholas V crowned Frederick III as Holy Roman emperor.

In the papal bull *Dum Diversas*, Pope Nicholas V authorized the king of Portugal to "attack, conquer, and subjugate Saracens, pagans, and other enemies of Christ wherever they may be found." He regarded all non-Christians as "enemies of Christ" and authorized hereditary slavery for captured Muslims and pagans.

The young sultan of the Ottomans, Mehmed II, set out to capture Constantinople. He raised an army of over one hundred thousand soldiers and constructed fortresses on the Bosporus, just a few miles from the city, in order to control navigation on the waterway. By the end of the year, Constantinople and its eight thousand defenders were entirely cut off from the rest of the Christian world.

The Byzantine emperor requested emergency help from the pope, but Nicholas V didn't see the urgency because he reportedly believed that God wouldn't allow Constantinople to fall to the infidels, and he wanted an iron-clad commitment of Church unification before he acted.

1453

After two months of besieging Constantinople, the Ottomans massed for an all-out attack. On the evening of Monday, May 28, whatever residents were not on duty on the walls attended Mass at the Hagia Sophia and prayed for their salvation. The next day, the Ottomans attacked using heavy cannons. When Genoese General Giovanni Giustiniani was wounded and appeared to flee the fight, his men, believing the battle was lost, followed him. As panic spread among the defenders, the Turks were able to pick their way through what remained of the land wall and enter the city, killing everyone they encountered. The last emperor of the Roman and Byzantine Empire, Constantine XI, charged into the maelstrom and was killed. The rescue fleet sent by Pope Nicholas V was delayed and never played a role. As was tradition, Sultan Mehmed II gave his troops three days to live out their fantasies of destruction and desecration in their new conquest. They looted, destroyed icons and libraries, and even obliterated the imperial archives, the written history of the city and the empire.

With the fall of Constantinople, Christian Europe was in panic. Pope Nicholas V called for a crusade against the Saracens, using Gutenberg's press to print flyers to spread the news. This call was not received with much enthusiasm because it not only involved reconquering Jerusalem but also retaking Constantinople. Scholars who fled Constantinople, and the books they brought with them, would help to fuel the Italian Renaissance.

Margaret, the granddaughter of Geoffrey de Charny, traded the Holy Shroud to the Royal House of Savoy for two castles.

1454

The Treaty of Lodi was signed between the Italian powers—Venice, Florence, Naples, Milan, and the Papal States—and the Hundred Years' War abruptly ended so a united Europe could prepare for the anticipated invasion by the Turks.

The archbishop of Krakow, Poland, invited an Italian monk to speak in his city. In speech after speech, the monk encouraged violence against Jews. As a result, residents demanded that King Casimir IV revoke the privileges he had given Jews, but he refused. Later, after Poland lost a battle against the Teutonic Knights, the archbishop blamed the defeat on the king's neglect of the Church. Popular pressure finally caused Casimir to revoke the Jewish charter.

Another one of Gutenberg's first projects was printing thousands of indulgences for the church to sell.

1455

Pope Nicholas V issued the papal bull *Romanus Pontifex*, which sanctioned Portugal to purchase African slaves in order that "the souls of many will be gained for Christ." It was essentially a green light for seizing land from non-Christians and conquering, converting, or enslaving native Africans. This policy was confirmed in bulls by three future popes with the excuse that forced conversion and slavery were blessings because they saved souls.

Gutenberg printed between 158 and 180 copies of Jerome's Vulgate Bible, which became known as the Gutenberg Bible. The older hand-copied Bibles of the scriptoriums had been available only to monks, the wealthy, and universities. The printed Bible made it possible for people literate in Latin to interpret scripture for themselves. Within fifty years, printers had outproduced what all the monks in history had copied by hand. Books were available in many languages, and now that people had something of interest to read, the literacy rate throughout Europe rose dramatically. The Church still clamped down on anyone writing or printing Christian scripture in any language other than Latin, so the common people still didn't have access to the Bible.

1456

The Ottomans set out to conquer Hungary. John Hunyadi, the Hungarian leader, and Giovanni de Capistrano, an Italian Franciscan friar and papal legate, hastily raised armies to confront them. The Christian armies traveled to Belgrade, which was by this time completely encircled by Turks. Hunyadi destroyed the Ottoman fleet, allowing him to enter the city. Heavy bombardment by the Turks breached the walls, and the Turks poured through, only to be driven back with heavy losses. The next morning the defenders went on the offensive and took the Turks by surprise. Things went so badly for the Turks that they withdrew that night, and the Ottoman advance into Europe was delayed for seventy years.

At the request of Inquisitor-General Jean Bréhal and Joan's mother, Pope Callixtus III granted permission to retry Joan of Arc. This year the panel of theologians declared that she was not a heretic but a true martyr and charged her prosecutor Pierre Cauchon with heresy because he had convicted an innocent woman in a secular dispute.

1457

c. Petr Chelcicky of Bohemia had long despised the entanglement of the Church in secular affairs. He believed that true Christianity was about brotherly love and pacifism, and his teachings established the foundation for the Unity of the Brethren, or the Moravians. This sect was an outgrowth of the Hussite movement.

1458

Franciscan monk Alfonso de Espina wrote *Fortalitium Fidei*. In this treatise, he called for the establishment of an official Spanish Inquisition to root out recent Jewish and Muslim converts who were not true to their new faith. The Jewish converts were known as *conversos,* and the Muslim converts as *moriscos.* The Spanish royalty would initiate this tribunal twenty years later.

1461

The Empire of Trebizond, on the Black Sea, fell to the Ottomans after a lengthy campaign. It was the last remnant of the Byzantine Empire in the region and the last Christian state in Asia.

Prince Vlad III of Wallachia (Romania) had been paying the required non-Muslim tax to the Ottoman sultan, Mehmed II, but this year he declined to pay it. He went by the nickname "Drakulya," meaning "dragon," and would earn another nickname "Vlad the Impaler." The fictional Dracula is based on him. When Turkish envoys came to collect the tax he owed and force him to pay homage to the sultan, he had them killed and impaled on stakes.

1462

In one of the first known uses of firearms, Prince Vlad III went on a campaign against all Turks and Turkish sympathizers in his region, massacring tens of thousands of Turks and allied Bulgarians. He was said to have killed over twenty-three thousand Turks, while apparently sparing Bulgarian Christians. The Christian world praised his accomplishments since his actions forced many Turks back into Anatolia.

Mehmed II prepared a great army to attack Vlad's army, but Vlad had used a scorched-earth policy to deprive the invaders of landing areas, food, water, and information and sent people infected with the plague to intermix with the Turks. Vlad raided the Turkish camp at night, killing many and creating terror throughout their army. The Turks marched on to Vlad's capital, which they found deserted with the gates open and thousands of Turkish soldiers impaled on poles. The Turks eventually retreated—winning several battles along the way and taking two hundred thousand cattle and horses with them—and considered the overall campaign a success.

1463

The Ottomans conquered most of Bosnia, but the full conquest wouldn't be completed until 1592. During that time, many Bosnian nobles converted to Islam.

1466

Pope Paul II revived one of the most depraved customs of the pagan Roman celebration of Saturnalia. This was the celebration of the winter solstice, which had been adapted to Christianity and rebranded as Christmas around AD 354. For the amusement of the Roman crowd,

Jewish men were forced to stuff themselves with food and then race naked through the streets.

Johannes Mentelin, one of the pioneers in book printing, produced a Bible in the high German language. This was the first Bible printed in any language other than Latin and became known as the Mentelin Bible.

1469

Ferdinand of Aragon and Isabella of Castile were married, uniting two huge provinces, and, in effect, creating the nation of Spain.

The town council in Frankfurt, Germany, ordered protection of the Jewish ghetto during the time of the Passion plays. These plays about the suffering Jesus went through in his last day were predicted to stir up such intense hatred against the so-called "Jesus killers" that Jews were not safe outdoors.

1470

c. The Vatican allowed local shrines to grant indulgences to raise money. For example, for a designated fee, the Canterbury Cathedral could release someone from a vow made to visit a pilgrimage site.

1471

Niccoló Malermi, an Italian biblical scholar, translated the Bible into Italian. The Malermi Bible was printed in 1490.

1475

A Franciscan preacher delivered a series of sermons in Trento, Italy, in which he vilified the local Jewish community. Shortly later, the body of a local two-year-old boy was found, and the townspeople blamed the Jews of ritual murder. The entire Jewish community was arrested and tortured until they confessed to the crime. Fifteen Jewish men were burned at the stake. This incident reignited anti-Jewish violence in neighboring towns.

1476

William Caxton established England's first printing press in London. One of his first printed works was *The Golden Legend*, a book about the lives of saints written around 1260. It included graphic detail about the martyrdom of saints, and the printed edition became enormously popular.

In Niklashausen, Germany, Hans Böhm said that the Virgin Mary spoke to him through visions. Once news of this got out, pilgrims flocked to the site of the apparitions—some estimate that between forty thousand to seventy thousand people were camped in the fields around the village at one point. Böhm, a layman and gifted speaker, controlled the mob, but because he enraged the local clergy by criticizing Church authority, he was seized and burned for heresy.

Pope Sixtus IV authorized the sale of indulgences to shorten the time family members or loved ones had to spend in purgatory. This was a new concept, since previously the sale of indulgences had been used only for the full or partial remission of one's own sins.

1478

Ferdinand and Isabella exhorted the pope to endorse the establishment of an Inquisition in Spain, but to be under their authority, not the pope's. Many Jews and Muslims appeared to have converted to Christianity only because of the threats on their lives, not out of true devotion. Some signs of backsliding included refusing to eat pork, refusing to work on Saturdays, and not observing Christian holidays. The goal of Ferdinand and Isabella's Inquisition was to establish the purity of an accused convert's true beliefs. The Inquisition would try not only Jews and Muslims but anyone who was suspected of heresy, later including Protestants and free thinkers, but more than 90 percent of the Inquisition's victims would be Jews. By 1492, the Inquisition drove 180,000 Jews from Spain, forcibly converted another 300,000, and burned 20,000 as heretics. The Spanish Inquisition wouldn't end until 1834.

1479

Pope Sixtus IV granted the head of the University of Cologne the authority to censure printers, sellers, and readers of heretical books.

1480

Sultan Mehmed II sent a fleet to Italy to conquer Rome and install himself as the new Roman emperor. The Muslims captured the city of Otranto, near Naples, and murdered thousands of residents, beheading eight hundred men who refused to convert to Islam. When Mehmed died the following year, the Muslim battle for succession took the momentum away from the Italian campaign. In 2013, Pope Francis bestowed sainthood on the eight hundred men who refused conversion.

1481

Pope Sixtus IV called for a crusade to free Otranto, but the Neapolitans expelled the Ottoman forces before a Spanish fleet arrived. The Ottomans never returned to mainland Italy.

By the time of his death, Mehmed II, the conqueror of Constantinople, had also added Albania, Moldavia, Bosnia, Wallachia, Trebizond, the Peloponnesian Peninsula of Greece, and much of Serbia to the Ottoman Empire.

1482

Pope Sixtus IV issued a bull of crusade to Ferdinand and Isabella of Spain. This was part of an all-out effort to finally drive the Moors out of the Iberian Peninsula.

Pope Sixtus IV informed the University of Tubingen that he had no objection to human anatomy studies if the bodies came from executed criminals and were given a Christian burial. This did not throw open the doors to the study of medicine since future popes would not agree with Sixtus.

Dominican friar Tomás de Torquemada was appointed grand inquisitor of Spain. He would become the stereotype of the sadistic inquisitor, calling his cohorts the "Militia of Christ" and executing more than two thousand people by 1500.

Pope Sixtus IV protested the excesses of the Spanish Inquisition, but the protests were basically ignored by King Ferdinand.

1484

Pope Innocent VIII issued the bull, *Summis desiderantes affectibus*, supporting the writings of Dominican friar Heinrich Kramer and authorizing German monks to investigate accusations of witchcraft. He also ordered pet cats to be burned along with the witches because they were considered demonic. Oddly, physicians also ordered cats and dogs to be killed during times of plague, thinking that this would halt the spread of infection—when the reverse was true.

1485

Opponents of the Spanish Inquisition assassinated Pedro de Arbués, a priest and high-ranking official of the Inquisition, in the Zaragoza cathedral. He had worn a helmet and chain mail for protection, but that wasn't enough to save his life. There is thought to be only one other incidence of an inquisitor being assassinated, and that was Juan Lopez Cisneros in 1657.

Italian adventurer Cristoforo Colombo, whose name was latinized to Christophorus Columbus (and anglicized to Christopher Columbus), visited King John II of Portugal with a plan to reach Asia by sailing west.

The king's experts rejected the idea because they believed Columbus had misjudged the distance to Asia.

1486

Heinrich Kramer and Jakob Sprenger wrote the manual *Malleus Maleficarum* (*Hammer of Witches*). It included a copy of the recent papal bull concerning witches. This book served as a guide on how to identify witches and systematize their persecution and extermination. It was a bestseller for almost two centuries, second only to the Bible. The authors wrote, "A belief that there are such things as witches is so essential a part of Catholic faith that obstinately to maintain the opposite opinion savors of heresy." One subject they focused on was sexual relations between witches and demons, underscoring an obsessiveness with sex.

Christopher Columbus, a passionate man with a strong Christian faith and a genius for ship handling, met with Spanish King Ferdinand II and Queen Isabella I. He proposed his plan to sail to Asia, today's Indonesia or Japan, via the Atlantic Ocean. This was the only way for Spain to tap the riches of eastern Asia because the 1479 Treaty of Alcacovas prohibited Spain from exploring the African coast, which was in Portugal's jurisdiction. Columbus's proposed journey had never been attempted before, and like the Portuguese, the queen's advisors rejected his plan because they didn't believe it was possible.

1487

Pope Innocent VIII called for a crusade against the Waldensians in southern France and northern Italy. This was the sect founded by Peter Waldo in the twelfth century and was related to the Cathars.

1488

Portuguese explorer Bartolomeu Dias was the first sea captain to reach the Indian Ocean by going around Cape Horn, South Africa.

1489

Turkish nobleman Cem failed in his quest for the sultan's throne and fled the Ottoman Empire. The new sultan, Bayezid II, paid Pope Innocent VIII to keep him in Italy and part of the payment was said to be the relic of the Holy Lance, which was reportedly found in Antioch during the First Crusade.

1490

c. Around this time, midwives, the most skilled people in child delivery, ran the risk of being accused of witchcraft. In this era of witch hysteria, they were sometimes accused of murdering babies in the womb, roasting them, or offering them to the devil.

Six Jews and five former Jewish converts were tried in Spain for allegedly kidnapping a Catholic child named Christobalico. They were accused of forcing him to go through the sadistic suffering that Jesus went through leading up to his crucifixion. Then they supposedly tore out his heart and used it with consecrated hosts to put a spell on the local inquisitors, and even Christianity in general. All eleven were burned at the stake, and Christobalico's supposed burial site became a shrine.

1491

After encountering Portuguese explorers, King Nzinga of the Kongo converted to Catholicism and took the Christian name João. His conversion was not popular with his subjects, but it greatly facilitated trade, especially slave trade with European countries. João's son and successor, Alfonso I, later sent his son to Europe to study how to combine Christianity with traditional African religion. The pope would appoint Alfonso as Bishop of Utica, in Tunisia, in 1518.

1492

The reconquest of Spain came to an end with the fall of Granada, end-ing seven centuries of Muslim rule on the Iberian Peninsula. Along with the Moors, 120,000 to 150,000 Jews had their properties confis-cated and were expelled from Spain. The Jewish community in Spain had been the largest, most tolerated, most prosperous, and most edu-cated in Europe. After their expulsion, the only haven for them seemed to be the Ottoman Empire, where the Muslims were rebuilding the population of Constantinople.

Columbus finally won approval from the king and queen of Spain to set out on his voyage across the Atlantic. Columbus hoped that his appearance in the East would precipitate events that would lead to the Second Coming of Jesus Christ. His ultimate objective was to meet the Great Khan in China, who was still thought to be favorable toward Christians. He hoped for the Mongols and Europeans to coordinate an attack on the Ottoman Turks, defeat them, and regain Jerusalem for Christendom. Columbus pledged that any gold he returned with would help finance that crusade. With the conversion of native inhab-itants in the lands he sought to discover and the return of Jerusalem to the Christians, he believed the conditions would be right for the Second Coming as foretold in the book of Revelation.

Columbus sailed from the port of Palos because the ideal staging port of Cadiz was filled with ships loading Jews for deportation. Two months after leaving Spain, Columbus began to discover the islands that would become known as the Bahamas, Hispaniola (present-day Dominican Republic and Haiti), and Cuba, but he thought they were off the Asian continent and was oblivious that the American continents even existed. The Roman doctrine of *terra nullius*, meaning "nobody's land," declared that any part of the world not occupied by "civilized" people was up for grabs and could be claimed by Europeans, no matter who was living there or how long they had been there. From his own diary and the writings of contemporaries, Columbus appears to have enjoyed the respect and company of most of the Indigenous people he met, and both he and Queen Isabella made it clear to the Spaniards that the native inhabitants were not to be harmed. The Spanish referred to them as Indios, thinking they were in the East Indies, and sought to convert them, especially because the Indios didn't seem to have their own gods to worship. Columbus reported that these inhabitants already behaved like Christians and their conversion to Christianity would be much easier if the Spanish treated them with respect and kindness. In his journal, Columbus wrote: "I believe that in the world there are no better people or better land. They love their neighbors as themselves, and they have the sweetest speech in the world; and gentle and always laughing." From them, he learned of another tribe, the Caribs, who were warlike and cannibalistic. Columbus seems to have placed them into a different category of human beings, who could only be converted if a few were captured, sent to Spain for Christian indoctrination, and then returned to evangelize their people.

In the town of Sternberg, Germany, Jews were accused of desecrating a host. As a result, sixty-five Jews were rounded up and tortured, with twenty-seven of them burned to death. The rest of the Jewish population was expelled.

1493

Portuguese explorer Pêro da Covilhã reached Ethiopia by land with the goal of establishing relations between his king and the Christian ruler of Ethiopia.

After news of Columbus's discoveries reached Europe, Pope Alexander VI issued the bull *Inter Caetera*, which officially divided the undiscovered world between Spain and Portugal. The one condition that the pope required was that the native populations be converted to Catholicism. By 1509, the navigator Martín Fernández de Enciso would claim: "The king has every right to send his men to the Indies to demand their territory from these idolaters because he had received it from the pope. If the Indians refuse, he may quite legally fight them, kill them, and enslave them, just as Joshua enslaved the inhabitants of the country of Canaan."

After a brief stay in Spain, Columbus returned to his settlement of La Navidad in Haiti with seventeen ships and 1,200 hundred men. He discovered that all the men he had left behind had been massacred. Some of the hot-headed aristocrats with him demanded immediate revenge, but Columbus investigated and found that those who had been killed had disobeyed practically every instruction he'd given them. They had quarreled among themselves, stolen from the native people, and raped and kidnapped their women. The Indios killed the Spaniards in a retaliatory raid. This was a turning point in how the Indios were viewed by many of the Spanish. Some, like Columbus, apparently wanted peace, conversion, and cooperation, and other Spaniards treated the native inhabitants like animals and would be ruthless in their quest for treasure. Those who hadn't previously sailed with Columbus resented him for being too strict, and when he left to explore other islands, those he left in charge treated the natives with indifference or cruelty. Aristocrats in the group had assumed they would take slaves to do their work and prepare their food, and since they had friends in high places, they would conspire against Columbus to make it look like he was the problem. The friar responsible for converting the Indios didn't even try to learn their language and seemed to believe that baptism alone made someone a Christian. Admittedly, there is much disagreement over the legacy of Christopher Columbus.

1494

Pope Alexander VI in the Treaty of Tordesillas set a specific degree of longitude as the dividing line between Spanish and Portuguese colonization of newly discovered lands. This became necessary when Portugal claimed Brazil, but the treaty gave Spain control of the rest of the Americas.

1495

Even though there was no strong animosity toward the Lithuanian Jews, they were unexpectedly expelled by the new king, Alexander Jagiellon. They were allowed to return eight years later.

Manuel I became king of Portugal. He saw the shipping route to India not only as an advantage for trade but also as an opportunity to launch a crusade against the Turks and recapture Jerusalem. When he died in 1521, his successor abandoned the crusade plan.

1497

England entered the age of exploration with Italian Giovanni Caboto (John Cabot), who believed a northern route to Asia would be shorter than the one Columbus took. He explored the North American coast from Labrador to New England without finding a passage.

King Manuel I of Portugal followed Spain's example and decreed that all Jews had to convert to Christianity or be expelled, and if they did keep their religion and emigrate, they had to leave their children behind.

The Dominican friar, prophet, and preacher Girolamo Savonarola held the first "bonfire of the vanities" in Florence. To cleanse the city of items inconsistent with orthodox Christian ideals, his supporters even raided homes. Anything they thought was inconsistent with a moral Christian life was taken and burned in an enormous bonfire. Poetry books, non-Christian artwork, cosmetics, fine clothing, playing cards, women's jewelry, and musical instruments all went up in flames.

1498

Leonardo da Vinci completed his famous painting *The Last Supper* on a dry plaster wall in a monastery in Milan. It depicted Jesus with his disciples after he told them one of them would betray him.

Girolamo Savonarola, who had held the bonfire of the vanities the previous year, was burned at the stake in Florence with two other friars. They had been found guilty of heresy and being schismatics for their work in trying to reform the Church. They had denounced clerical corruption, despotic rule, and the exploitation of the poor.

A Portuguese expedition commanded by Vasco da Gama reached India by sailing around South Africa. There, they encountered the Thomas Christians. Because these Indian Christians were being persecuted at that time, they welcomed an alliance with the Portuguese.

Columbus returned to Hispaniola on his third voyage. In his absence, his brother Bartholomew had been in charge. Many of the Spaniards resented Bartholomew's rules of poverty, chastity, and obedience. Various groups of Spaniards seized ships or just set out on foot to gain independence. They lived as they chose and often mistreated the Indios terribly. Those in charge of these rebellious groups also confiscated Indio land and gave it to Spanish soldiers.

1499

Michelangelo di Lodovico Buonarroti Simoni, better known simply as Michelangelo, completed his famous marble sculpture, the *Pieta*, which portrayed Mary cradling the dead body of Jesus. It is now on display in Saint Peter's Basilica in Rome.

c. The monotheistic religion of Sikhism developed on the Indian subcontinent. It was inspired by the spiritual teachings of Guru Nanak and emphasizes the link between spiritual development and truthful moral living. It is currently the fifth-largest organized religion in the world.

CHAPTER 16: SIXTEENTH CENTURY AD

Since then your serene majesty and your lordships seek a simple answer, I will give it in this manner, neither horned nor toothed: Unless I am convinced by the testimony of the Scriptures or by clear reason (for I do not trust either in the pope or in councils alone, since it is well known that they have often erred and contradicted themselves), I am bound by the Scriptures I have quoted and my conscience is captive to the Word of God. I cannot and I will not retract anything since it is neither safe nor right to go against conscience.

—Martin Luther

Here [a basket of gold and jewels] is the God the Spaniards worship. For these they fight and kill; for these they persecute us and that is why we have to throw them into the sea . . . They tell us, these tyrants, that they adore a God of peace and equality, and yet they usurp our land and make us their slaves. They speak to us of an immortal soul and of their eternal rewards and punishments, and yet they rob our belongings, seduce our women, violate our daughters. Incapable of matching us in valor, these cowards cover themselves with iron that our weapons cannot break.

—Chief Hatuey, as related by Bartolomé de Las Casas

It was a general rule among Spaniards to be cruel, not just cruel, but extraordinarily cruel so that harsh and bitter treatment would prevent Indians from daring to think of themselves as human beings or having a minute to think at all.

—Bartolomé de Las Casas

This was the century of the Protestant Reformation, the world's first successful heresy, which drastically changed the religious dynamics of Europe—a change fought by the Council of Trent and the Catholic Counter-Reformation. The Spanish continued to conquer the Americas by spreading disease and genocide. The trend of using rationalism to explain Christian theology continued, represented by Erasmus and others. Copernicus developed and published his theory of heliocentricity, which was incomprehensible to most Europeans, but marked the beginning of the Scientific Revolution. Anabaptists made their first appearance and were immediately rejected by both Catholics and Protestants. Old World rivalries and fears migrated to the New World and other colonies, and witch paranoia reached new heights. Crusades were still being organized and conducted, this time against the heretical sect of Waldensians.

1500

Spanish nobles in the Indies accused Columbus of incompetence and excessive brutality. When his replacement Francisco de Bobadilla arrived, Columbus's enemies presented false evidence that Columbus used torture and mutilation to maintain order, and he was returned to Spain as a prisoner in chains. According to Friar Bartolomé de Las Casas, who later became the main historian and advocate for the Indios, once Bobadilla arrived, the Spanish became crueler toward the Indios, killing many for no reason other than sport.

c. With the mass production and distribution of printed material, bookmaking and book selling became a trade, and monks no longer had to copy manuscripts by hand. Attempts to print the Arabic language were found unsatisfactory because Arabic letters flowed together, and that interconnection could not be duplicated with movable type. Because of this, the Muslims would not allow their holy book, the Koran, to be printed. Ironically, because of their beautiful flowing script, the Muslim world would not be able to keep up with the dissemination of scientific advances in Europe and would fall behind technologically. They wouldn't have an adequate printing press until 1727.

c. Christianity was steadily shrinking as a world religion. It was basically extinguished in China, Central Asia, and across most of the Muslim world. Middle Eastern, Mongolian, Indian, and African Christians existed in isolated pockets, but no longer had contact with each other.

c. The Portuguese arrival in India brought mixed fortune for the Thomas Christians. At the time, there were about thirty thousand Christian families with as many as two hundred thousand people. The Christians welcomed the Portuguese and sought their protection against local Muslims.

c. With the resurgence of scholarship and the invention of the printing press, books were distributed to more readers, and many forgeries that the Church had used to gain and maintain power began to be exposed. After this time, the Church was not able to fabricate forgeries without them likely being detected.

c. Following Columbus's discovery of the West Indies and da Gama's voyage to India, there was much renewed interest in the physical world. This included a fascination with geography, anthropology, botany, zoology, and geology. Explanations of unusual phenomena shifted away from miracles but provided a new appreciation of God's creation.

c. The German states of Gotha and Thuringia established the earliest public schools in modern Western society. As late as the eighteenth century, most Europeans received no formal schooling, and classroom schooling wouldn't become the most common means of education until the mid-nineteenth century.

c. By this time, 236 cities and towns in Europe had their own print shops.

c. Jewish people from Spain and Portugal became known as *Sephardic* Jews and retained the customs and rituals preserved mainly from Babylonian Jewish traditions. The Jewish people of eastern and central Europe, called *Ashkenazi* Jews, carried on Palestinian traditions.

c. The pope granted indulgences for attending the punishment of heretics. English Protestant martyrologist John Foxe later wrote that people who added wood to the pyre of a heretic were granted forty days of pardon. Large attendance at executions also increased the number of people who learned how unwise it was to oppose the Church.

Sandro Botticelli, a well-known Italian painter, wrote a caption on his painting *The Mystical Nativity* that stated that the end times were beginning. This was in line with the apocalyptic thinking of the time, shared by Columbus.

At this time, close to 95 percent of the world's Christians lived in Europe.

1501

The Spanish began to import African slaves from Europe to Hispaniola. Slaves who had converted to Christianity were treated the same as those who didn't.

1502

Columbus completed his *Book of Prophecies*, a collection of biblical passages and writings by Josephus, Augustine, and other philosophers. In the book, Columbus sought to demonstrate that the events that were unfolding were long predicted and would lead to the Apocalypse and Second Coming of Christ. He planned to present the book to the sovereigns, but for some reason, it was never published and was only discovered in 1892 in a library in Sevilla. He focused on four criteria for the Apocalypse—the spread of Christianity throughout the world; the rediscovery of the Garden of Eden, which he thought he may have found in Venezuela; a last crusade to win back the Holy Land; and the choice of the last world emperors, which he thought were Ferdinand and Isabella.

Columbus wrote to Pope Alexander VI to inform him that he wouldn't be able to visit the pope as intended because he was preparing for a fourth voyage to what he still thought were islands near China. In the letter, he reminded the pope that his voyages were made to obtain gold for the restoration of Jerusalem to the Church. He even predicted that the Second Coming would take place in 155 years.

1503

Columbus returned to Spain from his fourth and last voyage. Queen Isabella had died, and Ferdinand reneged on the original charter they had given Columbus in 1492 that presented him hereditary titles and a share of the profits from his discoveries. Spanish friar Bartolomé de Las Casas later wrote, "As for the Catholic King Ferdinand, I do not know why he was not only ungrateful in words and deeds but actually harmed Columbus whenever possible, although his words belied his actions."

Julius II was elected pope, winning the office through bribery and family influence. Julius became known as "the warrior pope" and greatly expanded his territorial jurisdiction by way of conquests. He was said to have chosen his name as a tribute to Julius Caesar.

1506

The Swiss Guard, who had served the popes occasionally since 1471, began providing continuous protective service to Pope Julius II. They also served as the pope's ceremonial unit.

Pope Julius II made plans to build a new basilica to Saint Peter over the old Constantine-era basilica and to finance it primarily with the sale of indulgences.

1508

Michelangelo began his four-year project of painting the ceiling of the Sistine Chapel, adjacent to Saint Peter's Basilica in Rome.

Russian monastic reformer Nilus of Sora died. He had advocated for small monastic groups instead of huge monasteries; for divestment of land ownership; for each monk to support himself through useful labor, such as copying and repairing old manuscripts; and for the demonstration of mercy to heretics.

Pope Julius II encouraged Emperor Maximillian I to attack Venice, and after Maximillian's coronation in Rome, he advanced on Venice. Venetian leader Bartolomeo d'Alviano not only routed the imperial army but seized more territory in Italy and Croatia. Venice then appointed its own bishop in the city of Vicenza, enraging the pope.

Pope Julius II formed the League of Cambrai to confront Venice. The alliance included the papal forces, France, the Holy Roman Empire, and Spain, and their plan was to carve up Venetian territories among themselves. The league defeated Venice, and Venice turned to the Vatican for a resolution of their differences while their lands were gradually being whittled away.

1509

Dutch humanist Desiderius Erasmus wrote *Praise of Folly*, which advocated a return to the moral concepts of early Christianity. He championed the ideals of Origen and Pelagius such as human free will, reason, skepticism, and curiosity. He shared Origen's optimistic approach to theology and thought it far superior to the pessimism, pageantry, and worldliness that had characterized Christianity since the days of Constantine and Augustine. During the Protestant Reformation, he would remain a Catholic and attempt to reform the Church as an insider.

Clerical advisors persuaded Holy Roman emperor Maximilian I to order the confiscation and burning of all Jewish books, except their scriptures. Johann Reuchlin, a German Christian scholar and humanist, protested and succeeded in having the ruling overturned. This seemed to have ended the dispute, but through pamphlet wars, the battle continued until 1520 when Pope Leo X finally condemned Reuchlin to silence.

1510

The first public Christmas tree was claimed to have been exhibited in Riga, Lativia.

The Portuguese defeated the regional militia and formed a permanent colony in Goa, on the southwest coast of India. One of their goals was to eventually dominate the Thomas Christians, who lived further south, and convert them to Catholicism.

The Council of Castile issued the *Requerimiento* to be read to the Indigenous people of American upon making first contact with them. It informed them of the truth of Christianity and their obligation to swear allegiance to the pope and the Spanish crown. If the natives refused, they were threatened with slavery and war. It was a written document and delivered in the Spanish language, so those who didn't speak Spanish, which was almost everyone they met, would not have had any idea what the *Requerimiento* meant. Additionally, the native people had no concept of land ownership, but they would realize the Spanish were taking their farmland and hunting grounds from them.

Martin Luther, an Augustinian monk and scholar, left Wittenberg, Germany, where he had been teaching, and traveled to Rome to present an appeal on behalf of his order. During his journey, while visiting monasteries, and in Rome itself, he was shocked by the luxurious living, loose morals, and impiety of the clergy.

Fearing French incursion into the Papal States, Pope Julius II allied with Venice and Swiss mercenaries to drive French forces from Italy, but they were unsuccessful.

The Spanish began to ship large numbers of African slaves to Santo Domingo, and then their other Caribbean colonies. In the tropics the Africans were in great demand as laborers compared to Europeans and Native Americans due to their immunity to malaria.

1511

Pope Julius II formed a Holy League, consisting of Spain, the Holy Roman Empire, Venice, and England. By the next year, they had greatly weakened French control of Italian territory, but when it came to dividing up newly won lands, the pope and Holy Roman emperor excluded Venice. Venice then formed an alliance with France, and the warring continued.

The native people of Puerto Rico, the Taíno, revolted against Spanish rule. By 1518, all Taínos on the island had been killed, captured, or escaped to other islands.

Beginning at this time, the Catholics in the Kerala region of India asked for the civil authorities to pressure the Thomas Christians to convert to Catholicism. In comparison, the Catholics put more effort into converting the lower castes than the Nestorians did.

Dominican friar Antonio de Montesinos openly rebuked the Spanish authorities governing Hispaniola because of their savage mistreatment of the Indigenous population.

The Spanish captured Taíno chief Hatuey after he led a rebellion against them on the island of Cuba. Before he was burned, the Spanish asked if he wanted to accept Jesus and go to heaven. He said that if heaven was where the Spanish went when they died, he would rather go to hell.

The first book about the Spanish experiences in the American colonies was printed in England. This was well before the first English
settlement in America. It painted a picture of the Indigenous people
as naked and vicious savages who ate each other. The book advised
the English and anyone who encountered them to treat the natives as
harshly as the Spanish did.

1513

The Portuguese reached China by sea, bringing a new wave of Christian
missionaries and eventually establishing the colony of Macau.

1516

The Venetians established a Jewish ghetto to contain and control the
Jewish population. These were basically urban prisons and were becoming more common throughout European towns and cities.

Martin Luther delivered a series of sermons that condemned idolatry,
including pilgrimage shrines. He noted that Christians had turned the
saints into their slaves and seemed to have returned to polytheism by
worshipping so many of them. He also raged against church practices
that he thought concealed the gift of grace offered by Christ. Like so
many reformers before him, he was trying to steer the Church back to
the Jesus of the Gospels.

Following ancient documents as closely as possible, Erasmus completed a new Latin translation of the New Testament from the original Greek. He wanted his Bible to be worded so that common people
could understand the message. This work became the basis for Martin
Luther's German translation, Tyndale's English translation, and the
King James Bible.

Italian philosopher Pietro Pomponazzi refuted Pope Leo X's bull that
the soul was immortal. Pomponazzi used Aristotle's reasoning that
the soul and body were connected, and the soul did not exist after
death. He had to write very carefully to escape the charge of heresy. He

also wrote about the power of the placebo effect—an improvement of a patient's condition based solely on the belief in the cure, even when the cure was not effective or possibly detrimental to one's health. He thought that could explain the miracle cures produced by relics.

Englishman Thomas More wrote the book *Utopia*, which discussed the use of land. He mentioned that if any "primitive" people had unoccupied or uncultivated land, it was permissible for colonists to use it, and if the native people objected, the settlers would be fully justified in killing or expelling them.

1517

The Ottomans, under Suleiman the Magnificent, took Jerusalem from the Mamluks and initiated a period of religious tolerance in the city.

Martin Luther's reaction to the sale of indulgences sparked the Protestant Reformation in Germany. He wrote his 95 Theses, which were charges against the Catholic Church and the pope, and he nailed them to the door of the Castle Church in Wittenberg. This document was copied, reprinted, and circulated with great enthusiasm around northern Europe. Because Luther's ideas became so widely known and discussed, Pope Leo X had to be careful how he dealt with him. A century earlier, Jan Hus had no printing presses to spread his ideas, so he, like so many other potential Church reformers, came to a tragic end.

1518

The Spanish brought many foreign microbes to the New World that the Indigenous people had no resistance to. By this time, waves of diseases had devastated the native population of the island of Hispaniola, killing up to 80 percent of the inhabitants. This was repeated wherever Europeans contacted native Americans. Once established, diseases spread from one tribe to another without any contact with Europeans being necessary. The most religious among the Spanish conquistadors saw this as not just unexpected good fortune but as an act of God that cleared the pagans from the land. According to Father Paul Le Jeune,

a later Jesuit missionary, many Indigenous people in New France—
French settlements in New England and Canada—associated all their
misfortune with the coming of the Christian religion to their land.

Pope Leo X ordered Martin Luther to appear in Rome, but Luther's
protector, Prince Frederick, objected to the summons because it would
be extremely hazardous for Luther to travel to Rome. They agreed instead that Luther would appear before Cardinal Cajetan in Augsburg,
Germany. When Luther discovered that the cardinal had no interest in
a reasonable discussion but only wanted him to retract his theses, he
refused to cooperate.

1519

By this time, only a few hundred Spanish remained on Hispaniola,
while the rest moved on to plunder other islands. Those who remained
on Hispaniola continued to import African slaves to work their sugar
plantations.

Hernán Cortés led an unauthorized expedition into central Mexico
to find precious metals, to capture slaves to mine the metals, and to
convert the native people to Christianity. He skillfully gained allies
from various tribes, with the ultimate plan of subduing the Aztecs, or
Mexica, as they called themselves. Cortés schemed his way into the
confidence of their chief, Moctezuma, who believed that he was the
returning Aztec god Quetzalcoatl. When Cortés met Moctezuma,
Spanish soldiers killed his bodyguards and placed him under house
arrest.

The Jewish inhabitants of Regensburg, Germany, having been persecuted for over forty years, were finally expelled from the city.
Regensburg was the site of the oldest Jewish settlement in Bavaria.
Their synagogue was destroyed, and five thousand tombstones were
removed from the cemetery for use as building materials.

1520

The Spanish had transported most of the population of the Bahamas to Hispaniola and other islands after the native laborers on those islands had died off. After that, little of the native population was left in the Bahamas, and the islands remain basically abandoned for 130 years.

While Cortés was away from the Aztec capital of Tenochtitlan on business his deputy, Pedro de Alvarado massacred thousands of Aztec nobles who were celebrating a festivity in honor of one of their gods. The victims were unarmed, and the massacre was unprovoked. The enraged Aztecs responded by driving the Spanish out of their capital, killing hundreds of Spanish soldiers, and reclaiming much of the treasure the Spaniards had looted.

1521

Cortés returned to Tenochtitlan with Spanish reinforcements and Indigenous allies, including the Tlaxcalan tribal nation, which supplied thousands of warriors. After a two-month siege, the Spaniards conquered the city and claimed the Aztec Empire for Spain, renaming the capital Mexico City. In the previous two years, the population of central Mexico had fallen precipitously due to war, smallpox, and famine. The city of Tenochtitlan, the most beautiful city the Spaniards had ever seen, even more impressive than Constantinople, was reduced to rubble and ashes. Cortés would govern Mexico for the next three years, and a Catholic cathedral would be built on the ruins of the Aztec temple, which was known as the Pyramid of the Sun. The one positive note in this tragic story was that Cortés made progress in bringing the Aztec practices of human sacrifice and cannibalism to an end.

The inhabitants of Mexico realized that diseases were killing off the native population but not affecting the Spanish, who had a significant degree of immunity to those diseases. This was an important factor in making them so easily accept the Christian God who had protected the Spaniards.

On his world-circling voyage, Ferdinand Magellan, sailing for Spain, became caught up in evangelism and tried to convert Philippine tribes to Christianity. The Mactan tribe on an island near his anchorage site refused to have anything to do with the Spanish and their religion. Magellan was determined to force the Mactan to accept Christianity, thinking this would demonstrate to other native people the superiority of the Spanish God. Things didn't go well for Magellan though, and he was killed in the skirmish.

At the Diet of Worms, Holy Roman emperor Charles V presided in the heresy trial of Martin Luther. Charles knew that if Christians could ignore the orders of a pope, they could also ignore those of an emperor. Since Luther didn't recant his criticism of the pope or Vatican policies, he was declared a heretic and an outlaw. Agents of Prince Frederick, his protector, abducted Luther and escorted him to the Castle Wartburg for safety.

While in seclusion, Luther began working on a German translation of the New Testament. He desperately wanted the German people to be able to read it for themselves and see how far the popes and the Church had strayed from the simple teachings of Jesus. It would be published the next year.

1522

William Tyndale acquired a copy of Luther's German translation of the New Testament and began to translate it into English with the aid of the Greek version compiled by Erasmus. The Latin Vulgate was still the only translation authorized by the Catholic Church, so the bishop of London forbade Tyndale from printing his Bible. Four years later, Tyndale would travel to Germany to have his Bible printed.

While Martin Luther was denouncing witches, Emperor Charles V enacted a criminal code distinguishing between black and white magic and stating appropriate punishments. It was believed that white witchcraft was the type that was helpful to individuals and the community, but black magic was used for selfish purposes and evil.

In Switzerland and Germany, Protestants began to destroy Catholic art and adornments, and this practice would spread throughout northern Europe.

Dutchman Adriaan Florensz Boeyens was elected Pope Adrian VI, the last non-Italian to hold the position until Pope John Paul II almost five centuries later.

Ulrich Zwingli led the Swiss Reformation from his position as the most influential priest in Zürich. Zwingli and his fellow reformers had learned much from Erasmus, and their relationship with him continued to be friendly despite their differences. One of Zwingli's biblical interpretations was that "Christians are free to fast or not to fast because the Bible does not prohibit the eating of meat during Lent." The "Affair of the Sausages" ignited the Swiss Reformation when the city's printer Christoph Froschauer invited many city leaders, including Zwingli, to a sausage feast during Lent. Since this was forbidden by the Church, Church authorities charged Froschauer with heresy, but he continued to print under the protection of Protestants.

After a five-month siege, the Ottomans forced the Knights Hospitaller, the only Christian military force in the eastern Mediterranean, to surrender their base on the island of Rhodes. Sultan Suleiman was so impressed by their bravery that he allowed them to leave peacefully. They boarded ships and sailed to Malta, where their headquarters remains. They became known as the Knights of Malta.

1523

Luther published a pamphlet entitled *That Jesus Christ Was Born a Jew*, in which he criticized the inhumane treatment of Jews by Christians. He passionately desired that Jews would understand the Christian scripture and convert.

Officials in Paris burned the Augustinian monk Jean Valliére for supporting Luther's doctrines.

1524

France entered the competition for foreign discoveries and acquisitions when Italian explorer Giovanni da Verrazzano surveyed the North American coast on behalf of the king of France.

At Cortés's request, Franciscan friars began to arrive in Mexico to convert and control the native population.

The German Peasants' War began when preachers such as Thomas Müntzer inspired peasants to demand more rights and freedoms from their nobles and landlords. Their thinking was that if religious oppression could be rejected, then so could an antiquated social system. The revolt received little support from the leaders of the Reformation, who were not interested in spreading the Reformation by physical violence, only by spiritual rebellion.

1525

The Anabaptist movement began in Switzerland. They insisted on the baptism of adult believers who understood and confessed their faith and claimed that infant baptism was not found in scripture and was meaningless since the infant didn't choose to be baptized and had no idea what baptism signified. Following a public debate between Anabaptists Conrad Grebel and Felix Manz and Swiss reformer Ulrich Zwingli, the Zürich town council mandated that all infants had to be baptized within eight days, paralleling the Jewish circumcision rite. Both Catholics and Protestants would bitterly persecute the Anabaptists because of the statements and actions of their more radical members. The Amish, Hutterites, and Mennonites would be future sects that originated from Anabaptists.

In Zürich, Zwingli introduced a new liturgy to replace the Catholic Mass, and the city council passed an ordinance to use assets taken from Catholic monasteries to help the poor and fund schools.

The Battle of Frankenhausen marked the end of the German Peasants' War. At least 150,000 poorly armed peasants were killed in the revolt.

Protestant leaders debated the use of the crucifix. Luther never abandoned its use in Lutheran churches. Andreas Karlstadt, another prominent German reformer, Zwingli, and later John Calvin, a reformer in Geneva, were strongly opposed to both the cross and crucifix. Their opposition was based on the Ten Commandments' prohibition of idolatry and the manufacture of graven images of God. As a result of this controversy, Catholic religious statues and images, including frescos and mosaics, were vandalized or destroyed by zealous Protestants, echoing the iconoclastic era.

It was about this time that the title *pastor,* meaning "shepherd," came into use. Calvin and Zwingli both began to use the title to differentiate them from priests.

1526

Pope Clement VII granted amnesty to all Lutherans who desired to return to the Roman Catholic Church without the severe penalties that his predecessor, Pope Leo X, had imposed.

The Spanish founded San Miguel de Guadalupe with six hundred settlers in what would become South Carolina. It was the first European settlement in the future continental United States. They brought African slaves to the colony, but the slaves revolted along with Indigenous allies, and the colony only lasted three months.

One year after Tyndale finished his translation, a printer in Worms, Germany, produced the first copies of the Tyndale English Bible. The English Church banned it and threatened to burn any that they found. It would later become the basis for the King James version of the Bible, with about 83 percent of the King James New Testament and 76 percent of the Old Testament coming from Tyndale's translation.

The Waldensians, a sect that had been persecuted for over three centuries by the Catholics, emerged from seclusion in the Alps and contacted Protestants in northern Europe.

The Ottomans defeated the Hungarians at the Battle of Mohács. Ottoman power was again on the rise, and the rest of Europe feared what would come next.

1527

The Zürich town council passed an ordinance that made rebaptism of an adult punishable by drowning. Felix Manz became the first victim of the edict, and the first Anabaptist martyr when Protestants drowned him in the Limmat River while he was rebaptizing Christian adults.

Swiss Anabaptists issued the Schleitheim Confession as the most representative statement of their principles. It concerned adult baptism and pacifism, among other subjects. Anabaptists didn't want anyone baptized until they were old enough to intelligently state their commitment to Jesus. They also wanted to separate the Church from politics, and with their belief in salvation by faith alone, they brought down the wrath of the Church on themselves.

The army of the Holy Roman Empire defeated the French army in Italy. After the thirty-four thousand imperial troops were not paid, they forced their commander, Duke Charles III of Bourbon, to lead them to Rome, where they burned two-thirds of the city and forced Pope Clement VII to flee through a secret corridor to Castel Sant'Angelo.

During the sacking of Rome, the Holy Foreskin was reportedly stolen. It would later be recovered, and indulgences would be offered to those who visited it.

Italian Dominican scholar Santi Pagnini created a system of numbered verses in the Bible, but his system was never widely adopted.

1528

The Capuchins founded their monastic order in Italy as an offshoot of the Franciscans. Like others before them, they wanted to return to the ascetic lifestyle of Saint Francis, the founder of their order. Their two guiding principles were poverty and service to humanity.

The Church had Hans Schlaffer, a former Catholic priest who became an Anabaptist, burned as a heretic after he refused to recant his objections to infant baptism.

1529

The Ottoman Turks besieged Vienna, but without their heavy artillery, which was left behind due to torrential rains and mud, they failed to take the city.

Martin Luther wrote the hymn "A Mighty Fortress Is Our God" as a paraphrase of Psalm 46. It became a very inspirational song during the difficult times to come and is still a popular hymn today.

Thomas Bilney, an English Catholic priest in good standing with the Church, began preaching a doctrine that denounced the veneration of saints and relics. He made many enemies in the Church and was later arrested and burned.

The French lawyer, activist, and civil servant Louis de Berquin was burned at the stake for attempting to reform the French Catholic Church.

The Abyssinian-Adal War began in Ethiopia. Ethiopian and Portuguese Christians attempted to halt the invading Muslims, but the Christians lost the war, and three-quarters of Abyssinia fell under Muslim control.

Juan de Valdés published *Dialogue*, which gave rise to the Valdesian movement in Spain and opened the way for Protestant ideas. Valdés had to flee the country to avoid the Inquisition.

Martin Luther wrote *Small Catechism* to assist pastors in teaching Lutheran doctrines to common people.

Swiss Protestant reformers George Blaurock and Hans Langegger were arrested, tortured, and burned at the stake in Innsbruck, Austria. A religious civil war in Switzerland was narrowly avoided when several Swiss states, or cantons, resisted the Reformation and remained Catholic.

Luther met with Zwingli at the Marburg Colloquy in Germany. They reached a consensus on fourteen theological points but differed on the concept of the Eucharist. Luther believed the host represented the true body and blood of Christ, whereas Zwingli did not.

1530

For the first time, Jews in the Ottoman Empire were accused of ritual murder. The accusers were Armenian Christians, and the charge stemmed from a missing child. The townspeople rioted, and the local governor arrested a rabbi and several other Jewish leaders. Under torture, the men confessed and were hanged. A few days later, the boy whose supposed murder had sparked the violence turned up alive and unharmed.

At the Diet of Augsburg, Protestant German princes presented a formal statement of their religious beliefs to Charles V, the Holy Roman emperor. They also showed him a copy of the charter that Emperor Frederick Barbarossa issued in 1157. It demonstrated the privileges Henry IV had granted to Jews before the First Crusade. Charles declared that the document was binding and renewed it a few years later.

Pope Clement VII issued a proclamation granting indulgences to anyone who made a pilgrimage to Charroux, France, to visit the foreskin of Jesus. This decree was intended to resolve a dispute concerning which town had the true foreskin. Clement declared Charroux to have the authentic foreskin because it produced drops of blood.

The Barnabite order was established in Lombardy, Italy, to reform the Catholic Church. The Barnabites pointed out many Church problems such as dioceses without bishops, clergy without adequate knowledge or training, and monasteries and convents that were failing. This monastic order still exists, devoting themselves to good works, and espousing the epistles of Saint Paul.

Jacques Lefèvre d'Étaples printed the first French translation of the Bible in Antwerp, Belgium.

1531

Michael Servetus published his book *On the Errors of the Trinity*, explaining conflicts he encountered in understanding the concept of the Trinity.

Juan Diego, a recent Mexican convert to Christianity, was said to have seen a bright light atop a hill and heard someone calling his name. The legend continues that he climbed the hill and encountered a young girl in a golden mist who identified herself as the Virgin Mary. The apparition told him to gather the flowers that were miraculously blooming in December. He took them to a disbelieving priest, and when the flowers fell from the cloak he had carried them in, the image of Mary appeared on the cloak's fabric. This began the tradition of Our Lady of Guadalupe, and Diego's cloak became one of Christianity's most visited sacred relics. This legend may be tied to an early fourteenth-century legend of Our Lady of Guadalupe in Extremadura, Spain.

c. French reformer John Calvin took up the Reform tradition begun by Zwingli, and it would later bear his name, Calvinism. The five tenets of this theology were the total depravity of human beings; unconditional election, or salvation of the few chosen by God; atonement by Jesus for the sins of the elect; the irresistible grace of God for those he chose to save; and perseverance of the saints, meaning those he chose will be with him for eternity.

1532

Francisco Pizarro led a Spanish expedition from Panama to Peru. Following the tactics of Cortés, he conquered Peru with a few hundred Spaniards, anti-Inca allies, and much deception. The Inca ruler Atahualpa refused to submit to the Spanish and pay homage to the Christian God or tribute to the Spanish king. Pizzaro fought and defeated the Incas at the Battle of Cajamarca, killing thousands for resisting him. He captured Atahualpa, and despite receiving a ransom of a room full of gold and two rooms full of silver, Pizzaro put the Inca ruler through a mock trial and sentenced him to be burned at the stake. Atahualpa agreed to be baptized if they would kill him in some other way, so the Spanish strangled Atahualpa and gave him a Christian burial.

Church leaders in Zürich executed Anabaptists Heinrich Karpfis and Hans Herzog by drowning them.

Waldensian pastors held a synod near Turin, Italy. They invited leaders of the German and Swiss Reform movements to attend in order to determine if the Waldensian doctrines agreed with those preached by Luther and Calvin.

Emperor Charles V issued *Constitutio Criminalis Carolina*, declaring harmful witchcraft to be punishable by death by fire but white witchcraft to have a lesser penalty.

Suleiman and the Ottomans again tried to capture Vienna, but the weather once more ruined their plans. Many people believed that Western Christianity being saved by the weather was a sign that God was protecting them.

1533

Henry VIII of England was married to Catherine of Aragon, the daughter of Ferdinand and Isabella of Spain and the aunt of Holy Roman emperor Charles V. For the last six years, Henry had been trying to have this marriage annulled because Catherine had not produced a male heir for him. Being a devout Catholic, he wanted the consent of Pope Clement VI, but the pope was trying to remain on good terms with the emperor so he would not grant it. Henry secretly married Anne Boleyn, but the pope wouldn't recognize the marriage, and by the end of the year, he had excommunicated Henry for his defiance. Henry then had his parliament prepare a declaration of ecclesiastical independence from Rome.

1534

With the Act of Supremacy, Henry VIII declared himself the supreme head of the Church of England and broke from the Roman Catholic Church. Henry's main religious advisor Thomas Cranmer, the arch-bishop of Canterbury, held a special court and granted Henry the annulment the pope would not allow. Although Henry declared his independence from the pope, the Church of England continued to op-erate as a Catholic Church and adopted few, if any, of the Protestant reforms that were occurring in northern Europe.

Martin Luther finished his translation of the Old Testament. This not only made scripture more accessible to the average German but also enabled the development of a standard version of the written German language.

Francis Xavier, then a teacher of Aristotelian philosophy at the University of Paris, met with Basque Catholic priest Ignatius of Loyola, Peter Faver of Savoy, and four other students. They swore a vow to go to the Holy Land and convert infidels. Five years later this seed would blossom into the Society of Jesus, better known as the order of Jesuits.

1535

In 1492, the island of Hispaniola had struck Columbus as a veritable paradise with a prosperous and untroubled population of around eight million Taínos. Only forty-three years later, due to Spanish-introduced diseases and the cruel treatment and starvation of the people, the native population was almost eliminated.

At the request of Henry VIII's Canterbury Convocation, Miles Coverdale translated the Bible into English and produced the first version printed in England. Tyndale's English-language Bible had been printed in Germany and had been derived from Hebrew and Greek texts, whereas the Coverdale Bible was compiled using Latin, English, and German sources.

Thomas Cromwell, the chief minister to Henry VIII of England, began closing Catholic monasteries and transferring their wealth to the king's treasury.

Catholic leaders such as John Fisher and Thomas More could not convince Henry VIII to change his mind about cutting ties with the pope. Neither could Robert Barnes or John Frith convince him to bring England more in step with what the reformers were doing on the continent. Henry had them all beheaded for their opposition to him. Three Carthusian monks and two Catholic priests were also hanged, drawn, and quartered in London for refusing to accept Henry VIII as the head of the Church.

Pierre Robert Olivétan, a Waldensian, revised and improved the French Bible that d'Étaples had first printed in 1530.

At the request of Henry VIII, William Tyndale was betrayed and seized in Antwerp. He was turned over to imperial Catholic authorities, who tried him on the charge of heresy and condemned him to death. He was strangled, and then his dead body was burned at the stake.

1536

c. Lutheran and Anglican theologians met to define a Protestant theology. Due to their different interpretations of the scriptures, they failed to find much common ground.

Anabaptists and Calvinists also had their own ways of viewing the Bible. Once the lid was removed from the boiling pot of forced Catholic conformity, almost every prior heresy would begin anew since there was no regulation by a centralized Church.

Menno Simons rejected the Catholic Church and the priesthood and became an Anabaptist. His followers became known as Mennonites and were committed to following the peaceful and loving ways of Jesus.

King John III established the Portuguese Inquisition. Like the Spanish Inquisition, its main targets were Jews who had converted to Catholicism. This Inquisition would remain viable until 1821.

In Münster, Germany, militant Anabaptists took over the city. They controlled the city for over a year and treated the non-Anabaptist population harshly. When Catholic troops besieging the city finally gained entry, they arrested and executed the Anabaptist leaders, hanging their bodies in cages from Saint Lambert's Church.

Dutch humanist reformer Desiderius Erasmus died. Unlike other reformers of his time, he had never left the Church. Like Origen, he argued that eternal damnation made nonsense of the idea of a loving and forgiving God.

French theologian, pastor, and reformer John Calvin published *The Institutes of the Christian Religion* in Latin, and later in French. It was an introductory textbook to the Protestant faith and a major document of the Reformation.

The bishop of Worcester, England, issued a sweeping denunciation of relics. He thought the precious metals and jewels in relics and statues should be used to help the needy and that pilgrimages lost their meaning when they became an unending journey from one image or relic to another. This was especially true because relics were often nothing more than the bones of farm animals. He also protested that the vast number of saint's days made it difficult for peasants to earn a living as too many feasts ended in drunkenness and made people unproductive.

The Church of England instituted reforms such as cancelling feasts held during the harvest season and forcing priests who continued to encouraged pilgrimages to recant.

1537

Pope Paul III appointed a committee of reform-minded cardinals. They issued the report *Commission for Reforming the Church*, which called for the papacy to focus on spiritual matters, not politics, the accumulation of wealth, or territorial matters. The cardinals also criticized the sale of offices and the incompetency of many bishops.

At the urging of Dominicans Bernardino de Minaya and Julián Garcés, Pope Paul III issued *Sublimus Deus*, a major pronouncement against atrocities and slavery in America. He called the native Americans "human beings who were not to be robbed of their freedom or possessions." This was believed to apply to native populations in the New World but not to the transatlantic African slave trade. Ironically, Pope Paul also authorized the purchase and possession of Muslim slaves within the Papal States.

Former Portuguese soldier João Duarte Cidade had a conversion experience followed by an apparent mental breakdown. In that weakened state, he had a vision of Mary that encouraged him to work with the poor, and he devoted the rest of his life to that cause, becoming known as John of God. In 1572, his disciples were recognized as the Brothers Hospitallers of Saint John of God and were entrusted with the medical care of the popes.

1538

c. Flemish physician Andreas Vesalius began to revolutionize medicine by clandestinely dissecting human cadavers. As the chairman of anatomy and surgery at the University of Padua, Vesalius believed the best medical education for his students was to dissect human bodies. The Church-imposed ban on human dissection as blasphemy had been relaxed, but it was still illegal in many countries. Vesalius took the study of anatomy well beyond that of Galen thirteen centuries earlier. Because of religious restrictions, Galen had dissected only animals, and his works were still the sole references for anatomical knowledge.

Approximately eight million Mexicans had been converted to the Catholic faith, largely due to the miracle of Our Lady of Guadalupe. The basilica built at the site of the miracle eventually became the most visited Catholic pilgrimage site in the world.

In Spain, the writings of Erasmus caused hostility between two rival groups, the Erasmistas and anti-Erasmistas. The king's own priest, Alonso de Virués, was arrested and sent to prison for four years because he supported the reformist views of Erasmus.

A writer in Toledo, Spain, describing the paranoia during the Inquisitions, wrote "preachers do not dare to preach, and those who preach do not dare to touch on contentious matters."

1539

Officials in Rome discontinued Passion plays because they were too often followed by civil unrest and the sacking of the Jewish ghetto.

Luther grew increasingly aggressive and abusive in his verbal attacks on Jews. He wrote *On the Jews and Their Lies*, in which he stated his belief that Jews would never convert to Christianity, calling them "children of the devil." If their conversion was not possible, then he saw no reason to tolerate them, and he campaigned for their expulsion from German and Western society. He also directed the same ire at Christians who treated Jews with compassion. In this treatise, he unknowingly helped lay the groundwork for the Holocaust four centuries later when it was recirculated in Germany by the Nazis.

German Protestant electors met to decide whether to expel Jews from their territories. In the defense of Jews, Philipp Melanchthon, author of the Augsburg Confession, said that when he was a young priest, thirty-eight Jews were convicted of desecrating the host. Just before their execution, their accuser confessed that he had lied about the incident. Melanchthon informed the Duke of Brandenburg of the accuser's confession but was ordered to remain silent. Rather than see himself and his Church embarrassed, the duke allowed the mass murder of those innocent people.

1540

Andreas Osiander, a Lutheran from Nuremberg, Germany, published essays defending Jews. He said that to imprison, torture, or execute Jews on charges that they stood against "God's word, nature, and human reason" was to do the work of the devil.

French officials arrested Collin Pellenc for heresy and burned him alive after a Waldensian Bible was found in his house.

Ignatius of Loyola, along with six of his companions, traveled to Rome to gain approval for their new monastic order to be known as the Society of Jesus. Other monastic orders considered the official name of the Jesuit order as blasphemous because it mentioned Jesus, but although the accusers tried, they could never get the Jesuits to change their name. Loyola believed in salvation through good deeds as well as faith. He was unconditionally obedient to the pope and became extremely active in the Catholic Counter-Reformation. The Jesuits would establish hundreds of colleges and seminaries and carry Christianity to India, Japan, China, Africa, and the Americas. They were stringent on their genealogical requirements and did not allow anyone with Jewish ancestry to join until 1946.

1541

William Farel convinced John Calvin to return to Geneva despite their expulsion three years earlier. There, they created a "Protestant Rome," driving out anyone who wasn't Protestant and training missionaries to spread the reformed message to other countries, especially France.

In Regensburg, Germany, Protestants and Catholic leaders met with the hope of reconciliation. They agreed that the Christian God was the only source of salvation and that good deeds were necessary to honor man's salvation by God.

Michelangelo completed his magnificent fresco *The Last Judgment* above the altar in the Sistine Chapel at the Vatican. His depiction of a clean-shaven, Apollo-like Jesus—instead of a bearded Jesus—brought him much criticism.

1542

With the Holy Roman Empire fighting the Turks in the Balkan states, typhus gained a bridgehead into Europe, killing some thirty thousand Christian soldiers. Four years later, the same disease struck the Ottomans, ending their siege at Belgrade.

The Roman Inquisition, or the Supreme Sacred Congregation of the Roman and Universal Inquisition, began as a series of tribunals. It was responsible for prosecuting individuals accused of a wide range of crimes relating to Catholic doctrine or alternate religious beliefs, mainly Protestantism. This office of the Vatican still exists as the Congregation for the Doctrine of the Faith, but without the barbarity of the past.

Henry VIII passed the first witchcraft act in England allowing for the confiscation of the property of an accused witch and execution if found guilty.

1543

Polish mathematician, astronomer, and clergyman Nicolaus Copernicus died at about the time his book *On the Revolutions of the Heavenly Spheres* was printed. This book is considered by many scholars to have launched the scientific revolution. Copernicus's theory was only possible because he had access to the printed writings of past astronomers and was able to see patterns that had been documented over the centuries. It wouldn't be long before scholars throughout Europe had access to his theory and could contribute their knowledge to help solve further scientific questions. The Church rejected Copernicus's theory of a sun-centered planetary system as blasphemy because, by not placing humans at the center of the universe, it conflicted with holy scripture. The Copernican concept was so radical and counter-intuitive that in his day very few people were able to understand it. As science historian Michael J. Crowe wrote about Copernicus in *A History of the Extraterrestrial Life Debate*, he "changed our Earth into a planet and inevitably, if gradually, transformed stars into other suns."

c. The Portuguese were the first Europeans to reach Japan, although probably not the first Christians since Nestorians or *Keikyoto* (as they were known in China) missionaries or soldiers may have arrived there as early as the eighth century. The Portuguese sought trade, not conquest, and a generation later, they founded the port of Nagasaki and acted as middlemen in European trade with Asia. In the first twenty-five years following the Portuguese arrival in Japan, Portuguese Jesuit missionaries may have converted as many as 250,000 Japanese to Christianity and established two hundred churches.

Andreas Vesalius wrote *On the Fabric of the Human Body* in response to the printed works of the second-century Greek physician Galen. He pointed out over two hundred anatomical errors that Galen had made because he had never dissected a human body. Copernicus and Vesalius were pushing the limits of knowledge thanks to the availability of printed writings from the past, and their ideas spread like wildfire, fueling the European Renaissance.

1544

Martin Luther wrote *Tischreden*, in which he criticized the Copernican theory of a sun-centered solar system. Luther, like most other Christians, viewed the concept as a violation of scripture.

Johannes Bugenhagen, a close associate of Martin Luther, began organizing new Lutheran churches in northern Germany, Denmark, and Norway.

1545

After the Waldensians came out of seclusion in Bohemia, France, and Germany, French King Francis I assembled an army to destroy them. In the area of Mérindol, Catholic troops massacred several thousand.

Pope Paul III convened the Council of Trent in response to the Protestant heresies. He formulated plans for a Counter-Reformation and charged the Jesuits with stemming the tide of Protestantism in Poland, Bohemia, Hungary, Bavaria, France, and the Netherlands.

1546

Jesuit co-founder Francis Xavier pleaded with the king of Portugal, John III, to begin an inquisition in the Portuguese colony of Goa, India.

Assassins killed Cardinal Beaton at his castle in Scotland to avenge his recent execution of reformer George Wishart.

Henry VIII sought an alliance with the Holy Roman emperor, but the price was ending the reforms of the Church of England. One victim of Henry's intransigence was Anne Askew, an English writer, poet, and Protestant. Inquisitors tortured her for weeks because she denied the doctrine of transubstantiation and refused to name other Protestants who held similar beliefs. She was eventually burned at the stake at the Tower of London.

1547

King Henry II of France condemned French Protestants, known as Huguenots. He ordered that those who would not repent be burned at the stake.

The archbishop of Toledo protested when Pope Paul III appointed a priest with Jewish ancestry to serve in Toledo's cathedral, arguing that he had "impure blood." The pope backed down and named a replacement to the post. The Spanish applied their purity laws not only to clergy, but the military, universities, guilds, and government offices. Any candidate for office had to divulge his place of birth and the names of his ancestors, and that information would be investigated for Jewish or Muslim ancestry.

1549

Spanish Jesuit missionary Francis Xavier reached Japan and later traveled to Indonesia, Malaysia, India, and China. Protestant missionaries would not reach these regions for another 150 years.

After Henry VIII's death, Thomas Cranmer, the archbishop of Canterbury, was able to institute changes to the Church of England that were more in line with the Reformation on the continent. He had images removed from churches; discontinued private confessions to priests; and abolished all superstitious practices, including processions of saints, healing with holy water, blessing candles, and the use of incense to drive away demons. Clergy were permitted to marry, and a new liturgy was adopted, but Mass continued in Latin.

1550

King Edward VI of England continued to eliminate Catholic influences from the island, but dissolution of monasteries resulted in the closure of almost all the hospitals in England. In 1600, even London would have only three functioning hospitals, and none were very large.

The Italian Renaissance reached its peak. It had been stimulated by refugees and progressive ideas from Constantinople and Spain, where ancient Greek writings and art had been preserved by Muslims, Nestorians, and Jews. This period allowed a rebirth of the classical learning and art that had been suppressed by Christians in the fourth and fifth centuries. The Renaissance would last until the seventeenth century when foreign invasions plunged Italy back into the familiar turmoil of war.

In Valladolid, Spain, Dominican friar Bartolomé de Las Casas and humanist scholar Juan Ginés de Sepúlveda debated over the rights and treatment of conquered Indigenous people. Las Casas argued that native Americans were free men and deserved the same human rights as the Spanish people and should not be forced to convert to Christianity but instead enticed to the religion based on the good examples that Christians set. He exposed the horrendous treatment of the native people in America by the Spanish. In response, Sepúlveda argued that because of their primitive nature and the crimes of human sacrifice and cannibalism, the Indigenous people should be suppressed at all costs, including war.

1551

French printer Robert Estienne developed the now widely adopted division of biblical chapters into numbered verses, making it easier for readers and congregations to locate specific passages. This was an improvement on the system created by Santi Pagnini in 1527, but an unintended result was that verses could easily be taken out of context and lose their original meaning when used alone.

Jews were officially expelled from most of Bavaria. They would return to Sulzbach in 1666 under the protection of Count Christian August.

1552

Leaders with different goals caused a schism in the Nestorian Church, and it branched into the Chaldean Catholic Church, the Assyrian Church of the East, and the Ancient Church of the East. The Chaldean Church came into full communion with Rome and establish its patriarchate in Mosul, Iraq. The other two churches remained independent.

1553

Pope Julius III declared that the Jewish Talmud was disrespectful to Christians and ordered all copies burned. Church officials burned Jewish books in Rome, Bologna, Florence, Venice, and other cities in Italy, just as had been done in France.

After King Edward VI of England's death, his chosen heir, Lady Jane Grey, a Protestant, became queen, but she reigned for only nine days before Edward's half-sister Mary, who was a Catholic, had her deposed. After Mary became queen, she saw to it that Lady Jane, her husband, and her father were convicted of high treason and executed. Jane was only sixteen or seventeen years old.

Michael Servetus published his major work *The Restoration of Christianity*. In refuting how the Holy Spirit enters the body, he put forth for the first time, the correct theory of pulmonary circulation. He reasoned that blood was the seat of the soul, which was breathed into man by God, so blood and air had to make contact in the lungs. However, orthodox Christians considered him a heretic for his views on the Trinity, and when he traveled to Geneva at John Calvin's invitation, he was arrested. Protestant officials tortured him, convicted him on the charge of denying the Trinity, and burned him at the stake along with his books.

1555

Queen Mary restored England to Roman Catholicism and was responsible for burning up to three hundred Protestants, including Archbishop Thomas Cranmer and clergyman and Bible translator John Rogers. For her ruthlessness she earned the name Bloody Mary.

English Protestant reformer John Hooper, who had declined the bishopric of Gloucester five years earlier, was another clergyman burned as a heretic.

In Rome, Giovanni Carafa, the cardinal in charge of the Roman Inquisition, became Pope Paul IV. He quarantined Jews in the ghetto, denying them most of the freedoms to which they had been accustomed. As with other ghettos, the one in Rome had only one gate, and it was locked in the evening. The pope's rationale was that the Jews' "own guilt has consigned them to perpetual servitude." The Jews were relentlessly pressured to convert and forced to wear special clothing if they didn't.

Holy Roman emperor Charles V declared the Peace of Augsburg, which decreed that every region, city, princedom, and kingdom should abide by the theological decisions and beliefs of its ruler, whether Catholic, Lutheran, or Calvinist. Subjects who could not accept this system would have to emigrate. This created unending problems when leaders vacillated between two religions, and the people had to go along with whatever they decided.

1556

When Spanish king Philip II organized an inquisition in the Spanish-ruled Netherlands, the Dutch revolted, demanding the right to follow their own religious beliefs with complete freedom of choice. The northern provinces gained their independence, but the southern provinces, present-day Belgium, remained under Spanish rule.

c. A cult devoted to Our Lady of Guadalupe came into existence in Tepeyac, Mexico. The image of the Virgin was placed at the shrine, and it became a popular pilgrimage site. Apparently, at that time, there was no mention to a supernatural origin concerning the image, but that would become part of the legend by the early seventeenth century.

1558

Elizabeth I was coronated as queen of England—after her half-sister, Mary Tudor, died—and returned the country to Protestantism. Realizing the threat of a Catholic crusade against England, she fostered a moderate Anglican Church but did execute many Catholic

priests who secretly continued to attempt to reestablish their church
in England.

1560

Pope Pius IV installed his nephew, the learned layman Charles
Borromeo, as cardinal, secretary of state to the pope, and archbishop
of Milan. Borromeo gave away much of his wealth and avoided the
comfort of earthly possessions. He became one of the great reformers
of the Catholic Church, fully devoted to his spiritual duties. He was
so passionate about reforming the laxity of the church and population
that he was either loved or hated by the people he served.

The Scottish Parliament adopted a Calvinistic profession of faith
drawn up by John Knox. Until this point, the Reformation had been
repressed in Scotland, and several reformers had been executed there.

A Portuguese established their inquisition in their colony of Goa,
India, to punished converts from Hinduism or Islam who were believed to have returned to their non-Christian beliefs and habits. This
inquisition did not end until 1812, and it "examined" approximately
sixteen thousand people, and executed fifty-seven of them.

1561

Mary, Queen of Scots—a Catholic who had been living in France as
the wife of King Francis II—returned to Scotland as a widow but made
no attempt to return the Scots to Catholicism.

In Zimbabwe, Portuguese Jesuit missionary Goncalo da Silveira baptized the king of Mutapa.

1562

The duke of Guise ordered that a barn full of Huguenots be set on
fire, killing all sixty worshippers inside. Another 1,200 Huguenots

were massacred at Vassey and Sens. A civil war began between French Catholics and Huguenots that would last until 1598.

1563

Queen Elizabeth I approved the Thirty-Nine Articles, which established the framework for the Church of England in relation to the Protestants, Anabaptists, and Catholic theologies.

Johann Weyer, the town doctor in Arnhem, Netherlands, wrote *On Conjuring Tricks of Demons*, in which he ridiculed witch hysteria. He stated that the devil had no power over the human body and that mentally ill people should be pitied and healed, not arrested and punished for witchcraft.

The Council of Trent ended with bishops adopting many canons to repress the heresy of the Protestant Reformation. They issued the Roman Catechism to define exactly what Catholics believed as far as sacred tradition, original sin, salvation, sacraments, and veneration of saints. They set new, tougher regulations for training priests and found failure to tithe as grounds for excommunication.

1564

c. The Puritans arose as a reform movement that sought to purify the Church of England from its quasi-Catholic practices.

Pope Pius IV issued the papal bull *Dominici gregis custodiae*, which placed Protestant writings on the banned book list, allowed for Old Testament translations only by learned men under the supervision of a bishop, and forbade any translations of the New Testament.

1565

The Spanish established the colony of Saint Augustine in Florida, and it became the first permanent European settlement in what would become the continental United States. The Spanish launched an expedition against French Huguenots who had settled in what is now South Carolina. They killed almost everyone in the colony, then tracked down the survivors and massacred them.

1567

Pope Pius V issued a papal bull against bullfighting and fighting any animal for sport. This document is often referenced as one of the earliest animal protection steps, but the pope's main purpose was protecting the moral welfare and salvation of the Christians who attended the fights.

1568

King Philip II of Spain ordered the duke of Alva to the southern Netherlands, still a Spanish possession, to conduct an inquisition to root out Protestants. The duke sought either complete submission or death and conducted many atrocities, including a mass drowning of six thousand to seven thousand people.

The Turks arrested Damian, a Greek monk, and charged him with preventing Christians from working or conducting business on Sundays. They fed him only bread and water and tortured him for fifteen days. Apparently, after he mocked the judge, Turkish officials hanged him and then burned him at the stake.

After the counts of Egmont and Horn protested the Spanish Inquisition in Flanders, both men were arrested for heresy and beheaded.

c. By this time the Spanish Inquisition had spread to Mexico and Peru. Officials executed up to fifty people in Mexico, mostly for being Jewish sympathizers. When the English ship *Jesus of Lubeck* wrecked on the coast of Mexico, the Spanish captured some of the Protestant crew members and subjected them to inquisition. The Spanish Inquisition wouldn't officially end until 1834.

In retaliation for the way they had been treated by Christians, Jews excluded Christians from their community in Kazimierz, Poland, a town built by Jews after their expulsion from Krakow.

1569

Pope Pius V issued a bull officially establishing the devotion to the rosary by introducing the Feast of Our Lady of the Rosary.

Dutch Anabaptist Dirk Willems escaped from his prison window by rope and then by crossing a frozen moat. When the heavy guard chasing him fell through the ice, the compassionate Willems turned back to help him. He was recaptured and burned at the stake.

Pope Pius V expelled all Jews from the Papal States, except for Rome and Verona, unless they converted to Christianity.

1570

Pope Pius V issued a bull excommunicating Protestant Queen Elizabeth I of England as a heretic and threatened to excommunicate any of her subjects who obeyed her.

The Ottoman Turks invaded Cyprus. At Nicosia, after a forty-day siege, they killed some twenty thousand townspeople and looted churches, public buildings, and the palace.

1571

After a heroic eleven-month defense, the Venetian fortress of Famagusta, Cyprus, fell to the Ottomans. The Turks lost approximately 52,000 of their 250,000 soldiers during their five assaults, and the Venetian defenders only lost 8,000 soldiers. After the surrender, the Christian population was protected for three days during their evacuation from the city, but then the Ottomans seized Venetian leader Marcantonio Bragadin. The Ottoman leader, Mustafa Pasha, accused Bragadin of having previously broken a promise of safe passage for a group of Muslim pilgrims. He had Bragadin flayed alive, and then quartered. The Turks also beheaded the Venetian governor and general and massacred any Christians who remained in the city.

Spaniards had kidnapped a teen-aged Native American boy from his home in Virginia and given him the baptized name Don Luis de Velasco. After eleven years living with the Spanish, he told his priest that he was ready to go home and returned as a guide and interpreter for a party of Jesuit missionaries. Once back home in Virginia, he later led an attack that wiped out the Jesuit mission. The Spanish would return and seek revenge, but that was the end of their plans to colonize Virginia.

Inspired by the bravery and martyrdom of Marcantonio Bragadin, Pope Pius V organized a fleet of the Holy League, his coalition of Catholic states, to attack the Ottomans. The fleet of more than 200 war vessels, flying the flag of the Crucifixion, met the Ottoman fleet off the coast of Greece. The Christians delivered a stunning defeat to the Turks at the Battle of Lepanto, where the Ottomans lost 113 ships and the Christians lost only 12. The Holy League captured another 117 Turkish ships and liberated some 15,000 Christian galley slaves.

Pope Pius V assigned Charles Borromeo, the archbishop of Milan, to institute reforms in the Humiliati monastic order. After one of the monks tried to kill Borromeo, Pius had the main conspirators executed, then he issued a bull suppressing the Humiliati order, which had existed since the twelfth century. He offered their dwellings and possessions to other religious orders, such as the Barnabites and Jesuits, or gave them to charity.

1572

Enraged by the wedding of her daughter to a Protestant, Queen Catherine of France, the mother of King Charles IX, ordered the Saint Bartholomew's Day Massacre in Paris and surrounding provinces. In these atrocities, lower-class Catholics murdered forty thousand to seventy thousand mostly prosperous Huguenots. Afterward, Pope

Gregory XIII wrote to King Charles IX, "We rejoice with you that with the help of God you have relieved the world of these wretched heretics."

Eastern Orthodox officials in Constantinople elected Jeremias II as patriarch of the Church. He interacted more with the Catholic Church than had most past patriarchs and approved full independence to the Russian Orthodox Church.

1573

The Spanish took the city of Haarlem in the Netherlands after a seven-month siege, then executed the entire Protestant military garrison, which included English, Germans, and French Huguenots.

1574

Lutherans, inspired by Matthias Vlacich, completed the *Magdeburg Centuries*. Begun in 1559, it was a multivolume set on Christian history covering a period of thirteen centuries. It documented the gradual corruption of the Catholic Church leading to the need for radical reformation.

The Portuguese founded the settlement of Luanda in Angola, southern Africa, and turned it into a major slave exporting port.

1576

Franciscan friar Girolamo Menghi wrote *The Devil's Scourge*, in which he argued that exorcisms should be performed in church in front of an audience because that's how Jesus exorcized demons in the Gospels.

1577

Catholic authorities in Antwerp executed Hans Bret, a young Anabaptist and a baker by trade. His crime was the heresy of being rebaptized. They tortured him for months, but he would not deny his faith. He was so passionate in his beliefs that when it was time for his burning, they clamped and seared his tongue so he wouldn't be able to preach to the crowd.

1578

Inquisitor Francisco Peña stated, "We must remember that the main purpose of the trial and execution is not to save the soul of the accused but to achieve the public good and put fear into others."

Duke Emmanuel Philibert of Savoy ordered the Holy Shroud be transferred from Chambéry, France, to Turin, Italy, where it remains.

Along Via Salaria in Rome, a resident accidentally discovered an entrance to the ancient subterranean cemeteries known as the catacombs.

1579

The Union of Utrecht was a treaty unifying the northern provinces of the Netherlands and giving the citizens freedom to hold whatever religious belief they chose. However, it did however not allow Lutherans or Jews to establish new churches.

1580

In the Portuguese colony of Goa, after the Inquisition declared Garcia de Orta a "crypto-Jew," his remains were exhumed and burned. De Orta was a physician of Jewish heritage who died twelve years earlier while studying tropical medicine in India. Many other Jewish converts changed their names and created false genealogies to avoid a similar fate.

1581

The Roman Inquisition began a witch hunt in Trier, Germany. Over the next twelve years at least 368 people, including some of the leading citizens, would be put to death in that city alone.

Protestant scholar Theodore Beza obtained a partial New Testament from the fifth century that had been in Lyon for centuries before being stolen by Huguenots and turned over to him. It became known as Codex Bezae, and since it was written in Greek and Latin, it was extremely valuable in facilitating translation.

1582

Spanish nun, mystic, and author Teresa of Ávila died. She had a significant influence in the Counter-Reformation and reformed the Carmelite Order, which consisted of both women and men. Her written works are still important in Christian mystical and meditation practices today.

Pope Gregory XIII instituted the Gregorian calendar, which refined the ancient Roman Julian calendar to reconcile the current date with the actual revolution of Earth around the sun (although at that time, it was mostly thought that the sun revolved around Earth) of 365 and a quarter days. The mathematical calculations necessitated skipping ahead twelve days. Since Easter is determined based on the full moon, this adjustment changed the date for Easter. The Gregorian calendar was adopted first by the Catholic regions but was not adopted by the British Empire until 1752. This is now the most widely used calendar in the world. Beginning about this time, the Vatican periodically operated its own celestial observatory.

Matteo Ricci, an Italian Jesuit friar, arrived in China and worked his way into the emperor's confidence. He had a long and successful ministry in China but became controversial to Europeans because he chose to dress in Chinese attire and adapt Christianity to their culture. He felt that Christianity had to integrate into local customs and traditions to be successful.

1584

English settlers landed on Roanoke Island in present-day North Carolina to establish a permanent colony. When a relief expedition landed in 1587, all the original inhabitants had vanished, leaving very little evidence of what had happened to them. They are remembered as the Lost Colony of Roanoke.

1586

Pope Sixtus V removed Clement of Alexandria, a Church Father who had lived in the second century, from the Roman Catholic list of saints. Sixtus questioned the orthodoxy of some of Clement's writings. Clement was closely associated with Origen, who had been Clement's student and had also fallen from the Church's grace.

For almost a century prior to this time, the patriarchate of the Eastern Orthodox Church had presided in the Church of Pammakaristos in Constantinople. This year, the Ottomans moved the patriarchate to the smaller Church of Saint George. By the end of the century, there would only be three Christian churches left in the entire city.

Spanish nun Maria de la Visitación exhibited signs of stigmata on her hands and side and crown-of-thorns-type puncture marks on her forehead. Inquisition investigators discovered that the marks on her hands could be rubbed off. They also discovered that two Dominican friars had put her up to the trick in hopes of benefiting from their association with a potential saint.

1587

Manteo, a member of the Croatoan tribal nation who had befriended the original Roanoke Island settlers and later had traveled to England, became the first Native American to be baptized as a Protestant, taking the baptismal name Jack Straw.

William Allen, the exiled cardinal of England's Catholic Church, exhorted King Philip II of Spain to invade England, where Allen assured Philip that the Spanish would find allies among the country's disgruntled Catholic population.

Toyotomi Hideyoshi became the ruler in Japan and was alarmed by the practices of the Portuguese Christians in Nagasaki, which included forced conversions, the garrisoning of troops, slavery, and eating horses and oxen flesh. He issued the Christian Expulsion Edict, banning Christianity and expelling all foreign missionaries.

Queen Elizabeth I had her Catholic cousin Mary, Queen of Scots, beheaded after Mary was found guilty of plotting to assassinate Elizabeth.

1588

The English navy defeated the Spanish Armada, preventing Spanish King Philip II from reinstating Catholicism in England. Philip took the role as main defender of Catholicism in Europe seriously, using his newfound riches from South American silver mines to finance attacks on Protestants in northern Europe.

Scottish authorities arrested Alison Pearson, a known healer, for the second time. Five years earlier, she had helped cure Patrick Adamson, the ailing archbishop of Saint Andrews, after no one else had been successful. The archbishop's enemies had claimed Alison was a witch and imprisoned her, but Adamson had helped her escape. This time she was retried, found guilty of using an herbal concoction to heal Adamson, and was burned at the stake for witchcraft.

1591

Spanish mystic, author, artist, priest, and reformer John of the Cross died. He had worked closely with Teresa of Ávila in reforming the Carmelite order. His books *Spiritual Canticle* and *Dark Night of the Soul* are still considered masterpieces of Spanish literature.

Twenty-three-year-old theology student Aloysius Gonzaga died in Rome after selflessly caring for victims of a plague. This was even after his superiors advised him not to take the risk.

1592

Father Cornelius Loos wrote of the inquisitions: "Wretched creatures are compelled by the severity of the torture to confess things they have never done, and so by cruel butchery, innocent lives are taken; and by a new alchemy, gold and silver are coined from human blood."

Spanish Franciscan friar Paschal Bayon had lived a life of austerity, humility, and self-imposed suffering. When he died, his followers covered his body with lime in the belief it would speed the body's decomposition and produce shiny white bones as relics. After eight months, his entire body was discovered to be miraculously preserved because they didn't realize that lime acted as a preservative.

1594

The faculty at the University of Tübingen, Germany, barred Johannes Kepler, one of the greatest scientists of his age, from teaching there due to his support of the heliocentric theory. Fortunately, he was a Lutheran and wasn't subject to the Roman Inquisition.

1595

Catholic attorney and witch-hunter Nicholas Rémy wrote *Demonolatry*, in which he discussed many cases of demon possession and claimed to have personally condemned over nine hundred witches to death. His career grew out of an obsession for vengeance because he believed his son had been killed by a witch's spell.

The population of central Mexico has been estimated at around 25 million people when the Spaniards arrived in 1519. By this time, there were only about 1.3 million remaining in the region.

1596

The Netherlands began their foreign explorations using Portuguese-trained Cornelis de Houtman as captain and reaching Java by sailing around Africa.

1597

Twenty-six Christians, including six Franciscan missionaries, were tortured and crucified outside Nagasaki, Japan, to discourage other Christians in the region. The Japanese persecution would last until 1632.

1598

Henry IV of France, seeking civil unity, signed the Edict of Nantes, which granted tolerance and equal rights to the Huguenots.

1599

Goa's catholic archbishop Alexis de Menezes called the Synod of Diamper, in which the Portuguese forced the Thomas Christians, who had been in communion with the Church of the East since AD 295, to accept the authority of the pope and Portuguese clergy. His synod passed 267 decrees against the Thomas Christians and collected and burned their scriptures. Their entire written history, 1,300 years of manuscripts, was destroyed. The Thomas Christians had received much more tolerance from the Hindus than their fellow Christians.

Officials sentenced Italian miller Domenico Scandella to prison for making atheistic statements in public. The availability of printed books allowed many ordinary people like Domenico to have access to knowledge that had in the past only been accessible to the highly educated people of the upper class. He was tortured to induce him to implicate others, then burned at the stake.

CHAPTER 17: SEVENTEENTH CENTURY AD

I do not feel obliged to believe that the same God who has endowed us with sense, reason, and intellect has intended us to forgo their use.

—Galileo Galilei

Puritanism: The haunting fear that someone, somewhere, may be happy.

—H. L. Mencken

A prisoner in the Inquisition is never allowed to see the face of his accuser, or of the witnesses against him, but every method is taken by threats and tortures, to oblige him to accuse himself, and by that means corroborate their evidence.

—John Foxe

The Christian religion not only was at first attended with miracles, but even at this day cannot be believed by any reasonable person without one.

—David Hume

This century continued the gradual emergence of Christendom from ignorance and superstition into an age of enlightened thinking. Arminianism was introduced as the antithesis to Calvinism, and the King James Bible and the Geneva Bible were created. Europe continued to export its religious disputes to America, and Protestant and

Catholics found commonality in witch hunts. Scientific study came into conflict with accepted theology and was condemned. The Thirty Years' War was fought between Catholics and Protestants and left central Europe and most of European society in ruins. Since the traditional authorities of Church and royalty had led Europe to this calamity, a new authority was sought on which to base European civilization. Since rationality had worked so well in the field of science, the stage was set for its use in human relations during the Enlightenment.

1600

Dominican friar, philosopher, and cosmological theorist Giordano Bruno had major disagreements with the Catholic Church. He denied the doctrines of the Trinity, eternal damnation, transubstantiation, and the virginity of Mary. He claimed that the universe was infinite, that stars were distant suns, and that Copernicus's theory of heliocentricity was true. Because of his progressive thinking and his courage to speak out, he was convicted of heresy and burned at the stake in Rome.

Pope Clement VIII approved a Portuguese law that forbade men of Jewish heritage from becoming priests.

By the end of the sixteenth century, Catholics had been successful in turning the tide of reformation in France, southern Germany, Belgium, Poland, Hungary, and Bohemia. Lutheranism was limited to northern Germany, Scandinavia, and the Baltic region. Reformed Protestantism (Calvinism) was active in Switzerland, southern Germany, Hungary, England, Scotland, and parts of France.

Michelangelo Merisi da Caravaggio began to change the style of Christian art. Before his time, Christian art almost always depicted biblical heroes and saints in an idealized world and in dreamlike states, with handsome features and gleaming countenances. Caravaggio had a different idea. Even when commissioned by the Church, he painted biblical heroes as average Romans with raw emotions, medieval clothing, and grimy bodies. He wanted average Christians to be able to identify with their heroes as real people, and his paintings were very popular with the populace, but often rejected by the Church and his patrons.

By the end of the sixteenth century, up to 90 percent of the native population of Spanish America had died due to disease and treatment by the Spanish. The same pattern would follow in North America as land was cleared of Indigenous people faster than it could be settled by Europeans.

c. The last of the Manichaeans who had tried to adapt their theology as close as possible to Buddhism were driven from China.

1601

c. At this time, most common people in Europe relied on capable women and men for the treatment of illness rather than churchmen, monks, and physicians. In the minds of literalist Christians, however, providing or accepting a cure at all was interpreted as humans determining the course of their lives rather than submitting to the will of God. Healing another person, especially with herbal medicines, or assisting in childbirth as a midwife could easily lead to an accusation of witchcraft.

c. The belief in the supernatural powers of words, or being misinterpreted, especially when speaking to God, was so strong that priests sometimes tried to keep their congregations from understanding their prayers.

The English defeated the Irish and their Catholic Spanish allies at the Battle of Kinsale. After the defeat, much of Ireland's Roman Catholic aristocracy fled to continental Europe, and Ireland was opened to colonization by Protestant English and Scottish settlers.

The English Parliament passed the Poor Relief Act, which provided aid to those who were poor, especially because of physical handicaps; work for the physically able; and incarceration for those who refused to work. It also helped the children of paupers by helping them find apprenticeships. These programs were administered by local parishes, which led to a wide range in the ways the programs were administered.

1603

Dutch theologian Jacobus Arminius was appointed professor of theology at Leiden University in the Netherlands, possibly the most prestigious university in the world at that time. Although he considered himself a Calvinist, he argued that Christ died for all people, not just those he predestined as "the elect," as staunch Calvinists believed.

1605

Francis Bacon published *Advancement of Learning*, which amounted to a declaration of independence on the part of scientific rationalism and sought emancipation from the myth that faith alone could provide humans access to the truth.

A group of English Catholics failed in their attempt to assassinate King James I and blow up Westminster Palace, the seat of English government. This became known as the Gunpowder Plot.

1606

John Smyth started a Separatist Church in England. Separatists were one of two reform groups, along with Puritans, that emerged in opposition to the Anglican Church, which they thought was too much like the Catholic Church. Separatists believed in the right of each congregation to determine its own affairs, independent of state control. After meeting too much resistance, Smyth and his congregation fled to Amsterdam.

The Ottomans signed a treaty of nonaggression with the Holy Roman Empire and proclaimed that the emperor and sultan were of equal status.

1607

The English established the colony of Jamestown on the James River in present-day Virginia. Their first permanent colony in the New World was begun as a commercial enterprise.

Ethiopian emperor Susenyos asked the pope and the king of Portugal for assistance in his war against the Oromo tribe. By 1622, he would convert to Catholicism, which was very unusual for an Ethiopian.

1608

The Sixth General Congregation of the Jesuit order voted that no candidate could enter the Society of Jesus unless his Gentile heritage could be traced back five generations.

1609

The Basque witch trials began after the monk Domingo de Sardo educated the local people about witchcraft and how to recognize witches. Although believing in witches was usually dismissed as superstitious in Spain, and the Inquisition mainly concerned itself with Protestants and conversos, the witch hunt in the Basque region was Spain's most ambitious attempt to root out the heresy. The inquisitors examined over seven thousand suspected cases and obtained confessions from two thousand people, mostly children. The next year, the bishop of Pamplona sent a letter to the Inquisition claiming that the witch hunt was based "on lies and self-delusion" and should be reevaluated. The Inquisition panel wasn't sure how to proceed, and five years later, they ended their trials and dismissed all remaining cases. A contemporary said that "there were neither witches nor bewitched until they were talked and written about."

German astronomer and mathematician Johannes Kepler published *Astronomia Nova*, the first book to state that planets orbit the sun in elliptical rather than circular paths. He also discovered that planets move faster the closer their orbits are to the sun. As a Lutheran, Kepler was free to pursue his theories, and as a Christian, he always searched for a divine plan in his celestial observations.

Representatives from various German Catholic states formed a military coalition known as the Catholic League. This countered the Protestant Union, a coalition of German states that had been formed the previous year.

The earliest Baptist church began in Amsterdam, and English Separationist John Smyth was its pastor. Like the Anabaptists, the Baptists rejected the baptism of infants and only baptized professing believers. The Baptists would come to emphasize the local church over any hierarchy and therefore would split into many denominations.

1610

Dutch Arminianism began when forty-five ministers articulated the theology of Jacobus Arminius and signed an agreement concerning their beliefs. They rejected the Calvinist theology of God electing only some people for salvation. The Calvinist accused them of Pelagianism (denying that humans inherited sin from Adam and believing humans had free will to do either good or evil). This split with the Calvinists was reminiscent of the fifth-century debate between Augustine and Pelagius over the depravity of humans and how Jesus's death served as an atonement for human sins.

Italian astronomer and physicist Galileo Galilei invented the telescope and discovered that Venus had phases like the moon. This was evidence that led him to support the Copernicus theory of a heliocentric solar system.

1611

The fifty-four scholars commissioned by King James I of England finished their new translation of the Bible. This was deemed necessary because of perceived inaccuracies in earlier translations. James wanted to rid himself of the Geneva Bible, a popular version published in 1560, which was too Calvinistic for him. The new version was very much influenced by Tyndale's Bible.

1612

Edward Wightman, a radical Anabaptist, was the last person burned at the stake for heresy in England. This was three weeks after Bartholomew Legate, a well-known anti-Trinitarian, was also burned in England for blasphemy.

Vincent Fettmilch reprinted Luther's *On the Jews and Their Lies*, with the goal of stirring up hatred against Jews in Frankfurt. Two years later, the people of Frankfurt would attack the Jewish ghetto and kill nearly three thousand people.

1613

In Jamestown, English colonists captured Pocahontas, the daughter of Chief Powhatan, and held her for ransom. While in captivity, she converted to Christianity and changed her name to Rebecca.

1615

Father Niccolò Lorini and the Roman Inquisition investigated Galileo's writings on heliocentrism, which agreed with Copernicus. Galileo had to travel to Rome to defend himself and his theory against an accusation of heresy.

1616

The Inquisition declared heliocentrism as "foolish and absurd in philosophy, and formally heretical since it explicitly contradicts in many places the sense of Holy Scripture." Galileo was ordered not to continue to pursue the theory, and the scientific writings of Copernicus and Galileo were added to the Catholic Church's list of banned writings.

In Scotland, an act demanded that every parish establish a school, and by 1633, the parliament would vote to fund them with money from taxation. This was originally intended for everyone to be able to read and interpret the Bible for themselves.

1618

The Dutch Reformed Church held the Synod of Dordrecht to settle the controversy between Calvinism and Arminianism. They rejected the Arminian view and decided that Christ's atoning work was only intended for a small percentage of people. The Arminians were ordered to sign an Act of Cessation, but they refused and were then exiled from the Netherlands. They would be allowed to return in 1625.

After Count Vilém Slavata forbade Bohemian Hussites from assembling, several of them bribed their way into the Catholic regent's office at Prague Castle. After an argument with the count, the Hussites threw him and an associate out the window, but both survived the fall. It was reported that either the two victims were protected by the Virgin Mary and the angels, or they fell into a pile of manure—or both. Slavata went into exile but would return to Bohemia in 1621 and became a major player in reestablishing Catholicism as the state religion.

The Thirty Years' War began with the removal of Count Slavata in Prague, although the conflict between Protestants and Catholics would mainly be fought in Germany. It began as a religious conflict but escalated into political alliances involving most of the Western European powers.

1619

Galileo clashed with Father Orazio Grassi, a professor of mathematics at the Jesuit Collegio Romano, over the nature of comets, alienating Jesuits that had previously been sympathetic to Galileo.

c. During the Thirty Years' War, in many regions, Jews were allowed to move to cities to help in the war effort, reversing a long-standing trend of their dispersal throughout the countryside.

The first African slaves were brought to Virginia. They arrived on a ship that had been captured from the Spanish. In 1625, there were twenty Africans in Virginia, and by 1690, there would be almost a thousand.

Lucilio Vanini, an Italian philosopher, physician, and free thinker, wrote the first recorded theory that humans evolved from ape-like primates, or at least shared a common ancestor with them. His ideas about natural laws, especially opposed to divine laws, were too radical for his time, and he had to flee countries on several occasions. Catholic officials hunted him down in Toulouse, France, and found him guilty of blasphemy and atheism. They had his tongue cut out and burned him at the stake.

Ferdinand II became the Holy Roman emperor, with an overriding goal of restoring Catholicism as the only acceptable religion in Europe. He nearly extinguished Protestantism in Bohemia and Austria and conducted campaigns in Poland, Germany, and Denmark as part of the Thirty Years' War.

1620

The army of Ferdinand II defeated the Bohemian army commanded by Prince Christian of Anhalt at the Battle of White Mountain, near Prague. This was a decisive battle and led to the end of two centuries of Protestantism in Bohemia.

English separatist Puritans, who had been living in exile in the Netherlands, left for America. They sailed aboard a ship called the Mayflower from Plymouth, England, to what is now Plymouth, Massachusetts. Once anchored north of Cape Cod, the men signed the Mayflower Compact, which was a social contract establishing a government under which both Puritans and the non-Puritan passengers could live harmoniously. They planned to rule themselves in the

New World without the aid of bishops or royalty and became known as "Pilgrims."

Catholic forces routed the Protestants in Bohemia. Jan Comenius led a group of the Unity of Brethren, Moravian heirs to Jan Hus's movement, across the border into Poland. Comenius was never allowed to return to his homeland, but he became a popular author and educator in Poland and is considered the father of modern education.

1621

To undercut the power of the Janissaries and gain the army's support, Osman II, the new Ottoman sultan, led an army into the Ukraine, at that time part of the Polish Empire. After losing forty thousand soldiers, Osman returned to Constantinople in shame, and was assassinated by Janissaries.

1622

Emperor Susenyos of Ethiopia converted to Catholicism. His relationship with the Catholic Church soured a few years later when his mentor's successor, another Jesuit priest, tried to change local customs.

1623

To return Bohemia to Catholicism, the Church turned the University of Prague over to the Jesuits, and education throughout the country became controlled by the Catholic Church. Conversion to Catholicism became the price of a pardon for participating in the recent revolt in Prague. The emperor stationed imperial troops in Protestant areas, heavily taxed Protestants, and drove around 150,000 Protestants from the country. Neighboring Hungary retained its religious liberty because the Church didn't want to risk upsetting the balance of power there because Hungary was the buffer between Christian Europe and the Ottomans.

1624

When a plague struck Palermo, Italy, the residents looked for a relic to protect them. They dug up the bones of Saint Rosalia, who had died in 1160. The plague soon passed, but the bones were discovered to be from a goat.

Within a few years of the Pilgrims landing in Plymouth, most of the Indigenous people in eastern North America had died from smallpox, typhus, measles, cholera, and plague.

The Portuguese Inquisition arrested Antonio Homem, a Portuguese Christian clergyman of Jewish ancestry, accused him of secret Jewish worship, and burned him at the stake.

Pope Urban VIII issued a bull that banned tobacco smoking and made the use of powdered tobacco in holy places punishable by excommunication. This was due to his perception that sneezing caused by snuff was like sexual ecstasy. His ban would be overturned a century later by Pope Benedict XIII, who was a fan of snuff.

The Dutch West India Company established the colony of New Netherland, present-day New York City and its surrounding territory. Their capital, New Amsterdam, would become the most tolerant and cosmopolitan colony in North America.

1625

c. By this time, stimulated by the Counter-Reformation, Augustinian, Dominican, and Jesuit missionaries had spread out from Europe and reached Mexico, Peru, Colombia, Chile, North America, India, China, Japan, Indonesia, Kenya, Arabia, Persia, Iraq, and Sri Lanka.

1626

The new Saint Peter's Basilica was inaugurated in Rome after 120 years of construction. It still is the largest Catholic church in Europe by square footage.

Portuguese Jesuit missionary Alfonso Mendes became patriarch of Ethiopia and began to condemn the practices of the traditional Ethiopian Church. This would lead to civil war, and in 1632, Emperor Susenyos would issue an act of tolerance declaring Catholicism optional, not mandatory. That signaled the end of Catholicism in Ethiopia.

1627

An entire version of a fifth-century Greek Bible, known as Codex Alexandrinus, was discovered in Constantinople and sent to King James in England.

1629

Many non-separating Puritans migrated from England to Massachusetts, landing at Massachusetts Bay and eventually founding the towns of Boston and Salem. They were not happy with the reformation of the Church of England but stayed loyal anyway. They wanted further reform but were not always in agreement among themselves with what that reform should be.

Following Catholic successes in the Thirty Years' War, Holy Roman emperor Ferdinand II issued the Edict of Restitution to Germany. This act nullified the Peace of Augsburg and the right for rulers to choose their own religion. Ferdinand's edict polarized the 1,800 various states of the empire into diverse groups with opposing interests. It also forced German Protestants to return Church land that they had purchased and set a precedent for an emperor being able to overturn treaties at will. Because of opposition to the edict, the war continued much longer than it should have.

1630

By this time, aggression by the Habsburg Holy Roman emperor and the Habsburg king of Spain had driven the papacy into sympathy with their Protestant enemies and Catholic France into a military alliance with the Protestants. The political aspect of the war had overcome the initial religious aspect.

1631

Jesuit Friedrich Spee wrote the anonymous *Precautions for Prosecutors* about the absurdity of witchcraft accusations and the unreliability of confessions under torture.

Pierre Gassendi, a French priest, astronomer, philosopher, and free-thinker, published the first data on the transit of the planet Mercury across the sun.

Armed forces of the Catholic League attacked the Protestant city of Magdeburg, one of the largest cities in Germany. They looted and burned the city and killed around twenty thousand residents. Pope Urban VIII was satisfied that the "nest of heretics" was destroyed.

The Protestant victory over the Catholic League at the Battle of Breitenfeld marked the first major victory for Protestant forces in the Thirty Years' War. King Gustavus Adolphus of Sweden led the Protestant army and gained many German states as allies.

1632

The Roman Inquisition again called Galileo before them after he publish a book on heliocentricity. They forced him to recant and remain silent about his beliefs. The Inquisition then sentenced him to house arrest for the rest of his life.

Antonio Bosio published *Roma Sotterranea*, detailing his explorations of the Roman catacombs. The book described his discovery of entrances to the underground cemeteries, how he learned their names, and how he determined who may have been buried in them.

1633

French priest Vincent de Paul and Louise de Marillac founded the Daughters of Charity, an organization that encouraged poor women to practice an apostolic life within the Catholic Church. These women served Jesus Christ by helping the poor through works of mercy.

1634

English Catholic Cecil Calvert, the Baron Baltimore, sent settlers to the Chesapeake Bay in the American colonies where they founded Saint Mary's City. He hoped to promote religious tolerance in his colony.

The Oberammergau Passion Play was first staged in Germany. This became the most popular and long-running of any Passion play due to its particularly moving portrayal of the Passion of Jesus and its extremely negative depiction of Jews.

1635

The town of Boston established the Boston Latin School as the first public school founded in the American colonies, and it is still in operation.

Puritan leaders of the Massachusetts colony passed a law requiring regular church attendance.

The leaders of the Massachusetts colony banished Roger Williams because of his opposition to what he saw as corruption in the colony. He believed that the Indigenous people should be paid for their land and that there should be a complete separation of the Church from secular life. He advocated for freedom of conscience to be extended to all and founded the colony of Providence as a haven for anyone who was persecuted for their religious beliefs. Providence became the first place in modern history where the Christian Church and the state were strictly separated.

1636

Angered that Massachusetts Puritans would not grant full voting privileges to all men, Reverend Thomas Hooker led a group of followers to the Connecticut River Valley where they founded the Hartford colony.

Immigrating Puritans led by Reverend John Davenport decided that the Massachusetts colony was too lax for their taste, so they sailed further and founded the Connecticut River Colony, which would become New Haven, possibly the most theocratic colony ever established in the New World.

The Massachusetts colonial legislature founded Harvard College as the first seminary in North America. It was named after clergyman John Harvard.

1637

King Charles I of England encouraged the clergy to introduce more decorations in their attire and their churches, edging closer to Catholic traditions. He tried to bring the Scots in line by introducing a new prayer book and liturgy that were also more Catholic.

Catholic peasants in Japan, upset over increased taxes, began the Shimabara Rebellion. The Tokugawa shogunate sent a large army to subdue the rebels, and after a four-month siege at Hara Castle, they defeated them. They beheaded the rebel leader and renewed the suppression of Christians. The official persecution would continue into the 1850s.

When the new settlers came into conflict with the Pequot tribe in Connecticut, killings and retaliations began. In what became known as the Mystic massacre, Puritans from the Connecticut River Colony, led by John Mason, attacked and destroyed the large Pequot settlement on Mystic River, killing more than six hundred Native Americans. One of the Puritan leaders, Lion Gardener, called the slaughter "a victory to the glory of God, and honor of our nation." John Underhill, a participant, justified his actions by referring to examples of God's wrath against the Canaanites in the Old Testament.

1638

William Chillingworth's book *The Religion of Protestants: A Safe Way to Salvation* sent shock waves through orthodoxy. He stated that ultimately it was the quest for truth, not its acquisition, that really mattered and that any belief, even if learned through scripture, was no more than just a hunch. He concluded that no one could ever be certain they found ultimate truth.

Roger Williams started the first Baptist congregation in the American colonies.

1639

At the Battle of the Downs, off the English coast, the Dutch navy won a major victory over a Spanish fleet sent to subdue the Netherlands. Spain lost most of its seventy-five ships, and this, in effect, ended Spain's long history as a great sea power.

1640

In the Bishops' War, Anglican rule in Scotland ended when the Scots defeated an English army. The resulting Presbyterian system had no bishops, only elders, so the Anglican bishops who had been appointed by the king were expelled.

1641

A rebellion started in Ireland as Catholic gentry tried to drive Protestant English government officials and residents out of the country. This began an ugly conflict known as the Irish Confederate Wars, with many atrocities committed by both sides.

1642

The first English Civil War, which was really a series of conflicts, began between Parliamentarians, known as "Roundheads," and Royalists, known as "Cavaliers." King Charles I ruled by what he considered divine right and, therefore, did not allow his decisions to be challenged or questioned. This brought him into conflict with those who wanted more power for Parliament. In addition, Charles's wife Henrietta Maria was a French Catholic, and the English citizens feared that she would persuade Charles to return the country to Catholicism. These wars would last until 1651.

The Massachusetts Bay Colony passed legislation requiring families to teach their children "to read and understand the principles of religion." Connecticut followed with a similar law in 1650. These laws would lead to the establishment of public schools.

René Goupil was a French Jesuit missionary with a passion for helping the sick and wounded. While traveling with a group of Hurons in New York, Mohawks captured him and his traveling companions. He was said to have been killed for teaching Mohawk children the sign of the cross.

1643

Massachusetts attempted to extend its influence over what it considered heretical settlements, such as Providence. This forced Roger Williams to travel to England to obtain a charter for his colony of Rhode Island.

1644

Sir William Berkeley, a Royalist and the governor of Virginia, expelled Puritans from his colony. They resettled across the Chesapeake Bay in Maryland, where they came into conflict with Lord Baltimore's Royalist settlers.

The Puritans of New England stopped enslaving members of the Pequot tribal nation because they continued to escape into the woods and instead turned to African slaves for free labor.

Officials in England executed Ralph Corbie, an Irish Jesuit, for confessing that he was a Catholic priest.

1645

The English government tried Archbishop William Laud of Canterbury for treason. They also accused him of Arminianism, favoring Catholics, and being too autocratic. His trial ended without a verdict, but the Puritan-controlled Parliament declared him guilty and had him beheaded.

Calvinists founded the Royal Society of London, the most prestigious scientific association in the world.

1646

In Massachusetts, Puritan missionary John Eliot preached the first worship service for Native Americans in the Wampanoag language.

Puritans established "praying towns" in New England to convert Native American tribes to Christianity. Native Americans moved to these towns voluntarily to learn farming techniques, and they were known as "praying Indians." By 1675, there were fourteen of these settlements. The English idea of full conversion to Christianity contrasted with the French Jesuits in Canada, who more often tried to merge Christianity with the Native Americans' existing religious beliefs.

Three years earlier, the English Parliament called for an assembly of "learned, godly, and judicious Divines" to determine matters of doctrine and worship for English churches. This year they published the

Westminster Confession of Faith, setting the Church of England on a course to abandon Episcopalianism in favor of Calvinism. This was a compromise to secure the help of the Scots against their king during the English Civil War.

1647

The predominantly Puritan English Parliament ordered that Christmas, along with other pagan holiday celebrations, cease to be observed. In New England, celebrating Christmas became a criminal offense.

The Massachusetts Bay Colony passed a law instructing towns with fifty or more households to appoint teachers of reading and writing. Towns with more than one hundred households were required to establish grammar schools. The main intent was for citizens to be able to read and understand their Bibles.

1648

In the Ukraine, Cossacks rebelled against the ruling Poles and attacked Polish nobles and Catholic priests. According to some sources, as many as one hundred thousand Jews—more than one-fourth of all Jews in Poland—were also killed in the war, and countless others were left homeless. As Polish influence disappeared, so did their charters that protected Jews. The Ottoman Empire was practically the only haven that remained for them.

The Peace of Westphalia ended the Thirty Years' War and essentially concluded the Reformation by recognizing Catholicism, Lutheranism, and Calvinism as valid religions. The war had brought devastation to Europe, with the loss of up to two-thirds of the population of central Europe. Germany alone suffered an estimated eight million fatalities. The competing countries had exhausted themselves, and there was a realization that they couldn't go on murdering each other over relatively minor religious differences, after all, they were all Christians. The ideal of religious toleration, dormant for over a thousand years,

was being gradually revived. Subjects were no longer required to follow the religious conversion of their rulers, and each state reverted
to its dominant religion from 1624. Another outcome of the treaty
was the establishment of the modern international order which partitioned Europe into sovereign states rather than a patchwork of jurisdictions nominally overseen by a pope or Holy Roman emperor, and
this spawned nationalism.

Puritans in Massachusetts wrote the Cambridge Platform, which became regarded as the religious constitution of the colony. It set the
guidelines for the sect of Congregationalism.

1649

Following their Civil War, the English established a republic under
the leadership of the Puritan Oliver Cromwell to replace their monarchy. He unleashed another wave of iconoclasm that left the many
architects, carvers, painters, glass painters, embroiderers, goldsmiths,
sculptors, and masons, whose livelihood was building and furnishing
churches and shrines, unemployed.

Oliver Cromwell invaded Catholic Ireland in what would be a disaster
for Ireland, resulting in great loss of life, famine, plague, and the capture of many Irish citizens to be used as indentured laborers.

The Puritan-dominated English Parliament outlawed Christmas seasonal plays and, two years later, would declare Christmas a day of
penance instead of feasting and reveling. Until 1656, government and
businesses remained open on Christmas Day.

1650

James Ussher, the Primate of All Ireland and a prolific author, published his *Annals of the Old Testament*, calculating the date of Creation
as nightfall on October 22, 4004 BC. This is still the date believed by
Young Earth Creationists.

Greek theologian and Vatican librarian Leo Allatius, in his *Discussion Concerning the Prepuce of Our Lord Jesus Christ*, speculated that the Holy Foreskin of Jesus had ascended into heaven and become the rings of Saturn.

Jordan of Trebizond, a Christian coppersmith who lived in Constantinople, jokingly mocked the prophet Muhammad during a card game with Muslims in return for mocking his religion. The next day authorities arrested him on the charge of blasphemy. Ottoman officials gave him the choice of converting to Islam or being beheaded, and he chose the latter.

The Japanese executed or expelled the last Catholic priests in the country. If any remained, they had to go deep into hiding.

c. Puritans in England began advocating for the restoration of Jews to Palestine in order to fulfill the end-times prophesy, but the idea wouldn't gain political traction until the early 1800s.

French philosopher Rene Descartes died. He had been one of Europe's first great Enlightenment thinkers. He rejected traditional authority and basically everything he had learned and started building his worldview anew with only "self-evident" truths. That led him to the bedrock proposition of "I think, therefore I am." His new authority was rationality, and he thought that, not myth or legend, should be the foundation for society.

1651

Thomas Hobbes published his book *Leviathan*, and its atheistic ideas sparked an outcry from Christians. He wrote that man's behavior was determined by physical laws and grounded in self-preservation, with no need for a god. He wrote that in nature nothing can be seen as just or unjust; it's simply nature. He envisioned all humans as equally born and rejected the divine rights of kings.

1652

George Fox had a vision in which Christ told him that it was possible to encounter God's immediate presence without the need for parish churches, salaried ministers, or the dispensing of sacraments. Based on his vision, he founded a new pacifistic sect, the Religious Society of Friends, more commonly known as Quakers.

Prominent French philosopher and physicist Blaise Pascal died. He is remembered for "Pascal's wager," which involved betting one's life on whether the Christian God exists or not. It goes like this: If someone bet that God did exist and lived according to Christian principles, and God really did exist, then he or she would be rewarded in heaven. But if someone bet that God didn't exist, and he really did, and they lived their lives based on disbelief, then they would go to hell. In the long run, Pascal argued, it was better to convince oneself that God did exist, thereby avoiding hell whether he exists or not. This same wager could be applied by Christians believing that Jesus Christ is the son of God. It's a simple concept, but all depends on believing the Christian God, not the god of any other religion, is the true God.

1653

The Thomas Christians of India, who been forced into the Roman Catholic Church, took a public vow known as the Coonan Cross Oath. The oath was a pledge to reject their church's latinization, which had begun in 1599. They split off from the Catholic Church and became the Malankara Orthodox Syrian Church and eventually other splinter groups. The Indians who held faithful to the Catholic faith became known as the Syro-Malabar Catholic Church. When the East Syrian patriarch sent Bishop Mar Ahatallah to the Thomas Christians, the Portuguese arrested him and turned him over to the Inquisition for execution.

1654

The capital of Dutch Brazil, Mauritsstad (now Recife) fell to the Portuguese. The Portuguese hostility toward resident Jews resulted in the first Jewish migration to North America, specifically New Amsterdam (present-day New York City).

1655

Oliver Cromwell allowed Jews back into England. His motives are unclear, but the act aligned with a European trend toward freedom of conscience.

The Duke of Savoy's army massacred an estimated four thousand to six thousand Waldensians in the upper valleys of Italy where they lived in exile. This became known as the Piedmontese Easter. Other Protestant countries offered sanctuary to the remaining Waldensians.

1656

Captain Kemble of Boston was sentenced to two hours in the public stocks for his "lewd" behavior, which involved kissing his wife in public on the Sabbath Day. This was a violation of the strict Puritan laws.

1660

After Cromwell's death, the English asked for Charles II to return from a nine-year exile. The restoration of Charles ended the Puritan ban on Christmas.

When Mary Dyer had left Boston for England, she was a Puritan. While in England, she had become a Quaker. When she returned to Boston, she was immediately arrested by the Puritan authorities and banished from the Massachusetts colony. Despite realizing the risk she was taking, this year she returned to Boston, where she was arrested and hanged. Mary was one of the four executed Quakers known as the "Boston martyrs."

c. German nobleman and later ascetic Lutheran missionary Baron Justinian von Welz is believed to have coined the term *Great Commission* to apply to the instructions Jesus gave to his disciples in Matthew 28.

1661

c. The Protestant Dutch arrived on the Malabar Coast of India and helped the Thomas Christians rid themselves of Portuguese dominance by expelling all Catholics from the territory the Dutch controlled. The pope didn't relent and sent Carmelite monks, who bribed and threatened many of the Thomas Christians back into submission. When the dust had settled there existed the Syrian Malankara Orthodox loyal to Antioch; the Syro-Malankara Church, being autonomous but recognized by Rome; and the Syro-Malabar Catholic Church, which had been established by the Portuguese.

1662

The new and improved Anglican Book of Common Prayer, an update of the original published in 1549, included requirements for worship and ritual. Most British Puritan ministers refused to accept it, and as many as two thousand left their positions rather than submit to it.

1664

The Order of Cistercians of the Strict Observance, or the Trappist order, was founded. The order was named after La Trappe Abbey in France, and their reform was based on penitence, including silence, manual labor, isolation, and a sparse diet. Most of this was not new to the order, but there was a need to return to stricter monasticism.

1665

Maria d'Agreda, a Spanish abbess and spiritual writer, died. Her best-known book was an obviously fictious (since so little is known about her) biography of the Virgin Mary. Titled *The Mystical City of God*, the book made a connection between Mary and the Trinity. The book was later censured and included in the Index of Forbidden Books.

1667

John Milton's epic poem *Paradise Lost* was first published. This was his masterpiece and concerned the biblical story of the Fall of man. There were two narrative tracts, one about Satan and the other about Adam and Eve. This poem, along with Dante's *Inferno*, would largely form the modern Christian concepts of the Fall of man, the rebellion of Satan against God, and hell itself.

1668

Pope Clement IX discontinued the sadistic "Jew races," which had been held in Rome each year during the Carnival celebrations preceding Lent.

1670

English colonists from the island of Barbados established a colony that would become Charleston, South Carolina. They had a long tradition of operating a slave state in the Indies and transported that concept to the mainland.

Benedict de Spinoza, a Dutch Jewish philosopher, published his *Theological-Political Treatise.* He is credited, along with Erasmus, with studying the Bible using historical criticism instead of a devotional approach. This incorporated information that ordinary Bible readers overlooked, such as comparison of facts, writing styles, word usage, and many other forensic tools. In the eighteenth century, this approach would become known as "higher criticism." Spinoza focused on the Old Testament because of his familiarity with it as the Jewish Bible. He proposed that revealed religion necessitated the use of reason and logical analysis to understand what was revealed, not simply blind faith; that the biblical books were written by many authors with diverse backgrounds; that the Torah was probably not composed entirely by Moses; that the Jews were not God's chosen people; and that the Torah applied only to ancient Israel.

1672

One of the earliest documentations of vampires was published in Croatia. As the folklore spread around Europe, it was believed that a crucifix, rosary, or holy water could be used for protection against them. It was also believed that vampires were not able to enter churches or temples.

1673

Jacques Marquette, a French Jesuit missionary to New France (present-day eastern Canada) joined the first European expedition down the Mississippi River, accompanied by explorer Louis Jolliet. Earlier, Marquette had been involved in missions along the Saint Lawrence River and had founded the first mission in Michigan territory.

The Common Doxology ("Praise God, from whom all blessings flow; Praise Him, all creatures here below; Praise Him above, ye heavenly host; Praise Father, Son, and Holy Ghost. Amen") was written by Thomas Ken as the final verse of a hymn. It is a normal part of many Protestant services even today.

1675

German theologian Philip Jacob Spener published *Pia Desideria* (*Heartfelt Desire for God-Pleasing Reform*), which presented a six-point doctrine that led to the movement known as Pietism. Spener criticized nobles, princes, ministers, and laypeople for their moral failures. Pietist guidelines included a deep understanding of the scriptures, small group meetings in homes, a priesthood of all believers, and an emphasis on applying scripture to everyday life. Although Pietism was a threat to the clergy, it stimulated many churches to begin Bible studies, group prayers, and local outreaches.

John Bunyan found himself in jail for the second time after another dispute with the Church of England. He began work on what became the world's best-selling devotional book, *The Pilgrim's Progress.*

Both colonists and American Indians distrusted and shunned the Praying Indians of Massachusetts. When King Philip's War broke out between the colonists and the Native Americans, the English rounded up the Praying Indians and shipped them to a prison camp on Deer Island in Boston Harbor. They had to leave most of their crops and farm animals behind and suffered terribly through the winter.

1676

In Massachusetts, a Native American raiding party took Mary Rowlandson prisoner and held her for the duration of King Philip's War. After she was freed, she wrote the first American best seller, *The Sovereignty and Goodness of God*, in which she described every detail of her capture and survival as part of God's plan.

1677

Antonie van Leeuwenhoek used a microscope to observe human sperm cells for the first time and thought they were microscopic animals. The ovum (egg cell) would not be discovered until the eighteenth-century, and an adequate understanding of human reproduction would have to wait until the nineteenth century. These discoveries often confused the issue of the humanness of Jesus and how he had entered his mother's womb.

1678

James Mitchell, a member of the Covenanters sect of the Scottish Presbyterian movement had been arrested in 1673 after attempting to assassinate Archbishop James Sharp of Saint Andrews, a determined persecutor of nonconformists. This year Mitchell was hung in Edinburgh.

1679

To avenge James Mitchell's death, a group of Covenanters ambushed James Sharp at a secluded site, dragged him from his carriage, and murdered him.

1681

The English executed Archbishop Oliver Plunkett of Armagh for treason because of his Catholic faith, making him the last Catholic executed in England for his religious belief.

1682

William Penn arrived in what would become Pennsylvania with a group of Quaker settlers. There he founded the village of *Philadelphia*, Greek for "brotherly love." Pennsylvania became the most religiously tolerant colony in the Americas. As long settlers believed in one almighty God and lived peaceably, they had religious freedom. Penn's tolerant and pacifistic Quaker principles also allowed for a long and peaceful relationship between colonists and American Indians.

1683

An enormous Ottoman army besieged Vienna. After eighteen Turkish assaults, the walls were breached, and only one-third of the original defenders were fit for combat. A combined army of Poles, Lithuanians, and Germans arrived to rescue the city just in time, and their counter-attack drove the Ottomans back so far that they lost territory they had conquered in Hungary and Greece. It was the Turks' most disastrous defeat in their empire's four-hundred-year history and ended the last Ottoman advance into Europe.

The Chaldean Catholic Church moved its patriarchate from Mosul, Iraq, to Baghdad.

1685

King Louis XIV of France revoked the Edict of Nantes, issued in 1598, and resumed the persecution of Huguenots.

1686

Russia joined Austria, Poland, and Venice to form a Holy League, an alliance against the Ottoman Empire.

1687

King James II of England issued the Declaration of Indulgence. It ended laws forcing conformity with the Church of England, allowed people to worship anywhere they chose, and eliminated the requirement to make religious oaths before gaining government jobs. The declaration was supported by Quaker William Penn but, not surprisingly, was opposed by the Church of England.

Isaac Newton published *Principia*, which revolutionized scientific thought by proposing three laws of motions that, when combined with gravitational attraction, could account for all the movement in the solar system. He wanted "to reduce the phenomena of nature to mathematical laws." He had done this through his own observations and original thinking, not by appealing to ancient scholars. He exposed the cosmos as not a divine mystery, but as running by predictable, universal rules. This fit well with the Enlightenment mentality of questioning all assumptions that had been handed down through history.

1688

With the aid of King William III of Holland, the English overthrew King James II in the "Glorious Revolution." James was England's last Catholic king, and William, who was James's nephew and husband of his daughter Mary, became King William III of England.

In a petition to the Quaker Church, Francis Daniel Pastorius, Garret Hendericks, and Derick op den Graeff led the Mennonites of Germantown, Pennsylvania, in the first public protest of slavery in America. Many others would speak out against slavery, but the Quaker Church would not formally denounce slavery until 1776, and Pennsylvania did not outlaw slavery until 1780.

Members of the Maliseet tribal nation attacked John Gyles's family homestead in Maine and captured young John. They held him as a slave for six years and treated him harshly. Contemporaries didn't consider capture or death by American Indians as the worst thing that could happen to someone on the frontier. To Protestant settlers, it was much worse to be captured by the French and converted to Catholicism, because then you lost more than your life, you lost your soul.

1689

c. With the fear of a Catholic takeover in England on his mind, English philosopher John Locke wrote his *Letters Concerning Toleration* about the evil of coercion in religion and the unassailable right to freedom of conscience. Like-minded thinkers concluded that Augustine, other Church Fathers, and thirteen centuries of Christian leadership had made an immensely tragic mistake in suppressing other forms of religion. His thoughts on individual freedom were influential to those who drafted the US Declaration of Independence.

1691

The Separatists of the Plymouth Colony merged with the Puritans of the Massachusetts Bay Colony to form the Province of Massachusetts.

1692

The constant threat of attacks by Native Americans in the new colonies caused much paranoia. As refugees from the frontier poured into towns such as Salem, Massachusetts, hysteria grew. In Salem, Samuel Parris gave sermons that increased the community's fear and sparked witch hunts that resulted in the execution of nineteen suspected witches.

1693

Jakob Ammann and his followers split from the Swiss Anabaptists, who they thought were spiritually lax, and became known as the Amish.

King Carlos II of Spain issued a decree that freed all slaves who escaped from English colonies to Spanish colonies, including Florida, if they accepted Catholicism.

1696

Irish poets Nahum Tate and Nicholas Brady created a book of Psalms that could be easily sung, the New Version of the Psalms of David. It replaced the more difficult Anglican Book of Common Prayer, which became known as the Old Version.

1697

French philosopher Pierre Bayle wrote the *Historical and Critical Dictionary*, in which he pointed out contradictions between theological axioms and rationality and pleaded for a return to religious tolerance. He argued that people had reasons for behaving morally other than a fear of burning in hell. This was one of the best-selling books of the eighteenth century and a great influence on the developing Enlightenment.

University of Edinburgh student Thomas Aikenhead openly criticized the scriptures and religion. Based on testimony from his fellow students, he was convicted of blasphemy and hanged. Incidents like this would be in the minds of the founders of the United States less than a century later when they decided there should be no national religion and there should be freedom of speech.

1698

Christian leaders in Prague accused local Jew Elias Backoffen of blasphemy because of a perceived show of disrespect to a statue of Jesus on the Charles Bridge. As punishment, he was forced to raise money to purchase a gold-plated banner, written in Hebrew, reading "Holy, Holy, Holy, the Lord of Hosts," a verse from the book of Isaiah referring to Almighty God. The city leaders affixed the sign to the statue as a way of humiliating the city's Jews. In the year 2000, as a gesture of reconciliation toward the Jewish community, plaques were added to the statue explaining the history of the inscription.

Italian natural philosopher Francesco Redi died. He had disproved the theory of spontaneous generation by demonstrating that insects didn't spontaneously generate from decayed matter, which was a popular belief at the time.

1699

Gottfried Arnold, a German theologian and historian, wrote the *Impartial History of the Church and of Heresy*. In the book, he suggested that heresy only existed because it served the vested interests of the orthodox and those in authority had used accusations of heresy to maintain their own positions of power and influence. Arnold had great sympathy for heretics and believed the worst thing that had happened in Church history was its domination and regulation by Constantine. This book became an important reference in the German Enlightenment.

CHAPTER 18: EIGHTEENTH CENTURY AD

I have examined all the known superstitions of the world, and I do not find in our particular superstition of Christianity one redeeming feature. Millions of innocent men, women, and children, since the introduction of Christianity, have been burnt, tortured, fined, imprisoned. What has been the effect of coercion? To make one half of the world fools, and the other half hypocrites; to support roguery and error all over the earth.

—Thomas Jefferson

In no instance have the churches been guardians of the liberties of the people.

—James Madison

Orthodoxy, or right opinion, is, at best, a very slender part of religion.

—John Wesley

If religion were true, its followers would not try to bludgeon their young into an artificial conformity; but would merely insist on their unbending quest for truth, irrespective of artificial backgrounds or practical consequences.

—H. P. Lovecraft

The European Enlightenment came into full bloom. One reaction to the Enlightenment was the First Great Awakening that occurred in England and its American colonies. European colonists continued to drive Native Americans from their land whenever they found their presence inconvenient. African slaves became omnipresent in many British, Spanish, French, and Portuguese colonies in America. Critical study of the Bible began in earnest, and superstitious beliefs were condemned by rational minds. The American and French Revolutions, products of the Enlightenment, confronted the issues of social justice and moral reform, and the United States of America was founded as a refuge from the horrors of European religious intolerance and political oppression.

1700

Judah he-Hasid led between five hundred and one thousand Jewish immigrants to Palestine. When they arrived in Jerusalem, they almost doubled the Jewish population in the city. This led to competition with the Ottomans for resources, and the ensuing animosity led to the Ottomans burning the Jewish synagogue.

The latest Catholic venture into China collapsed after the Vatican prohibited Jesuits from using Chinese customs and language in their liturgy.

At the end of this century, there were ninety thousand Franciscans, Capuchins, and Carmelites dedicated to the principles of the Franciscan order.

1701

Yale College was founded in Connecticut. Like Harvard College in 1636 and William and Mary College in 1693, its main goal was the education of clergy.

1702

After renewed persecution of Huguenots, the Camisard Rebellion broke out in central France. In the following year, over four hundred Protestant hamlets were burned, and their populations exiled. The uprising would last for thirteen years.

1704

Isaac Newton wrote his treatise *Opticks*. He sought to deduce causes from effects until he came to the very first cause, which he was certain was not mechanical but divine.

1705

Pennsylvania became the first North American colony to ban the importation and sale of Native American slaves.

In *Synopsis of the Astronomy of Comets*, British astronomer Edmund Halley wrote that comets are natural phenomena in the solar system, and they return to our region of the solar system at predictable intervals. This discovery eliminated another ominous and unexplainable event from the list of things humans had to fear and gave it a natural rather than supernatural explanation.

1709

While Anglicans had an aversion to hymns sung during worship services, Baptists did not. Englishman Isaac Watts published the songbook *Hymns and Spiritual Songs* to give his church hymns that included Christian elements not found in the Psalmic song books. Watts eventually wrote more than six hundred Christian songs, including "Joy to the World" and "When I Survey the Wondrous Cross."

The Quakers opened a hospital in Philadelphia, possibly the first hospital in the British colonies.

1712

African slaves rebelled in the village of New York, killing twenty white residents. In retaliation, the city leaders arrested seventy Blacks and executed twenty-one of them.

1715

By this time, Carolina colonists and their Indigenous allies had enslaved up to fifty-one thousand other indigenous people, as many as a quarter of the remaining population of the Southeast. Many of these slaves were shipped to the West Indies.

1717

An Egyptian mummy purchased by King Louis XIV of France as a gift to King Charles XII of Sweden had to pass through Constantinople. At a city gate, Ottoman guards stopped those who were transporting it and opened the sarcophagus. When they discovered the mummy, they assumed it was the body of the last Byzantine emperor, Constantine XI, and remembered the Greek legend that he would return from the spirit world to conquer the Turks. The guards decapitated the mummy, cut it in half, and then locked it in a tower in Yedikule Fortress.

1722

A small group of Moravian Brethren emerged from a clandestine church and visited Nikolaus Ludwig von Zinzendorf, a German nobleman and Lutheran Pietist. He allowed them to settle on his land, and they called their new village Herrnhut.

1726

Isaac Newton, the great English mathematician, astronomer, and physicist, died. Although he held strong religious beliefs, Newton was sure that natural forces could be understood and studied using mathematical formulas. Other scientists began to believe that science was a ural causes.

1727

In Herrnhut, Germany, people of several different religious backgrounds sought refuge, and this led to conflict. Count Zinzendorf committed himself to bringing peace to the colony. An "awakening," or spiritual revival, occurred and launched the Moravian Brethren to the forefront of the modern Protestant missionary movement. In addition to their other spiritual practices, the Moravians instituted a continuous, around-the-clock prayer vigil that lasted for more than a century.

The *New England Primer*, a book for Christian education, was first printed. It became the best-selling and most widely read book in the British colonies after the Bible.

1729

Jean Meslier, a French Catholic priest, died. After his death, his acquaintances discovered a book-length essay he had written about his hidden atheism. He called heaven and hell "nothing but delusions, errors, lies, fictions, and impostures." His essay became an important influence on Voltaire and other contributors to the Enlightenment.

Ursuline nuns founded the first North American orphanage in Natchez, Mississippi. It was founded for white children whose parents had been massacred by American Indians.

1730

The First Great Awakening, or the Evangelical Revival movement, began as a Protestant reaction to the Enlightenment. Jonathan Edwards of Connecticut and George Whitefield of England were the main leaders, and followers renewed their commitment to individual piety and religious devotion. Evangelicalism began to emerge as a trans-denominational movement and had an enormous impact. Especially in the American colonies, an emotional connection with Jesus, rather than knowledge of Christian dogma, became recognized as evidence of true faith.

1731

Pope Clement XII fixed the number of stations of the cross in Jerusalem at fourteen. The first station was where Pilate condemned Jesus to die, and the fourteenth was Jesus's tomb. Clement delegated Franciscan friars to administer the stations.

1734

After being expelled from the Catholic city of Salzburg, Austria, Protestant refugees sailed to what would become the colony of Georgia, where they founded Ebenezer, a village near Savannah. There pastor Johann Martin Boltzius sought to build a religious utopia that avoided slavery and plantation agriculture. Moravians would also settle in the area soon after.

1735

John Wesley and his brother Charles sailed from England to the American colonies as missionaries. In Georgia, they met and were heavily influenced by the Moravians. The Wesleys went on to develop the Methodist denomination as a sect of the Episcopal Church. Their ideology used logic and reason in all matters of faith and emphasized evangelism and mission work, promoted inclusiveness, and believed that music was an integral part of worship.

1736

The inquisition in Lima, Peru, burned Dona Ana de Castro alive after convicting her of practicing a Jewish mourning ritual. She had testified that she hadn't considered what she'd done to be in conflict with Christianity.

Because of complaints from neighboring nobles and what was seen as theological heresy, Lutheran authorities banished Count Zinzendorf from Saxony. He migrated to the American colonies as a missionary, and in 1741, he established the colony of Bethlehem in Pennsylvania as a base for Moravian mission work among the indigenous population.

1738

English Anglican evangelist George Whitefield arrived in the American colony of Georgia to serve as a parish priest. Once there, he decided to make the care of orphans his priority in life. He returned to England to raise money for his Bethesda orphan house by conducting revival meetings and giving speeches. Two years later, he would establish the Bethesda Academy near Savannah, which still exists today as a private day school for boys.

Pope Clement XII issued the first pronouncement against Freemasons, a secret fraternal order which made belief in God a requirement for membership. He viewed them as competing with the established Church for followers and accused them of teaching a naturalistic, deistic religion. At least eleven popes since then have tried to prevent Catholics from becoming involved in Freemasonry.

The ruins of the city of Pompeii had been discovered in the late sixteenth century but the systematic excavation began this year and can be considered the birth of modern archeology.

1739

A slave rebellion in South Carolina ended with thirty slaves and twenty-five others killed. It was the largest slave uprising on mainland North America, and as a result, many planters stopped importing slaves, preferring those who were locally born and raised. The owners believed that slaves were more content if they lived in bondage their entire lives.

At the urging of George Whitefield, John Wesley preached outdoors for the first time, to a group of English miners. This was unusual at that time, but he realized that by going outside church buildings, he could reach people who didn't attend church. That same year, John Wesley broke with the Moravians and started the Methodist Society of England.

Charles Wesley, aided by George Whitefield, wrote the Christmas carol "Hark! The Herald Angels Sing," using a melody by German composer Felix Mendelssohn.

1740

Upon George Whitefield's return to North American, he began preaching outdoor sermons across the country. This was a turning point in the Great Awakening. Over his career, Whitefield was said to have preached at least eighteen thousand times to audiences of more than ten million in Great Britain and the American colonies, and Benjamin Franklin became one of his loyal supporters. Because of his preaching, geographically and spiritually diverse colonists along the eastern seaboard began to develop a common bond, and this was a factor in paving the way for the American Revolution. Americans would fight to establish in the political realm the contentment and unity they had found in the spiritual realm.

In the Ambrosian Library in Milan, Italian priest and archeologist Lodovico Muratori discovered a fragment of a copy of the oldest known list of New Testament books. Scholars believe the original was written in about AD 170 in Greek. It's become known as the Muratorian Canon and is the second oldest list of New Testament books, after the Marcion Canon. It was very similar to the current New Testament but excluded James, First and Second Peter, and Hebrews—and it's not clear if it listed John's three epistles. Two of the gospels were unnamed, and it also included the *Apocalypse of Peter* and the *Wisdom of Solomon*.

1741

American revivalist preacher Jonathan Edwards delivered his most famous sermon, "Sinners in the Hands of an Angry God," in Enfield,
Connecticut. His image of a spider dangling over a fire effectively
scared people into converting and living Godly lives by threatening
them with the punishment of hell.

1742

German, later British, composer George Frideric Handel first performed *Messiah*, an English language oratorio, in Dublin, Ireland.

1743

Persians massacred 150 Christian monks at Saint Elijah's Monastery
in Mosul, Iraq, because they would not convert to Islam.

1744

Muhammad ibn Abd al-Wahhab and Prince Muhammad bin Saud
allied to unite the many states on the Arabian Peninsula by socio-
religious reforms. Saud conducted military operations while Wahhab
worked the socio-political front to encourage jihad and a return to
Islamic fundamentals to regain God's blessing.

1746

When the Chinese emperor became suspicious of European intentions
in his country, he issued an edict to deport Westerners. This policy
was not enforced uniformly throughout the country but was a serious
blow to the efforts of Christian missionaries there.

1747

The Shakers, officially known as the United Society of Believers in
Christ's Second Appearing, was founded in England. They were

originally known as the Shaking Quakers because of their overzeal-ous behavior during worship. Many of them would later immigrate to America, beginning in 1774.

1748

Henry M. Muhlenberg, a German missionary to Pennsylvania, founded the Ministerium of Pennsylvania, the first permanent Lutheran synod in America.

1749

Junípero Serra, a Franciscan priest and friar, landed in Veracruz, Mexico, with his missionary team. He was trained to work with the indigenous people and to conduct the Inquisition in his region.

Another nun accused Bavarian nun Maria Renata Singer of witchcraft and satanism, and she became the last woman burned as a witch in Europe.

Denis Diderot, a French philosopher and writer, published *Letter on the Blind*, in which he argued against the existence of God. It was writ-ten under a pseudonym, but the authorities traced the book back to him. They arrested him and sent him to prison for three months as a political prisoner.

1750

German composer Johann Sebastian Bach died. One of the greatest musical geniuses in history, he channeled much of his creative energy into church music.

c. Deistic thought was becoming extremely popular in English and American colleges. Its influence on many of the United States' Founding Fathers would become apparent in later years. Non-Christian Deists referred to "Providence," a "Creator," or "Nature's

God," rather than Judeo-Christian terms for God. It was a movement of reason and equality with a strong emphasis on social justice.

1751

Scottish philosopher David Hume wrote *An Enquiry Concerning the Principles of Morals*, demonstrating that morality did not depend on religious teachings. He saw the Bible simply as a product of ancient people trying to understand their origins.

1752

Benjamin Franklin supposedly performed his now-famous kite-flying experiment. The experiment may be a legend, but he did make the connection between lightning and electricity, understood the concept of grounding, and invented the lightning rod. His discoveries and inventions overturned the idea that lightning strikes were demonstrations of God's power.

Swedish botanist Carl von Linné, latinized to Carl Linnaeus, published *Species Plantarum*, in which he wrote about sexual reproduction in plants and apparently caused an outrage due to the sexual overtones of the book. Linnaeus and other "natural historians" were trying to reveal the systems of nature in order to reveal how God created it.

1753

The English Parliament passed a law allowing Jews to become naturalized citizens without taking a Christian oath. After subsequent rioting by Christians, Parliament repealed the law.

1755

A New York newspaper was the first to refer to the term *blue laws*. These laws restricted or prohibited various activities and commerce on Sundays in the Puritan colonies. They were originally enacted in the seventeenth century, and many are still valid today.

A destructive earthquake rocked Boston. According to some of the town's clergy, the earthquake was God's punishment for installing lightning rods.

1756

The Seven Years' War began between England and France, and in the American colonies, it was known as the French and Indian War. Many English Protestants saw religious overtones in the war and saw themselves as fighting satanic French Catholics with the pope in the role of Anti-Christ.

1758

The Quakers of Philadelphia banned anyone in the slave trade from church membership.

1759

Scottish economist, philosopher, and "Father of Capitalism" Adam Smith wrote the book *The Theory of Moral Sentiments*. Evidently an atheist, he theorized about the origin of human morality. Like David Hume, he saw it as a consequence of human interactions and relationships, not something derived from religion.

1760

François-Marie Arouet, better known as Voltaire, spoke out against the irrational and deadly persecution in European society. He refused to accept that one man could say to another, "Believe what I believe, or you will die."

Abbé Charles-Michel de L'Épée founded the world's first free school for the deaf in Paris, the National Institute for Deaf Children. In 1817, Congregational clergyman Thomas Gallaudet would start the first American school for the deaf in Connecticut.

Count Zinzendorf died at Herrnhut in Saxony. By this time, 266 Moravian Brethren missionaries were active around the world, from the Baltic Sea to South Africa and from South Carolina to Nicobar Islands in the Indian Ocean. The Moravians greatly inspired not only the Wesley brothers but also William Carey, another of the pioneers in modern Protestant missions.

1762

In *Emile*, or *On Education*, Jean-Jacques Rousseau wrote that rather than indoctrinating children in rules of good and evil, adults should allow children to interact with nature and learn by their own experiences. He said that if they damaged things, it was not from an intention to do harm or because of sin, but from their own innocence and ignorance. These ideas were revolutionary in child-rearing at a time when beating a child was thought to be necessary to exorcise evil forces.

1763

c. Prussia became one of the first countries in the world to establish a compulsory and free eight-year secular primary school system.

1764

Voltaire began a series of written attacks against Christianity by publishing one of his best-known philosophical works, the *Philosophical Dictionary*, which was an appeal for religious tolerance.

Milan economist and social scientist Cesare Baccaria wrote the best-selling *On Crimes and Punishment*, which influenced the major political thinkers of that time, including Voltaire, Thomas Jefferson, and John Adams. He argued that punishment should be proportional to the harm caused by the crime, not balanced against some subjective divine or cosmic scale of justice. He also insisted that criminal trials should be public, based only on evidence, and there should not be a death penalty. This book was placed on the papal Index of Forbidden Books and ridiculed by religious leaders for recklessly undermining their time-tested system. The Church advocated strong punishments were needed to counteract man's innate depravity and serve as an example to others.

1765

The first Magdalen Asylum for Penitent Females opened in Dublin, Ireland. These secretive Church-run institutions were originally designed to help prostitutes find new lines of work by learning a trade. Over the next two centuries, some of these asylums became veritable prisons where women could be sent without trial and against their will, and even incarcerated for the rest of their lives. Many of the women worked without pay in what were known as Magdalene laundries, so it was a very profitable arrangement for the Church.

1766

After noticing that Elohim and Yahweh, both names for the Jewish God, were mentioned in two different threads throughout the book of Genesis, French professor and scholar Jean Astruc proposed that the book was derived from several different sources.

Jean-Francois Lefebvre, a twenty-year-old French nobleman, was tortured, hung, and burned for the crime of slashing a wooden crucifix with a knife. This was one of the events that drove the writers of the US Constitution to want to separate Church ideology from government enforcement.

1767

King Charles III expelled the Jesuits from Spain and its possessions, ordering Jesuits in South America to return to Europe. This followed other expulsions of Jesuits in the past decade from the Portuguese Empire, France, Sicily, and Malta and would be followed by Austria and Hungary sixteen years later. Many governments thought these actions were necessary because of the Jesuits' alleged political maneuvering. They were seen as unwanted international influences within culturally evolving nations. As countries expelled Jesuits, they also confiscated their assets.

1768

German historian Hermann Reimarus died. He had argued that Jesus never claimed to be divine and that his ambitions had been entirely political. German scholars were applying the emerging techniques of literary analysis, archaeology, and comparative linguistics to gain deeper insight into the Bible and the conditions at the time it was written.

Refugees from Greece sought to escape poverty and oppression in their home country. They agreed to work as indentured servants in America. Of around one thousand that boarded ships for Florida, about two hundred died at sea. The rest arrived at New Smyrna, Florida, where they set up an indigo plantation. With them, Greek Orthodoxy was introduced to America.

Junípero Serra arrived in Baja California and began establishing a string of authoritarian Spanish missions from Baja to San Francisco. Indigenous converts were restricted to the premises unless they had special permission to leave. They served as conscripted labor and were beaten to assure they followed the rules. For these Native Americans, slavery became the price of salvation.

1769

Scottish inventor James Watt received a patent for his new steam engine. By employing it in machinery that graded land, mined coal, and cut roads, scientists could analyze the various layers of exposed soil. They discovered large numbers of fossils and developed an increasing interest in animals that had preceded humans on the planet.

1770

Baron d'Holbach, a French-German author, published his most famous book, *The System of Nature*, under a pseudonym. In it, he denied the existence of a deity and described the universe as purely materialistic. He saw Christianity as a major obstacle to the betterment of society. This would become one of the most widely read books of the eighteenth century.

The *Philosophical History of the Two Indies* was published anonymously but attributed to former Jesuit abbot Guillaume-Thomas Raynal. It argued that liberty was the birthright of all men, especially political liberty, and that women should not be oppressed. Raynal believed these goals were only possible with a retreat from hierarchical, anti-rational, traditional religions.

The Roman Catholic Church officially banned Passion plays across all of Europe, as many as three hundred of them in Bavaria and Austria alone. The Church found the mixture of religion and theater to be demeaning, especially when it involved portraying the suffering of Jesus. The popular play in Oberammergau was excluded from this policy because it was not sponsored by the Church.

1772

Denis Diderot completed his massive *Encyclopedie*, containing twenty-eight volumes, almost seventy-two thousand articles, and over three thousand illustrations on an enormous variety of subjects. He sought to make current knowledge available to everyone because of the many benefits of having an educated public. Many of the famous men in the French Enlightenment contributed to the work, which had to be published in secret to protect the authors from the Church's retribution.

Britain criminalized the practice of slavery but did not extend the law to its colonies. Their Atlantic slave trade still delivered an average of seventy-five thousand African slaves a year to the American colonies between 1750 and 1800.

1773

Scottish explorer James Bruce discovered the ancient Jewish *Book of Enoch* in Ethiopia. The authorship was attributed to Enoch, the great-grandfather of Noah but was probably written in the third century AD and was quoted in the New Testament epistle of Jude. The rediscovered manuscript was written in the Ge'ez language, and no Hebrew version is known to have survived. The book described the fall of the "Watchers," the angels or gods that fathered the Nephilim, giants mentioned in Genesis. Also mentioned are Enoch's travels to heaven and revelations about what he found there.

By the bull *Dominus ac Redemptor*, Pope Clement XIV dissolved the Society of Jesus, which included over eleven thousand priests and three thousand overseas missionaries. This was done in return for territorial concessions from France and Spain, who were threatening the Papal States. Jesuits took refuge in non-Catholic countries, particularly Prussia and Russia.

1774

King George III granted religious freedom to the French Catholics in Canada. In the minds of many American colonists, that made the king an accomplice to the pope, who they believed was the Anti-Christ.

American Universalists established their first church in Gloucester, Massachusetts. The sect had developed from the Pietist, Anabaptist, and Moravian movements in Europe, and what set them apart was the belief that was popular with early Christianity writers—that all people will eventually be saved and that loyalty to humanity is more important than national or religious allegiances.

1775

English Enlightenment enthusiast Thomas Paine, who had recently arrived in Philadelphia, was named editor of the *Pennsylvania Magazine*, and it soon became the best-selling magazine in the American colonies. He turned it in a political direction, running abolitionist essays and articles on workers' rights and animal cruelty.

In Philadelphia, Quakers founded the Society for the Relief of Free Negroes Unlawfully Held in Bondage, the first American abolition society. Thomas Paine was among its founders, and later Benjamin Franklin served as its president.

1776

Thomas Paine published *Common Sense*, a pamphlet advocating independence for the thirteen American colonies. He was very persuasive in convincing Americans that breaking away from the most powerful military power on Earth was what was necessary to attain the future they desired.

Members of the Second Continental Congress signed the US Declaration of Independence. Thomas Jefferson had composed the original draft, and although he was a slaveholder himself, he was reported to have included anti-slavery language that was later removed by the more pro-slavery delegates. There was to be a clear rejection of European influences, going so far as to use the deistic term *Creator* instead of *God* in the document. The new country proposed to rest on ideals that included a commitment to freedom of conscience and religious tolerance, so there would be no possibility of an inquisition in the United States. References to "laws of nature," "nature's God," and "self-evident truths" were the universal principles discovered by Isaac Newton and a reflection of the Enlightenment. Among the noble and respectable provisions was a statement that wasn't so enlightened in the description of Native Americans as "Indian Savages, whose known rule of warfare, is an undistinguished destruction of all ages, sexes, and conditions," a gross generalization if there ever was one.

Bavarians founded the secret society known as the Illuminati in order to oppose superstition, religious influence over public life, and abuses of state power. Due to lobbying by the Roman Catholic Church, the group was outlawed but not eliminated. Some conspiracy-minded people claim that the Illuminati is still active today.

The Spanish founded the mission of San Francisco in the northern part of their California territory. It was named after Saint Francis of Assisi. This continued a pattern of the Spanish giving Christian names to their colonies and geographical features. Other examples were Santo Domingo, Saint Augustine, San Juan, Veracruz (True Cross), Florida (Easter), Las Cruces (Crosses), Corpus Christi (body of Christ), Sacramento (holy sacrament), San Jose, San Diego, Santa Barbara, Los Angeles (angels), San Antonio, Santa Ana, Santa Fe (holy faith), and Sangre de Cristo Mountains (blood of Christ). This was also not unusual in Portuguese (Sao Paulo) and English and French colonies (Saint Paul, Saint Joseph, Saint-Domingue).

1777

Thomas Jefferson attempted to institute a statute on religious freedom in Virginia. It was not enacted until nine years later and would serve as the foundation for what later became the First Amendment to the US Constitution. Jefferson reasoned that the Creator, being omnipotent, could have made people all think the same way, but he chose not to. He said that we ought to have the sense to follow the Creator's example and that for anyone to dictate a certain religious faith was absurd.

Vermont was the first state to abolish slavery in its constitution. This practice spread to most of the states north of the Ohio River and the Mason-Dixon line, the line of latitude which divides Pennsylvania and Delaware from Maryland.

The US Congress officially approved the stars and stripes pattern for the country's flag. The name "United Colonies" was changed to "United States," and the Second Constitutional Congress issued a resolution which read: "Resolved, that the flag of the United States be thirteen stripes, alternate red and white; that the union be thirteen stars, white in a blue field, representing a new constellation." The stars and constellation seemed to make it a flag of the Enlightenment and its values.

1779

John Newton, a former English slave ship captain, wrote the song "Amazing Grace" after he realized his sin as a Christian in being part of the slave trade.

1780

Father Francisco Javier Clavijero published *History of Ancient Mexico*, a ten-volume set that reinforced the view that most of the indigenous Mexican population were peaceful and kind. The book strongly criticized the Spanish conquistadors.

Over the next ten years, the Holy Roman emperor Joseph II influenced the Church and his empire to be more in line with the Enlightenment. He granted religious freedom to Protestants, simplified the Catholic liturgy, closed many monasteries, and limited the power of the pope in Austria.

Robert Raikes organized Sunday schools in England as a way for poor children to receive an education and hopefully climb out of poverty. By 1787, there were 250,000 children attending Sunday schools in England, and the program crossed the ocean to America soon after. By the 1830s, there were 1.5 million children attending these schools, but as public education developed, Sunday schools would become more focused on the Bible and less on "the three Rs."

1781

In *Critique of Pure Reason*, German philosopher Immanuel Kant wrote that proving God's existence was impossible, since any deity was beyond the reach of human senses and therefore inaccessible to the human mind.

German historian and political writer Christian Wilhelm von Dohm published *On the Civil Improvement of the Jews*, an influential book calling for Jewish emancipation and full benefits of citizenship on humanitarian grounds.

1782

The first Unitarian church in America was founded in Boston. This sect interpreted God as one entity, not a trinity, and understood Jesus as a savior inspired by God. Unitarian origins were believed to be in Poland, Transylvania, and Britain.

Pennsylvania militiamen attacked the peaceful Lenape people at the Moravian mission of Gnadenhutten, Ohio, when they returned to their ancestral fields to harvest crops. This massacre of members of the Lenape tribe left twenty-eight men, twenty-nine women, and thirty-nine children dead. The militia was retaliating for the earlier kidnappings and deaths of frontier Pennsylvanians, crimes of which these Lenapes were completely innocent. Ironically, the Pennsylvania legislature, dominated by Quaker pacifists, was rarely anxious to fight the Native Americans and seemingly would never have approved such a violent action against any of them.

Austria's Edict of Tolerance permitted Jews to enter the Austrian economy, remove their stigmatizing clothing, retain Christian servants, have the option to leave their ghettos, show themselves in public during Christian holidays, and, for men, have the choice to no longer wear beards. The edict stopped short of allowing Jews to own land or shops outside the ghettos or to build public synagogues in Vienna, and it also forced Jews to pay a special tax for their protected status.

1783

Thanks to French military assistance, the American Revolution ended in victory for the United States. America's successful fight for freedom from British rule led to the establishment of the first secular republic in the modern world and a more just and tolerant social order. After more than two and a half centuries of European religious violence following the Protestant Reformation, the Thirty Years' War, the Huguenot wars, and the imprisonment, torture, and execution of people for the crimes of heresy and blasphemy, American leaders wanted no national religion, only the freedom for people to choose their own religious path.

Noah Webster published his *American Spelling Book*, and it became a best seller. As with most textbooks of its time, it was full of Bible quotations and other religious details. Along with the *New England Primer*, it is still reprinted and sold to this day.

1785

Catherine the Great of Russia sent an army to annex Chechnya, a former Persian province near the Caspian Sea. The Muslim Chechens and their allies defeated the Russians at the Battle of Sunja River.

1786

The four prince-archbishops of the Holy Roman Empire called the Congress of Ems, Germany, to protest papal interference in local affairs and more clearly define their relationship with the Vatican. This was in part a reaction to the papal documents that had become known as forgeries and that the Vatican had been using for centuries to retain power. The summary of the decisions of the congress were released in a document called the Punctuation of Ems and broke the bond between archbishops in the Holy Roman Empire and the Vatican. This caused the German Catholic Church to split because many bishops distrusted the archbishops and wanted to keep ties with the pope.

Thomas Jefferson disestablished the Anglican Church as the Church of Virginia. There was broad consensus in the United States that the old model, where religious establishments were funded through taxes, should be abandoned.

1787

The Society for Propagating the Gospel among the Indians and Others in North America was founded in Boston as the first missionary society in the United States.

The Constitutional Convention adopted the US Constitution. This document did not mention God, and it clearly kept religious influence out of government. One provision stipulated that there would be no religious test as a prerequisite to run for any governmental office. States that kept religious qualifications for office would later find those laws unenforceable.

Holy Roman emperor Joseph II issued the decree *Das Patent über die Judennamen*, which roughly translates to Charter for Jewish Names, which required Jews in his jurisdiction to adopt German surnames. Jews with more money to bribe officials obtained the more respectable names.

Louis XVI signed the Edict of Toleration, again granting religious freedom to French Huguenots but retaining Catholicism as the national religion.

The US Constitutional Congress agreed to the Three-Fifths Compromise. It counted three out of every five slaves as citizens in awarding the number of seats in the House of Representatives. Since slaves couldn't vote and few Southerners represented the slaves' best interests, the compromise only allowed slaveholding states to have more influence in government than non-slaveholding states until the Civil War in 1861.

1788

Edward Gibbon, an English historian, wrote the six-volume *The History of the Decline and Fall of the Roman Empire*. Gibbon asserted that Christianity helped lead to the fall of the western Roman Empire. His reasoning was that when Christians controlled the empire, their beliefs in an imminent return of Jesus and a heavenly realm to follow caused them to be more apathetic about the real world in which they lived, showing a criminal disregard for the public welfare because of their focus on God. Also, due to their pacifistic model of Jesus, many Christians may have avoided military service, weakening the empire's defense. In addition, Christians spent much of their resources on the Church rather than the needs of the empire. He believed that this focus on God resulted in a weakened empire, making it ripe for barbarian conquest.

1789

George Washington was sworn in as the first president of the United States. He placed his left hand on the Bible and ended his oath by kissing the Bible. The familiar phrase "so help me God" at the end of the presidential oath may not have been used before the twentieth century. The Judiciary Act of 1789 prescribed judges and elected officials to swear their oaths with God's name. It's interesting that this seemed to be a deviation of the overall deistic influence in the nation's founding documents.

The French Revolution began as an uprising of the common people against the aristocracy and the excessive wealth of the French Church. The momentum would grow from an attempt to separate the Church from secular life to the ruling Jacobin party attempting to suppress religion entirely. That government would shut down or nationalize many churches, close convents and monasteries that were not involved in educational or charitable work, require bishops to be chosen based solely on their competency, and sell prime Church lands to the public. For the first time in many centuries, God's existence could be openly questioned without fear of incarceration and death. In Paris, revolutionists would rename 1,400 streets that bore references to royalty or saints.

Thomas Jefferson was in Paris when the French Revolution began and consulted with Abbé Sieyès and the Marquis de Lafayette on the

Declaration of the Rights of Man and of the Citizen, which had many similarities to the US Declaration of Independence.

The document was approved by the French National Assembly.

Although many Jesuit universities had been founded in Hispanic America, Georgetown College in Washington, DC, was the first Jesuit college in the United States. By 1954, there would be twenty-seven more including prestigious names of Saint Louis University, Xavier, Fordham, Holy Cross, Saint Joseph's, Loyola, Boston College, Santa Clara, Saint Peter's, Creighton, Marquette, Gonzaga, and Seattle University.

Holy Roman emperor Joseph II issued a charter of religious toleration for the Jews in Galicia, between Poland and modern-day Ukraine. It ended Austrian control of Jewish affairs, promoted the Germanization of Jews, and allowed the wearing of non-Jewish clothing.

1790

Manuel Lacunza, a Jesuit priest in exile in Italy, completed the three-volume work *The Coming of the Messiah in Glory and Majesty*. Despite its prohibition by the Inquisition, he had the book printed in secret, and it was widely distributed in Europe and South America. Lacunza's writing became very influential in the development of the modern concept of end-times theology and greatly influenced John Nelson Darby, who would later popularize the idea in England.

The French National Assembly reaffirmed equal rights for Protestants and later voted to extend the same rights to Jews.

John Carroll of Baltimore became the first Catholic bishop in the US, and in 1805, he became the nation's first archbishop.

1791

The Bill of Rights, which consisted of the first ten amendments to the US Constitution, was ratified by the states and adopted by the federal government. The First Amendment declared religious freedom for all Americans, separating religion from government by prohibiting the creation of a national religion or forcing citizens to worship a religion other than the one of their own choosing. The First Amendment also guaranteed freedom of speech, freedom of the press, and the right to peaceful assembly. The Second Amendment allowed the right to own and house firearms to maintain a local militia. Since there was no national religion, a spiritual marketplace developed from which believers could choose the religion or denomination that best suited them. Many democracies around the world would eventually follow this model in their constitutions.

The French National Assembly required all elected clergy to swear an oath of loyalty to the national government. This oath implied the end of their loyalty to the pope, and Catholics vehemently resisted it. Pope Pius VI declared that those who signed the oath were heretics. The assembly also voted to place the papal enclave of Avignon under domestic rule, ending almost five hundred years of papal control. This seems to be where the French Revolution veered away from the American trajectory. France had a long history of being controlled by Rome. However, the US was basically Protestant and so had no revenge factor against religion, just a determination to keep it out of government.

John Wesley died, leaving an admirable legacy. He campaigned against slavery and excessive drinking and for the education of children. He had traveled roughly a quarter of a million miles and delivered nearly forty thousand sermons. His brother Charles, who died three years earlier, wrote nearly ten thousand hymns.

Slaves revolted against their French colonial masters in the colony of Saint Domingue, now known as Haiti, and at that time the most prosperous colony in the Caribbean region, and maybe even the world. Saint Domingue's population consisted of twenty-four thousand free

Blacks, thirty-two thousand Whites, and a hugely disproportionate five hundred thousand African slaves. It would be a long and bloody series of revolts with many unusual alliances and would last until 1804.

Olympe de Gouges, a French playwright and feminist, campaigned for women's rights, civil partnerships, and the abolition of slavery. This year she wrote *Declaration of the Rights of Women and of the Female Citizen*, in which she challenged the concept of male authority. Two years later she would be executed by the Revolutionary government.

1792

c. The Second Great Awakening, another Protestant revival movement, began in the United States. A series of incendiary Baptist and Methodist preachers, many of them untrained and illiterate, sermonized about reforming one's life, emphasizing individual salvation and free will over predestination.

By this time, five of the original thirteen states had followed the federal lead and changed their religious laws to align with the Constitution's more secular values.

The new French Legislative Assembly ordered all clergy who refused to take the loyalty oath to leave the country due to the disorder they were causing.

Mary Wollstonecraft published *A Vindication of the Rights of Woman* in England, advocating for the same opportunities as men in education, employment, and politics.

1793

The French government devised a new dating system, based not on Christ's birth, but on the founding of the French Republic. The Notre-Dame Cathedral became the site of a Temple of Philosophy during Paris's Festival of Reason. Among other works of art, it included busts of Voltaire, Rousseau, and Benjamin Franklin. Additionally, the assembly decided to erect a statue of Jean Meslier, the atheist Catholic priest who helped inspire the Enlightenment.

European countries from Great Britain to Russia were invading France to prevent their countries from being infected by the revolutionary zeal they saw in France. Abbé Claude Allier organized the Christian Army of the Midi, a French counterrevolutionary group that harassed Republican forces on their way to the front in France's war with Spain.

Missionary William Carey sailed from England to India. There he would translate the Bible into forty-four dialects, more new languages than had previously been produced in all Christian history, and he established many schools and mission stations.

The new French National Convention decreed that each parish could retain only one church bell, and the others were confiscated to make cannons, cannon balls, and bullets for the ongoing wars. Nationally, up to one hundred thousand bells from sixty thousand churches across the country were turned over and melted.

German philosopher Immanuel Kant wrote *Religion Within the Bounds of Bare Reason*. He strongly criticized basing belief on religious tradition, revelation, or superstition and wrote that truth must depend on what can be proven.

As an example of how much power Southerners had in the national legislature, the US Congress passed the Fugitive Slave Act, which required local and state governments to seize and return escaped slaves and imposed penalties on anyone who aided a slave in their flight. This act applied to anti-slavery states as well.

1794

Thomas Paine published *The Age of Reason*, which was an outright rejection of Christianity. Paine wrote that clergy had corrupted the religion for their own benefit and built an elaborate but false religion with illogical and dangerous doctrines. He advocated replacing

Christianity with Deism, which allowed free rational inquiry into all knowledge. Deists believed that a first cause had created the universe to allow humans to discover natural laws, but after that, the universe ran on its own without any supernatural interference. He argued that if the Creator had made a multitude of worlds, why would a unique savior only come to this one, let alone have to die because "one man and one woman had eaten an apple." Paine believed that the Creator would convince people of his existence in the language of the cosmos, which were the laws of nature, not in a book as confusing as the Bible. As expected, there was a vilification of Paine and his book by Christians, with more than thirty rebuttals and another religious revival.

During France's reign of terror, government officials drowned in the Loire River up to four thousand people who opposed the revolution. Many of the victims were priests and nuns. By this time, around twenty thousand French priests had left their positions and become ordinary citizens, with a large percentage of them marrying. Some leaders of the revolution tried to replace Catholicism with what they called the Cult of the Supreme Being, a Deist concept.

The first Russian missionaries arrived at the Russian colony on Kodiak Island, Alaska, introducing Russian Orthodoxy to what would become US territory.

The French National Convention abolished slavery in the French empire.

1795

Absalom Jones, a former slave, became a deacon and, later, America's first African American Episcopal priest.

Thomas Paine wrote an addendum to *The Age of Reason*, in which he addressed the inconsistencies, immoralities, and absurdities he found in the Bible.

Authorities arrested fifty-seven slaves and three white men in Pointe Coupee, Louisiana, after an insurrection. The local officials hanged twenty-three slaves, sentenced thirty-one others to flogging and hard labor, and deported the white men to Cuba.

American churches began to take sides over the slavery issue, with both sides quoting Bible verses to justify their stances. Many slave owners believed that Black Africans were the descendants of Ham, the son of Noah, and inherited the curse cast on Ham in Genesis.

Scottish scientist James Hutton published the book *Theory of the Earth*, in which he speculated, based on his studies of the processes of sedimentation and weathering, that Earth could be possibly millions of years old, much older than the six thousand years that religious scholars believed.

1796

The French government permitted emigrant priests to return to France, but only if they took the civic oath. They also made religious observance a private matter by forbidding the ringing of church bells and demonstrating outward signs of religion.

1797

In the Treaty of Tripoli, signed with Muslims in North Africa, US President John Adams affirmed "the government of the United States of America is not in any sense founded on the Christian religion—as it has in itself no character of enmity against the laws, religion or tranquility of [Muslims]." The US Senate unanimously ratified the treaty. Since many of the Founding Fathers were Deists, or deistic Christians, they did not follow orthodox Christian doctrines.

Young French General Napoleon Bonaparte led an army into Italy, and with Jewish soldiers in the vanguard, he captured Ancona, Italy. The Jewish soldiers entered the Jewish ghetto and tore off the yellow badges worn by the city's Jews, instead, offering them tricolor rosettes, symbols of the French Revolution. The French next conquered Venice and took their colonies in Albania and Corfu.

1798

The Church of England formed the Church Missionary Society as its foreign arm; it was the first evangelical missionary society to send its members to Africa.

Napoleon's army captured Rome, and after Pope Pius VI refused to renounce his temporal powers, he was taken to France as a prisoner. The pope died in captivity the following year after reigning longer than any other pope in history.

Napoleon's forces captured Malta and expelled the Knights Hospitaller, who had arrived there after already being forced out of Palestine, Cyprus, and Rhodes.

In Egypt, the Mamluks destroyed the ancient White Monastery, founded by Saint Pigol in AD 442.

The French army under Napoleon invaded Egypt in order to hinder the British, with whom they were at war. The native population resisted, and the French defeated the Mamluks at the Battle of the Pyramids. This was the beginning of the end for the Mamluks, who had ruled Egypt for seven centuries. The following year Napoleon's army invaded the coastal cities of Palestine, which were under Ottoman control. Through Muslim eyes, this was another Christian crusade, although it had nothing to do with the cross or Christianity.

In Egypt, one of Napoleon's soldiers discovered the Rosetta Stone. Originating in 204–180 BC, the artifact contained three scripts: common Egyptian, Greek, and hieroglyphics. This was a major archeological find for understanding both Egyptian and ancient Jewish culture and history.

The Irish rebelled against British rule. The revolt started with Presbyterians who were angry about Anglicans excluding them from power. They were joined by a small French army. The uprising was poorly organized and was quickly suppressed, with a death toll of ten thousand to thirty thousand.

1799

Cardinal Fabrizio Ruffo organized the Christian Army of the Holy Faith to fight against the Parthenopean Republic, which the French had established in Naples. With the aid of the British navy under Admiral Horatio Nelson, they captured Naples and ended the revolutionary republic.

When Napoleon occupied Siena, Italy, he emancipated the Jewish population. In retaliation, a few months later antisemitic rioters burned the Jewish ghetto and killed nineteen Jews.

Before George Washington died, he wrote his last will and testament. In it, he advocated for the establishment of a secular, publicly funded national university that would bring people together from all the states and hopefully dissolve prejudices. Washington had noticed how effective that kind of mixing was in establishing camaraderie in the Continental Army. At this time, the major US colleges were all religious institutions, none were secular. Congress rejected his request, and no such university was ever established. Also in his will, Washington freed his slaves.

CHAPTER 19: NINETEENTH CENTURY AD

The purpose of separation of church and state is to keep forever from these shores the ceaseless strife that has soaked the soil of Europe with blood for centuries.
—James Madison

When I told the people of Northern Ireland that I was an atheist, a woman in the audience stood up and said, "Yes, but is it the God of the Catholics or the God of the Protestants in whom you don't believe?"
—Quentin Crisp

The mentality of fundamentalism is by no means an exclusive property of orthodoxy. Its attitudes are found in *every* branch of Christendom: the quest for negative status, the elevation of minor issues to a place of major importance, the use of social mores as a norm of virtue, the toleration of one's own prejudice but not the prejudice of others, the confusion of the church with a denomination, and the avoidance of prophetic scrutiny by using the Word of God as an instrument of self-security but not self-criticism. The mentality of fundamentalism comes into being whenever a believer is unwilling to trace the effects of original sin in his own life. And where is the believer who is wholly delivered from this habit?
—Edward J. Carnell

We have men-stealers for ministers, women-whippers for missionaries, and cradle-plunderers for church members. The man who wields a blood-clotted cowskin during the week fills the pulpit on Sunday, and claims to be a minister of the meek and lowly Jesus. . . . The slave auctioneer's bell and the church-going bell chime in with each other, and bitter cries of the heart-broken slave are drowned in the religious shouts of his pious master.

—Frederick Douglass

This century introduced more of the concepts that we are familiar with today. Slavery ended bloodlessly in Britain but lethally in the US, and its end was not recognized or accepted in the former Confederate States of America. Even more new Christian sects emerged. Women's rights became a powerful movement, and many charitable and social justice organizations were established in Great Britain and the US. The last of the Native American land was taken over by white Americans. Amazing archeological discoveries were made, and Darwin introduced his theory of evolution. Conservative Christians continued to reject modern discoveries and theories, while the Industrial Revolution brought great demographic and technological changes to the Western world. European powers continued to colonize every part of the world, bringing Christian missionaries with them.

1800

c. In France, by the end of the eighteenth century, approximately three thousand clergy members had been killed, including 920 who were publicly executed as counterrevolutionaries. Without the Church's control, France became the first Western European country to decriminalize sexual acts between consenting adults, and birth control, forbidden for so long, became widespread.

c. Protestants in the US agreed to work together to combat the Catholic threat. Searching for some glue to bind them together, they found unity in the enforcement of personal morality.

c. The custom of dressing up in one's finest clothing to go to church became popular as the Industrial Revolution created a middle class wanting to establish a new image of success. This happened first in England and then in northern Europe and North America.

Gabriel Prosser, a Virginia slave, planned a large-scale slave rebellion in Virginia, but his plot was revealed by an informant, and he and twenty-five followers were hanged. This was the fourteenth significant slave revolt in the New World, but none had been successful.

c. "Altar calls," or people coming to the front of the church to proclaim their commitment to Jesus Christ, became more common.

1801

Partially as a reaction to the attacks by Thomas Paine and other enlightenment writers on Christianity, the Second Great Awakening gained momentum at a camp meeting at Cane Ridge, Kentucky. In these revival gatherings, the Calvinist doctrine of predestination was replaced with the Arminian doctrine that all are free to accept or reject the saving grace of Jesus. The individual played the leading role in determining his or her eternal destiny. This revival would remain strong until the mid-nineteenth century and caused church membership in the US to double.

The Ottomans and a British fleet ended Napoleon's Middle Eastern campaign at Acre, Palestine. The French army returned home, and the British took possession of the Rosetta Stone.

Napoleon and Pope Pius VII signed a concordant to reconcile French revolutionaries with the Catholic Church. It reaffirmed the Roman Catholic Church as the majority church of France.

c. Reported sightings of the Virgin Mary spiked. Visitations from the Virgin had been common in the sixteenth century but declined after that due to the Protestant Reformation's rejection of apparitions and miracles and the Inquisition's focus on witch-hunting, which made people hesitant to utter anything hinting at the occult.

1802

The French, under Napoleon's rule, reimposed slavery in Saint Domingue. The French invaded the island and introduced a reign of terror that left few Black citizens safe. Thousands of Polish soldiers sent to Saint Domingue by Napoleon turned against the French and aided the Haitians in their revolt.

1803

Ludwig van Beethoven's oratorio *Christ on the Mount of Olives* was first performed in Vienna, portraying the emotional turmoil Jesus suffered in the Garden of Gethsemane before his arrest.

The Massachusetts Society for Promoting Christian Knowledge became the first association in the country devoted to publishing exclusively religious literature.

After Napoleon Bonaparte realized his dream of a French empire in the Americas was not going to materialize, he sold the vast Louisiana Territory that stretched from Louisiana north to Canada, and west as far as Montana, to the US for fifteen million dollars.

1804

At Notre-Dame Cathedral in Paris, Pope Pius VII handed the crown to Napoleon, and he crowned himself emperor of the French. His self-crowning indicated he was subservient to no one. The format of the ceremony had been approved by the pope, but with changes made to suit a new kind of French ruler, one of destiny, not of heredity.

Thomas Jefferson completed the first part of a personal project known as the Jefferson Bible, which he titled *The Philosophy of Jesus of Nazareth*. He compiled this by cutting and pasting sections of the

New Testament with razor and glue, excluding all miracles and references to the supernatural.

In St. Louis, Missouri, minor chiefs of the Sauk tribe and William Henry Harrison, who represented the United States, signed the Quashquamme Treaty, or Treaty of St. Louis, which ceded fifty million acres of Native American land to the US. The chiefs were in Saint Louis for an entirely different matter and were not authorized to negotiate or make any agreements on behalf of their tribe. American representatives took advantage of their presence and supplied them with generous amounts of whiskey to get them drunk. They then declared the treaty legal and forcibly evicted the Sauks from their land. US courts of law refused to consider any appeal. The Sauk tribe and their allies, not surprisingly, would side with the British during the upcoming War of 1812, and still trying to return to his native homeland, Black Hawk, a Sauk leader, would fight the Black Hawk War in 1832.

Once the Haitians gained independence from France in what became the only truly successful slave revolt in world history, the Blacks and those of mixed race turned on the remaining white population. To avenge past French atrocities, the Haitian president, Jean-Jacques Dessalines, ordered the massacre of most remaining French-born citizens and saw that it was carried out. The Haitian Revolution influenced the British to end their slave trade, but because of the massacre of the French and the ruination of Haiti's economy, the US wouldn't recognize Haiti or end its trade embargo until 1862.

1805

Harvard College promoted Unitarian Henry Ware to professor of divinity, but Calvinist teachers, who upheld the doctrine of the Trinity, began to resign from the faculty. Ware kept his position, and his son would also become a professor of divinity at Harvard.

Napoleon's army defeated the Austrians and Russians at the Battle of Austerlitz, forcing Francis II to give up his title as Holy Roman emperor, and the thousand-year-old Holy Roman Empire ceased to exist.

1806

Henry Martyn, a young Anglican priest, arrived in India as a missionary. Over the next six years, he translated the New Testament into Urdu, Persian, and Judeo-Persian.

Napoleon announced that Jews in France would become full citizens of the republic. This was in fulfillment of the revolution's principles of liberty, equality, and fraternity.

Author Thomas Paine wrote in a letter to Andrew Dean: "The fable of Christ and his twelve apostles, which is a parody on the sun and the twelve signs of the zodiac, copied from the ancient religions of the eastern world, is the least hurtful part. Everything told of Christ has reference to the sun. His reported resurrection is at sunrise, and that on the first day of the week; that is, on the day anciently dedicated to the sun, and from thence called Sunday."

1807

After his twenty-seven-year campaign against the British slave trade, William Wilberforce finally achieved success with Parliament's passage of the Slave Trade Act, which forbade transport of slaves on British ships. This led to the establishment of Sierra Leone as a home for displaced Africans. However, even when former slaves were returned to Africa, they were not freed immediately but forced to work under a quasi-slavery institution called apprenticeship.

The Act Prohibiting Importation of Slaves was passed in the US, but ownership of slaves in the South continued to be legal until the US Civil War.

1808

Napoleon conquered Spain and ended the Spanish Inquisition. Although King Ferdinand VII would try to reinstate it, the Inquisition finally lost momentum and was finished by 1834.

1809

Charles-Francois Dupuis, an influential French professor of rhetoric, died. Along with Constantin Francois Chasseboeuf de Volney, he had developed the "Christ myth theory," which argued that Christianity was a combination of various ancient mythologies, and that Jesus was a mythological character like other ancient gods, not a real historical person.

French troops raided the Quirinal Palace in Rome and, after battling the Swiss guard, kidnapped Pope Pius VII and took him to Savona in northern Italy. Napoleon had him captured to make it easier for the emperor to carry out his plans.

1810

Friedrich Schleiermacher, a German theologian, philosopher, and bible scholar, took the theological chair at the University of Berlin. Schleiermacher became a pioneer in the discipline of higher criticism of the Bible, seeking historical confirmation of the events mentioned in the scriptures.

New England Congregationalists founded the American Board of Commissioners for Foreign Missions, one of the first American societies of its kind, and they later became active in Hawaii.

Inspired by the American and French Revolutions, Miguel Hidalgo y Costilla, a Mexican Roman Catholic priest, led a revolt of poor, native-born Mexicans against their Spanish rulers. This became the Mexican War of Independence.

1811

Russia annexed the neighboring nation of Georgia and assimilated the Georgian Orthodox Church into the Russian Orthodox Church. Georgia's Church would remain in that status until 1917 and only regain full independence in 1991.

Two Oxford students, Thomas Jefferson Hogg and Percy Bysshe Shelley, wrote a pamphlet entitled *The Necessity of Atheism*, borrowing from Baron d'Holbach's *System of Nature*. Oxford expelled both students, but their parents were well-connected, and so Hogg and Shelley did not face legal action or religious damnation.

Slaves in Louisiana revolted in what is known as the German Coast uprising. This was possibly the largest slave insurrection in US history with two hundred to five hundred participants. The slaves did little more than march twenty miles and burn plantations along the way, but the white militia and national troops that pursued them killed ninety-five slaves while losing only two of their own men.

1812

Presbyterians established the Princeton Theological Seminary as the second Protestant seminary in the United States. Andover Theological Seminary had been founded five years previously.

Congregationalist missionaries Adoniram and Ann Judson sailed for India as two of the first foreign missionaries sent from the United States. Another young missionary, Harriet Newell, gave birth at sea, but the infant died, and Harriet would also die soon after the ship landed, making her the first American to lose her life in the mission field.

1814

Napoleon allowed Pope Pius VII, who had been a French prisoner since they invaded the Papal States in 1809 and the second consecutive pope to be kidnapped and imprisoned by Napoleon, to return to Rome. It didn't take the pope long to reinstitute confinement of Rome's Jews to the ghetto and lock it at night.

After Paris surrendered to a coalition of armies and Napoleon's generals would no longer follow him, he was forced to abdicate his throne and go into exile on the island of Elba, off the coast of Tuscany.

Orthodox monk Euthymius had converted from Christianity to Islam but then reverted to Christianity and became a monk at Mount Athos. When he traveled back to Constantinople, he was arrested and beheaded for his apostasy.

Because he needed their help in rebuilding Church influence and schools after the Napoleonic wars, Pope Pius VII restored the Jesuit order after forty-one years of official suppression.

1815

Napoleon escaped from his exile on Elba and restored his army but was defeated by a coalition at Waterloo, Belgium. His hopes of re-establishing his empire ended, and he was exiled again, this time to the island of Saint Helena, off the southern African coast, where he died six years later. The rights he had granted to European Jews were withdrawn except in France and Holland.

By this time, scientists were determining that fossils in the uppermost layers of the earth's soil resembled present-day species, while those below progressively changed, making it obvious that life had altered dramatically over time. It was also about this time that natural scientists began to reject the book of Genesis as a source of authority on science.

1816

Pope Pius VII officially ended torture as a tool of the Roman Inquisition. Despite this decree, the Papal States were reported to secretly use torture until 1870 when the pope's jurisdiction became limited to Vatican City.

Former President John Adams wrote to his son John Quincy Adams: "An incarnate God! An eternal, self-existent, omnipresent omniscient Author of this stupendous Universe, suffering on a Cross! My Soul starts with horror at the Idea, and it has stupefied the Christian World. It has been the Source of almost all the Corruptions of Christianity."

1817

English Quaker Elizabeth Fry and her team began a ministry to incarcerated women. She became a model for social compassion and involvement with the underprivileged.

Pope Pius VII granted an indulgence for anyone who climbed the Holy Stairs outside the Sancta Sanctorum of the Church of Saint Lawrence in Rome. They had to ascend the twenty-eight steps on their knees and recite a prayer on each one. This equated to nine years less in purgatory for every step climbed in the appropriate manner.

Gordon Hall and Samuel Newell, who had lost his wife and baby traveling to India, were American missionaries in Bombay. They co-wrote the book *The Conversion of The World: Or the Claims of Six Hundred Millions of Heathens, and the Ability and Duty of the Churches Respecting Them.* They proposed a strategy to reach every person on Earth by sending out thirty thousand Protestant missionaries from the United States and Europe over a twenty-one-year period.

1818

In Austria, Franz Xavier Gruber composed the melody for "Silent Night! Holy Night!" ("Stille Nacht, Heilege Nacht") to lyrics written by Joseph Mohr two years earlier.

France again declared slavery illegal, but this law was unenforceable, and French ships still covertly carried Africans to slave markets in Cuba and Brazil.

1819

When a professor at the University of Würzburg urged an end to discrimination against Jews, his outraged students physically attacked him, then took to the streets to join other townspeople who were attacking Jewish homes and businesses. They killed Jewish residents and drove many more from their homes. As was the usual case, this type of purge, or pogrom, spread to other German towns.

English authorities fined publisher Richard Carlile and sent him to prison for the crime of blasphemy. His offense had been publishing the book *The Age of Reason* by Deist Thomas Paine. The book was extremely popular in the United States, France, and Britain.

1820

Thomas Jefferson completed *The Life and Morals of Jesus of Nazareth*, book two of what is known as the Jefferson Bible, using the same cut and paste method as used in book one.

The first Protestant missionaries arrived in Hawaii, having sailed from Boston.

The citizens of Boston founded the first public high school in the US. One of the main goals was to Americanize the student population, which was multiethnic and multireligious due to a growing Catholic population. Public education was not established in the southern states until after the Civil War.

The first freed slaves from the US arrived in what would become Liberia, West Africa. The following year, the American Colonization Society, including many prominent Americans, founded the colony as a homeland and refuge for former slaves. The name *Liberia* came from the word *liberty*, and its capital of Monrovia was named after US president James Monroe.

1821

The Greeks revolted against the Ottoman Turks, who had occupied their country since the sixteenth century. The revolt would last until 1832, with the Greeks being assisted by Russia, Great Britain, and France. There were large-scale atrocities and massacres on both sides.

American educator Elizabeth Ann Seton died. She had founded the country's first Catholic girls' school in Baltimore and organized the Sisters of Charity, the first congregation of religious sisters in the US. In 1975, she became the first native-born American to be canonized as a saint.

The Russian Empire had acquired a significant Jewish population by taking land from the Polish-Lithuanian Commonwealth and the Ottoman Empire. This Jewish population was often subjected to terrible treatment. The first major *pogrom,* the Russian word for "wreaking havoc," occurred in Odessa where fourteen Jews were killed.

1822

Lott Carey, a former slave and the first American missionary to Africa, established Providence Baptist Church in Monrovia, Liberia.

c. Jean-Francois Champollion deciphered Egyptian hieroglyphs by using the Rosetta Stone. This was a monumental historical accomplishment because it allowed scholars to understand not only the ancient Egyptian writings but also their culture. Quite unexpectedly, it would lead to evidence that some aspects of Judaism and Christianity appeared to have evolved from Egyptian mythology.

1823

Eighteen-year-old New York farmer and handyman Joseph Smith said he was visited by an angel named Moroni, who spoke of gold plates buried in a nearby hillside. Smith claimed that he had found and translated the plates and then returned them to Moroni, without anyone else seeing them. Smith said the text, which would become the Book of Mormon, revealed that American Indians were descended from the Lamanites of ancient Israel, who God cursed and turned dark. Smith said the Indians wouldn't be turned white, by which he meant they wouldn't become civilized, until they accepted Christ's teachings.

1824

Despite all the hopes of the Enlightenment and emancipation from the grip of religious influence, France was reverting to its prerevolution situation. The new government established a secret committee that removed books from libraries that encouraged Enlightenment thoughts.

In England, compassionate Christians and Jews founded The Society for the Prevention of Cruelty to Animals, the first animal welfare organization in the world.

1825

Russia began to draft Jewish boys as young as twelve years old into the army to convert them to Christianity. Jewish conscripts were required to spend twenty-five years in service and were often forced into the front lines for use as "cannon fodder." Jewish boys in agricultural areas were not affected by this policy, but even so, many were kidnapped and forced into the army. Jews were not allowed to become officers.

William Buckland, a British geologist, visited Palermo (modern-day Italy) and discovered that the relics of Saint Rosalia, which had been venerated since the twelfth century, were the bones of a goat. Apparently, the bones had cured so many diseases over the centuries that the people didn't even care what animal they came from.

1826

Cayetano Ripoll was the last person executed by the Spanish Inquisition, which would formally end eight years later. In total, between 150,000 and 340,000 persons may have been examined and tortured, and 5,000 to 32,000 of them burned.

1827

New York ended the practice of slavery after a twenty-eight-year period of gradual abolition.

Massachusetts passed a law prohibiting the use of public funds to buy schoolbooks that favored any specific Christian denomination.

German scientist Karl Ernst von Baer discovered the mammalian oocyte, or egg cell. The following year he wrote *Developmental History of Animals*, in which he discussed the similarities in the fetuses of fish, birds, and mammals, including humans—dramatic evidence of evolution being reproduced during gestation since it showed humans going through a stage where they had gill slits and tails.

1829

After Greece was liberated from Turkish control, Greeks sought revenge by destroying the minarets that Muslims had used for centuries to call their faithful to prayer.

At the insistence of Christian missionaries, the British banned the practice of *sati* in India. This was the tradition of widows being burned alive in the cremation fires of their husbands.

Felix Mendelssohn performed Bach's *Saint Matthew's Passion* for the first time in Berlin exactly one hundred years after Bach composed it.

1830

President Andrew Jackson signed the Indian Removal Act, which forced tens of thousands of indigenous Americans in the Southeast to give up their traditional homes, fields, and hunting grounds and move to designated locations west of the Mississippi River.

In western New York, Joseph Smith published the Book of Mormon. He also organized a church named the Church of Christ, or Church of Jesus Christ of Latter-day Saints, but today known to outsiders as the Mormon Church. The new faith was based on the revelations Smith said he received from the angel, and therefore his followers considered him a prophet. Mormons usually self-identify as Christians, but they have enough differences—such as not accepting the Trinitarian concept, using alternate scriptures, believing in the continuing revelation from God—that many Christians see them as a different religion.

A wave of Catholic immigrants from Ireland arrived in the predominantly Protestant United States, deepening the religious animosity that had been Europe's trademark since the Protestant Reformation.

c. The US was in the midst of the Industrial Revolution, and with shifting populations from small towns to the larger cities, education reform was in progress. At this time, ministry remained the most popular career choice for college graduates in the United States, but things were changing to suit the current industrial, legal, and medical needs of society.

In Paris, Sister Catherine Labouré said she was visited by the Virgin Mary, who presented herself within an oval frame. Mary instructed her to have a medal struck, using the way the apparition appeared and specific symbolism as the model for a devotional medal. Two years later, goldsmith Adrien Vachette created large quantities of the Miraculous Medal of Our Lady of Graces, which were circulated around the world.

In Scotland, Margaret MacDonald had a vision of Jesus making a two-stage return to Earth. Part of her prophecy later became popularized by Anglo-Irish Bible teacher John Nelson Darby as the "Rapture."

France invaded and conquered Algeria, at the time a province of the Ottoman Empire. Although the Ottomans were quickly defeated, popular resistance went on for another forty-five years.

Queen Ka'ahumanu of Hawaii converted to Christianity. Since the Puritan missionaries thought hula dancing had heathen roots and celebrated physical enjoyment, they compelled the queen to forbid public performances of the traditional dance. The hula would not experience a revival until 1883 under King Kalakaua.

Because they considered such literature heretical, Catholic missionaries threw thousands of ancient Nestorian books and manuscripts from the library in Mosul into the Tigris River.

1831

American preacher William Miller founded the Millerite movement and predicted the Second Coming of Christ in 1844. This was based on Miller's reading of the book of Daniel and using the day-year principle, meaning that when biblical prophecy referred to "days," that should really be interpreted as years.

William Garrison, a New England journalist, began publishing *The Liberator*, a weekly paper advocating the complete abolition of slavery in the US.

The Mormons moved from New York to Ohio and then to Missouri.

Ten years after he invited missionaries from the London Missionary Society to his country, King Radama I declared the attempt to bring Christianity to Madagascar a failure. When Queen Ranavalona I gained the throne, she relaxed anti-Christian measures and encouraged conversion, baptism, and church attendance. However, this year, she became suspicious of the political and cultural aspects of Christianity and reversed direction. By 1835, the queen would formally forbid Christian practice among her people, and Christians were persecuted until she died in 1861.

In Virginia, Nat Turner led the largest and deadliest slave uprising in US history, killing fifty-five to sixty-five white people. In retaliation, 120 slaves and freed African Americans were murdered by militias and mobs. Following this rebellion, many Southern states passed laws prohibiting the education of Blacks, limiting their right to assemble, and requiring white ministers to be present for all their worship services.

While traveling through the US, French social scientist Alexis de Tocqueville wrote "The Americans combine the notions of Christianity and liberty so intimately in their minds, that it is almost impossible to make them conceive of one without the other."

1832

After eight years of fighting, the Black War ended in Tasmania with the extermination of the entire indigenous population of the island.

Prominent abolitionist and former slave Frederick Douglass later wrote that this year his master, Thomas Auld, became a Christian. Douglas hoped that his conversion would make him kinder, but the opposite happened. Auld became more cruel and hateful and was able to justify his behavior by quoting Bible verses.

1833

In France, lawyer, author, and professor Frédéric Ozanam founded the Society of Saint Vincent de Paul to provide aid and advocacy for the poor.

Massachusetts was the last state to allow full religious freedom by disestablishing the state Anglican Church. Without state support, churches were forced to fund themselves in other ways, and the weekly passing of the collection plate became more important in America.

Activist, orator, and escaped slave, Frederick Douglass helped found the American Anti-Slavery Society in Philadelphia.

Inspired by Christian revivals, Presbyterians John Jay Shipherd and Philo Stewart founded Oberlin College in Ohio. Believing that "slavery was America's most horrendous sin" and hoping to bring on the millennium, or end times, Oberlin became the first college in the United States to admit African Americans. A few years later it was the first to admit women.

John Nelson Darby began to popularize the "Rapture" that would precede the return of Christ. The notion was derived from First

Thessalonians 4:16–17: "For the Lord himself will come down from heaven . . . with the trumpet call of God, and the dead in Christ will rise first. After that, we who are still alive and are left will be caught up together with them in the clouds to meet the Lord in the air. And so, we will be with the Lord forever." The epistle writer Paul had cobbled together several Old Testament verses and local tradition to create this image. The concept of the Rapture took off with US evangelicals, who for centuries had tried to guess when Jesus physical return might occur. Even to the present day, outside of evangelicals, there are serious concerns among Christians that focusing too much on the Rapture motivates many to wish for it, and some to actively try to hasten the event, out of a desire to meet Jesus face-to-face.

The British House of Commons passed the Slavery Abolition Act, freeing all slaves in the British empire. The government agreed to financially compensate the owners of the eight hundred thousand freed slaves.

Britain passed the Factory Act, which limited the number of hours a person could work to forty-eight hours per week and declared that a child under thirteen years of age could not be forced to work.

J. D. Paxton was the minister of the Cumberland and College Church congregations in a region of Virginia where there was much controversy over slavery. When he discovered that his salary was mostly paid from money earned by hired out slaves, he expressed his disgust. Paxton had freed his own slaves and sent them to Liberia, so he felt justified to speak out against slavery. After writing the abolitionist article "Letters on Slavery" for a religious newspaper, his hate-filled congregants forced Paxton to resign from his parish and move north.

1834

The Knights Hospitaller had evolved into the Sovereign Military Order of Malta and acquired a new headquarters in Rome, where they are still active.

Slavery was abolished in the British Empire, but Canada had already taken steps to end the practice and was a haven for runaway slaves from the US.

1835

The US Humane Society founded the secular National Federation of Child Rescue agencies to investigate the mistreatment of children.

1836

At a time when few existed, German Lutheran pastor Theodor Fliedner opened a hospital and a deaconess training center in Kaiserswerth, Germany. British social reformer and nurse Florence Nightingale would receive her medical training there in 1850.

German scholar David Friedrich Strauss published *The Life of Jesus Critically Examined*, in which he focused on the historical Jesus. He argued that all of Jesus's miracles were myths and pointed out the lack of coherence and the numerous contradictions in the Gospels. Strauss traced two strains of theology back through time, one originating from Paul's epistles about the divine Christ and the other stemming from the Gospels and their emphasis on the human Jesus. He believed it took heavy editing of the scriptures in the second century to make these two themes intertwine and seem compatible.

The US Senate passed the Pinckney Resolutions, with one resolution known as the "gag rule." This prevented anti-slavery petitions from being read or discussed in Congress and stated that federal representatives had no constitutional authority to interfere with slavery in individual states.

Alabama was the first state to make Christmas a legal holiday, but the US Congress still would meet on Christmas Day until 1855, and Boston public schools were open on Christmas Day until 1870. These traditions were holdovers from the Puritan de-emphasis of Christmas two centuries earlier.

The Jewish community in Rome sent a petition to Pope Gregory XVI begging him to stop the annual Saturnalia, or Christmastime, abuse of the Jewish community, but the pope refused, so apparently, the tradition had been reestablished.

The *McGuffey Reader* was printed in the US. By 1890, it became the standard school reader in thirty-seven states. Like other American educational books, it focused on the teaching of morality, prayers, and Bible quotations.

Friedrich Froebel returned to Germany after supervising an orphanage in Switzerland and devoted himself to preschool education, calling his teaching facilities *kindergartens*.

After his five-year voyage on the HMS *Beagle*, Charles Darwin wrote of the fact that various types of plants and animals had similar body plans, but they used similar structures for different functions, another clue that life had evolved from simpler forms and was branching out in its diversity.

In his book *Geology and Mineralogy Considered with Reference to Natural Theology*, Reverend William Buckland of Oxford tried to explain the "problem of pain" in nature. He wrestled the dilemma of why a benevolent God would allow creatures to suffer.

1837

Presbyterian minister and journalist Elijah Parish Lovejoy became a martyr to the cause of abolitionism when pro-slavery radicals murdered him in his printing office in Alton, Illinois.

Influenced by the Enlightenment and the French Revolution, the Spanish government seized Church land and sold it to the middle class. The Spanish Church responded by becoming more defensive and traditional.

1838

English military consul Henry Rawlinson was the first Westerner to transcribe the Old Persian portion of the Behistun cuneiform inscriptions. Other inscriptions were written in the Elamite and Babylonian languages. His work was instrumental in unlocking the secret of these ancient writings. This process was very much like deciphering the Rosetta Stone to understand Egyptian hieroglyphics.

Up until 1830, the "Five Civilized Tribes"—Cherokee, Chickasaw, Choctaw, Muscogee (Creek), and Seminoles—had been living as self-governing nation in southeastern US. As part of Andrew Jackson's Indian Removal Act's policy, these tribes were forced to relocate to Oklahoma so white settlers could confiscate their land. By this time, the last of them were being uprooted and led away and many thousands died of exposure, disease, starvation, and mistreatment. Four thousand Cherokees were said to have died just this year alone in what became known as the "Trail of Tears."

Ralph Waldo Emerson addressed the senior class of the Harvard Divinity School, assaulting the traditions and activities of the established church.

German philosopher Christian Hermann Weisse refined the earlier ideas of Friedrich Schleiermacher and suggested that the writers of the Gospels of Luke and Matthew used a second source other than the Gospel of Mark. This other source, believed to have been written around AD 50, eventually came to be known as Q, an abbreviation for the German word *Quelle*, meaning "source."

The Missouri Mormon War began when local citizens tried to prevent Mormons from voting in an election. The Mormons had used their growing population to influence election outcomes in their region of Missouri, and other residents feared that the Mormons would establish a theocracy there. That same year, Joseph Smith fled Missouri and went to Illinois to evade the legal charges of threatening a public official and treason.

Abner Kneeland, a Massachusetts evangelist, theologian, publisher, and debater, became more skeptical and outspoken about revealed religion. He was the last person arrested and jailed in the United States for the crime of blasphemy.

Englishman Samuel Birley Rowbotham conducted the Bedford Level experiment and concluded that Earth was flat, not round. Over the years, due to a literal interpretation of the Bible and the rejection of all evidence to the contrary, those who believed Rowbotham formed Flat Earth societies.

1839

In France, a newspaper announced that the death warrant of Christ, supposedly issued by Pontius Pilate, had been rediscovered. It was said to have been discovered in 1280 in Italy, then lost, and rediscovered when the French occupied Naples from 1806 to 1815. It was later exposed as a fraud.

Slaves aboard the Spanish slave ship *Amistad* rebelled off the coast of Long Island, New York. US authorities captured the ship and imprisoned the Africans in Connecticut, which had not yet abolished slavery. This event drew worldwide attention with both the United States and Spain arguing that the captives should be sent to Cuba, where the Spanish would probably execute them for the insurrection. After a Hartford court ruled that the Africans had been kidnapped from Africa illegally, a dispute developed between President Martin Van Buren and former President John Quincy Adams, who defended the Africans before the US Supreme Court. Following their many months in Spanish captivity, and then eighteen more months in the Connecticut jail, the surviving Africans were freed. With no help from the US government, abolitionists raised the money to resettle them in Sierra Leone, West Africa.

Having been arrested months earlier during anti-Mormon hostilities, Joseph Smith was transferred to a Missouri jail, where this year he escaped. He and his Mormon followers fled Missouri and settled in Nauvoo, Illinois.

The Ottoman Empire abolished their strict Sharia law, the codes of conduct for Muslim life and Islam's legal system. As a result, the empire eliminated taxes on non-Muslims and opened positions to them in the government and military. Newly integrated schools did not teach the Koran but did teach science and language. This was still a Muslim empire, but it was experimenting in Westernization largely because the Ottomans owed much money to Western creditors who they needed to appease.

1840

c. The *Book of Jubilees*, written as early as 160 BC and known also as the *Book of Division*, was rediscovered in Ethiopia. This was an ancient well-known Jewish writing that early Christian writers had referenced. Both the Ethiopian Orthodox Christians and Ethiopian Jews considered it canonical. The manuscript was written in the Ge'ez language but was faithful to the version that would be found in the Dead Sea Scrolls a century later.

David Livingstone, a medical doctor, missionary, and explorer, left England to provide medical care in Central Africa.

c. About this time in America, pew rentals began to fall out of favor. The renting of pews, or box pews, was introduced in sixteenth-century Britain as a source of income for churches after state funding dried up. Because of this policy, there was no longer a feeling of equality among church members; choice seats went to the highest bidders, and money bought status.

c. The Methodist Church became the largest Christian denomination in the US.

1841

Theodore Parker, a prominent reform minister in the Massachusetts Unitarian Church, delivered a memorable sermon about Christianity entitled "A Discourse on the Transient and Permanent in Christianity." In it, he insisted that the church was more concerned with monitoring the petty details of people's lives than living the eternal truths of Jesus's teaching.

British Anglicans and German Lutherans founded a joint Protestant bishopric in Jerusalem.

1842

George Jacob Holyoake was an English secular newspaper pioneer who coined the term *secularism* to define his ideology. This year he was convicted of blasphemy and spent six months in jail. He was quoted as saying "Secularism is not an argument against Christianity, it is one independent of it. It does not question the pretensions of Christianity, it advances others."

1843

Because of perceived encroachment of the government on the Church of Scotland, Thomas Chalmers led 473 Church of Scotland clergy to form the new Free Church of Scotland.

Kurds attacked Assyrian and Nestorian Christians in Hakkari, Iraq, killing as many as ten thousand Nestorians over the next three years. This persecution was thought to have been a retaliation against the unwanted intrusion of Christian missionaries into the region. An Ottoman army eventually had put an end to the massacres.

Charles Dickens wrote *A Christmas Carol*, which revived and reinterpreted Christmas in England and the United States as a special day for family gatherings and good will.

John Hersey, an evangelical pastor in Baltimore, wrote *An Appeal to Christians on the Subject of Slavery*, an article advocating the emancipation of slaves. After its publication and hostile reception in Maryland, Hersey was compelled to move further north. There seemed to be little tolerance for his ideas in the South.

1844

George Williams founded the Young Men's Christian Association (YMCA) in London. Its aim was to put Christian principles into practice by developing healthy bodies, minds, and spirits. The organization grew rapidly and branched out to include humanitarian work and athletic events.

Alarmed by the growing Catholic population, especially those coming from Ireland, native-born American Protestants organized anti-Catholic factions. The Philadelphia Prayer Riots erupted when rumors spread that Catholics were trying to remove Protestant Bibles from public schools. The riots resulted in some deaths and the destruction of several Catholic churches.

Constantin von Tischendorf, one of the world's leading biblical scholars, discovered the Codex Sinaiticus at Saint Catherine's Monastery near Mount Sinai, Egypt. The codex dated to the mid-fourth century and contained half of the Greek Old Testament along with an entire New Testament including the *Epistle of Barnabas* and portions of *The Shepherd of Hermas*.

American anti-Catholics founded the secretive anti-immigrant and xenophobic Native American Party, commonly known as the Know-Nothing Party. The party was associated with violent acts of intimidation around the times of US elections.

William Miller's 1831 prophesy concerning the return of Jesus failed and became known as the "Great Disappointment." Miller's followers assumed that the expected date of the Advent (October 22, 1844) must have really signified the beginning of Jesus's final work of atonement leading up to the event of his Second Coming.

A newly established newspaper, the *Nauvoo Expositor*, was critical of Joseph Smith and other Mormon leaders. As the elected mayor of Nauvoo, Smith declared the newspaper a public nuisance and had the printing press destroyed. The county justice of the peace issued a warrant for Smith's arrest for inciting a riot, causing Smith to flee to Illinois. There he was tracked down and returned to face justice, but he and his brother were killed by an angry mob who broke into the Illinois jail where they were held. Smith was reported to have been arrested at least thirty times, and possibly as many as forty-two times, during his short lifetime.

Scottish journalist Robert Chambers published *Vestiges of the Natural History of Creation*. This book presented the view that an almighty Creator could design a system such as evolution that would drive continuing creation over millions of years. He thought that was even more clever than a designer making one species at a time out of thin air as in Genesis. This concept today is known as *theistic evolution*.

The Bahá'í Faith began in Iran with the teachings of Bahá'u'lláh, who was believed to be a messiah. He taught the universality of all humanity and all religions, but his teachings were unpopular with most Muslims. Since then, the religion has spread throughout the world.

1845

Newspaper editor John O'Sullivan coined the term *manifest destiny* to describe the conviction that it was God's intent for the United States to spread from the Atlantic Ocean to the Pacific Ocean while spreading Christian values in whatever land it took control of.

The Southern Baptist Convention began when Baptists in slave states broke away from the northern Baptists (today known as American Baptist Churches USA) over the issue of slavery. Both sides were able to defend their positions with verses from the Bible. For example, slave owners justified their behavior based on passages from the Old and New Testaments, including the Book of Philemon, which addressed runaway slaves and the scriptural year of the Jubilee, when the Bible said slaves should be freed. Exodus 21:20–21 gave slaveowners permission to beat their slaves as long as they didn't die within two days of the beating. On the other hand, Deuteronomy 23:15 states "If a slave has taken refuge with you, do not hand him over to his master," or Galatians 3:28, "There is neither Jew nor Greek, slave nor free, male nor female, for you are all one in Christ Jesus."

The Great Famine began in Ireland when a blight struck the Irish potato crop, the main source of food for Irish peasants. More than a million people died due to famine and typhus, and another million Irish migrated to Britain, the US, and Australia.

c. Alexander von Humboldt, a German freethinker, published the first book in his series of ground-breaking *Cosmos* books deliberating on the environment. His writings stressed the interconnectedness of all of nature and issued a strong warning about the harm Humboldt already saw humans causing to the environment. Some Christians branded his books as blasphemous not only for their audacity of trying to comprehend the cosmos, but also for thinking humans could change the environment. The German Church said he had made "a pact with the devil."

Balkan rabbi Judah ben Solomon Chai Alkalai began seriously advocating for the return of Jews to Palestine.

1846

After the Mormons, now led by Brigham Young, were forced out of Illinois, they traveled west to Utah, which was then part of Mexico and inhabited only by Native Americans.

1847

Pope Pius IX reestablished a Latin Patriarchate in Jerusalem for the first time since the Crusades.

Adolphe Adam, a French composer, wrote the Christmas hymn "O Holy Night."

Scottish obstetrician James Simpson demonstrated on some of his female patients the effectiveness of chloroform as an anesthetic and sleep-inducing drug. Many Christian clergymen thought it was against God's will to ease the suffering of women during childbirth because of the curse that God had placed on Eve in the Garden of Eden in Genesis. Earlier in the century, many Christians also opposed the smallpox vaccine because it usurped God's right to decide when we should die. It's interesting that wars and slavery were acceptable, but vaccines and general anesthetics were not.

1848

John Thomas founded the Christadelphian sect in England after he began to question orthodox beliefs. His denomination rejected the preexistence of Christ but believed in his resurrection and expected him to return to Earth eventually.

In Beirut, Lebanon, Arabic-speaking Christians established the first evangelical church to use Arabic as the language of worship.

German philosophers Karl Marx and Friedrich Engels published the *Communist Manifesto*, calling for a "forcible overthrow of all existing social conditions," which included organized religion.

Women at the Seneca Falls Convention in New York began a campaign for their right to vote. Many men and women from strict male-dominant sects felt that progress in voting rights would conflict with the biblical injunctions in First Timothy and First Corinthians that women should submit to male authority. Interestingly, no one knows who wrote those verses of the Bible. Most modern scholars do not believe that Paul wrote the epistles of Timothy or the verses in First Corinthians 14:34–35 about women being submissive and inquiring about issues only through their husbands. There is strong evidence that those verses were added later by more misogynistic writers because they are inconsistent with Paul's cooperation with female co-workers such as Priscilla, Junia, and Phoebe.

Illustrated London News published an image of Queen Victoria, Prince Albert, and their children gathered around a decorated tree on Christmas. As a result, the Christmas tree became very popular in British and American societies. Victoria and Albert, both of German descent, found it natural to celebrate this symbol of winter, which traces back to ancient pagan times as a symbol of eternal life.

The US and Mexico went to war two years earlier over border disputes after the US annexed Texas. This year the Treaty of Guadalupe Hidalgo was signed, ceding California, Nevada, Utah, most of Arizona, and parts of three other states to the US. Many believed this was a further sign what was believed to be a divine right to expand westward, or Manifest Destiny.

1849

A book titled *The Crucifixion of Jesus, by an Eyewitness* had supposedly been found in a Greek monastery in Alexandria and translated into German and other languages. It focused on the life of Jesus up to his crucifixion, which the book said Jesus survived. The writing was later exposed as a fraud.

English archaeologist Austen Henry Layard recovered the *Enuma Elis*, the Mesopotamian creation myth, in the ruins of the Ashurbanipal library in Nineveh, near Mosul, Iraq. Prior to the discovery of this and the *Epic of Gilgamesh*, the Hebrew Bible was thought to possibly be the oldest preserved writings in the world. Both Babylonian writings confirmed that many biblical stories originated in Mesopotamia, and tens of thousands of those writings are older than the oldest texts in the Hebrew Bible.

1850

c. Following the lead of the Baptists, American Methodist and Presbyterian Churches split into regional churches over the issue of slavery.

c. Youth organizations became common in US churches as many young adults moved to cities seeking jobs provided by the Industrial Revolution.

The Taiping Rebellion began in China. Its roots can be traced to Hong Xiuquan, who began reading Christian books at the encouragement of an American missionary. Xiuquan became convinced that he had been chosen to be God's son, the brother of Jesus, and the savior of the Chinese. He was charismatic and persuasive enough to gain an enormous following, and he and his followers established the Taiping Heavenly Kingdom of Great Peace. The movement eventually gained control over most of southern China before it was finally subdued by imperial troops in 1864, after an astonishing ten to thirty million Chinese died in the ensuing bloodshed, plague, and famine.

c. A member of the Temperley clan in Somerset, England, discovered and then re-buried a fossilized dinosaur, a fish-lizard known as Ichthyosaurus. Apparently, this person didn't know how to deal with the conflict between the evidence he found and his religious teachings. Even though Charles Darwin had not introduced his theory of evolution at that time, belief in dinosaur fossils seemed to be a denial of the Bible and God. In 2019 Julian Temperley exhumed the fossil, restored it, and not only put it on display, but used the image on the label of his company's brandy cider.

Muslim rioters in Aleppo, Syria, attacked Christians, destroying their property and forcing the emigration of many Greek Antioch Christians to Smyrna, Anatolia, and Beirut in present-day Lebanon.

c. The women's rights movement continued to gain strength in the US despite the patriarchal mindset of American Christians. The women's movement was led by women who had given up traditional religious beliefs. Susan B. Anthony and Elizabeth Cady Stanton were agnostics, and Frances Wright and Ernestine Rose were atheists.

c. Alcohol consumption had been a normal part of Western life until some Protestant sects, particularly the Methodists, began to advocate abstinence from alcoholic drinks. They considered consumption of alcohol a sin because excessive use often led to immorality and domestic disputes.

1851

A religious census in England found that half of all adults were not in church on a given Sunday, startling news at the time.

In New York, the Congregational Church gave Antoinette Brown a license to preach. The following year she became the first woman ordained as a Protestant minister in a well-known sect.

A concordat between Queen Isabella II of Spain and Pope Pius IX maintained Catholicism as the only recognized religion in Spain. This agreement lasted until it was renounced by the Second Spanish Republic in 1931. In 1953, a similar concordat would be signed, but it would also be reversed.

1852

Harriet Beecher Stowe's book *Uncle Tom's Cabin* became one of the most influential works in raising anti-slavery awareness and compassion in the US.

The First Plenary Council of Baltimore urged every Catholic parish in the US to establish its own parochial school system. They feared that Catholic children would be indoctrinated by Protestant teachers in the public schools. By 1895, over 750,000 Catholic children would be enrolled in 4,000 Catholic schools, and the system continued to grow to over 12,000 elementary and secondary schools, serving 5 million students by 1965.

British physician Henry Nelson reported observing a sperm cell from a nematode worm enter a worm ovule. This was a breakthrough in understanding reproduction in animals.

1853

The Ottomans declared a formal "status quo" at nine holy sites in Jerusalem and Bethlehem. Under this arrangement, nothing in the common territory held by Muslims, Jews, and Christians could be modified without the consensus of all three religions.

Hormuzd Rassam discovered the 3,600-year-old *Epic of Gilgamesh*. Written on clay tablets, it is considered the earliest surviving important work of literature.

The people of New York founded the secular Children's Aid Society to protect abandoned and orphaned children, not by confining them to institutions, but by finding foster parents for them.

1854

British Protestant missionary and medical doctor James Hudson Taylor arrived in China and established the China Inland Mission. He would spend fifty-one years there, and his society brought 800 other missionaries to China, founded 125 schools, and created around 300 places of employment. Still unusual among missionaries, Taylor wore traditional Chinese clothing to be accepted more easily by the people.

Pope Pius IX defined the doctrine of the Immaculate Conception, which explained that Mary, being the mother of Jesus and therefore the mother of God, as defined by the Trinity, was also conceived free from the original sin that tainted the rest of humankind. Her lack of original sin from the moment of her conception was necessary so that she could give birth to sin-free Jesus. This idea that the embryo is a person from the moment of conception would evolve into a complex controversy a century later with the abortion debate.

Danish philosopher and theologian Søren Kierkegaard published attacks on Christianity, particularly, the Church of Denmark. He wrote about Christian ethics, lack of proof as to the validity of Christianity, the distinction between man and God, and the quality of Christian love. He insisted that Christianity was not a set of rules to follow, but a life that affirmed the ethics of Jesus in the Gospels.

1855

Yellow fever struck Portsmouth, Virginia, a town of 3,200 inhabitants, killing a quarter of the population. James Chisholm, an Episcopal priest, was one of the few who did not leave. For seven months, he worked closely with Reverend Francis Devlin, caring for those who remained, until he succumbed to the fever himself.

US-backed Mexican politician and future president Benito Juárez ensured the passage of the Juárez Law, which removed special privileges from the Catholic clergy and military to apply Mexican law equally to all Mexican citizens. Juárez nationalized Church property, separated the Church from the government, and made the Church subject to secular law.

After a brief stay near Buffalo, New York, German Pietists, who left Germany due to persecution by Lutherans, founded seven communal Amana Colonies in Iowa.

Abolitionist John Gregg Fee founded Berea College in Kentucky as the first racially integrated college in the South. Four years later, a mob of his fellow Kentuckians attacked Fee, causing him and the other teachers to flee to Ohio.

Canadian preacher Joseph M. Scriven composed the hymn "What a Friend We Have in Jesus" to comfort his mother while they were separated.

1856

Augustinian friar, scientist, and abbot Gregor Johann Mendel began experiments with pea plants that would evolve into the science of genetics. His work was not of much public interest in his time, but it would be rediscovered in 1900.

David Livingstone returned to England after sixteen years in Africa. He gained worldwide notoriety for his outspoken condemnation of the Portuguese slave trade in Central Africa.

Britain and France helped repulse the Russian invasion of Turkey, ending the three-year-long Crimean War. The British ambassador then pressured the Ottoman sultan into issuing an edict granting religious freedom in Turkey. This edict also ended the tradition of Christian women who had been raped by Ottomans being forced to convert and marry their assailants. As would be expected, in much of the Ottoman Empire, local authorities were less than enthusiastic about implementing these new policies.

1857

David Livingstone published *Missionary Travels and Researches in South Africa*, an account of his journeys as missionary, physician, explorer, and opponent of the African slave trade. The book became a best seller in Great Britain.

The US Supreme Court ruled that Dred Scott, a slave who lived with his owner in the non-slave states of Illinois and Wisconsin, was not entitled to his freedom while living there. The court also declared that African Americans were not, and could never become, citizens of the United States.

The Mormons controlled Utah under martial law and, after their history of persecution, were very suspicious of strangers in their land. When the California-bound Baker-Fancher wagon train passed through their territory, a Mormon militia attacked them, killing 120 people and sparing only seventeen young children. This event became known as the Mountain Meadows Massacre. Some of the Mormon attackers had dressed as American Indians, and when the public learned about the massacre, the Mormon hierarchy tried to shift the blame to the Paiutes.

The Iglesias Law in Mexico regulated the collection of clerical fees from the poor and prohibited clerics from charging money for baptisms, marriages, or funeral services.

The Vatican finally allowed the oldest surviving manuscript of the entire Greek Bible, the fourth-century Codex Vaticanus, to be transcribed. When the entire text was translated from its 759 leaves of vellum, scholars found it to be very different from the fourth-century Vulgate, still the standard Catholic Bible. The Codex Sinaiticus and the Codex Vaticanus are the oldest and therefore most accurate Greek texts of the New Testament.

1858

Members of the papal guard in Bologna, Italy, arrived at the home of a Jewish couple and presented them with a written order from the local priest for custody of their child. They told the parents that the boy had been secretly baptized five years earlier, and since Jews were not allowed to raise Christian children, the boy had to be taken from his parents. This story made headlines in cities around Western Europe.

With the Government of India Act, the British government took control of India from the British East India Company. Queen Victoria proclaimed religious freedom and equal rights for the Indians, intending to eliminate the caste system. It wasn't that easy, and the caste system remains in effect in rural India.

A fourteen-year-old girl, Bernadette Soubirous, and her companions repeatedly witnessed an apparition of the Virgin Mary in a cave near Lourdes, France. Up to nine thousand people were said to have been present for the fifteenth appearance, and water and mud obtained from the grotto were said to have brought miracle cures of afflictions. The grotto was opened to the public, and it developed into one of the most popular pilgrimage destinations in Europe. Bernadette died at the young age of thirty-five and was proclaimed a saint.

Catholic missionaries had been in Vietnam since the sixteenth century, and a significant Christian population had developed there. The French used decades of Vietnamese harassment of Christians as a pretext to invade the country. Vietnamese Christians did not join the French, as hoped, and the war dragged on for four years before the French and their Spanish and Filipino allies defeated the Vietnamese and gained a valuable colony.

The Young Women's Christian Association (YWCA) began in New York City with the goal of integrating Christian values and beliefs into young women, mainly on college campuses.

1859

Charles Darwin published his book *On the Origin of Species*. This is considered the introduction to evolutionary biology, but many readers saw his theory as an alternative to a Creator God. The book did not address the initiation of life on Earth. Instead, it focused on the gradual adaptations that life-forms had made over at least a hundred million years through a process of natural selection—the ability for organisms to adapt to their environments the best ways possible to survive, reproduce, and therefore improve the gene pool. Darwin speculated that humans were part of this tree of evolution, which had begun with the most primitive forms of life, and therefore humans were not a separate creation by God. Many Christians then and now have vilified Darwin and his writings and dismissed them as heresy because those Christians chose to believe that God created man "in his image," in fact, a very vague statement because it could mean physical, spiritual, or similar in some other quality. Besides, in the minds of Darwin-disbelieving Christians, if the world is only six thousand years old as they believe, there hasn't been enough time for evolution to occur as Darwin presented it.

Scottish preacher John Duncan wrote "Christ either deceived mankind by conscious fraud, or he was himself deluded and self-deceived, or he was divine. There apparently was no getting out of this trilemma. It is inexorable." C. S. Lewis popularized this argument in the twentieth century by saying that Jesus was either a liar, a lunatic, or Lord. Skeptics bring up a fourth possibility, that he was a legend.

1860

The lyrics of the hymn "Jesus Loves Me" were written by Anna Bartlett Warner. The tune was added two years later by William Batchelder Bradbury.

Maronite Christians in Syria revolted against their Druze overlords. Tension had been building in Syria since the partition of the country into Christian and Druze regions in 1842. The rioting spread throughout the country as a religious civil war. Hundreds of Christian villages were destroyed, and thousands of Christians were massacred, including eleven thousand in Damascus alone.

Jewish leaders met in Paris to establish an organization known as the Universal Israelite Alliance. It was intended to advocate for Jewish human rights since the Jewish people had no country or society to represent them.

c. V. Van Dyck completed the work begun by Eli Smith, a Protestant missionary, of translating the Bible into Arabic.

Seven prominent Anglican theologians began the process of incorporating historical criticism, geology, and biology into Christian studies in the book *Essays and Reviews*. Controversy over this book overshadowed that of Darwin's newly published book on evolution, and two of the Anglican authors were indicted by the Church for heresy.

After defeating the papal army at the Battle of Castelfidardo, King Victor Emmanuel II of Italy seized all papal territories except for Rome, which was still under French protection.

1861

The Confederate States of America came into existence when southern states in the US succeeded from the country to retain legalized slavery. A civil war began when the Confederate Army attacked federally held Fort Sumter in South Carolina. Whether warriors or pacifists, Northerners or Southerners, all could turn to the Bible to justify their cause and ease their consciences.

Reginald Heber, a minister in the Church of England, wrote the hymn "Holy, Holy, Holy! Lord God Almighty." The music was added by John B. Dykes after Heber's death.

Charles Spurgeon founded the Metropolitan Tabernacle in Southwark, England. It was the largest church of its time, seating five thousand people. He preached there for thirty-one years.

Julia Ward Howe wrote the "Battle Hymn of the Republic," using the music from the song "John Brown's Body." The song linked the judgment of the wicked with the American Civil War.

The Treaty of Fort Wise followed a pattern of gathering tribal chiefs together, whether the US representatives had authority or not, and then coercing the chiefs into signing over their tribe's land. In this case, it was a large section of eastern Colorado. Any Native Americans who didn't abide by these treaties would be considered hostile and hunted down.

1862

English Congregational minister Andrew Reed died in London. He had founded asylums for orphans, fatherless children, and the mentally ill; he also built a hospital for incurables, what we would now call a hospice. These kinds of institutions were uncommon at the time.

1863

The Seventh-day Adventist movement began in Battle Creek, Michigan. It grew from the Millerite movement and branched off from Protestant orthodoxy because they wanted to observe the true Sabbath on Saturdays. Adventists also believed, as Miller had, in the imminent Second Coming of Jesus, but they declined to set another date for the event.

Abraham Lincoln issued the Emancipation Proclamation, declaring freedom for all slaves in the United States, including those in the Confederate states. The Southerners did not recognize this executive order, but the proclamation received much praise in the North.

Pope Pius IX issued the Syllabus of Errors, listing subjects that no Catholics should believe. Included on this list were the modern ideas of rationalism, socialism, civil marriages, and religious tolerance.

Jean-Henry Dunant and his associates in Switzerland founded the International Committee for Relief to the Wounded. Although the founders of what later became the International Committee of the Red Cross were nominal Christians, this humanist organization was not founded as a Christian organization. The following year Dunant's example inspired the first Geneva Convention, which produced the Humanitarian Law of Armed Conflicts to promote the humane treatment of wounded soldiers and prisoners of war and provide protection for medical personnel and civilians.

Abraham Lincoln established Thanksgiving Day as an annual holiday. This tradition stemmed from the 1600s and the early American colonists in Virginia and Massachusetts as a day of thanks to God and a celebration of good fortune.

1864

A group of prominent Protestant ministers asked President Lincoln to support a constitutional amendment to make God and Christ the source of American authority. They hoped this would compensate for the fact that the name "God" was left out of the US Constitution. Lincoln never acted on this proposal.

An act of Congress allowed the motto *In God We Trust* to appear on US coins for the first time.

John Henry Newman wrote *A Defense of One's Life*. Newman stated that "the Greek fathers thought that when the cause was just, an untruth need not be a lie." The idea that one could be dishonest if it convinced another person to convert to Christianity was acceptable to many Christians, going back to Eusebius of Caesarea, because they believed conversion by any method would provide someone eternal life.

At Sand Creek, Colorado, a force of US cavalry attacked and destroyed a peaceful American Indian village, even though the village was flying an American flag and a white flag of submission. The soldiers massacred and mutilated over 150 people, mostly Cheyenne and Arapaho women and children.

1865

After one unsuccessful vote and extensive legislative maneuvering by the Lincoln administration, the US Congress passed the Thirteenth Amendment to the Constitution. The amendment officially abolished slavery and was the first of three Reconstruction amendments adopted near the end of the Civil War.

English scholar Sabine Baring-Gould wrote the lyrics to "Onward, Christian Soldiers" as a marching song for children. The music was composed by Arthur Sullivan in 1871. It celebrated the spirit of the Crusades and the more militant side of Christianity.

c. Science emerged as a popular curriculum of study in US universities, vying with other subjects to displace theology as the main discipline of study.

Despite political gridlock that prevented him from assisting the poor in other ways, William Booth and his wife, Catherine, established a mission in London to provide material aid to the poor and save their souls. In 1878, their mission became the Salvation Army, complete with uniforms, officers, marching brass bands, and a magazine named *The War Cry*.

Following the Civil War, Confederate veterans in Tennessee established the Ku Klux Klan. Their goal was to "reestablish Protestant Christian values in America by any means possible," and believed Jesus was the first Klansman. With terrorism and violence, the Klan targeted African Americans, Jews, Catholics, and any other social and ethnic minority they hated.

After the South's defeat in the Civil War, Southern church leaders struggled to help their congregants make sense of their loss. This resulted in the ideology of the "Lost Cause," a mythology that ennobled the Confederacy's struggle and idealized the antebellum South as a bastion of Christian piety and chivalric virtue and emphasized happy slaves and Northern aggression and Southern victimization. This fusion of religious and cultural values was preached in churches over the next twenty years, legitimizing the righteousness of the Southern cause and reinforcing the social order of white supremacy. The Confederate battle flag became their idol, and the Ku Klux Klan was credited with rescuing the southern way of life. Many adopted an increasingly fundamental form of Christianity.

1866

Persecution of Christians in Korea resulted in the death of eight thousand Korean Catholics and nine French missionaries.

Henry Bergh, a former US diplomat, founded the American Society for the Prevention of Cruelty to Animals (ASPCA) after being inspired by Lord Harrowby, the president of the Royal Society for the Prevention of Cruelty to Animals, in England. The ASPCA addressed issues such as slaughterhouse practices, the dissection of living animals, cock fighting, and dog fighting.

1867

A Presbyterian publishing company in Scotland began to publish a ten-volume series entitled *Ante-Nicene Fathers*. This was in response to the concurrent publication *Library of the Fathers*, which they thought was too biased toward the Catholic perspective on the early Church.

New Jersey became the first state in the US to ban corporal punishment in public schools, and thirty other states followed over the next 150 years. This fell along regional lines, with all southeastern states and a few western states still allowing this kind of punishment in 2021.

British surgeon Joseph Lister published "Antiseptic Principle of the Practice of Surgery," partly based on the work of French biologist Louis Pasteur. After contemporaries made discoveries in cellular pathology, the practice of medicine changed dramatically. The discovery of the role of micro-organisms in disease changed everything from treating wounds to preventing disease, and this was the birth of modern medicine.

The Russians sold Alaska to the US for seven million dollars to prevent it from falling into British hands.

1868

The states adopted the Fourteenth Amendment to the US Constitution. It granted citizenship to all people born or naturalized in the United States and offered them equal protection under the laws. It was presented in response to issues faced by former slaves and was bitterly contested by the Southern states. A similar battle was fought two years later when the Fifteenth Amendment gave all male citizens the right to vote regardless of "race, color, or previous condition of servitude."

1869

Thomas Henry Huxley coined the term *agnostic* meaning "without knowledge." As applied to God, Huxley meant that nothing is or can be known about the existence or nature of a spiritual being, unless it is irrefutably revealed by that being.

The First Vatican Council was convened in response to rationalism, liberalism, and materialism. Pope Pius IX proclaimed the doctrine of papal infallibility in all matters of faith and morality, seeking to establish that he, as pope, had full and direct power over every aspect of the Church. He said that when he spoke as pope, based on sacred tradition and sacred scripture, he was infallible. This was based on his interpretation of Matthew 28:18, where Jesus said, "All authority in heaven and on earth has been given to me." The pope was losing his territorial control as Italy was becoming unified, so he was attempting to hold onto power in the spiritual world. The following year, those opposed to the idea of papal infallibility founded what was known as the Old Catholic Church.

Cincinnati's Board of Education voted to outlaw the singing of hymns, the reading of the Bible, and religious education in its public schools.

An investigation of the Protestant Orphan Asylum in St. Louis found that only 27 percent of children were really orphans. Most had been removed from their families for various reasons such as poverty, unfitness for parenthood, or sickness. At the time, conditions in the one thousand US orphanages were so bad that progressive activists began to shut them down and place the children with foster families. This established the compassionate modern concept of caring for children by addressing their individual needs and preparing them for life within a family setting.

On a trip to Europe, humanitarian Clara Barton became familiar with the Red Cross. She was inspired to create the American Red Cross to respond to national crises such as war and natural disasters.

Swiss scientist Friedrich Miescher accidentally discovered DNA as a distinct molecule after extracting it from a cell nucleus. By 1881, it would be named and have its building blocks identified by German biochemist Albrecht Kossel. In 1882, Walther Flemming would discover mitosis, or the process of cell division. DNA would be seen as the code for life, and its origin is still being debated.

1870

When the Franco-Prussian War began, French forces were recalled from protecting the pope in Rome. This allowed the united Italian army to advance on Rome and take the city. Pope Pius IX, although not physically confined, claimed that he was a prisoner in the Vatican. After more than one thousand years of ruling the Papal States, the pope was stripped of all his territories except for Vatican City. The Italian government ended the Roman Inquisition and liberated Jews from the ghetto, where they had been forced to live for over three hundred years. Jews were allowed citizenship in the new nation and entitled to the full protection of the law.

The current US census showed that Catholics were the largest Christian denomination. There were still more Protestants than Catholics in total, but they were fragmented into numerous denominations.

In a Tibetan monastery, someone discovered *The Gospel of the Nazarenes*, a manuscript written in Aramaic before AD 200. It was translated and published as *The Gospel of the Holy Twelve*. Some theologians consider it the elusive *Gospel of Q*.

c. Antisemitism was increasing in Russia. Many Russians had been conditioned to believe that Jewish people had too many privileges and that the presence of Jewish students in state schools would lead to Jewish domination of law, engineering, medicine, and architecture.

c. In America, the academic study of the Old Testament was changing from the scriptures being seen as revelations by God to stories of the Semitic cultures that existed before the Hebrews and had continued through them. Evangelical Christians were forced to defend the Bible against legitimate criticism.

Australian Museum staff member Gerald Krefft was the first person to describe the Australian Lungfish, a living fish with lungs that can breathe air in addition to gills and believed to be an intermediary species between fish and amphibians.

In the US, the Fifteenth Amendment was ratified, giving African American men the right to vote.

1871

The Italians approved the Law of Guarantees, giving popes the use of the Vatican but not sovereignty over its territory. The Law of Guarantees also gave the Vatican the right to send and receive ambassadors and establish a set budget for its government. The pope responded by rejecting the offer, refusing to recognize the new kingdom of Italy, and excommunicating the nation's leaders.

The US Army supplied twenty-five wagons and all necessary supplies for a group of wealthy Americans to try to exterminate bison, the main source of food, shelter, and clothing for the Plains Indians. The Indigenous people had to be cleared out of the region so that railroads, stagecoaches, and telegraph lines could be built and operated without molestation and so that resources, such as gold and other minerals, could be extracted more easily from their lands.

The *Lost Chapter of Acts of the Apostles* was published in London, claiming to be the continuation of the Book of Acts. It was said to have originally been written in Greek, and it described the apostle Paul traveling to England to preach to a tribe of Israelites who were living there. It is classified as modern pseudepigraphon, or fraud.

The Universities Test Act in the United Kingdom abolished religious restrictions for colleges. Until this time, all applicants at Oxford, Cambridge, and Durham had to be members of the Church of England.

The Reconstructionist Congress passed the Force Acts that allowed President Ulysses S. Grant to use military force to protect African American rights in the South. Some South Carolina counties were placed under martial law and thousands of suspected terrorists were arrested. Due to this use of force, the Ku Klux Klan went into hiding.

1872

German Chancellor Otto von Bismarck banned Jesuits from his newly united Germany because he saw them as an obstacle to his secular government.

Composer Lowell Mason died in New Jersey. He had composed over 1,500 songs for church, including the popular hymns "Nearer, My God to Thee" and the musical adaptation of "When I Survey the Wondrous Cross."

US President Ulysses S. Grant signed a bill creating the world's first national park—Yellowstone. This was the beginning of a new movement to preserve and protect the beautiful and historic regions of the country and to provide a place for animals to thrive and humans to experience untouched nature. This signified a new interpretation of the biblical command for humans to have dominion over the Earth; they were meant to protect it.

Children in the United Kingdom began to be protected by infant protection organizations and the Infant Life Protection Acts. The laws were enacted because of the abuses of "baby farming," in which children were turned over to another woman to nurse, care for, and possibly even raise as their own.

1873

Philotheos Bryennios found the Codex Hierosolymitanus, an eleventh-century Church order, in a Greek monastery in Constantinople. It contained perhaps the earliest reference to a Christian canon, which is known as the Bryennios List, dating from the first or second century AD. The codex also contained a list of twenty-seven Old Testament books and the Didache, or *The Teaching of the Twelve Apostles*. This codex was an example of the holy scripture of one early group of Christians and demonstrated the ways new converts had to modify their lives to become Christians.

US women founded the Women's Christian Temperance Union in Ohio with the goal of controlling or eliminating the consumption of alcohol.

The US Congress passed the Comstock Act, making it a crime to send erotica, contraceptives, or any medication that could induce miscarriage through the mail. This allowed religious organizations to control even newspapers that mentioned contraceptives.

The US Supreme Court weakened the Fourteenth Amendment by modifying the Privileges or Immunities Clause, giving the states more power to decide the legal rights of former slaves.

1874

In his book *What is Darwinism?* Charles Hodge described Darwin's theory of evolution as an attack on the literalness of the Bible. This stimulated much debate, and more liberal Christians, such as Henry

Ward Beecher, became open to the idea of evolution being directed by God, called "theistic evolution."

George Custer led a government-sanctioned expedition into the Black Hills of South Dakota to search for gold. This was in direct violation of the Fort Laramie Treaty, which gave the Sioux tribes a sense of security that white people would never interfere with their traditional hunting grounds. Once gold was discovered there, the treaty had no chance of surviving, and the Sioux were eventually driven out of the Black Hills.

In response to a Russian law that ordered all males under Russian jurisdiction into the military at the age of twenty, 1,265 Hutterites immigrated to the United States and established a community in the Dakota Territory. They were a communal and pacifistic organization that had originated in Germany in 1527 and were associated with the Anabaptists, Mennonites, and Amish.

1875

Henry Bergh, aided by Quaker philanthropist John D. Wright, founded the New York Society for the Prevention of Cruelty to Children after the initial success of his New York Society for the Prevention of Cruelty to Animals.

US Congress issued the Blaine Amendment with the support of President Ulysses Grant. It was written to prevent direct government aid to educational institutions with religious affiliations. It passed the House with a 180–7 vote but failed by four votes in the Senate and never became law. Eventually, all but ten states passed similar laws, but many have also tried to repeal them since.

c. The Jehovah's Witnesses grew out of a home church started by Charles Taze Russell in Pittsburgh, Pennsylvania, after disputes with mainstream denominations over the immortality of the soul, hellfire, predestination, and the return of Jesus in the flesh. They were non-Trinitarian, believed that the destruction of the world was imminent, and preached that the establishment of God's rule over Earth would solve all of humanity's problems.

Mary Baker Eddy's book *Science and Health with Key to the Scriptures* described sickness as an illusion that could be corrected with prayer alone, and she proposed that medical care was usually not needed for health problems. Four years later, in New England, the Christian Science denomination evolved from these concepts.

Kersey Graves published *The World's Sixteen Crucified Saviors*, which listed sixteen deities or combinations of gods and humans, who were understood as saviors. They were all said to have ascended into heaven or its equivalent. Many of these saviors predated Christianity, had miraculous births, were born on December 25, and had twelve disciples. It's possible that all these godmen stemmed from a common legend from ancient Egypt or the Middle East. This book is still used by present-day skeptics who see it as correlation that Jesus of Nazareth was a mythical figure, or at least his legend is heavily influenced by ancient gods.

Great Britain became the largest shareholder in the Suez Canal, which opened in 1869. This led to British financial and cultural domination of Egypt, a Muslim country.

The Civil Rights Act of 1875 was passed "to protect all citizens in their civil and legal rights," giving African Americans the right to equal treatment in all aspects of public life. It was signed into law by President Ulysses Grant.

1876

The Ottomans ruthlessly extinguished revolts in Bulgaria and Serbia, forcing Russia to again consider declaring war on the Ottomans. This war was temporarily postponed when the Ottomans said they would institute a Western-style constitution and make plans for a free election the following year.

The Red Crescent Society, allied with the Red Cross and the Turkish government, began to use ambulances with red crescents rather than red crosses. The organization would grow and ultimately be recognized by thirty-three Muslim countries.

German embryologist and zoologist Oscar Hertwig proved that fertilization in humans occurred when a sperm entered an ovum.

1877

Brigham Young died after leading the Mormon Church for thirty years. He was an authoritarian leader, a racist, and a polygamist with fifty-five wives. He excluded Blacks from positions of leadership in the church, proposed that Utah introduce slavery, and called for the death penalty for interracial marriages.

Charles Bradlaugh and Annie Besant republished the American birth control manual *The Fruits of Philosophy* (written by Charles Knowlton) for married couples in England. They were prosecuted for obscenity and sentenced to six months in prison, but their sentences were dismissed on a technicality.

As a result of the Bradlaugh and Besant trial, English progressives formed the Malthusian League to educate the public about the importance of family planning and to advocate for the end of legal penalties for promoting birth control.

The US experiment in interracial democracy, known as the Reconstruction Era, came to an end when the federal government backed away from its role of protecting the rights of former slaves. The Compromise of 1877 was an unwritten agreement worked out by US congressmen to decide the disputed election of 1876. The result was that Rutherford B. Hayes became president, and the last federal troops were pulled out of the South. Without the troops, there was no way to enforce antidiscrimination laws, and the Southern states chose their own courses in dealing with the freed slaves.

1878

Julius Wellhausen, a German biblical scholar, proposed that the Hebrew Torah, the first five books of the Old Testament, had originated in four separate lines of tradition that were later combined into one. His theory, known as the Documentary Hypothesis, is today the dominant theory in explaining the Torah's composition.

German scholar Paul de Lagarde suggested that European Jews be relocated to Madagascar. The idea generated interest, but no definitive action until 1940.

1879

The *McGuffey Reader* was revised. Public schools were still using it extensively, but whereas a third of the lessons had been focused on religion in the 1830s edition, by this time, only two religious passages remained, the Lord's Prayer and the Sermon on the Mount.

German journalist Wilhelm Marr founded the League of Anti-Semites to combat the imagined paranoia of world Jewish domination.

In *Reynolds v. United States*, the Supreme Court upheld a criminal conviction of a Mormon who broke federal law by practicing polygamy.

1880

Charles Bradlaugh, an atheist elected to the British Parliament, refused to take a religious Oath of Allegiance. After much debate about letting him "affirm" instead of taking the oath, Parliament voted him down, and after he protested, they escorted him from the building to a prison cell. His seat in Parliament became vacant for that term, but he would be reelected, and in 1888, he secured the passage of the Oaths Act, which allowed future members of Parliament the right to affirm their allegiance without the religious oath.

c. Mendele Mocher Sforim began to reestablish the Hebrew language, in disuse since the second century AD. It had long been the scriptural, hymnal, and prayer language of the Jewish people but never a comprehensive language for common use in dialogue.

c. Anglican clergymen started wearing detachable clerical collars as a way of setting themselves apart from the secular world. Previously, they had worn black shirts with white ties.

Former US Civil War general and New Mexico governor Lewis Wallace wrote *Ben Hur: A Tale of the Christ*, and it made him the best-selling religious author of his day.

c. The New Thought movement in the US popularized the belief in the power of the mind to achieve mental and physical health and material success. This movement still exists and is an important influence on the Christian Church International and its seminary.

1881

Francis Edward Clark founded the United Society of Christian Endeavor in Portland, Maine. The members, mostly young Christians, pledged to try to make some useful contribution to the world via their faith. The movement spread rapidly in the US, and seventy-five thousand delegates attended their 1896 convention.

Sixty-five scholars from various Protestant denominations began work on the English Revised Version of the Bible. Their goal was to adapt the King James Bible to the modern English language and current standards of Bible scholarship. It would take them until 1894 to complete their work.

After someone assassinated Russian emperor Alexander II, rumors spread that Jews were responsible, initiating a wave of anti-Jewish pogroms in the Russian Empire and forcing a mass migration of Jews from Russia. Most fled to the United States, and thousands more settled in Western Europe and Palestine. Within three years, more than two hundred anti-Jewish riots occurred in Russia. This ignited the Zionist movement, which sought a Jewish homeland to escape persecutions and establish self-rule.

On Christmas Day, Christian leaders whipped Polish masses into an antisemitic frenzy, leading to riots across the country. In Warsaw, twelve Jews were murdered, many were wounded, and many Jewish women were raped.

The French invaded Tunisia, part of the Ottoman Empire. Since that empire was gradually weakening, it was ripe for colonization and land takeovers. The next year the British carried out a military occupation in Egypt.

1882

A. B. Simpson founded the Missionary Training Institute, which later became Nyack College. It was an interdenominational fellowship devoted to serving unreached people and has been called the first Bible college in the United States.

The Edmunds Act declared polygamy a felony, and it became federal law in the US. In the next ten years, more than one thousand Mormons would be convicted of "unlawful cohabitation."

1883

William Smith founded the Boys Brigade in England. It combined games and sports with hymns and prayers, transforming the traditional Sunday schools.

The US Supreme Court eviscerated the Civil Rights Act of 1875, by declaring it unconstitutional. The 1875 act had outlawed racial discrimination in public accommodations and transportation, but the court decided that Congress lacked the power to regulate private affairs, leaving each business owner to treat African Americans any way they wished. The decision also signaled an end to the federal government's ability to set penalties for the crimes of assault and murder as it had done in confronting racial terrorism since 1871.

1884

Charles Eliot, the president of Harvard College, instituted a wide-ranging elective system in literature and science for undergraduates. The school's motto had originally been *In Christi Gloriam*, meaning "for the glory of Christ." In the eighteenth century, it was changed to *Christo et Ecclesiae*, meaning "for Christ and Church." This year, Eliot changed the motto to *Veritas*, meaning "truth." Two years later, he ended compulsory chapel services for students. This was a gradual shift from an institution established exclusively to train clergy to a more secular school looking beyond the Bible for truth.

The Berlin Conference was held to regulate European and US colonization and trade in Africa. This was followed by the "Scramble for Africa" in which the conference participants jostled for control of the continent.

1886

Dwight Moody founded what would later become the Moody Bible Institute in Chicago. Its purpose was to train young Americans for service in the Church and the mission field.

The Original Church of God started in Tennessee and became one of the first Pentecostal denominations in America. The sect believed in baptism by immersion, feet washing, divine healing, and speaking in tongues.

Former Canadian Catholic priest Charles P. Chiniquy published the book *Fifty Years in the Church of Rome* as an indictment of the Catholic Church. In 1855, early in his career, he had been sued for libel and was defended by Abraham Lincoln.

Urbain Bouriant discovered copies of the *Gospel of Peter, First Enoch* and the *Apocalypse of Peter* buried with a monk in the Egyptian city of Akhmim. The *Gospel of Peter* was the first noncanonical gospel to be rediscovered. It contained stories of the trial, death, and resurrection of Jesus. It was claimed to be written by the apostle Peter but was dated to around the second century. It stated that the spiritual Christ entered the man Jesus only temporarily and remained with him during his ministry. Since the author didn't use biblical Gospel material, it seems that he may not have been aware of that information and relied on oral transmission alone. The discovery site was sixty miles north of Nag Hammadi, where another sensational discovery would occur in 1945.

1887

In New Jersey, former Seventh-day Adventist minister Charles B. Reynolds stood trial for blasphemy. He had distributed a pamphlet denying the infallibility and divine authorship of the Bible. Reynolds was defended by Robert Green Ingersoll, the most prominent American freethinker of his time. Ingersoll defined blasphemy as "what an old mistake says to a new discovered truth" and "what a withered last year's leaf says to this year's bud." Reynolds was found guilty but only fined a small sum, which Ingersoll paid. Even today, at least six states still have laws that reference blasphemy.

An unknown American wrote the lyrics to the Christmas carol "Away in the Manger," and it was set to music a few years later.

Owners of professional baseball teams in the US made a "gentleman's agreement" to exclude Black ballplayers by 1900.

1888

Representatives from 139 missionary organizations met at the Conference on the Protestant Missions of the World in London. Almost 1,600 missionaries attended.

Brazil ended slavery, which had existed in the country since the Portuguese founded the first colony in 1532. Brazil imported more African slaves than any other country in the Americas and was the last American nation to end the practice.

Anglican missionaries had been working in India since 1843, trying to reform the churches there. This year, their efforts resulted in another schism and the founding of the Mar Thoma Syrian Church of Malabar.

1889

Andrew Carnegie wrote an article entitled "The Gospel of Wealth." In it, he advocated the responsibility of the rich to redistribute their surplus wealth wisely and reduce the stratification between the rich and the poor. Carnegie wrote this during a time of great financial difficulty in the country, yet he believed that poor people were in poverty because of their own laziness, and this laziness stemmed from a moral failure. He wrote that money should not be given directly to the poor but, instead, to causes that would aid them if they demonstrated that they deserved the aid. His concept would reassure many Americans that getting rich was a religious obligation, and it would help lay the groundwork for "prosperity theology."

While reading his Bible as a child, American clairvoyant Edgar Cayce had a vision of a woman with wings who asked him what he wanted most of all. He said that he wanted to be a missionary and to help others, especially sick children. Cayce would become known as the "sleeping prophet," who supposedly could diagnose people's ailments while in a trance, even when they weren't in his presence. His mental powers became legendary and resulted in the founding of the Association for Research and Enlightenment, known as A.R.E., in 1931.

The British Parliament passed the Children's Charter, which permitted the government to legally intervene in unhealthy relationships between parents and children.

A Syrian priest succeeded in making a copy of Nestorius's main work, a twelfth-century Syriac manuscript of the *Bazaar of Heracleides*, which had recently been found in Kurdistan. It was written just before Nestorius died in AD 451 and was assumed to have been burned along with all of his other writings. The manuscript refuted the accusations against him that led to his exile and pointed to the fact his theologically was not much different than those who banished him.

1891

Pope Leo XIII issued an encyclical addressing the condition of the working class. It supported their right to form unions, rejected socialism and unrestricted capitalism, and affirmed the right to hold private property.

The Presbyterian Church tried and convicted Charles Briggs, a New York minister, of heresy and suspended him from the Church due to his public defense of higher criticism of the Bible. He claimed that the Bible was full of errors and contradictions, saying "There is nothing divine in the text, in its letters, words, or clauses." Although Briggs's Union Theological Seminary was open to his ideas, his Church wouldn't tolerate them, so he converted to Episcopalian.

In Cincinnati, the Northern Pacific Railway dedicated the first of several Baptist rail cars, called "chapel cars." These cars were coupled with other train cars and designed to provide space for religious services, with altars, pews, and, in some cases, stained glass windows. They could seat one hundred worshippers and served as living quarters for missionaries.

Scottish American naturalist John Muir founded the Sierra Club in the United States. It was one of the world's first modern environmental protection organizations, with a goal of protecting natural habitat and making it available to people who want to get more in touch with nature.

1892

Mary Baker Eddy and her followers founded the First Church of Christ, Scientist, in Boston. The church was based on her Christian Scientist textbook *Science and Health with Key to the Scriptures*. For medical treatment, their members depended on faith healers called practitioners, whose treatment was limited to prayer. Believers risked their lives and the lives of their children by not seeking proper medical care for treatable diseases.

American Christian socialist minister Francis Bellamy wrote the first version of the US Pledge of Allegiance.

1893

Construction began on the Sagrada Familia Basilica, a unique, visionary structure in Barcelona, Spain, designed by architect Antoni Gaudí. It is still under construction, with a proposed completion date of 2026, the centennial of Gaudí's death. When finished, it will be the tallest and assuredly the most unusual church in the world.

A World Parliament of Religions was held in Chicago. Different faiths from around the world met and engaged in respectful conversation, a very significant milestone at that time or any time.

American sugar planters overthrew Queen Liliuokalani of Hawaii and established their own government. In 1898, Hawaii would be annexed by the US.

1894

The French government found Alfred Dreyfus, a French army officer and a Jew, guilty of treason, although much of the evidence against him had been fabricated. After spending twelve years incarcerated on Devil's Island, off the coast of French Guiana, the ruling would be overturned. The "Dreyfus Affair" helped crushed the optimism of many Jews in Western Europe. They had hoped to one day assimilate into

European society, but if they couldn't be accepted in even the most progressive country in Europe, they realized that they would never be accepted as equals by any Christian society. They would have to look somewhere other than Europe to realize peace and self-respect.

Tulane professor William Benjamin Smith wrote *Ecce Deus: The Pre-Christian Jesus*. Smith wrote that the earliest written Christian sources, Paul's epistles, emphasized the divinity of Christ with no mention of his human personality, and this would have been implausible if Jesus had been the real human portrayed in the Gospels.

The British government modified the British Children's Charter to allow children to give evidence in court. They also monitored for emotional abuse, as well as physical abuse, and made it a crime to deny medical attention to a sick child.

Nicholas Notovitch wrote *The Unknown Life of Jesus Christ*. In the book, he claimed that Jesus had traveled to India and studied under Hindu gurus before he began his ministry in Galilee. Notovitch mentioned that the book was based on *The Life of Saint Issa*, a document that he had seen in India. The book is now believed to be a hoax.

Ottoman Sultan Abdul Hamid II initiated the massacre of Armenian Christians in an act of desperation and paranoia when he tried to save his collapsing empire by eliminating the non-Islamic population, who were asking for more rights. The results of the two-year Hamidian massacre were an estimated eighty thousand to three hundred thousand Armenians killed and over fifty thousand children orphaned. Over the next twenty-three years, the Ottomans would kill more than one and a half million Armenians in a genocide that reached its peak during World War I. Often overlooked in these accounts are the concurrent massacres of the Assyrians Christians, with around three hundred thousand killed, and Greek Christians, with possibly five hundred thousand killed or deported.

American eugenics enthusiasts established the Immigration Restriction League to stop the dilution of "the superior American racial stock"—meaning upper-class Anglo-Saxons—by preventing southern Europeans from immigrating into the country.

The Canadian Parliament passed the Indian Act to establish a comprehensive plan for the indigenous inhabitants of the country. The first provision was to define who was an Indian. The act made school attendance mandatory for Indigenous children, forcing many children in rural areas to leave their families and relocate to "residential schools" where they were indoctrinated into European-American culture. Most of these children were placed under the control of the Catholic Church and were forbidden to speak their native languages or wear the clothing with which they were accustomed. The last of these schools wouldn't close until 1996.

1895

Thomas Huxley, the English biologist and anthropologist who coined the term *agnostic*, died in England. He was known as "Darwin's bulldog" because of his strong advocacy of Charles Darwin's theory of evolution. In his time, he was the main proponent for choosing between religion or science, meaning supernatural or natural explanations, because he believed those realms were mutually exclusive.

In New York, the Niagara Bible Conference affirmed five "essentials" of Christian faith: inerrancy of scripture, the virgin birth and deity of Christ, substitutionary atonement, the physical resurrection, and bodily return of Christ.

1896

Pope Leo XIII issued the encyclical *Satis Cognitum* to address the unity of orthodox Christianity. He called for non-Catholics to reunite with the Catholic Church under his authority.

What is known as the Berlin Codex, or Akhmim Codex, was discovered near Akhmim, Egypt. It contained the *Apocryphon of John*, the *Sophia of Jesus Christ*, the *Gospel of Mary*, and a summary of the

Acts of Peter. The codex was written in Coptic and dated to the fifth century. Due to the World Wars, it wasn't translated and published until 1955.

English Egyptologist Flinders Petrie discovered the Merneptah Stele in Thebes, Egypt. Outside the Bible, it contains the oldest reference to a country named Israel.

In the wake of the demoralizing Dreyfus Affair, European Jews released the Zionist Manifesto, which outlined their new strategy to emigrate to Palestine. These Zionist Jews privately planned to saturate the region with Jewish immigrants but to not declare a Jewish state until they had more power than the five hundred thousand Arabs who already lived there.

Following their subjective criteria for aiding the survival of the fittest, the Connecticut legislature enacted marriage laws to prohibit anyone who was "epileptic, imbecile, or feeble-minded" from being married.

In the case of *Plessy v. Ferguson*, the US Supreme Court ruled 7–1 to allow racial segregation to continue as the norm for public businesses under the "separate but equal" doctrine.

1897

The Oxyrhynchus Papyri, or Oxyrhynchus Gospels, consisted of fragments of parchment discovered in a rubbish dump in Egypt. The manuscripts date from as early as the third century BC. The cache contained many canonical and noncanonical texts, as well as Christian hymns, prayers, and letters from around the seventh century AD. These later writings contained a story about Jesus found in no other gospel regarding a Pharisee who tried to order Jesus and his disciples out of the Jerusalem Temple because they were ritually unclean.

American Congregationalist minister Charles M. Sheldon wrote the book *In His Steps* and introduced the expression "What would Jesus do?"

After his conversion in a Russian monastery, Grigori Rasputin became a mystic and traveling holy man who was said to have performed miracles. Within ten years, he would serve as spiritual healer and political advisor to Tsar Nicholas II and his family.

1898

British forces had entered Egypt to prop up the Egyptian economy, which was being drained by a war with neighboring Sudan. Since the British basically controlled Egypt due to their interests in the Suez Canal, Egypt's fate was vital to British interests. The British reasserted Egypt's claim on Sudan by invading and conquering the country.

American social activist Elizabeth Cady Stanton and a committee of twenty-six women published a collection of essays written by women and called *The Woman's Bible*. It challenged the traditional belief in Christian orthodoxy that women should keep silent in church and be subservient to men. Many activists who worked with Stanton were opposed to the book because their focus was not on attacking religion but only on winning the right to vote.

The Vatican newspaper *L'Osservatore Romano* villainized Jews, calling them vampires thirsting for Christian blood and conspiring to destroy Christianity. The paper demanded more legal discrimination against Jews.

Vasily Ivanovich Bellavin was appointed bishop of the Aleutian Islands and Alaska. He eventually became an American citizen and expand his jurisdiction to all North America. In 1907, he would be recalled to Russia and become Tikhon, patriarch of Moscow and All Russia.

The US sent the battleship *Maine* to Havana, Cuba, to protect American interests during the Cuban War of Independence against Spain. The *Maine* suffered a major explosion in the harbor, and the US government blamed the Spanish, although the real cause of the explosion is still not certain. In retaliation, the US declared war on Spain and quickly defeated them. Staying true to its belief in Manifest

Destiny, the United States forced Spain to relinquish their colonies of Cuba, Puerto Rico, Guam, and the Philippine Islands. These colonies became US possessions, and the United States became an empire.

In England, Sir William Blake Richmond established the Coal Smoke Abatement Society to address air pollution caused by coal burning. It is one of the world's oldest nongovernmental environmental organizations.

1899

English physicists and astronomers William and Margaret Huggins published an atlas of stellar spectra, summarizing their finding on the light spectrometry analysis of various stars. With their work, the science of astrophysics was born. They were able to understand the life cycles of stars and to realize that all the elements in our bodies, or any form of life, are derived from those created inside stars. Along with corresponding discoveries in geology, it became clear that the heavens and Earth were not thousands, but millions, or even billions, of years old. Those who believed the literalness of the Bible would find ways to dismiss this evidence.

Christian Herald magazine editor Louis Klopsch published the first red-letter Bible. He based the concept on Luke 22:20: "This cup is the new testament in my blood, which is poured out for you." He printed all of Jesus's quotes in red to represent his blood. He was also influenced by some medieval scriptures which used red ink in the opening letters of text. The red-letter Bibles gained instant popularity among Christians because Jesus's quotes were easier to locate.

Robert Ingersoll died. He had been known as the Great Agnostic and was one of, if not the, most popular public speakers in the United States. His mockery of the more ridiculous aspects of Christianity influenced mainstream Protestant denominations to drop many of their rigid theological positions. To Ingersoll, there were no social injustices in which religion did not play a major role. He attacked the delusions that God intended some people to remain poor throughout their lives;

that only those who could afford a decent education deserved one; that religion-based laws and customs allowed marital violence and the denial of educational access to women; and that debtors' prisons, animal and child cruelty, and inhumane treatment of the insane and criminals could be justified and excused. These were all social issues Ingersoll fought against, and they were all defended with biblical passages, which could be used by those in power to rationalize their mistreatment of the powerless. Because of people like Ingersoll, the champions of evangelical fundamentalism vilified freethinkers and were fearful of them, equating them with anarchy, socialism, and communism.

The Boxer Rebellion—an anti-foreign, anti-colonial, and anti-Christian uprising—began in China. In 1900, the Eight-Nation Alliance, including the United States, brought twenty thousand armed troops to Peking and broke a siege of the compounds of Westerners that had lasted fifty-five days. The Rebellion took the lives of 136 Protestant missionaries, 47 Catholic priests and nuns, 30,000 Chinese Catholics, 2,000 Chinese Protestants, and at least 200 Russian Orthodox Christians.

Albert von Schrenck-Notzing claimed to have converted a homosexual man to heterosexuality with hypnosis and trips to a brothel. Homosexual orientation was considered sinful by some and a disease by others. Schrenck-Notzing introduced a series of techniques to make homosexual individuals conform to normal heterosexual expectations. His ideas led to other practices of treating homosexuality, such as electroconvulsive therapy and even lobotomies. It would not be until the twenty-first century that those kinds of procedures would be deemed ineffective as conversion tools by the general psychological community and that human homosexuality appears to fall into the normal range of sexual behavior seen in many animal species.

CHAPTER 20: TWENTIETH CENTURY AD

Education, you know, means broadening, advancing; and if you limit a teacher to only one side of anything, the whole country will eventually have only one thought, be one individual. I believe in teaching every aspect of every problem or theory.

—John T. Scopes

God proved His love on the Cross. When Christ hung, and bled, and died, it was God saying to the world, "I love you."

—Billy Graham

We can find no evidence that there is any type of illness cured by "spiritual healing" alone which could not have been cured by medical treatment.

—Archbishop Randall Davidson

Jackie Robinson made my success possible. Without him, I would never have been able to do what I did.

—Dr. Martin Luther King Jr.

Conservative Christians continued to be wary of anything new, especially scientific and societal advancements. End-times theology continued as fundamentalists waited for the return of Jesus. The Great War began as a chain of events that would ripple across the entire world and the entire twentieth century. Two millennia

of Christian antisemitism culminated with Nazi Germany targeting Jewish people in the Holocaust, and later with many surviving
European Jews returning to their ancestral homeland as refugees.
Communism developed and spread rapidly due to people rejecting the traditional forms of society and religion. American fear of
Communism led to another Christian revival calling on God for
protection, while the United States struggled mightily with the
separation of predominantly Christian moral influence from secular society. Apparitions of the Virgin Mary became more common;
the US finally could no longer procrastinate in confronting its continuing sin of racism; and many exciting archeological discoveries were made as archeologists combed the ancient world and we
began to learn more about early civilizations than even the people
who lived at that time.

1900

Another holy foreskin was "discovered" in France. By this time, the
Church had grown tired of these hoaxes since there had been twelve of
them reported over the centuries. The pope decreed that anyone who
continued to discuss the Holy Prepuce would be excommunicated.

c. US Christian fundamentalism gained unity in responding to
the increasingly popular belief in evolution and other modernist
concepts, such as questioning the truthfulness of the Bible and its
relevance to modern life. So dedicated were fundamentalists to a
literal interpretation of the Bible, that rationality and scientific discoveries held no truth to them if they were perceived to contradict
scripture.

c. Sixty-eight percent of the world's Christians lived in Europe, and 25
percent lived in the Americas, leaving only 7 percent in the entire rest
of the world.

c. Due to the rapid and unregulated development of industry, both liberal and conservative Christians in the US became involved in social
programs to protect those who were being left behind by the march of

progress. Many conservatives later became critical of the "social gospel" and argued that it was pointless to try to improve a world that was predestined by God for destruction.

In the Mogao Caves in China, which had been walled off since 1036 when the region was ruled by the Tibetan Empire, a Taoist monk discovered the Dunhuang manuscripts. These consisted of tens of thousands of writings, mostly in Chinese, but also in nine other languages. Some of the writings were Nestorian Christian, including *The Messiah Sutra* and *On One God*, both presumed to have been written by Alopen in the seventh century and providing valuable insight into early Asian Christianity.

The US took possession of eastern Samoa and obtained a Deed of Cession to make it a US territory.

1901

Speaking in tongues was an important aspect of Pentecostalism, and the practice gained momentum when a church in Topeka, Kansas, experienced a spontaneous outpouring of the phenomenon. The Pentecostals assumed this was evidence of a direct connection to the Holy Spirit, like what had happened in first-century Jerusalem on the fiftieth day after the resurrection of Jesus, an event Christians refer to as the Pentecost.

The American Standard Version, an Americanization of the English Revised Version of the Bible, was published.

After twenty-three years as a missionary to New Guinea, James Chalmers and his companion Reverend Oliver Tomkins were clubbed to death and eaten by cannibals when they entered an unfamiliar part of the island.

1902

Pope Leo XIII appointed cardinals to the Pontifical Biblical Commission, which was established to ensure the proper interpretation and defense of the Bible.

French theologian and professor Alfred Loisy attempted to apply biblical criticism to the study of scripture in the Catholic Church. For this audacity, he was excommunicated and dismissed from his position as a professor at the College of France.

1903

A document entitled *The Protocols of the Elders of Zion* was circulating in Russia. It described a Jewish plot for world domination to be implemented by controlling the world's economy and the press. This "secret" document was considered proof of Jewish intentions, but in fact, the document was invented and printed by the Russian secret police. *The Times* of London would expose the fraud in 1921.

US intervention in Colombia's province of Panama led to the independence of Panama and gave the US possession of the *Canal Zone*, a ten-mile-wide slice of Panamian territory that now contains the Panama Canal.

1904

Anglican priest Kenneth Sylvan Guthrie published the *Long-Lost Second Book of Acts*, describing Mary, the mother of Jesus, and her teachings about reincarnation. It also told what became of the apostle Paul after the book of Acts ended. The work was later declared a hoax.

President Theodore Roosevelt introduced the "Roosevelt Corollary" that justified the intervention of the US to represent European interests in conflicts between them and Latin American countries. Roosevelt claimed that this was an extension of the Monroe Doctrine of 1823. As a result, the United States militarily and politically intervened in

Honduras in 1905, Cuba in 1906, Nicaragua in 1912, Mexico in 1914, Haiti in 1915, the Dominican Republic in 1916, Cuba again in 1917, Panama in 1918, and Guatemala in 1920.

1905

Scottish author, poet, and minister George MacDonald died. He is remembered as a pioneer in fantasy literature who influenced Lewis Carroll, C. S. Lewis, and J. R. R. Tolkien, among others. He is also remembered as a believer and proponent of universal reconciliation and a loving God who would endlessly forgive those who repented and not sentence anyone to eternal torment in hell.

German sociologist Max Weber coined the term *Protestant work ethic* in his book *The Protestant Ethic and the Spirit of Capitalism*. This was also known as the Calvinist or the Puritan work ethic. It emphasized discipline, hard work, and prudent use of one's resources. The attainment of prosperity and wealth was considered a divine blessing.

Antisemitic pogroms in Odessa and other Russian cities took over eight hundred Jewish lives and resulted in thousands of Jewish homes being burned. It's believed that the Russian secret police and the military allowed these riots to occur, if not outright sponsored them.

German physicist Albert Einstein was helping to develop a new view of the universe with his theories on relativity. He saw time and space as interrelated, not as two separate variables, and held a view of an infinite universe far beyond what Isaac Newton ever envisioned. Every major advancement in scientific thought had repercussions in theology, and God being seen outside space and time seemed to be acceptable to most Christians.

c. New Zealand British physicist Ernest Rutherford and British radiochemist Frederick Soddy introduced the science of radiometric dating. Using the predictable breakdown of radioactive elements, they found that they could measure the elements to determine the age of rocks. This led to the age calculation of many geological formations. This kind of dating technique led scientists to discard the Bible as a basis for any accurate information about the age of Earth.

1906

Albert Schweitzer, the Alsatian theologian, writer, humanitarian, and physician, wrote *The Quest for the Historical Jesus*, a critical look at Jesus that helped establish Schweitzer's reputation as a New Testament scholar.

William J. Seymour, an African American preacher, led a prayer meeting on Azusa Street in Los Angeles. Revivalist Christians prayed for an outpouring of the Holy Spirit, and some of them proceeded to speak in tongues. The revival lasted until 1915 and was a source of what became modern Pentecostalism.

Prominent Americans became interested in eugenics, which was the improvement of the gene pool by selective breeding, and many corporate foundations contributed to the studies. This year J.H. Kellogg funded the Race Betterment Foundation in Battle Creek, Michigan.

1907

The Indiana legislature passed a sterilization law. Thirty other states followed within the next few years.

Pope Pius X issued the decree A Lamentable Departure Indeed, condemning the modernist intellectual movement within the Catholic Church and denouncing sixty-five modernist propositions that conflicted with Church doctrine.

Gerald Massey, a British Egyptologist, published *Ancient Egypt: The Light of the World.*

He had learned to read hieroglyphics and decipher ancient Egyptian texts, and he found that many events and concepts in the canonical Christian Gospels had first been written about in Egyptian mythology, often based on the mythical god Horus. Massey accused fourth-century Christian historian Eusebius of facilitating the destruction of this body of evidence.

1908

Gideons International, an organization started by two American Protestant salesmen in 1899, began a free distribution of Bibles. They modeled themselves after Gideon, an Old Testament figure who the organization says "was willing to do exactly what God wanted him to do, regardless of his own judgment as to the plans or results. Humility, faith, and obedience were his great elements of character." Their Bibles are now omnipresent, appearing in hotel rooms, hospitals, and doctor's offices in over a hundred languages and in around two hundred countries.

Pope Pius X granted an indulgence of seven years to everyone who looked at the body and blood of Christ and said, *"Dominus meus et Deus meus,"* meaning "my Lord and my God," the words of Saint Thomas when he encountered the risen Jesus. He also granted one year for every time a Catholic ascended the Holy Stairs in Rome after confession and Holy Communion.

British Army General Robert S. S. Baden-Powell founded the Boy Scouts Association in England to set young boys on a course of unselfish morality and adventure. Two years later the Boy Scouts of America organization was established, and it would become the largest youth organization in the country. In their oath, the scouts state "duty to God and my country," but they were not an overtly religious organization.

Amendments to the British Children's Charter established juvenile courts and mandated the registration of foster parents. The Punishment of Incest Act put family sex abuse cases under state, rather than clerical jurisdiction.

American preacher Levi H. Dowling published *The Aquarian Gospel of Jesus the Christ* after he had supposedly tapped into a spiritual plane of existence. In the book, Dowling chronicled the eighteen unknown years in Jesus's life, how the man Jesus allowed the Christ to dwell in him, the actuality of reincarnation, how all souls evolve to perfection, and the trinity consisting of strength, love, and wisdom. Dowling's gospel spawned the Aquarian Christine Church Universal.

Geologist George Bernard Reynolds was the first geologist to discover oil in the Middle East. He found it in Persia (modern-day Iran). Oil would subsequently be discovered in Iraq, Saudi Arabia, Kuwait, and the United Arab Emirates. Middle Eastern oil became highly coveted and fought over, and by 1954, a Western cartel would control Persia's oil industry.

1909

Immigrating Jews founded Tel Aviv as a Jewish suburb of the ancient port city of Jaffa, which had a mostly Arab population.

Fundamentalist Christians published the Scofield Reference Bible, and it became a widely circulated study Bible based on the King James Version. It had printed commentaries on pages alongside the verses being commented on. Since the Geneva Bible in 1560, commentaries had been printed only in separate volumes. The Scofield Bible also cross-referenced related verses to allow readers to follow various themes.

Pope Pius X established a board of censors to discover and report on writings and persons tainted with the heresy of Modernism. The censors were suspicious of those who believed reason was needed to discover truth; thought miracles were legendary, not real; opposed the temporal power of the pope; and held many other new and popular beliefs. Pius also imposed an oath against Modernism on Catholic clergy and scholars, which stifled scholarship in the Roman Catholic Church until 1967.

1910

The Methodist Minister Association gathered two hundred ministers together in San Francisco to disrupt the heavyweight boxing match between African American Jack Johnson and white champion James Jeffries. At that time, there reportedly had never been so many US ministers gathered to protest other controversial events, such as lynchings, and the reason this fight triggered their interest is noteworthy. The perception of white supremacy was at stake. The clergy were successful in stopping the fight in San Francisco, so it was moved to Reno, Nevada. After Johnson defeated Jeffries for the heavyweight title, the United Society of Christian Endeavor, who had never protested prizefighting before, launched a campaign against showing fight films in movie theaters, and their fight film protest spread worldwide. The clergy were concerned that the film of that particular fight would ignite race riots, but in the few cities where the film was shown, there were no such disturbances, only pride was felt in Black communities.

George Went Hensley, a Tennessee minister, believed that Mark 16:16–18 and Luke 10:19 commanded Christians to handle serpents. He introduced snake handling practices into the Church of God's Holiness, and the tradition eventually led to some churches in Appalachian America requiring snake handling as evidence of true belief. The type of snake and the methods of handling them aren't specified in the Bible, so the practice was open to the interpretation of individual pastors. Hensley would die of a snake bite in 1955.

The White-Slave Traffic Act, or Mann Act, made it a felony in the US to transport a woman across state lines for the purpose of prostitution or for any other "immoral" purpose. The intent was good, but the ambiguous use of the word *immoral* could be twisted to apply to almost anything. In 1913, heavyweight boxing champion Jack Johnson's enemies used the Mann Act to try him after he crossed a state line with his white girlfriend. When that didn't work, he was tried for crossing with another white woman in 1909 and found guilty, even though the Mann Act hadn't been passed at that time. He spent a year in prison, and this law was not amended until 1978.

The Testimony Publishing Company of Chicago published a series of essays, known as *The Fundamentals: A Testimony to the Truth*. The ninety essays reflected a concern about liberal Christianity, especially higher biblical criticism. It warned Christians against believing in evolution, questioning the authority of the Bible, and challenging the accepted identity of Christ. The essays are considered the foundation of modern Christian fundamentalism.

c. There were approximately eleven million Jews in the world. In order of population, they resided in the Russian Empire, the United States, Poland, Austria-Hungary, Germany, Ottoman Empire (Turkey and Bulgaria), North Africa, Romania, and the United Kingdom.

1912

The last three of the four-volume *Catholic Encyclopedia* were published in New York, with the intent to present information related to Christianity from a specifically Catholic perspective.

Bulgaria, Serbia, Greece, and Montenegro fought the First Balkan War to completely free themselves from three centuries of Ottoman rule. The Balkan allies were victorious, and the Ottomans lost almost all their European territory. The Bulgarian advance was stopped just twenty-five miles from Constantinople.

Juliette Gordon Low, after meeting with Robert Baden-Powell, the founder of Boy Scouts, founded Girl Scouts of America in Savannah, Georgia.

The Chinese criminalized the practice of foot binding, the intentional altering of the shape of women's feet. It had begun as a sign of status in the tenth century, because men liked the way it made women walk, and the practice was forced on young girls between the ages of four and nine. A driving force behind overturning this practice came from Christian missionaries.

1913

Based on his studies of the age of rocks using radioactive decay, British geologist Arthur Holmes published *The Age of the Earth*. He said he had found samples that were 1.6 billion years old.

1914

The Assemblies of God denomination was founded in Arkansas following a conference of white Pentecostal ministers who wanted to detach themselves from the Church of God in Christ, which was dominated by African Americans. The AOG eventually became the world's largest Pentecostal denomination.

The First World War, known in Europe as the "Great War," began. When the Ottoman Empire entered the war on the side of Germany and Austria-Hungary, their leader Sultan Mehmed V declared it a holy war and urged Muslims worldwide—including those in Turkey's enemy countries of Britain, France, Russia, and Serbia—to take up arms against their Christian neighbors.

On Christmas Eve, in the trenches on one stretch of the Western Front, French, German, and British troops laid down their weapons in an unofficial ceasefire. They exchanged holiday greetings and gifts and sang Christmas hymns together. They also conducted prisoner exchanges and allowed for the recovery of the dead and their burial. The next day they went back to killing each other. The army commanders from those three countries would assure that such a fraternal event, known as the Christmas Truce, would never happen again.

1915

The Ottoman and Russian governments continued to persecute vulnerable minorities in their empires and suspect them of being disloyal or treasonous. The Ottomans targeted Armenian Christians and Assyrians, while the Russians singled out the Jews. Armenians were slaughtered on an even larger scale than in the 1890s. When some

Muslim governors refused to kill helpless Armenians, they were re-placed with "patriots" who were willing to carry out the massacres. The death squads were ordered to spare no one, not even "babes in the cradle." Ottoman Interior Minister Talat Pasha was responsible for the massacre of more than 1.5 million Armenians, and the Russians relo-cated over six hundred thousand Jews to other parts of the country.

Austrian neurologist Sigmund Freud was popularizing the theory that the "unconscious mind" drives much of human behavior. He described the mind as being divided into three levels, the conscious, the pre-conscious, and the unconscious. The unconscious mind, he wrote, was inaccessible to the conscious mind and influenced feelings, impulses, and behaviors. If this was true, introspective Christians would be left to wonder whether their impulses, dreams, and revelations came from their own unconscious minds or from the Holy Spirit, the indwelling divinity that supposedly guided their lives.

In the United States, inspired by the movie *Birth of a Nation*, Methodist preacher William Joseph Simmons led fifteen other men up Stone Mountain, Georgia. Once at the top, they built an altar, took an oath, and set a cross on fire. This event signified the rebirth of the Ku Klux Klan, a terrorist organization that President Grant had suppressed in 1871. The Klan and its ceremonies were steeped in Christian rituals and members were required to be white Christians. In the aftermath of this event, KKK membership continued to grow to around four million.

American mission worker, poet, and songwriter Fanny Crosby died. She was known as the "queen of gospel songwriters." Her life's work included more than eight thousand hymns and gospel songs, including the well-known "Blessed Assurance," "To God Be the Glory," and "Pass Me Not, O Gentle Savior."

1916

Great Britain and France signed a secret treaty known as the Sykes-Picot Agreement, designed to carve up the Ottoman Empire following

World War I and give the two countries control of the Middle East. The British planned to control Palestine, Jordan, and southern Iraq, and the French would control southeastern Turkey, northern Iraq, Syria, and Lebanon. To the Arabs, this was a betrayal since the British had led the Arabs to believe that by allying with the British against the Turks, they would be granted an independent Arab country without arbitrary borders drawn by Westerners.

Authorities in Waco, Texas, lynched Black teenager Jesse Washington in front of city hall after declaring him guilty of murdering a white woman. Around ten thousand spectators watched and celebrated as he was hanged, mutilated, burned, then dragged through the town. A *New York Times* editorial read: "In no other land even pretending to be civilized could a man be burned to death in the streets of a considerable city amid the savage exultation of its inhabitants."

The Russians launched the Erzurum Offensive against the Turks. Since Turkey was focused to a large extent on their Armenian genocide, they were not prepared for this winter offensive. The Russians were victorious, spoiling Turkey's celebration over their defeat of the allied forces at Gallipoli.

Lithuanian American Unitarian minister Michael X. Mockus was convicted of blasphemy in Connecticut after making statements in public that were perceived to be atheistic. This charge and conviction were based on a law adopted in 1642. He was again convicted for the same charge in Maine the following year, but he never served prison time.

1917

Assyrian Christian men who survived the Turkish genocide joined with the Russians in an attempt to link up with the British, who were in Palestine. The British had promised the Assyrians, Kurds, and Armenians, just as they had the Arabs, that they would be rewarded with an independent state if they help the British defeat the Turks. The Russian army folded when their revolution began, and when the

Assyrians finally met up with the British, the British disarmed them and placed them in refugee camps.

Germany, desperate for materials to continue their war, confiscated over ten thousand church bells. Like in the French Revolution, many of those bells were centuries old and beloved in their towns, where people had heard them ring every day of their lives. The Germans also melted organ pipes to produce more guns and ammunition. Churches were restricted from burning oil in lamps since the oil was also needed in the war effort.

Pope Benedict XV directed the updating of Codex Juris Canonici, the official comprehensive codification of Latin canon law. It was the most significant update since the 1150s and would be revised again in 1983.

Due to Western Pentecostal influences, Chinese Christians established the True Jesus Church. This sect is still active with some one and a half million members in fifty-eight countries.

From their base in Cairo, British forces captured Jerusalem from the Ottomans. Christians were temporarily back in control of the city, with the British Army accomplishing what King Richard the Lionhearted was unable to in 1192.

As World War I ended and the Ottoman Empire struggled through its final days, British Foreign Secretary Arthur James Balfour issued the Balfour Declaration, which in part declared, "the establishment in Palestine of a national home for the Jewish people." Hebrew prophets had foretold that the Jews would return to their homeland before the end of time, so this announcement had several layers of meaning. The Zionist desire for a homeland was presented to the Palestinian Arabs in terms of a refuge for European Jews, not a takeover of the region, so the Arabs mostly accepted the gradual assimilation of Jews into their population as the Turks had done after Spain expelled their Jews in 1492.

In Fatima, Portugal, three shepherd children reported seeing a sudden flash of lightning followed by an apparition of a beautiful woman, radiantly lit and hovering in the air. One of the children, named Lucia, spoke with the apparition, who said she would reveal her identity in six months and told the children to return to the site on the thirteenth day of every month. The children returned with more people the next month. Lucia again talked to the apparition, but only she could see it. At the sixth gathering, between thirty thousand and seventy thousand people were in attendance. The figure appeared again, but only to the children, and identified herself as the "Lady of the Rosary." She directed the children and the crowd to look at the sun, where many saw a silvery disk emerge from behind clouds. It allegedly spun and dove and did other strange phenomena. It was the sun miracle that would become part of many sightings of the Virgin Mary and put Fatima on the pilgrimage map as a place of miraculous healing. The site is now so popular that its square can hold five hundred thousand people at a time.

The Bolsheviks came to power in Russia. Since Leon Trotsky, the leader of the Red Army, and Karl Marx, the architect of Communist ideology, were both of Jewish descent, many non-Bolsheviks blamed the Jews for the rise of Communism and targeted them with a new wave of pogroms, killing 1,200 Jewish inhabitants just in the town of Proskurov. More than 2,000 pogroms took place in eastern Europe between 1917 and 1921, resulting in the deaths of an estimated 75,000 Jews and leaving at least another 500,000 homeless.

Vladimir Illyich Ulyanov, better known as Vladimir Lenin, organized a new government in Russia that eliminated clerical privileges and religious influence. It put marriages and divorces under civil control and severed the connections between the state and school system and the Russian Orthodox Church. Lenin nationalized church property and granted freedom of religion to Russian citizens.

The Anglican Church licensed women to read scripture during church services but stopped short of ordaining them to preach.

Mexico enacted a new constitution that lessened the power of the Roman Catholic Church. The Mexican government nationalized church property, outlawed monastic orders, and allowed individual states to dismiss priests in their jurisdiction.

Edward J. Flanagan, a Roman Catholic priest, founded Boys Town in Nebraska as a refuge and educational facility for abused, runaway, and delinquent boys.

The US purchased many of the Caribbean Virgin Islands from Denmark.

1918

US automaker Henry Ford purchased his hometown newspaper, the *Dearborn Independent*, and began publishing a series of articles that claimed the US was being infected by a vast Jewish conspiracy. The series continued in the next ninety-one issues. He bound these articles into a four-volume set named *The International Jew* and distribution five hundred thousand copies through his car dealerships and subscribers.

By the end of the World War I, the Ottoman Empire had lost most of its remaining territory outside Anatolia, including Syria, Palestine, and the Persian Gulf region. Constantinople was split into three zones of occupation, controlled by the French, British, and Italians.

The US Congress attempted to impose a tax on businesses that employed children under the age of sixteen, but the Supreme Court would overturn the law in 1922.

Irving Berlin, a Jewish American, wrote the patriotic song "God Bless America" while serving in the US Army. He would revive it in 1938 when Hitler began to threaten Europe. Antisemitic groups protested the song because of Berlin's ethnicity. In the 1960s, conservative Christians used the same song to inspire liberals and dissenters, who they thought weren't being patriotic enough.

1919

The Eighteenth Amendment to the US Constitution outlawed the production, transport, and sale of "intoxicating liquors" but not the possession or consumption of them. This law was the result of 140 years of intensive campaigning by women's groups who were mainly Christian.

A Greek army landed in Turkey with the goal of restoring the old Byzantine Empire under Christian rule. Three years later, the Greeks forces were driven out by the Turks.

1920

c. Belgian priest Georges Lemaître was the first person to popularize the Big Bang theory for the birth of the universe. He postulated that the entire universe was created in an explosion of a magnitude beyond description. Forty years later, cosmic radiation would be discovered that echoed and seemed to confirm this event. This theory was rejected by fundamentalist Christians who believed in a six-day creation.

The Nineteenth Amendment to the US Constitution gave American women the right to vote. Although this became the law of the land, local laws blocked women from minority groups from voting in the South and in a few other states.

c. At this time, Constantinople was still populated by mainly Eastern Orthodox, but by 2010, this total would drop to only four thousand due to population exchanges between Turkey and Greece, a wealth tax, and religious persecution.

British papyrologist Bernard Grenfell acquired a fragment of papyrus in an Egyptian marketplace. It was written in Greek and would not be translated until 1934. It turned out to be a piece of the Oxyrhynchus Papyri containing the Gospel of John. It most likely dates from the early to mid-second century and mentions Jesus's crucifixion in Jerusalem. It is one of the earliest surviving New Testament documents.

Due to a devastating famine in Russia, government forces ransacked Orthodox churches, Catholic churches, synagogues, and mosques to seize valuables to sell in order to feed the hungry.

The newly established League of Nations partitioned Greater Syria, giving mandates to the French and English in accordance with their Sykes-Picot Agreement of 1916.

A committee of prominent American humanitarians founded the American Civil Liberties Union (ACLU) with the initial goal of protecting freedom of speech, especially for war protesters. Since then, its scope has grown to include addressing injustices to many groups who face persecution from our society because of race, color, gender, sexual orientation, birth control and abortion choices, opposition to the death penalty, and more.

Arab leader Faisal I bin Hussein bin Ali al-Hashemi, despite British duplicity, established an independent Arab state in Greater Syria. The state didn't last long, as the French brushed the Arabs aside in order to establish the mandate they had been given by the League of Nations. Following the Battle of Maysalun, French General Gouraud visited the tomb of Sultan Saladin in Damascus, walked over to it, and kicked it, saying "Awake, Saladin. We have returned. My presence here consecrates the victory of the Cross over the Crescent."

Pope Benedict XV canonized Joan of Arc as a saint in the Roman Catholic Church.

1921

Zionist Jews had been trickling into Palestine for years, and there was intense debate among them about how they should maintain peace with Arabs, whose families had lived there for centuries. Some wanted to gradually establish themselves, helping the Arabs economically and thus winning their respect and acceptance, but others thought the land already belonged to the Jewish people from biblical times and sought to remove the Arabs and establish a Jewish state. This year a riot broke out in Jaffa as a confrontation between two opposing Jewish groups, but it soon escalated to involve Arabs, Christians, and British soldiers who were trying to keep peace.

The British Parliament partitioned Ireland. Most of the Protestant population of Northern Ireland remained loyal to Great Britain, and the southern part of the island, which was almost entirely Catholic, sought independence.

Many conservative Christians in the US viewed the introduction of the radio with some anxiety, as they did with many modern technical advances, because it seemed supernatural, like channeling voices from who-knows-where. But radios would be accepted and later play an important role in the evangelical Christian movement, beginning in Pittsburgh where the first Christian radio broadcast was a church service.

A riot broke out in Tulsa, Oklahoma, when a white mob attacked Black residents and businesses. During the Tulsa Race Massacre, whites destroyed more than thirty-five blocks of one of the most prosperous Black communities in the country. An unknown number of Blacks were killed, over eight hundred injured people were admitted to hospitals, and thousands were left homeless.

1922

Greece and Turkey signed the Treaty of Lausanne, which led to the forced resettlement of five hundred thousand Turks who had been living in land that the Ottoman Empire lost and one and a half million Greeks who had been living in the Ottoman Empire. Some of these families had lived in their hometowns since 1000 BC. Turkey moved their capital from Constantinople to Ankara in the heart of the new country, and Constantinople was renamed Istanbul, a name derived from the ancient Greek phrase *is tim 'polin* meaning "to the city."

Ida Scudder, an American missionary and physician, witnessed the first class of her medical school graduate in Vellore, India. Her school, the Christian Medical College, became one of the best teaching hospitals in Asia.

1923

President Calvin Coolidge presided over the first national Christmas tree lighting on White House grounds.

Thomas Chisholm, a humble Kentuckian who struggled with health problems, wrote the hymn "Great Is Thy Faithfulness."

George McCready Price wrote *The New Geology*, a book that explained evidence for Earth being only a few thousand years old and its present geology being indicative of the great flood in Genesis. This was an effort to reconcile what he observed with a literal interpretation of the Bible, in opposition to the modern scientific understanding of Earth's geology as having developed over billions of years.

Hungarian linguist Edmond Bordeaux Szekely reportedly discovered the Hebrew version of the *Essene Gospel of Peace* in the scriptorium at the Benedictine monastery of Monte Cassino and the Aramaic version in the Vatican library. His claims were rejected by many biblical scholars because the originals were seen by only Szekely.

A white mob burned the Black town of Rosewood, Florida to the ground as revenge for a supposed assault on a white woman by a Black man. At least six people were killed. This followed other violent racial incidents in Colfax, Louisiana; Wilmington, North Carolina Elaine, Arkansas; and Ocoee, Florida.

1924

After the Russians invaded Georgia, the Soviets imprisoned Patriarch Ambrosius, an outspoken critic of communists, for concealing historic treasures to prevent them from falling into Soviet hands.

President Calvin Coolidge signed the National Origins Act, which restricted immigration into the US. The new law set national quotas that mainly affected southern and eastern Europeans and basically excluded Asians.

When the Turkish government ended their caliphate, Constantinople was no longer the center of the Muslim world. The Arabs who had helped defeat the Turks regained that honor. To stifle religious opposition to westernization, Turkish president Mustafa Kemal, aka Atatürk, closed hundreds of religious schools and colleges. He directed independent secular courts rather than religious courts to administer Turkish law and even urged Turkish women to shed their veils and dress in a modest Western manner.

American astronomer Edwin Hubble discovered that what he thought were clouds of gas in outer space were in fact galaxies. This demonstrated that our own Milky Way galaxy was just one of millions of others in the universe. He conjectured that the universe had an utterly spectacular beginning with an even more amazing and mysterious cause, which he could only speculate on.

1925

Adolf Hitler published his autobiography *Mein Kampf*. In it, he expressed his deep admiration for Martin Luther, his intense disgust for Jews, and his future hopes for Germany. It became a best seller in Germany during the 1930s. He wrote, "Hence today I believe that I am acting in accordance with the will of the Almighty Creator; by defending myself against the Jew, I am fighting for the work of the Lord."

The American Civil Liberties Union defended John Scopes, who had been accused of violating Tennessee's law against teaching evolution in public schools. Clarence Darrow defended Scopes in what became known as the Monkey Trial, and William Jennings Bryan, a former presidential candidate and anti-evolution activist, served as prosecutor. Scopes was found guilty, but the verdict was overturned by the Tennessee Supreme Court. Christian fundamentalists were ridiculed in newspapers across the country, and Scopes's career was sabotaged by those fundamentalists.

From forty to sixty thousand Ku Klux Klan members in their white robes marched along Pennsylvania Avenue in Washington DC.

1926

An English translation of Nicolas Notovitch's *The Unknown Life of Jesus Christ* was published and caused great commotion in the US, even though it had been exposed as a fraud in Europe thirty years earlier.

The religion of Caodaism began in Vietnam. It is a syncretism of other religions, including Christianity, and is characterized by nonviolence, vegetarianism, and veneration of ancestors, with the goal of a union with God.

1927

The US Supreme Court decided 8 to 1 to allow states to forcibly sterilize those they judged "unfit to procreate." This ruling upheld the Virginia Sterilization Act, which called for compulsory sterilization of patients in mental institutions. As many as sixty-four thousand Americans would be forcibly sterilized by 1963, and this court decision has never been overturned.

1928

Turkey began converting Arabic script to Roman letters as the country continued to westernize. Other significant changes followed, such as Sunday becoming a day of rest and the Hagia Sophia, Emperor Justinian's masterpiece, being transformed into a museum.

After he experienced a vision, Spanish priest Josemaría Escrivá founded the Prelature of the Holy Cross and Opus Dei, later shortened to Opus Dei. It became an institution of the Catholic Church in

1950, with its own bishop. Their mission was social work, charity, and training in the application of Catholic spirituality to daily life. In 2018, there were nearly ninety-five thousand members in ninety countries, mostly lay persons.

1929

Pope Pius XI issued the encyclical *Divini Illius Magistri* (*On the Christian Education of Youth*), in which he stated that the goal of a Christian education should be eternal salvation, not the matters of the world. This educational responsibility belonged to the Church, the family, and society, but not to public schools.

The Cardinal Secretary of State Pietro Gasparri and the Italian head of state Benito Mussolini signed the Lateran Treaty, creating the independent country of Vatican City.

1930

Works by English religion scholars George Milligan and the late James Hope Moulton were published as *The Vocabulary of the Greek Testament*. This book summarized what had been learned about ancient Greek vocabulary from the vast number of papyri and inscriptions found in Egypt in the nineteenth century. The goal of their work was to define words that were used in the New Testament, and most New Testament dictionaries and concordances today are based on their work.

At the Seventh Lambeth Conference in Canterbury, the Anglican Church issued a statement permitting birth control "where there is a clearly felt moral obligation to limit or avoid parenthood." The Church of England therefore became the first Protestant denomination to officially accept the morality of birth control, but only under certain circumstances.

The Vatican's International Commission on the revision of the Bible decided that Exodus 20:5 had been mistranslated and proposed a revised text with a completely opposite meaning to make God seem more loving. The passage originally read "For I the Lord thy God am a Jealous God, visiting the iniquities of the fathers upon the children unto the third and fourth generation of them that hate me." The updated version read, "For I, the Lord thy God, am a God of loving-kindness and mercy, considering the errors of the fathers as mitigating circumstances in judging the children unto the third and fourth generations." This was just the latest in the thousands of mistakes or mistranslations the Church had corrected in the Vulgate.

Zealous Kenyans from the Kikuyu tribe murdered and mutilated the body of American missionary Hulda Stumpf. This crime was thought to have been carried out because of the Africa Inland Mission's opposition to female genital mutilation, a cultural and tribal rite of passage.

Charles Coughlin, a Detroit-based Catholic priest, broadcasted a weekly radio program that reached more than thirty million homes across the nation. He was an anti-Semite, whose *Social Justice* magazine reprinted *The Protocols of the Elders of Zion*, the forged anti-Jewish document from 1903.

Alfred Rosenberg wrote *The Myth of the Twentieth Century*, a treatise on the ideology of Nazism. He described the religion the Nazis were embracing as "Positive Christianity," a return to the original and purer teachings of Christ. He understood Jesus's true work not as promoting universal love but promoting a love for his race, which Rosenberg believed was Aryan, not Jewish.

c. At this time, the Roman Catholic Index of Prohibited Books contained over five thousand books.

1931

Chiang Kai-shek, the ruler of the Republic of China, became a Christian after reading the Bible twice and seeing the moral teachings of Jesus echoing those of Confucius. He was baptized into the Methodist Church of his wife's family.

Mexico was the first country in the world to legalize abortion in cases of rape.

The Spanish established a democratic secular republic and declared a distinct separation between church and state. It abolished Catholic schools and charities and expelled Jesuits from the country. Waves of violence followed in which Spanish mobs attacked Christians and their churches, monasteries, and convents.

1932

Turkey began broadcasting the *adhan*, or call to prayer, in the Turkish language rather than in Arabic. This experiment was neither popular nor successful, and in 1950, they shifted back to Arabic.

As a result of the Great Depression, millions of Americans couldn't find jobs. Seventeen thousand World War I veterans and their families, totaling more than forty-three thousand people, established a homeless camp in Washington, DC to demand the early payment of a promised bonus to veterans, rather than waiting until 1945, when their certificates were redeemable. This became known as the "Bonus Army." President Herbert Hoover ordered the camp destroyed, and General Douglas MacArthur cleared it with the use of tanks. The homeless and their supporters suffered several deaths, and over one thousand were injured.

1933

States ratified the Twenty-First Amendment to the US Constitution, repealing the Eighteenth Amendment and ending America's failed experiment with alcohol prohibition.

Pastors in Hamburg, Germany, issued the Altona Confession, which advised Lutherans on how to conduct themselves when encountering unwanted Nazi influence on their Church. It declared that no political party could claim to be ruled by the word of God.

Shortly after coming to power, Chancellor Adolf Hitler met with Bishop Wilhelm Berning and Monsignor Steinmann of the Roman Catholic Church in Germany. He reminded them of the Christian persecution of Jews throughout their history and told them that he merely intended to do it more effectively than the Church had been able to. He called it "doing Christianity a great service."

Hitler's new Nazi government held a one-day boycott of Jewish businesses, apparently as an experiment. No Christian leaders publicly condemned it, and many openly supported it.

Hitler appointed a Reich bishop, Ludwig Müller, to lead the German Christian movement. This new sect combined Protestant traditions with Nazi ideology, including the notion that Jesus was not actually a Jew but really an enemy of the Jews. Hitler also maintained that conversion did not turn a Jew into a Christian. In response, Protestant clergy who opposed these racial ideas organized what was called the Confessing Church.

When Jews were expelled from the German civil service, the German Christian movement also announced converted Jews, as well as Protestants who were married to "non-Aryans," were forbidden to hold church office or serve as pastors. The German Christians would later apply racial restrictions not only to their clergy but to their congregations.

Pope Pius XI and Cardinal Eugenio Pacelli, the pope's ambassador to Germany and later secretary of state for the Vatican, signed an agreement with Hitler to protect the freedoms and rights of German Catholics. It was one of Hitler's first foreign-policy successes, and it greatly enhanced his prestige.

The Trier Cathedral in Germany displayed the robe supposedly worn by Jesus prior to his crucifixion, and it drew two million pilgrims.

One year after gaining independence from Great Britain, Iraq's army attacked 95 Assyrian Christian villages, destroying 65 them and massacring three thousand unarmed Assyrian Christians who refused to convert to Islam. The Iraqis would later ally with Germany in World War II and declare war on Great Britain.

With the US mired in the Great Depression, the new administration of President Franklin Roosevelt sought ways to help poverty-stricken Americans. When Archbishop George Mundelein was unable to adequately help the poor in Chicago, he convinced Roosevelt to funnel money from the Federal Employment Relief Administration (FERA) through his archdiocese. This was against FERA policy but was done for expediency.

The US Bonus Army renewed their efforts for veteran's benefits once Franklin Roosevelt became President. Roosevelt offered the protesters jobs in the new Civilian Conservation Corp, which most accepted, and allowed them to live at Fort Hunt, Virginia. He made sure they were supplied with field kitchens, bus transportation, and entertainment. Their bonuses were finally paid three years later.

President Franklin Roosevelt announced the "Good Neighbor Policy" that reversed the Roosevelt Corollary of 1904 and opened the path to more peaceful relationships between the US and the countries of Latin America.

1934

Nazis controlled the Oberammergau Passion Play and made sure the play depicted Jews in the worst possible way. Hitler attended the play and praised the performance. The following year, the committee that produced the play was no longer elected by the villagers, but instead appointed by the Nazi party.

The Confessing Church in Germany issued the Barmen Declaration, the strongest anti-Nazi statement made during the Hitler years. It stressed that Christians had to stand unified against forces that were gathering against them and the country. Nothing was mentioned about antisemitism, though by this time, thirty-seven thousand Jews, including scientist Albert Einstein, had fled the country.

The *Egerton Gospel*, or *Unknown Gospel*, was discovered in Egypt, and experts dated the fragments of papyrus to the end of the second century. It contained four stories similar to those in the canonical Gospels.

German theologian Walter Bauer wrote *Orthodoxy and Heresy in Earliest Christianity*, which put forth the previously little-known theory that contemporary Christian orthodoxy was just one of many forms of Christianity that existed in the earliest centuries of the religion. This "orthodox" form of Christianity succeeded where others went extinct because the Roman Empire funneled money and political power into its Church. Bauer also stated that orthodox Christians in the fourth century rewrote history to make it appear that their version of Christianity had always been the only one and attempted to destroy any writing that supported other versions of Christianity. Because of World War II, this book was not translated into English, and its ideas did not spread into English-speaking countries until 1971.

The Vatican urged the Fascist government in Italy to restrict public gatherings of Protestants, including private worship in homes.

President Franklin Roosevelt tasked his Labor Secretary, Frances Perkins, with creating a pension program for retirees, an unemployment insurance program, and a national health care program to address the needs of the working class. These were social programs, or socialist measures, for the good of the nation and were to be paid for by periodic contributions from workers and subsidized by the federal government. These programs could be seen as socialist because they attempted to equalize the inequities between the rich and the poor and raise the overall standard of living for a healthy economy.

1935

The German government expelled Swiss theologian and Barmen Declaration author Karl Barth because of his opposition to Hitler's distortion of the German Church.

Iceland became the first Western country to legalize therapeutic abortion under limited circumstances.

Two alcoholics in Akron, Ohio, founded Alcoholics Anonymous to help other alcoholics remain sober. Their twelve-step program was largely based on a model from the Christian-based Oxford Group and focused on the need for a higher power to achieve recovery from alcoholism.

After a decade persecuting Catholic clergy in Mexico, seventeen of the thirty-two Mexican states were left without any priests.

The Social Security Act became law, making the United States the last modern industrial country to institute such a policy of giving workers a sense of financial security in their retirement years.

c. British engineer Guy Stewart Callendar began to sound the alarm that the atmosphere was beginning to be affected due to industrial pollution. Most people were skeptical of his conclusion that the atmosphere was beginning to warm.

1936

The Confessing Church, under the leadership of Martin Niemöller, sent Hitler a memorandum that protested the regime's anti-Christian tendencies and denounced the regime's antisemitism. The Nazis responded by arresting several hundred dissenting pastors, confiscating funds from the Confessing Church, and forbidding them from collecting offerings.

A US federal appeals court ruled that the government could not interfere with doctors providing contraceptives to their patients.

The Spanish Civil War began after reports of a rigged election and resultant rioting. Myths became the stimulus for a military coup, and the country descended into anarchy. The Nationalists were fascist insurgents supported by Mussolini and Hitler. They opposed both the Republicans, who were mainly urban and agricultural workers, and those Galicians and Catalonians who sought independence from Spain. Within the first two days, the "Red Terror" began with Republican forces burning more than fifty churches in Madrid alone.

Nazi propaganda defended the right to sterilize people against their will by using the United States as an example.

1937

Minnie Vautrin, an American missionary to China and president of Ginling College, refused evacuation during the Japanese invasion and stayed in Nanking. Her small campus became a refugee camp holding as many as ten thousand women. Vautrin returned to the US in 1940 in severe emotional distress and committed suicide the following year.

Pope Pius XI issued the encyclical *On the Church and the German Reich*. It was smuggled into Germany and read in German Catholic churches on Palm Sunday. The pope condemned many aspects of Nazi dogma, especially the exaltation of race to an idolatrous level. German Cardinal Bertram sought to dilute its impact by ordering certain passages not to be read aloud, but the Gestapo still raided churches the next day and shut down the printers of the encyclical.

As Shanghai, China, was being destroyed by fighting between Japanese invaders and Chinese defenders, French Jesuit Robert Jacquinot de Besange negotiated with both sides to establish a Safe Zone where civilians could escape the horrors of modern urban warfare. This concept was later used by other Chinese cities and probably saved the lives of over a half million people.

1938

People passionate about eugenics and wanting to eliminate harmful elements from the human gene pool in the United States founded the Euthanasia Society of America, calling not only for voluntary euthanasia for the terminally ill but also for involuntary euthanasia for the mentally ill. When they attracted less support than expected, they turned their attention to forced segregation and sterilization.

Hitler required German clergy, military members, and civil servants to sign a loyalty oath. It was a pledge of personal loyalty to Hitler, not to the constitution of Germany.

Benito Mussolini reinstituted the 1555 papal edict against Jews, renewing persecution against them in Italy. His government fired all Jewish public-school teachers and blocked Jewish children from attending schools. They expelled all Jews who had moved to Italy since the end of the World War I, even naturalized citizens who had converted to Catholicism.

A Nazi report indicated that 51 percent of the Schutzstaffel, or SS members, were Protestants, 23 percent were Catholics, and 26 percent were nondenominational Christians known as Gottglaubig, or God-believers. In the years to come, the SS would be responsible for the Nazis' mass extermination of the Jews and other groups.

The Nazis arrested Confessing Church leader Martin Niemöller for his outspoken opposition to their policies. He would spend seven years in confinement in a prison and a concentration camp.

Delegates from thirty-two nations met in Évian, France, to discuss the growing refugee crisis. They intentionally did not refer to it as a Jewish crisis because most of the countries were reluctant to admit more Jews.

Nazi storm troopers looted thousands of Jewish homes and businesses, set fire to more than three hundred synagogues, killed about ninety Jewish citizens, and shipped around thirty thousand Jews to concentration camps. Kristallnacht, or Night of Broken Glass, began on November 9, the eve of the birthday of Martin Luther, whose anti-Jewish writings were being used to inspire the Nazis. President Franklin Roosevelt recalled the US ambassador from Germany after this hate-filled incident, but Americans who were suffering through extreme unemployment due to the Great Depression were not ready to welcome more refugees.

German Christians founded the Institute for Study and Eradication of Jewish Influence in German Church Life. Their purpose was to eliminate anything that even hinted of Jewishness from Christian scripture and hymnals, in order to create a "pure" Aryan Christianity.

After Germany invaded western Czechoslovakia, the Nazis named Jozef Tiso, an influential and antisemitic Catholic priest, to lead the new state of Slovakia. He allied his country with Germany and cooperated in their plans against the Jews, all the while still actively participating in Church affairs. Tiso would be executed for war crimes in 1947.

1939

As a result of a three-year-long Arab revolt in Palestine, the British limited the number of Jews allowed to immigrate there to fifteen thousand per year for five years.

Reich Minister of Church Affairs Hanns Kerrl gathered German Protestant church leaders together to formulate and sign the Godesberg Declaration, which they adopted as official church policy. It stated that "the Christian faith is the irreconcilable religious opposite of Judaism" and that National Socialism, or Nazism, carried on the work of Martin Luther and would lead the German people to the true understanding of the Christian faith.

Emanuel Hirsch, a German professor of religion, argued that Jesus was not Jewish, but an Aryan, the Nazi idea of a pure, idealized Caucasian.

He believed the earliest Christians knew that but concealed the information.

Pope Pius XI died the day before he was due to issue a worldwide encyclical condemning racism and the persecution of Jews and other minorities in Germany, Austria, and Czechoslovakia. His successor, Pope Pius XII, the former envoy to Germany, would never publicly criticize the repressive policies of Hitler or Mussolini. There is suspicion that Pius XI was poisoned by someone, possibly at the instigation of Mussolini, who didn't want the encyclical issued.

Czechoslovakian Oskar Schindler, a former Nazi spy, acquired an enamelware factory in Poland that employed many Jews. After being outraged after witnessing the liquidation of the Kraków ghetto, where many of his employees lived, he protected his Jewish workers the best he could. Over the course of the war that followed, he bribed officials and regularly broke the law to help his employees evade Nazi roundups and arrests. Schindler saved over 1,200 lives and sacrificed his entire fortune in the process.

After a month in the United States, Confessing Church leader Dietrich Bonhoeffer returned to Germany after saying, "I will have no right to participate in the reconstruction of Christian life in Germany after the war if I do not share the trials of this time with my people."

George Orwell was the first writer to use the term *Judeo-Christian values* to describe the origin of Western ethics.

Workers digging beneath Saint Peter's Basilica in Rome found many previously unknown tombs containing human bones. Thirty years later, the bones found in one prominent location would be proclaimed the actual bones of Saint Peter.

American Unitarian minister Waitstill Sharp and his wife, Martha, arrived in Prague, where they helped desperate refugees escape from Nazi Germany.

The Spanish Civil War ended with General Francisco Franco and his Nationalists victorious. It was a multifaceted war, with possibly the worst anticlerical violence in modern history, including the execution of 12 bishops, 283 nuns, 6,832 priests, and the death of many hundreds of thousands of citizens.

1940

Chiune Sugihara, the Japanese vice-consul to Lithuania, defied his superiors and helped some six thousand Jews escape the Nazis by issuing them visas to travel to Japan via Russia. The Russians let them pass through their territory only if they purchased extraordinarily expensive tickets on the Trans-Siberian Railway.

The German Eisenach De-Judaization Institute produced a de-Judaized version of the New Testament, known as Die Botschaft Gottes, and the de-Judaized hymnal, Grosser Gott Wir Loben Dich, which both sold very well.

In Poland, the Nazis brutally suppressed the Catholic Church. One year after the German invasion, there were few priests left in their parishes, with the Nazis killing an estimated three thousand clergy and sending another 1,800 to concentration camps. Thousands of churches and monasteries were either closed or destroyed.

German Protestant theologian Wolfgang Stroothenke published *Genetic Cultivation and Christianity*, a book that sought to justify Nazi eugenics, the theory that populations could be improved with controlled breeding. Stroothenke put race at the core of what the Nazis called "Positive Christianity."

In 1932, there were only five antisemitic organizations in the United States. By this year, there were over 120 such groups. Many used articles and books that Henry Ford published in the 1920s, especially the bogus *The Protocols of the Elders of Zion*, to support their verbal and literary attacks on Jews.

The Nazis seriously considered the idea of transferring all European Jews to Madagascar, at that time a French colony. Germany had defeated France, so they could have taken over Madagascar and run the island as a police state, controlling every aspect of life. Later events in the war, such as the catastrophe following their invasion of Russia, caused Germany to abandon this plan.

1941

Bishops in the German Catholic Church tried to obtain permission from the Gestapo, or German secret state police, to allow Jewish Catholics to attend church without the yellow Star of David on their clothing, but the Gestapo refused.

As German forces entered Muslim-populated territories in the Balkans and North Africa they did everything possible to secure good relations with the Muslims. They sought to form alliances with the Muslims against their professed common enemies—Russia, America, the British Empire, and Jews. Interestingly, in Albania, Muslims saved around two thousand Jews from deportation to German death camps.

Hitler's SS began to systematically round up and deport Jews to extermination camps. In just a two-day period, 33,771 Jewish men, women, and children were shot and buried in a Ukrainian ravine known as Babi Yar.

Maximillian Kolbe, a Polish Franciscan friar who helped shelter Jews, was sent to Auschwitz-Birkenau concentration camp for helping to distribute anti-Nazi publications. There he volunteered and was allowed to die in place of a man who had a wife and children and had been selected randomly for execution to deter escape attempts.

In France, Catholic priest Jacques Loew began working at the docks in Marseilles. His was a worker-priest movement in which the Church placed young priests into secular jobs to regain the confidence of the French working class. The program was approved by Pope Pius XII and ended in 1954.

An Egyptian worker discovered a cache of sixth- and seventh-century Greek codices in a quarry near Toura, not far from Cairo, Egypt. There was a pile of these about a meter high, and the workers divided them amongst themselves, but only a fraction of them were preserved. Much of what we know about Origen and Didymus the Blind, a Christian theologian of the fourth century, was discovered in these writings. Some related fragments still occasionally find their way to the antiquities market.

1942

After the Japanese carried out a surprise attack on the US Naval Station at Pearl Harbor, Hawaii, President Franklin Roosevelt issued Executive Order 9066, which authorized the deportation and incarceration of 120,000 Japanese Americans living on the US Pacific coast. Most of these people were second- or third-generation Americans, but little thought seemed to be given as to who might be a true security threat. Eleven thousand Americans of German ancestry and three thousand Americans of Italian ancestry were also imprisoned.

German civilian and SS officials held the Wannsee Conference near Berlin. With the war on the Russian front going badly for Germany, the participants had to put their Final Solution to their "Jewish problem" into action without further delay. They decided to prevent Jews from leaving Germany and to ship all Jews in German-occupied Europe to Poland for extermination in order to hide the genocide from Germans. Since the legitimate Polish government was in exile, the Nazis had complete freedom there.

The Dutch Bishops' Conference issued a public statement condemning Nazi racism, which was read in all the nation's churches. In retaliation, the Nazis ordered the arrest of all Jewish converts and arrested and deported 243 former Jews, among them Edith Stein, a Carmelite nun who would later become a saint in the Catholic Church.

Kurt Gerstein, an SS colonel, was tasked with the technical aspects of mass murder using Zyklon B. After witnessing a fatal gassing of Jews, he attempted to inform the Vatican about the incident. He had also informed Swiss and Swedish diplomats, but his reports apparently received little notice and didn't stimulate the reaction he had hoped for.

The White Rose was a nonviolent, anti-Nazi organization consisting of five students and a professor at the University of Munich. They distributed several pamphlets, one describing the killing of three hundred thousand Jews in Poland and asking why their fellow Germans were apathetic in the face of these horrendous crimes. Students Sophie Scholl, Hans Scholl, and Christoph Probst were arrested, convicted of treason, and executed.

The Germans pressured Bulgaria to deport its Jewish citizens to the extermination camps. Bulgarian Tsar Boris III canceled the order after protests from thousands of his citizens, leaders of the parliament, and the Bulgarian Church. Because of this, most of Bulgaria's Jews survived the Holocaust.

The American priest Charles Coughlin sided with the Nazis and continued to attack Jews and Communists via his US radio broadcasts. His direct superior, Bishop Michael Gallagher, refused to terminate his show, but when Gallagher died, his replacement, Archbishop Edward Mooney of Detroit, with the backing of the federal government, instructed Coughlin to stop all nonpastoral activities or be defrocked. Coughlin complied and continued to serve as a parish priest until 1966.

The reported mass murders of Jews and other minorities in Europe seemed too incredible to be true, so most journalists were reluctant to publish stories about them. However, American radio reporter Edward R. Murrow did report on what he knew regardless of the consequences.

Pope Pius XII declared the establishment of the Institute for the Works of Religion, now known as the Vatican Bank. It is a secretive organization overseen by cardinals with a mission "to provide for the safekeeping and administration of movable and immovable property transferred or entrusted to it by physical or juridical persons and intended for works of religion or charity." Its assets were not intended to be the property of the papacy, but its surplus could be used by the papacy.

C. S. Lewis wrote *The Screwtape Letters*, a fictional work examining the devil's attempts to win human souls for hell. The following year, Lewis wrote the nonfiction *Mere Christianity* to show the sensibility of the religion he had recently adopted.

US evangelicals founded New Tribes Mission, now known as Ethnos360, as a missionary organization. As of 2015, they had more than 3,300 missionaries in over twenty countries.

The Wycliffe Bible Translators organization was formed in the US with the goal of translating the Bible into every language on Earth, thus allowing unreached people groups around the world to have access to Christian scripture.

Quakers and social activists in Oxford, England, established the Oxford Committee for Famine Relief, or Oxfam. Their purpose was to address the causes of poverty and other injustices and remedy them by working through responsible local organizations.

The US Pledge of Allegiance, which had been written by Francis Bellamy in 1892, was adopted by Congress.

The National Association of Evangelicals was founded as an organization to inform and inspire US evangelicals to influence American society. It would grow to represent more than forty denominations and forty-five thousand churches.

1943

Germans rounded up the Jewish population in Rome, but by that time, most of the seven thousand Roman Jews had gone into hiding, many aided by clergy of the Catholic Church. Of the country's forty-nine thousand Jews, around forty-one thousand evaded extermination by an "underground railroad" that led to neutral Switzerland. Pope Pius XII had the option to threaten excommunication for all German Catholics involved in the Nazi Holocaust, but he was reluctant to do that. He had served as the papal representative to Germany for twelve years and reportedly did not want to undermine Germany's war against Russia since he distrusted the Communists more than the Nazis.

The nation of Lebanon peacefully achieved independence from France. This enclave in Syria had been created after World War I to protect Syrian Christians.

1944

In the Netherlands, a neighbor betrayed Corrie ten Boom's family, who were devout Christians and were hiding Jews. The Nazis arrested the family, but the six people hidden in their house were not discovered and were later rescued. Ten Boom's father and sister died in a concentration camp, but she survived to write the popular book, *The Hiding Place*.

American bombers destroyed the historic monastery of Monte Cassino, founded by Saint Benedict in the sixth century. Since it was on the highest ground in the region and of great strategic importance, German soldiers occupied it, and it had been impossible to dislodge them with land forces.

Raoul Wallenberg, a Swedish special envoy to Hungary, saved tens of thousands of Jews by issuing protective passports and sheltering them in buildings he rented in Budapest.

Joseph Stalin deported everyone from the Muslim Republic of Vainakh, now Chechnya and Ingushetia. Nearly 100,000 of the 496,000 people involved in this expulsion died while being relocated to work camps in Central Asia.

1945

As Germany's defeat became imminent, sympathetic Christian clergy helped many Nazis escape to safer places such as South America to avoid prosecution for war crimes. One notable facilitator was Austrian Bishop Alois Hudal, who was based in Rome during the war and viewed helping Nazis escape as a charitable act. The Argentine government also worked closely with Catholic cardinals Antonio Caggiano and Eugene Tisserant to expedite the transportation of Nazis.

Just weeks before the war ended, the Nazis hanged Dietrich Bonhoeffer, the German Confessing Church pastor, author, and diplomat who had actively opposed Nazism. He had been arrested in 1943 for helping to smuggle fourteen Jews into Switzerland, and he was one of the few German Christian clergymen who tried to help Jews who had not converted to Christianity. His book *The Cost of Discipleship* called Christians to a stringent, self-denying faith because far too many of them had accepted "cheap grace," or reward without risk.

An Egyptian peasant discovered sealed jars containing twelve leather-bound codices in a desert graveyard near Nag Hammadi, Egypt. They were written in Coptic and included the only complete text of the *Gospel of Thomas* ever found. This became known as the Nag Hammadi Library or the Gnostic Gospels. The *Gospel of Thomas* was a collection of the sayings of Jesus, and the original may have been written in Greek before the New Testament Gospels. Before this discovery, the Gnostic Christians had been known only from rebuttals in the writings of their orthodox detractors.

In the Stuttgart Declaration of Guilt, German Lutherans publicly stated their responsibility for antisemitic propaganda leading to the Holocaust. They pledged to eradicate myths about Jews that had led to the genocide, such as the belief that Jesus was not really a Jew, the claim that Jews were Christ-killers or God-killers, the belief that the Jews were not worthy of salvation because of their denial of Jesus as the Messiah, and all of the superstitious charges brought against them throughout the Middle Ages and into the present century.

At the end of World War II, experts estimated that the Holocaust had resulted in six million Jewish deaths, along with countless Poles, Slavs, Jehovah's Witnesses, homosexuals, physically and mentally disabled, Roma (Gypsies), and members of political opposition groups. These victims were systematically eliminated because they didn't fit with Nazi ideology.

American humanitarian and environmentalist Arthur Cuming Ringland and associates founded the organization CARE, the Cooperative for American Remittances to Europe. It is based in Geneva, Switzerland, and originally intended as a temporary agency to provide relief to those starving in Europe after the war. It would later expand its mission to fight world hunger as the Cooperative for Assistance and Relief Everywhere.

The United States went against the traditional ways that a conqueror dealt with the vanquished and spent precious resources helping former enemies—Germany and Japan—rebuilt their destroyed countries in a manner approved by the US. The main goals were to build stable economies, prevent remilitarization, and establish buffers against Communism.

1946

Although Syria had declared its independence two years earlier, the country truly became free when the last French troops withdrew.

In Kielce, Poland, townspeople killed forty-two Jews, believing that they had kidnapped and ritually murdered a young boy and possibly other Polish children. In later years, this alleged kidnapping was revealed to be a lie perpetrated by the boy's father, and ritual murders were exposed to be consistently imagined or fabricated in order to punish Jews. This was nearly seven hundred years after Pope Innocent IV became the first of many popes to declare that Jews should not be blamed for ritual murder, because such murders were only legends and myths.

The country we now know as Jordan gained its independence from Great Britain and became the Hashemite Kingdom of Transjordan. This was accomplished peacefully by the Treaty of London.

1947

Three Bedouin boys entered a cave at Qumran, near the Dead Sea in Palestine, and discovered the first batch of scrolls that became known as the Dead Sea Scrolls. Eleven more caves would be found containing scrolls, and this Essene collection eventually grew to 972 documents. Some of these texts were relatively complete, some were severely damaged, and hundreds had been reduced to desiccated fragments. The writings spanned from 200 BC to AD 70 and included much from the Hebrew Bible.

Sixty-five Christian and Jewish leaders and scholars from nineteen different nations met in Seelisberg, Switzerland, to express their concern about continued antisemitism after the war.

The British relinquished their control of India after almost two centuries of domination. In their quest for independence, the Indians, led by Mahatma Gandhi, used the nonviolent strategy that Gandhi so admired in the teachings of Jesus. Gandhi was later assassinated by someone who could not conceive of a world without violence.

Michel 'Aflaq, a Christian, helped found the Ba'ath Party, which would rule Iraq and still holds power in Syria. The party called for Arab unification and freedom from non-Arab control in the region.

United Nations Resolution 181 partitioned Palestine into Jewish and Arab zones, precipitating an Arab holy war against the Jews. The battle for Jerusalem, which was part of the Arab zone, began.

A major exodus of Jews from Muslim countries started. The Jewish population in the Middle East and North Africa would be reduced from nine hundred thousand to less than eight thousand. About six hundred thousand of these refugees immigrated to Palestine.

The Brooklyn Dodgers broke the race barrier in major league baseball by signing Jackie Robinson to a contract. Previously, African Americans had to play in their own segregated leagues. In the sphere of sports, some Black athletes would finally find some parity with whites and gain fame, respect, and a decent standard of living.

1948

The British ended their mandate in Palestine, and the Jewish people proclaimed the birth of the State of Israel. The next day neighboring Arab countries invaded Israel. They saw the Jewish state as a land grab from the Palestinian Arabs who had lived there for centuries, and as a continuation of unwanted European influence in their region. Following a stalemate in the battle for Jerusalem, the city, like Palestine was partitioned between Israel and Jordan.

War between the Jews and Palestinians caused the exodus of up to 650,000 Palestinian Muslims and 55,000 indigenous Christians from Israel.

The flow of Jews into Palestine signaled to British and American Christian fundamentalists that end-times events were in motion. Many pro-Zionist Christians sought to aid the Jews in bringing on these apocalyptic events by attempting to convert Jews and even aiding Israelis in schemes to blow up the mosques in Jerusalem.

President Truman signed Executive Order 9981, committing US military to integrate its forces. During World War II, African American soldiers, as well as soldiers of Japanese and Chinese descent, served in segregated regiments.

The US government initiated the Marshall Plan, or European Recovery Program, to rebuild war-torn regions of Europe, remove trade barriers, and prevent the spread of Communism.

In *McCollum v. Board of Education*, the US Supreme Court ruled that religious education in public schools was a violation of the First Amendment.

Alan Turning, an English mathematician and computer scientist, who was influential in breaking German military codes in World War II, ran into religious objections when he proposed that it was possible for a machine to show intelligent behavior.

Representatives from 147 Christian churches met in Amsterdam and founded the World Council of Churches, an organization that promoted Christian unity and Christian presence in society. It had no centralized power but existed as a resource through which various sects could cooperate with each other.

Sayyid Qutb, an Egyptian author, educator, and Islamic theorist, became active in the Muslim Brotherhood and developed a radical interpretation of the Koran that required armed resistance to the recurring Christian incursions into the Muslim world. He had been a witness to European colonialism in the Middle East and what he viewed as cultural decadence in the US. He was very influential in the development of a militant extremist group founded forty years later, which we know as Al-Qaeda.

Four-year-old Marjoe Gortner was ordained as an evangelical preacher and performed his first marriage ceremony in California. He became a celebrity in the new US revival movement, a reaction to Communism.

The Hungarian government arrested Cardinal József Mindszenty, an outspoken critic of Communism, on the charge of treason. He was tortured and spent eight years in prison and then fifteen more years in asylum in the American embassy in Budapest. The government finally allowed him to leave the country in 1971 to go into exile in Vienna.

The Church of Denmark became the first Lutheran body to ordain women.

The Cold War was characterized by covert US intervention in many countries with one goal being to stifle Communism. Activity began this year with CIA involvement in Italian politics, and continued later with coups and conspiracies in Syria, Iran, Guatemala, Indonesia, Cuba, Cambodia, the Congo, Vietnam, Brazil, Haiti, Ghana, Bolivia, Chile, Argentina, Afghanistan, Angola, Chad and Iraq. Many of the leaders the US supported were authoritarian dictators.

1949

The Geneva Convention continued its work to try to make wars more humane. It defined the basic rights of prisoners of war, created guidelines for the protection for the sick and wounded, and tried to establish protection for civilians near war zones. This was an outgrowth of Henry Dunant's Red Cross in Geneva.

Following World War II, the US experienced the "Red Scare." Communism was being demonized as the enemy of God, the family, and the American way of life.

Christianity and patriotism became interwoven in fear of Communist infiltration and subversion. This threat became much more serious when Russia tested an atomic bomb, since many believed it would lead to Armageddon and the end of the world. Many Christians saw the ensuing Cold War as a battle between the forces of good and evil.

Christian evangelist Billy Graham's Los Angeles crusade catapulted him to national fame. In 1954, a trip to London would make him an international celebrity also. He hosted a radio show called the *Hour of Decision*, co-founded *Christianity Today* magazine, and served as an advisor to US presidents.

The Kirchentag, an assembly of lay members of the German Protestant Church, was held for the first time. It has since been held every two years in different German cities and consists of Bible studies, lectures, discussions, and concerts.

Aaron J. Smith, the dean of the People's Bible College in North Carolina, led an unsuccessful expedition to locate Noah's ark. This was the first expedition since 1876, and to date, these expeditions have turned up no conclusive evidence of the ark.

1950

c. US bishops began to refer sexually abusive priests to church-run medical facilities to be evaluated without disclosing their crimes outside the Church organization.

Albanian nun Mary Teresa Bojaxhiu, better known as Mother Teresa, had arrived in India in 1929. This year she founded the Missionaries of Charity, which would eventually administer hospices, orphanages, and schools in 133 countries. Mother Teresa became a household name but also a controversial figure. The Missionaries of Charity received millions of dollars in donations but drew criticism for not providing for the basic needs of their patients, such as physician care, proper nutrition, or analgesics for those in pain. Mother Theresa herself had her critics who condemned her stand against birth control and abortion in India, the most populous country on Earth. Her clinics were said to be like medieval hospitals in the type of care they provided, basically seen as places to die. She was quoted as saying "There is something beautiful in seeing the poor accept their lot, to suffer it like Christ's Passion. The world gains much from their suffering."

The United States had a larger Jewish population than any other country, with 4.5 to 5 million Jewish citizens.

American Baptist minister Robert Pierce founded World Vision Inc. as a Christian humanitarian organization to meet the needs of missionaries in crisis areas of the world. It would later become World Vision International, add developmental work and child sponsorship to its objectives, and become active in almost one hundred countries.

Billy Graham took advantage of the new technology of television to bring his message of salvation to a national audience. In his televised addresses, he warned that Americans would experience a nuclear holocaust unless they turned to Jesus Christ.

c. About this time, the Sinner's Prayer, or Salvation Prayer, became popular in evangelical churches. This was a prayer of repentance stemming from a desire to form or renew a personal relationship with God through Jesus Christ. It came in various forms and was often accompanied with calling congregants to the altar to recite it.

The subject of religion began to return to the college curriculum with the popularization of religious studies and comparative religion.

c. Hand raising during worship gained popularity in charismatic churches in the US. There are Biblical antecedents for the custom.

Pope Pius XII wrote the apostolic constitution *Munificentissimus Deus*, exercising his supposed papal infallibility and promoting the doctrine that Mary was assumed bodily into heaven at the end of her earthly life. Accounts of her assumption were not biblical but had been mentioned in Christian writing since the fourth century.

1951

Bill Bright started Campus Crusade for Christ International at the University of California, Los Angeles. It is an interdenominational organization for the promotion of evangelism among college students.

Rosalind Franklin, using X-ray diffraction photographs, showed DNA's spiraling double helix structure. This was confirmed by James Watson and Francis Crick two years later. Christians would understand DNA as the language, or code, invented by God to serve as the blueprint for life.

1952

The US Congress formalized the National Day of Prayer. Each year since its inception, the president has signed a proclamation encouraging all Americans to pray for the country and whatever else they choose to pray for on this day.

1953

In a rally in Chattanooga, Tennessee, Billy Graham tore down the ropes separating the Black audience from the white audience. This was symbolic as a rejection of racism, but Graham did not support the civil rights movement. After Martin Luther King Jr.'s "I Have a Dream" speech, Graham would say, "Only when Christ comes again will the little white children of Alabama walk hand in hand with little Black children." Graham would also choose not to participate in the landmark 1963 March on Washington.

The Vatican returned the relic (right arm) of Saint Thomas to India. The relic had been removed from India and taken to Edessa in AD 370.

With the financial assistance of the US Central Intelligence Agency (CIA) the Iranian military overthrew their premier, Mohammad Mosaddeq and installed Mohammed Reza Pahlevi as Shah. The new Shah thanked the Americans by signing over 40 percent of Iran's oil fields to them.

1954

L. Ron Hubbard's Hubbard Dianetics Research Foundation declared bankruptcy due to lawsuits for practicing medicine without a license. With the psychiatric profession strongly criticizing his mental health philosophy known as Dianetics, Hubbard transformed his philosophy into a religion he called Scientology.

With President Eisenhower's encouragement, Congress added the phrase "under God" to the US Pledge of Allegiance, which had previously read "I pledge allegiance to the Flag of the United States of America and to the Republic for which it stands, one nation, indivisible, with liberty and justice for all."

In *Morals and Medicine*, Joseph Fletcher advocated allowing patients to decide on medical ethics, including contraceptives, artificial insemination, sterilization, and euthanasia, rather than basing these issues on specific biblical or Christian principles.

Trans World Radio, the largest Christian media organization in the world, started as the Voice of Tangier. It later moved to Monaco and added transmitters in Swaziland, Guam, Bonaire, Sri Lanka, and Cyprus. Their programs can now be heard in 160 countries in 230 languages.

1955

The Communist government of East Germany prohibited church services, Bible studies, and celebrations of the Eucharist, or communion.

American evangelist Francis Schaeffer and his wife Edith founded L'Abri, an evangelical Christian study retreat in the Swiss Alps.

The Chinese government imprisoned Catholic Bishop Kung Pin-Mei of Shanghai, along with several hundred priests and church leaders, for not cooperating with the Communist program to subjugate churches. The bishop would spend the next thirty years in prison.

After receiving false news that Greeks had bombed the Turkish consulate in Thessaloniki, Turks attacked Greeks living in Istanbul. Following this, emigration of ethnic Greeks from Turkey would result in a further decrease in the Greek population in Turkey from 119,822 in 1927 to 7,000 in 1978.

1956

Chinese authorities forced more than twenty-two thousand members of the "Little Flock" to denounce their Christian faith. This sect began in 1922 with men named Watchman Nee and Witness Lee and was overseen by the Plymouth Brethren in the United Kingdom.

The United States officially changed its motto from *E pluribus Unum* ("from many, one") to In God We Trust. The phrase has appeared on US paper currency since 1957.

When Elvis Presley first appeared on "The Ed Sullivan Show," it attracted some sixty million viewers, which was 82 percent of the nation's TV audience. Many conservative Christians were shocked by Elvis's music, lip curls, and hip gyrations. Many feared the cultural "perversion" that was taking place in American youth.

Missionaries Nate Saint, Ed McCully, Jim Elliot, Peter Fleming, and Roger Youderian were murdered in a remote part of Ecuador by an indigenous tribe who saw all outsiders as enemies.

The Ten Commandments, a film about Moses and the Exodus of the Jewish people from Egypt, shot to the top of the box office rankings. At the time, it was the most expensive movie ever made.

Scottish obstetrician Ian Donald and engineer Tom Brown developed the first ultrasound device for clinical use. It wouldn't be in wide use until the 1970s, but from the start, it gave a surreal glimpse into the development of human fetuses. The information from the images is often a factor in deciding whether to keep the fetus to full term or have the pregnancy ended.

1957

The Soviet Union allowed Chechens to return from exile, but when they arrived back in their homeland, they found that the Russians had closed all their mosques.

One hundred thousand people turned out to see Billy Graham preach at Yankee Stadium, and more than ten thousand were turned away. It was the largest crowd in the stadium's history.

Reverend Martin Luther King Jr. invited sixty Black ministers to Atlanta, where they founded the Southern Christian Leadership

Conference to try to achieve civil rights for African Americans through nonviolent means, the technique that Gandhi had successfully used in India. The ministers elected King as the organization's first president.

1958

Morton Smith, a professor of ancient history, discovered the *Secret Gospel of Mark* in a monastery near Jerusalem. It was thought to have been written by Clement of Alexandria around the second or third century. The document disappeared from the museum where it was kept before it could be scientifically dated, and there is an ongoing debate about whether the document is authentic or a hoax.

The Jehovah's Witnesses held a Divine Will convention and packed Yankee Stadium with a crowd of 123,707, a new record attendance.

After Pope Pius XII died, Pope John XXIII began a new era of church reform.

The Hollywood movie *Ben Hur* was released. Like *The Ten Commandments* it had an underlying religious theme, with Jesus and his Passion in the background. At the time, it was the most expensive movie ever made and won eleven Academy Awards, including best picture.

1960

Madalyn Murray's son had been harassed by school officials for refusing to participate in Bible readings. She filed a lawsuit in Baltimore, Maryland, to protect his right not to participate. This case, *Murray v. Curlett*, led to a Supreme Court ruling against prayer and Bible reading in public schools, and it also led three years later to Murray's founding of American Atheists, a nonprofit organization created to defend the civil liberties of atheists.

Leonard Woolley, a preeminent British archeologist, died. He was one of the first modern archeologists to excavate in a methodical way and use his findings to reconstruct ancient life. He was one of the first archeologists to propose that the flood account in Genesis was based on regional legends, not a global catastrophe.

Archbishop Geoffrey Fisher of Canterbury, the leader of the Church of England, visited Pope John XXIII. This was the first formal meeting of these two Churches since the Henry VIII broke with the Roman Catholic Church in the sixteenth century.

Twenty-year-old American college graduate Loren Cunningham founded Youth with a Mission (YWAM)—an international missionary organization intended to send young people out into the world after high school to give them a sense of purpose. YWAM currently has over 15,000 full-time volunteers at 1,100 locations in 180 countries.

The rapidly growing Christian population of Africa surpassed what it had been at its peak in the eleventh century. In 1900, there had been around nine million Christians in Africa, but by 2000, there would be 380 million.

The people of Quebec elected reform-minded Jean Lesage as their leader, and the province turned in a secular direction, greatly restricting the power of the Catholic Church. In what is called the "Quiet Revolution," the Quebec government removed control of education and health care from the Catholic Church and placed them under the control of the provincial government. At the same time, the rest of Canada also underwent secularization, greatly easing religious conflict in the country.

Americans elected John F. Kennedy as president. Many Americans were afraid that since he was Catholic, he would be under the pope's influence. His opponent, Richard Nixon, had been closely aligned with the evangelical Billy Graham. Graham had met with twenty-four other American Protestant leaders in Montreux, Switzerland, to try to block Kennedy's election. This meeting was only disclosed by a historian in the early 1990s.

With the world's focus on the conflict between Israel and the Palestinian Arabs, little attention was paid to the approximately 875,000 Jews who lived outside Palestine but in Arab-dominated areas in the Middle East and North Africa. Most of them had descended from families that had lived in those regions for more than 2,500 years, and by this time, all but a few of them were being forced out of their homelands.

Calvinist philosopher, missionary, and theologian Rousas John Rushdoony began advocating homeschooling to combat what he saw as the secular nature of the public school system in the United States. Rushdoony was a controversial figure, also supporting white supremacy and traditional gender roles.

After police in Nowa Huta, Poland, removed a cross that had been erected without a permit, Christians protested, and this led to rioting. The Communists finally relented and granted permission to construct a church.

Greek Cypriot Archbishop Makarios III became the president of Cyprus. He would serve three terms and survive four assassination attempts and a coup.

The US Food and Drug Administration approved the first birth control pill after a hard-fought battle between American couples who desperately wanted birth control and Christians who opposed it in any artificial form.

Frenchman Pierre Plantard created a fictitious secret organization known as the Priory of Sion and even planted a false family tree in the national library to "prove" his claim to Frankish royalty. The Priory was said to have been created in 1099 by Godfrey of Bouillon, one of the leaders of the First Crusade, and was later referred to in the book *The DaVinci Code*. This hoax would not be discovered until 1993.

Jack Chick began to evangelize through graphic art. His first effort was called a "tract" and titled *Why No Revival?* Chick would produce many full-size comic books containing evangelical Christian themes, which have generated much criticism from Catholics and moderate to progressive Christians.

University of Chicago professor Willard Libby was awarded the Nobel Prize in Chemistry for developing radiocarbon dating. It is a precise scientific method to determine the age of preserved organic substances. This breakthrough was a boon to archeologists because it allowed them to date their findings much more accurately.

This year was referred to as the Year of Africa because seventeen African countries won their independence from European colonial rule.

1961

Southern Baptist minister Pat Robertson founded the Christian Broadcasting Network, the first television network in the US devoted solely to Christianity.

The American Unitarian Association merged with the Universalist Church of America to form the Unitarian Universalist Association.

In Caesarea Maritima, Israel, archeologists discovered the Pilate Stone, a block of limestone with an engraving mentioning Pontius Pilate. This was confirmation that Pilate was an actual historical person.

Orthodox churches from Europe's Communist bloc joined the World Council of Churches at the New Delhi Assembly.

Israeli agents captured Adolf Eichmann, one of the main organizers of the Holocaust, in Argentina and smuggled him out of the country. In Israel, he was put on trial for war crimes, convicted, and hanged. After the trial, the World Council of Churches issued a document condemning antisemitism and reiterating that contemporary Jews were in no way responsible for the death of Jesus. James Parkes, an Anglican priest and expert on Christian history, stated, "There is an unbroken chain which goes back from Hitler's death camps to the denunciations of Jews by the early Church."

In *Torcaso v. Watkins*, the US Supreme Court decided that neither state nor federal governments can impose laws forcing someone to declare a belief in God as a prerequisite for holding public office.

The United Nations established the World Food Program as an extension of the US Food for Peace Program. Its goal was to end world hunger and malnutrition and ultimately eliminate the need for food aid entirely.

Henry Morris and John Whitcomb published the book *The Genesis Flood: The Biblical Record and its Scientific Implications*, in which they proposed that creation took place in six days and that all the findings that pointed to the appearance of an ancient Earth, such as geological formations and fossils, could be explained by the worldwide flood in Genesis. This book was said to have affixed "Young Earth" creationism to fundamentalist orthodoxy.

1962

The US Supreme Court, in *Engel v. Vitale*, decided that it was unconstitutional to compose an official school prayer and encourage students in public schools to recite it.

The US civil rights movement gained momentum, and many Black Americans identified with the Jewish slaves of Exodus, in exile but awaiting a return to the promised land. The promised land they sought was a land of not only freedom but respect, which few had experienced in the United States. Reverend Martin Luther King Jr. led the movement and remained faithful to its nonviolent roots.

Pope John XXIII called the Second Vatican Ecumenical Council into existence to revitalize the Catholic Church and make it more relevant in the modern era. The council strove for more lay participation, the use of languages other than Latin in worship, open dialogue with other religions, recognition of Protestant and other denominations as fully Christian, and the removal of religion from the political sphere. They also instituted a more modernized approach to scripture analysis and interpretation, made scripture the primary basis of divine truth, and did away with the rote memorization of the Baltimore Catechism.

The Vatican issued *Crimen Sollicitationis*, establishing procedures for the investigation of child sexual abuse by priests. It also addressed those priests who solicited sex during confessions and stated that anyone discovered discussing testimony from these investigations was to be excommunicated. Fearing the repercussions of public accusations and having to confront repressed emotions, even today many victims are reluctant to discuss their cases.

The US established the Peace Corps as a volunteer organization to provide less developed countries with technical assistance to improve their standard of living. The Peace Corps is basically a secular missionary outreach.

Dr. C. Henry Kempe published the article "The Battered Child Syndrome" in the *Journal of the American Medical Association*. It was the first published work emphasizing the need for physicians to identify cases of child abuse and neglect and report them to civil authorities.

The United Lutheran Church appointed a commission of medical doctors and theologians to investigate faith healing performed by certain practitioners. In their report, the commission stated that the healers had exploited those who were desperate, avoided proven scientific treatments, and blamed failures on the patient's lack of faith.

c. With the recording of rising carbon dioxide levels in the atmospheric and the onset of computer modeling, the "greenhouse effect" was being tracked and began to draw some concern.

1963

The Roman Catholic Church lifted its ban on cremation primarily because relying only on traditional burials was creating sanitation risks, overcrowded cemeteries, and financial strain on the families of the deceased. Three years later, another ruling allowed priests to officiate at cremation ceremonies.

Pope John XXIII created a commission to examine overpopulation, including a study of artificial birth control. The commission completed this study in 1966 under Pope Paul VI, who issued an encyclical that restated the traditional opposition of the Church to artificial contraception, as well as sterilization and abortion. This was extremely disappointing to liberal Catholics, many of whom would ignore Church policy.

German playwright Rolf Hochhuth published the five-act play *The Deputy, a Christian Tragedy*. The play condemned Pope Pius XII for failing to speak out or act against the Nazis when he knew what they were doing during the Holocaust. The play has been translated into more than twenty languages.

The US Supreme Court banned devotional Bible readings in public schools, quoting the freedom of religion clause in the First Amendment.

1964

Pope Paul VI and Patriarch Athenagoras I of the Eastern Orthodox Church met in Jerusalem where they repealed their churches' mutual excommunications from 1054. This was the first meeting between the two offices since the Council of Florence in 1439. Pope Paul VI became the first pope to leave Italy since 1809. Over a six-year period, he would visit Israel, India, the United States, Portugal, Turkey, Columbia, Switzerland, Uganda, the Far East, and Australia.

Reverend Martin Luther King Jr. received the Nobel Peace Prize for his efforts to end racial injustice in the United States by peaceful means.

President Lyndon Johnson signed the US Civil Rights Act, outlawing any discrimination based on a person's race, color, religion, sex, or national origin. This officially ended the Jim Crow era of segregation for African Americans. A little-known and complicated aspect of this act was that private businesses could be forced to end discrimination because of the Commerce Clause of the US Constitution, which prevented citizens from restricting interstate commerce. The rationale was that if private businesses could prevent travelers from staying at certain hotels or eating at certain restaurants because of their race or other demographic criteria, then such businesses would be impeding interstate commerce.

British scientists established the International Union for Conservation of Nature (IUCN) in the United Kingdom to preserve endangered animal species in the wild and in captivity. Through a grading system, they prioritized how much attention to give each threatened species.

The Ancient Church of the East split from the Assyrian Church of the East with one of the main areas of contention being the calendar. The Assyrian Church decided to adopt the Gregorian calendar, but the Ancient Church continued to use the Julian calendar.

Conservative activist Phyllis Schlafly published *A Choice Not an Echo*, a book that helped insert the modern Christian conservative movement into the Republican Party.

1965

US President Johnson signed the Voting Rights Act to overcome the legal barriers at state and local levels that had for almost a century prevented certain African Americans from voting.

In order to refocus their movement on peace following the shooting death of civil rights activist Jimmie Lee Jackson by a state trooper, American civil rights leaders led eight thousand demonstrators on a proposed march from Selma to Montgomery, Alabama. It ended in bloodshed when state troopers and local vigilantes attacked the peaceful marchers with tear gas and clubs. This attack received world-wide attention and became known as Bloody Sunday. Two days later, Martin Luther King Jr. led a second march in Selma, but this time when they reached the bridge on the county line, they stopped to pray. Even though the police stepped aside, King led the marchers back to the church where the march had begun so as not to disobey a court order preventing them from making the full march. That night, members of the KKK beat three white Unitarian Universalist ministers with clubs, killing one of them, James Reeb from Boston. A week later, after a judge ruled in favor of the protesters' First Amendment rights, a third march drew extensive media coverage and twenty-five thousand people. President Johnson federalized the Alabama National Guard to escort the marchers out of Selma. Four days later, they arrived at the state capitol building in Montgomery.

The US Congress passed the Immigration and Nationality Act, abolishing national origins formulas that had been in use since the 1920s and had restricted immigration mainly to northwestern Europeans. The new law allowed more Buddhist, Hindus, Sikhs, and Muslims to immigrate to the United States, forever changing the religious and cultural demographics of the country and further angering those who wanted to keep the country purely white, Anglo-Saxon, Protestant.

The Oriental Churches Conference, representing the Armenian, Coptic, Ethiopian, Malankara, and Syriac Churches, met in Addis Ababa, Ethiopia. This was the first meeting since the fifth or sixth century of the heads of the Monophysite Churches, those that found themselves ostracized from orthodox Christianity after the Council of Chalcedon.

The Second Vatican Council approved a document known as *Nostra Aetate* (*In Our Time*). It renounced the myth that Jews, neither those who lived at the time of Jesus nor those who are alive today should be blamed for his death. The council also reaffirmed the Church's belief that God has an "eternal covenant" with the Jewish people.

In *Griswold v. Connecticut*, the US Supreme Court ruled that it was unconstitutional for state governments to prohibit married couples from using birth control.

The Second Vatican Council issued *Dei verbum* (*Word of God*), a dogmatic constitution on divine revelation. It declared that sacred scripture had been the result of the Holy Spirit's divine revelation to biblical authors and that all divine knowledge had been revealed at that time. The age of divine revelation had ended. The bishops decided that God still helps Christians interpret scripture today, and the Catechism of the Catholic Church states, "Christianity is the religion of the 'Word' of God, a word which is not a written and mute word, but the Word is incarnate and living. If the Scriptures are not to remain a dead letter, Christ, the eternal Word of the living God, must, through the Holy Spirit, open [our] minds to understand the Scriptures."

Chuck Smith founded Calvary Chapel in Costa Mesa, California. Smith's goal was to bring hippies and surfers to Jesus through a charismatic style of worship. Calvary Chapel went on to become the mother church of a thousand churches worldwide.

1966

The American Jewish Congress encouraged a boycott of the 1970 Oberammergau Passion Play until the producers agreed to change the script to make it less antisemitic. Due to certain members on Oberammergau's community council, it would take until 1990 to finally eliminate all traces of antisemitism from the play.

The Roman Catholic Church required meatless fasting days on Ash Wednesday and Fridays during Lent for anyone over fourteen years of age. Prior to this, the Church had required all Catholics over the age of seven to abstain from meat every Friday.

Pope Paul VI formally abolished the Catholic Index of Prohibited Books after four hundred years of existence. The list was no longer considered binding, and the penalty of excommunication for reading any of the books was lifted.

As many as 250 foreign missionaries were expelled from Burma, and the Burmese Protestant Church itself grew to become an active missionary-sending organization.

John Lennon of the British rock band the Beatles publicly said, "Christianity will go. It will vanish and shrink. I needn't argue about that; I'm right and I will be proved right. We're more popular than Jesus now; I don't know which will go first—rock 'n' roll or Christianity." Statistically, he may have been correct about their popularity, but he still caused a huge uproar in the Christian world. Although many Christians turned to the old tradition of burning what they didn't like—in this case, Beatles albums—Lennon was eventually forgiven by the Vatican in 2008.

The American music group the Crusaders cut the record *Make a Joyful Noise with Drums and Guitars*, marking the beginning of Christian rock music. The Crusaders were followed many popular Christian rock groups and solo artists over the ensuing decades.

The Chinese Cultural Revolution began. For ten years, all aspects of religious life were banned, churches and temples were desecrated or destroyed, and missionaries were expelled.

Catholics began a nonviolent civil rights campaign in Northern Ireland, but by the end of the year, it had turned violent, unleashing centuries of repressed hatred and lasting until 1998.

Mississippi became the first US state to allow abortion in cases of rape.

1967

US and Canadian women formed the first women's liberation organizations in major cities with the goal of ending sexual discrimination and gaining socio-economic equality with men. In the last century, the women's suffrage movement had grown out of abolitionism, and at this time, the women's liberation movement was an extension of the African American quest for civil rights. Like any attempt to shed traditional roles, women were opposed by conservative Christian men and women who believed that since Eve's Fall in the Garden of Eden, it was God-ordained for men to rule over women and relegate women to child-bearing and domestic chores.

The era of colonization and its associated genocides had mostly been consigned to history, but not in Brazil where the Minister of the Interior's *Figueiredo Report* revealed crimes again Brazil's indigenous population. Since 1900, eighty indigenous tribes had been destroyed, and the overall indigenous population had been reduced from one million to two hundred thousand by incursions into the Amazon rain forest for mining, logging, money crops, and cattle ranching.

In the case of *Loving v. Virginia*, the US Supreme Court found inter-racial marriage to be legal. Before this decision, marrying someone of a different race was illegal in southeastern states, Missouri, West Virginia, and Delaware.

Gamal Abdel Nasser, Egypt's president, closed the Straits of Tiran to shipping to or from Israel and demanded that United Nations troops leave the Sinai Peninsula. These acts convinced the Israelis that war was inevitable, so they preemptively started the Six-Day War. Israel took full control of the city of Jerusalem, and with the confiscation of Arab land, they provided Christians and Jews access to the Tomb of the Patriarchs in Hebron—the traditional burial site of Abraham, Sarah, Isaac, Rebecca, Jacob, and Leah—for the first time in seven hundred years.

Around 1915, German geophysicist Alfred Wegener had proposed the theory of plate tectonics causing continental drift. By the 1960s, this was proven and accepted by almost all scientists. Fundamentalist Christians mostly accepted the theory because they interpreted Genesis 1:9–10 to imply that all land was once connected. They explained the spreading of the continents by believing that at the time of the worldwide flood, molten rock blasted up from the depths and split Earth's crust into separate bodies of land.

New York state passed a law allowing no-fault divorces. Prior to this, due to the powerful Catholic lobby, adultery had been the only grounds for divorce in the state.

The Macedonian Orthodox Church declared full independence from the Serbian Orthodox Church.

Anglican nurse, physician, and social worker Cicely Saunders founded the world's first modern hospice in England for the palliative care of patients approaching death. The Saint Christopher's program would expand to the US in 1971.

US history professor William Storey and graduate student Ralph Kiefer launched a charismatic renewal in the Catholic Church that involved a personal relationship with Jesus and expressed the gifts of the Holy Spirit.

The Abortion Act legalized the termination of pregnancies by registered practitioners under certain conditions in the United Kingdom.

1968

With great fanfare, Pope Paul VI returned the relics of Saint Mark to the Coptic Pope Kyrillos VI after they had been stored in Venice for eleven centuries.

Pope Paul VI issued *Humanae Vitae* (*On Human Life*), in which he renewed the condemnation of all forms of birth control except the rhythm method.

Four Spanish schoolgirls said they saw an apparition of the Virgin Mary near Palmar de Troya. One of the early witnesses, Clemente Domínguez y Gómez, claimed that Mary gave him her personal instructions on how to purge the Catholic Church of "heresy and progressivism." Later, miracles began to be associated with the site, and this initiated the Order of Carmelites of the Holy Face and the Palmarian Church.

Catholic priest Daniel Berrigan, his brother Philip, and seven other Catholic protesters burned draft files in Catonsville, Maryland, to protest US involvement in the Vietnam War.

The chair of Saint Peter, a wooden throne that had been a gift from the Holy Roman emperor to Pope John VIII in AD 875, was examined and scientifically dated to the sixth century. Before this, the prevailing belief was that the chair had been used by Peter when he served as the first bishop of Rome, even though it was extremely unlikely that Peter sat on a throne while meeting with his small congregation.

An archeological excavation under Saint Peter's Basilica in 1942 had uncovered human bones, which were then hidden away for safekeeping. This year, Pope Paul VI declared that they were the bones of Saint Peter and had been identified to his satisfaction.

The Italian government revoked the Vatican's tax-exempt status on income from its Italian investments.

US soldiers massacred and mutilated as many as 504 unarmed men, women, and children in the village of My Lai, South Vietnam. This revelation sickened average Americans, but due to the influence of President Richard Nixon, only one platoon leader, Lieutenant William Calley Jr., served any time incarcerated for the crime, and his sentence was only three and a half years under house arrest.

Many US evangelicals interpreted the woman's liberation movement, the hippie culture, and protestors of the Vietnam war as threats to traditional authority and an assault on the God-ordained social order. They gradually came to shift their attention from their theological differences to uniting in opposition to this crisis of cultural values.

1970

c. With contemporary worship music not suitable for church organs, many Protestant churches introduced worship teams, or praise teams, to lead the musical aspects of worship, using guitars, drums, and other nontraditional instruments.

The US Supreme Court upheld the constitutionality of the New York statute that exempted church property from taxation.

The US Congress removed contraceptives, and references to them, from the list of federal obscenity laws.

Some Christian organizations alleged that popular vinyl records had Satanic messages embedded in them that could only be heard if the record was played backwards on a turntable. The fear from this allegation led to boycotts and burnings of suspected records.

Hal Lindsay and Carole C. Carlson published *The Late, Great Planet Earth*, comparing biblical end-times prophecy with current events. The book inspired widespread interest in the end times and led to fear-based conversions by readers who believed the rapture and return of Christ was imminent.

c. At this time, the youth-oriented Jesus movement grew as a reaction to the prevailing US culture of war and racism and sought a return to the original communal life and morality of the early Christians. Many popular secular songs from the time either directly or obliquely mentioned Jesus, such as "Mrs. Robinson," "Jesus is Just Alright," "Spirit in the Sky," "Put Your Hand in the Hand," "Day by Day," "One Toke Over the Line," "Levon," "American Pie," "I Don't Know How to Love Him," and many others. The movement had its own popular singers, such as Randy Stonehill, Larry Norman, Chuck Girard, Keith Green, and Phil Keaggy.

Andrew Lloyd Webber and Tim Rice released their rock opera *Jesus Christ Superstar*. It offered another interpretation of the psychology of

Jesus and other related characters during the last week of Jesus's life in Jerusalem.

Proposed by Wisconsin Senator Gaylord Nelson, the first "Earth Day" took place as a day to focus on the environmental issues facing the US and the world.

The US congress passed the National Environmental Policy Act and two other environmental acts. The Environmental Protection Agency was also established this year.

The US congress passed the Clean Air Act, designed to regulate emissions from industrial and mobile sources in order to keep toxins out of our air and reduce the problems associated with smog and acid rain.

1971

American theologian Jim Wallis established Sojourners as a Christian social justice organization, and he became editor of their monthly magazine.

American minister Bill Gothard began youth conflict seminars, which provided ways for parents and teenagers to resolve problems. In 1989, the organization evolved into the Institute in Basic Life Principles and developed a purity culture that provided guidelines on topics from marriage to national morality.

1972

Elvis Presley recorded his seventeenth album, *He Touched Me*. This was his third album devoted entirely to gospel music, and it won him a second Grammy Award.

In an extensive study of glossolalia, the phenomena of "speaking in tongues," linguist William Samarin concluded that the sounds made during those occasions are meaningless human utterances, though the speakers usually believe them to be a real spiritual language. He discovered that those who spoken in tongues used only sounds from their native language.

Campus Crusade for Christ sponsored Explo '72 in Dallas, Texas. Dubbed the "Christian Woodstock," this was one of the most visible events of the 1970s Jesus movement. It included many celebrities, including Billy Graham, Johnny Cash, Kris Kristofferson, Chuck Girard and Love Song, Andraé Crouch and the Disciples, and Larry Norman. On the final day alone, over two hundred thousand young, mostly white, Christians attended.

Mike Warnke's book *The Satan Seller* was released. Warnke wrote of his own battles with Satan and Satanism before finding Jesus and becoming an evangelist. The book became a religious best seller and reinforced a belief that there was a vast underground network of Satanists in control of secular society. In 1992, *Cornerstone* magazine exposed Warnke's story as an embellished work of fiction.

The movie *Marjoe* won the Academy Award for best documentary feature. It followed the last preaching tour of Marjoe Gortner and showed how he manipulated crowds into donating money and believing that he performed miracles. The movie was suppressed in the US South because of the fear of the consequences of evangelical outrage.

On Stone Mountain, Georgia, work was completed on an enormous carving of three Confederate Civil War generals. This was the same place where the KKK had been reenergized in 1915.

The US Congress passed the Clean Water Act to regulate the discharge of pollutants into American's water systems.

The US experienced a major political scandal after a break-in at the Democratic National Committee headquarters in the Watergate Office Building in Washington, D.C. was tied to the Nixon administration. The scandal resulted in 69 government officials being charged, 48 being found guilty, Richard Nixon resigning the presidency in 1974.

1973

The Yom Kippur War began when an Arab coalition, including Egypt and Syria, attacked on two fronts, the Suez Canal and the Syrian Golan Heights. The war ended three weeks later with Israel still in control of the lands it had taken in 1967, but the war made some Israeli leaders realize that they needed to seek a lasting peace with the Arabs.

The Muslim Brotherhood perceived the defeat of the Arabs in the two wars with Israel as evidence that Arab leaders had strayed from the "pure teaching of Islam." This fear of losing God's blessing led to even more fundamentalist Islamic thinking and tactics.

The US Supreme Court decision in *Roe v. Wade* legalized abortion in the US. This action would become one of the most divisive in modern US Christian history. The Republican Party and the founders of the Moral Majority would use the issue of abortion to draw evangelicals into politics to overturn this ruling. Prior to *Roe v. Wade*, thirty states prohibited abortions, sixteen allowed them in certain situations, and four states allowed abortions on request.

Over a 3.2 million people attended Billy Graham's five-day "crusade" in South Korea. It was the largest gathering of Christians in history.

The movie *The Exorcist* was released in the US, leading to a revival in the belief of demon possession. Because of a renewed demand for exorcisms as a result of the movie, some clergy advertised themselves as "deliverers."

Elizabeth Clare Prophet founded Church Universal and Triumphant as a covering organization for other projects such as Summit Lighthouse and Summit University. Ten years later, she would predict the end of the world, and she and her followers would move to a remote region of Montana.

Following their interpretation of Mark 16:16–18, Pentecostals Jimmy Ray Williams and Buford Pack claimed that they could drink poison without harm because they had true faith. They died after drinking strychnine during a worship service in Tennessee.

The US Congress passed the Endangered Species Act to identify and protect species in threat of extinction.

1974

The Middle East Council of Churches held their first general assembly in Nicosia, Cyprus. It was a major ecumenical event, bringing the Eastern Orthodox Church and Oriental Orthodox Churches in the Middle East together for discussions. These churches didn't argue over doctrine but instead discussed how to deepen their spiritual fellowship and coordinate their resources to provide humanitarian assistance.

The Chicago Declaration of Evangelical Social Concern was the founding document for Evangelicals for Social Action. It was inspired by Ron Sider, author of the book *Rich Christians in an Age of Hunger*, who saw fighting against social injustice as part of his responsibility as a Christian. Some critics from the Christian Right saw Sider's book as contrary to biblical teachings.

American missionary Ralph D. Winter created the course Perspectives on the World Christian Movement to educate Christians about the history of Protestant missionary work and the needs that are still unfulfilled in spreading the message of Jesus to all the people in the world.

Kenn Gulliksen combined two Bible study groups that had been meeting at the houses of singers/songwriters Larry Norman and Chuck Girard. They met in Beverly Hills, California, and formed a church known as the Association of Vineyard Churches. Their meetings attracted many celebrities.

In the wake of the racial unrest of the past decade, West Virginia sought to introduce new textbooks that were more multicultural. After the Kanawha County school board approved the new books, fundamentalist Christian opponents rose in protest. This resulted in a boycott of public schools, violence against families who didn't participate in the boycott, and attacks on schools and school buses.

1975

In Lebanon, the flood of Arab refugees from Israel swung the national balance of power decidedly in Arab favor, outnumbering the native Maronite Christians. A civil war ignited between the Arab Palestine Liberation Organization (PLO) and Maronite forces. Over the next fifteen years, Israel, Syria, the United States, France, Italy, and many other countries would be drawn into the conflict, which would result in 120,000 deaths. Beirut, possibly the most beautiful and cosmopolitan city in the Middle East, was left in ruins, and thousands of Christians fled the country as refugees, further shrinking the Lebanese Christian population to about 40 percent.

Synods of the dioceses in West Germany issued stronger declarations assuming responsibility for Nazi crimes than the Vatican had at the Second Vatican Council.

For the first time since its founding in 1927, the Christian fundamentalist Bob Jones University in South Carolina admitted Black students but prohibited interracial dating.

1976

In 1976, President Ford rescinded Executive Order 9066, which had relocated Japanese Americans and Japanese nationals to camps as a national security precaution during World War II. In 1988, the US Congress would authorize reparations, but few of the original detainees were still living to benefit from these attempts at reconciliation.

Anne Nicol Gaylor, and Annie Laurie Gaylor founded the Freedom from Religion Foundation, a nonprofit organization that promotes separation of church and state and educates the public from a secular perspective. The organization began to publish a monthly newspaper named *Freethought Today*. The paper has evolved and not only delivers news on the free thought or atheist front but has a regular section called Black Collar Crime that lists two full pages of clergy members or church workers who have been charged with a crime, arrested, convicted, or sentenced. It also lists church-related civil lawsuits filed and settled and church financial crises—basically any religious figure or organization that made the news for their failure to follow the moral rules of society.

Francis Schaeffer's published his book *How Should We Then Live? The Rise and Decline of Western Thought and Culture*. It, as well as a ten-episode film series that supported the book, were extremely influential in motivating conservative Christians in the US to reject modern progressive philosophy and scientific discoveries.

The movie *The Omen* was released in the US. It, and its sequels, told a story of the birth and early life of the son of Satan, who as the Anti-Christ had been inserted at birth into an unaware and very influential American family.

Ralph Winter established the US Center for World Mission in Pasadena, California, with the goal of sending missionaries to "hidden peoples," those who up until then had not heard of Jesus. The organization later changed its name to Frontier Ventures.

Translations of fifteen volumes of the papyri uncovered in the 1897 Oxyrhynchus discovery in Egypt were published for the first time. Each new release of documents brought new insight into the ancient Christian era. The Bibles we are using today usually don't incorporate findings since the 1930 book *Vocabulary of the Greek Testament* so now technical journals shed a vastly different light on the early Christian period. Scholars are learning that many words in the New Testament have been mistranslated from the original Greek and therefore misunderstood.

California became the first US state to legally recognize living wills, which state a person's wishes for whether they will accept life-sustaining medical procedures. In 1984, the state would recognize durable powers of attorney for health care, which allowed the delegation of health care decisions to a designated individual if someone was unable to make these decisions for themselves. Many conservative Christians saw these practices as infringements on God's authority to determine the time of a person's death.

1977

With the outbreak of a civil war in Rhodesia (present-day Zimbabwe), several white Catholic missionaries disappeared or were found murdered. Seven missionaries were killed at Saint Paul's Mission, but the Black staff and native Christians were not targeted.

James Dobson founded Focus on the Family; a fundamentalist Christian organization concerned with the preservation of the traditional family. They support creationism, abstinence before marriage, school prayer, and traditional gender roles.

British missionaries Malcolm and Jean Hunter began to establish the Adopt-a-People program for North American churches to allow them to develop intimate relationships with non-Christian cultural-linguistic groups. They believed doing this would carry out the Great Commission of Jesus, which they interpreted to mean reaching all the world's twenty-four thousand ethnic groups.

In *Ingraham v. Wright*, the US Supreme Court ruled that corporal punishment is constitutional and left it to the individual states to decide how to control it.

1978

When Pope Paul VI died, Pope John Paul I was elected, but he too died shortly later. The cardinals then elected a Polish cardinal who became Pope John Paul II, the first non-Italian pope in 456 years. He traveled to Poland the following year and encouraged the Poles in their fight against Communism.

Members of the Palmarian Catholic Church of Spain claimed they had witnessed apparitions that declared that all popes after Paul VI were excommunicated and that the Holy See had been transferred to the Palmarian Church. The sect's founder, Clemente Domínguez y Gómez, became their first pope, calling himself Gregory XVII.

The Church of Scotland had begun allowing women as deaconesses to preach in 1949 but did not ordain women as pastors until this year, with Mary Levison being the first.

The US Internal Revenue Service eliminated the tax-exempt status of segregated Christian schools.

Jim Jones, a former Disciples of Christ minister, died along with 918 of his followers when they committed mass suicide, or were murdered, at their Peoples Temple compound in Jonestown, Guyana. Three hundred and four of the victims were children. Jones coerced them into drinking a fruit juice concoction laced with cyanide poison. This led to the phrase "drinking the Kool-Aid" to describe someone who had totally accepted an ideology, no matter how bizarre.

Jim Peters, the music director at the Zion Christian Life Center in St. Paul, Minnesota, instigated a campaign of burning and destruction of rock albums, claiming they were satanic and calling them "graven images." This protest spanned a wide range of popular music from John Denver and Linda Ronstadt to the Beatles and Electric Light Orchestra. Two years later he would again ignite a wave of fear by condemning the Proctor and Gamble corporate logo.

Maria Rubio of New Mexico was making burritos when she noticed a burn mark on a tortilla that looked to her like the face of Jesus Christ. She had a priest bless the tortilla and then created a shrine for it in her home. Thousands flocked there to witness the "miracle" and pray for divine assistance.

1979

In Israel, Gabriel Barkay discovered tiny silver scrolls that were originally worn as amulets around the neck. They were dated around 586 BC and, when closely examined, were found to contain the oldest Old Testament writing ever found—the priestly benediction from Numbers 6:24–26: "The Lord bless you and keep you; the Lord make his face shine on you and be gracious to you; the Lord turn his face toward you and give you peace."

Militant Muslims destroyed the fifth-century Coptic Church of Saint Mary the Virgin in Cairo.

Ted and Peggy Fletcher founded Pioneers, an evangelical missionary organization focused on reaching unreached people. In 2018, they sponsored over three thousand missionaries serving in one hundred countries.

US Baptist minister Jerry Falwell Sr. founded the Moral Majority, closely aligned with the Republican Party. He urged Protestant evangelicals to get involved in politics and challenge issues that pushed a "secular humanist" agenda. It appeared that if evangelicals couldn't fend off change with reasonable dialogue, they would do it by trying to legislate their preferred morality. That was exactly what the United States' Founding Fathers warned against because of what forcing one group's morality on a population did in Europe.

The US Fifth Circuit Court of Appeals, in *O'Hair v. Blumenthal*, upheld the use of In God We Trust on currency and coins, affirming that the "primary purpose of the slogan was secular," not religious.

Through Vineyard Ministries, folk singer Bob Dylan converted from his Jewish roots and became a born-again Christian. Over the next few years, he produced three Christian-themed albums and refrained from playing his earlier secular hits in concert. Over time, he would return to more of his original song lineup and avoid public displays of Christianity.

Dan O'Neill established Save the Refugees Fund as a secular humanitarian organization to provide relief to displaced people following the
Cambodian genocide. Over the years, it expanded its mission under
the name of Mercy Corps and has given assistance to people in 122
countries.

The secular humanitarian organization Action Against Hunger was
established in France with a commitment to end world hunger. As of
2020, it was active in forty-six countries with a staff of 8,500.

Sweden became the first country to ban corporal punishment of children. Since then, forty-nine countries have passed similar prohibitions. The United States is not one of them.

Following the Iranian revolution and the founding of an Islamic government, over 250 thousand Christians left the country, and those
who remained were discriminated against and persecuted.

The United State began aiding the rebels in Afghanistan who were
fighting against the invading Soviets. One of the recipients of US aid
was fundamentalist Muslim leader Osama bin Laden.

1980

As the Satanic panic was nearing its peak, the more conspiracy-
minded Christians accused Proctor and Gamble of using Satanic
imagery in the company's logo—a man in the moon and thirteen
stars. The symbol was believed to have been from ancient Egypt and
shown in English Egyptologist E. A. Wallis Budge's book *Amulets and
Superstitions*. Despite repeated denials of any connection, the paranoia wouldn't diminish and in 1985 the company announced that it
would change the logo.

The US Supreme Court overturned a Kentucky law that required
the Ten Commandments to be posted in Kentucky public school
classrooms.

Former California Governor Ronald Reagan embraced evangelicals in his bid for the White House. Later, after a series of high-profile sex and money-related scandals involving prominent Christian televangelists, Reagan reportedly distanced himself from the evangelicals and didn't seriously advance their agenda while in office.

A right-wing sniper killed Salvadoran archbishop Óscar Romero as he was conducting mass. He was a major figure of the Latin American liberation movement and had been a champion for social justice and a critic of El Salvador's military.

c. The issue of euthanasia gained national attention in the US in a debate over the ability and responsibility of physicians to artificially extend life. In the 1990s, the debate would grow to the legality of physician-assisted suicide, often called "death with dignity." Conservative Christians believed that physicians usurped God's prerogative when they assisted a patient in ending their own life.

Marjorie Matthews was consecrated as the first female bishop in the United Methodist Church.

The best-selling book *Michelle Remembers* chronicled a woman's repressed memories from Satanic ritual abuse. It was written by the patient Michelle Smith and her psychiatrist Lawrence Pazder. The book inspired other people to say they'd also had similar repressed memories. The problem was that the claims in the book didn't hold up to scrutiny and could not be proven to have happened.

1981

Francis Schaeffer published *A Christian Manifesto*, addressing the philosophical struggle between devout Christians and secular humanists. He urged the end of legalized abortion and influenced many conservative leaders to become more active in politics. "It is not too strong to say that we are at war, and there are no neutral parties in the struggle. One either confesses that God is the final authority, or one confesses that Caesar is Lord." He stressed that Christians could not afford to lose this war.

American televangelist Robert Schuller completed his opulent Crystal Cathedral in Garden Grove, California. It seated 2,736 people and at the time was the largest glass building in the world. Schuller became known for his weekly television program *Hour of Power.*

Near the town of Medjugorje, in present-day Bosnia, six children between the age of ten and seventeen reported being startled at dusk by a bright light. At its center was a beautiful woman who held an infant and floated above the ground. The figure visited them again the next day and identified herself as the Blessed Virgin Mary. After that, she appeared to the children almost daily at the same time but at different places. In 1984, she began to give messages to them for the parish and three years later began giving them messages for the entire world. When the Bosnian Civil War started in 1991, the children stopped meeting for the daily visits, but others saw the figure. The Vatican sanctioned Medjugorje as a pilgrimage site in 2019.

In *McLean v. Arkansas Board of Education*, the equal treatment of creation science and evolution science was challenged since it was said to violate the First Amendment. Judge William Overton ruled that creationism is religion, not science. Six years later, the US Supreme Court ruled similarly, making the ruling applicable nationwide.

1982

Christian antiabortion extremists established the Army of God, and members began a series of attacks against doctors and abortion clinics in the US.

The Vatican Bank was accused of channeling money through the Italian Banco Ambrosiano to various anti-Communist organizations. Roberto Calvi, who ran Banco Ambrosiano and was known as "God's Banker," was later found dead, most likely murdered.

Keith Green, one of the most popular American Christian singers and songwriters of his generation, died in a plane crash with two of his children and nine other people while on a tour of land owned by Green's Last Days Ministries.

Greg Livingstone developed Frontiers as a mission organization to spread Christianity to Muslims. They are currently active in thirty countries.

US evangelical pastor John Wimber left the Calvary Chapel organization and started the Anaheim Vineyard Christian Fellowship. Kenn Gulliksen merged his Vineyard churches with Wimber and began the Vineyard Movement.

1983

In Rome, Pope John Paul II made the first known papal visit to a Lutheran church in celebration of the five hundredth anniversary of the birth of Martin Luther.

During the Lebanese Civil War, militants exploded truck bombs at a peacekeeper's barracks in Beirut, killing 241 American and 58 French soldiers and marines. The troops were in Lebanon to try to restore order after an Israeli invasion that had apparently been sanctioned by the US.

The *Gospel of Judas*, a Gnostic gospel consisting of conversations between Jesus and Judas Iscariot and thought to have been composed in the second century, was found in a cave in Egypt.

Hillsong Church was established in Australia as a charismatic Pentecostal congregation with a strong emphasis in music. It would grow into an international megachurch with as many as 150,000 attending weekly.

The Family Research Council was founded as an American fundamentalist activist group very much involved in lobbying. It would become a division of Focus on the Family in 1988, before becoming independent again in 1992. It opposes stem cell research, abortion, divorce, and LGBT rights.

1984

Pope John Paul II and Syriac Orthodox Patriarch Ignatius Zakka I affirmed their bond as fellow Christians, calling their beliefs "one and the same faith."

The Italian government announced that Catholicism was no longer the state religion and officially declared themselves a secular state.

Survivors of sexual abuse by American Catholic priest Gilbert Gauthe refused hush money that had been offered by the Church and publicly testified against him. Gauthe confessed to abusing thirty-seven children in the diocese of Lafayette, Louisiana.

At the Saint John of God Church in Chicago, witnesses reported that a thirty-nine-inch-tall wooden statue of the Virgin Mary began to weep. Within days, thousands of people came to witness the event. An investigation later concluded that no miracle was involved but did not explicitly claim the phenomenon was a hoax. This was one of several incidents of crying or bleeding statues that have been reported since the 1950s.

A committee of European doctors studying reported incidents of healing at the Lourdes grotto in France decided that sixty-four cases were possibly miraculous, but six thousand others were not. A few years before, British psychologist Donald West determined that all the cures were the result of psychosomatic influences.

1985

The National Family Violence Resurvey found that 8.7 million US married couples experienced violence in their relationship over the past year. This prompted James Alsdurf of the Fuller Seminary to conduct a survey of 5,700 American and Canadian evangelical pastors to deter-mine their feelings about spouse abuse in Christian families. The sur-vey found that 27 percent of the pastors would tell an abused wife that she should submit to her husband and "trust that God would honor her actions by either stopping the abuse or giving her the strength to endure it." The survey also reported that 71 percent of pastors would never advise a battered wife to leave her husband. Alsdurf and his wife Phyllis later wrote the book *Battered into Submission: The Tragedy of Wife Abuse in the Christian Home.*

Granger Westberg, a Lutheran pastor and professor, started the Parish Nursing Program in Illinois. This organization encouraged the merg-ing of religion and medicine in the healing process. By 2015, they had more than fifteen thousand participating nurses in many countries.

The Quiverfull movement began after the publication of Mary Pride's book *The Way Home: Beyond Feminism, Back to Reality.* She encour-aged Christian wives to submit to their husbands, promoted unlim-ited procreation, and encouraged abstinence from all forms of birth control.

Desmond Tutu became the first Black Anglican bishop of Johannesburg, South Africa, which at the time was racially segregated under their apartheid system.

The Westar Institute hosted the first Jesus Seminar. The seminar's goal was to better understand the historical Jesus by establishing which verses of the Gospels were most likely authentic. In 1993, the semi-nar would publish a book called *The Five Gospels*, which included the *Gospel of Thomas* along with the four canonical Gospels and rated all the biblical sayings of Jesus as to their probability of being authen-tic. Although members were reputable scholars, the seminar was very controversial among Christians.

In the Philippines, Amparo Santos, known as Mother Paring, allowed herself to be physically crucified—literally nailed to a cross—to model Jesus's suffering. She carried out this act of devotion annually for fifteen years. When asked why, she said that the Virgin Mary asked her to do it.

The Iraqi army, on the orders of Saddam Hussein, conducted what is known as the Anfal genocide in Kurdistan, which is partly in Iraq. Human Rights Watch reported the extermination of between fifty thousand and nearly two hundred thousand Kurds and the destruction of over two hundred Assyrian Christian villages, churches, and monasteries.

The Iran-Contra scandal occurred. It was a covert operation by the Reagan administration to sell missiles to the Islamic Republic of Iran—then under an arms embargo, and use the money to fund rebels in Nicaragua—against the wishes of the US Congress. Most of those indicted were pardoned by George H. W. Bush when he became president.

1987

Randall Terry led hundreds of pro-life Christians from Operation Rescue as they blocked access to an abortion clinic in Cherry Hill, New Jersey. By the time Terry left the group four years later, he had been arrested more than forty times.

In Virginia, Christian broadcaster Pat Robertson founded the Christian Coalition of America as a nonprofit, voter-based organization designed to elect Christian candidates to political offices. The expected result was the Christianization of the federal government, which would lead to US society being controlled by Christian morality.

American televangelist Jim Bakker, who headed Praise the Lord Ministries, resigned following a sex scandal. He was later convicted of financial fraud and sentenced to prison.

The US Supreme Court struck down a Louisiana law that required public schools teaching evolutionary theory to provide equal time to "creation science."

Charismatic televangelist and faith healer Oral Roberts made head-lines when he appealed to his supporters for $8 million, saying that if he didn't receive it in three months, God was going to "call me home," meaning end his life. His congregation came through and raised over $9 million for him.

Charles Thaxton used the engineering term *intelligent design* to de-scribe a new kind of creationism in which the appearance of design in living beings and in the natural world pointed to an intelligent de-signer or creator. The term *God* is not mentioned in intelligent design but is implied.

Peter Popoff, a well-known Christian faith healer, went bankrupt after skeptics proved that he received information about certain audience members through an earpiece.

Irish Catholic priest Alec Reid attempted to bring peace to Northern Ireland where there had been a violent revolt by the Irish Republican Army (IRA) against British rule since the late 1960s. His efforts would pay off eleven years later.

1988

Pat Robertson, the fundamentalist Christian media celebrity, ran for president. He got off to a good start in Iowa, finishing ahead of George H.W. Bush, but was not competitive after that and returned to his broadcasting career.

Scientists at Oxford University used carbon dating to determine that the Shroud of Turin was made in the thirteenth or fourteenth century. If so, it couldn't have been the actual Holy Shroud of Jesus, but how the images were imprinted on the cloth is still not fully understood.

The Assemblies of God denomination defrocked televangelist Jimmy Swaggart after he admitted to having a sexual affair with a prostitute. Three years later, he was found with a prostitute again, but despite all of that, his Jimmy Swaggart Ministries is still active.

After forty years of inaction, and over one hundred other countries signing, the United States conditionally ratified the United Nations Genocide Convention. South African sociologist Leo Kuper speculated that the long delay had been from the "fear that [the US] might be held responsible, retrospectively, for the annihilation of Indians in the United States, or its role in the slave trade, or its contemporary support for tyrannical governments engaging in mass murder."

Edgar C. Whisenant wrote *88 Reasons Why the Rapture Will Be in 1988*. He predicted it on October 4, but when it failed to occur, Whisenant said the fault must have been due to biblical errors.

Scientists had enough evidence to sound the alarm that the accumulation of carbon dioxide in Earth's atmosphere was causing the surface of the planet to get hotter. People who believed this was a real and imminent danger began to act, but the critical mass for a worldwide response has not occurred.

1989

Operation Rescue staged an abortion confrontation at a clinic in Los Angeles. Police arrested 700 members of the group for blocking entrance to the medical clinic.

After a series of lawsuits and scandals, Oral Roberts was forced to close his City of Faith medical center, sell his homes in Palm Springs and Beverly Hills, and sell his three Mercedes cars.

1990

The United States led an international coalition of military allies to war against Iraq in response to its invasion of Kuwait and the threat to the global oil supply. Because of the war, thousands of Western forces were stationed in Saudi Arabia. Since this was the Islamic Holy Land, their presence was intolerable to militant Muslims, and this helped in recruiting new members for terrorist organizations such as Al-Qaeda.

Pakistani officials arrested Tahir Iqbal, a Christian living in Pakistan, for blasphemy after he had underlined passages and made marginal notes in a copy of the Koran. He died in prison two years later from poisoning.

Bill McCartney founded Promise Keepers as an evangelical organization to help Christian men grow in their faith. Seven years later, the organization staged an event at the National Mall in Washington, DC, which attracted at least six hundred thousand men.

The National Cathedral in Washington, DC, was completed after eighty-three years of construction.

Pope John Paul II consecrated the Basilica of Our Lady of Peace in Yamoussoukro, Ivory Coast. By square footage, it is the largest church in the world.

The US launched the Hubble Space Telescope into orbit. With no atmospheric interference, its clarity began to change our concept of the universe. It helped scientists determine the age of the universe and its rate of expansion, discover that every major galaxy has a black hole in its center, measure elements in the atmosphere of a planet orbiting another star, and show various stages of star formation and decline.

1991

The Muslim enclave of Chechnya declared its independence from Russia, but Russia would not allow it and invaded the breakaway republic two years later.

Croatia seceded from Yugoslavia, causing a civil war between native Croatians and Serbs who lived there. The country of Yugoslavia had been cobbled together after World War I from independent Balkan states and lacked unity. The Balkan states were the ancient boundary between the eastern and western halves of the Roman Empire and more recently between Christian Europe and the Ottoman Empire. This was an area of mixed ethnicities and religions with most Serbs being Orthodox Christians, most Croatians Catholic, and half of the Bosnians Muslim. Once the Croatians declared their independence, Yugoslavia began to split apart along the former religious and ethnic lines.

Polish president Lech Walesa apologized to the Israeli Parliament for Poland's role in the Jewish Holocaust since many of the death camps had been in Poland and many Poles participated to some degree. Auschwitz-Birkenau, Sobibor, Majdanek, Chelmno, Belzek, and Treblinka were all in Poland.

The US Senate threatened to eliminate or reduce funding for a Smithsonian Institution project that referred to what the US had done to the Native Americans as "genocide."

On a ranch in Tlacote, Mexico, a dog was reported to have been miraculously cured of an ailment after drinking the water from a well. People began to drink the water to see if it helped them. What began as a trickle of people turned into a flood as lines grew so long that people had to sometimes wait days for their chance to get some of the free "healing" water. When tested, the water was found to be high in mineral content, but otherwise normal. Despite the analysis, the ranch's owner began to sell the product after concluding "All God's creatures have the right to sell. It's the divine right of commercialism."

Laurel Rose Willson, writing as Lauren Stratford, published *Satan's Underground*. The book chronicled Lauren's nightmarish story of being raised by a Satanist cult and surviving only because of her unwavering faith in God. Later, Willson changed her name again and claimed to be a Holocaust survivor. Her frauds were later debunked by *Cornerstone* magazine, but *Satan's Underground* is still available today as a book of nonfiction.

With the fall of the Soviet Union and the decreasing threat from Communism, the Religious Right found their new primary threat to be the New World Order. This was based partly on scriptural prophesies of an Antichrist and a distrust of any unifying force in world government.

The Teen Mania organization introduced Acquire the Fire, a twenty-seven-hour youth gathering of music and teaching. They would go on to hold over five hundred of these events in the US.

1992

With the ending of the Soviet Union, members of the Ukrainian Catholic Church began to emerge from hiding and seek the pope's protection. They developed an intense rivalry with the Ukrainian Orthodox Church for the power and property that was being returned to the Churches after the Communist collapse.

Bosnia and Herzegovina voted for independence from Serbian-dominated Yugoslavia. A three-year-long war followed as Bosnian Serbs, supported by the now-independent country of Serbia, conducted a program of ethnic cleansing including mass extermination of Bosnian Muslims and Croatians. More than 104,000 people were killed, and 2.2 million were forced to flee their homes.

After a thirteen-year investigation, the Vatican officially admitted that Galileo had been right about the structure of the solar system and the location of our world within that system. The pope apologized for condemning and imprisoning him in 1633. This was an admission that the Church had misinterpreted the scriptures.

After a rabbi spoke at a middle school graduation in Rhode Island, the parents of Deborah Wiesman filed a lawsuit against the school's principle. In *Lee v. Weisman*, the US Supreme Court prohibited clergy-led prayer at public schools.

In Massachusetts, victims accused Father James Porter of sexually abusing more than one hundred children, creating a national outcry. His diocese was eventually forced to settle lawsuits and adopt a policy on how to handle similar accusations. This scandal was later portrayed in the 2015 movie *Spotlight*.

The leader of the Dami Mission in Seoul, South Korea, predicted that the rapture would occur on October 28, and this news spread to the US. Some followers took the prediction seriously and sold their houses, quit their jobs, and abandoned worldly possessions. When the day came and went, many who had taken the advice seriously took their rage out on local pastors, forcing the mission to disband.

1993

Muslim terrorists exploded a truck bomb under the World Trade Center in New York City, hoping to bring the north tower crashing into the south tower, but their plan failed. Six people were killed, and over one thousand were injured.

The Branch Davidians, led by David Koresh, were a religious cult and an offshoot of the Davidian Seventh-day Adventist Church. Because it was believed that they had a stockpile of illegal weapons, federal Alcohol, Tobacco, and Firearms (ATF) agents attempted to serve a search warrant at their compound near Waco, Texas. The raid was intended to surprise the Davidians and confiscate their weapons, but they were tipped off, and a two-hour gun battle ensued. After a stand-off lasting fifty-one days, the federal agents assaulted the compound, but tragedy occurred when complex caught fire and seventy-six of the Davidians died in the conflagration.

Archeologists found a stone engraved with the inscription "House of David" at Tel Dan, Israel. This was the first non-biblical confirmation that King David was an actual historical person.

US forces found themselves fighting in another Muslim country, this time as part of a United Nations attempt to defuse a civil war in Somalia. After only limited success, the UN withdrew all their re-sources two years later.

The Vatican established diplomatic relations with Israel. This had been delayed because of the Vatican's disapproval of Israel's treatment of Palestinian Christians. Both parties agreed to the protection of Church property and traditional sacred sites in Israel, freedom to teach and train Christians, and freedom of religion.

During the Algerian Civil War, Islamic militants killed twelve technicians from Croatia and Bosnia, adding to the growing number of foreigners killed in Algeria that year. The militants would go on to conduct terrorist attacks in Europe, and the war would not end until 2004.

American televangelist Robert Tilton's television program *Success-N-Life* went off the air after it was disclosed that Tilton threw away prayer requests but kept whatever money or valuables viewers sent him, amounting to about $80 million a year.

The Southern Baptists launched the True Love Waits campaign to promote sexual abstinence for Christian youth by having them take a purity pledge. They stressed virginity as the ideal nature for teens. Later, it was discovered that these pledges only introduced more shame concerning their bodies and sex. Many teens were taught that even physical attraction and desires were a threat to salvation.

1994

At the United Nations, 180 countries met to draft a proposal about the coming crisis of overpopulation. The Catholic Church opposed the plan, thereby allying itself with Islamic countries such as Iran and Libya.

Pope John Paul II and Patriarch Dinkha IV of the Assyrian Church of the East signed a declaration reestablished connection for the first time since the fifth century.

Fundamentalist Christians Michael and Debi Pearl created considerable controversy with their book *To Train Up a Child*. They advocated corporal punishment to guide a children's moral development in ways that many viewed as child abuse. Focus on the Family, along with numerous states, also currently allow for, but may stop short of encouraging, corporal punishment. There are many Old Testament verses that support physically disciplining children, such as Proverbs 22:15: "Folly is bound up in the heart of a child, but the rod of discipline will drive it far away."

In Pakistan, paleontologists found fossils that were transitional between land mammals and whales. The ancestors to whales returned to an aquatic environment from land, so these findings were a true missing link. During this decade, at other locations, fossils were also discovered of a fish-like four-legged creature with internal gills, and even a fish containing digits (fingers) in its fins. While these transitions were unknown as recently as 1980, today they are better understood and are answering questions about extinct transitional species in the evolutionary process.

The Toronto Blessing, a charismatic revival said to have been inspired by revivals in other countries, began at the Toronto Airport Vineyard Church. It was characterized by holy laughter, rolling on the floor in ecstasy, and miracles. By the following year, *Charisma Magazine* would report that four thousand English churches and seven thousand North American churches were influenced by this movement.

1995

Swiss astronomers Didier Queloz and Michel Mayor confirmed the existence of a planet beyond our solar system, approximately fifty light years from us in the constellation Pegasus. Its orbit was so unusual that it necessitated the rethinking of theories of planetary formation.

The Joshua Project began in Colorado as an organization to coordinate the work of missionary organizations in evangelizing non-Christian ethnic groups around the world.

Domestic terrorists Timothy McVeigh and Terry Nichols blew up the federal building in Oklahoma City, Oklahoma, killing 168 people.

They were motivated in part by the federal government's handling of standoffs with reclusive families at Ruby Ridge, Idaho, and with the Branch Davidians at Waco, Texas.

Tim LaHaye and Jerry B. Jenkins began publishing their *Left Behind* series of sixteen best-selling novels that gave a fantasized version of what they believed was the coming Apocalypse. It brought the themes of the Anti-Christ, the Rapture, and tribulation together in a frightening way.

Scientists at the Institute for Genomic Research published the first complete genome of a living organism, a bacterium. As DNA sequencing, starting in the 1970s, became more widely used, it's been another way to compare the relationship between various species. This type of comparison has shown that humans and chimpanzees share about 98 percent of their DNA.

Proctor and Gamble sued Amway distributors because they used voice mail to tell customers that P&G profits were going to a satanic cult. Proctor and Gamble eventually won nineteen million dollars in damages and reintroduced the moon to their logo.

1996

The journal *Science* carried an article by American laser chemist Richard Zare and his team describing what seemed to be evidence of bacterial life on Mars. This evidence was seen in a meteorite found in Antarctica that was billions of years old and had apparently once been part Mars. Zare would have to temporarily suspend his website due to religious fundamentalists claiming that his discovery conflicted with the Bible.

The leaders of the Roman Catholic and the Armenian Churches signed a declaration to reconcile their differences.

The US Congress passed the Defense of Marriage Act, and twenty-five states banned same sex marriage.

Assyrian Church Patriarch Dinkha IV and Chaldean Catholic Church Patriarch Raphael I signed an agreement to end their historical differences.

1997

Oregon was the first US state to pass a Death with Dignity Act that allowed doctors to prescribe lethal medications to terminally ill people so they could end their lives in comfort. In 1990, Jack Kevorkian, a medical pathologist, had begun the practice of assisting terminally ill patients to end their lives with medication, but he was eventually found guilty of murder and spent several years in prison. Many Christians opposed the procedure because of the sanctity of life and their belief that only God has the right to decide when a person should die.

Joshua Harris published his book *I Kissed Dating Goodbye*. This was a bestseller aimed at evangelical youth and emphasized sexual purity as the best way to ultimately attain a happy marriage. In 2019 he and his wife would separate, and he would reveal that he no longer was a Christian. He also apologized for the fear and harm his book had caused.

1998

The Vatican apologized for not taking more decisive action in challenging the Nazis' treatment of the Jews during World War II. The apology stopped short of condemning Pope Pius XII or any antisemitic behavior that could be traced to the teachings of the Church and its clergy.

Ireland's thirty-year-long nationalist-religious conflict, commonly known as "The Troubles," ended with the Belfast Good Friday Agreement.

Serbia, which is predominantly Orthodox Christian, prevented Kosovo, a region largely populated by Muslim Albanians, from gaining independence. In the war that ensued, NATO air support was deployed to prevent a humanitarian disaster there like there had been in recent Balkan wars. By the time the war ended the following year, between 1.2 million and 1.4 million Albanians had been displaced, and Serbs were accused of killing thousands of civilians.

Islamic terrorists bombed US embassies in Nairobi, Kenya, and Dar es Salaam, Tanzania, killing 224 people. These attacks occurred exactly eight years after US troops entered Saudi Arabia in response to Iraq's invasion of Kuwait.

Westboro Baptist Church of Topeka, Kansas, began to picket at the funerals of a homosexuals. They eventually expanded their efforts to disrupt the funerals of military service members killed in the wars in Iraq and Afghanistan. Examples of some of their signs were God Hates Fags and Thank God for Dead Soldiers. This church became a symbol of the hatred that judgmental Christians can exemplify with remarks like this news release: "JEWS KILLED JESUS! Yes, the Jews killed the Lord Jesus . . . Now they're carrying water for the fags; that's what they do best: sin in God's face every day, with unprecedented and dispro-portionate amounts of sodomy, fornication, adultery, abortion and idolatry! God hates these dark-hearted rebellious disobedient Jews."

The first Harry Potter book, *Harry Potter and the Sorcerer's Stone*, was released in the US. Some evangelical churches told their congregations to avoid the book because of its wizards and magic. A few years later, an evangelical gospel tract by Jack Chick declared "the Potter books open a doorway that will put untold millions of kids in hell."

1999

Between sixty and eighty members of the Christian terrorist organi-zation Concerned Christians were discovered to be missing from their Colorado homes. The next time they were heard from, they were in Israel where they were arrested and deported on suspicion of plan-ning attacks on Muslim holy sites in Jerusalem, including the Al-Aqsa Mosque. They reportedly believed the destruction of the mosque and their possible deaths were necessary for the return of Jesus at the end of the millennium.

Fueled by the fear of computer failures and end-of-the-world scenarios, many people began to panic when Y2K, the year 2000, approached.

The US Internal Revenue Service denied the Christian Coalition tax-exempt status because it engaged in political activities. This forced the organization to relocate their headquarters to Texas because the Christian Coalition of Texas had received tax-exempt status as a social welfare organization.

European Christians concluded a Reconciliation Walk from Cologne, Germany, to Jerusalem to mark the nine hundred years since the conquest of the city by crusaders. They sought to apologize and seek forgiveness for the barbaric actions of the crusaders.

At a symposium on Jan Hus held in Rome, Pope John Paul II issued an apology for the Czech reformer's execution by the Catholic Church in 1415.

CHAPTER 21: TWENTY-FIRST CENTURY AD

If one has the answers to all the questions—that is the proof that God is not with him. It means that he is a false prophet using religion for himself. The great leaders of the people of God, like Moses, have always left room for doubt. You must leave room for the Lord, not for our certainties; we must be humble.

—Pope Francis

Many churches of all persuasions are hiring research agencies to poll neighborhoods, asking what kind of church they prefer. Then the local churches design themselves to fit the desires of the people. True faith in God that demands selflessness is being replaced by trendy religion that serves the selfish.

—Billy Graham

We don't have to protect the environment; the Second Coming is at hand.

—James Watt

The New Right, in many cases, is doing nothing less than placing a heretical claim on Christian faith that distorts, confuses, and destroys the opportunity for a biblical understanding of Jesus Christ and of his gospel for millions of people.

—Mark Hatfield

Progressing into the current century, we seemed to have no better idea of how to define a "real Christian" than they had in the first century AD. After the horrendous actions of a few militant Muslims, many Americans overreacted against the religion of Islam. American evangelicals became even more identified with the Republican Party and with a Christian nationalist movement that seemingly wanted to rewrite the US Constitution. People with nontraditional sexual relationships were better accepted by sympathetic Christians but hated and condemned by conservative Christians, as more Europeans and Americans tired of religious irrationality and intolerance. Sexual and financial scandals involved both Catholic and Protestant clergymen.

2000

The Catholic Church held a Great Jubilee for the entire year. It celebrated many events, drawing attention to everything from prison reform to senior citizen issues. On the Day of Pardon, Pope John Paul II begged for forgiveness for sins committed by Catholics throughout their history, especially if committed in the name of the Church.

US evangelicals decisively supported Republican George W. Bush, a born-again Christian, in his run for the presidency.

After a series of lawsuits aimed at Bob Jones University's racial policies and tax-exempt status, the university finally ended its ban on interracial dating.

Joseph Ratzinger, who would become Pope Benedict XVI, signed the declaration of *Dominus Iesus* (*The Lord Jesus*), which restated the doctrine that the Catholic Church is the sole true Church of Christ and that non-Christians are seriously deficient when it comes to a means of salvation. The declaration was approved by Pope John Paul II, who said, "This confession does not deny salvation to non-Christians, but points to its ultimate source in Christ, in whom man and God are united."

c. What became known as "Gabriel's Revelation" was found, consisting of eighty-seven lines of Hebrew text written on a stone slab near the Dead Sea. Most scholars believe it to be authentic and dated between the first century BC and the early first century AD, the pre-Christian era. It contains sayings with the theme of a Messiah ben Joseph, meaning "son of Joseph." There is a vague statement about a possible resurrection of someone who is thought by some scholars to have been Simon of Peraea, who was killed by the Romans in 4 BC, but much of this is inconclusive.

The Oberammergau Passion Play went through a radical makeover with some ancient Jews portrayed in the positive role of defending Jesus, while others, but not all, were portrayed as supporting the religious leaders against him. Also, Muslims performed in the play for the first time.

Patrick Henry College was founded in Virginia as a Christian liberal arts college. Currently, it promotes itself as an institute for students who have been homeschooled, with 78 percent of the student body falling into that category.

By this year, more than a quarter of the world's Christians would identify themselves as Pentecostals or Charismatics.

2001

John Eldredge published his book *Wild at Heart*. It encouraged Christian men to rediscover their innate wildness and masculinity and use those traits to better serve God. This book helped influence a generation of young Christian men toward a more confrontational and patriarchal Christianity.

Nineteen terrorists from the militant Islamic organization Al-Qaeda hijacked commercial airliners and flew them into the World Trade Center in New York City and the Pentagon in Washington, DC, then attempted to strike another target. These strikes killed 2,977 people and caused an unprecedented wave of anger and fear across the US, with repercussions around the world. In response, the US attacked Al-Qaeda training sites in Afghanistan and drove the Taliban, the ruling party who had harbored Al-Qaeda, from power. Two days later, Pat Robertson had fellow televangelist Jerry Falwell on his show, and they agreed that God allowed the attacks due to the "moral decay" in our country, mentioning the ACLU, abortionists, feminists, and gays as examples of our moral depravity.

After the terrorist attacks in the US and the resulting Islamophobia, the militant, conservative wing of our society had a new evil enemy to replace the Soviet Union.

The Holy Land Experience theme park opened in Orlando, Florida. It included the Scriptorium—a museum containing a large collection of artifacts from biblical times—along with a restaurant, retail shops, theaters, facilities for bible studies, a two-thousand-seat auditorium for church services, and Smile of a Child Adventure Land. By 2021, with declining revenue, the property would be sold for redevelopment.

2002

Jewish, Islamic, and Christian religious leaders signed the Alexandrian Declaration, which declared the Holy Land in Israel to be a sanctuary for all three faiths and called for an end to violence in that region.

A Barna Group survey showed that despite relentless efforts by Christian clergy in the United States, only 3 percent of adults contributed the anticipated tithe of ten percent or more of their household income to the church.

2003

Begun in 1990, the Human Genome Project completed its work of revealing the genetic blueprint for human beings. Subsequent research would demonstrate how similar human DNA is to the DNA of other species of animals, and even plants, a further confirmation of the process of evolution because it indicated that all life can be traced back a single source.

Charles Dyer's book *The Rise of Babylon: Sign of the End Times* portrayed Iraqi president Saddam Hussein as the Anti-Christ. According to Dyer, Hussein was rebuilding Babylon, signaling the approaching Armageddon.

President George W. Bush's administration fabricated and exaggerated information to justify a US invasion of Iraq and convince Congress to support the invasion. They used the imagined threat of Iraq's possession of weapons of mass destruction to support their case for war. The outpouring of international sympathy for the US after the 9/11 attacks dissolved with this controversial war as it dragged on for over eight years. The war reduced many parts of Iraq to ruins and turned the populace to anarchy, destabilized most of the Middle East, did not disclose any weapons of mass destruction, subjected Iraqi Christians to the wrath of anti-Christian mobs, and encouraged more sympathy for the militants and their causes.

The Episcopal Diocese of New Hampshire elected Gene Robinson, a priest living in a committed gay relationship, as bishop. Consequently, conservative Episcopalians sought to disassociate themselves from the Episcopal Church of the United States.

In Iraq, radical clerics, such as Muqtada al-Sadr, not only denounced moderate Muslim opponents but declared them un-Islamic. Like other powerful clerics, he surrounded himself with an armed militia, reminiscent of the bishops of Alexandria in the fifth century.

Over one thousand Christians attended the Heal Our Land conference in Winterthur, Switzerland. Its purpose was to seek God's help in healing broken relationships between Christian sects. Some Reformed pastors carried remorse for the way their church's founder, Ulrich Zwingli, and his associates and descendants had persecuted the Anabaptists for several hundred years.

American author Dan Brown published *The Da Vinci Code*, which concerned a two-thousand-year cover-up of the fact that Jesus and Mary Magdalene had a child together and had a descendent that was still alive. It earned the label of blasphemy and created a huge disturbance throughout the evangelical Christian community.

2004

Sam Harris's book *The End of Faith: Religion, Terror, and the Future of Reason* became a best seller in the United States. Motivated by the 9/11 attacks, Harris was one of several modern atheist writers who used the term *new atheism* to describe a renewed social movement toward atheism and secularism as the way to end religious violence. They believed that religion should not be granted blanket respect and toleration because too often it crosses the line into controlling the lives of others. Instead, it should be countered, criticized, and exposed by rational argument wherever its influence arises. The new atheists were reminiscent of the freethinkers at the end of the nineteenth century.

The United Methodist Church passed resolutions to discourage parents using child beating as a form of discipline. The organization also called upon states to prohibit corporal punishment in schools, day cares, and residential facilities.

The Eastern Orthodox patriarch in Istanbul accepted an apology, offered by Pope John Paul II in 2001, for the sacking of Constantinople by crusaders in 1204.

After watching TV coverage of the genocide in Rwanda, prominent Oklahoma minister Carlton Pearson said he received an epiphany from God. This led him to state that he no longer believed in hell as a place of eternal torment but rather what we can experience on Earth. Because of his declaration, he was branded a heretic, his congregation shrank from six thousand to under a thousand, and the church eventually closed in 2006. Pearson found like minds in the Unitarian denomination.

2005

In Pennsylvania, the civil trial *Kitzmiller v. Dover Area School District* challenged the teaching of "intelligent design" in schools. The plaintiffs successfully argued that intelligent design is a form of religious creationism and that teaching it in public schools violated the First Amendment.

Pope John Paul II died. Over the course of his papacy, he had made 104 international trips to 130 countries, though he had never been invited to Russia or China. He had renewed dialogue with formerly schismatic Christian Churches, Jews, and Muslims. John Paul II is remembered as a voice against violence and war and was widely respected during his twenty-seven years in office, even forgiving the man who shot him during an assassination attempt.

The international organization Human Rights Watch revealed evidence that US Army personnel were ignoring the Geneva Convention and torturing prisoners captured in its war on terrorism. Human Rights Watch held many American leaders, including President George W. Bush, responsible for these actions because the administration bypassed any international laws they considered too restrictive. Prisoners were held for years in secret prisons without formal charges or trials, and many were tortured and humiliated to obtain information, although information obtained through these means has been repeatedly found to be unreliable and often further radicalizes the victim.

The US Supreme Court ruled in *McCreary County v. ACLU of Kentucky* that the display of the Ten Commandments on courthouse property was unconstitutional. On the same day, in *Van Orden v. Perry*, the same court decided it was constitutional to keep another monument inscribed with the same Commandments in place at the Texas State Capitol.

Terri Schiavo, a woman who had been in an irreversible vegetative brain state for years, was finally taken off a feeding tube and died in

Florida. This followed a long religious and legal battle about when life ends and what extremes to go to extend a life. The Catholic Church came down against removing the tube if she was still breathing.

At this time, the Assyrian Church of the East had only four hundred thousand remaining members, the Ancient Assyrian Church had fifty to seventy thousand, and the Chaldean Catholic Church around six hundred thousand.

2006

Ted Haggard, a Colorado pastor and president of the National Association of Evangelicals, made national headlines when he was accused of paying a male prostitute for sex and using methamphetamine. He resigned his leadership roles and later confessed to both accusations.

A federal court convicted Kent Hovind, a prominent American Baptist minister and vocal advocate for Young Earth Creationism, on 58 federal tax offenses.

2007

Former US presidential candidate Al Gore was awarded the Nobel Peace Prize for his efforts to alert the world to the dangers of human-caused climate change. Even at this point, anti-science conservative Christians still rejected the idea because they believed that a loving God wouldn't let harm come to them or their descendants, mere humans had no power to change the atmosphere, the Rapture was imminent, Earth had been through worse crises in the past and survived okay, and other completely unscientific thinking. Their rejection of scientists' warnings assured that the US would not lead the way out of the coming crisis and obscured the meaning of stewardship of Earth.

Leaders of the Russian Orthodox Church and the Russian Orthodox Church Outside of Russia officially ended a division that had begun in 1927.

The Taliban captured twenty-three South Korean Christian mission-aries in Afghanistan. They executed two of them and eventually freed the rest.

Muslim students killed and burned their teacher Christiana Oluwasesin, a Nigerian Christian, for allegedly desecrating the Koran after she unintentionally threw a copy of it on the ground with a student's other books. Then they beat up the school's principal and burned part of the school.

There were over 1,200 megachurches in the US with weekly attendance of two thousand or more. This was up from only 350 of these churches in 1990.

Leaders of the Coptic Orthodox Church and the Ethiopian Orthodox Church declared their unity of faith and an interest in expanding cooperation.

Australian-born fundamentalist Ken Ham opened the Creation Museum in Kentucky to promote a biblical explanation of the origin of the universe and life on Earth. Ham and his backers were Young Earth Creationists who assumed the universe was roughly six thousand years old. Being almost completely unscientific, and clearly biased toward the Bible, the museum has received its share of criticism.

Frank Schaeffer, the son of Francis and Edith Schaeffer, published the book *Crazy for God: How I Grew Up as One of the Elect, Helped Found the Religious Right, and Lived to Take All (or Almost All) of It Back.* As the titles implies, Schaeffer spent his childhood in his parents' Christian enclave in Switzerland, rubbing shoulders with the who's who of American Christian celebrities, but eventually rejected the evangelical movement he had helped to build via cooperative efforts with his father and became a secular writer.

Kalen Fristad and Eric Stetson founded the Christian Universalist Association to advocate that universalism is the main theme of the Gospels and that belief in a retributive God and hell was mistaken.

2008

René Salm published *The Myth of Nazareth: The Invented Town of Jesus*. Based on all available archeological evidence, Salm concluded that the town of Nazareth was uninhabited at the time of Jesus, and therefore, he could not have lived there. The term *Nazarene* is still confusing.

The city council in Demre, Turkey, removed a bronze statue of native-born Saint Nicholas wearing a halo and holding a Bible and replaced it with him in the guise of Santa Claus, in red winter clothes, carrying a sack over his shoulder and ringing a bell. The new statue would be removed during construction work in 2017 and replaced with a more traditional bronze statue of Nicholas in native attire, holding a child's hand and carrying another child on his shoulder.

2009

A meeting of the Fellowship of Middle East Evangelical Churches unanimously approved the ordination of women as pastors.

English bishop Richard Williamson had been consecrated in 1988 without the permission of the pope and was subsequently excommunicated. But this year, Pope Benedict XVII lifted his excommunication. Williamson was a Holocaust denier who repeatedly referred to the forged *Protocols of the Elders of Zion* as proof that the Jews were preparing the Anti-Christ's throne in Jerusalem. In Germany, where it is illegal to deny the Holocaust, a court convicted Williamson of Holocaust denial and fined him several times. His excommunication was reimposed, and in 2019, the European Court of Human Rights would rule against his attempt to overturn the conviction.

Tony Alamo Christian Ministries' namesake leader, who had previously been convicted for tax evasion, was convicted on ten counts of transporting minors across state line for sexual purposes, along with other crimes. Alamo was sentenced to 175 years in prison.

2010

After a suit was brought against the US by the Freedom from Religion Foundation, US district judge Barbara Crabb ruled that the National Day of Prayer was unconstitutional and that it was "an inherently religious exercise that serves no secular function."

Italian authorities investigated the Vatican Bank for money laundering, but no charges were filed. Two years later, the bank was investigated again for not complying with European Union standards.

2011

A Pew Research Center Forum on Religion determined the distribution of Christians around the world: 804 million lived in the Americas, 565 million in Europe, 516 million in Sub-Saharan Africa, 285 million in the Asia-Pacific region, and only 12 million lived in the Middle East and North Africa, the previous heart of Christianity.

US promoters held the first Wild Goose Festival in North Carolina to focus on social justice, spirituality, and other contemporary issues through seminars, music, and art. It has since become an annual event modeled after England's Greenbelt Festival, founded in 1974. The event is most popular among progressive Christians but is open to anyone regardless of their religious beliefs.

Florida pastor Terry Jones gained media notoriety by overseeing the burning of the Koran on the tenth anniversary of the September 11, 2001, attacks. His vengeful and disrespectful action made him feel good but caused worldwide outrage.

After eighteen years in effect, the US Congress repealed the "Don't Ask, Don't Tell" policy concerning homosexuality in the US military. This made it acceptable for military personnel to be open about their sexual orientation without fear of punishment.

A circuit court of appeals overturned the ruling on the unconstitutionality of the National Day of Prayer. It found that the Freedom from Religion Foundation, which originally filed the lawsuit, could not show that they were in any way harmed by this event, even though it appeared to violate the Constitution.

The Clergy Project began as a confidential, online community for clergy members who had lost their faith and want to transition to a new career. As of 2020, it had around a thousand participants.

A Gallup survey reported that 30 percent of Americans say the Bible is the actual word of God and must be interpreted literally.

Pastor and author Rob Bell published his book *Love Wins*, which questioned whether hell exists. As was predictable, his use of reason came under heavy attacks from conservative Christians.

Customs officials in Memphis, Tennessee, intercepted a package of ancient cuneiform tablets like those looted from war-ravaged Iraq. The confiscated shipment belonged to Steve Green, a billionaire evangelical, who was collecting exhibits for his new Museum of the Bible in Washington, DC.

A crisis developed at Sovereign Grace Ministries; a suburban DC megachurch founded in the late 1970s as Covenant Life Church. At the time, the church had around twenty-eight thousand followers worldwide. The head pastor CJ Mahaney was accused by his church of deceit and abuse of authority, and the church was accused of not reporting cases of sexual molestation of children. Since the scandal, Mahaney, other pastors, and more than thirty churches have left the ministry and one former youth leader was convicted of sexual abuse. Complaints and investigations are still in progress.

Bart Campolo, the son of one of the best-known evangelical preachers in the US, Tony Campolo, and a pastor in his own right, announced that he no longer believed what he had been preaching and left his ministry. He began a new career as the first humanist chaplain at the University of Southern California.

The membership in the Indian Christian churches broke down to 2,345,911 Syro-Malabar Catholics; 932,733 Latin Catholics; 493,858 in the Malankara Orthodox Syrian Church; 482,762 Jacobite Syrian Christians; 465,207 Syro-Malankara Catholics; and 405,089 in the Mar Thoma Church.

2012

Roy Bourgeois, a priest for forty years, was dismissed from the Catholic priesthood because of his participation in the ordination of a woman in Lexington, Kentucky, in 2008.

A Gallup survey showed that 46 percent of Americans believed that God created humans in their present form within the last ten thousand years.

Montgomery County, Maryland, sued Sovereign Grace Ministries for conspiracy to cover up child sex abuse after founder C. J. Mahaney and other leaders failed to report accusations to the police, saying they weren't required to. The church issued a statement saying, "Allowing courts to second-guess pastoral guidance would represent a blow to the First Amendment."

Dan Wallace of the Dallas Theological Seminary announced the discovery of a papyrus fragment from the Gospel of Mark dating from the first century. If true, the papyrus, which had been found in the papier-mâché material inside a mummy's mask, would be the earliest surviving Christian text. Later, the papyrus was found to be the property of the Egypt Exploration Society and dated to the late second or early third century. It was apparently obtained illegally by the Museum of the Bible.

2013

In Shelby County v. Holder, the US Supreme Court invalidated what some see as the heart of the Voting Rights Act of 1965, the preclearance clause, a rule that prevented states from passing discriminatory voting laws against minority groups by requiring preapproval by the federal government. This decision opened the door to states passing restrictive laws that would have to be fought in court *after* they were enacted, and it's much more difficult to overturn an existing law than to prevent one from being brought to a vote. An example of what this ruling has resulted in is the 2021 Texas law that restricts abortions.

A YouGov survey indicated that 57 percent of US adults believed in the devil.

Exodus International, an interdenominational organization, was founded in 1976 to treat the perceived sinful condition of homosexuality. It grew to four hundred local ministries in nineteen countries. This year its president Alan Chambers dissolved the organization, believing conversion therapy was ineffective and harmful to those who participated. Many of the ministries and ex-members are still aligned with other organizations such as the Exodus Global Alliance, Restored Hope Network, and Living Hope Ministries.

2014

The Islamic State of Iraq and the Levant, often called ISIL or ISIS, took over parts of northern Iraq and began a genocide of Assyrian Christians. These were the same people who had been targeted by Islamic militants of the Ottoman Empire, and more recently during the US-Iraq War. When the Assyrian Christians fled Mosul, it marked the end of 1,600 years of continuous Christian presence in that city. Over one hundred thousand Assyrians took refuge in Kurdistan.

The board of Mars Hill Church asked Mark Driscoll, the founder and charismatic pastor, to step down from leadership during an investigation of alleged abusive behavior. He then resigned his position. Within three months of his resignation, his replacement announced plans to dissolve the thirteen other Mars Hill Churches and let them become autonomous.

In the northeastern region of Nigeria, the extremist, Al Qaeda-trained Boko Haram terrorist organization attacked several villages and killed over one hundred Christian men. They also kidnapped 276 young girls from their school.

A Pew Research Center poll showed that 25 percent of the US population was evangelical, 21 percent was Catholic, and 15 percent was mainline Protestant, leaving around 40 percent as non-Christian.

2015

Islamic State militants inflicted major damage on a Greco-Roman archeological site in Palmyra, Syria, and severely damaged the statue known as the Lion of Al-lat. Ironically, the Lion had been discovered in the Palmyra ruins in 1977 and then restored after likely being destroyed by a Christian mob during the time of Theodosius I in the fourth century. The following year ISIS would destroy the statue of Athena in the Palmyra Museum, another statue that had been heavily damaged by a Christian mob. In their spasm of destruction of almost anything non-Islamic, the Islamic State also obliterated Saint Elijah's Monastery, the oldest Christian monastery in Iraq.

Following the Charleston, South Carolina, church shooting in which 9 African Americans were killed by a white man during a Bible study, momentum built to remove monuments and other symbols of the Confederacy, considering them representative of white supremacy, and treachery against the US. The Charlottesville rally in 2017 and George Floyd's murder in 2020 only added to this movement. Since then, around 140 such statues have been removed from public places, but several states still retain laws that prevent their removal.

2016

The Vatican issued new guidelines on cremation, directing Catholics to store cremated remains in a sacred place (such as a church cemetery) and not to scatter them on the ground or in water, not to keep them in an urn at home, and not to divide them up among family members or make them into jewelry or other objects.

After presidential candidate Donald Trump held a closed-door meeting with nine hundred evangelical Christian leaders, he announced a new Evangelical Executive Advisory Board consisting of twenty-five influential right-wing Christians leaders. This board would continue to meet in secret after he was elected, clearly in violation of the church-state separation.

Eighty-one percent of white American evangelicals voted for Donald Trump in the presidential election. Over 74 percent of evangelicals had voted as a block for the Republican candidates in all presidential elections since 2004. It's reported that many of these voters believed that Trump, who was endorsed by most of their clergy, was a holy warrior battling against the "demonic" influences of political liberals and the media.

A survey by Focus on the Family, Francis A. Schaeffer Institute of Church Leadership Development, and Fuller Seminary discovered that 80 percent of pastors felt unqualified or discouraged in their roles, 50 percent of their marriages ended in divorce, 50 percent of them admitted they would leave the ministry if they could, 80 percent of graduates from seminaries and Bible schools left the ministry within their first five years, 70 percent of pastors constantly fight depression, and 70 percent said the only time they studied the Bible was when they were preparing sermons.

In recent surveys, 62 percent of religious households said they gave to charity, compared to 46 percent of households with no religious affiliation. Thirty-one percent of all charitable giving in the US ($127 billion) went to religious organizations. Only about 5 percent of church attendees tithed 10 percent of their income, with the average Christian giving 2.5 percent. Of regular attendees, 37 percent didn't give any money to their church. Percentagewise, Muslims gave more to charity than other religions.

The Ark Encounter opened in Kentucky as a kind of Christian creationist theme park. It features an ark built to the dimensions mentioned in the Bible, and its purpose is to educate people about the "truth" of the biblical story of Noah's ark, including the supposed transporting of dinosaurs as passengers. This attraction was partially funded with tax-payer money.

The movie *Spotlight* released to critical acclaim. It was a fact-based depiction of the *Boston Globe* newspaper's uncovering of sexual abuse by Catholic clergy in the Boston vicinity. The film went on to win two Academy Awards, including Best Picture.

A study of abortions in the US since 1980 found that the rate had dropped from around thirty per one thousand women in the age group 15–44 to nearly twelve per thousand. Sixty-six percent of abortions were performed in the first eight weeks of pregnancy, and 91 percent were performed in the first thirteen weeks. The significant drop in the abortion rate was credited to better family planning options.

2017

The Trump administration changed the existing law and allowed US employers to opt out of offering birth control assistance in their employee's health coverage. The former policy had saved women $1.4 billion on birth control in its first year in effect and resulted in the lowest abortion rate since the procedure became legal in 1973.

Irish officials located a mass grave on the grounds of Bon Secours Mother and Baby Home in Tuam. The home, which closed in 1961, had been run by Catholic nuns and was a shelter for orphans, unmarried mothers, and children of unwed mothers. A burial site containing the remains of almost eight hundred babies and children is still being investigated.

The Unite the Right rally was a gathering of white supremacists in Charlottesville, Virginia, to protest the removal of a statue of Confederate General Robert E. Lee. The rally was characterized by racial and antisemitic mantras, torches, openly carried weapons, and violence.

The Museum of the Bible opened in Washington, DC. Although it claims to be nonsectarian, every member of the board of directors was required to sign a statement of faith. The museum's main donors were the Green family, whose money came from their chain of Hobby Lobby stores, and the National Christian Foundation.

2018

Billy Graham died. During his lifetime, he conducted more than four hundred "crusades" in 185 countries and territories and influenced many millions of people to accept Jesus as their savior or become stronger Christians.

The Trump administration ordered border officials to separate immigrant children from their undocumented parents at the Mexican border. Children were confined to detention centers while their parents were held in federal jails awaiting prosecution. The number of affected children ran into the thousands, and haphazard record keeping impeded or prevented family reunions.

2019

In Illinois, a law firm accused 395 Catholic priests and deacons of sexual misconduct. Church officials had only informed the public of a fraction of those allegations.

New York State legislature passed the Child Victims Act, increasing the maximum age for suing for sexual abuse during childhood from twenty-three to fifty-five years of age. The law gave people of any age a one-year window from the date it was enacted to sue for child sexual abuse. The Catholic Church reportedly spent nearly $3 million to block the law's passage and over $10 million lobbying against similar legislation elsewhere.

Pope Francis I issued an edict that mandated all Catholic priests and nuns report sexual abuse and its cover-up to church authorities and promised protection for whistleblowers.

Pope Francis I expelled Washington, DC, archbishop and cardinal Theodore E. McCarrick from the clergy after a decades-long pattern of sexual abuse. He was the highest-ranking American official to be removed for this crime. According to the *Washington Post*, during this year alone there were 4,434 allegations of clergy sexual abuse of minors in the US.

After stating his opinion that Satan "exists as a symbolic reality, not a personal reality," Father Arturo Sosa, the superior general of the Jesuit order, incurred the wrath of the International Association of Exorcists along with many non-exorcists because his remarks opposed Catholic catechism. Four months later he reversed himself by saying that Satan is real.

2020

A deadly pandemic known as COVID-19 made its appearance. Many anti-science and conspiracy-minded conservative Christians tried their best to ignore the advice of public health officials and continued to closely associate indoors at church functions, refuse to wear masks, or even get vaccinated to protect themselves and others from contracting the disease. Their politicizing of the pandemic and refusal to practice the necessary precautions to defeat it drove the wedge between them and science-believing Americans even deeper. Despite their disregard for public health measures to contain the disease, many would complain when businesses and schools remained closed and the economy suffered due to the tenacity of the disease.

British police arrested Dirk Obbink, an Oxford professor and world expert in papyrology, for the theft of papyrus fragments from Oxford's Sackler Library. The archaeological treasure had turned up in a collection belonging to the Museum of the Bible. Obbink was the head of the Oxyrhynchus Papyri Project, which deciphered the stash found in Egypt starting in 1896, but he no longer has access to it.

In the midst of a peacefully protest of police brutality against African Americans near the White House President Trump ordered the protest disrupted by active-duty military using tear gas. Then, protected by bodyguards, he walked across the street to have his picture taken in front of Saint John's Episcopal Church while holding up a Bible, apparently linking the Bible to a tough military response against a perceived enemy. The stunt didn't go over well with the bishop of the Episcopal Diocese, who expressed regret that Trump didn't instead come inside to pray for the welfare of the country.

Eight states in the U.S. still had statutes that prevented professed Atheists from holding public office, and two, Arkansas and Maryland, prohibited non-believers from serving as jurors or witnesses in court.

Over one hundred Christian pastors objected to the practice of yoga in Ohio public schools because they said it coerced students to practice Eastern religion, and that violated the First Amendment. The public schools complied.

A study by political scientists Paul A. Djupe and Ryan P. Burge found that 49 percent of US white Protestants who attended church weekly believed that God chose Donald Trump to be president.

Jerry Falwell Jr. left his position as president of Liberty University, a Christian college founded by his father, after the disclosure of a sexual affair that involved him, his wife, and another man.

The Vatican's Congregation for the Doctrine of the Faith, the modern name for the Inquisition, decided that any baptism carried out with the priest saying the words "we baptize you" instead of "I baptize you" was invalid. To affected Catholics, invalid baptisms meant they were not considered true Christians.

Pope Francis I shocked the world by making a statement endorsing same-sex civil unions but also said that priests could not officiate at or bless same-sex marriages.

The US House of Representative passed House Resolution 512 by a 386 to 3 margin, calling for the global repeal of blasphemy, heresy, and apostasy laws. It's uncertain what impact this resolution will have.

By this year, the Christian Bible had been translated into 700 languages, the New Testament into 1,548 more, and portions of the Bible into 1,138 more, making at least some Christian scripture available in 3,386 languages.

2021

After being energized and directed by the president himself, Trump supporters broke into and ransacked the US Capitol Building to overturn the election of Joe Biden and keep Donald Trump in power. Many in the mob carried items with Christian symbolism and chanted Christian rhetoric in justifying their actions. Trump-supporting Christians also held a Jericho March that day. This tradition is based on the biblical concept of a prayer walk circling a threatening site— in this case the US Capitol—with the hope of God bringing about a miracle—in this case overturning what they believed to be a fraudulent election.

The Survey Center on American Life found a wide gap between White Evangelical Republicans and Nonevangelical Republicans when it came to belief in political conspiracies. The evangelicals expressed much more belief in voter fraud in the 2020 presidential election, a "Deep State" undermining the Trump administration, and the antifascist activist group, Antifa, being responsible for the domestic terrorism at the US Capitol. There was a narrower difference in the belief

that Donald Trump was secretly fighting a group of child sex traffick-
ers that included prominent Democrats and Hollywood elites.

An investigation into prominent Christian apologist Ravi Zacharias,
who died the previous year, uncovered a long pattern of sexual misconduct involving women who worked in health spas. In response to
the findings, his ministry, Ravi Zacharias International Ministries
(RZIM)—once the largest apologetics organization in the world according to *Christianity Today*—is in damage control mode and will
restructure itself into a grant-making charity.

The Alabama legislature passed a law that overturned a 30-year ban
on the practice of yoga in public schools. It was reported that conservative Christians who supported the ban were afraid yoga would
open the door for people to convert to Hinduism. The bill states that
"Chanting, mantras, mudras, use of mandalas, induction of hypnotic
states [meditation], guided imagery, and namaste greetings shall be
expressly prohibited." It also requires English names for all poses and
exercises.

Ground-penetrating radar revealed mass graves containing 1,300 bodies on the grounds of four Canadian residential schools. These were
the mainly schools administered by Roman Catholics, and intended
to extract Indian culture from the children and convert them to
European ways. Since there were 130 of those schools throughout the
country, there is no telling how many similar graves will be found. The
outrage over what happened to those children has led to the vandalism
and burning of at least a dozen Canadian Catholic churches and even
churches mistaken for being Catholic.

A report issued by France's National Institute of Health and Medical
Research documented an estimated 330,000 cases of sexual abuse of
children by some 3,000 priests and church workers over the last 70
years.

Hillsong Church of Australia, with 131 churches in 30 countries, was rocked by various scandals including financial impropriety, moral failings of pastors, and sexual abuse and its concealment.

CONCLUSION

Any time scientists disagree, it's because we have insufficient data. Then we can agree on what kind of data to get; we get the data; and the data solves the problem. Either I'm right, or you're right, or we're both wrong. And we move on. That kind of conflict resolution does not exist in politics or religion.

—Neil deGrasse Tyson

As I mentioned in the introduction, I have always admired Christians who tried their best to live by the morality found in Matthew's Sermon on the Mount, Luke's parable of the Good Samaritan, and the Golden Rule. Whether by their innate disposition or through a great deal of conscious effort, these people took those teachings of love, respect, and compassion to heart and tried their best to live a life consistent with them. I can't help but imagine what the world would be like now if all Christians had devoted themselves to living by those principles. Humanity may have attained those seemingly impossible goals of establishing world peace, ending poverty and hunger, and protecting our environment from harm—my interpretation of a kingdom of God

Now I realize I was using what is known as *confirmation bias* to affirm the teachings that resonated with me while I gave less thought to the rest of the Gospels. If this was true for me, the same was probably true for the multitudes of Christians throughout history who chose to live their lives based on other teachings they found in the Bible. I have known many people who practiced other religions—Hindus, Muslims, Jews, Sikhs, and those who rejected religion entirely—who did adhere to the compassionate teachings of Jesus and other teachers of morality without a Bible. All humans have so much in common regardless of the manmade divisions that we think separate us and make one group think they are superior to another.

REACHING MY GOALS

Throughout Christian history many forgeries, frauds, and lies were used to win converts and gain power for the Church. Since it's not known who wrote many of the books of the New Testament, or what any authors' true motives were, it seems reasonable to treat all biblical accounts with a good deal of skepticism.

Through my research, most of my questions about Christianity have been answered to my satisfaction. The discoveries I've made in this study have finally quieted my restless mind and brought me some semblance of peace. It's probably more accurate to say that I am now comfortable with the many questions I cannot answer, and that may never be answered at all.

I realize that no two people would come away with the exact same conclusions after putting in the same amount of effort in reviewing the evidence. To me, commitment and an inquisitive mind are essential for learning truth. Answering questions about Christian history and doctrine by quoting scripture may make some people feel successful and satisfied, but it won't bring them any closer to the truth without historical context. Since there is no proof that any scripture was written or inspired by a god, it is more likely that religion is just something religious leaders have used to control the behavior of others.

An example is Saint Paul, who led Christianity out of Judaism. He wrote that his knowledge of Jesus came not from any person who knew Jesus, but from the spiritual Christ himself. His communications with a spiritual being can't be proven false, but they can't be proven true either; therefore, we can only guess at the accuracy of the mystic's supposed revelations, or the reliability of any other biblical author.

In the introduction, I set out several questions that I hoped to answer based on my research. This is how I would answer them now.

To trace the evolution of Christianity:

This was accomplished to the best of my ability by the timeline itself.

To determine what "real Christians" are and if these people are really recognized by the love and forgiveness they show each other—John 13:34-35, and their "neighbors."—Matthew 22: 37-39

Christianity has been represented by every type of person imaginable. There were those like Francis of Assisi who rejected materialism and devoted themselves to the compassionate care of the poor, but also those like Andrew Carnegie and the promoters of the prosperity gospel who interpreted their scripture to justify the accumulation of wealth. There was the German Christian Church that supported the Nazis and their antisemitic and imperialist agendas opposed by Dietrich Bonhoeffer, who called for all true Christians to stand up to the Nazi evil and protect those who were vulnerable. There were the Marcionites, who believed that there were two gods—accepting the loving God of Jesus and rejecting the wrathful Jewish God of the Old Testament contrasted with the Ebionites, who wanted Christianity to retain every single one of its Jewish traditions. Some Christians have heeded Jesus's teachings of nonviolence and pacifism, such as Martin Luther King Jr., the Quakers, and the Anabaptists, but others who were warmongers like Justinian, Charlemagne, the crusaders, and those who initiated our country's recent wars in Afghanistan and Iraq. There were those who admired the compassionate side of Jesus, while others who thought they were wimps and instead emulated and worshipped a machismo Jesus. There were charismatics who were ecstatic for Jesus, and Puritans who tried to be as reverent and pious as possible. There were those Christians who whipped slaves mercilessly and tore the slave families apart versus abolitionist Christians who couldn't stand to see any human remain in captivity. There are also those who respect each person's right to their own religious beliefs and those who want to force their beliefs on others. These examples could go on ad infinitum. Just about any behavior imaginable has been demonstrated by Christians, and then justified in the name of their God. Due to these inconsistencies, I see no way to define a "real Christian," and think those who do have been deceived.

Tracing Christianity as an imperial religion:

From what I've learned, there was little to set the Roman Empire, Byzantine Empire, or Holy Roman Empire apart from the brutality of any other empire of their ages, although it seems they were less brutal than the Mongols. I did encounter empires that at times practiced religious intolerance, and persecution of those who wouldn't convert to the state religion, such as the Sassanid Empire in the fourth century and the Chinese Ming Dynasty in fourteenth century. Christian empires, however, seemed to practice this suppression of other religions and heresies over a much longer time span. From what I've learned, religious persecution by Christian empires went far beyond that of the Islamic Empire that splintered in the thirteenth century. At least those Muslims tolerated people with other religious beliefs and Christians thrived in that empire for centuries. Later, the Ottomans tolerated Christians living in their empire but did eventually carry out horrendous massacres of certain groups of Christians in the late nineteenth and early twentieth centuries.

I am not qualified to make further comparisons, so I'll leave those to trained historians. I can safely say that Christian empires were not characterized by the compassionate teachings of Jesus.

Tracing the history of the United States as a "Christian nation":

Apparently, those who say the United States is a Christian nation are confused. They have been led to believe that our country had a unique blessing from the Judeo-Christian God, and in their minds, they have somehow mistakenly equated the New World colonists with the Israelites of the Old Testament. Like the biblical accounts of the Israelites who entered Canaan, took the land, and slaughtered the inhabitants, many of the colonists thought they were justified in intruding onto the American continents and doing the same to the Native

Americans. Their leaders convinced them that it was God's plan, and that led to the belief that the US was an especially hallowed nation. Fortunately, most reputable scholars believe those Old Testament accounts of invasion and genocide are fictional. So, it appears those who believe in this concept—Christian nationalists—think this is a Christian nation because it was first settled by European Christians, some using tactics learned from fictitious accounts of ancient Israelites.

The truth is that the Americas were originally settled by people of Asian descent, and European colonists who took the land from those people and destroyed their civilizations must be judged on the morality of their behavior and the God they represent.

What the Christian nationalists don't seem to accept is the truth—that many of the influential people who founded our country in 1776 rejected Christianity because of its wide-ranging failures in Europe. They were instead inspired by the Enlightenment, which came about as a result of the total breakdown of Church-controlled European society during more than a century of horrible wars between Protestants and Catholics. Most of our Founding Fathers were determined to keep religion out of our government and politics. Our constitution was as much as anything else a repudiation of Christianity and the establishment of a secular—meaning unreligious—state. Regardless of their patriotic beliefs and justifications, Christian nationalists are working against the best wishes of our Founding Fathers, the US Constitution, and the flag they claim to love and respect. Since the nation's founding, the actions of many of its past Christian leaders and citizens make it clear that this nation had no unique blessing from any loving God.

Determining if the world is a better or worse place because of the existence of Christianity:

All I can say concerning this is that from my limited vantage point I believe Christianity's major mistake was providing too many ways to practice the religion. By including the Jewish scripture—Old Testament, and the always controversial book of Revelation, those who determined which writings were canonical in the fourth century left too many options for Christians. If people believe that the genocides of the Old Testament or the end times of Revelation represent their God's will, their worldview and actions will be based on those examples. Certainly, the degree of harm that religious persecution; the religious wars and crusades; the domination of the lives of Europeans, Middle Easterners and North Africans for over a millennium; colonialism; and the spiritual abuse that Christian beliefs have caused millions of people cannot be quantified.

On the positive side, the actions of individual Christians have eased suffering and provided encouragement to multitudes of people. However, these individual events must be scrutinized as to how many of these compassionate acts were due to the Christian religion, or to people who were innately compassionate. Surely, compassion is found in all current religions; it is not an invention of Christianity. I believe that most people will help those in need because most people have a sense of empathy and compassion, not because their religion tells them to. Conversely, when any group of people intentionally inflicts harm on others, that seems to be because of some malignant ideology and leadership that incited them to fear and hate that other group. Whether the harm caused by the perpetrators of those ideologies can be quantified and weighed against the good done by compassionate Christians acting because of their Christian faith is something that I'll also have to rely on the experts to answer.

RECONCILIATION

After years of research and contemplation, I personally have chosen to reject any ideology that doesn't emphasize kindness, respect, and reason as its guiding principles. I think Dietrich Bonhoeffer was right when he wrote that for Christians there is a cost to discipleship. If the prize of being saved and going to heaven is won by doing nothing more than believing and saying the right things, then Christianity is cheap, effortless, and maybe even meaningless. We must judge people by their actions, and as seen throughout history, Christians can act any way imaginable and still attribute their behavior to their God. The "you're not a real Christian" accusation only demonstrates the exclusionist mentality of those who voice it.

Like many others, I believe the real heaven and hell are here on Earth right now, ultimately defined by how we treat each other, how we treat our fellow creatures, and how we care for this planet from which we evolved, and on which we live, die, and our bodies will return to. The line between goodness and evil does not run between cultures, religions, or any other manmade divisions, nor does it originate in the spiritual world. It runs through every single one of us. The ideologies we accept, the decisions we make, and how we conduct our lives will affect others for the better or worse and determine our legacy. We should all measure ourselves as to whether we brought more happiness or misery into our world.

I refuse to accept that what we are doing as a human race is the best we are capable of. All of us were born into this world without our consent. We are all trying the best we can to survive, stay healthy, protect our offspring, hopefully be protected by them in our old age, and experience more pleasure than grief before our lives end. Throughout my study of history, I continued to wonder why it was so seemingly impossible for people in any age to live in peace and cooperation and it kept leading me back to the same conclusion. It's egomania—the need for wealth, power, influence, and attention; or some other mental affliction. Unfortunately, many humans are so utterly selfish that their only goal seems to be to get what they can from this world and to hell with everyone else. And they can be charming and persuasive enough to get others to do their dirty work for them. They've used the concept of "survival of the fittest" to justify behaving like the most despicable of animals. Most people have the brainpower to overcome their primitive instincts but are often convinced by others not to bother trying. This is very important—it's up to the average follower to see through the selfish schemes of divisive leaders. Unfortunately, if those followers were thoroughly indoctrinated into their leader's religious or political culture and convinced to leave all the thinking to their leaders, the followers will usually remain submissive and loyal.

If someone finds themself accepting and defending the persecution, deceit, and violence in Christianity's past, then they, like Eusebius of Caesarea or Augustine of Hippo, apparently condone spreading their version of Christianity by any means available and that means their religion has nothing to do with compassion.

If you are a Christian and are troubled by much of Christian history or present-day Christian behavior, then please find opportunities
to share what you may have learned from this book with others. We
know that many people won't change their attitudes or actions because of anything you tell them, but at least you can try, and that's better than doing nothing. Every positive action you take is one little step
closer to gaining a critical mass for change. I've learned that arguing
with people with opposing beliefs gets you nowhere, whereas just asking questions about why people believe what they do can open doors
to reasonable discussion.

Also, if you are a Christian, ask yourself if there is anything you can
do to atone for any harm you feel your religion has caused in the past.
Some popes have been honest and courageous enough to apologize
for the past abuses of Christians and the Church as a whole, so surely
you could use them as role models. Every time you meet an African
American, Jewish person, Muslim, Native American, Asian American,
Pacific Islander, member of the LGBTQ+ community, or member of
another previously persecuted Christian denomination is an opportunity. Apologies and reconciliation take a great deal of courage, but afterward, you know you did something worthwhile. You can't atone for
what your ancestors did to the ancestors of others, and people know
that, but I'll bet they will still appreciate your thoughtfulness.

With that said, I'd like to share the words of Rabbi Gamaliel when
he addressed Jewish leaders in the Sanhedrin in Acts 5:38–39. After
he had given examples of past men who had been thought to be the
long-awaited Messiah but had disappeared into oblivion, he said of the
followers of Jesus:

> Therefore, in the present case I advise you: Leave these
> men alone! Let them go! For if their purpose or activity
> is of human origin, it will fail. But if it is from God, you
> will not be able to stop these men; you will only find
> yourselves fighting against God.

From what I've learned, Christianity has staggered forward over
its entire existence with no unity. It has experienced periods of tremendous growth and tremendous decline and many times gained and

retained prominence through dishonesty and violence. It has often been represented by self-centered authoritarian leaders, tenacious apologists, vigilantes, exhibitionists, and others who were mentally unstable. People who practiced the religion missed endless golden opportunities to accomplish good by prioritizing the welfare of all people. With that in mind, I must conclude that the answer to the good rabbi's observation is that Christianity, like every religion throughout history, is much more likely to be the creation of men than of gods.

If religions originated from tribal morality which is learned through living in harmony with a group of fellow humans, then morality should not be attributed to a god or a holy book. Scriptures are just codified versions of tribal culture and mythology. Through our God-given or nature-given ability to reason, we can understand that religion does not teach us how to live in peace and cooperation. It more often does the opposite. The necessity of living cooperatively with other humans originally inspired morality, but since then religions have been used to separate groups of humans for millennia.

I'm just echoing good advice that I've heard and taken to heart, and that is—to live in harmony, we must free ourselves from the primitive doctrines and narrow-minded rivalries of our religions, enjoy the blessing of loving those who are unloved, and make that the central issue in our lives. Sure, it's difficult, but when is the easy route through life ever the best one? If we live with this as our worldview, it really will transform lives. The Christian Gospels presented us with a loving Jesus who said those things about loving our neighbors, and I still believe them. And the reason I believe them is not because they're in the Bible, but because they've been proven effective in the real world. Being motivated by hate harms everyone involved, including those who carry it inside them, whereas treating others with kindness and respect is a blessing for everyone.

ACKNOWLEDGMENTS

My deep dive into Christian history began around 2008 with a con-fluence of events. One of those events was the discovery that someone in my Christian home group was as confused about Christian founda-tions and doctrines as I was. He was expressing the same doubts and asking the same questions to try to understand the evidence that sup-ported Christian beliefs. Later, after we both found our group much too restrictive, we sought others like us who wanted to honesty dis-cuss our religion without being judged on our level of faith. The new group loved studying Christian history and encouraged me to write a book about my personal timeline studies.

Another event that occurred about that time was the publication of *Pagan Christianity: Exploring the Roots of our Church Practices*, by Frank Viola and George Barna, concerning the many pagan influences on Christianity. I was amazed by all that I learned in that book.

Those two fortunate occurrences and my discovery of podcasts set me on a course correction. I became addicted to the *Unbelievable* pod-cast which presented debates between Christians and non-Christians or between Christians of different sects. Thank you Justin Brierley for your very courageous and illuminating podcast.

Next, I discovered biblical historian Bart Ehrman's books such as *Misquoting Jesus: The Story Behind Who Changed the Bible and Why* and was absolutely fascinated by the way he conveyed information that had been available in the academic arena for decades and made it understandable to the average non-academic reader. My reading list snowballed as I discovered books by Philip Jenkins, Charles Freeman, Karen Armstrong, John Dominic Crossan, and many other writers focused on Christian history. Without my spark of inspiration being ignited by these people, this book would never have been researched and written.

During the weaving of thousands of diverse threads of historical information into one hopefully coherent manuscript I had to rely on many trusted friends and family members. I came close to giving up on publishing many times, but they encouraged me to persevere because they saw the value in my work that I occasionally lost sight of while focusing on the individual bits of information and trying to nail down names and dates. I bounced ideas off them and they kept me in bounds and held me to my intended parameters of historical accuracy, high level of relevancy and interest, and neutrality. Jan, Michael, Nathan, Nancy, Heather, Rik, and others, you have been such a tremendous help to me in that area.

Then I went pro. I want to shout a huge thank you to my editors, Beth Jusino and Kathy Burge. Without their observant eyes, professional knowledge, encouragement, and the patience to point out or correct all my many writing blunders, this book would have been unreadable. Thank you so very much Beth and Kathy.

I owe a tremendous debt of gratitude to the wonderful staff at Girl Friday Productions for all the various ways they've worked so diligently to magically turn my manuscript into a book. This wonderful team consisted of Mari Kesselring, Reshma Kooner, Abi Pollokoff, Katie Meyers, and Paul Barrett.

I've always felt a need to write and teach and all these people have finally helped me accomplish one of my life's goals.

Above all, I owe so much to my wonderful wife, who was with me throughout this entire project, encouraging me and helping me process what I was learning. Honey, I couldn't have put the pieces together without the hundreds of conversations we had trying to understand their meanings. Thank you so very much.

GLOSSARY

abbey: A religious community that is usually larger than a monastery, containing many buildings. It is led by an abbot or an abbess.

Adoptionism: The belief that Jesus was the son of God only by adoption. He received the Holy Spirit at baptism, and it may have left him when he was crucified.

agnostic: A person who believes that nothing is known or can be known of the existence or nature of God or anything beyond the material world.

Albigensian: A member of a heretical sect known as the Cathars. They were mainly located around the town of Albi, in southern France, in the twelfth and thirteenth centuries.

Anabaptism: The concept of a quasi-Protestant denomination that arose during the Protestant Reformation. They believed in baptism once a person was old enough to understand Christian doctrine, so they conflicted with the prevailing practice of infant baptism.

Anatolia: The western peninsula of Asia, which is present-day Turkey. This area is also referred to as Asia Minor.

Anglican: The Protestant sect identified with the Church of England.

antipope: A person established as pope in opposition to one who has been chosen through the accepted church system.

antisemitism: Hatred or prejudice against Jews. Anti-Jewish is another word for antisemitism.

Apocalypse: A term related to end times, the Second Coming of Jesus, or Armageddon.

Apocrypha: Biblical or related writings that are not accepted as canonical scripture.

Apollinarianism: The Christological concept that proposes Jesus had a normal body but a divine mind instead of a normal human soul.

apostate: A person who renounces a religious belief or principle.

apostle: Someone sent out on a mission with a message or as a delegate. In Christian tradition, an apostle was a man Jesus trained.

Arab: A member of the Semitic people originally from the Arabian Peninsula.

archbishop: The chief bishop responsible for multiple dioceses or pastoral districts.

Arianism: A theology that refuted the Trinity and asserted that Christ was begotten by God but not of the same substance as God. It was extremely popular in Europe from the fourth to seventh centuries and is still an element of some present-day Christian denominations.

Arminianism: A theology related to the doctrines of Jacobus Arminius in opposition to Calvinist predestination.

ascetic: Practicing severe self-discipline and abstention from pleasurable activities.

atheist: A person who lacks belief in the existence of gods.

augustus: Meaning "majestic" or "venerable," the title applied to Roman emperors who were senior to caesars, their expected successors.

authoritarian: Showing lack of concern for the wishes or opinions of others, dictatorial.

barbarian: A member of a community or tribe not belonging to one of the great civilizations of Greeks, Romans, or Christians.

Beghard: A male counterpart to a Beguine.

Beguine: A member of the Roman Catholic lay sisterhood not bound by vows. They are mainly located in Belgium and the Netherlands.

belief: A state of mind in which a person thinks something is true.

bishop: The clergyman responsible for a diocese or pastoral district.

brainwashing: Making someone adopt radically different beliefs by using systematic and often forceful pressure.

bull: An edict issued by a pope, from the Latin *bulla*, meaning leaden "seal."

Byzantine Empire: The Roman Empire's eastern section, established in Constantinople on the site of the ancient Greek city of Byzantium.

caesar: A title use by Roman emperors, but at times the title of a successor to an augustus.

canon or canonical: Writings which have been accepted as sacred.

cardinal: A leader within the Roman Catholic Church, nominated by a pope.

Carolingian: Referring to family name Karlings, the dynasty that ruled the Franks during the eighth and ninth centuries.

Cathars: Members of a heretical Christian sect that sought great spiritual purity and professed a form of Manichaean dualism. (see Albigensian)

Catholic: The word comes from the Greek *katholikos*, which means "universal" or "in general." All major Christian sects—including Eastern Orthodox, Oriental Orthodox, Church of the East, and major Protestant denominations—feel that they are the true catholic church, derived from the original Christian movement. In modern times, most people are more familiar with the Roman Catholic Church and associate the word *catholic* with that church.

Chalcedonian: The Christology determined at the Council of Chalcedon in AD 451 that became the definition of orthodoxy. Christ is fully divine and fully human, both natures united, but also distinct. The term is basically synonymous with Dyophysitism.

Charismatic: The Christian movement that emphasizes gifts believed to be from the Holy Spirit, such as prophesy, speaking in tongues, and spiritual healing.

Christ: English for the Greek word *Christos*, meaning "the Anointed One." The equivalent Hebrew word is *Messiah*. Jesus Christ means "the Anointed One, Jesus."

Christendom: The regional or worldwide body of people united under Christianity.

Church Fathers: Ancient and influential Christian theologians who established the intellectual and doctrinal foundations of Christianity.

Circumcellion: A group of Christian extremists in North Africa active in the fourth century.

clergy: Those persons who are ordained for religious leadership roles.

codex: Ancient manuscript with the pages bound together as a book. Plural is *codices*.

Congregationalism: A system of organization among Christian churches where individual congregations are mostly self-governing.

conservative: Holding to traditional attitudes and values while cautious about change or innovation.

convent: Building or campus occupied by Christian nuns living under monastic rules.

copyist: A person who makes copies, especially of handwritten documents.

creed: A statement of the shared beliefs of a religious community.

crusade: A military expedition instigated by the Church for alleged religious goals. The word stems from the Latin and French words for cross. Also, an organized campaign concerning a political, social, or religious issue.

cultural Christian: A nonreligious person who adheres to Christian values and appreciates Christian culture.

Dead Sea Scrolls: Ancient Jewish religious writings found in caves near the Dead Sea beginning in 1947.

Deism: Belief in the existence of a supreme being, specifically a creator who does not intervene in the universe.

diaspora: The dispersion of people from their original homeland. Often applied to the Jews who left the area that became Palestine.

diet: A legislative assembly in certain countries.

divine: Supernatural qualities, related to God or gods.

Docetism: The doctrine associated with Gnosticism that believes Christ's body was not human but made of a substance that made it appear physical. Because of this, he could not suffer like a normal person.

Dominican: A member of the Roman Catholic monastic order founded by Domingo de Guzmán.

Donatism: A schismatic Christian group in North Africa. They condemned the orthodox clergy who had submitted to the Roman persecution in the early fourth century.

Dualism: Conceptualizes things as balanced opposites. This could mean body versus soul or good entities versus evil entities. As opposed to monotheists, dualists believe that evil is a separate power with its own origins. Manichaeans and Zoroastrians are examples.

Dyophysitism: The belief held by the Byzantine, Roman, and Nestorian Churches that Jesus is of two natures, fully human and fully divine. This term is basically synonymous with Chalcedonian, or what the Byzantine Church found to be orthodox Trinitarian theology.

Eastern Orthodox: Christian Churches evolving from the original Greek Church in Constantinople, such as Greek, Russian, Serbian, Romanian, or Bulgarian Orthodox.

Ebionites: An early Christian sect that conformed to traditional Jewish practices but accepted Jesus as the Messiah.

ecumenical: Promoting unity among the world's Christian churches.

elect: Those who God has chosen for eternal salvation.

Episcopal: The Anglican Church in the US and Scotland.

epistle: A type of letter used by Paul and others in the New Testament to communicate with churches and other entities.

Essene: A member of the ancient ascetic Jewish sect that lived in isolated communities and produced the Dead Sea Scrolls.

eugenics: The science of improving a human population by controlled selective breeding.

evangelical: The tradition within Protestantism of emphasizing the authority of the Bible, personal conversion, spreading Christianity, and salvation by faith in Jesus's atonement for the sins of mankind.

evangelism: The spread of Christian belief by public preaching or personal witness.

evidence: The body of information used to determine whether a belief or proposition is true or valid.

faith: Confidence or trust in something based on sufficient justification, which does not require tangible evidence.

forgery: A document or work of art which is produced with the intent to deceive an audience. Similar to fraud or hoax.

Franciscan: A member of the monastic order founded by Francis of Assisi in 1209.

Franks: The Germanic people who conquered Gaul in the sixth century and controlled much of Western Europe for centuries.

Freemasons: An international order that holds elaborate secret ceremonies.

freethinker: A person who, based on evidence or lack thereof, rejects accepted opinions, especially those concerning religious belief.

fundamentalist: A person who believes in the strict, literal interpretation of religious scripture.

Gentile: To Jews, anyone who is not Jewish.

Gnosticism: The belief in mystical knowledge or knowledge obtained by divine revelation. Gnostics believe that a divine Christ temporarily inhabited the human Jesus.

god: A superhuman or spiritual being worshipped as having power over nature or human events.

heliocentrism: Accepting the sun as the center of the solar system.

Hellenization: The historical spreading of ancient Greek culture.

heresy: Deviation from the accepted or traditional way of thinking, a heretic. In early Christianity, it was the worst sin that someone could commit since it was thought to disrespect orthodoxy and therefore God.

Holy Roman Empire: The empire established in Western Europe by the medieval papacy in an attempt to unite Western Christendom under one ruler.

Holy See: The papacy or papal court, associated with the pope in the government of the Roman Catholic Church at the Vatican.

humanism: A system of thought attaching prime importance to human rather
than divine or supernatural matters.

Hussite: A follower of Jan Hus, the fifteenth-century church reformer.

Hutterites: An Anabaptist sect practicing an old-fashioned communal way
of life. Like the Amish and Mennonites, who are also descendants of the
Anabaptists.

iconoclasm: The rejection or destruction of religious images as being heretical.

indulgence: A grant issued by a pope for remission of time in purgatory still
due for sins committed.

Jehovah: The proper name of the God of Israel in the Hebrew Bible.

Jesuit: A member of the Society of Jesus, a Roman Catholic order of priests
founded by Ignatius of Loyola in the sixteenth century.

Knights Hospitaller: A military monastic order founded in Jerusalem during
the Crusades to provide care for sick and injured pilgrims.

Knights Templar: A military monastic order founded at the Temple of
Solomon in Jerusalem during the Crusades.

laity: The members of a congregation, not the clergy or leaders.

Latins: Another name for crusaders from Europe who spoke Latin.

Levant: The eastern shore of the Mediterranean Sea, including the islands
there, basically covering Syria, Lebanon, Palestine, Jordan, and Cyprus.

liberal: Open to new behavior or opinions and willing to discard traditional
values if seen as obsolete.

Logos: Greek term meaning "word" or "reason." In Christianity, the name is
applied to Jesus, through whom it is said that all things were made.

Lombard: Germanic people who invaded Italy in the sixth century.

Manichaeism: A religious system containing Christian, Gnostic, and pagan
elements, founded by Mani in Persia in the third century AD. They
believed in dualism, meaning that Christ was two coexisting persons,
human and divine.

Marcionism: The belief system which saw Jesus as the savior sent by God, with
Paul as his chief apostle. They rejected the Hebrew Bible and the God of
the Old Testament, who they thought was a wrathful, lower entity than
the true God of Jesus.

Miaphysitism: The Christological doctrine that Christ has a blend of both
human and divine nature, but not two distinct natures as Dyophysites

believe. Although similar, this term is considered more accurate than the term Monophysitism, which the Byzantines used to describe the Syrian, Coptic, and Armenian churches.

Middle East: The large region of southwestern Asia and northern Africa that basically extends from the Mediterranean Sea to Pakistan.

Mithraism: The cult of the god Mithras, which was popular with Roman soldiers and the main rival to Christianity for the first three centuries AD.

monastery: Building or campus occupied by a community of monks living under religious vows.

monastic order: Monks who live under specific religious vows and rules, whether in monasteries or not.

Monophysitism: The belief that there is only one nature to Jesus Christ, and it is divine. This term was apparently misapplied to the Miaphysites of Egypt and Syria, who believe in a blend of divine and human qualities into one nature.

Monothelitism: An adherence to the doctrine that Jesus had only one will.

Montanism: A heretical, apocalyptic, and ascetic Christian sect that heavily relied on prophecy and was founded by the priest Montanus in the second century.

Moravian: A region in the Czech Republic and the name given to members of the Protestant Church founded in Saxony by emigrants from Moravia holding views derived from the Hussites.

Mormon: A member of the Church of Jesus Christ of Latter-day Saints, founded in 1830 by Joseph Smith.

Nestorianism: The doctrine credited to Nestorius, the fifth-century patriarch of Constantinople, that maintained that Christ was two separate persons, one human and the other divine. They rejected the idea that the Virgin Mary was the mother of God.

New Testament: The second part of the Christian biblical canon, related to the life and teachings of Jesus and events in early Christianity.

Old Testament: The part of the Christian Bible based on the Hebrew Bible, or Tanakh. The books that comprise this section differ between Jews and Christians, and even between some Christian denominations.

orthodox: Conforming to what is generally or traditionally accepted as right or true. The name became attached to the "right way" of theology but now mainly is attached to the Eastern Orthodox Church, which grew out of the Byzantine Empire and divided into Greek, Russian, and other versions.

paganism: A term used by Christians to describe those who were not Christian or Jewish.

parchment: Durable writing material made from the prepared skins of animals, often sheep.

patriarch: A man who is the oldest and most respected member of a group. In Christianity, it referred to the head of one of the five major sees.

Paulician: A religious sect that started in Armenia in the seventh century, teaching a form of Manichaeism.

Pelagianism: The belief advanced by Pelagius in the fifth century that human nature is not tainted by original sin and people are capable of choosing good or evil without divine assistance.

Pentecostalism: A Christian movement that emphasizes baptism in the Holy Spirit, evidenced by prophecy, healing, exorcism, and speaking tongues. Derived from the Pentecost in Act 2:9–11.

Pharisee: A member of a political party, social movement, and school of thought from 536 BC to 70 AD. They were strong supporters of Jewish law, and their beliefs became the foundation of Rabbinic Judaism, based on the laws that God gave to Moses in the scripture.

pilgrims: A person who journeys to a sacred place for religious reasons. May also refer to the specific group of English Puritans who sailed to Massachusetts to escape religious persecution.

pope: An affectionate term derived from the Greek word *papa*, meaning "father." The title now is used by the bishop of Rome, but in the past, the title was applied to other bishops who served in father roles. From this word comes *papal* and *papacy*.

preorthodox or proto-orthodox: A sect of Christianity descended from the teachings of the apostle Paul and the early Western Church that eventually came to dominate the religion. This sect formed the Church organization, scripture, and doctrines that most Christians are familiar with today, and they often tried to do away with any competing sects and any written proof of those sects' existence.

pseudepigraphon: Anonymous writing attributed to a well-known person. A pseudepigraphon differs from a forgery when an admirer seeks to honor the departed person by writing in his or her name with the sincere belief that they are expressing the honored person's views.

Puritan: A member of a group of English Protestants of the sixteenth and seventeenth century who thought the Reformation of the Church of England was incomplete.

Quaker: A member of the Religious Society of Friends, a Christian movement founded by George Fox in 1650.

regent: The person appointed to administer a royal's realm when the royal is too young or incapacitated to perform the duties of ruler.

relic: An object surviving from an earlier time, especially one of historical, sentimental, or supposedly supernatural value, such as part of a deceased holy person's body or belongings.

reliquary: A container for holy relics.

sacrament: A Christian rite having certain significance because God is felt to be present.

Saracen: A name used during the Crusader era, referring to Arabs or Muslims.

Sassanid: Referring to the dynasty that ruled Persia from the early third century until the Arab conquest in the seventh century.

schism: A significant break in the ties that used to bind entities together.

scripture: The sacred writings considered authoritative by a religion.

sectarian: Someone who rigidly follows the doctrines of a sect.

secular: Denotes attitudes and activities that have no basis in religion or spirituality.

secular humanism: The belief that humanity is capable of morality and self-fulfillment without a belief in God.

Septuagint: The ancient Greek translation of the Hebrew Bible.

Shakers: An American sect that lived simple lives in celibate mixed communities. They were named after the wild, ecstatic movements they engaged in during worship.

syncretism: The blending of different religions, cultures, or philosophies.

synoptic: From Greek, meaning "together." Describes observations that give a broad view of a subject. Referring to the canonical Gospels: Mark, Matthew, and Luke are grouped together as synoptic because they have so much in common.

Teutonic Knights: The Order of Brothers of the German House of Saint Mary in Jerusalem were a military monastic order founded in 1190.

Torah: The first five books of the Hebrew Bible or Christian Old Testament, specifically the books of Genesis, Exodus, Leviticus, Numbers, and Deuteronomy. The Greek version is called the Pentateuch.

Trinitarian: A term referring to the orthodox church after the adoption of the Nicene Creed and the belief in the Trinity. Their opponents were the Arians, who believed that Jesus was inferior to God and therefore there was no Trinity.

Trinity: The term used to mean the three distinct persons sharing the single divine essence of God (Father, Son, and Holy Spirit).

Unitarian: A sect of Christians who assert that Jesus did not claim to be God and who reject the doctrine of Trinity.

universal reconciliation: The doctrine that everyone, no matter how sinful, will eventually be reconciled to God. It mostly dismisses the concept of hell. Also called "universal salvation."

Universalist: Christians who believe that all of humanity will eventually be saved by God.

unreached people: Those groups of people who have never been successfully evangelized by Christians.

Vulgate: The main Latin version of the Bible which was prepared mainly by Jerome in the fourth century. Revised in 1592, it is the official text for the Roman Catholic Church.

Zionism: The belief that the return of Jews to Israel was in accordance with biblical prophecy.

Zoroastrianism: A monotheistic religion founded in sixth-century BC Persia, based on the teachings of Zoroaster.

BIBLIOGRAPHY

Abelard, Peter, Blanche Beatrice Boyer, and Richard Peter McKeon. *Sic Et Non.* Chicago: University of Chicago Press, 1976.

Adomnan of Iona. *Life of St. Columba.* Translated by Richard Sharpe. London: Penguin, 1995.

Armstrong, Karen. *Fields of Blood.* New York: Alfred A. Knopf, a division of Random House, 2014.

Armstrong, Karen. *The Battle for God: Fundamentalism in Judaism, Christianity and Islam.* London: Harper Perennial, 2004.

Attwell, Lionel. *Jesus Christ the Counterfeit Christian Messiah—Incorporating "What Really Happened in the Garden of Eden" and God, Genes and Evil.* Self-published, Lulu.com, 2007.

Bailey, Betty Jane, and J. Martin Bailey. *Who Are the Christians in the Middle East?* Grand Rapids, MI: William B. Eerdmans Publishers, 2010.

Baillon, Eleanor. *Life of Saint John of God.* London: Thomas Richardson and Son, 1884.

Bald, Margaret, and Ken Wachsberger. *Banned Books: Literature Suppressed on Religious Grounds.* New York: Facts on File, 2006.

Barber, Malcolm. *The Trial of the Templars.* Cambridge: Cambridge University Press, 2012.

Barnes, Timothy D. *Constantine and Eusebius.* Cambridge, MA: Harvard University Press, 1981.

Barton, John, and John Muddiman. *Oxford Bible Commentary.* Oxford/New York: Oxford University Press, 2001.

Bator, Robert, and Chris Rothero. *Daily Life in Ancient and Modern Istanbul.* Minneapolis, MN: Runestone Press, 2000.

Baumer, Christoph. *The Church of the East: An Illustrated History of Assyrian Christianity.* London: I. B. Tauris & Co. Ltd, 2016.

Bautista, Julius. *The Way of the Cross: Suffering Selfhoods in the Roman Catholic Philippines.* Honolulu: University of Hawaii Press, 2019.

Beinart, Haim. *Carta's Atlas of the Jewish People in the Middle Ages*. Jerusalem: Carta, 1981.

Bergad, Laird. *The Comparative Histories of Slavery in Brazil, Cuba and the United States*. Vancouver, BC: Access and Diversity, Crane Library, University of British Columbia, 2013.

Bergreen, Laurence. *Over the Edge of the World: Magellan's Terrifying Circumnavigation of the Globe*. New York: William Morrow, an imprint of HarperCollins Publishers, 2019.

Blunt, Anthony. *Artistic Theory in Italy*. N.p.: Read Books, 2008.

Bonpane, Blase. *The Nicene Heresy—Christendom and War: Reverence and Critique*. Los Angeles: Office of the Americas, 2016.

Bossy, John. *Christianity in the West 1400–1700*. Oxford: Oxford University Press, 2010.

Bouley, Bradford. *Pious Postmortems: Anatomy, Sanctity, and the Catholic Church in Early Modern Europe*. Philadelphia: University of Pennsylvania Press, 2017.

Brent, Allen. *A Political History of Early Christianity*. London: T & T Clark, 2009.

Bruce, David Forbes. *Christmas: A Candid History*. Berkeley, CA: University of California Press, 2008.

Brundage, James A. *Law, Sex and Christian Society in Medieval Europe*. New York: ACLS History E-Book Project, 2005.

Bushman, Richard Lyman, and Jed Woodworth. *Joseph Smith: Rough Stone Rolling*. New York: Vintage Books, 2007.

Campbell, Joseph, and Bill Moyers. *The Power of Myth*. New York: Random House, 1988.

Cahill, Thomas. *How the Irish Saved Civilization: The Untold Story of Ireland's Heroic Role from the Fall of Rome to the Rise of Medieval Europe*. New York: Anchor Books, a division of Random House, 1995.

Camp, Michael. *Craft Brewed Jesus: How History We Never Knew Taps a Spirituality We Really Need*. Eugene, OR: Resource Publications, An Imprint of Wipf and Stock Publishers, 2016.

Carrier, Richard. *Not the Impossible Faith: Why Christianity Didn't Need a Miracle to Succeed*. Self-published, Lulu.com, 2009.

Carroll, James. *Constantine's Sword: The Church and the Jews*. New York: Houghton Mifflin Harcourt Publishing, 2001.

Charlesworth, James H. *The Historical Jesus: An Essential Guide*. Nashville, TN: Abingdon Press, 2008.

Chiat, Marilyn J., and Kathryn L. Reyerson. *The Medieval Mediterranean: Cross-Cultural Contacts*. Minneapolis, MN: University of Minnesota Press, 1988.

Cohen, Richard. *The Avengers*. London: Jonathan Cape, 2000.

Collins, Adela Yarbro. *Crisis and Catharsis: The Power of the Apocalypse*. Philadelphia: Westminster Press, 1984.

Conze, Edward. *Buddhism and Gnosis*. Leiden, Netherlands: Brill, 1967.

Covey, Herbert C. *The Smallest Victims: A History of Child Maltreatment and Child Protection in America*. Santa Barbara, CA: Praeger, an imprint of ABC: CLIO, 2018.

Cross, F. L., and E. A. Livingstone. *The Oxford Dictionary of the Christian Church*. Oxford, UK: Oxford University Press, 1997.

Crossan, John Dominic, and Jonathan L. Reed. *Excavating Jesus: Beneath the Stones, Behind the Texts*. New York: HarperCollins Publishers, 2001.

Crouzel, Henry. *Origen: The Life and Thought of the First Great Theologian*. San Francisco: Harper & Row, 1989.

Delaney, Carol Lowery. *Columbus and the Quest for Jerusalem*. London: Duckworth, 2013.

Doherty, Earl. *Challenging the Verdict*. Ottawa, ON: Age of Reason Publications, 2001.

Doherty, Earl. *Jesus Puzzle: Did Christianity Begin with a Mythical Christ?* Ottawa, ON: Age of Reason Publications, 2005.

Duchesne, Louis. *Fastes épiscopaux de l'ancienne Gaule*, Vol. 1. Elibron Classics Replica. Boston: Adamant Media Company, 2002.

Dugard, Martin. *Into Africa: The Dramatic Retelling of the Stanley-Livingstone Story*. London: Bantam Books, 2012.

Du Mez, Kristin Kobes. *Jesus and John Wayne: How White Evangelicals Corrupted a Faith and Fractured a Nation*. New York: Liveright Publishing Corporation, 2020.

Earls, Irene. *Renaissance Art: A Topical Dictionary*. New York: Greenwood Press, 1987.

Eckert, Allan W. *Twilight of Empire*. Ashland, KY: Jesse Stuart Foundation, 2004.

Ehrman, Bart D. *Did Jesus Exist?: The Historical Argument for Jesus of Nazareth*. New York: HarperOne, 2013.

Ehrman, Bart D. *Forged: Writing in the Name of God—Why the Bible's Authors Are Not Who We Think They Are*. New York: HarperOne, 2012.

Ehrman, Bart D. *Forgery and Counterforgery: The Use of Literary Deceit in Early Christian Polemics*. New York: Oxford University Press, 2014.

Ehrman, B. D. *Lost Christianities: The Battles for Scripture and the Faiths We Never Knew*. New York: Oxford University Press, 2005.

Ehrman, Bart D. *The Triumph of Christianity: How a Forbidden Religion Swept the World*. New York: Simon & Schuster, 2019.

Eisner, Peter. *The Pope's Last Crusade: How an American Jesuit Helped Pope Pius XI's Campaign to Stop Hitler*. New York: William Morrow, 2014.

Engelman, Peter C. *A History of the Birth Control Movement in America*. Santa Barbara, CA: Praeger, 2011.

Evans, James Allan. *The Emperor Justinian and the Byzantine Empire*. Westport, CT: Greenwood Press, 2005.

Fenster, J. M. *The Case of Abraham Lincoln: A Story of Adultery, Murder, and the Making of a Great President*. New York: Palgrave Macmillan, 2009.

Finkelstein, Israel, and Neil Asher Silberman. *The Bible Unearthed: Archaeology's New Vision of Ancient Israel and the Origin of its Sacred Texts*. New York: Touchstone, trademark of Simon& Schuster, 2001.

Foss, Michael. *People of the First Crusade*. New York: Arcade Publishing, 1997.

Freeman, Charles. *A.D. 381: Heretics, Pagans, and the Christian State*. London: Pimlico, an imprint of Random House, 2009.

Freeman, Charles. *The Closing of the Western Mind: The Rise of Faith and the Fall of Reason*. Paw Prints, 2008.

Freeman, Charles. *Holy Bones, Holy Dust*. New Haven, CT: Yale University Press, 2012.

Ferguson, Everett. *Encyclopedia of Early Christianity*, 2nd ed. New York: Routledge, imprint of Taylor & Francis Group, 1999.

Gerli, E. Michael. *Medieval Iberia: An Encyclopedia*. New York: Garland, 2002.

Glazier, Michael, and Monika K. Hellwig. *The Modern Catholic Encyclopedia*. Collegeville, MN: Liturgical Press, 2004.

Goldstein, Phyllis, and Harold Evans. *A Convenient Hatred: The History of Antisemitism*. Brookline, MA: Facing History and Ourselves National Foundation, 2012.

Gregg, Robert C. *Athanasius: The Life of Antony and the Letter to Marcellinus*. New York: Paulist Press, 1980.

Guscin, Mark. *The Image of Edessa*. Leiden, Netherlands: Brill, 2009.

Harpur, Tom, and John Callen. *The Pagan Christ: Is Blind Faith Killing Christianity?* Auckland, NZ: Royal New Zealand Foundation of the Blind, 2006.

Harris, Stephen L. *Understanding the Bible*. New York: McGraw-Hill, 2010.

Harris, William V. *The Spread of Christianity in the First Four Centuries: Essays in Explanation*. Leiden, Netherlands: Brill, 2005.

Harrison, Guy P. *50 Reasons People Give for Believing in a God*. Amherst, NY: Prometheus Books, 2008.

Hefele, Charles Joseph. *A History of the Councils of the Church*, Vol. 2. Edinburgh: T. & T. Clark, 1876.

Heller, Henry. *Iron and Blood: Civil Wars in Sixteenth Century France*. Montreal: McGill-Queen's University Press, 2014.

Herbermann, Charles, G. *The Catholic Encyclopedia: An International Work of Reference on the Constitution, Doctrine, Discipline, and History of the Catholic Church*. New York: Catholic Encyclopedia Incorporated, 1913.

Hinzie, W. C. *Secrets of the 12 Disciples: The Stories You Do Not Hear in Sunday School*. Bloomington, IN: WestBow Press, 2011.

Hornung, Erik. *The Secret Lore of Egypt: Its Impact on the West*. Ithaca, NY: Cornell University Press, 2001.

Hume, Lynne, and Nevill Drury. *The Varieties of Magical Experience: Indigenous, Medieval, and Modern Magic*. Santa Barbara, CA: Praeger, 2013.

Jacoby, Susan. *Great Agnostic: Robert Ingersoll and American Freethought*. New Haven, CT: Yale University Press, 2014.

Jedin, Hubert, and John Patrick Dolan. *History of the Church: From the High Middle Ages to the Eve of the Reformation*. New York: Crossroad, 1982.

Jenkins, Philip. *Jesus Wars: How Four Patriarchs, Three Queens, and Two Emperors Decided What Christians Would Believe for the Next 1,500 Years*. New York: HarperOne, 2011.

Jenkins, Philip. *The Lost History of Christianity: The Thousand-Year Golden Age of the Church in the Middle East, Africa, and Asia—and How It Died*. New York: HarperOne, 2009.

Jones, Timothy Paul. *Misquoting Truth: A Guide to the Fallacies of Bart Ehrman's "Misquoting Jesus."* Downers Grove, IL: IVP Books, 2007.

Jusino, Beth. *Walking to the End of the World: A Thousand Miles on the Camino De Santiago*. Seattle, WA: Mountaineers Books, 2018.

Keller, Werner, William Neil, Joachim Rehork, and B. H. Rasmussen. *The Bible As History*. New York: William Morrow, an imprint of HarperCollins Publishers, 2015.

Kelly, J. N. D. *Early Christian Creeds*. London: Routledge, an imprint of Taylor & Francis, 2017.

Kertzer, David I. *The Pope and Mussolini: The Secret History of Pius XI and the Rise of Fascism in Europe*. New York: Random House, 2014.

King, Daniel. *The Syriac World*. London: Routledge, an imprint of Taylor & Francis, 2018.

Kitto, John. *An Illustrated History of the Holy Bible: Being a Connected Account of the Remarkable Events and Distinguished Characters Contained in the Old and New Testaments, and in Jewish History during the Four Hundred Years Intervening between the Time of Malachi and the Birth of Christ*. Norwich, CT: Henry Bill, 1894.

Krahl, Joseph. *Chinese Missions in Crisis: Bishop Laimbeckhoven and His Times*. Rome: Gregorian University Press, 1964.

Krupp, E.C. *Echoes of the Ancient Skies: The Astronomy of Lost Civilizations*. Mineola, NY: Dover Publications, 1994.

Kuhn, Alvin Boyd. *Shadow of the Third Century: A Revaluation of Christianity*. Surrey, BC, Canada: Eremitical Press, 1949.

Küng, Hans. *The Catholic Church: A Short History*. New York: Modern Library, 2003.

Kurian, George Thomas. *A Quick Look at Christian History*. Eugene, OR: Harvest House Publishers, 2015.

Lapidge, Michael. *The Anglo-Saxon Library*. New York: Oxford University Press, 2006.

Lea, Henry Charles. *A History of the Inquisition of the Middle Ages*, Vol 2. New York: Harbor Press, 1955.

Life Application Bible: New International Version. Wheaton, IL: Tyndale House Publishers, 1995.

Lipinski, Edward. *Itineraria Phoenicia*. Leuven, Belgium: Peeters Publishers, 2004.

Lodge, Richard. *The History of England from the Restoration to the Death of William the Third: 1660–1702*. New York: AMS Press, 1969.

Loftus, John W. *The Christian Delusion: Why Faith Fails*. New York: Prometheus Books, 2010.

Louden, Bruce. *Homer's Odyssey and the Near East*. Cambridge: Cambridge University Press, 2011.

Lowrie, Walter. *Monuments of the Early Church*. New York: The Macmillan Company, 1901.

Luttikhuizen, Frances. *Underground Protestantism in Sixteenth Century Spain: A Much Ignored Side of Spanish History*. Gottingen: Vandenhoeck & Ruprecht, 2017.

Macdonald, Dennis R. *The Homeric Epics and the Gospel of Mark*. New Haven, CT: Yale University Press, 2000.

MacMullen, Ramsay. *Christianizing the Roman Empire*. New Haven, CT: Yale University Press, 1984.

MacMullen, Ramsay. *Enemies of the Romans Order: Treason, Unrest, and Alienation in the Empire*. London: Harvard University Press, 1975.

Mack, Burton L. *Who Wrote the New Testament?: The Making of the Christian Myth*. San Francisco: HarperOne, an imprint of HarperOne, 2015.

Madden, Thomas F. *Istanbul: City of Majesty at the Crossroads of the World*. New York: Penguin Books, 2017.

Madden, Thomas F. *Venice: A New History*. New York: Penguin Books, 2012.

Marchant, Jo. *The Human Cosmos: Civilization and the Stars*. New York: Dutton, an imprint Penguin Random House, 2020.

Marjanen Antti, and Petri Luomanen, eds. *A Companion to Second-Century Christian "Heretics."* Leiden, Netherlands: Brill, 2005.

Mayer, Arno J. *Why Did the Heavens Not Darken: The "Final Solution" in History*. London: Verso, 2012.

McCartney, Dan G. *James* (Baker Exegetical Commentary on the New Testament). Grand Rapids, MI: Baker Books, 2009.

McGuckin, John Anthony. *The Westminster Handbook to Origen*. Louisville, KY: Westminster John Knox Press, 2004.

Mcphee, Peter. *Liberty or Death: The French Revolution*. New Haven: Yale University Press, 2017.

Meyers, Robin. *Underground Church: Reclaiming the Subversive Way of Jesus*. San Francisco: Jossey-Bass, an imprint of Wiley, 2012.

Michaud, Joseph. *History of the Crusades*. London: Routledge, 1881.

Miller, Kenneth R. *Finding Darwin's God: A Scientist's Search for Common Ground between God and Evolution*. New York: HarperCollins, 1999.

Morison, Samuel Eliot. *Admiral of the Ocean Sea: A Life of Christopher Columbus*. Boston: Little, Brown & Co., 1942.

Moss, Candida R. *The Myth of Persecution: How Early Christians Invented a Story of Martyrdom.* New York: HarperOne, 2014.

Muir, William. *The Mameluke or Slave Dynasty of Egypt: 1260–1517 A.D.* New York: AMS Press, 1973.

Nickell, Joe. *Looking for a Miracle: Weeping Icons, Relics, Stigmata, Visions & Healing Cures.* Amherst, NY: Prometheus Books, 1999.

Nixey, Catherine. *The Darkening Age: The Christian Destruction of the Classical World.* Boston: Mariner Books, an imprint of Houghton Mifflin Harcourt, 2019.

Noll, Mark A. *Turning Points: Decisive Moments in the History of Christianity.* Grand Rapids, MI: Baker Academic, 2012.

Nyland, A. *The Gospel of Thomas: Translation with Commentary.* N.p.: Ancient Mysteries Publishing, 2011. E-book.

Oast, Jennifer. *Institutional Slavery: Slaveholding Churches, Schools, Colleges, and Businesses in Virginia, 1680–1860.* New York: Cambridge University Press, 2016.

Offit, Paul A. *Bad Faith: When Religious Belief Undermines Modern Medicine.* New York: Basic Books, a member of the Perseus Books Group, 2015.

Oman, Charles. *The Dark Ages 476–918.* London: Rivingtons, 1898.

Orr, James. "The Apostles' Creed." In *International Standard Bible Encyclopedia* 2011.

Ott, John S. *Bishops, Authority and Community in Northwestern Europe, c.1050–1150.* Cambridge: Cambridge University Press, 2015.

Papandrea, James Leonard. *Novatian of Rome and the Culmination of Pre-Nicene Orthodoxy.* Eugene, OR: Pickwick Publications, 2012.

Pater, Walter. *Miscellaneous Studies: A Series of Essays.* London: Macmillan, 1920.

Paulkovich, Michael. *Beyond the Crusades: Christianity's Lies, Laws, and Legacy.* Cranford, NJ: American Atheist Press, 2015.

Perry, Mary Elizabeth, and Anne J. Cruz. *Cultural Encounters: The Impact of the Inquisition in Spain and the New World.* Berkeley: University of California Press, 1991.

Pinker, Steven. *The Better Angels of Our Nature: Why Violence Has Declined.* New York: Penguin Books, 2012.

Porter, Roy. *The Greatest Benefit to Mankind.* London: The Folio Society, 2016.

Pritchard, James B. *Archaeology and the Old Testament.* Princeton, NJ: Princeton University Press, 1958.

Prothero, Stephen. *Religious Literacy: What Every American Needs to Know—and Doesn't.* New York: HarperOne, 2008.

Reyes, E. Christopher. *In His Name.* N.p.: Trafford Publishing, 2018.

Rivera, Luis N. *A Violent Evangelism: The Political and Religious Conquest of the Americas.* Louisville, KY: Westminster/John Knox Press, 1992.

Roach, Andrew P., and James R. Simpson. *Heresy and the Making of European Culture: Medieval and Modern Perspectives.* New York: Routledge, imprint for Taylor & Francis Group, 2013.

Roellig, Harold F. *The More Excellent Way: 2000 Years of Jesus' New Way of Life.* Independence, OR: Crucifer Press, 2006.

Roseman, Mark. *The Villa, the Lake, the Meeting: Wannsee and the Final Solution.* London: Penguin, 2003.

Ruiz, Ramon Edouardo. *Triumphs and Tragedy: A History of the Mexican People.* New York: Norton, 1994.

Russell, Bertrand. *Why I Am Not a Christian and Other Essays on Religion and Related Subjects.* London: Routledge, an imprint of Taylor & Francis Group, 2017.

Ryholt, K. S. B. *The Political Situation in Egypt During the Second Intermediate Period, c. 1800–1550 BC.* Copenhagen: University of Copenhagen Museum Tusculanum Press, 1997.

Sanderson, Stephen K. *Religious Evolutions and the Axial Age: From Shamans to Priests to Prophets.* London: Bloomsbury Academic, 2018.

Schäfer, Peter. *Judeophobia: Attitudes Toward the Jews in the Ancient World.* London: Harvard University Press, 1998.

Schiller, Gertrud. *Iconography of Christian Art.* London: Lund Humphries, 1972.

Schmidt, Alvin J. *How Christianity Changed the World.* Grand Rapids, MI: Zondervan, 2004.

Schneemelcher, Wilhelm, and R. McL. Wilson. *New Testament Apocrypha.* Louisville, KY: Westminster John Knox Press, 2003.

Shapiro, James. *Oberammergau: The Troubling Story of the World's Most Famous Passion Play.* New York: Vintage Books, 2001.

Sharf, Andrew. *Byzantine Jewry: From Justinian to the Fourth Crusade.* London: Routledge & K. Paul, 1971.

Shoemaker, Stephen J. *Mary in Early Christian Faith and Devotion.* New Haven, CT: Yale University Press, 2016.

Shorto, Russell. *The Island at the Center of the World: The Epic Story of Dutch Manhattan and the Forgotten Colony That Shaped America.* London: Abacus, 2014.

Simpson, Lesley Byrd. *Cortes: The Life of This Conqueror by His Secretary Francisco López de Gómara.* Berkeley, CA: University of California Press, 1964.

Smith, Christian. *The Bible Made Impossible: Why Biblicism is not a Truly Evangelical Reading of Scripture.* Grand Rapids, MI: Brazos Press, 2011.

Stark, Rodney. *The Triumph of Christianity: How the Jesus Movement Became the World's Largest Religion.* New York: HarperOne, 2012.

Stephens, Mitchell. *Imagine There's No Heaven: How Atheism Helped Create the Modern World.* New York: Palgrave Macmillan, 2014.

Strobel, Lee. *The Case for Christ: A Journalist's Personal Investigation of the Evidence for Jesus.* Grand Rapids, MI: Zondervan Publishing House, 1998.

Strobel, Lee. *The Case for Faith: A Journalist Investigates the Toughest Objections to Christianity.* Grand Rapids, MI: Zondervan Publishing House, 2000.

Sumption, Jonathan. *The Albigensian Crusade.* London: Faber and Faber, 2011.

Swanson, R. N. *Indulgences in Late Medieval England: Passports to Paradise?* Cambridge: Cambridge University Press, 2011.

Taylor, Robert. *The Diegesis: Being a Discovery of the Origin, Evidences, and Early History of Christianity.* Boston: J.P. Mendum, 1853.

Taylor, Wilma Rugh, and Norman Thomas Taylor. *This Train is Bound for Glory: The Story of America's Chapel Cars.* Valley Forge, PA: Judson Press, 1999.

Tice, Paul. *Jumpin' Jehovah: Exposing the Atrocities of the Old Testament God.* Escondido, CA: Book Tree, 2000.

Van den Broek, Roelof. *Pseudo-Cyril of Jerusalem on the Life and Passion of Christ: A Coptic Apocryphon.* Leiden, Netherlands: Brill, 2013.

Van Voorst, Robert E. *Jesus Outside the New Testament: An Introduction to the Ancient Evidence.* Grand Rapids, MI: Eerdmans, 2000.

Viola, Frank, and George Barna. *Pagan Christianity?: Exploring the Roots of Our Church Practices.* Carol Stream, IL: Barna, 2012.

Waddingon, George. *A History of the Church, from the Earliest Ages to the Reformation.* New York: Harper and Brothers, 1843.

Waterfield, Robin. *Dividing the Spoils: The War for Alexander the Great's Empire.* Oxford: Oxford University Press, 2013.

Wedgwood, C. V. *The Thirty Years War.* London: Methuen, 1981.

Weidensaul, Scott. *The First Frontier: The Forgotten History of Struggle, Savagery, and Endurance in Early America.* Boston: Houghton Mifflin Harcourt, 2012.

Wells, George A. *The Historical Evidence for Jesus.* Buffalo, NY: Prometheus Books, 1988.

Wheless, Joseph. *Forgery in Christianity: A Documented Record of the Foundations of the Christian Religion.* Minneapolis, MN: Filiquarian Publishing, 2007.

Wheless, Joseph. *Is It God's Word?: An Exposition of the Fables and Mythology of the Bible and the Fallacies of Theology.* Montana, US: Tetra Press, 1997.

White, Andrew D. *A History of the Warfare of Science with Theology in Christendom.* Amherst, NY: Prometheus Books, 1993.

Wigram, W. A. *An Introduction to the History of the Assyrian Church or the Church of the Sassanid Persian Empire, 100–640 A.D.* Piscataway, NJ: Gorgias Press, 2004.

Wilhelm, August. *Meyer's Commentary on the New Testament.* Peabody, MA: Hendrickson, 1983.

Wilken, Robert L. *The Christians as the Romans Saw Them.* New Haven, CT: Yale University Press, 1984.

Wills, Garry. *Future of the Catholic Church with Pope Francis.* New York: Penguin Books, 2015.

Wilson, Ian. *The Bleeding Mind: An Investigation into the Mysterious Phenomenon of Stigmata.* London: Weidenfeld and Nicolson, 1988.

Winn, Albert C. *Ain't Gonna Study War No More: Biblical Ambiguity and the Abolition of War.* Louisville, KY: Westminster, 1993.

Wood, Diana. *Clement VI: The Pontificate and Ideas of an Avignon Pope.* Cambridge: Cambridge University Press, 2002.

Woodward, Colin. *American Nations: A History of the Eleven Rival Regional Cultures of North America.* New York: Penguin Books, 2012.

Woolfenden, Gregory W. *Daily Liturgical Prayer: Origins and Theology.* New York: Routledge, an imprint of Taylor & Francis, 2016.

Wright, Jonathan. *Heretics: The Creation of Christianity from the Gnostics to the Modern Church.* Boston: Houghton Mifflin Harcourt, 2011.

Wulf, Andrea. *The Invention of Nature: The Adventures of Alexander von Humboldt, the Lost Hero of Science.* New York: Vintage Books, 2015.

Zank, Michael. *Byzantine Jerusalem.* Hoboken, NJ: Wiley, 2018.

Zindler, Frank R., and Robert M Price. eds. *Bart Ehrman and the Quest of the Historical Jesus of Nazareth: An Evaluation of Ehrman's Did Jesus Exist?* Cranford, NJ: American Atheist Press, 2013.

Zindler, Frank R. *The Jesus the Jews Never Knew: Sepher Toldoth Yeshu and the Quest of the Historical Jesus in Jewish Sources.* Cranford, NJ: American Atheist Press, 2003.

JOURNALS

Albright, William F. "From the Patriarchs to Moses II: Moses Out of Egypt." *The Biblical Archaeologist* 36, no.2 (May 1973): 48–76.

Barber, Malcolm. "The Crusades of the Shepherds in 1251," Proceedings of the Tenth Annual Meeting of the Western Society for French History, 1982. Lawrence, 1984.

Barr, James. "The Question of Religious Influence: The Case of Zoroastrianism, Judaism, and Christianity." *Journal of the American Academy of Religion* 53, no. 2 (June 1985): 201–235.

Hill, Richard S. "Not So Far Away in a Manger: Forty-One Settings of an American Carol." *Notes* 3, no. 1 (December 1945): 12–36.

Wright, N. T. "Farewell to the Rapture." *Bible Review* (August 2001).

PODCASTS

Bolelli, Daniele. *History on Fire*, various episodes. Podcast. http://historyon firepodcast.com/.

Carlin, Dan. *Hardcore History*, various episodes. Podcast. https://www .dancarlin.com/hardcore-history-series/.

Cooper, Darryl. *Martyrmade*, various episodes. Podcast. https://www.martyr made.com/.

Duncan, Mike. *Revolutions*, various episodes. Podcast. https://thehistoryof rome.typepad.com/revolutions_podcast/.

Harris, Brad. *How It Began*, various episodes. Podcast. https://howitbegan .com/.

Price, Robert M. *The Bible Geek*, various episodes. Podcast. https://www .robertmprice.mindvendor.com/biblegeek.php.

Wyman, Patrick. *Tides of History*, various episodes. Podcast. https://wondery
.com/shows/tides-of-history/.

VIDEOS

Jacoby, Oren, dir. *Constantine's Sword*. 2008; New York: First Run Features.
Film.
Christianity: The First Thousand Years. 2001; Los Angeles: A&E Television
Networks. TV mini-series.

WEBSITES

About Jesus, http://www.about-jesus.org/.
Academia, https://www.academia.edu.
Aeon, https://aeon.co/.
All About Archaeology, https://www.allaboutarchaeology.org/.
American Survey Center, https://www.americansurveycenter.org/.
Ancient History Encyclopedia, https://www.ancient.eu/.
Ancient Wisdom Foundation, http://www.ancient-wisdom.com/.
Answers in Genesis, https://answersingenesis.org/.
Atlas Obscura, https://www.atlasobscura.com/.
Bart D. Ehrman, https://www.bartdehrman.com/.
Be Thinking, https://www.bethinking.org/.
Bible Hub, https://biblehub.com/.
Bible Odyssey, http://bibleodyssey.org/.
Bible Probe for Christians and Messianic Jews, http://bibleprobe.com/.
BibleWise, https://biblewise.com/.
Biblical Archeology, http://www1.biblicalarcheology.org/?tm=1&subid4=
1612585797.0010875990.
Biblical Archaeology Society Online Archive, https://www.baslibrary.org/.
BioLogos, https://biologos.org/.
Catholic Answers, https://www.catholic.com/.
Catholic News Agency, https://www.catholicnewsagency.com/.
Christianity Today, https://www.christianitytoday.com/.

Christianity Today—Christian History, https://www.christianitytoday.com/
    history/.

Christian Post, https://www.christianpost.com/.

Cistercian Publications, https://litpress.org/CP/Index.

The Conversation, https://theconversation.com/us.

CopticChurch.net, https://copticchurch.net/.

Crystalinks, https://www.crystalinks.com/.

Desiring God, https://www.desiringgod.org/.

Domain of Man, http://domainofman.com/.

Early Christian Writings, http://earlychristianwritings.com/.

Encyclopaedia Britannica, https://www.britannica.com/.

English Language Notes, https://muse.jhu.edu/.

The Flavius Josephus Home Page, http://josephus.org/.

Fordham University: Internet History Sourcebooks Project, https://source-
    books.fordham.edu/.

Forum Ancient Coins, https://www.forumancientcoins.com/.

Fourth-Century Christianity, https://www.fourthcentury.com/.

Gates of Nineveh, https://gatesofnineveh.wordpress.com/.

The Gospel Coalition, https://www.thegospelcoalition.org/.

Historum, https://historum.com.

History Discussion, https://historydiscussion.net.

HistoryNet, https://www.historynet.com/.

History of Information, https://historyofinformation.com/.

History Today, https://www.historytoday.com/.

History World, http://historyworld.net/.

The Holocaust Chronicle, http://holocaustchronicle.org/.

Home of Heroes, https://homeofheroes.com.

HuffPost, https://www.huffpost.com/.

Human Religions, http://www.humanreligions.info/.

International Catacomb Society, http://www.catacombsociety.org.

Jewish Virtual Library, https://www.jewishvirtuallibrary.org/.

JSTOR, https://about.jstor.org/.

Live Science, https://www.livescience.com/.

Malankara World: Baselios Church Digital Library, http://malankaraworld
    .com/.

Martin Luther King, Jr. Research and Education Institute of Stanford
    University, https://kinginstitute.stanford.edu/.

My Jewish Learning, https://www.myjewishlearning.com/.

Mythicist Papers, http://www.mythicistpapers.com/.

National Geographic, https://www.nationalgeographic.com/.

New Advent, https://www.newadvent.org/.

New York Times, https://www.nytimes.com/.

New World Encyclopedia, https://www.newworldencyclopedia.org.

Oxford Bibliographies, https://www.oxfordbibliographies.com/.

Patheos, https://www.patheos.com/.

Pete Enns, https://peteenns.com/.

Pravmir: Orthodox Christianity and the World, https://www.pravmir.com/.

Quora, https://www.quora.com/.

Rational Christianity, http://rationalchristianity.net/.

Realm of History, https://realmofhistory.com/.

Roman Empire & Colosseum, http://www.tribunesandtriumphs.org/.

Simple to Remember: Judaism Online, https://www.simpletoremember.com/.

Simply Bible, https://www.simplybible.com/.

Slate, https://slate.com/.

Space, https://www.space.com/.

That the World May Know, https://www.thattheworldmayknow.com/.

Thesaurus Precum Latinarum, https://www.preces-latinae.org/index.htm.

Twelve Tribes, http://twelvetribes.org/.

Vision, https://www.vision.org/.

The Washington Post, https://www.washingtonpost.com/.

The Well, https://www.well.com/

Wikipedia: The Free Encyclopedia, https://www.wikipedia.org/.

ADDITIONAL INFORMATION

One thing that I've really found helpful in understanding the ebb and flow of Christianity are the animated maps available online. Good examples are "Christianity in Europe (30-2019)," "The Spread of Christianity part one (30-1000 AD) and part two (1000-2016)," and the "Spread of the Gospel."

ABOUT THE AUTHOR

J. Steven Paul spent much of his life trying to be more than just a cultural Christian by attending church, reading the Bible, seeking divine guidance through prayer, and immersing himself in broader church culture of community outreach and overseas missions. Over time, realizing there was no consistent way that Christians behaved, he began questioning the origins of the practices and beliefs that characterized the religion he was raised in. He then spent more than a decade delving into the history of Christianity to fully understand those practices and the mindsets that support them.

www.ingramcontent.com/pod-product-compliance
Lightning Source LLC
Chambersburg PA
CBHW030346130626
46549CB00004B/1391